ERNEST HEMINGWAY:

A COMPREHENSIVE BIBLIOGRAPHY

ERNEST HEMINGWAY

A COMPREHENSIVE

BIBLIOGRAPHY

BY AUDRE HANNEMAN

PRINCETON, NEW JERSEY

PRINCETON UNIVERSITY PRESS

1967

FOR MY MOTHER AND FATHER,

NETTIE AND *HOMER HANNEMAN*

FOREWORD

As the U.S. publishers of Ernest Hemingway for over forty years we regard the completion of this Bibliography with very special interest. It is difficult to imagine a more gratifying corroboration of the importance of a writer to scholars and book-lovers (perhaps "bibliophiles" is a more exact word to use here but I believe "book-lovers" is a more inclusive one). The compiler of the work tackled and completed a task comparable to one of the fabled labors of Hercules. Indeed it has been a minor labor of Hercules for us to furnish her with acceptable answers to the many questions she raised about the editions of Hemingway's books: when did we change the binding of this or that book? Why did we "re-set" it? How large was the first printing?

I might explain here that even an old firm like Scribners, which has had an ample opportunity to develop a respect for the past, does not always have the answers to such questions at its finger-tips. Our primary responsibility is to bring each book we publish to as many readers as we can. This easily defined, but not always easily achieved, objective often results in the issuing of different editions at different prices, and the changing of jackets as frequently as one changes one's wardrobe to keep up with contemporary fashions. In all this a publisher is not always so much motivated by a long-range strategy as by the natural and often opportunistic tactics of his trade. Consequently a publisher views the whole catalog of what he may have done for one particular book with something close to surprise. We did not realize what complex bibliographical history was being made by our year-to-year business decisions, much as Molière's character did not realize he had been speaking prose all his life. Take *The Old Man and the Sea* as an example. The Bibliography shows in how many editions it has already been published, but I venture to predict that there will be many more editions of this great work in the years to come.

I am sure that Miss Hanneman does not at this moment view with complete equanimity the labor of preparing a second edition of her work but I can almost assure her that new editions and, I hope, new unpublished works by Hemingway will be coming along. Of making many books there is no end!

Charles Scribner, Jr.

July 13, 1967

PREFACE

This book is organized into three parts. Part One is a descriptive and enumerative bibliography of Hemingway's work. The first section is comprised of descriptions of Hemingway's books, from *Three Stories and Ten Poems*, published in Paris in 1923, to *A Moveable Feast*, published posthumously in 1964. These descriptive entries begin with the first edition of each book and continue through all reprint editions known to the bibliographer. Each of the seven instances where the bibliographer was unable to locate a reprint edition is noted. A search in nearly forty libraries and as many secondhand bookshops, publishing company files, and advertising in national publications failed to unearth these editions. This section concludes with descriptions of the first English editions and brief mention of subsequent English editions.

Section B comprises the first appearance in book form of short stories, articles, dispatches, and poems, as well as original contributions, introductions to works of fiction and nonfiction, and appraisals of artists' work in exhibition catalogues. Also included is Hemingway's anonymous epigraph for Martha Gellhorn's novel *A Stricken Field*, which is credited to a "Medieval Chronicle." Hemingway accomplished a similar feat when he wrote the epigraph for *Winner Take Nothing* as though it was quoted from an antique book of rules for gaming.

Section C comprises a chronological listing of Hemingway's work in newspapers and periodicals. Both first appearances and reprinted work are included. The contributions begin with those published in his high school newspaper, *Trapeze*, and the high school literary magazine, *Tabula*, and articles in the *Toronto Daily Star* and the *Toronto Star Weekly*. While Hemingway preferred not to be judged by this early work, its inclusion here clearly shows the diversity of experience that constituted his literary apprenticeship.

Section D lists translations of Hemingway's books, giving wherever possible the date of the first translated edition. Section E lists anthologies containing work by Hemingway. Explications of the selected works are mentioned in those instances where they appear. Section F is comprised of several parts. The first part lists library holdings of Hemingway's manuscripts and letters. Also, published facsimiles of pages of Hemingway's manuscripts. The second part lists 110 Hemingway letters which have been published in full or partially quoted. They are preceded by a copy of Hemingway's request regarding the publication of his letters. This section concludes with ephemera, including nine book blurbs by Hemingway.

PREFACE

Part Two is an enumerative bio-bibliography. The first half, Section G, is an alphabetical listing of books on Hemingway and books in which he or his work is significantly discussed. Over sixty books devoted entirely to Hemingway are listed. The remainder are biographies, autobiographies, collections of letters, literary criticism, books of poetry, and reference books. This check list encompasses a history of American literature from the 1920s to the 1960s.

The last half of Part Two, Section H, is comprised of newspaper and periodical material on Hemingway during the period from 1918 through 1965. It is inclusive rather than selective. The chronological list includes everything from critiques, interviews, and news items to parodies, poems, and caricatures. This list also includes short excerpts from reviews of all of Hemingway's books. These excerpts were selected to indicate the critics' reception to his work and to present various definitions of the Hemingway style.

Part Three, the appendix, lists the place of publication of newspapers and periodicals cited in this work.

Most of the sections are preceded by a brief introductory note covering usage, sources, and acknowledgments.

Where the text of Hemingway's books is referred to, the reference is always to the first edition.

The first draft of this bibliography was compiled in 1959, after a five-year period of research on Hemingway. An enlarged second draft was completed in 1962, and a revised and enlarged third draft was completed in 1965. Final revisions were made during 1966. During these various drafts, the work benefited from more than twenty research trips I made to various parts of the country to examine library holdings and private collections, and from my voluminous correspondence with many people both here and abroad. It would be impossible to list my correspondents but I wish to express my appreciation for their gracious cooperation.

I am indebted to Louis Henry Cohn's *A Bibliography of the Works of Ernest Hemingway*, which has been of invaluable aid regarding the early books to 1930, and to Lee Samuels for the numerous items of interest in *A Hemingway Check List*.

I owe a special debt of gratitude to Mrs. Mary Hemingway for allowing me to quote various materials and for granting me permission to reproduce the holograph page from the manuscript of *A Moveable Feast*; to Charles Scribner, Jr., for his courtesy and generosity in making bibliographical information accessible to me, and for his foreword to this book; to Mrs. Louis Henry Cohn, of House of Books, Ltd., who allowed me to examine her late husband's Hemingway collection, kept me informed of new items of interest, and also put me in touch with other notable Hemingway collections, of which I might otherwise have remained unaware; to

Professor William White, who was helpful regarding many aspects of this work, including advice on bibliographical form, and for allowing me to examine his Hemingway collection; to Professor Carlos Baker for his many helpful suggestions and his generous encouragement.

I also wish to express my thanks to George McKay Schieffelin and L. H. Brague, Jr., at Charles Scribner's Sons, Milton H. Altman of St. Paul, Minnesota, Mrs. Morris R. Buske of Oak Park, Illinois, Benjamin Swann of New York, Professor Fraser B. Drew of Buffalo, New York, Mrs. Mary M. Hirth of Austin, Texas, Signora Fernanda Pivano of Milan, Waring Jones of Wayzata, Minnesota, Leicester Hemingway of Miami, Florida, John Doohan of Kansas City, Missouri, Jasper Wood of Cleveland, Ohio, C. Waller Barrett of Charlottesville, Virginia, David A. Randall of Bloomington, Indiana, Miss Barbara Ballinger of Oak Park, Illinois, and William F. Nolan of Los Angeles.

I would also like to thank the staff of Princeton University Press; especially Herbert S. Bailey, Jr., Director, Mrs. Polly Hanford, my editor, and Marshall Henrichs, who designed this book.

I am grateful to the librarians and staffs of all the libraries in which I worked, and would particularly like to express my thanks to the librarians and staffs of the New York Public Library, the Donnell Library in New York, the Library of Congress, the Kansas City Public Library, the University of Kansas City Library, the Oak Park Public Library, the Firestone Library at Princeton University, the Lilly Library at Indiana University, the Barrett Library at the University of Virginia, the University of Texas Libraries, and the Beinecke Rare Book and Manuscript Library at Yale University.

I especially want to thank my family and my friends for their unflagging interest and encouragement. And to express my deep appreciation to my sister, Marjorie Hanneman, whose advice and encouragement have contributed to this book in so many ways.

Audre Hanneman

New York, N.Y.
September, 1967

CONTENTS

ABBREVIATIONS
USED IN THIS WORK

AMF	A Moveable Feast
ARIT	Across the River and Into the Trees
Baker	Hemingway: The Writer as Artist by Carlos Baker
Baker anthology	Hemingway and His Critics: An International Anthology. Edited by Carlos Baker
Baker critiques	Ernest Hemingway: Critiques of Four Major Novels. Edited by Carlos Baker
Cohn's Bibliography	A Bibliography of the Works of Ernest Hemingway by Louis Henry Cohn
DIA	Death in the Afternoon
First 49	The Fifth Column and the First Forty-nine Stories
FTA	A Farewell to Arms
FWBT	For Whom the Bell Tolls
GHOA	Green Hills of Africa
iot	in our time (Paris, 1924)
IOT	In Our Time
Macomber	The Short Happy Life of Francis Macomber
McCaffery	Ernest Hemingway: The Man and His Work. Edited by John K. M. McCaffery
MWW	Men Without Women
OMATS	The Old Man and the Sea
SAR	The Sun Also Rises
TFC	The Fifth Column
THAHN	To Have and Have Not
TOS	The Torrents of Spring
TSTP	Three Stories & Ten Poems
Weeks collection	Hemingway: A Collection of Critical Essays. Edited by Robert P. Weeks
WTN	Winner Take Nothing

PART ONE
THE WORKS
OF ERNEST HEMINGWAY

CHRONOLOGICAL LIST
OF HEMINGWAY'S BOOKS

1923 *Three Stories & Ten Poems*. Short stories and poems

1924 *in our time*. Short chapters

1925 *In Our Time*. Short stories and inter-chapters

1926 *The Torrents of Spring*. Novel

1926 *Today is Friday*. Play (Pamphlet)

1926 *The Sun Also Rises*. Novel

1927 *Men Without Women*. Short stories

1929 *A Farewell to Arms*. Novel

1932 *Death in the Afternoon*. Treatise on bullfighting

1933 *God Rest You Merry Gentlemen*. Short story

1933 *Winner Take Nothing*. Short stories

1935 *Green Hills of Africa*. Nonfictional account of big game
hunting

1937 *To Have and Have Not*. Novel

1938 *The Spanish Earth*. Commentary for the film of the same name

1938 *The Fifth Column and the First Forty-nine Stories*. Play and
short stories

1940 *For Whom the Bell Tolls*. Novel

1942 *Men at War*. Anthology. Edited by Hemingway

1950 *Across the River and Into the Trees*. Novel

1952 *The Old Man and the Sea*. Novella

BOOKS PUBLISHED POSTHUMOUSLY:

1962 *The Wild Years*. *Toronto Star* articles. Edited by Gene Z.
Hanrahan

1964 *A Moveable Feast*. Nonfictional sketches of Paris in the
twenties

SECTION A

BOOKS AND PAMPHLETS

This section is comprised of descriptions of Hemingway's books and pamphlets, beginning with the first edition of each and including all reprint editions known to the bibliographer. It is followed by descriptions of the first English editions and brief mention of subsequent English editions. The bibliographer gratefully acknowledges her debt to Charles Scribner's Sons, Jonathan Cape Ltd., Crown Publishers, Inc., The Viking Press, Inc., Random House Inc., Penguin Books Ltd., and P. F. Collier, Inc. for information regarding various editions of Hemingway's books.

No attempt has been made here to include a textual study of Hemingway's manuscripts in their various forms. However, deletions, additions, and revisions in the text are noted in many instances and it is hoped that these will be helpful to whoever undertakes the much needed full-scale textual study of Hemingway's work.

In the following descriptions, the endpapers are white and the lettering is black unless otherwise noted. The page size is given and, of course, can be only approximate for untrimmed pages. On books published by Scribner's since 1930, first editions are indicated with a capital "A" on the copyright page.

A1 Three Stories and Ten Poems

A. First limited edition:

THREE STORIES | Up in Michigan | Out of Season | My Old Man | & TEN POEMS | Mitraigliatrice | Oklahoma | Oily Weather | Roosevelt | Captives | Champs d'Honneur | Riparto d'Assalto | Montparnasse | Along With Youth | Chapter Heading | ERNEST HEMINGWAY

7 x 4½. Published by Robert McAlmon at the Contact Publishing Co., Paris, during the summer (probably July) of 1923, at $2.00. The first and only limited edition consisted of 300 copies. Issued in grayish-blue paper covers which fold over the first and last blank leaves at the top, bottom, and fore edge. The black lettering on the front cover is identical with the title page, as shown above. The backstrip is blank. Printed in black on the back cover: BY ERNEST HEMINGWAY | IN OUR TIME— (THREE MOUNTAINS PRESS). All edges untrimmed.

COLLATION: [i]–[xii] + [1]–[64], as follows: [i]–[iv] blank; [v] star in lower right corner; [vi] Copyright, 1923, by the author | Published by | Contact Publishing Co.; [vii] title page as above; [viii] blank; [ix] dedication: THIS BOOK | IS FOR HADLEY; [x] blank; [xi] CONTENTS and acknowledgment; [xii] blank; [1] divisional half title: UP IN MICHIGAN; [2] blank; 3–58 text; [59] colophon: PRINTED AT DIJON | BY | MAURICE DARANTIERE | M.CM. XXIII; [60]–[64] blank.

PREVIOUS PUBLICATION: The acknowledgment, on p. [xi], states: "Five of these poems were first printed in *Poetry* A Magazine of Verse." This is incorrect. Six of the poems were printed, under the general heading "Wanderings," in *Poetry*, XXI (Jan. 1923). In the magazine, "Mitraigliatrice" was spelled "Mitrailliatrice." This is the first appearance of "Oklahoma," "Captives," "Montparnasse," "Along With Youth," and the three stories.

NOTE: "Out of Season" and "My Old Man" were included in *IOT* (1925). However, "Up in Michigan" was not reprinted until 1938 when it was included, with some revisions, in the *First 49*.

NOTE: As shown by the advertisement on the back cover, it was expected that *in our time* would be published first. According to Hemingway's inscription to Dr. Guffey in a copy of *in our time*, William Bird had that manuscript "long before" Robert McAlmon had this book set up, but because *in our time* was sixth in a series it did not appear until 1924. [See *The Library of Dr. Don Carlos Guffey*, New York, 1958, p. 32. This inscription is quoted in full in Charles Norman's *Ezra Pound*, New York, 1960, p. 256.]

2 in our time

A. First limited edition:
in our time | *by* | ernest hemingway | A GIRL IN CHICAGO: Tell us about | the French women, Hank. What are | they like? | BILL SMITH: How old are the French | women, Hank? | [publisher's device] | paris: | *printed at the* three mountains press *and for sale* | *at* shakespeare & company, *in the rue de l'odéon;* | *london*: william jackson, *took's court, cursitor street, chancery lane.* | 1924

10 1/4 x 6 1/2. Published by William Bird, Paris, in the Spring (probably mid-March) of 1924, at $2.00. The first and only limited edition consisted of 170 copies. Issued in tan boards, with black lettering and publisher's device printed over a collage of red-lettered newspaper items, headlines, and a map on the front cover. All edges untrimmed.

COLLATION: [1]-[32], as follows: [1]-[2] blank; [3] half title; [4] frontispiece: the author *wood-cut from portrait by* henry strater; [5] title page as above; [6] blank; [7] dedication: to | robert mcalmon and william bird | *publishers of the city of paris* | and to | captain eric edward dorman-smith, m.c., | *of his majesty's fifth fusiliers* | this book | is respectfully dedicated; [8] note: *of 170 copies* | *printed on* | rives *hand-made paper* | *this is number*   ; 9-30 text; [31] colophon; [32] blank.

CONTENTS: Eighteen short untitled chapters. chapter 1 | Everybody was drunk . . . chapter 2 | The first matador got the horn . . . chapter 3 | Minarets stuck up in the rain . . . chapter 4 | We were in a garden at Mons . . . chapter 5 | It was a frightfully hot day . . . chapter 6 | They shot the six cabinet ministers . . . chapter 7 | Nick sat against the wall of the church . . . chapter 8 | While the bombardment . . . chapter 9 | At two o'clock in the morning . . . chapter 10 | One hot evening in Milan . . . chapter 11 | In 1919 he was traveling on railroads in Italy . . . chapter 12 | They whack whacked the white horse . . . chapter 13 | The crowd shouted all the time . . . chapter 14 | If it happened right down close . . . chapter 15 | I heard the drums coming down the street . . . chapter 16 | Maera lay still . . . chapter 17 | They hanged Sam Cardinella . . . chapter 18 | The king was working in the garden.

PREVIOUS PUBLICATION: The first six chapters appeared in the *Little Review*, IX (Spring 1923). For book publication, minor revisions were made in all of the chapters (most notably in Ch. 2) except Ch. 6; the title was omitted from Ch. 5.

COLOPHON on p. [31]: Here ends *The Inquest* into the state | of contemporary English prose, as | edited by Ezra Pound and printed at | the Three Mountains Press. The six | works constituting the series are: | Indiscretions of Ezra Pound | Women and Men by Ford

Madox Ford | Elimus by B. C. Windeler | with Designs by D. Shakespear | The Great American Novel | by William Carlos Williams | England by B.M.G.-Adams | In Our Time by Ernest Hemingway | with Portrait by Henry Strater. Note: Ezra Pound's duties as editor consisted of his selecting and securing the manuscripts for inclusion. [See Donald Gallup's *A Bibliography of Ezra Pound*, London: Hart-Davis, 1963, p. 57.] For Hemingway's comments on his inclusion in this series and his reference to the fact that William Bird had the manuscript for this book before Robert McAlmon had *TSTP* set up, see *The Library of Dr. Don Carlos Guffey*, New York, 1958, p. 32.

NOTE: In a broadside distributed by the Three Mountains Press late in 1922, this book is listed as "BLANK by Ernest M. Hemingway." [See Gallup's *A Bibliography of Ezra Pound*, p. 381.]

NOTE: The title is apparently an ironic allusion to the twelfth line of the Episcopalian "Evening Prayer": "Give peace in our time, O Lord."

NOTE: Facsimiles of the cover, frontispiece, title page, and first page of the text are reproduced in *Ezra Pound*: *Perspectives*: *essays in honor of his eightieth birthday*, ed. Noel Stock, New York: Regnery, 1966, pp. 152-153.

NOTE: A color reproduction of the portrait of Hemingway by Henry Strater, from which a printer's woodcut was made for the frontispiece, appears in *Art in America*, XLIX, iv (1961). The original portrait is in the Ogunquit Museum of Art, in Ogunquit, Maine.

3 In Our Time

A. First edition:

IN OUR TIME | *STORIES BY* | ERNEST HEMINGWAY | [publisher's device] | *NEW YORK* | BONI & LIVERIGHT | 1925 [title page enclosed in a triple black border, with a thin rule between a heavy inner rule and an ornamental outer border]

7 7/16 x 5 1/8. Published October 5, 1925, at $2.00. The first printing consisted of 1335 copies. Issued in smooth black cloth with gold lettering on front cover and backstrip. Front cover: In Our Time | Ernest Hemingway | [geometric design stamped in gold]. Backstrip: In Our | Time | [ornament] | Ernest | Hemingway | [publisher's device, blind-stamped] | BONI & | LIVERIGHT. Top edges stained yellow; bottom and fore edges untrimmed.

COLLATION: [i]–[ii] + [1]–[222], as follows: [i]–[ii] blank; [1] half title; [2] blank; [3] title page as above; [4] notice of copyright and publisher's device; [5] dedication: To | HADLEY RICHARDSON HEMINGWAY; [6] acknowledgment; [7] CONTENTS; [8] blank; [9] epigraph; [10] blank; [11] half title; [12] blank; [13]-[215] text; [216]-[222] blank.

7

ACKNOWLEDGMENT on p. [6]: *For permission to reprint some of the stories in this volume | acknowledgments are due to the editors of The Little | Review, The Transatlantic Review and This Quarter.*

EPIGRAPH on p. [9]: A girl in Chicago—*Tell us about the French | women, Hank. What are | they like?* | Bill Smith:—*How old are the French | women, Hank?* This epigraph appeared on the title page of *in our time.*

CONTENTS: The short chapters of *in our time* are printed as inter-chapters in this volume and are indicated here by the arabic numerals in parentheses. I (1)/Indian Camp/II (3)/The Doctor and the Doctor's Wife/III (4)/The End of Something/IV (5)/The Three Day Blow/V (6)/The Battler/VI (7)/A Very Short Story (10)/VII (8)/Soldier's Home/VIII (9)/The Revolutionist (11)/IX (2)/Mr. and Mrs. Elliot/X (12) /Cat in the Rain/XI (13) /Out of Season/XII (14) /Cross Country Snow/XIII (15)/My Old Man/XIV (16)/Big Two-Hearted River, Part I /XV (17)/Big Two-Hearted River, Part II/L'Envoi (18).

PREVIOUS PUBLICATION: Sixteen of the short chapters from *iot* are included as inter-chapters. Two of the *iot* chapters have been included as short stories: Ch. 10 has been titled "A Very Short Story" and Ch. 11 has been titled "The Revolutionist." Ch. 18 of *iot* has been titled "L'Envoi" but left as an inter-chapter. "Out of Season" and "My Old Man" first appeared in *TSTP.* "Soldier's Home" was first published in *Contact Collection of Contemporary Writers,* Paris, 1925. "Indian Camp" first appeared in the *Transatlantic Review,* I (April 1924), under the heading "Work in Progress." "The Doctor and the Doctor's Wife" first appeared in the *Transatlantic Review,* II (Dec. 1924). "Mr. and Mrs. Elliot" first appeared in the *Little Review,* x (Autumn-Winter 1924-1925). "Cross Country Snow" first appeared in the *Transatlantic Review,* II (Jan. 1925). Both parts of "Big Two-Hearted River" first appeared, in English, in *This Quarter,* I (May 1925). The four stories which appear for the first time are: "The End of Something," "The Three Day Blow," "The Battler," and "Cat in the Rain."

NOTE: Minor revisions were made in both the inter-chapters and the short stories before publication in this volume. The most notable changes were in "Mr. and Mrs. Elliot," which was later changed back as it appeared in the *Little Review* when it was published in the Scribner's edition of *IOT* (1930).

NOTE: Hemingway had originally submitted "Up in Michigan" as the second story in this volume, but the publisher, Horace Liveright, eliminated it as censorable and Hemingway replaced it with "The Battler."

NOTE: The dust jacket is light gray, printed in dark blue and brown. The front cover is ruled off into nine sections. The title and author's name appear in the center section. The top corner sections have an ornamental design. In the remaining six sections are appreciations of Hemingway's work by Edward J. O'Brien, Sherwood Anderson, Gilbert Seldes, Donald Ogden Stewart, Waldo Frank, and Ford Madox Ford. These quotations are excerpts from longer appreciations which appear on the front flap and the back cover of the dust jacket. An appreciation by John Dos Passos also appears on the back cover.

NOTE: The book was reprinted in March 1927, October 1928, and had a fourth printing in December 1929. The various printings are indicated on the copyright page. The publishing rights were sold to Scribner's on June 19, 1930.

B. Second American edition, revised:

IN OUR TIME | STORIES BY | ERNEST HEMINGWAY | WITH AN INTRODUCTION | BY EDMUND WILSON | NEW YORK | CHARLES SCRIBNER'S SONS | 1930

7 3/8 x 5 3/16. Published October 24, 1930, at $2.50. The first printing consisted of 3240 copies. Issued in smooth black cloth with gold paper labels, printed in black, on the front cover and backstrip. Backstrip label: [triple rule] | IN OUR | TIME | [ornament] | ERNEST | HEMINGWAY | [ornament] | SCRIBNER'S | [triple rule]. Front label: IN OUR TIME | [three ornaments] | ERNEST HEMINGWAY. Enclosed in a triple-ruled border with a thin rule between two thick rules. Top and bottom edges trimmed, fore edges untrimmed.

COLLATION: [i]-[xvi] + [3]-[214], as follows: [i] blank; [ii] BOOKS BY ERNEST HEMINGWAY; [iii] half title; [iv] blank; [v] title page as above; [vi] notice of copyright, note of origin, and printer's device; [vii] dedication: To | HADLEY RICHARDSON HEMING-WAY; [viii] blank; ix-xv INTRODUCTION BY EDMUND WILSON; [xvi] blank; [the pagination is incorrect, pp. [1]-[2] are lacking]; [3] CONTENTS; [4] blank; [5] legal disclaimer and acknowledgment; [6] blank; [7] half title; [8] blank; 9-12 INTRO-DUCTION BY THE AUTHOR; [13]-[213] text; [214] blank.

LEGAL DISCLAIMER on p. [5]: Note | In view of a recent tendency to identify characters in | fiction with real people, it seems proper to state that there | are no real people in this volume: both the characters and | their names are fictitious. If the name of any living per- | son has been used, the use was purely accidental.

CONTENTS: The short stories and inter-chapters in *IOT* (1925) appear in the same order in this edition. An "Introduction by the Author" has been added, on pp. 9-12; this was retitled "On the Quai at Smyrna" and included as a short story in the *First 49*. The epigraph, which appeared on the title page of *iot* and on p. [9] of the 1925 edition, has been omitted. Some revisions were made in the text. In "A Very Short Story," the setting was changed from Milan to Padua and the girl's name from "Ag" to "Luz." "Mr. and Mrs. Elliot," which was revised in *IOT* (1925), is printed almost as it originally appeared in the *Little Review*, x (Autumn-Winter 1924-1925).

NOTE: The original blue dust jacket is printed in gold and black, with a design by "Cleonike" on the front cover.

NOTE: Scribner's bought the plates, bound stock, and reprint rights to this book from Boni & Liveright, on June 19, 1930.

NOTE: Reprinted in December 1930 in an edition of 1035 copies.

c. Reprint edition:

In | Our Time | Stories by | Ernest Hemingway | PARIS | Crosby Continental Editions | 2, Rue Cardinale | 1932

6 7/16 x 4 7/8. Published by Caresse Crosby, at the Black Sun Press, Paris, at 12 francs. Issued in white paper covers, with flaps, printed in orange on the front cover and backstrip. Front cover: Modern Masterpieces in English | In Our | Time | by | Ernest Hemingway | [publisher's device] | Crosby Continental Editions | Paris. Backstrip: No 6 | In Our | Time | [publisher's device] | Hemingway | 12 fr. |. Back cover: *Not to be introduced | into the British Empire or U.S.A. | Sole distributors Hachette, Paris.* The list on the front flap, under the heading ALREADY APPEARED, includes: *THE TORRENTS | OF SPRING* | by Ernest HEMINGWAY | open letter by Caresse Crosby.

COLLATION: [1]-[224], as follows: [1] half title; [2] blank; [3] title page as above; [4] blank; [5] dedication; [6] blank; [7] NOTE [legal disclaimer]; [8] blank; [9]-12 INTRODUCTION BY THE AUTHOR; [13]-[221] text; [222] blank; [223] note: *Each volume of the C.C.E. | is published with Continen- | tal rights acquired from the | author or his representative.*; [224] colophon: PUBLISHED BY | THE BLACK SUN PRESS | 2, RUE CARDINALE | PARIS | PRINTED BY | F. PAILLART | PARIS-ABBEVILLE | JUNE 1932.

CONTENTS: This edition follows the same order and the same text as the 1930 Scribner edition of *IOT*.

D. Reprint edition:

ERNEST HEMINGWAY | [wavy line] | IN OUR TIME | *With an Introduction by | Edmund Wilson* | [design of a rising sun] | SUN RISE EDITION | *Volume One* | [wavy line] | *CHARLES SCRIBNER'S SONS* | NEW YORK

7 7/8 x 5 3/8. Published in May 1938, at $15.00 for a six-volume set. 3020 sets were printed. Issued in bright blue buckram, with the author's signature blind-stamped on the front cover. Stamped in gold on the backstrip: [decorative band] | HEMINGWAY | [short

rule] | IN | OUR | TIME | I | [decorative band] [all on indented block] | design | [decorative band] | THE | SUN RISE | EDITION | [decorative band] [all on indented block] | [design] | [decorative band] | SCRIBNERS | [decorative band] [all on indented block]. The top and bottom edges are trimmed, fore edges untrimmed.

COLLATION: [i]-[xvi] + [3]-[214]. The same as the 1930 Scribner edition, except that the list of books on p. [ii] has been omitted. The copyright page shows the original copyright dates only.

NOTE: Also issued in a variant binding of red buckram.

NOTE: This is Vol. I of a six-volume set. The other volumes are: Vol. II *SAR*; Vol. III *MWW*; Vol. IV *FTA*; Vol. V *WTN*; Vol. VI *THAHN*.

E. Uniform edition:

IN OUR TIME | STORIES BY | ERNEST HEMINGWAY | NEW YORK | CHARLES SCRIBNER'S SONS | 1955

7 5/16 x 5 1/8. Published in 1955, at $3.00. Issued in light green cloth. Stamped in gold on the front cover: [ornament] IN OUR TIME [ornament]. Backstrip: the title is stamped in gold on a black block; the author's name and publisher's name are stamped in black on gold blocks. All edges trimmed.

COLLATION: [i]-[ii] + [1]-[214], as follows: [i] half title; [ii] *Books by*; [1] title page as above; [2] notices of copyright, change of title, note of origin, and reservation of rights; [3] dedication; [4] Note (legal disclaimer); [5] CONTENTS; [6] blank; [7] half title; [8] blank; 9-[213] text; [214] blank.

NOTE: The green dust jacket is printed in the uniform design, in blue, white, green, and black.

F. Paperback edition:

IN OUR TIME | STORIES BY | ERNEST HEMINGWAY | NEW YORK | CHARLES SCRIBNER'S SONS

8 x 5 3/8. Published in 1962, at $1.25, as No. SL 56 of the Scribner Library series. Issued in gray stiff paper covers, printed in black, white, and purple. The same pagination as the 1955 uniform edition.

4 The Torrents of Spring

A. First edition:

The | Torrents of Spring | A Romantic Novel in Honor of the | Passing of a Great Race | BY | ERNEST HEMINGWAY | AUTHOR OF "IN OUR TIME" | And perhaps there is one reason why a comic | writer should of all others be the least excused | for deviating from nature, since it may not be | always so easy for a serious poet to meet with | the great and the admirable; but life every- | where furnishes an accurate observer with the | ridiculous. |

HENRY FIELDING. | NEW YORK | CHARLES SCRIBNER'S SONS | 1926

7 7/16 x 5 3/16. Published May 28, 1926, at $1.50. The first printing consisted of 1250 copies. Issued in smooth dark green cloth, stamped in red on the front cover and backstrip. Backstrip: THE | TORRENTS | OF | SPRING | [ornament] | HEMINGWAY | SCRIBNERS. Front: THE TORRENTS OF | SPRING | [ornament] | ERNEST HEMINGWAY. Blind-ruled border around the front cover. Top edges trimmed, bottom and fore edges untrimmed.

COLLATION: [i]-[viii] + [1]-[144], as follows: [i] half title; [ii] blank; [iii] title page as above; [iv] notice of copyright, note of origin, and printer's device; [v] dedication: To | H. L. MENCKEN AND S. STANWOOD MENCKEN | IN ADMIRATION; [vi] blank; [vii] CONTENTS; [viii] blank; [1] divisional half title: Part One | Red and Black Laughter | [illustration]; [2] quotation from Henry Fielding; 3-143 text; [144] blank.

CONTENTS: Part One: Red and Black Laughter/Part Two: The Struggle for Life/Part Three: Men in War and the Death of Society/Part Four: The Passing of a Great Race and the Making and Marring of Americans/Author's Final Note to the Reader. Note: Quotations from Henry Fielding precede each of the four parts.

NOTE: The title is taken from Ivan Turgenev's *The Torrents of Spring*, written in 1870, which in turn was taken from an old folksong: *Years of gladness,* | *Days of glee,* | *Like torrents of spring,* | *They flee, they flee!*

NOTE: S. Stanwood Menken's name was misspelled in the dedication. This error remained uncorrected in later printings. For an explanation of Hemingway's choice of H. L. Mencken, critic and iconoclast, and S. Stanwood Menken, wealthy vice crusader, as dedicatees, see *Baker*, p. 41.

NOTE: The dark green binding appears almost black in artificial light and has been described as black in booksellers' catalogues.

NOTE: The dust jacket is tan with black lettering. On the front cover, a drawing, by "M. F.," in orange, black, and tan, depicts a scene at a lunch counter.

PRINTING HISTORY: Reprinted in July 1928, March 1930, and September 1930.

NOTE: *TOS* is included complete in *The Hemingway Reader* edited by Charles Poore, 1953, pp. 25-86. See (A25).

B. Reprint edition:

The | Torrents | of | Spring | A Romantic Novel in Honor of the | Passing of a Great Race | by | Ernest Hemingway | PARIS | Crosby Continental Editions | 2, Rue Cardinale | 1932

6 1/16 x 4 3/4. Published by Caresse Crosby at the Black Sun Press, Paris, at ten francs. Issued in heavy white paper covers printed in green, with flaps along the fore edge which fold over the first and last blank leaves. Front cover: World-wide Masterpieces in English | The | Torrents | of Spring | by | Ernest Hemingway | [publisher's device] | Crosby Continental Editions | Paris |. Backstrip: No 1 | Torrents | of | Spring | [publisher's device] | Hemingway | 10 fr. |. Back cover: Not to be introduced | into the British Empire and U.S.A. | Sole distributors Hachette, Paris.

COLLATION: 1 leaf + i-[viii] + [1]-[180], as follows: [blank leaf]; i-vii OPEN LETTER | TO ERNEST HEMINGWAY (by Caresse Crosby) *Paris, December,* 1931; [viii] blank; [1] half title; [2] blank; [3] title page as above; [4] quotation from Henry Fielding; [5] dedication; [6] blank; [7] CONTENTS; [8] blank; [9] divisional half title; [10] quotation from Henry Fielding; 11-176 text; [177] note: Each volume of the C.C.E. | is published with Continen- | tal rights acquired from the | author or his representative.; [178] colophon: PUBLISHED BY | THE BLACK SUN PRESS | 2, RUE CARDINALE | PARIS | PRINTED BY F. PAILLART | PARIS-ABBEVILLE | DECEMBER 1931; [179]-[180] blank.

NOTE: A large paper edition, 7 1/2 x 5 5/8, was issued at 125 francs.

5 Today is Friday

A. First edition:

Today is Friday [Caption title only. No title page.]

7 1/2 x 5. Published by The As Stable Publications, Englewood, N.J., in the summer of 1926, at $1.50, as No. IV of The As Stable Pamphlets. The publishers were: Edith Finch, George Platt Lynes, and Adlai Harbeck. Issued in white paper wrappers, of slightly heavier weight than the leaves, measuring 7 7/8 x 5 1/8. Drawing by Jean Cocteau on the front cover, signed "Jean," and below it, in script: "L'impuissance à convaincre." The pages are sewn into the wrappers with white silk thread. Top and bottom edges trimmed; fore edges untrimmed. Enclosed in a white envelope with a geometric design in black on the front.

COLLATION: [1]-[8] pages, as follows: [1] caption title and stage instructions; [1]-[7] text; [8] blank.

NOTE: The notices of copyright and reservation of rights appear on the back cover.

COLOPHON on the back cover: *Three hundred numbered copies printed. | Two hundred and sixty for sale. | Number |.*

NOTE: This was the first appearance of this one-act play, which was published the following year, with only minor changes in punctuation, in *MWW*.

NOTE: A facsimile of Cocteau's drawing on the front cover is reproduced in *Cohn's Bibliography*, p. [24].

NOTE: The other pamphlets in this series, as listed on the back cover, were: I. GENESIS OF PEACE *by* Paxton Howard, | with drawing by A.E.H. | II. DESCRIPTIONS OF LITERATURE *by* Gertrude Stein, | with drawing by Pavel Tchelitchew. | III. 1830 *by* René Crevel, | with drawing by H. Phelan Gibb.

6 The Sun Also Rises

A. First edition:

THE SUN ALSO RISES | By | ERNEST HEMINGWAY | Author of "The Torrents of Spring," "In Our Time" | [design by Cleon] | NEW YORK | CHARLES SCRIBNER'S SONS | 1926

7 1/2 x 5 3/16. Published October 22, 1926, at $2.00. The first printing consisted of 5090 copies. Issued in smooth black cloth with gold paper labels, lettered and ruled in black, on the front cover and backstrip. Backstrip label: [triple rule] | THE SUN | ALSO | RISES | [ornament] | ERNEST | HEMINGWAY | [ornament] | SCRIBNERS | [triple rule]. Front label: THE SUN ALSO | RISES | [three ornaments] | ERNEST HEMINGWAY [enclosed in a triple-ruled border with a thin rule between two thick rules]. Top and bottom edges trimmed, fore edges untrimmed.

COLLATION: [i]-[viii] + [1]-[260], as follows: [i]-[ii] blank; [iii] half title; [iv] blank; [v] title page as above; [vi] notice of copyright, note of origin, and printer's device; [vii] dedication: THIS BOOK IS | FOR HADLEY AND FOR JOHN HADLEY | NICANOR; [viii] quotations from Gertrude Stein and Ecclesiastes; [1] divisional half title: THE SUN ALSO RISES | [short rule] | *BOOK I*; [2] blank; 3-259 text; [260] blank.

Quotations on p. [viii]: "You are all a lost generation."| —*Gertrude Stein in conversation.* | "Vanity of vanities, saith the Preacher, vanity of | vanities; all is vanity. . . . One generation passeth | away, and another generation cometh; but the earth | abideth forever. . . . The sun also ariseth, and the | sun goeth down, and hasteth to the place where he | arose. . . . The wind goeth toward the south, and | turneth about unto the north; it whirleth about con- | tinually, and the wind returneth again according to | his circuits. . . . All the rivers run into the sea; yet | the sea is not full; unto the place from whence the | rivers come, thither they return again." | —*Ecclesiastes.* [I: 2, 4-7.]

NOTE: In the third issue and all later issues, the second verse, regarding vanity, was omitted.

NOTE: In the first issue a typographical error appears on p. 181, line

26. The word "stopped" is spelled "stoppped." This was corrected in the second issue.

NOTE: The dust jacket is printed in gold, black, and tan, with a gold apple on either side of the title. A design by Cleon depicts a seated classical figure. The same design appears on the title page. A misprint on the front cover lists *In Our Time* as "IN OUR TIMES." The back cover carries a drawing of Hemingway by John Blomshield, dated Paris, 1925. Hemingway's facsimile signature appears below the drawing.

PRINTING HISTORY: Reprinted in November 1926, December 1926, January 1927, February 1927 (twice), March 1927, February 1928, July 1928, and November 1929 (tenth printing).

NOTE: *Publishers' Weekly*, CLXXX (July 10, 1961), 49, reported that *"The Sun Also Rises* has sold an estimated 1,037,000 copies."

NOTE: *The Sun Also Rises* is included complete in the Viking Portable *Hemingway*, ed. Malcolm Cowley, 1944, pp. 5-243; in *The Hemingway Reader*, ed. Charles Poore, 1953, pp. 89-289; and in *Three Novels of Ernest Hemingway*, 1962, pp. 3-247, with an introduction by Malcolm Cowley.

B. Reprint edition:
THE SUN ALSO RISES | [long rule] | BY | ERNEST HEMING-WAY | [long rule] | INTRODUCTION BY | HENRY SEIDEL CANBY | [long rule] | [publisher's device] | [long rule] | THE MODERN LIBRARY | PUBLISHERS : NEW YORK [title page enclosed in a double-ruled border, with a thin inner rule and a thick outer rule]

6 1/2 x 4 1/4. Published February 25, 1930, at ninety-five cents, as No. 170 of The Modern Library of the World's Best Books. Issued in four shades of cloth: red, blue, green, and maroon. Publisher's device stamped in gold on the front cover. Blind-stamped rule around the top, bottom and fore edge of front cover. Stamped in gold on the backstrip: THE SUN | ALSO RISES | [rule] | ERNEST | HEMINGWAY | [design] | MODERN | LIBRARY. All edges trimmed. Top edges stained to match the color of the cloth. Printed endpapers.

COLLATION: [i]-[xii] + [1]-[260], as follows: [i] half title: THE MOD-ERN LIBRARY | OF THE WORLD'S BEST BOOKS | [double rule] | THE SUN ALSO RISES; [ii] publisher's note regarding catalogue; [iii] title page as above; [iv] notice of copyright, *First Modern Library Edition* | 1930, note of origin, and binder's note; [v]-ix INTRODUCTION by Henry Seidel Canby; [x] blank; [xi] dedication; [xii] quotations; [1] divisional half title; [2] blank; 3-259 text; [260] blank.

The Introduction by Henry Seidel Canby, on pp. [v]-ix, is dated: New York | *January*, 1930.

NOTE: The quotation, on p. [xii], from Ecclesiastes, begins with the fourth verse.

NOTE: The dust jacket is white with black lettering and a red border. An illustrative drawing by "Wuyts," in black and white, is on the front cover.

NOTE: Reissued, [date unknown], at $1.25. 7 x 4 5/8. THE SUN | ALSO | RISES | BY | ERNEST | HEMINGWAY | INTRODUC-TION BY | HENRY SEIDEL CANBY [all enclosed in a thin-ruled border] | THE | MODERN LIBRARY | NEW YORK [publisher's device] [title page enclosed in thick-ruled border]

Issued in red cloth with gold lettering and ruling, on a black background, and publisher's device stamped in gold on the front cover and backstrip. All edges trimmed; top edges stained dark gray. Printed gray endpapers.

Same pagination as the first Modern Library edition except in this edition the publisher's note is on p. [i]; p. [ii] is blank. The original copyright date only is given. Note on revised copyright page: *Random House* IS THE PUBLISHER OF | THE MODERN LIBRARY.

c. Reprint edition:

The Sun Also | Rises | By | ERNEST HEMINGWAY | Author of "Farewell to Arms" | [design by Cleon] | *Grosset & Dunlap, Publishers | by arrangement with* | CHARLES SCRIBNER'S SONS [title page enclosed in a decorative red border within a double-ruled red border, with a thin inner rule and a heavy outer rule]

7 3/4 x 5 1/4. Published in September 1930, at $1.00, in the Novels of Distinction series. Issued in black cloth with red paper labels lettered and ruled in black on the front cover and backstrip. The lettering is identical to the first edition except for the substitution of GROSSET | & DUNLAP in place of SCRIBNERS on the backstrip. Publisher's device blind-stamped on lower right corner of front cover. Bottom and fore edges untrimmed; top edges stained red.

COLLATION: [i]-[viii] + [1]-[264]. The same as the first edition except there are two blank leaves at the end. The original copyright date only is given. The quotation from Ecclesiastes begins with the fourth verse.

NOTE: The white dust jacket is printed in red, green, and purple.

NOTE: Grosset & Dunlap issued *FTA* in an identical binding. See (A8d).

d. Reprint edition:

ERNEST HEMINGWAY | [wavy line] | THE | SUN ALSO RISES | [design of a rising sun] | SUN RISE EDITION | *Volume Two* | [wavy line] | *CHARLES SCRIBNER'S SONS* | NEW YORK

7 7/8 x 5 3/8. Published in May 1938 in a six-volume set, which sold for $15.00. 3020 sets were printed. Issued in blue buckram with the author's signature blind-stamped on the front cover. Gold lettering and designs on the backstrip: [decorative line] | HEMING-WAY | [short rule] | THE | SUN ALSO | RISES | II | [decorative line] [all on indented block] | [design] | [decorative line] | THE | SUN RISE | EDITIONS | [decorative line] [all on indented block] | [design] | [decorative line] | SCRIBNERS | [decorative line] [all on indented block]. Top and bottom edges trimmed; fore edges untrimmed.

COLLATION: [i]-[viii] + [1]-[264]. The same as the first edition except this edition has two blank leaves at the end. Original copyright date only. The quotation from Ecclesiastes begins with the fourth verse.

NOTE: Also issued in a variant binding of red buckram.

NOTE: The other volumes in this set are: Vol. I *IOT*; Vol. III *MWW*; Vol. IV *FTA*; Vol. V *WTN*; Vol. VI *THAHN*.

E. Reprint edition:

The Sun Also Rises | *by* | ERNEST HEMINGWAY | [publisher's device] | P. F. Collier & Son Corporation | PUBLISHERS [dot] NEW YORK

8 x 5 1/4. Published in 1942 as part of a six-volume set. Issued in dark blue cloth with the design of a quill pen and the author's name blind-stamped on the front cover. Lettered in gold with the quill design blind-stamped on the backstrip. All edges trimmed.

COLLATION: [i]-[viii] + [1]-[264]. The same as the first edition except this edition has two blank leaves at the end. Original copyright date only. Publisher's "TU" on copyright page.

PRINTING HISTORY: The first printing consisted of 5000 sets. 20,000 sets were printed in 1943; 20,000 in 1944; 10,000 in 1945; 20,000 in 1947. A total of 75,000 sets (450,000 books) were printed.

NOTE: The other volumes in this set are: *FTA, DIA, THAHN, TFC & First 49* and *FWBT*. The set was sold as an alternative part of a combination involving various reference titles, which included the Harvard Classics and the National Encyclopedia.

F. Reprint edition:

ERNEST HEMINGWAY | *The Sun* | *Also* | *Rises* | [decorative line] | [publisher's device] | GROSSET & DUNLAP | *Publishers* | NEW YORK

7 7/16 x 5 3/16. Published in [1948?], at $1.29. Issued in bluish-gray cloth, stamped in gold on the backstrip only. [Double rule] | ERNEST | HEMINGWAY | *The* | *Sun* | *Also* | *Rises* | [double rule] | [long design] | [double rule] | GROSSET | & DUNLAP | [double rule]. Top edges stained bluish-gray; bottom edges trimmed, fore edges untrimmed. Pictorial dust jacket printed in red, black, white, yellow, green, and brown.

COLLATION: [viii] + [264] pages. The same as the 1930 Grosset & Dunlap edition. Original copyright date only on the copyright page.

G. Paperback edition:
THE SUN | ALSO RISES | by | ERNEST HEMINGWAY | [publisher's device] BANTAM BOOKS | NEW YORK
6 7/16 x 4 1/4. Published by Bantam Books, Inc., in September 1949, at twenty-five cents, as No. 717. Issued in a stiff paper cover: [publisher's device] 717 [in yellow] | COULD HE LIVE WITHOUT THE POWER TO LOVE? [in yellow] | Ernest Hemingway [in script, in white] | THE SUN ALSO RISES [in orange] | "You gave more than | your life," the Colonel | had said. It was a rotten | way to be wounded. [in white] | [illustrative drawing by Ken Riley] | A BANTAM BOOK, Complete and Unabridged [in yellow]. All edges stained red.
COLLATION: [i]-[vi] + 1-[218], as follows: [i] blurb about the book; [ii] *About* THE COVER; [iii] title page as above; [iv] notices of publication arrangement, date of publication, copyright, and note of origin; [v] dedication; [vi] quotations; 1-212 text; [213]-[218] advertisements for other Bantam Books.
PRINTING HISTORY: Second printing, October 1949; third printing, December 1949.
NOTE: A note at the bottom of p. 212 states: "This BANTAM BOOK contains the complete text of the original edition. Not one word has been changed or omitted. . . ." However, more than ten anti-Semitic references were either changed or omitted and the derogatory term for Negro was deleted. For commentary regarding these omissions, see David A. Randall's article in *Papers of the Bibliographical Society of America*, LVI (1962), 346-353.
NOTE: A new edition was published in August 1954, at thirty-five cents, as Bantam Giant No. A 1249. 7 x 4 1/8. 202 pages. Issued in blue stiff paper covers, printed in black and white, with an illustrative drawing on the front cover. The anti-Semitic references, which were changed or omitted from the first Bantam edition, were replaced as they appear in the first Scribner edition.
NOTE: The covers were changed for the fifth printing, in April 1955, to gray with black and red lettering and a photograph of Hemingway on the front cover.

H. Uniform edition:
[Decorative line] | ERNEST HEMINGWAY | [short graduated line, long graduated line, short graduated line] | THE SUN | ALSO RISES | *New York* | CHARLES SCRIBNER'S SONS | 1953
8 5/16 x 5 3/8. Published in April 1953, at $3.00. Issued in light brown cloth with a row of ornaments and the title blind-stamped on the front cover. Stamped in gold on the backstrip: ERNEST |

in our time

by

ernest hemingway

A GIRL IN CHICAGO: Tell us about
the French women, Hank. What are
they like?
BILL SMITH: How old are the French
women, Hank?

paris:

printed at the **three mountains press** *and for sale*
at shakespeare & company, *in the rue de l'odéon;*
london: william jackson, *took's court, cursitor street, chancery lane.*

1924

Having no faculty for
speech making and no command
of oratory nor any domination of
rhetoric I wish to thank the
administrators of the generosity of
Albert Nobel for this prize. x

No writer who knows the great
writers who did not receive the prize
can receive it other than with
humility. There is no need to
list these writers. Everyone here
may make his own list according
to his knowlege and his
conscience.

It would be impossible for me
to ask the Ambassador of my
country to read a speech in
which I said all of the
things which are in my heart.
But I will try to write them. x

Holograph page from first draft of Nobel prize
acceptance speech. Courtesy of the Rare Book
Division of the New York Public Library

HEMINGWAY | The Sun | Also Rises | SCRIBNERS. All edges trimmed.

COLLATION: [i]-[viii] + [1]-[248], as follows: [i] blank; [ii] *Books by*; [iii] half title; [iv] blank; [v] title page as above; [vi] notices of copyright, note of origin, publisher's notation; [vii] dedication; [viii] quotations; [1] divisional half title: BOOK I; [2] blank; 3-247 text; [248] blank.

PRINTING HISTORY: Reprinted with the date 1954 on the title page.

NOTE: The word "horns" was changed to the original scatological term, on p. 175 | line 18, and on p. 176 | lines 13, 17. This change has also been made in later printings of other editions.

NOTE: The brown dust jacket is printed in the uniform design, in dark blue, white, and black.

I. Student's edition:

THE SUN | ALSO RISES | BY ERNEST HEMINGWAY | CHARLES SCRIBNER'S SONS | NEW YORK

8 x 5 5/16. Published in August 1957, at $1.45. Issued in dark gray stiff paper covers. Cover: THE SUN | ALSO RISES [on yellow block] | A NOVEL BY | Ernest Hemingway [on white block] | STUDENT'S EDITION [in yellow, on solid gray block].

COLLATION: [i]-[viii] + [1]-[248]. The same as the 1953 uniform edition. The publisher's "A-8.57 [C]" appears below the copyright notes.

J. Paperback edition:

[Decorative line] | ERNEST HEMINGWAY | [short graduated line, long graduated line, short graduated line] | THE SUN | ALSO RISES | *New York* | CHARLES SCRIBNER'S SONS

8 x 5 3/8. Published in 1960, at $1.45, as No. SL 5 of the Scribner Library series. Issued in gray stiff paper covers printed in black, yellow, and white. The same pagination as the 1953 uniform edition.

K. Reprint edition:

ERNEST | HEMINGWAY | [ornament] | The Sun | Also Rises | CHARLES SCRIBNER'S SONS | *New York*

8 1/4 x 5 1/2. Published in July 1966 as part of a three-volume set which was offered as an introductory selection by the Literary Guild of America, Inc. Issued in dark blue cloth. Stamped on the front cover: THE | SUN ALSO | RISES [title in gold] | [broken rule, in bright blue] | [design of a quill pen, in silver] | [author's signature, in silver]. Backstrip, reading downwards: THE SUN ALSO RISES [top line, in gold] | HEMINGWAY [bottom line, in silver] | [horizontal rule, in bright blue] | SCRIBNERS [horizontal, in gold]. Top and bottom edges trimmed, fore edges untrimmed. Light blue endpapers.

COLLATION: [i]-[viii] + [1]-[248], as follows: [i] half title; [ii] blank; [iii] title page as above; [iv] notices of copyright, reservation of rights, note of origin; [v] dedication; [vi] blank; [vii] quotations; [viii] blank; [1] divisional half title: BOOK I; [2] blank; [3]-247 text; [248] blank.

NOTE: The other two volumes in this set are *FTA* and *FWBT*.

7 Men Without Women

A. First edition:

MEN | WITHOUT WOMEN | By | ERNEST HEMINGWAY | [design: silhouette of a white bull charging, in a black circle] | NEW YORK | CHARLES SCRIBNER'S SONS | 1927

7 7/16 x 5 3/16. Published October 14, 1927, at $2.00. The first printing consisted of 7650 copies. Issued in smooth black cloth with gold paper labels, stamped in black, on the front cover and backstrip. Backstrip label: [triple rule] | MEN | WITHOUT | WOMEN | [ornament] | ERNEST | HEMINGWAY | [ornament] | SCRIBNERS | [triple rule]. Front label: MEN WITHOUT | WOMEN | [three ornaments] | ERNEST HEMINGWAY. Enclosed in a triple-ruled border with a thin rule between two thick rules. Top edges stained orange; bottom edges trimmed, fore edges untrimmed. The endpapers are yellow with three deeper yellow bands, which are centered with the silhouette of a charging bull, in a yellow circle.

COLLATION: [i]-[xii] + 1-[236], as follows: [i] half title; [ii] BOOKS BY ERNEST HEMINGWAY; [iii] title page as above; [iv] notices of copyright, note of origin and printer's device; [v] dedication: TO | EVAN SHIPMAN; [vi] blank; [vii] acknowledgments; [viii] blank; [ix] CONTENTS; [x] blank; [xi] half title; [xii] blank; 1-232 text; [233]-[236] blank.

CONTENTS: The Undefeated/In Another Country/Hills Like White Elephants/The Killers/Che Ti Dice La Patria?/Fifty Grand/A Simple Enquiry/Ten Indians/A Canary for One/An Alpine Idyll/ A Pursuit Race/To-day Is Friday/Banal Story/Now I Lay Me.

PREVIOUS PUBLICATION: Ten of the fourteen stories were previously published. "The Undefeated" first appeared in English in *This Quarter*, 1 (Autumn-Winter 1925-1926), and also appeared in *The Best Short Stories of 1926*, ed. Edward J. O'Brien, New York, 1926. "In Another Country" and "A Canary for One" appeared in *Scribner's Magazine*, LXXXI (April 1927). "Hills Like White Elephants" first appeared in *transition*, v (Aug. 1927). "The Killers" first appeared in *Scribner's Magazine*, LXXXI (March 1927). "Che Ti Dice La Patria?" appeared as an article in *New Republic*, L (May 18, 1927), under the title "Italy, 1927." "Fifty Grand" first appeared in the *Atlantic*, CXL (July 1927). "An Alpine Idyll" was originally published in the anthology *American Caravan*, ed. Van Wyck Brooks *et al.*, New York, September 1927. "Today Is Friday" was originally published by The As Stable Publications, Englewood, N.J., in 1926. "Banal Story" first appeared in the *Little Review*, XII (Spring-Summer 1926). The four previously unpublished stories are: "A Simple Enquiry," "Ten Indians," "A Pursuit Race," and "Now I Lay Me."

ACKNOWLEDGMENTS on p. [vii]: Some of these stories were first published | in the following periodicals: *The American | Caravan, The Atlantic Monthly, The Little | Review, The New Republic, La Nouvelle | Revue Française, This Quarter, Der Quer- | schnitt, Scribner's Magazine, Transition.*

NOTE: The original dust jacket was tan, with black lettering and three plain orange bands across the front. [In the second printing, excerpts from reviews appear on the top and bottom bands.] The blurb on the front flap contains two errors: there are fourteen stories, not "thirteen" stories in this volume, and only four of them are previously unpublished, not "six."

NOTE: There were no typographical changes or corrections made in the second printing. However, it was printed on thinner paper. The first edition was printed "on 80 pound stock with the exception of 2200 copies in which 70 pound stock was used in the printing of 128 pages. . . . The first edition copies weigh 15½ ounces, or in the case of the 2200 copies . . . about 15 ounces." The second printing was "on 65 pound stock and weighs between 13 and 14 ounces." [See *Cohn's Bibliography*, p. 29.]

PRINTING HISTORY: Reprinted, with the date appearing on the title page, in 1928, 1932, and 1943.

B. Reprint edition:

Men Without Women, published by Peter Smith, New York, 1931, at $1.00. 222 pages. Note: This book has not been examined by the bibliographer.

C. Reprint edition:

ERNEST HEMINGWAY | [wavy line] | MEN | WITHOUT WOMEN | [design of a rising sun] | SUN RISE EDITION | *Volume Three* | [wavy line] | *CHARLES SCRIBNER'S SONS* | NEW YORK

7 7/8 x 5 3/8. Published in May 1938 in a six-volume set, which sold for $15.00. 3020 sets were printed. Issued in blue buckram with the author's signature blind-stamped on the front cover. Stamped in gold on the backstrip: [decorative line] | HEMINGWAY | [short rule] | MEN | WITHOUT | WOMEN | III | [decorative line] [all on indented block] | [design] | [decorative line] | THE | SUN RISE | EDITION | [decorative line] [all on indented block] | [design] |

[decorative line] | SCRIBNERS | [decorative line] [all on indented line]. Top and bottom edges trimmed, fore edges untrimmed.

COLLATION: [i]-[xii] + 1-[236]. The same as the first edition except in this edition the list of books by Hemingway on p. [ii] has been omitted. Original copyright date only.

NOTE: Issued in a variant binding of red buckram.

NOTE: The other volumes in this set are: Vol. I *IOT*; Vol. II *SAR*; Vol. IV *FTA*; Vol. V *WTN*; Vol. VI *THAHN*.

D. Reprint edition:

MEN | WITHOUT WOMEN | By | ERNEST HEMINGWAY | [publisher's device for Forum Books] | THE WORLD PUBLISH-ING COMPANY | CLEVELAND AND NEW YORK

8 x 5 1/2. Published in November 1944, at $1.00, as No. F-83 of the Forum Books series. Issued in smooth black cloth, lettered and ruled in black on an indented gold block on the front cover and backstrip. The lettering is identical to that on the first edition; it is enclosed in a double-ruled border. The publisher's device and WORLD are stamped in gold on the lower backstrip. Bottom edges trimmed, fore edges untrimmed; top edges stained red.

COLLATION: [i]-[xii] + 1-[236]. The same as the first edition except in this edition the list of books by Hemingway, on p. [ii], is omitted.

PRINTING HISTORY: Reprinted in January 1945 and December 1945.

NOTE: The dust jacket, designed by Leo Manso, is blue with gray and white lettering on black and red backgrounds.

E. Illustrated edition:

ERNEST HEMINGWAY | Men Without Women | [drawing of two men seated at a counter] | ILLUSTRATED BY John Groth | With a Note on the Author by the Artist | CLEVELAND AND NEW YORK | THE WORLD PUBLISHING COMPANY

7 1/4 x 4 7/8. Published in October 1946, at $1.00, as No. L-19 of The Living Library series. Issued in red cloth, lettered in gold with a drawing stamped in black on the front cover. Cover: [drawing] | Men | Without | Women. Backstrip: HEMINGWAY [in gold, on black block] | Men | Without | Women [lettered in black, on gold block] | [publisher's device, in black and gold]. All edges trimmed; top edges stained red. Yellow endpapers.

COLLATION: [1]-164, as follows: [1]-[2] free endpaper; [3] publisher's device | THE LIVING LIBRARY | GENERAL EDITOR: Carl Van Doren; [4] blank; [5] title page as above; [6] FIRST PRINT-ING OCTOBER 1946, publisher's "WPC," notices of copyright and note of origin; [7] dedication; [8] blank; [9] Contents; [10] blank; 11-16 Foreword by John Groth; [17] acknowledgments; [18] blank; 19-164 text.

NOTE: A NOTE ON ERNEST HEMINGWAY by John Groth is on pp. 11-16. A drawing of Hemingway, dated September 8, 1944, appears on p. 11.

NOTE: The dust jacket is yellow, with a drawing by Groth on the front cover, in red and black.

F. Uniform edition:
MEN | WITHOUT WOMEN | By | ERNEST HEMINGWAY | [design: silhouette of a white bull charging, in a black circle] | NEW YORK | CHARLES SCRIBNER'S SONS | 1955
7 3/8 x 5 1/8. Published in 1955, at $3.00. Issued in gray cloth. Stamped in gold on the front cover: [ornament] MEN WITHOUT WOMEN [ornament]. Backstrip: the title is stamped in gold on a black block; the author's name and the publisher's name are stamped in black on gold blocks. Top and bottom edges trimmed, fore edges untrimmed. The same pagination as the first edition.

NOTE: The gray dust jacket is printed in the uniform design, in red, white, gray, and black.

8 A Farewell to Arms

A. First edition:
A FAREWELL TO ARMS | By | ERNEST HEMINGWAY | NEW YORK | CHARLES SCRIBNER'S SONS | 1929
7 3/8 x 5 3/16. Published September 27, 1929, at $2.50. The first printing consisted of 31,050 copies. Issued in smooth black cloth with gold paper labels, lettered and ruled in black, on the front cover and backstrip. Backstrip label: [triple rule] | A | FARE-WELL | TO | ARMS | [ornament] | ERNEST | HEMINGWAY | [ornament] | SCRIBNERS | [triple rule]. Front label: A FARE-WELL | TO ARMS | [three ornaments] | ERNEST HEMING-WAY. Enclosed in a triple-ruled border with a thin rule between two thick rules. Top and bottom edges trimmed, fore edges untrimmed.

COLLATION: [i]-[x] + [1]-[358], as follows: [i]-[iii] blank; [iv] BOOKS BY ERNEST HEMINGWAY; [v] half title; [vi] blank; [vii] title page as above; [viii] notice of copyright, note of origin, and printer's device; [ix] dedication: TO | G. A. PFEIFFER; [x] blank; [1] divisional half title: A FAREWELL TO ARMS | [short rule] | *BOOK I*; [2] blank; 3-355 text; [356]-[358] blank.

PREVIOUS PUBLICATION: *FTA* first appeared serialized in *Scribner's Magazine*, LXXXV (May-June 1929); LXXXVI (July-Oct. 1929). There were no major textual revisions made for the book publication. The deletion form ("———— ————") is the same as in the magazine. In a few instances the words were inserted. See James B. Meriwether's "The Dashes in Hemingway's *A Farewell to Arms*," *Papers of the Bibliographical Society of America*, LVII (Oct.-Dec. 1964), 449-457.

NOTE: The dedicatee was the uncle of Pauline Pfeiffer Hemingway.

NOTE: The white dust jacket is printed in blue and orange. A drawing by "Cleon" is on the front cover. The front flap carries a blurb on the book in which the name of the heroine, Catherine Barkley, is misspelled "Katharine Barclay."

PRINTING HISTORY: Reprinted twice in September, once in October, and three times in November 1929. By February 14, 1930, sales stood at 79,251 [see *Baker*, p. 301]. *Publishers' Weekly*, CLXXX (July 10, 1961), 49, reported that "*A Farewell to Arms* has sold 1,383,000 copies."

NOTE: The second printing contains a legal disclaimer on p. [x]. This note, inserted at Hemingway's request, states: None of the characters in this book is a living | person, nor are the units or military organiza- | tions mentioned actual units or organizations. | — E. H. This note, which did not arrive in time for the first printing, was omitted after the second printing. [See *Cohn's Bibliography*, p. 31.] See also the "Bastard Note," a limited edition of the foundry proof of this disclaimer (F150).

NOTE: *FTA* appeared on "*The Bookman's* Monthly Score" of bestsellers for the first time in February 1930, in seventh place. From April through June 1930, it was in third place; and it appeared for the last time in July, in ninth place.

NOTE: *FTA* was adapted by Laurence Stallings and produced by A. H. Woods at the National Theatre, in New York. The play opened on September 22, 1930, and ran for twenty-four performances.

NOTE: For "The Original Conclusion to *A Farewell to Arms*," see *Ernest Hemingway: Critiques of Four Major Novels*, ed. Carlos Baker, New York, 1962, p. 75 (B59).

B. Limited edition:
A FAREWELL TO ARMS | BY | ERNEST HEMINGWAY | [ornament, in bluish-green] NEW YORK | CHARLES SCRIBNER'S SONS | 1929 [title page enclosed in a light bluish-green decorative border]

9 1/16 x 6 1/16. Published September 27, 1929, at $10.00, in a limited edition of 510 numbered copies. Issued in light bluish-green boards with white vellum backstrip and corners. A black leather label on the backstrip is lettered and decorated in gold: A | FAREWELL | TO | ARMS | [ornament] | ERNEST | HEMINGWAY [all enclosed in a decorative border]. All edges untrimmed. Light bluish-green endpapers. Issued in a decorative gold, black,

and red board slip-case with a red paper label, lettered and ruled in black, on the front.

COLLATION: [i]-[x] + [1]-[356], as follows: [i] blank; [ii] colophon: THIS EDITION IS LIMITED TO FIVE | HUNDRED AND TEN COPIES OF WHICH | FIVE HUNDRED ARE FOR SALE AND | TEN FOR PRESENTATION | No. ———; [iii] half title; [iv] blank; [v] title page as above; [vi] notice of copyright, note of origin, printer's device; [vii] dedication; [viii] blank; [ix] half title; [x] blank; [1] divisional half title; [2] blank; 3-355 text; [356] blank.

NOTE: This edition was signed by the author and issued simultaneously with the first regular edition.

c. Reprint edition:

A FAREWELL TO | ARMS | BY | ERNEST HEMINGWAY | *COPYRIGHT EDITION* | [rule] | BERNHARD TAUCHNITZ [slanted line] LEIPZIG | 1930

6 1/2 x 4 1/2. Published in June 1930, at 2 marks, as Vol. 4935 of the Tauchnitz Editions. Issued in cream-colored heavy paper wrappers, lettered and ruled in black.

COLLATION: [1]-320 + 32, as follows: [1] half title: COLLECTION OF BRITISH AND | AMERICAN AUTHORS | VOL. 4935; [2] blank; [3] title page as above; [4] legal disclaimer; [5]-320 text [printer's imprint at the bottom of p. 320]; 32 pages of advertisements for other Tauchnitz Editions.

NOTE: The price on the backstrip varies: M. 2 or Fs. 12.50.

NOTE: A note on the back cover states that this edition is published with Continental copyright acquired directly from the author or his representative.

d. Reprint edition:

A Farewell | to Arms | By | ERNEST HEMINGWAY | *Author of* "The Sun Also Rises" | [drawing by Cleon] | *Grosset & Dunlap, Publishers* | *by arrangement with* | CHARLES SCRIBNER'S SONS [title page enclosed in a decorative red border within a double-ruled red border, with a thin inner rule and a thick outer rule]

7 3/4 x 5 1/4. Published in August 1931, at $1.00, in the Novels of Distinction series. Issued in black cloth with red paper labels, ruled and lettered in black, on the front cover and backstrip. The lettering is identical to the labels on the first edition except that on the backstrip GROSSET | & DUNLAP has been substituted for SCRIBNERS. Publisher's device blind-stamped on lower right corner of the front cover. Bottom and fore edges untrimmed; top edges stained red.

COLLATION: [1]-[viii] + [1]-[358], as follows: [i]-[ii] blank; [iii] half title; [iv] blank; [v] title page as above; [vi] notice of copyright, note of origin, printing history of the Scribner edition only; [vii] dedication; [viii] blank; [1] divisional half title; [2] blank; 3-355 text; [356]-[358] blank.

NOTE: The dust jacket is printed in black, silver, and red. A list of the Novels of Distinction appear on the front and back flaps.

NOTE: *SAR* is also in this series in identical binding. See (A6c).

E. Reprint edition:
A | FAREWELL TO ARMS | [long rule] | BY | ERNEST HEMINGWAY | [long rule] | INTRODUCTION BY | FORD MADOX FORD | [long rule] | [publisher's device] | [long rule] | BENNETT A. CERF [dot] DONALD S. KLOPFER | THE MODERN LIBRARY | NEW YORK [title page enclosed in a double-ruled border, with a thin inner rule and a thick outer rule]
6 1/2 x 4 1/4. Published May 25, 1932, at ninety-five cents, as No. 19 of The Modern Library of the World's Best Books. The first printing consisted of 7000 copies. Issued in four shades of cloth: red, green, gray, and blue. The publisher's device is stamped in gold on the front cover, which is enclosed in a blind-ruled border. Stamped in gold on the backstrip: A | FAREWELL | TO ARMS | [rule] | HEMINGWAY | [design] | MODERN | LIBRARY. All edges trimmed. Top edges stained to match the color of the cloth. Printed endpapers.

COLLATION: [i]-xx + [1]-[364], as follows: [i] half title: THE MODERN LIBRARY | OF THE WORLD'S BEST BOOKS | [double rule] | A FAREWELL TO ARMS; [ii] publisher's note regarding list of Modern Library titles; [iii] title page as above; [iv] notices of copyright, First Modern Library Edition | 1932, note regarding *SAR* in this series, note of origin, and binder's note; [v] dedication; [vi] blank; [vii] half title; [viii] blank; ix-xx INTRODUCTION by Ford Madox Ford; [1] divisional half title; [2] blank; 3-355 text; [356] blank; [357]-[361] list of Modern Library titles; [362]-[364] blank.

NOTE: Ford Madox Ford's introduction, on pp. ix-xx, is dated: Paris, *January*, 1932.

NOTE: The white dust jacket is printed in red and black.

NOTE: This edition was reissued, date unknown, at $1.25. 7 x 4 3/4. Issued in three shades of cloth: brown, green, and blue. Stamped in gold on colored blocks on the front cover and backstrip. Top edges stained to match the color of the binding. Printed endpapers. The revised copyright page states that Random House is the publisher of the Modern Library. The original copyright date only is given.

F. Reprint edition:
A FAREWELL | TO ARMS | By | ERNEST HEMINGWAY | GROSSET & DUNLAP | Publishers [dot] *New York* | BY ARRANGEMENT WITH CHARLES SCRIBNER'S SONS

8 x 5 1/4. Published in 1932, at seventy-five cents. Issued in red cloth, stamped in black on the front cover and backstrip. Cover: A FAREWELL | TO ARMS | Ernest Hemingway. Backstrip: A | FAREWELL | TO | ARMS | ERNEST | HEMINGWAY | GROS-SET | & DUNLAP. All edges trimmed; top edges stained black.

COLLATION: [i]-[viii] + [1]-[358]. The same as the 1931 Grosset & Dunlap edition. Original copyright date only. Publisher's "CL" on copyright page.

NOTE: The red dust jacket is printed in red, white, and black.

NOTE: Also issued with black and white pictorial endpapers and the following note on the title page, between the author's name and the publisher's name: *With scenes from the | Paramount Production | with Helen Hayes | and Gary Cooper.*

G. Reprint edition:

ERNEST HEMINGWAY | [wavy line] | A FAREWELL | TO ARMS | [design of a rising sun] | SUN RISE EDITION | *Volume Four* | [wavy line] | *CHARLES SCRIBNER'S SONS* | NEW YORK

7 7/8 x 5 3/8. Published in May 1938 in a six-volume set, which sold for $15.00. 3020 sets were printed. Issued in blue buckram with the author's signature blind-stamped on the front cover. Stamped in gold on the backstrip: [decorative line] | HEMINGWAY | [short rule] | A | FAREWELL | TO ARMS | IV | [decorative line] [all on indented block] | [design] | [decorative line] | THE | SUN RISE | EDITION | [decorative line] [all on indented block] | [design] | [decorative line] | SCRIBNERS | [decorative line] [all on indented block]. Top and bottom edges trimmed; fore edges untrimmed.

COLLATION: [i]-[x] + [1]-[358]. The same as the first edition except that the list of books by Hemingway, on p. [iv], has been omitted from this edition. Original copyright date and reprint dates of the first six impressions on the copyright page.

NOTE: Issued in a variant binding of red buckram.

NOTE: The other volumes in this set are: Vol. I *IOT*; Vol. II *SAR*; Vol. III *MWW*; Vol. V *WTN*; Vol. VI *THAHN*.

H. Reprint edition:

A Farewell to Arms, published by Grosset & Dunlap, New York, in October 1940, at fifty cents, as one of the Madison Square Books. 370 pages. Hardcover edition with dust jacket. Note: This book has not been examined by the bibliographer.

I. Reprint edition:

A Farewell to Arms | *By* | ERNEST HEMINGWAY | [publisher's device] | P. F. Collier & Son Corporation | PUBLISHERS [dot] NEW YORK

8 x 5 1/4. Published in 1942 as part of a six-volume set. Issued in dark blue cloth with the design of a quill pen and the author's

name blind-stamped on the front cover. Lettered in gold with the quill design blind-stamped on the backstrip. All edges trimmed.
COLLATION: [i]-[viii] + [1]-[356], as follows: [i]-[ii] blank; [iii] half title; [iv] blank; [v] title page as above; [vi] notice of copyright, original copyright date only, publisher's "TC"; [vii] dedication; [viii] blank; [1] divisional half title; [2] blank; 3-355 text; [356] blank.
NOTE: For the printing history of this set, see *SAR* (A6e).
NOTE: The other volumes in this set are: *SAR, DIA, THAHN, TFC & First 49*, and *FWBT*. The set was sold as an alternative part of a combination involving various reference titles, which included the Harvard Classics and the National Encyclopedia.

J. Illustrated edition:
A | FAREWELL | TO ARMS | BY | ERNEST HEMINGWAY | WITH ILLUSTRATIONS BY | DANIEL RASMUSSON | *CHARLES SCRIBNER'S SONS, NEW YORK* | *1948*
9 3/16 x 6 1/4. Published November 15, 1948, at $6.50. The first printing consisted of 5300 copies. Issued in gray cloth with a cream-colored paper label, lettered and ruled in dark blue, on the back-strip only. Backstrip label: [triple rule] | A | FAREWELL | TO ARMS | ERNEST HEMINGWAY | WITH ILLUSTRATIONS BY | DANIEL RASMUSSON | [triple rule] | *SCRIBNERS* | [triple rule] [all triple rules have a thick rule between two thin rules]. Top and bottom edges trimmed, fore edges untrimmed. Light gray endpapers. Issued in a gray board slip-case with a cream-colored label, printed in dark blue, on one side only.
COLLATION: [i]-[xii] + [1]-[364] including 29 wash drawings, as follows: [i] half title; [ii] blank; [iii] title page as above; [iv] notices of copyright, note of origin, reservation of rights, Scribner's "A" and printer's device; [v] dedication; [vi] blank; vii-xi INTRODUCTION by Hemingway; [xii] blank; [1] divisional half title: BOOK | I | [ornament]; [2] illustration; 3-363 text; [364] blank.
NOTE: Hemingway's Introduction, on pp. vii-xi, is dated: Finca Vigia, San Francisco de Paula, Cuba | June 30, 1948.
NOTE: Issued in the same gray cloth binding, with an orange paper label, printed in orange, black, and white, on the backstrip only. Issued in a gray board slip-case with white paper labels, printed in black and orange, with an illustration from the book, in black and white, on both sides of the slip-case. Number of copies and date issued are unknown.
NOTE: Reissued, after 1954, at $3.75. Issued in a red dust jacket with an illustration from the book, in black and white, on the front cover.

K. Paperback edition:

A | FAREWELL | TO ARMS | ERNEST HEMINGWAY | [publisher's device] | BANTAM BOOKS NEW YORK

6 5/16 x 4 1/8. Published by Bantam Books, Inc. in January 1949, at twenty-five cents, as No. 467. Issued in stiff paper covers, printed in black and red, with an illustrative scene by C. C. Beall on the front cover. All edges stained red.

COLLATION: [i]-[vi] + 1-[278], as follows: [i] blurb on the book; [ii] note regarding the cover; [iii] title page as above; [iv] notice of copyright, Published January 1949, and note of origin; [v] half title; [vi] blank; 1-277 text; [278] note on the author.

PRINTING HISTORY: Reprinted April 1951.

NOTE: Reissued in a new edition, in August 1954, at thirty-five cents, as Bantam Giant No. A 1240. Title page: A | FAREWELL | TO | ARMS | [design of leaves] | by | Ernest Hemingway |.

7 x 4 3/16. Issued in dark blue stiff paper covers, printed in orange, black, and white on the front cover. All edges stained pale orange.

COLLATION: [i]-[vi] + 1-[250]. Text on pp. 1-249. Printing history of all editions on the copyright page.

NOTE: Reissued in April 1955 in black stiff paper covers, printed in yellow and white, with a photograph of Hemingway by A. E. Hotchner on the front cover. All edges stained yellow. Same collation as the 1954 Bantam paperback edition.

L. Reprint edition:

MODERN STANDARD AUTHORS | A FAREWELL | TO ARMS | BY | ERNEST HEMINGWAY | WITH AN INTRODUCTION BY | ROBERT PENN WARREN | CHARLES SCRIBNER'S SONS | NEW YORK CHICAGO ATLANTA SAN FRANCISCO | 1949

8 1/4 x 5 1/2. Published May 16, 1949, at $1.75, in the Modern Standard Authors series. The first printing consisted of 5000 copies. Issued in a green cloth backstrip over light blue covers. The author's signature is stamped in silver on the green cloth section of the front cover. Stamped in silver on the backstrip: [thick rule] | A | FAREWELL | TO | ARMS | [ornament] | ERNEST | HEMINGWAY | [ornament] | *SCRIBNERS* | [thick rule]. All edges trimmed.

COLLATION: 1 leaf + [i]-[xxxviii] + [1]-[344], as follows: [blank leaf]; [i] half title; [ii] blank; [iii] title page as above; [iv] notices of copyright, note of origin, Scribner's "A," and printer's device; [v] dedication; [vi] blank; vii-xxxvi INTRODUCTION by Robert Penn Warren; xxxvi-xxxvii SUGGESTED READINGS; [xxxviii] blank; [1] divisional half title: *BOOK ONE*; [2] blank; 3-[343] text; [344] blank.

PRINTING HISTORY: Reprinted with 1953 on the title page.

NOTE: Robert Penn Warren's Introduction, on pp. vii-xxxvi, was reprinted in *Three Novels*. See (A29).

NOTE: Reissued in variant bindings of green cloth backstrip over gray covers, stamped in silver; and black cloth backstrip over light green covers, stamped in dark green.

M. Uniform edition:

A FAREWELL | TO | ARMS | BY | ERNEST HEMINGWAY | NEW YORK | CHARLES SCRIBNER'S SONS | 1953

8 3/16 x 5 1/2. Published March 4, 1953, at $3.00. Issued in rose-red cloth with a row of ornaments and the title blind-stamped on the front cover. Stamped in gold on the backstrip: ERNEST |HEMINGWAY | A Farewell | to Arms | SCRIBNERS. All edges trimmed.

COLLATION: [i]-[viii] + [1]-[344], as follows: [i] blank; [ii] Books by; [iii] half title; [iv] blank; [v] title page as above; [vi] notice of copyright, note of origin, reservation of rights, and printer's device; [vii] dedication; [viii] blank; [1] divisional half title: *BOOK ONE*; [2] blank; 3-[343] text; [344] blank.

NOTE: The red dust jacket is printed in the uniform design, in dark blue, white, and black.

PRINTING HISTORY: Reprinted in September 1953 and December 1953. Reissued with 1954 on the title page.

N. Paperback edition:

A FAREWELL | TO ARMS | BY | ERNEST HEMINGWAY | CHARLES SCRIBNER'S SONS | NEW YORK

8 x 5 3/8. Published in 1962, at $1.65, as No. SL 61 of the Scribner Library series. Issued in gray stiff paper covers, printed in black, red, and white. The same pagination as the 1953 uniform edition, except that the list of books by Hemingway is on p. [iv] and p. [ii] is blank.

O. Reprint edition:

ERNEST | HEMINGWAY | [ornament] | A Farewell | to Arms | CHARLES SCRIBNER'S SONS | *New York*

8 1/4 x 5 1/2. Published in July 1966 as part of a three-volume set which was offered as an introductory selection by the Literary Guild of America, Inc. Issued in dark blue cloth. Stamped on the front cover: A | FAREWELL | TO ARMS [title in gold] | [broken rule, in bright blue] | [design of a quill pen, in silver] | [author's signature, in silver]. Backstrip, reading downward: A FAREWELL TO ARMS [top line, in gold] | HEMINGWAY [bottom line, in silver] | [horizontal rule, in bright blue] | SCRIBNERS [horizontal, in gold]. Top and bottom edges trimmed, fore edges untrimmed. Light blue endpapers.

COLLATION: [i]-[vi] + [1]-314, as follows: [i] half title; [ii] blank; [iii] title page; [iv] notices of copyright, reservation of rights, note of origin; [v] dedication; [vi] blank; [1] divisional half title: BOOK I; [2] blank; [3]-314 text.

NOTE: The other two volumes in this set are *SAR* and *FWBT*.

9 Introduction to Kiki of Montparnasse

ERNEST HEMINGWAY | *Introduction* | *to* | KIKI of MONT-PARNASSE | [ornament] | NEW YORK, 1929 | EDWARD W. TITUS | *at the Sign of the Black Manikin*

9 1/2 x 6 1/2. This pamphlet was published January 22, 1930, in an edition of 25 copies to secure copyright. Issued in white paper covers of the same weight as the leaves. The front cover serves as the title page. All edges trimmed. Wire stitched.

COLLATION: [1]-[8], as follows: [1] cover-title as shown above; [2] notice of copyright: *Copyrighted, 1930, by* | EDWARD W. TITUS | *New York*; [3]-[6] text; [7]-[8] blank.

NOTE: This introduction appeared in *Kiki's Memoirs*, Paris, 1930. See (B7).

10 Death in the Afternoon

A. First edition:

DEATH IN THE | AFTERNOON | By | Ernest Hemingway | [silhouette of a black bull] | CHARLES SCRIBNER'S SONS | NEW YORK [dot] LONDON | 1932

9 1/4 x 6 3/8. Published September 23, 1932, at $3.50. The first printing consisted of 10,300 copies. Issued in smooth black cloth with the author's signature stamped in gold on the front cover. Gold lettering, ruling, and decoration cover the entire length of the backstrip: [thick rule] | [decorative band] | [thick rule] | DEATH | IN THE | AFTERNOON | [thick rule] | [double decorative band] | [thick rule] | ERNEST | HEMINGWAY | [thick double rule] | SCRIBNERS | [thick double rule]. All edges trimmed.

COLLATION: [i]-[xiv] + 1-[518] including 81 photographs, as follows: [i] blank; [ii] BOOKS BY; [iii] half title; [iv] blank; [v] blank; [vi] frontispiece, in color; [imprinted on verso of tissue guard: THE BULLFIGHTER | BY | JUAN GRIS]; [vii] title page as above; [viii] notice of copyright, note of origin, Scribner's "A," and printer's device; [ix] dedication: TO | PAULINE; [x] blank; [xi] CONTENTS; [xii] blank; [xiii] half title; [xiv] blank; 1-278 text; [279] ILLUSTRATIONS; 280-[407] photographs with descriptive letterpress on versos facing plates; 408 photograph credits to Vandel and Rodero; [an unnumbered leaf, containing divisional half title:

31

AN EXPLANATORY GLOSSARY with verso blank, not included in the pagination]; [409]-[493] glossary; [494] blank; 495-501 SOME REACTIONS OF A FEW INDIVIDUALS TO THE INTEGRAL SPANISH BULLFIGHT; [502] blank; [503]-[506] A SHORT ESTIMATE OF THE AMERICAN, SIDNEY FRANKLIN, AS A MATADOR; 507-515 DATES ON WHICH BULLFIGHTS WILL ORDINARILY BE HELD IN SPAIN, FRANCE, MEXICO, AND CENTRAL AND SOUTH AMERICA; [516] blank; [517] BIBLIOGRAPHICAL NOTE (signed "E. H.") ; [518] blank.

NOTE: The painting, "TOROS," on the dust jacket cover is by Roberto Domingo. The dust jacket is pale orange with black lettering on white blocks.

NOTE: "A Natural History of the Dead," from Ch. XII, was included, with revisions, as a short story in *WTN*. "A Short Estimate of the American, Sidney Franklin, as a Matador" was reprinted in *Bullfighter From Brooklyn* by Sidney Franklin, New York, 1952, pp. 241-245.

NOTE: In 1933, Hemingway described *DIA* as "a rather technical book, which sold, or rather was offered for sale, at $3.50." [See footnote on p. 137, *WTN*.] Carlos Baker has pointed out that the depression caused the low sale of both *DIA* and *GHOA*. [See *Baker*, p. 302.]

NOTE: Three footnotes, on pp. 6, 55, 184, have been retained in later editions.

NOTE: Prior to the publication of the book Scribner's printed a dummy in an issue of twenty-five copies. Title page: DEATH IN THE | AFTERNOON | By | Ernest Hemingway | CHARLES SCRIBNER'S SONS | NEW YORK [dot] LONDON | 1932 9 x 6 1/2. Issued in black cloth with the author's signature stamped in gold on the front cover. Decorations and lettering in gold, on an orange background, on the backstrip, which owing to the narrowness of the dummy appears on the back cover.

COLLATION: [i]-[viii] + 1-8 + 4 plates, as follows: [i] half title; [ii] Books by; [iii] blank; [iv] frontispiece, in color; [tissue guard imprinted: THE BULLFIGHTER | BY | JUAN GRIS]; [v] title page as above; [vi] notice of copyright, note of origin, Scribner's "A" and printer's device; [vii] half title; [viii] blank; 1-8 text; 4 "aquatone" photographs.

NOTE: The type-face on the title page differs from that used on the title page in the book.

B. Reprint edition:
DEATH | IN THE | AFTERNOON | *Ernest Hemingway* | ILLUSTRATED | [publisher's device] | [long rule] | HALCYON HOUSE | NEW YORK | The Bullfighter *by Juan Gris, frontispiece*

9 1/8 x 6 3/8. Published by Halcyon House, a division of Blue Ribbon Books, Inc., in October 1937, at $1.89. Issued in shimmery black cloth with the author's signature stamped in gold on the front cover. Stamped in black on the backstrip: [zig-zag line, in gold] | DEATH | IN THE | AFTERNOON | Ernest | Hemingway [name in script] [all on gold background] | [design of a red cape, crossed gold swords and black pics] | [zig-zag line, in gold] | HALCYON HOUSE [in gold] | [zig-zag line, in gold]. All edges trimmed; top edges stained red. Blue endpapers.

COLLATION: [i]-[xiv] + 1-[518]. The same as the Scribner's edition, except in this edition the appendices are numbered; the leaf that precedes the Explanatory Glossary is not included in the pagination. The tissue guard is omitted. Original copyright date only.

NOTE: Printed by the Cornwall Press, Inc., Cornwall, N.Y.

c. Reprint edition:
DEATH IN THE | AFTERNOON | *by* | ERNEST HEMINGWAY | [silhouette of a black bull] | P. F. Collier & Son Corporation | PUBLISHERS [dot] NEW YORK
8 x 5 1/4. Published in 1942 as part of a six-volume set. Issued in dark blue cloth with the design of a quill pen and the author's name blind-stamped on the front cover. Lettered in gold with the quill design blind-stamped on the backstrip. All edges trimmed.

COLLATION: [i]-[x] + 1-[372], as follows: [i] half title; [ii] blank; [iii] title page as above; [iv] notice of copyright, original copyright date, publisher's "TU"; [v] dedication; [vi] blank; [vii] CONTENTS; [viii] blank; [ix] half title; [x] blank; 1-278 text; [279]-[365] Explanatory Glossary; [366] blank; [367]-[370] A Short Estimate of Sidney Franklin; [371] Bibliographical Note; [372] blank.

NOTE: The frontispiece, the photographs and two of the appendices, Reactions of a Few Individuals to the Bullfight and Dates of Bullfights, were omitted from this edition.

NOTE: The other volumes in this set are: *SAR, FTA, THAHN, TFC & First 49* and *FWBT*. The set was sold as an alternative part of a combination involving various reference titles, which included the Harvard Classics and the National Encyclopedia. For the printing history, see *SAR* (A6e).

d. Reprint edition:
DEATH IN THE | AFTERNOON | By | Ernest Hemingway |[silhouette of a black bull] | CHARLES SCRIBNER'S SONS | NEW YORK [dot] LONDON | 1953
9 1/8 x 6 1/4. Published in 1953, at $6.50. Issued in smooth black cloth, stamped in gold on the backstrip only. The backstrip is identical to that of the first edition. All edges trimmed.

COLLATION: [i]-[xii] + 1-[518], as follows: [i]-[ii] blank leaf; [iii] half

33

title; [iv] blank; [v] title page as above; [vi] notice of copyright with the original copyright date only, note of origin, reservation of rights, and printer's device; [vii] dedication; [viii] blank; [ix] contents; [x] blank; [xi] half title; [xii] blank; 1-278 text; [279]-408 illustrations (photographs); [409]-[493] glossary; [494] blank; 495-501 reactions by individuals to the bullfight; [502] blank; [503]-[506] short estimate of Sidney Franklin; 507-515 dates of bullfights; [516] blank; [517] BIBLIOGRAPHICAL NOTE; [518] blank.

NOTE: The dust jacket is printed in pink, black, and white.

NOTE: Reissued in 1961, at $10.00. The dust jacket is printed in black, yellow, and white, with the painting from the original dust jacket on the front cover, and a portrait of Hemingway by Russell E. Roberts on the back cover.

11 God Rest You Merry Gentlemen

A. First limited edition:
GOD REST YOU | MERRY | GENTLEMEN | [ornament] | ERNEST | HEMINGWAY | [ornament] | [small crown] | HOUSE OF BOOKS, LTD. | NEW YORK [dot] 1933

7 1/2 x 5. Published by Louis Henry Cohn in mid-April 1933, at $2.75. The first and only limited edition consisted of 300 copies. Issued in red cloth, stamped in gilt on the front cover and in gold on the backstrip. Cover: GOD REST YOU | MERRY | GENTLE-MEN | [ornament] | ERNEST | HEMINGWAY | [ornament]. Back-strip, reading upward: GOD REST YOU MERRY GENTLE-MEN [dot] HEMINGWAY. Tan paper throughout. Stitched with beige thread. Top and bottom edges trimmed; fore edges untrimmed from front to center stitching. Endpapers untrimmed.

COLLATION: [1]-[20], as follows: [1] blank; [2] THIS FIRST EDITION IS LIMITED TO | THREE HUNDRED COPIES. | THIS IS   ; [3] title page as above; [4] Copyright 1933 by Ernest Hemingway | (legal disclaimer); [5]-[16] text; [17] blank; [18] colophon: THIS IS NUMBER TWO OF | The Crown Octavos [Gothic] PUBLISHED BY HOUSE OF BOOKS, LTD. | 555 MADISON AVENUE, NEW YORK | AND MADE BY THE WALPOLE | PRINTING OFFICE | [small crown]; [19]-[20] blank.

NOTE: This is the first appearance of this short story, which was published, with some revisions, later in the same year in *WTN*.

NOTE: This book was designed by Peter Beilenson of the Walpole Printing Company.

NOTE: Louis Henry Cohn later noted that: "With all the banks in the United States closed, I sent out a press release to a few newspapers and announcements to a few book-stores and received over a thousand orders for an edition of 300 copies." [See *Avocations,* 1 (Jan. 1938), 353.]

12 Winner Take Nothing

A. First edition:

Winner Take Nothing | By | ERNEST HEMINGWAY | "Unlike all other forms of lutte or | combat the conditions are that the | winner shall take nothing; neither | his ease, nor his pleasure, nor any | notions of glory; nor, if he win far | enough, shall there be any reward | within himself." | CHARLES SCRIBNER'S SONS | NEW YORK : : : LONDON | 1933

7 5/16 x 5 1/8. Published October 27, 1933, at $2.00. The first printing consisted of 20,300 copies. Issued in smooth black cloth with gold paper labels, lettered and ruled in black, on the front cover and backstrip. Backstrip label: [triple rule] | WINNER | TAKE | NOTHING | [ornament] | ERNEST | HEMINGWAY | [ornament] | SCRIBNERS | [triple rule]. Front label: WINNER | TAKE NOTHING | [three ornaments] | ERNEST HEMING-WAY. Enclosed in a triple-ruled border with a thin rule between two thick rules. Bottom edges trimmed, fore edges untrimmed; top edges stained red.

COLLATION: [i]-[x] + [1]-[246], as follows: [i]-[ii] blank; [iii] half title; [iv] BOOKS BY; [v] title page as above; [vi] notice of copyright, note of origin, Scribner's "A," and printer's device; [vii] dedication: TO | A. MacLEISH; [viii] blank; [ix] CONTENTS; [x] blank; [1] divisional half title: AFTER THE STORM; [2] blank; 3-244 text; [245]-[246] blank.

CONTENTS: After the Storm/A Clean, Well-Lighted Place/The Light of the World/God Rest You Merry, Gentlemen/The Sea Change/ A Way You'll Never Be/The Mother of a Queen/One Reader Writes/Homage to Switzerland/A Day's Wait/A Natural History of the Dead/Wine of Wyoming/The Gambler, the Nun, and the Radio/Fathers and Sons.

PREVIOUS PUBLICATION: "After the Storm" first appeared in *Cosmopolitan,* XCII (May 1932). "A Clean, Well-Lighted Place" first appeared in *Scribner's Magazine,* XCIII (March 1933). "God Rest You Merry, Gentlemen" was first published by House of Books in April 1933. Several revisions were made for publication in this volume. A dash was substituted for a scatological term on p. 48 | line 1. Numerous commas were added, most notably in the title; the spelling of "Savior" was changed to "Saviour"; and the last sentence, on p. 48, was shortened. "The Sea Change" first appeared in *This Quarter,* IV (Dec. 1931). "Homage to Switzerland" appeared in

35

Scribner's Magazine, XCIII (April 1933). "A Natural History of the Dead" is reprinted from Ch. XII of *DIA*. In this volume the dialogue between the author and the "Old Lady" has been omitted, and the description of death by Spanish influenza has been revised. A footnote, on p. 137, states: This story was published in a rather technical book called | *Death in the Afternoon*, which sold, or rather was offered for sale, | at $3.50. It is reprinted here in case any one not caring to spend that | appreciable sum for a rather technical book should care to read it. This footnote was omitted from the *First 49* and later collections. A second footnote, regarding humanists, on p. 146, has been retained in later editions. "Wine of Wyoming" first appeared in *Scribner's Magazine*, LXXXVIII (Aug. 1930). "The Gambler, the Nun, and the Radio" appeared in *Scribner's Magazine*, XCIII (May 1933), under the title: "Give Us a Prescription, Doctor." Several revisions were made for book publication. Four references to "Portland, Oregon" were changed to "Seattle, Washington." In the magazine, the story ends: "The opiums are for before and for after." Three sentences were added to this ending in the book.

This was the first appearance of six of the fourteen stories: "The Light of the World"/"A Way You'll Never Be"/"The Mother of a Queen"/"One Reader Writes"/"A Day's Wait"/and "Fathers and Sons."

NOTE: "The title derives from the epigraph of the book. This epigraph, ostensibly drawn from an antique book of rules for gaming, was actually written by Hemingway himself." [See *Baker*, p. 142.]

NOTE: The dedication in the first English edition reads: *To Ada and Archibald MacLeish*. See (A38).

NOTE: The dust jacket is printed in red, white, and black. An excerpt from a review of *DIA*, by Laurence Stallings, appears on the back cover.

NOTE: Prior to the publication of the book Scribner's printed around 30 copies of a dummy for use by their salesmen. Title page: STORIES | (TITLE TO BE DETERMINED) | By | ERNEST HEMINGWAY | [design] | NEW YORK | CHARLES SCRIBNER'S SONS | 1933.

7 3/8 x 5 1/4. Issued in black cloth with blank gold paper labels on the front cover and backstrip. Due to the narrowness of the dummy the backstrip appears on the back cover. The dust jacket is gray with blue lettering.

COLLATION: [i]-[iv] + 1-8, as follows: [i] half title; [ii] blank; [iii] title page as above; [iv] copyright page; 1-8 text: beginning of "Give Us a Prescription, Doctor." As noted above, this story was retitled "The Gambler, the Nun, and the Radio" in *Winner Take*

Nothing, which was the title that was finally selected for this collection of stories.

B. Reprint edition:
ERNEST HEMINGWAY | [wavy line] | WINNER | TAKE
NOTHING | [design of a rising sun] | SUN RISE EDITION | *Volume Five* | [wavy line] | *CHARLES SCRIBNER'S SONS* | NEW YORK

7 7/8 x 5 3/8. Published in May 1938 in a six-volume set, which sold for $15.00. 3020 sets were printed. Issued in blue buckram with the author's signature blind-stamped on the front cover. Stamped in gold on the backstrip: [decorative line] | HEMINGWAY | [short rule] | WINNER | TAKE | NOTHING | V | [decorative line] [all on indented block] | [design] | [decorative line] | THE | SUN RISE | EDITION | [decorative line] [all on indented block] | [design] | [decorative line] | SCRIBNERS | [decorative line] [all on indented block]. Top and bottom edges trimmed, fore edges untrimmed.

COLLATION: [i]-[x] + [1]-[246]. The same as the first edition except that the list of books by Hemingway has been omitted from p. [iv]. The copyright page is the same as the first edition, including Scribner's "A." The epigraph does not appear in this edition.

NOTE: Also issued in a variant binding of red buckram.

NOTE: The other volumes in this set are: Vol. I *IOT*; Vol. II *SAR*; Vol. III *MWW*; Vol. IV *FTA*; Vol. VI *THAHN*.

C. Uniform edition:
Winner Take Nothing | By | ERNEST HEMINGWAY | [epigraph] | CHARLES SCRIBNER'S SONS | NEW YORK : : : LONDON

7 3/8 x 5 1/8. Published in 1955, at $3.00. Issued in blue cloth. Stamped in gold on the front cover: [ornament] WINNER TAKE NOTHING [ornament]. Backstrip: the title is stamped in gold on a black block; the author's name and publisher's name are stamped in black on gold blocks. Top and bottom edges trimmed; fore edges untrimmed.

COLLATION: [i]-[x] + [1]-[246]. The same pagination as the first edition.

NOTE: The blue dust jacket is printed in the uniform design, in red, white, and black.

13 Green Hills of Africa

A. First edition:
GREEN HILLS | OF AFRICA | By | Ernest Hemingway | [decoration: head of a kudu encircled with stars] | Decorations by ED-

WARD SHENTON | [long rule] | CHARLES SCRIBNER'S SONS, NEW YORK | Charles Scribner's Sons, Ltd., London | 1935

8 3/16 x 5 9/16. Published October 25, 1935, at $2.75. The first printing consisted of 10,550 copies. Issued in smooth light green cloth, with the author's signature stamped in gold on the front cover. Stamped in gold on the backstrip: [decorative band] | GREEN HILLS | OF AFRICA | HEMINGWAY [all on black block] | [double rule] | [double rule] | SCRIBNERS [on black block] | [decorative band]. Top and bottom edges trimmed, fore edges untrimmed.

COLLATION: [i]-[viii] + [1]-[296], as follows: [i] half title; [ii] BOOKS BY; [iii] title page as above; [iv] notice of copyright, note of origin, Scribner's "A," and printer's device; [v] dedication: TO PHILIP, TO CHARLES, | AND TO SULLY; [vi] blank; [vii] FOREWORD by Hemingway; [viii] blank; [1] divisional half title: GREEN HILLS OF AFRICA | [decoration] | PART I | Pursuit and Conversation; 2-[295] text; [296] blank.

PREVIOUS PUBLICATION: *GHOA* first appeared serialized in *Scribner's Magazine*, XCVII (May-June 1935) ; XCVIII (July-Nov. 1935) . The sectional headings were changed for book publication.

FOREWORD on p. [vii]: Unlike many novels, none of the char-|acters or incidents in this book is | imaginary. Any one not finding suf- | ficient love interest is at liberty, while | reading it, to insert what-ever love in- | terest he or she may have at the time. | The writer has attempted to write an | absolutely true book to see whether the | shape of a country and the pattern of a | month's action can, if truly presented, | compete with a work of the imagination. Note: This prefatory note was omitted from the first English edition and a letter to "Mr. J. P." was used in its place. See (A39a) .

PRINTING HISTORY: Reprinted in October 1935.

NOTE: The dedicatees are Philip Percival, who is "Jackson Phillips" in the book; Charles Thompson, a Key West friend, who is "Karl" in the book; and Jim Sullivan, an ironworker friend in Key West.

NOTE: "The working title through 1934 was *The Highlands of Africa*. Hemingway decided on the present title sometime in Jan-uary 1935." [*Baker*, p. 165.] For Maxwell Perkins' suggestions re-garding the title, see his letter to Hemingway (dated: November 28, 1934) in *Editor to Author*, New York, 1950, pp. 96-97.

NOTE: The dust jacket is black with white lettering, with a wide decorative green band on the left side of the front cover. The back cover carries a photograph of Hemingway, taken in Africa in 1934, and a blurb on the book. The front flap lists *The People in the Book*.

NOTE: Prior to the publication of the book Scribner's printed around 30 copies of a dummy for use by their salesmen. Title page:

[design] | GREEN HILLS | OF AFRICA | By | ERNEST HEM-
INGWAY | [design] | [rule] | CHARLES SCRIBNER'S SONS |
NEW YORK [dot] LONDON | 1935

8 1/4 x 5 3/4. Issued in green cloth with the author's signature
stamped in gold on the front cover. The green and black dust jacket
has the same layout but a different type face than the one issued
with the first edition of the book.

COLLATION: [i]-[x] + 1-6 + 1 photograph, as follows: [i] blank; [ii]
Books by; [iii] half title; [iv] blank; [sepia photograph: GLASSING
ACROSS TO THE EDGE OF THE FOREST FOR RHINO]; [v]
title page as above; [vi] copyright page; [vii] FOREWORD by Hem-
ingway; [viii] blank; [ix] divisional half title; [x] The People in the
Book; 1-6 text.

NOTE: The photograph and the cast of characters were omitted in
the book.

B. Reprint edition:
Green Hills of Africa, published by Sun Dial Books, Garden City,
N.Y., October 3, 1938, at ninety-eight cents. 295 pages. Decorations
by Edward Shenton. Note: This book has not been examined by
the bibliographer.

C. Uniform edition:
GREEN HILLS | OF AFRICA | By | ERNEST HEMINGWAY |
[decoration] | Decorations by EDWARD SHENTON | [long rule] |
CHARLES SCRIBNER'S SONS, NEW YORK | *1953*

8 5/16 x 5 7/16. Published in March 1953, at $3.50. Issued in green
cloth with a row of ornaments and the title blind-stamped on the
front cover. Stamped in gold on the backstrip: ERNEST | HEM-
INGWAY | Green Hills | of Africa | SCRIBNERS. All edges
trimmed. Same pagination as the first edition.

NOTE: The green dust jacket is printed in the uniform design, in
brown, white, and black.

D. Paperback edition:
GREEN HILLS | OF AFRICA | *Ernest Hemingway* | [decoration] |
DECORATIONS BY EDWARD SHENTON | PERMABOOKS |
A division of Doubleday & Company, Inc. | *Garden City, New York*

7 1/8 x 4 3/16. Published in April 1954, at thirty-five cents, as Permabook No. P-296. Issued in white stiff paper covers printed in red,
green, blue, and black. A photograph of Hemingway by A. E.
Hotchner and a photograph of Kilimanjaro by Ylla are on the front
cover. All edges stained green.

COLLATION: [1]-[200], as follows: [1] brief excerpts from reviews of
the book; [2] BOOKS BY; [3] title page as above; [4] dedication,
PRINTING HISTORY, foreword, notice of copyright and note of

origin; [5] divisional half title; 6-199 text; [200] advertisement for the Permabook edition of *THAHN*.

NOTE: A new edition was published in June 1956, at twenty-five cents, as Permabook No. M-3056. 6 3/8 x 4 1/4. 202 pages. Issued in green stiff paper covers printed in black, yellow, and white, with a drawing of Hemingway by Robert Schulz on the front cover. All edges stained red.

E. Paperback edition:
GREEN HILLS | OF AFRICA | By | ERNEST HEMINGWAY | [decoration] | Decorations by EDWARD SHENTON | [long rule] | CHARLES SCRIBNER'S SONS, NEW YORK
8 x 5 3/8. Published in 1962, at $1.45, as No. SL 50 of the Scribner Library series. Issued in blue stiff paper covers, printed in green, black, and white. Same pagination as the first edition.
PRINTING HISTORY: Reprinted in August 1963.
NOTE: This edition was bound by Peter Smith in 1962. 7 3/4 x 5 3/16. $3.50. Issued in red cloth, stamped in black on the backstrip only. Backstrip, reading downward: GREEN HILLS OF AFRICA — — — HEMINGWAY | PETER [horizontal] | SMITH [horizontal]. All edges trimmed.

14 To Have and Have Not

A. First edition:
TO HAVE | AND | HAVE NOT | ERNEST | HEMINGWAY | NEW YORK | CHARLES SCRIBNER'S SONS | 1937
8 x 5 3/8. Published October 15, 1937, at $2.50. The first printing consisted of 10,130 copies. Issued in smooth black cloth with the author's signature stamped in gold on the front cover. Stamped in gold on the backstrip: [dotted line] | [thick rule] | TO | HAVE | AND | HAVE | NOT | [four rules] | HEMINGWAY | [thick rule] [all on a green block] | [thick rule] | [dot] SCRIBNERS [dot] | [thick rule] | [dotted line] [all on a green block]. Bottom edges trimmed, fore edges untrimmed; top edges stained beige.
COLLATION: [i]-[viii] + [1]-[264], as follows: [i] blank; [ii] *Books by*; [iii] half title; [iv] blank; [v] title page as above; [vi] notices of copyright, note of origin, reservation of rights, Scribner's "A," and printer's device; [vii] legal disclaimer; [viii] blank; [1] divisional half title: PART ONE | HARRY MORGAN | (*Spring*) ; [2] blank; 3-262 text; [263]-[264] blank.
LEGAL DISCLAIMER on p. [vii]: NOTE | *In view of a recent tendency to identify characters* | *in fiction with real people, it seems proper to state* | *that there are no real people in this volume: both the* |

characters and their names are fictitious. If the name | of any living person has been used, the use was | purely accidental.

PREVIOUS PUBLICATION: Two of the three parts concerning Harry Morgan were previously published as short stories. Part I first appeared as "One Trip Across" in *Cosmopolitan*, XCVI (April 1934). It was reprinted in book form with only minor revisions. However, the magazine story ends with the last line of p. 63 in the book; all of p. 64 was added for book publication. Part II first appeared as "The Tradesman's Return" in *Esquire*, V (Feb. 1936). Numerous revisions were made for publication in book form. For example: the main character is identified only as "Harry" not "Harry Morgan"; " 'That's enough Harris,' the man called Doctor said" [p. 194 | second column, lines 66 and 67] was changed to " 'That's enough, Willis,' Frederick Harrison said" [p. 80 | line 26], with the two new names used in that part of the story; the last five paragraphs of Ch. VII are condensed from a much longer magazine version. The deletion form ("————") used in the magazine is not used in the book. Note: The magazine version was reprinted in *The Esquire Treasury*, ed. Arnold Gingrich, New York, 1953, pp. 89-98.

NOTE: The dust jacket, designed by "Neely," is gold, black, and white. A photograph of Hemingway, "taken at the front in Spain," by Joris Ivens, appears on the back cover.

NOTE: On the *Publishers' Weekly* National Best Sellers list, *THAHN* was in fifth place in October, sixth place in November, and ninth place in December 1937.

PRINTING HISTORY: Reprinted twice in October and once in November 1937. By March 10, 1938, the book had sold 36,000 copies. [See *Baker*, p. 205.]

NOTE: Prior to the publication of the book Scribner's printed around 30 copies of a dummy for use by their salesmen. Title page: TO HAVE | AND TO | HAVE NOT | ERNEST | HEMINGWAY | NEW YORK | CHARLES SCRIBNER'S SONS | 1937

8 x 5 3/8. Issued in black cloth with gold paper labels on the front cover and the backstrip, which due to the narrowness of the dummy appears on the back cover. The dust jacket is yellow, red, and black.

COLLATION: [i]-[iv] + [1]-8, as follows: [i] half title; [ii] Books by; [iii] title page as above; [iv] copyright page; [1] half title; [2] blank; 3-8 text.

NOTE: The second "TO" in the title was deleted before book publication.

B. Reprint edition:

ERNEST HEMINGWAY | [wavy line] | TO HAVE | AND HAVE NOT | [design of a rising sun] | SUN RISE EDITION | *Volume*

Six | [wavy line] | *CHARLES SCRIBNER'S SONS* | NEW YORK
7 7/8 x 5 3/8. Published in May 1938 in a six-volume set, which
sold for $15.00. 3020 sets were printed. Issued in blue buckram with
the author's signature blind-stamped on the front cover. Stamped in
gold on the backstrip: [decorative line] | HEMINGWAY | [short
rule] | TO HAVE | AND | HAVE NOT | VI | [decorative line]
[all on indented block] | [design] | [decorative line] | THE | SUN
RISE | EDITION | [decorative line] [all on indented block] | [de-
sign] | [decorative line] | SCRIBNERS | [decorative line] [all on in-
dented block]. Top and bottom edges trimmed; fore edges untrimmed.

COLLATION: [i]-[viii] + [1]-[264]. The same as the first edition except
in this edition the list of books by Hemingway has been omitted
from p. [ii]. Original copyright date only.

NOTE: Also issued in a variant binding of red buckram.

NOTE: The other volumes in this set are: Vol. I *IOT*, Vol. II *SAR*,
Vol. III *MWW*, Vol. IV *FTA*, Vol. V *WTN*.

c. Reprint edition:
TO HAVE | AND | HAVE NOT | ERNEST | HEMINGWAY |
GROSSET & DUNLAP | Publishers [two dots] New York | *By ar-
rangement with Charles Scribner's Sons*
7 1/2 x 5. Published in February 1939, at $1.00, as part of the Novels
of Distinction series. Issued in red cloth with the author's signature
stamped in black on the front cover. Lettered and ruled in black on
the backstrip: [dotted line] | [thick rule] | TO | HAVE | AND |
HAVE | NOT | [four rules] | HEMINGWAY | [thick rule] | GROS-
SET | & DUNLAP. Bottom edges trimmed, fore edges untrimmed;
top edges stained black.

COLLATION: [i]-[viii] + [1]-[264]. The same as the first edition except
in this edition the list of books by Hemingway has been omitted
from p. [ii]. Original copyright date only. Scribner's "A" appears
on the copyright page.

PRINTING HISTORY: First printing, November 1938; second, February
1941; third, May 1941; fourth, August 1942; fifth, April 1943;
sixth, June 1944; seventh, April 1945; eighth, July 1945; ninth,
December 1945; tenth, March 1947; eleventh, October 1947; twelfth,
October 1950.

NOTE: Reissued in a variant binding of orange cloth with the author's signature stamped in black on the cover and black lettering
and ruling on the backstrip. Top edges stained blue. Publisher's
"TC" on copyright page.

NOTE: The front cover and backstrip of the dust jacket are the same
as the original Scribner's jacket, with the substitution of GROSSET
| & DUNLAP on the lower backstrip.

D. Reprint edition:

To Have and | Have Not | *by* | ERNEST HEMINGWAY | [publisher's device] | P. F. Collier & Son Corporation | PUBLISHERS [dot] NEW YORK

8 x 5 1/4. Published in 1942 as part of a six-volume set. Issued in dark blue cloth with the design of a quill pen and the author's name blind-stamped on the front cover. Lettered in gold with the quill design blind-stamped on the backstrip. All edges trimmed.

COLLATION: [i]-[viii] + [1]-[264]. The same as the first edition except in this edition the list of books by Hemingway has been omitted from p. [ii]. Original copyright date only. Publisher's "TC" on copyright page.

NOTE: The other volumes in this set are: *SAR, FTA, DIA, TFC &* *First 49* and *FWBT*. The set was sold as an alternative part of a combination involving various reference titles, which included the Harvard Classics and the National Encyclopedia. For the printing history, see *SAR* (A6e).

E. Armed services edition:

[On the right-hand side of title page:] TO HAVE | AND | HAVE NOT | by | Ernest Hemingway | *Editions for the Armed Services, Inc.* | A NON-PROFIT ORGANIZATION ESTABLISHED BY | THE COUNCIL ON BOOKS IN WARTIME, NEW YORK [On the left-hand side of title page: notices of publication arrangements, reservation of rights, and copyright] [the two sections of the title page are separated by a vertical line; the entire page is enclosed in a double ruled border with a thin inner rule and a heavy outer rule] 667 [below border in left-hand bottom corner]

3 7/8 x 5 1/2. Published in [1945?], as No. 667 of the Armed Services Editions. Issued in stiff paper covers, printed in blue, black, white, red, and yellow. The book is bound along the short edge and printed two columns to a page.

COLLATION: [1]-[256], as follows: [1] title page as above; [2] legal disclaimer and note of origin; 3-[256] text.

NOTE: This is one of a series of "pocket-size" reprints which were published for free distribution to members of the American armed services, mainly overseas, and were "not to be resold or made available to civilians." Each book was issued in a printing of 57,000 copies. See also *Selected Short Stories* (A20).

F. Uniform edition:

TO HAVE | AND | HAVE NOT | ERNEST | HEMINGWAY | NEW YORK | CHARLES SCRIBNER'S SONS | 1953

8 3/16 x 5 3/8. Published March 1, 1953, at $3.00. Issued in light blue cloth. Blind-stamped on the front cover: [row of ornaments] | To Have and Have Not. Stamped in gold on the backstrip:

ERNEST | HEMINGWAY | To Have and | Have Not | SCRIB-
NERS. All edges trimmed.

COLLATION: [i]-[viii] + [1]-[264]. The same as the first edition. Original copyright dates only on the copyright page.

NOTE: The blue dust jacket is printed in the uniform design, in
rose, white, and black.

NOTE: Reissued (date unknown) in blue cloth stamped in gold on
the front cover and in gold and black on the backstrip.

G. Paperback edition:

To Have | *and* | *Have Not* | BY ERNEST HEMINGWAY | *Perma-
books, a Division of* | *Doubleday & Company, Inc., Garden City,
New York*

7 1/8 x 4 3/16. Published in November 1953, at twenty-five cents, as
Perma Star paperback No. 253. Issued in white stiff paper covers,
with red, purple, and black lettering, and an illustrative scene in
color on the front cover. All edges stained blue.

COLLATION: [1]-[200], as follows: [1] brief excerpts from three reviews of the book; [2] books by; [3] title page as above; [4] publication arrangement, printing history, notices of copyright, note of
origin; [5] legal disclaimer; [6] blank; [7] divisional half title; [8]
blank; 9-195 text; [196]-[200] advertisements for other Permabooks.

PRINTING HISTORY: Reprinted in January 1954.

15 The Spanish Earth

A. First edition:

THE | SPANISH EARTH | [ornament] | ERNEST HEMINGWAY
| [ornament] | With an introduction by Jasper Wood | Illustrations
by Frederick K. Russell | THE J. B. SAVAGE COMPANY | CLEVE-
LAND [dot] 1938

7 1/2 x 5. Published by Jasper Wood, June 15, 1938, at $3.50, in a
limited edition of 1000 numbered copies. Issued in tan cloth, let-
tered in black on the front cover and backstrip. Cover: THE |
SPANISH | EARTH | ERNEST HEMINGWAY [the lettering partly
covers a large clenched fist and three small airplanes, all stamped in
orange]. Backstrip, reading downward: THE SPANISH EARTH
[dot] HEMINGWAY. All edges trimmed. Tan paper throughout.
Enclosed in a glassine jacket.

COLLATION: [1]-[64], including 7 illustrations, as follows: [1] half
title; [2] colophon: This book was published in a limited | edition
of 1000 numbered copies on | Linweave paper with Caslon type. |
THIS COPY IS NUMBER ——— | [at bottom of page:] FIRST EDI-
TION; [3] title page as above; [4] Copyright June 1938 | in the |
United States and Canada | by | Ernest Hemingway | Verve 1938;

[5] dedication: *To all | the friends of | Loyalist | Spain*; [6] AC-KNOWLEDGMENTS; [7] TABLE OF CONTENTS; [8] film credits; 9-15 INTRODUCTION *by* JASPER WOOD; [16] blank; 17 illustration, divisional half title: REEL ONE; [18] blank; 19-52 text; 53 illustration; [54] blank; 55-60 Afternote: The Heat and The Cold by Hemingway; [61]-[64] blank.

NOTE: This book contains a transcript of Hemingway's narration for the sound track for the film "The Spanish Earth." The film was directed by Joris Ivens, photographed by John Ferno and presented by Contemporary Historians, Inc. Its purpose was to raise money for the Loyalist cause. The sound-script is divided into six reels. The afternote, "The Heat and The Cold," is reprinted from *Verve*, I (Spring 1938).

NOTE: Jasper Wood's Introduction, on pp. 9-15, is dated: *May 17, 1938. Cleveland Heights, O*[hio].

NOTE: There are two issues of the first edition. The first issue has pictorial endpapers, front and back, showing a large F.A.I. [Federación Anarquista Iberica] banner, in orange, flying over the heads of advancing soldiers. In a letter to the bibliographer, Jasper Wood estimated that there were between 50 and 100 copies of the first issue. The second issue has plain tan endpapers with a statement printed on the rear lining paper. It states that Hemingway "had nothing to do with the preparation of this book, never saw the proof, furnished no material for the introduction, and has just wired . . . protesting that he considers the introduction inaccurate and in bad taste" because it gave him credit for the film which he felt should have gone to Joris Ivens and John Ferno. Also, Hemingway protested against the F.A.I. banner on the endpapers. The statement ends with Hemingway's request that all money to be paid to him from the book go directly to the widow of Dr. Werner Heilbrun, who was killed in action in Spain. Although this statement is signed by Jasper Wood, the young high school student who published the book, it was taken directly from the second page of a telegram sent to him by Hemingway, from Key West, Florida, on July 19, 1938. Only the punctuation was changed. In the telegram, Hemingway insisted that the statement be affixed inside the cover in a manner in which it could not be removed without mutilating the F.A.I. banner. Instead, the endpapers were changed to plain tan paper and the excerpt from Hemingway's telegram was printed, in orange, on the inside of the back cover. The original telegram is among the holdings of the University of Texas.

NOTE: A full-page advertisement in *Publishers' Weekly*, CXXXIV (July 2, 1938), 16, announced the publication date as July 9; however, it was published earlier, on June 15, 1938.

45

16 The Fifth Column and the First Forty-nine Stories

A. First edition:
THE FIFTH COLUMN | AND THE FIRST | FORTY-NINE |
STORIES | By | ERNEST | HEMINGWAY | NEW YORK |
CHARLES SCRIBNER'S SONS | 1938

8 1/4 x 5 5/8. Published October 14, 1938, at $2.75. The first print-
ing consisted of 5350 copies. Issued in red cloth with the author's
signature stamped in black on the front cover. Stamped in gold on
the backstrip: [double rule] | [thick black rule] | [double rule] |
[decorative line] | [double rule] | THE FIFTH | COLUMN | AND
| THE FIRST | FORTY-NINE | STORIES [all lettering on a black
block] | [double rule] | HEMINGWAY [on a black block] | [triple
rule] | [triple rule] | SCRIBNERS [on a black block] | [double rule]
| [decorative line] | [double rule] | [thick black rule] | [double rule].
Top and bottom edges trimmed, fore edges untrimmed.

COLLATION: [i]-x + [1]-[598], as follows: [i] half title; [ii] *Books by*;
[iii] title page as above; [iv] notices of copyright, note of origin,
reservation of rights, Scribner's "A," and printer's device; v-vii
PREFACE by Hemingway; [viii] blank; ix-x CONTENTS; [1] half
title; [2] blank; 3-101 text of *TFC*; 102-597 text of the stories; [598]
blank.

CONTENTS: *The Fifth Column*/The Short Happy Life of Francis Ma-
comber/The Capital of the World/The Snows of Kilimanjaro/Old
Man at the Bridge/Up in Michigan/On the Quai at Smyrna/Indi-
an Camp/The Doctor and the Doctor's Wife/The End of Some-
thing/The Three-Day Blow/The Battler/A Very Short Story/Sol-
dier's Home/The Revolutionist/Mr. and Mrs. Elliot/Cat in the
Rain/Out of Season/Cross-Country Snow/My Old Man/Big Two-
Hearted River: Part I/Big Two-Hearted River: Part II/The Unde-
feated/In Another Country/Hills Like White Elephants/The Kil-
lers/Che Ti Dice La Patria?/Fifty Grand/A Simple Enquiry/Ten
Indians/A Canary for One/An Alpine Idyll/A Pursuit Race/To-
day Is Friday/Banal Story/Now I Lay Me/After the Storm/A
Clean, Well-Lighted Place/The Light of the World/God Rest You
Merry, Gentlemen/The Sea Change/A Way You'll Never Be/The
Mother of a Queen/One Reader Writes/Homage to Switzerland/
A Day's Wait/A Natural History of the Dead/Wine of Wyoming/
The Gambler, the Nun, and the Radio/Fathers and Sons. Note: The
inter-chapters from *iot* precede the short stories in this volume in
the same order as in *IOT*.

PREVIOUS PUBLICATION: This volume comprises the contents of *IOT*,
MWW, and *WTN*, the first printing of the play *The Fifth Column*,

and four previously uncollected stories. Three of the stories appear for the first time in book form: "The Short Happy Life of Francis Macomber" first appeared in *Cosmopolitan,* CI (Sept. 1936); "The Capital of the World" appeared in *Esquire,* V (June 1936), under the title "The Horns of the Bull"; and "Old Man at the Bridge" first appeared in *Ken,* I (May 19, 1938), as "The Old Man at the Bridge." "The Snows of Kilimanjaro" first appeared in *Esquire,* VI (Aug. 1936). It was reprinted in *The Best Short Stories of 1937,* ed. Edward J. O'Brien, Boston, 1937, as it appeared in magazine form. Several revisions were made for publication in the *First 49,* including corrections in spelling and punctuation. The most notable revision is the deletion of Scott Fitzgerald's name, in a reference to his "romantic awe" of the rich, and the insertion of the name "Julian" in its place [p. 170 | line 23]. "On the Quai at Smyrna" appeared in *IOT* (1930) under the title "Introduction by the Author." "Up in Michigan" was first published in *TSTP*. It was rejected by Boni & Liveright for inclusion in *IOT* (1925). When it was being considered for inclusion in the 1930 Scribner edition, Hemingway changed several of the characters' names; for example, he changed "Liz" to "Mary" and "Jim Gilmore" to "Jim Dutton." Scribner's rejected it at that time. For inclusion in the *First 49,* the original names of the two main characters were retained; however, "A. J. Smith" or "Alonzo" was changed to "D. J. Smith" and "Fox's house" was changed to "Dillworth's house."

NOTE: Hemingway's preface, on pp. v-vii, is not dated. He notes in the preface that: "The first four [stories] are the last ones I have written. The others follow in the order in which they were originally published" [i.e., the order in which they appeared in *IOT, MWW,* and *WTN*]. The preface is partly recorded on "Ernest Hemingway Reading" (Caedmon, TC 1185). See (F154).

NOTE: The dust jacket is printed in red, white, and gold. A photograph, by Joris Ivens, of Hemingway and Herbert Matthews observing artillery bursts during the Spanish Civil War, appears on the back cover.

PRINTING HISTORY: Reissued with 1939 on the title page.

NOTE: Prior to the publication of the book Scribner's printed around 30 copies of a dummy for use by their salesmen. Title page: THE FIRST | 48 | ERNEST | HEMINGWAY | NEW YORK | CHARLES SCRIBNER'S SONS | 1938
8 1/4 x 5 5/8. Issued in black cloth with the author's signature stamped in gold on the front cover. Issued in a white dust jacket with blue lettering, marked: PERMANENT JACKET IN PREPARATION across the lower front cover.

COLLATION: 1 leaf + [i]-[viii] + 1-[6], as follows: [blank leaf]; [i] half title; [ii] blank; [iii] title page as above; [iv] notice of copyright, note of origin, reservation of rights, Scribner's "A," and printer's device; v-vii CONTENTS; [viii] blank; 1-4 text: beginning of "Up in Michigan"; [5]-[6] blank.

NOTE: The contents are listed in the chronological order in which the stories first appeared, whether in magazine or book form. "Old Man at the Bridge" is not included; "Big Two-Hearted River" is not separated into two parts; the inter-chapters of *iot* are printed together and included as one unit.

NOTE: Scribner's advertisement in *Publishers' Weekly*, CXXXIII (June 4, 1938), 2202, announced that *The First 48*, collected short stories of Ernest Hemingway, "including three new ones," would be published in September, at $2.50. The advertisement included an announcement that *The Fifth Column: A Play* would be published in September, at $2.50. [A dummy copy of *TFC* was also made up, see (A17).]

NOTE: As early as November 28, 1934, Maxwell Perkins wrote to Hemingway in regard to a collected volume of his work, of which the working title was "The First Fifty-Seven." [See *Editor to Author*, New York, 1950, pp. 97-98.]

B. Reprint edition:

The Fifth Column | *And the First* | Forty-nine Stories | *By* | ERNEST HEMINGWAY | [publisher's device] | P. F. Collier & Son Corporation | PUBLISHERS [dot] NEW YORK

8 x 5 1/4. Published in 1942 as part of a six-volume set. Issued in dark blue cloth with the design of a quill pen and the author's name blind-stamped on the front cover. Lettered in gold with the quill design blind-stamped on the backstrip. All edges trimmed.

COLLATION: [i]-x + [1]-[598]. The same as the first edition except that the list of books by Hemingway was omitted from p. [ii]. Original copyright date only. Publisher's "TE" on the copyright page.

NOTE: Hemingway's Preface, on pp. v-vii, is reprinted from the first edition.

NOTE: For the printing history of this set, see *SAR* (A6e).

NOTE: The other volumes in this set are: *SAR, FTA, DIA, THAHN*, and *FWBT*. The set was sold as an alternative part of a combination involving various reference titles, which included the Harvard Classics and the National Encyclopedia.

C. Reprint edition:

[Decorative line] | THE SHORT STORIES OF | ERNEST HEMINGWAY | THE FIRST FORTY-NINE STORIES | AND THE PLAY *THE FIFTH COLUMN* | [decorative line] | [publisher's device] | [decorative line] | THE MODERN LIBRARY | NEW YORK

8 x 5 1/4. Published by Random House, Inc., September 15, 1942,

at $1.45, as Modern Library Giant No. G 59. The first printing consisted of 10,000 copies. Issued in gray cloth with the publisher's device stamped in gold on a black oval, bordered in gold, on the front cover. Stamped in gold on the backstrip: [double rule] | *THE* | SHORT STORIES | *OF* | ERNEST | HEMINGWAY | *Modern Library* | [double rule] [all on a black block] | [publisher's device in gold, on a black oval, bordered in gold]. All edges trimmed; top edges stained black.

COLLATION: [i]-x + [1]-[598]. The same as the first edition except that the following wording appears above the half title, on p. [i]: THE MODERN LIBRARY | *of the World's Best Books*; and a publisher's note regarding their illustrated folder was substituted for the list of books by Hemingway, on p. [ii]. The copyright page states: First Modern Library Giant Edition | 1942.

NOTE: Hemingway's preface, on pp. v-vii, is reprinted from the first edition.

NOTE: In "The Snows of Kilimanjaro," the name of a minor character, which appears as "Barker" in the original manuscript, in *Esquire*, VI (Aug. 1936), and in the *First 49*, has been changed to "Gardner" [p. 155 | lines 1, 3] in this edition. Inexplicably, the name was changed to "Johnson" in the second English edition (Cape, 1944).

NOTE: Issued in variant bindings of gray cloth, stamped in gold on a red background and top edges stained red; and in green cloth, stamped in gold on a black background and top edges stained black.

D. Uniform edition:

THE SHORT | STORIES | of Ernest Hemingway | [ornament] | NEW YORK | CHARLES SCRIBNER'S SONS | 1954

8 3/16 x 5 7/16. Published November 22, 1954, at $4.75. Issued in black cloth with a row of ornaments and the title blind-stamped on the front cover. Stamped in gold on the backstrip: The Short | Stories | of | Ernest | Hemingway | SCRIBNERS. All edges trimmed.

COLLATION: [i]-[viii] + [1]-[504], as follows: [i] half title; [ii] *Books by*; [iii] title page as above; [iv] notices of copyright, change of title, note of origin and reservation of rights; v-vi PREFACE, dated 1938; vii-viii CONTENTS; [1] half title; [2] blank; 3-499 text; [500]-[504] blank.

PRINTING HISTORY: Reissued with 1955 on the title page.

NOTE: The dark gray dust jacket is printed in the uniform design, in gold, white, and black.

E. Reprint edition:

MODERN STANDARD AUTHORS | THE | SHORT STORIES | of Ernest Hemingway | CHARLES SCRIBNER'S SONS | NEW YORK

8 1/4 x 5 1/2. Published in October 1956, at $2.75. Issued in black cloth backstrip over light brown covers. The author's signature is stamped in gold on the black cloth section of the front cover. Lettered, decorated, and ruled in gold on the backstrip. Top and bottom edges trimmed; fore edges untrimmed.

COLLATION: [i]-viii + [1]-[500]. Same pagination as the 1954 uniform edition, except the two blank pages at the end have been omitted. The publisher's symbols "A-8.56 (MH)" appear on the copyright page.

17 The Fifth Column

A. First separate edition:
THE FIFTH COLUMN | A PLAY IN THREE ACTS | By | ER-NEST HEMINGWAY | NEW YORK | CHARLES SCRIBNER'S SONS | 1940
8 1/2 x 5 1/2. Published June 3, 1940, at $1.75. The first printing consisted of 1174 copies. Issued in gray cloth, stamped in red on the front cover and backstrip. Cover: *ERNEST HEMINGWAY* | [design] | THE FIFTH COLUMN | [design] | *A PLAY IN THREE ACTS*. Backstrip, reading downward: [design] *THE FIFTH COL-UMN* [dot] *HEMINGWAY SCRIBNERS* [design]. All edges trimmed.

COLLATION: 1 leaf + [i]-[viii] + [1]-[102], as follows: [blank; verso, *Books By*]; [i] half title; [ii] blank; [iii] title page as above; [iv] notices of copyright, printing, reservation of rights, and printer's device; v-vi PUBLISHERS' NOTE; vii Contents; [viii] blank; [1] half title; [2] blank; 3-101 script, in three acts and ten scenes; [102] blank.

PUBLISHERS' NOTE on pp. v-vi: "This is the original version as written by Ernest Hemingway of the play, *The Fifth Column*, which, as adapted by Benjamin Glaser [*sic*], was produced in the winter of 1940 with great success by the Theatre Guild of New York. The play was first published in 1938 in a volume entitled *The Fifth Column and the First Forty-nine Stories*. . . ." The paragraphs regarding the play are quoted from Hemingway's preface to the *First 49*.

NOTE: The gray dust jacket is printed in red and gray. The back cover carries excerpts from reviews of the play when it first appeared in book form, in 1938.

NOTE: *The Fifth Column*, adapted by Benjamin Glazer, was produced by the Theatre Guild, Inc., and opened March 6, 1940, at the Alvin Theatre in New York. The play closed on May 18, 1940, after eighty-seven performances.

NOTE: Scribner's issued around 30 copies of a salesman's dummy in 1938, when the play was first planned as a separate volume but in-

THREE STORIES

Up in Michigan

Out of Season

My Old Man

& TEN POEMS

Mitraigliatrice

Oklahoma

Oily Weather

Roosevelt

Captives

Champs d'Honneur

Riparto d'Assalto

Montparnasse

Along With Youth

Chapter Heading

ERNEST HEMINGWAY

Title page of first edition. Courtesy of Princeton
University Library

and then go on from there. It was easy then because there was always one true sentence that you knew or had seen or had heard someone say. If I started to write elaborately or like some one introducing or presenting something I found that I could cut that scroll work or ornament out and threw it away and start with the first true simple declarative sentence I had written. Up in that room I decided that I would write one story about each thing that I knew about. I was trying to do this all the time I was writing and it was very good and severe discipline. It was in that room too that I learned not to think about anything that I was writing from the time I stopped writing until I started again the next day That way my subconscious would be working on it and at the same time I would be listening to other people, noticing everything, I hoped, learning, I hoped, and I would

---

Holograph page from manuscript of *A Moveable Feast.* Courtesy of Mrs. Mary Hemingway

stead was included with the short stories. Title page: The Fifth Column | A PLAY IN THREE ACTS | By | ERNEST HEMING-WAY | 1938 | CHARLES SCRIBNER'S SONS [dot] NEW YORK | CHARLES SCRIBNER'S SONS [dot] LTD [dot] LONDON

8 1/4 x 5 3/4. Issued in black cloth with the author's signature stamped in gold on the front cover.

COLLATION: [i]-[iv] + 1-8, as follows: [i] half title; [ii] blank; [iii] title page as above; [iv] copyright page, with Scribner's "A"; 1-8 script: Act One, Scene One and part of Scene Two.

18 For Whom the Bell Tolls

A. First edition:

FOR WHOM | THE BELL TOLLS | By | ERNEST | HEMING-WAY | NEW YORK | CHARLES SCRIBNER'S SONS | 1940

8 1/4 x 5 5/8. Published October 21, 1940, at $2.75. The first printing consisted of 75,000 copies. Issued in nubby beige cloth with the author's signature stamped in black on the front cover. Stamped in black on the backstrip: [four rules on indented red block] | FOR WHOM | THE BELL | TOLLS | [short rule] | HEMINGWAY [all on indented red block] | [four rules on indented red block] | [two rules, in red] | SCRIBNERS [on indented red block] | [two rules, in red]. Bottom edges trimmed, fore edges untrimmed; top edges stained brown.

COLLATION: [i]-[x] + 1-[472], as follows: [i] blank; [ii] *Books by*; [iii] half title; [iv] blank; [v] title page as above; [vi] notice of copyright, note of origin, reservation of rights, and Scribner's "A"; [vii] dedication: *This book is for* | *MARTHA GELLHORN*; [viii] blank; [ix] half title; [x] quotation from John Donne; 1-471 text; [472] blank.

Quotation on p. [x]: No man is an *Iland*, intire of it selfe; every man | is a peece of the *Continent*, a part of the *maine*; if a | *Clod* bee washed away by the *Sea, Europe* is the lesse, | as well as if a *Promontorie* were, as well as if a *Mannor* | of thy *friends* or of *thine owne* were; any mans | *death* diminishes *me*, because I am in- | volved in *Mankinde*; And therefore | never send to know for | whom the *bell* tolls; It | tolls for *thee*. | JOHN DONNE | [ornament]. Note: This quotation is from Donne's seventeenth Meditation in "Devotions Upon Emergent Occasions," written in 1624.

NOTE: This 211,000-word novel is Hemingway's longest work.

NOTE: The black dust jacket is printed in red, white, blue, and gray. A photograph of Hemingway appears on the back cover. On later states of the dust jacket, the name of the photographer, [Lloyd] "Arnold," appears below the photograph.

NOTE: By December 28, 1940, sales stood at 189,000 copies and by

April 4, 1941, sales had risen to 491,000 copies. [See *Baker*, p. 302.]
NOTE: Prior to the publication of the book Scribner's printed around 30 copies of a dummy for use by their salesmen. Title page: FOR WHOM | THE BELL TOLLS | By | ERNEST | HEMING-WAY | NEW YORK | CHARLES SCRIBNER'S SONS | 1940
8 x 5 1/2. Issued in plain black cloth. *Collation*: [i]-[viii] + 1-6, as follows: [i]-[ii] blank; [iii] half title; [iv] blank; [v] title page as above; [vi] copyright page; [vii] quotation [from John Donne]; [viii] blank; 1-6 text.
NOTE: An advance issue of 15 copies, which measure 8 5/8 x 5 3/4, were bound uncut in the same cloth as the first edition.
NOTE: *FWBT* was chosen as the Book-of-the-Month Club selection for November 1940. The first printing consisted of 135,000 copies. An unrevised proof was issued in a brown paper cover for the Book-of-the-Month Club judges. 7 3/4 x 6 1/2. 476 pages, printed on the right side only. A note explains that the last two chapters are omitted because the author wished to read the proofs up to that point "before perfecting the end."

B. Reprint edition:
For Whom | The Bell Tolls | *by* | ERNEST HEMINGWAY | [publisher's device] | P. F. Collier & Son Corporation | PUBLISHERS [dot] NEW YORK
8 x 5 1/4. Published in 1942 as part of a six-volume set. Issued in dark blue cloth with the design of a quill pen and the author's name blind-stamped on the front cover. Lettered in gold with the quill design blind-stamped on the backstrip. All edges trimmed. COLLATION: [i]-[x] + 1-[472]. The same as the first edition except that the list of books by Hemingway is omitted from p. [ii]. Original copyright date only. Publisher's "TP" on the copyright page.
NOTE: For the printing history of this set, see *SAR* (A6e).
NOTE: The other volumes in this set are: *SAR, FTA, DIA, THAHN* and *TFC & First 49*. The set was sold as an alternative part of a combination involving various reference titles, which included the Harvard Classics and the National Encyclopedia.

C. Limited illustrated edition:
For whom the bell tolls [in script] | BY ERNEST HEMINGWAY | WITH AN INTRODUCTION BY SINCLAIR LEWIS | ILLUS-TRATED WITH LITHOGRAPHS | BY LYND WARD | PRINTED FOR THE MEMBERS OF THE LIMITED | EDI-TIONS CLUB [ornament] PRINCETON UNIVERSITY PRESS | NINETEEN HUNDRED FORTY TWO [ornament] PRINCE-TON | [drawing: a tolling bell with men fighting in the mountainous background]
10 x 6 11/16. Published in October 1942, in a limited edition of

1500 copies. Issued in a dark green backstrip over nubby, yellow cloth covers. Stamped in gold on the entire length of the backstrip: [design] | For | Whom | the | Bell | Tolls | [design] | ERNEST | HEMINGWAY | [design] | LITHOGRAPHS BY | LYND WARD | [design]. All edges trimmed; top edges stained rust. Enclosed in a rust-colored board slip-case, printed in green on the backstrip only: ERNEST | HEMINGWAY | For | Whom | the | Bell | Tolls | LYND WARD

COLLATION: [i]-[xii] + [1]-[500] + 29 pages of illustrations, as follows: [i]-[ii] blank; [iii] quotation; [iv] blank; [v] title page as above; [vi] notices of copyright; [vii] dedication; [viii] blank; ix-xi *INTRO-DUCTION* by Sinclair Lewis; [xii] blank; [1] half title; [2] blank; [unnumbered leaf, with illustration]; 3-498 text; [499] blank; [500] colophon.

COLOPHON on p. [500]: THIS EDITION OF FOR WHOM THE BELL TOLLS | MADE FOR | THE MEMBERS OF THE LIMITED EDITIONS CLUB | AT THE PRINCETON UNIVERSITY PRESS | WAS DESIGNED BY ELMER ADLER AND P. J. CONKWRIGHT | THE LITHOGRAPHS PRINTED BY GEORGE C. MILLER | WERE DRAWN ON STONE BY LYND WARD | THIS COPY IS NUMBER | SIGNED BY THE ILLUSTRATOR

NOTE: 15 copies for presentation by the author were imprinted with a circular seal beneath the colophon, stating: ONE OF 15 PRESENTATION COPIES "OUT OF SERIES."

NOTE: Hemingway was awarded the Limited Editions Club Gold Medal on November 26, 1941. The *Monthly Letter of the Limited Editions Club*, No. 149 (Sept. 1942), was issued with this edition. See (H496).

D. Overseas edition:

For Whom | The Bell Tolls | [long rule] | *BY ERNEST HEMING-WAY* | [ornament] | OVERSEAS EDITIONS, INC. | NEW YORK 6 3/8 x 4 1/2. Published in [1945?], as No. E 19 of the Overseas Editions. Issued in white stiff paper covers, printed in red and blue, with the outline of the Statue of Liberty on the front cover.

COLLATION: [i]-[viii] + 1-[472], as follows: [i] half title; [ii] publisher's notice; [iii] title page as above; [iv] notices of original publisher, reservation of rights, copyright, and note of origin; [v] quotation; [vi] blank; [vii] half title; [viii] blank; 1-470 text; [471]-[472] blank.

NOTICE on p. [ii]: This book is published by Overseas Editions, Inc., a non- | profit organization established by the Council on Books in | Wartime, which is made up of American publishers, | librarians, and booksellers. It is the sole purpose of Overseas | Editions, Inc., to make available representative American | books of recent years until such time as normal publishing | activities are resumed in Europe and Asia. This edition will | not be sold in the continental United States or Canada.

E. Reprint edition:
For Whom the Bell Tolls, published by Grosset & Dunlap, New York, in July 1944, at $1.49. Note: This book has not been examined by the bibliographer.

F. Reprint edition:
For Whom the Bell Tolls, published by Doubleday, New York, in July 1944, in the Doubleday Dollar Book Club edition. Note: This book has not been examined by the bibliographer.

G. Reprint edition:
For Whom the Bell Tolls, published by Sun Dial Books, Garden City, N.Y., in September 1944, at $1.49. 410 pages. Reissued in [1952?], at $1.98. Note: This book has not been examined by the bibliographer.

H. Reprint edition:
FOR WHOM | THE BELL TOLLS | By | ERNEST | HEMING-WAY | THE BLAKISTON COMPANY | *Philadelphia*
7 7/8 x 5 1/2. Published September 11, 1944, at $1.00. Issued in black paper-covered boards with the author's signature blind-stamped on the front cover. Stamped in gold on the backstrip: [four rules] | FOR WHOM | THE BELL | TOLLS | [short rule] | HEMINGWAY | [four rules] | BLAKISTON. Bottom edges trimmed, fore edges untrimmed; top edges stained red.
COLLATION: [i]-[vi] + [1]-410, as follows: [i] title page as above; [ii] notice of original copyright, note of origin, reservation of rights; [iii] dedication; [iv] blank; [v] half title; [vi] quotation; [1]-410 text.
NOTE: The dust jacket is the same as the Scribner's dust jacket on the first edition, except for the substitution of BLAKISTON on the lower backstrip.
NOTE: Issued in a variant binding of dark red paper-covered boards, with the top edges stained yellow.

I. Paperback edition:
[On the left-hand page:] For Whom the | *by* | [publisher's device]. [On the right-hand page:] Bell Tolls | *Ernest Hemingway* | BANTAM BOOKS [dot] New York
6 3/8 x 4 1/8. Published in March 1951, at thirty-five cents, as Bantam Giant No. A 883. Issued in stiff paper covers with an illustrative scene in color covering the front and back covers and backstrip. Lettered in red and black on the front cover.
COLLATION: [i]-[viii] + 1-502. A printing history of *FWBT* appears

on the copyright page, p. [iv]. A note, on p. 502, states that this Bantam Book contains the complete text of the original edition.

J. Reprint edition:

MODERN STANDARD AUTHORS | FOR WHOM | THE BELL TOLLS | By | ERNEST | HEMINGWAY | NEW YORK | CHARLES SCRIBNER'S SONS

8 1/4 x 5 1/2. Published in [April] 1957, at $2.75. Issued in black cloth backstrip over silvery-gray covers. The author's signature is stamped in silver on the black cloth section of the front cover. Stamped in silver on the backstrip: [thick rule] | FOR WHOM | THE BELL | TOLLS | [ornament] | ERNEST | HEMINGWAY | [ornament] | *SCRIBNERS* | [thick rule]. All edges trimmed.

COLLATION: [i]-[viii] + 1-[472], as follows: [i] half title; [ii] *Books by*; [iii] title page as above; [iv] notice of copyright, note of origin, publisher's notation, and reservation of rights; [v] dedication; [vi] blank; [vii] half title; [viii] quotation; 1-471 text; [472] blank.

NOTE: The dust jacket is red, white, and black, with a photograph of Hemingway on the front cover.

K. Paperback edition:

FOR WHOM | THE BELL TOLLS | By | ERNEST | HEMING-WAY | NEW YORK | CHARLES SCRIBNER'S SONS

8 x 5 3/8. Published in 1960, at $1.95, as No. SL 4 of the Scribner Library series. Issued in gray stiff paper covers printed in black, red, and white. The same pagination as the Modern Standard Authors edition.

L. Uniform edition:

FOR WHOM | THE BELL TOLLS | By | ERNEST | HEMING-WAY | NEW YORK | CHARLES SCRIBNER'S SONS

8 x 5 1/2. Published in 1962, at $4.95. Issued in rose cloth. Stamped in gold on the front cover: [ornament] FOR WHOM THE BELL TOLLS [ornament]. Backstrip: the title is stamped in gold on a black block; the author's name and publisher's name are stamped in black on gold blocks. All edges trimmed. The same pagination as the Modern Standard Authors edition.

NOTE: The rose dust jacket is printed in the uniform design, in purple, white, and black.

M. Reprint edition:

ERNEST | HEMINGWAY | [ornament] | For Whom | the Bell Tolls | CHARLES SCRIBNER'S SONS | *New York*

8 1/4 x 5 1/2. Published in July 1966 as part of a three-volume set offered as an introductory selection by the Literary Guild of America, Inc. Issued in dark blue cloth. Stamped on the front cover: FOR WHOM | THE BELL TOLLS [title in gold] | [broken rule, in

bright blue] | [design of a quill pen, in silver] | [author's signature, in silver]. Backstrip, reading downward: FOR WHOM THE BELL TOLLS [top line, in gold] | HEMINGWAY [bottom line, in silver] | [horizontal rule, in bright blue] | SCRIBNERS [horizontal, in gold]. Top and bottom edges trimmed, fore edges untrimmed. Light blue endpapers.

COLLATION: [i]-[iv] + [1]-[508], as follows: [i] half title; [ii] blank; [iii] title page as above; [iv] dedication, notices of copyright, reservation of rights, note of origin; [1] half title; [2] quotation; [3]-507 text; [508] blank.

NOTE: The other volumes in this set are *SAR* and *FTA*.

19 Men at War

A. First edition:

MEN AT WAR | *The Best War Stories* | *of All Time* | EDITED | *with an Introduction* | BY | ERNEST HEMINGWAY | Based on a plan by William Kozlenko | CROWN PUBLISHERS | NEW YORK

8 1/4 x 5 5/8. Published October 22, 1942, at $3.00. The first printing consisted of 20,500 copies. Issued in smooth black cloth, lettered in gold on the backstrip only: MEN | AT | WAR | EDITED | *with an Introduction* | BY | ERNEST | HEMINGWAY | CROWN. All edges trimmed; top edges stained yellow.

COLLATION: [i]-[xxxii] + [1]-1072, as follows: [i] half title; [ii] blank; [iii] title page as above; [iv] notice of copyright, 1942, publisher's "A," note of origin; [v] dedication: *To* | John, Patrick and Gregory Hemingway; [vi] blank; vii-ix Table of Contents; [x] Editor's Note and Publisher's Note; xi-xxxi Introduction by Hemingway; [xxxii] note regarding subtitles and quotations; [1] divisional half title: *WAR IS PART OF THE INTERCOURSE* | *OF THE HUMAN RACE*; [2] quotation from von Clausewitz; 3-1072 text.

EDITOR'S NOTE on p. [x]: *The editor wishes to thank Colonel Charles Sweeny,* | *Lt. Col. John W. Thomason, and Maxwell E. Perkins* | *for the invaluable aid and advice they have given in the* | *editing of this book.*

PUBLISHER'S NOTE on p. [x]: *Acknowledgments are due to William Kozlenko for the* | *plan from which this book was developed, and for the* | *suggestion of a number of the stories; also to Edmund* | *Fuller, Fred C. Rodewald, Albert Seadler and the many* | *others whose suggestions and contributions helped to* | *make this book.*

NOTE on p. [xxxii]: *The subtitles and quotations at the beginning of the* | *first seven sections of this book are from ON WAR by* | *General Karl von Clausewitz: Kegan Paul, Trench,* | *Trubner & Co., London; E. P. Dutton & Co., New York.*

CONTENTS: Eighty-two war stories. Hemingway included the following three selections from his own work: Ch. xxvii, here titled "The Fight on the Hilltop," from *For Whom the Bell Tolls*, in [Section 2]: War Is the Province of Danger, and Therefore Courage Above All Things Is the First Quality of a Warrior, on pp. 238-250; Chs. xxix-xxx, here titled "The Retreat from Caporetto," from *A Farewell to Arms*, in [Section 6]: War Is the Province of Friction, on pp. 698-711; and "The Chauffeurs of Madrid," a North American Newspaper Alliance (NANA) dispatch, which appeared in the *N.Y. Times* (May 23, 1937), in [Section 8]: War Is Fought By Human Beings, on pp. 993-997.

NOTE: The black dust jacket is printed in gray and red.

NOTE: *Men at War* appeared on the *N.Y. Times Book Review*'s list of The Best Selling Books, Here and Elsewhere, under nonfiction, in New York and Chicago, during November and December 1942. It was in first place, in New York, on December 13, 1942.

B. Paperback edition:

MEN | AT | WAR | Edited by, and with a | special introduction by | ERNEST HEMINGWAY [all enclosed in a decorative border] | Based on a plan by William Kozlenko | [publisher's device] | All stories complete and unabridged as | they appeared in the original edition. | AVON PUBLISHING CO., INC. | 575 Madison Avenue, New York 22, N.Y. [title page enclosed in a decorative border]

6 1/4 x 4 3/8. Published in June 1952, at fifty cents, as Avon paperback No. G 1006. Issued in stiff paper covers, printed in black, yellow, red, white, and gray. All edges stained yellow.

COLLATION: [i]-[xviii] + 19-[640]. Publisher's note on p. [vii]. Hemingway's "Introduction to the Original Edition" appears on pp. ix-xiv.

CONTENTS: Thirty-seven of the stories from the original hardcover edition are reprinted, including two by Hemingway. "The Fight on the Hilltop," from *FWBT*, on pp. 142-159, and "The Retreat from Caporetto," from *FTA*, on pp. 451-471. The NANA dispatch was omitted in this edition.

C. Reprint edition:

MEN AT WAR | The Best War Stories | of All Time | EDITED | with an Introduction | BY | ERNEST HEMINGWAY | *Based on a plan by William Kozlenko* | New Complete Edition | CROWN PUBLISHERS, INC. | NEW YORK

8 x 5 3/8. Published May 5, 1955, at $4.95. Issued in smooth black cloth with white lettering on the backstrip only. The lettering is identical with the backstrip on the first edition. All edges trimmed; top edges stained red.

COLLATION: [i]-[xxviii] + [1]-[1076], as follows: [i] half title; [ii]

blank; [iii] title page as above; [iv] notice of copyright, New Edition Published, 1955; [v] dedication; [vi] Editor's Note and Publisher's Note; vii-ix Table of Contents; [x] Publisher's Foreword; xi-xxvii Introduction by Hemingway; [xxviii] note regarding subtitles and quotations; [1] divisional half title; [2] quotation from von Clausewitz; 3-1072 text; [1073]-[1076] blank.

NOTE: The Publisher's Foreword to the New Complete Edition, on p. [x], dated: New York, March 1955, states: "This book . . . was permitted to go out of print in 1946. . . . When the Korean war began . . . we arranged for a paper-back edition, containing about one-third of the material in the complete book." This edition contains Hemingway's introduction "as it was written in 1942, complete except for a few topical references, and the entire contents of the original edition."

NOTE: Hemingway's introduction, on pp. xi-xxvii, is marked "Edited for the 1955 edition." Hemingway authorized the editing of the original introduction for this edition. An error appears in the introduction [p. xv | line 33], "unpunishable" should read "unpublishable."

D. Reprint edition:

MEN AT WAR | The Best War Stories | of All Time | EDITED | with an Introduction | BY | ERNEST HEMINGWAY | *Based on a plan by William Kozlenko* | New Complete Edition | BRAMHALL HOUSE | NEW YORK

8 x 5 3/8. Published by Bramhall House, a division of Clarkson N. Potter, Inc., New York, in 1955. The binding is identical to the 1955 Crown edition, except for the substitution of "BRAMHALL HOUSE" for "CROWN" on the lower backstrip. Top edges stained red. Same pagination as the 1955 Crown edition.

E. Second paperback edition:

MEN | AT | WAR | EDITED | *with an Introduction* | BY | ERNEST HEMINGWAY | *Based on a plan by William Kozlenko* | [publisher's device] | A BERKLEY MEDALLION BOOK | published by | THE BERKLEY PUBLISHING CORPORATION

7 1/16 x 4 3/16. Published in June 1958, at seventy-five cents, in New York, as Berkley Medallion paperback No. S 426. Issued in white stiff paper covers printed in red and black. All edges stained red.

COLLATION: [i]-[iv] + [1]-[508], as follows: [i] blurb on the book; [ii] blank; [iii] title page as above; [iv] notices of copyright, publication arrangement, acknowledgments, publisher's address, and note of origin; [1]-[3] contents; [4] dedication, EDITOR'S NOTE, PUBLISHER'S NOTE; 5-20 Introduction by Hemingway "Edited for the 1955 edition"; 21-505 text; [506]-[508] advertisements for other Berkley books.

CONTENTS: This edition contains thirty-seven of the stories that appeared in the original hardcover edition. It includes Hemingway's "The Fight on the Hilltop," from *FWBT*, on pp. 118-133, and "The Retreat from Caporetto," from *FTA*, on pp. 360-376. The NANA dispatch was omitted.

PRINTING HISTORY: Reissued in July 1960. Fifth printing in April 1963.

20 Selected Short Stories

A. Armed services edition:

[On the right-hand side of title page:] SELECTED | SHORT | STORIES | of | ERNEST HEMINGWAY | *Editions for the Armed Services, Inc.* | A NON-PROFIT ORGANIZATION ESTABLISHED BY | THE COUNCIL ON BOOKS IN WARTIME, NEW YORK [On the left-hand side of title page: notices of publication arrangements and reservation of rights] [the two sections of the title page are separated by a vertical rule; the entire page is enclosed in a double-ruled border] K-9 [below the border in left-hand bottom corner]

3 7/8 x 5 1/2. Published in [1945?], as No. K-9 of the Armed Services Editions. Issued in stiff paper covers printed in red, yellow, blue, black, and white. The book is bound along the short edge and printed two columns to a page.

COLLATION: [i]-[iv] + 1-[252], as follows: [i] title page as above; [ii] notices of copyright and note of origin; [iii] contents; [iv] blank; 1-[251] text; [252] biographical note on Hemingway.

CONTENTS: The Short Happy Life of Francis Macomber/The Snows of Kilimanjaro/Indian Camp/Mr. and Mrs. Elliot/Cat in the Rain /My Old Man/The Undefeated/Fifty Grand/A Canary for One/ An Alpine Idyll/Now I Lay Me/A Day's Wait.

NOTE: This is one of a series of "pocket-size" reprints published for free distribution to men of the American armed forces, mainly overseas. Each book was issued in a printing of 57,000 copies. *THAHN* was also in this series, see (A14e).

21 Voyage to Victory

VOYAGE | TO VICTORY | AN EYE-WITNESS REPORT OF THE BATTLE | FOR A NORMANDY BEACHHEAD | BY | *ERNEST HEMINGWAY* | Collier's correspondent on | the Invasion Front | [dot] | *in the July 22nd issue* | Collier's—The National Weekly | *on newsstands Friday, July 14th*

8 1/2 x 5 1/2. Published by the Crowell-Collier Publishing Co., New York, in July 1944, as a promotion booklet. Issued in mottled gray paper covers, lettered in black. Wire-stapled. The yellow dust jacket is printed in red, black, and white. A small photograph of Hemingway appears on the back flap.

COLLATION: 12 unnumbered pages, as follows: [1] title page, as shown above; [2] notice of copyright, notice of dispatch being radioed from London, and a note regarding the circumstances under which Hemingway wrote the dispatch; [3] cast of characters, place of action and time; [4] prologue; [5]-[12] text.

NOTE: Hemingway's dispatch appeared in *Collier's*, CXIV (July 22, 1944). It was originally titled "War Ferry to France," but the title was changed to "Voyage to Victory" just before publication.

NOTE: The prologue, on p. [4], consists of the last two lines of the dispatch: *Real war is never like paper war,* | *nor do accounts of it read much the* | *way it looks. But if you want to* | *know how it was in an LCV (P) on* | *D-Day when we took Fox Green* | *beach and Easy Red beach on the* | *sixth of June, 1944, then this is as* | *near as I can come to it.* | E. Hemingway [signature].

NOTE: Reprinted in *The United States Navy in World War II*, ed. S. E. Smith, New York, 1966, pp. 603-616. See (B62).

22 Hemingway

A. First edition:
The Viking Portable Library [in script] | [long rule] | HEMING-WAY | [decorative line and rule] | Edited by Malcolm Cowley [in script] | [long rule] | NEW YORK [dot] THE VIKING PRESS | 1944

6 7/16 x 4 1/4. Published September 18, 1944, at $2.00, as No. 6 of the Viking Portable Library. The first printing consisted of 20,000 copies. Issued in red cloth with a large decorative black "H" on the front cover. Stamped in black on the backstrip: [thick rule] | [thin rule] | [star] | [thin rule] | [thick rule] | Heming- | way | [thick rule] | [thin rule] | [star] | [thin rule] | [thick rule] | THE | VI-KING | PORTABLE | LIBRARY | [thin rule] | [thick rule] | EDITED | BY | Malcolm | Cowley | [thick rule] | [thin rule] | THE | VIKING | PRESS | [thin rule] | [thick rule]. All edges stained yellow.

COLLATION: 1 leaf + [i]-xxxiv + [1]-[646], as follows: [blank leaf]; [i] half title; [ii] *Other Books in The Viking Portable Library*; [iii] title page as above; [iv] notices of compliance with the War Production Board conservation orders, copyright, reservation of rights, printing, and note of origin; v-vi CONTENTS; vii-xxiv INTRO-DUCTION by Malcolm Cowley; [1] divisional half title: [decorative line] | THE NOVELS | [decorative line]; [2] blank; 3-642 text; [643]-[646] blank.

CONTENTS: *The Sun Also Rises*/Chs. I-VII, here titled "Caporetto," from *A Farewell to Arms*/Ch. XVIII, here titled "A Boatload for Cuba," from *To Have and Have Not*/Ch. XXVII, here titled "El Sordo on the Hilltop," from *For Whom the Bell Tolls*/*In Our Time*, complete with inter-chapters/In Another Country/Hills Like White Elephants/The Killers/Today Is Friday/A Clean, Well-Lighted Place/The Light of the World/A Way You'll Never Be/The Short Happy Life of Francis Macomber/The Snows of Kilimanjaro/Ch. XX, the last chapter of *Death in the Afternoon,* here titled "Epilogue." Note: Ten Editor's Prefaces precede the various sections of the book.

NOTE: The dust jacket is printed in red, white, and yellow.

PRINTING HISTORY: Reprinted in September 1944, October 1944, and October 1949.

23 Across the River and Into the Trees

A. First American edition:

ACROSS THE RIVER | AND | INTO THE TREES | BY | *ER-NEST HEMINGWAY* | *CHARLES SCRIBNER'S SONS* | *NEW YORK* | *1950*

8 1/4 x 5 1/2. Published September 7, 1950, at $3.00. The first printing consisted of 75,000 copies. Issued in black cloth with the author's signature stamped in gold on the front cover. Stamped in gold on the backstrip: [four rules] | ACROSS | THE | RIVER | AND | INTO | THE | TREES | [triple rule] | ERNEST | HEM-INGWAY | [four rules] | SCRIBNERS. Top and bottom edges trimmed, fore edges untrimmed.

COLLATION: [i]-[xii] + 1-308, as follows: [i] blank; [ii] *BOOKS BY*; [iii] half title; [iv] blank; [v] title page as above; [vi] notice of copyright, note of origin, reservation of rights, Scribner's "A," and printer's device; [vii] dedication: To Mary With Love; [viii] blank; [ix] Note (legal disclaimer) ; [x] blank; [xi] half title; [xii] blank; 1-308 text.

"NOTE" on p. [ix]: In view of a recent tendency to identify characters in fiction | with real people, it seems proper to state that there are no real | people in this volume: both the characters and their names are | fictitious. The names or designations of any military units are | fictitious. There are no living people nor existing military units | presented in this book.

PREVIOUS PUBLICATION: *ARIT* first appeared serialized in *Cosmopolitan*, CXXVIII (Feb. 1950–June 1950). Numerous changes, additions, and omissions were made prior to book publication. For example: "Conte Carlo" was changed to "Count Andrea"; the passages regarding "the Honorable Pacciardi," on pp. 39-41, were added; the passages regarding d'Annunzio, on pp. 49-51, were added; the whole of Ch. xxxvii was added; the deletions were filled in; etc.

NOTE: The title is taken from the last words of General Thomas J. (Stonewall) Jackson, which are quoted on p. 307: "Let us cross over the river and rest under the shade of the trees."

NOTE: The English edition was published September 4, 1950, preceding the American edition by three days. See (A44a).

NOTE: The dust jacket is black with yellow lettering and a drawing of Venice, by "A. Ivancich," in white, yellow, and orange. A photograph of Hemingway by Paul Radkai appears on the back cover. In a later state the dust jacket has orange lettering on the backstrip.

PRINTING HISTORY: Reprinted in September 1950.

NOTE: *ARIT* appeared on the *N.Y. Times Book Review*'s Best Seller List from September 24, 1950 to February 11, 1951. During the twenty-one weeks that it appeared, it was in first place for seven weeks, from October 15 to November 26, 1950.

NOTE: 25 "advance copies," issued in blue cloth, were printed from discarded plates *after* the first edition was run off. [See David A. Randall's "Dukedom Large Enough: ii. Hemingway, Churchill, and the Printed Word," *Papers of the Bibliographical Society of America*, LVI (July–Sept. 1962), 351.] These "advance copies" contain the following errors: On p. 21, line 26, "Papadopohi" should read "Papadopoli." On p. 24, line 5, there should be a period after "got" and "o" made a capital in "One." On p. 80, line 21, the second "how" should be omitted. A penciled note by David A. Randall, dated August 7, 1950, on the flyleaf of the "advance copies" mentions the first and third corrections. The note is reprinted and the additional correction is mentioned in Randall's article, pp. 350-351.

B. Reprint edition:

Across the River and into the Trees, published by Garden City Books, New York, in October 1951, at $1.49. Note: This book has not been examined by the bibliographer.

C. Paperback edition:

[On the left-hand page:] ACROSS the RIVER [On the right-hand page:] and INTO the TREES | by | ERNEST HEMINGWAY | Author of | THE OLD MAN AND THE SEA | FOR WHOM THE BELL TOLLS | TO HAVE AND HAVE NOT | A FAREWELL TO ARMS, etc. | A DELL BOOK

6 3/8 x 4 1/4. Published by the Dell Publishing Co., Inc., New

York, January 2, 1953, at thirty-five cents, as Dell Book No. D 117. Issued in dark blue stiff paper covers printed in red and yellow, with an illustrative scene in color, by Griffith Foxley, on the front cover. All edges stained red.

COLLATION: [1]-320, as follows: [1] blurb on the book; [2]-[3] title page as above; [4] publisher's address, executives' names, notices of original copyright, reservation of rights, publication arrangement, and note of origin; [5] legal disclaimer; [6] dedication; [7]-320 text.

D. Uniform edition:
ACROSS THE RIVER | AND | INTO THE TREES | BY | *ER-NEST HEMINGWAY* | *CHARLES SCRIBNER'S SONS* | *NEW YORK*
8 3/16 x 5 1/2. Published in October 1956, at $4.50. Issued in yellow cloth. Stamped in gold on the front cover: ACROSS THE RIVER | [ornament at either end] | AND INTO THE TREES. Backstrip: the title is stamped in gold on a black block; the author's name and publisher's name are stamped in black on gold blocks. All edges trimmed.

COLLATION: [i]-[xii] + 1-308. The same pagination as the first edition.

NOTE: The yellow dust jacket is printed in the uniform design, in dark blue, white, and black.

24 The Old Man and the Sea

A. First edition:
THE OLD MAN | AND | THE SEA | ERNEST HEMINGWAY | CHARLES SCRIBNER'S SONS, NEW YORK | 1952
8 x 5 3/8. Published September 8, 1952, at $3.00. The first printing consisted of 50,000 copies. Issued in light blue cloth with the author's signature blind-stamped on the front cover. Stamped in silver on the backstrip: ERNEST HEMINGWAY [reading downward] | THE | OLD | MAN | AND | THE | SEA [title horizontal] | SCRIBNERS [reading downward]. Top and bottom edges trimmed, fore edges untrimmed.

COLLATION: [i]-[ii] + [1]-[142], as follows: [i] blank; [ii] *BOOKS BY*; [1] half title; [2] blank; [3] title page as above; [4] notices of copyright, note of origin, reservation of rights, Scribner's "A," and Scribner's press device; [5] dedication: TO CHARLIE SCRIBNER | AND | TO MAX PERKINS; [6] blank; [7] half title; [8] blank; 9-140 text; [141]-[142] blank.

PREVIOUS PUBLICATION: Eleven days in advance of the book's publication the full text of the 27,000-word novella appeared in twenty pages of *Life*, XXXIII (Sept. 1, 1952). See (C370).

63

NOTE: The blue dust jacket is lettered in black and white, with a drawing, by "A," in blue and brown on the front cover. A photograph of Hemingway, by Lee Samuels, appears on the back cover. The deep blue ink in the photograph was changed to olive in later states of the dust jacket. Two lines of small production symbols appear at the end of the text on the back flap of the original dust jacket. These symbols were later omitted and the back cover was changed to include mention of Hemingway winning the Nobel prize.

NOTE: The first 30 sets of sheets were bound uncut in black buckram for presentation only. The author's signature is blind-stamped on the front cover. Stamped in gold on the backstrip.

NOTE: *OMATS* appeared on the *N.Y. Times Book Review*'s Best Seller List from September 14, 1952, to March 8, 1953. During the twenty-six weeks that it appeared on the list, it did not reach higher than third place.

NOTE: *OMATS* was half of the dual selection of the Book-of-the-Month Club in September 1952. The first printing consisted of 153,000 copies. Issued in light blue cloth covers identical to the first edition. The Kingsport Press [Tennessee] imprint appears on the copyright page. The Book-of-the-Month Club trademark appears on the front flap of the dust jacket. Later printings of the book were in a variant binding of dark blue cloth.

NOTE: An abridged version of *OMATS* was published in English as a German textbook by Silva-Verlag, in Iserlohn, in 1953. Abridgment and preface by Paul Kämmer. 72 pages. [See William White's article in *Papers of the Bibliographical Society of America*, LX (Jan.–March 1966), 89-90].

NOTE: *OMATS* was published unabridged in English in Nan'un-do's Contemporary Library series, by Nan'un-do, in Tokyo, in [1957]. Edited with Notes (in English and Japanese) by Kōzō Hayashibara. 130 pages.

NOTE: *OMATS* was reprinted in full in *Three Novels of Ernest Hemingway*, 1962, pp. 1-72, with an introduction by Carlos Baker. See (A29).

B. College edition:

[Drawing] | The Old Man and the Sea | *by* | ERNEST HEMINGWAY | CHARLES SCRIBNER'S SONS | *597 Fifth Avenue, New York 17, New York*

7 x 4 5/8. Published in September 1960, at $1.60. Issued in bright blue cloth backstrip over light blue covers. Design of a fish and the author's signature stamped in gold on the light blue front cover. Stamped in gold on the backstrip: HEMINGWAY [reading downward] | The | Old | Man | and | the Sea | SCRIBNERS [reading

downward]. Stamped in gold on the light blue back cover: [publisher's device] | COLLEGE | EDITION. All edges trimmed.

COLLATION: [1]-[128], as follows [1] half title; [2] blank; [3] title page as above; [4] dedication, notice of copyright, note of origin, reservation of rights, publisher's symbols; [5]-127 text; [128] blank.

NOTE: The light blue dust jacket is printed in dark blue. The front flap is marked: *SPECIAL STUDENT'S EDITION.*

c. Illustrated edition:

[Drawing] | The Old Man [red] | and the Sea [red] | BY ERNEST HEMINGWAY | ILLUSTRATED EDITION [red] | CHARLES SCRIBNER'S SONS | *New York*

8 1/2 x 5 7/8. Published in October 1960, at $5.00. Issued in black cloth backstrip over bright blue covers. Design of a fish stamped in gold on the blue front cover. Stamped in gold on the backstrip, reading downward: HEMINGWAY The Old Man and the Sea SCRIBNERS. The publisher's device is stamped in gold on the blue back cover. All edges trimmed; top edge gilt. Light blue endpapers with drawings in dark blue.

COLLATION: [1]-[144], as follows: [1] blank; [2] *Books by*; [3] half title [4] frontispiece: drawing; [5] title page as above; [6] notices of copyright, reservation of rights, publisher's "A-9.60 (Q) " and note of origin; [7] dedication; [8] blank; [9] PUBLISHERS' NOTE (regarding illustrations) ; [10] blank; 11-138 text; [139] drawing; [140]-[144] blank.

PUBLISHERS' NOTE on p. [9]: "The drawings in this illustrated edition of *The Old Man and the Sea* are the work of Raymond Sheppard and C. F. Tunnicliffe." The note is followed by a listing of the pages on which the work of each artist appears.

NOTE: The dust jacket is printed in three shades of blue with black and white lettering. An illustration from the book appears on the front cover and another on the back cover.

d. School edition:

[Drawing] | The Old Man and the Sea | *by* | ERNEST HEMING-WAY | CHARLES SCRIBNER'S SONS | *597 Fifth Avenue, New York 17, New York*

7 x 4 5/8. Published in June 1961, at $1.60. Issued in light green cloth with a drawing stamped in black on the front cover. Stamped in white on the front cover: The Old Man and the Sea | *by ERNEST HEMINGWAY*. Backstrip: *Ernest* | *Hemingway* [two lines, in black, reading downward] | THE | OLD | MAN | AND | THE | SEA [title in black] | *SCHOOL* | *EDITION* [two lines, in white, reading downward] | SCRIBNERS [in black, reading downward]. All edges trimmed.

COLLATION: [1]-[160], as follows: [1] half title; [2] blank; [3] title page as above; [4] dedication, notices of copyright, study guide copyright, reservation of rights, publisher's symbols, and note of origin; [5]-127 text; [128] blank; [129] divisional title: *STUDY GUIDE | by |* MARY A. CAMPBELL; [130] blank; 131-148 text of study guide; 149-154 *NOTES ON THE TEXT*; 155-157 *QUESTIONS FOR STUDY AND DISCUSSION*; 158 *THE NOVEL AS A WHOLE— TOPICS FOR | DISCUSSION AND WRITING*; 159 *BOOKS ABOUT HEMINGWAY* [a checklist of five studies]; [160] blank. NOTE: A dust jacket was not issued with this edition.

E. Paperback edition:
ERNEST HEMINGWAY | THE OLD MAN | AND THE SEA | [ornament] | CHARLES SCRIBNER'S SONS, NEW YORK
8 x 5 3/8. Published in January 1965, at $1.25, as No. SL 104 of the Scribner Library series. Issued in gray stiff paper covers, printed in blue, white, and black.
COLLATION: [1]-[128], as follows: [1] blank; [2] *Books by*; [3] half title; [4] blank; [5] title page as above; [6] notices of copyright, reservation of rights, Scribner's "A-165 (Col.)" and note of origin; [7] dedication; [8] blank; 9-127 text; [128] blank.

25 The Hemingway Reader

A. First edition:
Ernest Hemingway | THE | HEMINGWAY | READER | *SE-LECTED | with a Foreword and twelve Brief Prefaces | by* CHARLES POORE | [publisher's device] | CHARLES SCRIB-NER'S SONS | NEW YORK 1953
8 5/16 x 5 5/8. Published in September 1953, at $5.00. The first printing consisted of 15,850 copies. Issued in rust-colored cloth, stamped in gold on the front cover and backstrip. Cover: [row of ornaments] | THE HEMINGWAY READER. Backstrip: Ernest | Hemingway | THE | HEMINGWAY | READER | SCRIBNERS. The publisher's device is blind-stamped on the back cover. Top and bottom edges trimmed, fore edges untrimmed.
COLLATION: [i]-xx + [1]-652, as follows: [i] blank; [ii] BOOKS BY; [iii] half title; [iv] blank; [v] title page as above; [vi] notices of copyright, change of title, reservation of rights, note of origin, Scribner's "(A)"; vii-viii CONTENTS; [ix] half title: *THE HEM-INGWAY READER | FOREWORD | by Charles Poore*; [x] blank; xi-xx *FOREWORD*; [1] divisional title: *from* IN OUR TIME | BIG TWO-HEARTED RIVER; [2] brief preface; 3-652 text.
CONTENTS: Big Two-Hearted River/*The Torrents of Spring*/*The Sun Also Rises*/Book Three (Chs. XXV-XXXII), here titled "The Retreat from Caporetto," and Chs. XXXV-XXXVII, here titled "Stresa,"

from *A Farewell to Arms*/A Way You'll Never Be/Fifty Grand/A Clean, Well-Lighted Place/The Light of the World/After the Storm/Ch. VII, here titled "The Bullfight," and Ch. XX, here titled "The Last Chapter," from *Death in the Afternoon*/Ch. I from *Green Hills of Africa*/Part One (Chs. I-V), here titled "One Trip Across," from *To Have and Have Not*/Ch. XXVII, here titled "Sordo's Stand," from *For Whom the Bell Tolls*/The Short Happy Life of Francis Macomber/The Capital of the World/The Snows of Kilimanjaro/Old Man at the Bridge/The Fable of the Good Lion/Chs. IV-VI, here titled "Venice and the Veneto," from *Across the River and Into the Trees*/an excerpt from *The Old Man and the Sea*, here titled "The Fight with the Sharks." Note: Twelve short prefaces precede the various selections.

PREVIOUS PUBLICATION: *The Torrents of Spring* is reprinted here for the first time since 1932. This is the first appearance in book form of "The Fable of the Good Lion," which appeared in *Holiday*, IX (March 1951), as "The Good Lion."

NOTE: An errata slip is inserted between pp. 86-87, regarding four transposed lines in *SAR*, which appear on pp. 112, 170, 175, and 255.

NOTE: The gold-colored dust jacket is printed in the uniform design, in red, white, and black.

NOTE: *The Hemingway Reader* was offered as a book dividend by the Book-of-the-Month Club in August 1953. The book club's trademark appears on the front dust jacket flap.

B. College edition:

Ernest Hemingway | THE | HEMINGWAY | READER | SE-LECTED | *with a Foreword and twelve Brief Prefaces* | *by* CHARLES POORE | [publisher's device] | CHARLES SCRIB-NER'S SONS | NEW YORK 1953

8 5/16 x 5 5/8. Published in July 1954, at $2.75. Issued in a red cloth backstrip over gray covers. The author's signature is stamped in silver on the red cloth section of the front cover. Stamped in silver on the gray front cover: MODERN | STANDARD | AU-THORS | EDITION. Stamped in silver on the backstrip: Ernest | Hemingway | THE | HEMINGWAY | READER | SCRIBNERS. Same pagination as the first edition. The dust jacket is printed in red and gray.

NOTE: Reissued in variant bindings of black cloth backstrip over red covers, stamped in gold; and in black cloth backstrip over bluish-gray covers, stamped in dark blue.

C. Paperback edition:

Ernest Hemingway | THE | HEMINGWAY | READER | SE-LECTED | *with a Foreword and twelve Brief Prefaces* | *by*

CHARLES POORE | [publisher's device] | CHARLES SCRIB-
NER'S SONS | NEW YORK
8 x 5 3/8. Published in June 1965, at $2.95, as No. SL 119 of the
Scribner Library series. Issued in blue stiff paper covers, printed
in black and white. Same pagination as the first edition.

26 The Collected Poems

A. Pirated edition:

NUMBER ONE OF | The Library of Living Poetry | THE COL-
LECTED POEMS | *of* | ERNEST HEMINGWAY [the title and author's
name are enclosed in a ruled border with a thick second rule at
top and a broken thick rule and an ornamental design at the bot-
tom] | ORIGINALLY | PUBLISHED IN PARIS
9 x 6. Unauthorized pamphlet: no place, date, publisher, or copyright. Issued in white paper covers of the same weight as the leaves,
printed in black. Wire stapled.

COLLATION: 24 unnumbered pages, including the paper covers: [1]
front cover, which serves as the title page, as above; [2] blank; [3]
divisional title: MISCELLANEOUS POEMS; [4]-[11] text; [12]
divisional title: TEN POEMS | from | *Three Stories and Ten
Poems,* | Paris, 1923.; [13]-[23] text; [24] blank.

CONTENTS: [Part One:] ULTIMATELY/THE ERNEST LIBER-
AL'S LAMENT/THE SOUL OF SPAIN (*In the manner of Gertrude
Stein*)/Part Two of THE SOUL OF SPAIN/THE LADY POET
WITH FOOTNOTES/THE AGE DEMANDED/NEO-THOMIST
POEM. [Part Two:] MITRAIGLIATRICE/OKLAHOMA/OILY
WEATHER / T. ROOSEVELT / CAPTIVES / CHAMPS D'HON-
NEUR / RIPARTO   D'ASSALTO / MONTPARNASSE / ALONG
WITH YOUTH/CHAPTER HEADING/VALENTINE: For a Mr.
Lee Wilson Dodd and Any of His Friends Who Want It.

PREVIOUS PUBLICATION: "Ultimately" is reprinted from the *Double
Dealer*, III (June 1922). "The Ernest Liberal's Lament" is reprinted
from *Querschnitt*, IV (Autumn 1924); the original spelling was
"Earnest." "The Soul of Spain" is reprinted from *Querschnitt*, IV
(Autumn 1924). This poem was originally titled "The Soul of
Spain with McAlmon and Bird the Publishers," without the subheading in parentheses. "Part Two of The Soul of Spain" is reprinted from *Querschnitt*, IV (Nov. 1924); it includes Part Two,
Part III, Part IV, and two Part V's. "The Lady Poet with Footnotes"
is reprinted from *Querschnitt*, IV (Nov. 1924); the original title has
"Poets" and "Foot Notes" in two words. "The Age Demanded" is
reprinted from *Querschnitt*, V (Feb. 1925). "Neo-Thomist Poem"
is reprinted from *Exile*, No. 1 (Spring 1927) ; it was originally misspelled "Neothoemist Poem." A footnote has been added in this

pamphlet: "The title 'Neo-Thomist Poem' refers to temporary embracing of church by literary gents—E. H." The footnote is taken from a letter from Hemingway to Louis Henry Cohn, which is quoted in *Cohn's Bibliography*, p. 89. The ten poems from *TSTP* are reprinted as they first appeared, with the exception of the added "T." [for Theodore] to the title of "Roosevelt." "Valentine" is reprinted from the *Little Review*, XII (May 1929).

B. Pirated edition:

NUMBER ONE OF | The Library of Living Poetry | THE COLLECTED POEMS | *of* | ERNEST HEMINGWAY [the title and author's name are enclosed in a ruled border with a thick second rule at top and a broken thick rule and an ornamental design at the bottom] | ORIGINALLY | PUBLISHED IN PARIS

7 1/4 x 5. Unauthorized pamphlet: no place, date, publisher, or copyright. Issued in white paper covers the same weight as the leaves. The cover is identical to the cover of the first edition. Wire stapled. 24 unnumbered pages, including the cover which serves as the title page. The pagination is the same as the first edition, except for two illustrations: the frontispiece, on the inside front cover, is a drawing of Hemingway by [John Blomshield], which appeared on the original dust jacket of *SAR*; and a photograph of Hemingway, which appeared in *Flair*, 1 (Feb. 1950), appears on the back cover.

CONTENTS: The same as the first edition, except the first part is in a different order: ULTIMATELY/THE LADY POET WITH FOOTNOTES/THE AGE DEMANDED/THE ERNEST LIBERAL'S LAMENT/THE SOUL OF SPAIN (*In the manner of Gertrude Stein*)/Part Two of THE SOUL OF SPAIN/NEO-THOMIST POEM.

C. Pirated edition:

ORIGINALLY | PUBLISHED IN PARIS | The | COLLECTED | POEMS | of | Ernest Hemingway | PIRATED EDITION | SAN FRANCISCO | 1960

7 x 5. Unauthorized pamphlet: no publisher or copyright. Issued in paper covers of the same weight as the leaves, printed in black, gray, and white. Wire stapled. The back cover is blank except for the price: 50 | cents.

COLLATION: 28 pages (+ paper covers) : [1] half title; [2] frontispiece: drawing of Hemingway by [John Blomshield]; [3] title page as above; [4] designed by Brayton [vertical, in upper left-hand corner, facing the fore edge]; [5] contents; [6] blank; [7] divisional title: MISCELLANEOUS POEMS; [8] blank; 9-16 text; [17] divisional title: TEN | POEMS | from | *Three Stories and Ten Poems,* | Paris, 1923.; 18-28 text.

CONTENTS: The same poems and in the same order as the second edition of The Library of Living Poetry, Number One.

27 Two Christmas Tales

A. Privately printed, limited edition:

Two [drawing] | CHRISTMAS | [drawing] *Tales* | by | ERNEST | HEMINGWAY | THE HART PRESS :: CHRISTMAS 1959

9 1/2 x 6 1/2. Published by Ruth and James D. Hart in Berkeley, Calif. Issued in blue paper covers slightly larger than the leaves. Printed in dark brown on the front cover: TWO CHRISTMAS TALES | [line] | [two drawings, separated by a vertical line] | [line] | [ornament] by ERNEST HEMINGWAY [ornament] [all enclosed in an unruled border]. Stitched with white thread. Printed on Arches Buff paper.

COLLATION: [i]-[iv] + [1]-[8], as follows: [i]-[ii] blank; [iii] title page as above; [iv] blank; [1]-3 A NORTH OF ITALY CHRISTMAS; 3-[5] CHRISTMAS IN PARIS; [6] colophon; [7]-[8] blank.

COLOPHON, on p. [6]: These tales, originally published in *The Toronto Star* | *Weekly*, December 22, 1923, are now reprinted for | the first time. Illustrated by Victor Anderson, print- | ed by Ruth & James D. Hart, Berkeley, Mcmlix.

NOTE: 150 copies of this pamphlet were printed as a Christmas booklet for friends; no copies were sold.

28 The Snows of Kilimanjaro and Other Stories

A. First edition:

THE SNOWS | OF KILIMANJARO | AND OTHER STORIES | *by Ernest Hemingway* | *CHARLES SCRIBNER'S SONS* | *New York*

8 x 5 3/8. Published in January 1961, at $1.25, as No. SL 32 of the Scribner Library series. Issued in dark gray stiff paper covers, printed in green, black, and white.

COLLATION: [i]-[vi] + [1]-154, as follows: [i] half title; [ii] *Books by*; [iii] title page as above; [iv] notices of copyright, reservation of rights, Scribner's "A-1.61 (C) ," and note of origin; [v] CONTENTS; [vi] blank; [1] half title; [2] blank; 3-154 text.

CONTENTS: The Snows of Kilimanjaro/My Old Man/Big Two-Hearted River (Parts I and II)/In Another Country/The Killers/A Way You'll Never Be/Fifty Grand/The Short Happy Life of Francis Macomber.

B. Revised, hard-cover edition:

THE SNOWS | OF KILIMANJARO | AND OTHER STORIES | *by Ernest Hemingway* | *CHARLES SCRIBNER'S SONS* | *New York*

8 x 5 9/16. Published in September 1962, at $3.50. Issued in smooth green cloth printed in gold on the backstrip only. Backstrip, reading downward: HEMINGWAY THE SNOWS OF KILIMANJARO [top line] | AND OTHER STORIES SCRIBNERS [bottom line]. All edges trimmed.

COLLATION: [i]-[vi] + [1]-154. The same pagination as the original paperback edition.

CONTENTS: The Snows of Kilimanjaro/A Clean, Well-Lighted Place/A Day's Wait/The Gambler, the Nun, and the Radio/Fathers and Sons/In Another Country/The Killers/A Way You'll Never Be/Fifty Grand/The Short Happy Life of Francis Macomber.

NOTE: Two stories in the original paperback edition have been omitted from this edition and four new stories have been added. This change was made due to publication of *IOT* in the Scribner Library series, thereby causing a duplication of "My Old Man" and "Big Two-Hearted River" in both paperback editions.

NOTE: The green dust jacket is printed in black and white.

C. Second paperback edition:

The Snows of Kilimanjaro and Other Stories was reprinted in September 1962, at $1.25, as No. SL 32 of the Scribner Library series. Issued in the same gray stiff paper covers as the original paperback edition. The title page and pagination are the same as the two previous editions. The contents are the same as the revised hardcover edition.

29 Three Novels of Ernest Hemingway

A. First edition:

MODERN STANDARD AUTHORS | [graduated line] | THREE NOVELS OF ERNEST HEMINGWAY | *The Sun Also Rises* | WITH AN INTRODUCTION BY | MALCOLM COWLEY | *A Farewell to Arms* | WITH AN INTRODUCTION BY | ROBERT PENN WARREN | *The Old Man and the Sea* | WITH AN INTRODUCTION BY | CARLOS BAKER | CHARLES SCRIBNER'S SONS | [graduated line] | NEW YORK

8 3/16 x 5 7/16. Published in May 1962, at $4.50, in the Modern Standard Authors series. Issued in a black cloth backstrip over green covers. The author's signature is stamped in gold on the black cloth section of the front cover. Stamped in gold on the back-

strip: [thick rule] | THREE NOVELS | [ornament] | THE SUN | ALSO RISES | A FAREWELL | TO ARMS | THE OLD MAN | AND THE SEA | [ornament] | ERNEST HEMINGWAY | [thick rule] | *SCRIBNERS*. All edges trimmed. Printed on 40-pound basis English finish.

COLLATION: [752] pages, as follows: [i] half title; [ii] blank; [iii] title page as above; [iv] notices of copyright, Scribner's "A-5.62 [Col]," note of origin, Library of Congress number; [v] CONTENTS (without pagination); [vi] blank; [vii] introductory title; [viii] blank; ix-xxviii INTRODUCTION *"Commencing with the Simplest Things"* by Malcolm Cowley; [xxix] divisional title: *The Sun Also Rises*; [xxx] blank; [xxxi] dedication; [xxxii] blank; [xxxiii] quotations; [xxxiv] blank; [1] *BOOK I*; [2] blank; 3-247 text of *SAR*; [248] blank; [i] introductory title; [ii] blank; iii-xl INTRODUCTION by Robert Penn Warren; [xli] divisional title: *A Farewell to Arms*; [xlii] blank; [xliii] dedication; [xliv] blank; [1] BOOK ONE; [2] blank; 3-332 text of *FTA*; [i] introductory title; [ii] blank; iii-xvii INTRODUCTION by Carlos Baker; [xviii] blank; [xix] divisional title: *The Old Man and the Sea*; [xx] blank; [xxi] dedication; [xxii] blank; 1-72 text of *OMATS*.

NOTE: Robert Penn Warren's introduction to *FTA* is reprinted from Scribner's Modern Standard Authors edition of *FTA* (1949).

30 Hemingway: The Wild Years

A. First edition:

THE WILD YEARS | ERNEST HEMINGWAY | *Edited and Introduced by* GENE Z. HANRAHAN | *an original volume* [slanted line] A DELL FIRST EDITION

6 3/8 x 4 1/4. Published by the Dell Publishing Co., Inc., New York, in December 1962, at sixty cents, as a Dell First Edition, No. 3577. The first printing consisted of 127,673 copies. Issued in black stiff paper covers printed in red, white, pink, and gray. Front cover: DELL | [short rule] | FIRST | EDITION [all in black, on a gray background] | 3577 [gray] [all in left-hand corner] | 60¢ [in pink, in right-hand corner] | Never before published in book form— | 73 articles by America's greatest writer [all in white] | HEMING-WAY [red] | THE WILD YEARS [white] | [photograph of Hemingway, taken in Africa in 1934]. All edges stained blue.

COLLATION: [1]-288, as follows: [1] blurb on the book; [2] frontispiece: unsigned woodcut of Hemingway; [3] title page as above; [4] publisher's address, notice of copyright, date of first printing, and note of origin; [5]-9 *INTRODUCTION* by Gene Z. Hanrahan; [10] blank; [11]-[13] CONTENTS; [14] blank; [15]-281 text; [282]-288 *APPENDIX: SOURCE OF HEMINGWAY'S WRITINGS*.

CONTENTS: Seventy-three articles by Hemingway, which appeared in the *Toronto Star Weekly* and the *Toronto Daily Star* between March 6, 1920, and January 12, 1924. The articles are arranged in twelve related sections, with a brief head note by the editor preceding each section and a concluding commentary which comprises section thirteen.

PRINTING HISTORY: Reprinted in March 1963.

31 A Moveable Feast

A. First edition:

ERNEST HEMINGWAY | *A Moveable Feast* | [ornament] | If you are lucky enough to have lived | in Paris as a young man, then wherever you | go for the rest of your life, it stays with | you, for Paris is a moveable feast. | ERNEST HEMINGWAY | *to a friend, 1950* | CHARLES SCRIBNER'S SONS, *New York*

8 3/16 x 5 7/16. Published May 5, 1964, at $4.95. The first printing consisted of 85,000 copies. Issued in a rust cloth backstrip over gray-green covers. The author's signature is stamped in gold on the gray-green front cover. Stamped in gold on the backstrip, reading downward: HEMINGWAY [ornament] *A Moveable Feast* [ornament] SCRIBNERS. The publisher's device is stamped in gold on the gray-green back cover. All edges trimmed; top edges stained gray-green. Gray-green endpapers.

COLLATION: [i]-[xii] + [1]-[212] + 8 pages of photographs, as follows: [i] *BOOKS BY*; [ii] blank; [iii] half title; [iv] blank; [v] title page as above; [vi] notices of copyright, reservation of rights, Scribner's "A-3.64 (H)," PICTURE ACKNOWLEDGMENTS, note of origin, and Library of Congress number; [vii] *Contents*; [viii] blank; [ix] *Preface* by Hemingway, dated: San Francisco de Paula, Cuba | 1960; [x] blank; [xi] *Note* by "M.H." [Mary Hemingway]; [xii] blank; [1] divisional title: *A Good Café | on the Place St.-Michel |* [ornament]; [2] blank; 3-211 text (9 photographs, on eight pages, are inserted between pp. 180-181) ; [212] blank.

CONTENTS: A Good Café on the Place St.-Michel/Miss Stein Instructs/"Une Génération Perdue"/Shakespeare and Company/ People of the Seine/A False Spring/The End of an Avocation/ Hunger Was Good Discipline/Ford Madox Ford and the Devil's Disciple/Birth of a New School/With Pascin at the Dome/Ezra Pound and His Bel Esprit/A Strange Enough Ending/The Man Who Was Marked for Death/Evan Shipman at the Lilas/An Agent of Evil/Scott Fitzgerald/Hawks Do Not Share/A Matter of Measurements/There Is Never Any End to Paris.

PREVIOUS PUBLICATION: Selected passages from eleven of the sketches appeared in *Life*, LVI (April 10, 1964). See (C420).

NOTE: Part of a sentence was omitted on p. 198. The sentence, beginning on line 27, reads: You climbed | on seal skins that you attached to the bottoms of the skis. In the Cape edition, p. 178, line 8, the sentence reads: You climbed on foot carrying your skis and | higher up, where the snow was too deep, you climbed | on sealskins that you attached to the bottom of the skis. The complete sentence also appears in the Bantam paperback edition, pp. 196-197.

NOTE: The "friend" to whom the epigraph on the title page was spoken, in 1950, was A. E. Hotchner. [See *Papa Hemingway*, New York, 1966, p. 57.]

NOTE: Mary Hemingway's *Note*, on p. [xi], begins: "Ernest started writing this book in Cuba in the autumn of 1957. . . ." Her note in the Cape edition begins: "Ernest started writing this book in Cuba in the summer of 1958. . . ." According to Mary Hemingway, her original note read "the summer of 1958" but Leonard Lyons noticed the error and it was corrected to "the autumn of 1957." Inadvertently, the Cape edition was not changed.

NOTE: For the extent of Mary Hemingway's editing of Hemingway's first posthumously published work, see her article "The Making of the Book: A Chronicle and a Memoir," *N.Y. Times Book Review* (May 10, 1964) p. 27.

NOTE: The painting of Pont Neuf, Paris, on the cover of the dust jacket is by Hildegard Rath. Below it, on a dark blue band, is the title in pale orange, subheading in pale blue: SKETCHES OF THE AUTHOR'S LIFE | IN PARIS IN THE TWENTIES, and the author's name in white. On the back cover is a portrait of Hemingway by Henry Strater and a brief reminiscence by the artist on the occasion of his painting Hemingway, in Rapallo, Italy, during the winter of 1922-1923.

PRINTING HISTORY: Reprinted twice in May 1964.

NOTE: *AMF* appeared on the *N.Y. Times Book Review's* General Best Seller List from May 24 to December 6, 1964; it was in first place for nineteen weeks, from June 14 to October 18, 1964.

NOTE: A Book-of-the-Month Club edition was published in June 1964, when it was chosen as the selection for that month. The first printing consisted of 204,000 copies.

B. Paperback edition:
[Long rule] | ERNEST | HEMINGWAY'S | A MOVEABLE | FEAST | [long rule] | *If you are lucky enough to have lived | in Paris as a young man, then wherever you go | for the rest of your life, it stays with | you, for Paris is a moveable feast.* | *ERNEST HEMINGWAY* | *to a friend, 1950* | [publisher's device encircled by:] [dot] BANTAM BOOKS [dot] TORONTO NEW YORK LONDON

7 x 4 3/16. Published by Bantam Books, Inc., New York, in November 1965, at ninety-five cents, as No. N 3048. Issued in stiff white paper covers printed in brown and black. All edges stained yellow.

COLLATION: [i]-[xii] + [1]-[212], as follows: [i] epigraph, blurb on the book, half title, and review excerpt; [ii]-[iii] six brief excerpts from reviews of the book; [iv] Books by; [v] title page as above; [vi] publication arrangement, printing history, reservation of rights, notice of copyright, publisher's address, and note of origin; [vii] *Contents*; [viii] blank; [ix] *Preface* by Hemingway; [x] blank; [xi] *Note* by "M. H." [Mary Hemingway]; [xii] blank; [1] divisional title; [2] blank; [3]-209 text; [210] blank; [211] *About the Author*; [212] blank.

ENGLISH

EDITIONS

32 A. First English edition:

IN OUR TIME | *STORIES BY* | ERNEST HEMINGWAY | [publisher's device] | LONDON: | JONATHAN CAPE 30 BEDFORD SQUARE

7 3/8 x 4 7/8. Published September 23, 1926, at 6s. Issued in green cloth, stamped in gold on the backstrip only. Blind-ruled border around the front cover and publisher's device blind-stamped on the center of the back cover. All edges trimmed. Signatures are in 16s with printer's marks.

COLLATION: [1]-[256], as follows: [1]-[2] blank; [3] half title; [4] blank; [5] title page as above; [6] notice of first English publication only; [7] dedication: To | HADLEY RICHARDSON HEMINGWAY; [8] blank; [9] CONTENTS; [10] blank; [11] epigraph; [12] blank; [13] half title; [14] blank; [15]-[249] text; [250] printer's note; [251]-[256] blank.

NOTE: The order of the *iot* inter-chapters and the stories is the same as in the first edition. See (A3a). Textual changes were made in several of the stories, most notably in "Mr. and Mrs. Elliot" and the ending of "A Very Short Story."

NOTE: The white dust jacket, printed in blue and black, states that this volume is No. 5 of THE STORY SERIES.

NOTE: Reissued in 1947 in *The Essential Hemingway*.

33 A. First English edition:

FIESTA | By | ERNEST HEMINGWAY | [publisher's device] | LONDON | JONATHAN CAPE 30 BEDFORD SQUARE

7 1/2 x 5. Published June 9, 1927, at 7s. 6d. Issued in blue cloth, stamped in gold on the backstrip only. Publisher's device blind-stamped on the center of the back cover. All edges trimmed. Signatures are in 16s with printer's marks.

COLLATION: [1]-[288], as follows: [1] half title; [2] BY THE SAME AUTHOR | IN OUR TIME—*Stones*; [3] title page as above; [4] notices of first English publication and press work; [5] dedication: THIS BOOK IS FOR | HADLEY AND JOHN HADLEY NICANOR; [6] No character in this book is the portrait of any actual person; [7] divisional half title: BOOK I; [8] blank; 9-286 text; [287]-[288] blank.

NOTE: The word *Stones* on p. [2] is a typographical error for *Stories*.

NOTE: This novel was published by Scribner's under the title *The Sun Also Rises*. The quotations from Ecclesiastes and Gertrude Stein are omitted in this edition.

NOTE: The white dust jacket is printed in blue, green, and black.

SUBSEQUENT EDITIONS:

(B) Issued by Guild Books, London, in 1941.

79

(C)   Issued by Pan Books, London, January 16, 1952, at 2s., as No. 96. 7 x 4 1/2. 192 pages.

(D)   Reissued by Cape, May 3, 1954, at 12s. 6d. 7 1/2 x 5. 286 pages.

34 A. First English edition:

MEN WITHOUT WOMEN | Stories by | ERNEST HEMING-WAY | [publisher's device] | LONDON | JONATHAN CAPE 30 BEDFORD SQUARE

7 1/2 x 5 1/16. Published April 20, 1928, at 6s. Issued in blue cloth, stamped in gold on the backstrip only. Publisher's device blind-stamped on the back cover. Top and fore edges untrimmed, bottom edges trimmed. Signatures are in 16s with printer's marks.

COLLATION: [1]-[224], as follows: [1] half title; [2] *By the same author*; [3] title page as above; [4] notices of first English publication and presswork; [5] dedication: To | EVAN SHIPMAN; [6] blank; [7] CONTENTS; [8] blank; [9] half title; [10] blank; 11-[222] text; [223]-[224] blank.

NOTE: The fourteen stories appear in the same order as in the first Scribner's edition. There were slight textual changes in this edition.

NOTE: The white dust jacket, designed by J. L. Carstairs, is printed in rose, green, and black. The blurb on the front flap erroneously refers to "thirteen stories" instead of fourteen stories.

SUBSEQUENT EDITIONS:

(B)   Issued by Cape, in May 1931, at 3s. 6d., in the Travellers' Library edition. 7 x 4 3/4. 222 pages.

(C)   Issued by Cape, in April 1934, at 2s. 6d., as No. 4 in the Flexibles edition. 6 1/2 x 4 1/2. 222 pages.

(D)   Reissued by Cape, May 9, 1955, at 12s. 6d. 224 pages.

(E)   Issued by Penguin Books, Harmondsworth, June 30, 1955, at 2s. 6d., as No. 1067. 7 1/8 x 4 3/8. 160 pages.

35 A. First English edition:

A FAREWELL TO ARMS | BY | ERNEST HEMINGWAY | [publisher's device] | JONATHAN CAPE | THIRTY BEDFORD SQUARE, LONDON

7 1/2 x 5. Published November 11, 1929, at 7s. 6d. Issued in magenta cloth, stamped in gold on the backstrip only. Publisher's device blind-stamped on the center of the back cover. All edges trimmed. Signatures are in 16s with printer's marks.

COLLATION: [1]-[352], as follows: [1] half title; [2] BY THE SAME AUTHOR; [3] title page as above; [4] notices of publication, origin, and presswork; [5] legal disclaimer: None of the characters in this book is a living person, nor | are the units or military organizations mentioned actual | units or organizations. | E. H.; [6] blank;

[7] dedication: TO | G.A.P.; [8] blank; [9] divisional half title: BOOK I; [10] blank; 11-[350] text; [351]-[352] blank.

NOTE: In the Scribner's edition the last name of the dedicatee, G. A. Pfeiffer, is given.

NOTE: Deletions are indicated by a dash (—).

NOTE: The white dust jacket, designed by Lee Elliott, is printed in blue, green, and black.

NOTE: A review copy, 7 3/8 x 5, was issued in gray wrappers.

SUBSEQUENT EDITIONS:

(B)   Issued by Cape, in September 1932, at 2s., as No. 30 in the Florin Books edition. 7 1/4 x 4 3/4. 288 pages.

(C)   Issued by Cape, in April 1934, at 2s. 6d., in the Half-crown Fiction series. 7 3/4 x 5. 350 pages.

(D)   Issued by Penguin Books, Harmondsworth, in July 1935, at 6d. 7 x 4 1/2. 288 pages.

(E)   Issued by Cape, in 1944, in the Six Shilling edition. 336 pages.

(F)   Issued by the Continental Book Company, Stockholm and London, in 1945. [Zephyr Books. A Library of British and American Authors. Vol. I.] 288 pages.

(G)   Issued by Cape, in June 1950, at 4s. 6d., as No. 224 in the Travellers' Library edition. 7 x 4 3/8. 336 pages.

(H)   Reissued by Penguin Books, Harmondsworth, June 30, 1955, at 2s. 6d., as No. 2. 7 1/8 x 4 3/8. 256 pages.

36 A. First English edition:

DEATH | IN THE AFTERNOON | By | ERNEST | HEMING-WAY | [publisher's device] | WITH A FRONTISPIECE FROM A PAINTING | By JUAN GRIS: THE BULLFIGHTER | AND EIGHTY-ONE REPRODUCTIONS FROM PHOTOGRAPHS | [graduated line] | JONATHAN CAPE 30 BEDFORD SQUARE | LONDON

8 3/4 x 5 3/4. Published in November 1932, at 15s. Issued in orange cloth, stamped in black on the front cover and backstrip. Publisher's device blind-stamped on the back cover. All edges trimmed; top edges stained black. Signatures are in 16s with printer's marks. COLLATION: [1]-[360] + [63 unnumbered leaves + frontispiece], as follows: [1] blank; [2] Also by | ERNEST HEMINGWAY; [3] half title; [4] blank; [blank; verso, frontispiece by Juan Gris, unnumbered]; [5] title page as above; [6] notices of first publication, publisher (with addresses), origin, presswork, paper, and binding; [7] half title; [8] blank; 9-261 text; [262] descriptive text of first photograph; [63 unnumbered leaves: photographs]; 263-340 AN EXPLANATORY GLOSSARY; 341-346 SOME REACTIONS OF A FEW INDIVIDUALS TO THE INTEGRAL SPANISH BULL-

FIGHT; 347-350 A SHORT ESTIMATE OF THE AMERICAN, SIDNEY FRANKLIN, AS A MATADOR; 351-358 dates of bullfights; [359] BIBLIOGRAPHICAL NOTE by "E. H."; [360] blank.

NOTE: The white dust jacket is printed in black and red.

NOTE: An advance proof copy was issued in green wrappers. 7 3/4 x 5 3/8.

SUBSEQUENT EDITIONS:

(B)   Reissued by Cape, in April 1950, at 25s. 9 x 5 7/8. 360 pages + plates.

(c)   Issued by Penguin Books, Harmondsworth, in October 1966, at 7s. 6d., as No. 2421. 348 pages.

37   A. First English edition:

The | TORRENTS| of | SPRING | A | Romantic Novel in Honour of | the Passing of a Great Race | *by* | Ernest | Hemingway | [publisher's device] | *Introduced by* | David Garnett | London | Jonathan Cape, 30 Bedford Square

7 1/2 x 5. Published in February 1933, at 5s. Issued in yellow cloth, stamped in blue on the backstrip. Signatures are in 16s with printer's marks.

COLLATION: [1]-[174], as follows: [1] half title; [2] Books by; [3] title page as above; [4] notices of first English publication, publisher (with addresses), origin, presswork, paper, and binding; [5] Contents; [6] blank; [7] dedication: To | H. L. Mencken | and | S. Stanwood Mencken | in admiration; [8] blank; 9-20 Introduction by David Garnett; [21] half title; [22] quotation by Henry Fielding; 23-173 text; [174] blank.

NOTE: The introduction states, on p. 12, that this novel was published as Hemingway's "second book in 1925." However, it was published by Scribner's in 1926.

SUBSEQUENT EDITIONS:

(B)   Reissued by Cape, October 29, 1964, at 16s. 7 1/2 x 5. 156 pages. Issued in dark green cloth, stamped in gold on the backstrip. A new introduction by David Garnett is on pp. 9-17.

(c)   Issued by Penguin Books, Harmondsworth, in May 1966, at 3s. 6d., as No. 2424. 112 pages.

38   A. First English edition:

Winner | Take Nothing | *by* | Ernest Hemingway | [publisher's device] | *'Unlike all other forms of lutte or | combat the conditions are that the | winner shall take nothing; neither | his ease, nor his pleasure, nor any | notions of glory; nor, if he win far | enough, shall there be any reward | within himself.'* | Jonathan Cape | Thirty Bedford Square London

7 5/8 x 5. Published in February 1934, at 7s. 6d. Issued in yellow cloth, stamped in black on the front cover and backstrip. Top and

fore edges trimmed, bottom edges untrimmed. Signatures are in 16s with printer's marks.

COLLATION: [i]-[ii] + [1]-[254], as follows: [i]-[ii] blank; [1] half title; [2] *By the same Author*; [3] title page as above; [4] notices of first publication, publisher (with addresses), origin, presswork, paper, and binding; [5] dedication: *To Ada and Archibald Mac-Leish*; [6] blank; [7] CONTENTS; [8] blank; [9] divisional half title: AFTER THE STORM; [10] blank; 11-250 text; [251]-[254] blank.

NOTE: The fourteen stories appear in the same order as in the first Scribner edition.

NOTE: In the Scribner's edition the dedication is: To A. MacLEISH.

NOTE: The white dust jacket is printed in black and orange.

39 A. First English edition:

GREEN | HILLS OF AFRICA | *by* | ERNEST HEMINGWAY | [publisher's device] | JONATHAN CAPE | THIRTY BEDFORD SQUARE | LONDON

7 7/8 x 5 5/16. Published April 3, 1936, at 8s. 6d. Issued in green cloth, stamped in gold on the backstrip. Top edges stained green; fore edges trimmed, bottom edges untrimmed. Signatures are in 16s with printer's marks.

COLLATION: [i]-[ii] + [1]-[286], as follows: [i]-[ii] blank; [1] half title; [2] *By the same author*, decoration; [3] title page as above; [4] notices of first English publication, origin, presswork, paper, and binding; [5] CONTENTS (erroneously marked "7") ; [6] blank; [7] dedicatory letter to "Mr. J. P."; [8] blank; [9] divisional half-title: PART I | PURSUIT AND CONVERSATION, decoration; 10-284 text; [285]-[286] blank.

NOTE: The dedication and the prefatory note which appear in the Scribner's edition have been omitted and the following dedicatory letter to "Jackson Phillips" [i.e., Philip Percival] appears on p. [7]: Dear Mr. J. P. | *Just tell them you are a fictional character | and it is your bad luck to have a writer put | such language in your speeches. We all know | how prettily the best brought up people speak | but there are always those not quite out of the | top drawer who have an 'orrid fear of vulgar- | ity. You will know, too, how to deal with anyone | who calls you Pop. Remember you weren't | written of as Pop. It was all this fictional | character. Any-way the book is for you and we | miss you very much. | E. H.* This note appears in the Italian translation, Turin, 1948, p. 11, and in the Hungarian translation, Budapest, 1961, p. [5].

NOTE: Illustrated with decorations by Edward Shenton.

SUBSEQUENT EDITIONS:

(B) Issued by Cape, in November 1940, at 5s., in the Odyssey edition. 8 x 5 1/2. 284 pages.

(c)   Reissued by Cape, February 22, 1954, at 12s. 6d. 8 x 5 1/2. 284 pages.

(D)   Issued by Penguin Books, Harmondsworth, in May 1966, at 5s., as No. 2422. 248 pages. Hemingway's dedicatory letter to "Mr. J. P." is on p. [4].

40   A.   First English edition:

TO HAVE AND | HAVE NOT | *by* | ERNEST | HEMINGWAY | [publisher's device] | JONATHAN CAPE | THIRTY BEDFORD SQUARE | LONDON

7 1/2 x 5. Published in October 1937, at 7s. 6d. Issued in blue cloth, stamped in gold on the backstrip. Top edges stained blue; fore edges trimmed, bottom edges untrimmed. Signatures are in 16s with printer's marks.

COLLATION: [1]-[264], as follows: [1] half title; [2] *By the same author*; [3] title page as above; [4] notices of first publication, publisher (with addresses), origin, presswork, paper, and binding; [5] NOTE (legal disclaimer) ; [6] blank; [7] divisional title: PART ONE | HARRY MORGAN | *Spring*; [8] blank; 9-256 text; [257]-[264] a list of novels published by Cape, including three by Hemingway, on p. [260].

NOTE: The black dust jacket, designed by Aufseeser, is printed in yellow, white, and orange.

SUBSEQUENT EDITIONS:

(B)   Issued by Cape, in April 1950, at 4s. 6d., as No. 220 in the Travellers' Library edition. 7 x 4 3/4. 256 pages.

(c)   Reissued by Cape, October 4, 1954, at 10s. 6d. 256 pages.

(D)   Issued by Penguin Books, Harmondsworth, June 30, 1955, at 2s. 6d., as No. 1065. 7 1/4 x 4 3/8. 206 pages.

41   A.   First English edition:

THE | FIFTH COLUMN | AND THE FIRST | FORTY-NINE STORIES | *by* ERNEST HEMINGWAY | [publisher's device] | JONATHAN CAPE | THIRTY BEDFORD SQUARE | LONDON

7 7/8 x 5 1/4. Published in June 1939, at 10s. 6d. Issued in light brown cloth, stamped in black on the front cover and the backstrip. Top edges stained red; fore edges trimmed, bottom edges untrimmed. Signatures are in 16s with printer's marks.

COLLATION: [1]-[592], as follows: [1] half title; [2] *Books by*; [3] title page as above; [4] notices of first English publication, publisher (with addresses), origin, presswork, paper, and binding; [5]-[6] CONTENTS; 7-9 PREFACE by Hemingway; [10] blank; [11] half title; [12] blank; 13-106 text of the play; 107-590 text of the short stories; [591]-[592] blank.

NOTE: The contents are in the same order of appearance as in the

1938 Scribner's edition. Hemingway's preface is reprinted from the Scribner edition.

SUBSEQUENT EDITION:

(B) Issued by Cape, in September 1944, at 10s. 6d., as *The First Forty-Nine Stories*. 7 7/16 x 5. 472 pages. Hemingway's preface, with the paragraphs regarding the play omitted, is on pp. 7-8.

SEPARATE EDITIONS:

(C) *The Snows of Kilimanjaro and Other Stories*, published by Penguin Books, Harmondsworth, February 21, 1963, at 3s. 6d., as No. 1882. 7 1/4 x 4 3/8. 160 pages.

(D) *The Short Happy Life of Francis Macomber and Other Stories*, published by Penguin Books, Harmondsworth, August 29, 1963, at 3s. 6d., as No. 1982. 7 1/4 x 4 3/8. 192 pages.

(E) *The Fifth Column*, published by Penguin Books, Harmondsworth, in May 1966, at 3s. 6d., as No. PL 64. 96 pages.

42 A. First English edition:

FOR WHOM | THE BELL TOLLS | *by* | ERNEST | HEMING-WAY | [publisher's device] | JONATHAN CAPE | THIRTY BEDFORD SQUARE | LONDON

7 7/8 x 5 1/4. Published March 7, 1941, at 9s. Issued in blue cloth, stamped in gold on the backstrip. Top edges stained blue; fore edges trimmed, bottom edges untrimmed. Signatures are in 16s with printer's marks.

COLLATION: [1]-[464], as follows: [1] half title; [2] *Books by*; [3] title page as above; [4] notices of first English publication, publisher (with addresses), origin, presswork, paper, and binding; [5] dedication: *This book is for* | *MARTHA GELLHORN*; [6] blank; [7] half title; [8] quotation from John Donne; 9-462 text; [463]-[464] blank.

NOTE: The black dust jacket, designed by Tisdall, is printed in red and white.

SUBSEQUENT EDITION:

(B) Issued by Penguin Books, Harmondsworth, June 30, 1955, at 3s. 6d., as No. 1066. 7 1/8 x 4 7/8. 444 pages.

43 A. First English edition:

THE ESSENTIAL | HEMINGWAY | *Containing* | One complete novel, extracts from | three others, twenty-three Short | Stories and a chapter from | *Death in the Afternoon* | by | ERNEST HEM-INGWAY | [publisher's device] | JONATHAN CAPE | THIRTY BEDFORD SQUARE | LONDON

7 3/4 x 5 1/4. Published in October 1947, at 12s. 6d. Issued in red cloth, stamped in gold on the backstrip. All edges trimmed. Signatures are in 32s with printer's marks.

COLLATION: [1]-[448], as follows: [1]-[2] blank; [3] half title; [4] *By the same author*; [5] title page as above; [6] list of titles and reprint rights of nine previous Hemingway books, notices of first publication of *The Essential Hemingway*, origin, and presswork; 7-8 CONTENTS; [9] divisional half title: THE NOVELS; [10] blank; 11-447 text; [448] blank.

CONTENTS: THE NOVELS: *Fiesta* (*The Sun Also Rises*)/"Caporetto," an extract from *A Farewell to Arms*/"A Boatload for Cuba," an extract from *To Have and Have Not*/"El Sordo on the Hilltop," an extract from *For Whom the Bell Tolls*. THE STORIES: *In Our Time* complete/In Another Country/Hills Like White Elephants/The Killers/To-day is Friday/A Clean, Well-Lighted Place/The Light of the World/A Way You'll Never Be/The Short Happy Life of Francis Macomber/The Snows of Kilimanjaro. "Epilogue," the last chapter from *Death in the Afternoon*.

SUBSEQUENT EDITIONS:

(B) Issued by Cape, in [November] 1947, for members of the Reader's Union. 7 3/4 x 5 3/8. 448 pages. Issued in gray cloth, stamped in blue, with the Reader's Union device, on the backstrip.

(C) Issued by Penguin Books, Harmondsworth, in June 1964, at 6s., as No. 2117. 472 pages.

44 A. First edition:

ERNEST HEMINGWAY | [line, star, line] | ACROSS THE RIVER | AND | INTO THE TREES | [publisher's device] | JON-ATHAN CAPE | THIRTY BEDFORD SQUARE | LONDON

7 1/2 x 5. Published September 4, 1950, at 9s. 6d. Issued in green cloth with a design stamped in red on the front cover. Stamped in silver, on a red background, on the backstrip. Top and fore edges trimmed, bottom edges untrimmed. Signatures are in 16s with printer's marks.

COLLATION: [1]-[256], as follows: [1] half title; [2] *By the same author*; [3] title page as above; [4] notices of first publication, origin, presswork, and binding; 5-254 text; [255]-[256] blank.

NOTE: The English edition preceded the American edition by three days.

NOTE: Deletions are indicated by a star enclosed in parentheses.

NOTE: The blue dust jacket, designed by Hans Tisdall, is printed in red, white, and yellow.

NOTE: An advance copy was bound in the same dust jacket that was issued with the first edition. 7 1/2 x 5.

SUBSEQUENT EDITIONS:

(B) Issued by Cape in 1950, in the Star Editions (to be sold on the continent of Europe only). 254 pages. Paperbound.

(c)   Issued by Cape, in 1952, for members of the Reader's Union. 182 pages. Issued in black cloth stamped in silver and red.

(d)   Issued by Penguin Books, Harmondsworth, in May 1966, at 5s., as No. 2425. 240 pages.

45   A. First English edition:

ERNEST HEMINGWAY | *The* | OLD MAN | *&* | THE SEA | [publisher's device] | JONATHAN CAPE | THIRTY BEDFORD SQUARE LONDON

7 1/2 x 5. Published September 8, 1952, at 7s. 6d. Issued in blue cloth with a design stamped in red on the front cover. Stamped in red on the backstrip. All edges trimmed. Signatures are in 16s with printer's marks.

COLLATION: [1]-[128], as follows: [1] half title; [2] by the same author; [3] title page as above; [4] notices of first publication, origin, presswork, and binding; 5-127 text; [128] blank.

NOTE: The dust jacket is printed in white, blue, red, yellow, green, and orange.

SUBSEQUENT EDITIONS:

(b)   Illustrated edition issued by the Reprint Society [London], in 1953. 8 1/2 x 5 7/8. 118 pages. Issued in bluish-green cloth with the design of a fish stamped in silver on the front cover. Stamped in silver, in part on a red background, on the backstrip. All edges trimmed; top edges stained red. Illustrative endpapers. Publishers' Note, on p. [5], regarding the sixteen illustrations by C. F. Tunnicliffe and the eighteen illustrations by Raymond Sheppard. The yellow dust jacket is printed in green, white, and red.

(c)   Illustrated edition issued by Cape, October 31, 1955, at 10s. 6d. 8 1/2 x 5 7/8. 120 pages. Issued in black cloth backstrip over white covers. Illustration, stamped in black, on the front and back covers. Stamped in white on the backstrip. All edges trimmed; top edges stained black. Illustrative endpapers. Publisher's Note, on p. [5], regarding the illustrations by C. F. Tunnicliffe and Raymond Sheppard. Reissued, type reset, March 11, 1957.

46   A. First English edition:

Ernest Hemingway | A MOVEABLE FEAST | [publisher's device] | *Jonathan Cape* | THIRTY BEDFORD SQUARE LONDON

7 3/4 x 5. Published May 21, 1964, at 18s. Issued in brown paper-covered boards, stamped in gold on the backstrip. All edges trimmed; top edges stained orange. Brown endpapers. Signatures are in 32s with printer's marks.

COLLATION: [1]-[192], as follows: [1] half title; [2] by the same author; [3] title page as above; [4] notices of first publication, copyright, origin, presswork, paper, and binding; [5] Contents; [6]

87

Hemingway's quotation from which the title is taken, Mary Hemingway's note; [7] *Preface* by Hemingway, dated: *San Francisco de Paula, Cuba* | 1960; [8] blank; 9-[192] text.

NOTE: For differences in the text of Mary Hemingway's note in the American and English editions, see (A31a).

NOTE: The sentence beginning on line 8, p. 178, was partially omitted from the American edition. See (A31a).

NOTE: An advance copy, marked "uncorrected proof," was issued in green wrappers. 7 3/4 x 5.

NOTE: A promotional piece was issued by Cape, containing extracts from *AMF*. Issued in blue wrappers. 9 1/2 x 7 1/4.

SUBSEQUENT EDITION:

(B)   Issued by Penguin Books, Harmondsworth, in May 1966, at 3s. 6d., as No. 2423. 160 pages.

SECTION B

CONTRIBUTIONS

AND FIRST

APPEARANCES

IN BOOKS

AND PAMPHLETS

B1 The Best Short Stories of 1923

THE | BEST SHORT STORIES | OF 1923 | AND THE | YEAR-BOOK OF THE AMERICAN | SHORT STORY | EDITED BY | EDWARD J. O'BRIEN | [publisher's device] | BOSTON | SMALL, MAYNARD & COMPANY | PUBLISHERS

7 5/16 x 5. xviii + 544 pages. Published in January 1924, at $2.00. Issued in blue cloth, lettered in gold on the front cover and the backstrip. Cover: THE | BEST SHORT STORIES | OF 1923 | And the | Yearbook of the American | Short Story | Edited by | Edward J. O'Brien | [blind-ruled border around cover]. Backstrip: [blind-ruled band] | THE | BEST | SHORT | STORIES | OF | 1923 | [rule] |O'Brien | SMALL | MAYNARD | & COMPANY | [blind-ruled band]. All edges trimmed.

This was the first book published in the United States to contain work by Hemingway. "My Old Man," on pp. 263-276, is reprinted from *TSTP*. It is the only title in the table of contents that is not followed by the magazine from which it was reprinted. Martha Foley commented, in *Fifty Best American Short Stories, 1915-1965*, Boston, 1965, p. 49, that "My Old Man" is "the only story in the entire series which did not first appear in a magazine." For Hemingway's comments, see *AMF*, p. 73.

NOTE: With one exception, on p. 464, Hemingway's name is misspelled throughout the book, including the dedication, on p. [v]: TO | ERNEST HEMENWAY. The incorrect spelling was partially corrected in the second and third editions.

NOTE: An English edition was published in 1924, by Jonathan Cape, under the title *The Best Short Stories of 1923. II: American.*

2 The Best Poems of 1923

THE BEST POEMS | OF 1923 | EDITED BY | L. A. G. STRONG | Author of "Dublin Days" | [publisher's device] | BOSTON | SMALL, MAYNARD & COMPANY | PUBLISHERS

6 1/2 x 4 5/16. xx + 228 pages. Published in [April?] 1924, at $2.00. Issued in dark blue cloth, stamped in gold on the front cover and backstrip. Cover: The Best Poems | of | 1923 [enclosed in a decorative gold border]. Backstrip: The Best | Poems | of | 1923 | SMALL | MAYNARD | AND | COMPANY. All edges trimmed. The gray dust jacket is printed in blue.

Hemingway's poem, "Chapter Heading," on p. 104, first appeared in *Poetry, A Magazine of Verse*, XXI (Jan. 1923). This was the first book containing a poem by Hemingway to be published in the United States.

NOTE: Second printing in April 1924.

3 Contact Collection of Contemporary Writers

CONTACT COLLECTION OF | CONTEMPORARY WRIT-
ERS | Djuna Barnes | Bryher | Mary Butts | Norman Douglas |
Havelock Ellis | F. M. Ford | Wallace Gould | Ernest Hemingway |
Marsden Hartley | H. D. | John Herrman | James Joyce | Mina Loy |
Robert McAlmon | Ezra Pound | Dorothy Richardson | May Sin-
clair | Edith Sitwell | Gertrude Stein | W. C. Williams

7 1/2 x 5 1/2. xii + 344 pages. Published by the Three Mountains
Press, Paris, in June 1925, at $3.00. Issued in gray paper wrappers,
lettered and ruled in black, which are turned under at the top, bottom and fore edges over the first and last blank leaves. Cover:
CONTACT COLLECTION OF | CONTEMPORARY WRIT-
ERS | [followed by list of contributors as shown above on the title
page]. Backstrip, reading upward: [thick rule, thin rule] Contact
Collection of Contemporary Writers [thin rule, thick rule]. All
edges untrimmed.

"Soldiers Home," on pp. 77-86, is subtitled "A Story."

NOTE: This Contact Edition was edited by Robert McAlmon,
who, with William Bird, also published the book. Printed at Dijon,
France, in an edition of 300 copies.

4 The Best Short Stories of 1926

THE | BEST SHORT STORIES | OF 1926 | AND THE | YEAR-
BOOK OF THE AMERICAN | SHORT STORY | EDITED BY |
EDWARD J. O'BRIEN | [publisher's device] | DODD, MEAD
AND COMPANY | NEW YORK : : : : 1926

7 3/8 x 5. xviii + 466 pages. Published in December 1926, at $2.50.
Issued in blue cloth with a blind-stamped border around the front
cover. Lettered and ruled in gold on front cover and backstrip.
Cover: THE | BEST SHORT STORIES | OF 1926 | And the |
Yearbook of the American | Short Story | Edited by | Edward J.
O'Brien Backstrip: [blind rule] | THE | BEST | SHORT |
STORIES | OF | 1926 | [short line] | O'Brien | DODD, MEAD |
& COMPANY | [blind rule]. All edges trimmed, top edges stained
orange.

"The Undefeated," on pp. 127-155, is reprinted from *This Quarter,*
I (Autumn–Winter 1925–1926).

5 The American Caravan

[Ornamental double rule] | THE AMERICAN | CARAVAN | [ornamental double rule] | A YEARBOOK | OF AMERICAN LITERATURE | Edited by | VAN WYCK BROOKS LEWIS MUMFORD | ALFRED KREYMBORG PAUL ROSENFELD | [two ornaments] | NEW YORK | THE MACAULAY COMPANY

9 1/4 x 6 1/4. xviii + 846 pages. Published in September 1927. Issued in dark green cloth with gold lettering, ruling and decoration on front cover and backstrip. Cover: [ornament] | [short rule] | THE | AMERICAN | CARAVAN | [long broken rule] | [rule] | [short rule] | [shorter rule]. Backstrip: [ornament] | [thick rule] | THE | AMERICAN | CARAVAN | [rule] | [broken rule] | [short rule] | [rule] | MACAULAY |. Top edges stained green; bottom and fore edges untrimmed. Printed gray and green endpapers.

"An Alpine Idyll," on pp. 46-51, was collected in *MWW*, in October 1927. A brief biographical note, on p. 838, erroneously gives the year of Hemingway's birth as 1896.

NOTE: A Literary Guild edition was issued simultaneously. Issued in black cloth with gold lettering, ruling, and decoration on the front cover and backstrip. Top edges stained orange. Printed brown and orange endpapers. Same pagination as the Macaulay edition.

6 Creating the Short Story

CREATING THE | SHORT STORY | A SYMPOSIUM-AN-THOLOGY | WITH AN INTRODUCTION | *by* | HENRY | GOODMAN | INSTRUCTOR IN ENGLISH | (EXTENSION TEACHING AND SUMMER SESSION) | HUNTER COLLEGE OF THE CITY OF NEW YORK | [publisher's device] | HARCOURT, BRACE AND COMPANY | NEW YORK [title page enclosed in a double-ruled border with a thin inner rule and a thick outer rule]

8 x 5 3/8. xiv + 514 pages. Published in February 1929, at $2.75. Issued in blue cloth with publisher's device and double-ruled border blind-stamped on front cover. Lettered and ruled in gold on the backstrip: [rule] | CREATING | THE | SHORT | STORY | [rule] | *Edited by* | HENRY | GOODMAN | HARCOURT, BRACE | & COMPANY | [rule]. All edges trimmed. The white dust jacket is printed in dark blue.

"Who Knows How?" on p. 121, is a humorous account of Hemingway's writing habits in Paris and Madrid. The title was chosen by the editor [see *Cohn's Bibliography*, p. 70]. The original two-page letter, dated January 16, 1928, from Gstaad, Switzerland, is among the holdings of the Rare Book Division of the New York Public Library.

"The Killers," on pp. 121-134, was collected in *MWW*.

7 Kiki's Memoirs

KIKI'S | MEMOIRS | TRANSLATED FROM THE | FRENCH BY SAMUEL | PUTNAM. INTRODUCTION BY | ERNEST HEMINGWAY. FULL | PAGE REPRODUCTIONS OF | TWENTY PAINTINGS BY | KIKI. WITH PORTRAITS | BY MAN RAY, FOUJITA, | KISLING, PER KROGH, | HERMINE DAVID, ETC. | [publisher's device] | EDWARD W. TITUS | At The Sign Of The Black Manikin Press | 4, rue Delambre, Montparnasse | PARIS, MCMXXX. |

9 x 7 1/8. 192 pages. Published in June 1930, at $5.00, in an edition of 1000 copies. Printed by Imprimerie Darantiere, at Dijon, France. Issued in cream color stiff paper covers, printed in red and black. A reproduction of a portrait of Kiki (Alice Prin) by Kisling is pasted on the front cover. All edges trimmed. Signatures in 16s with printer's marks.

Hemingway's Introduction, on pp. 9-14, was previously issued in pamphlet form, under the title *Introduction to Kiki of Montparnasse*. See (A9).

See also the translator's notes, on pp. 17-23, and the publisher's notes, on pp. 24-32, for references to Hemingway.

NOTE: 150 copies were intended for distribution in the United States by Random House. However, "the book was barred from entry by the U.S. Customs on the grounds of obscenity." [See *Cohn's Bibliography*, p. 38.]

NOTE: Reissued by Boar's Head Books, New York, in 1950, under the title *The Education of a French Model: The Loves, Cares, Cartoons and Caricatures of Alice Prin*. Issued in rust cloth, stamped in black on the front cover and backstrip. 9 x 6. 192 pages. Hemingway's introduction appears on pp. 9-14. Also issued in a variant binding of yellow cloth, stamped in purple.

NOTE: Reissued in a paperback edition, under the title *The Education of a French Model*, by Crest Books (Fawcett Publications, Inc.), New York, in March 1956, at twenty-five cents, as No. 127. 144 pages.

NOTE: Reissued in a paperback edition by Belmont Books, New York, in January 1962, at fifty cents, as No. L 525. 128 pages. Hemingway's introduction appears on pp. ix-xi.

NOTE: Reissued by Continental Books, New York, in May 1966, at $4.95. 160 pages.

8 Modern Writers at Work

MODERN WRITERS | AT WORK | *Edited* | BY | JOSEPHINE K. PIERCY | INSTRUCTOR IN ENGLISH, | INDIANA UNIVERSITY | New York [Gothic] | THE MACMILLAN COMPANY | 1930
7 5/8 x 5 1/8. xx + 994 pages. Published in September 1930, at $4.00. Issued in purple cloth, stamped in silver on the front cover and backstrip. Cover: MODERN | [rule] | WRITERS | [rule] | AT WORK | [rule] | [dot] | PIERCY [vertical band the length of the lettering] | [design, lower right corner]. Backstrip: MODERN | WRITERS | AT WORK | [dot] | PIERCY | [design] | MACMIL-LAN | [three dots]. All edges trimmed.
An excerpt on writing prose from Hemingway's reply to an inquiry by the editor appears on pp. 488, 490. Note: The original letter is among the holdings of Lilly Library, at the University of Indiana. A facsimile of a holograph page of manuscript from *FTA*, showing how Hemingway revised a sentence, is reproduced on p. [489]. "Cat in the Rain" is reprinted on pp. 491-494.
NOTE: A College Edition was issued simultaneously, at $2.75.

9 A Bibliography of the Works of Ernest Hemingway

A Bibliography of the Works of | ERNEST | HEMINGWAY | [graduated line] | LOUIS HENRY COHN | [publisher's device separates R and H and 19 and 31] | RANDOM HOUSE [dot] NEW YORK
9 5/16 x 6 1/4. [2 leaves] + 116 pages + [5 leaves]. Published in August 1931, at $6.00. Issued in shimmery black cloth, stamped in gold on the backstrip only. Bibliog- | raphy | of | Ernest | Heming- | way | [ornament] | COHN | RANDOM | HOUSE. Top and bottom edges trimmed, fore edges untrimmed.
The folded frontispiece is a facsimile of a holograph page of manuscript, titled "Death of the Standard Oil Man," with a typewritten note across the top of the page addressed to "Captain Cohn," signed "E. H."
CONTENTS: THE BOOKS AND PAMPHLETS, on pp. [13]–58, including collations, previous appearances, title page facsimiles, and numerous informative notes on Hemingway's first nine works; also details on the English, French, Norwegian, German, and cheap editions. BOOKS CONTAINING ORIGINAL WORK, on pp. [59]–78, including title page descriptions, collations, and notes. PERIODICAL CONTRIBUTIONS NOT REPRINTED, on pp. [79]–83. REPRINTED PERIODICAL CONTRIBUTIONS, on

pp. [85]–93. PERIODICAL INDICES, on pp. 94-96. CRITICAL (articles and references in books), on pp. 97-105. REVIEWS, listing of reviews of *IOT, TOS, SAR, MWW,* and *FTA,* on pp. 106-111. FROM THE COMPILER'S NOTE-BOOK, on pp. 112-116, includes a long quote from a letter from Hemingway, on p. 112, regarding his views on listing his early newspaper work.

The colophon, on p. [4], states: *Of this book there have been printed five hundred numbered and | five lettered copies at The Harbor Press for* RANDOM HOUSE *in | the month of August 1931. This is |.* Note: According to Mrs. Louis Henry Cohn, no lettered copies were issued.

10 The New Yorker Scrapbook

THE NEW YORKER | SCRAPBOOK | [publisher's device] | DOUBLEDAY, DORAN & COMPANY, INC. | GARDEN CITY, NEW YORK, 1931

8 x 6. xii + 354 pages. Published in November 1931; at $2.50. Issued in red cloth with the *New Yorker* symbol stamped in black on the front cover. Backstrip, lettered in black, reading downward: THE NEW YORKER SCRAPBOOK [enclosed in a wide black border]. All edges trimmed; top edges stained yellow. The dust jacket is printed in white, black, and red.

"My Own Life: After Reading the Second Volume of Frank Harris' 'My Life'," on pp. 154-158, is reprinted from the *New Yorker,* II (Feb. 12, 1927).

11 Salmagundi

SALMAGUNDI [red] | *By* | WILLIAM FAULKNER | *and a Poem* [red] *by* | ERNEST M. HEMINGWAY | MILWAUKEE : | *The* CASANOVA PRESS | MCMXXXII [red]

9 1/4 x 6 1/8. 54 pages. Published in a limited edition of 525 numbered copies, in May 1932, at $3.00. Issued in stiff tan paper covers slightly larger than the buff colored leaves. The front and back covers and the backstrip are printed in black and red. All edges untrimmed.

Back cover: ULTIMATELY [red] | *by* | ERNEST M. HEMINGWAY | [four-line poem in italics] | June, 1922.

Paul Romaine explains in a "N.B." to the preface, on p. 9, that he included Hemingway's poem on the back cover because it appeared on the same page with Faulkner's poem "Portrait" in the *Double Dealer,* III (June 1922).

The colophon, on p. [54], notes that this is the first book published by this firm.

NOTE: The lining papers in the copies numbered one to twenty-five are flush at the top edge and an eighth of an inch from the bottom edge, both front and back.

12 The Cantos of Ezra Pound

THE CANTOS | *of* | EZRA POUND | *Some Testimonies by* | ERNEST HEMINGWAY | FORD MADOX FORD | T. S. ELIOT | HUGH WALPOLE | ARCHIBALD MacLEISH | JAMES JOYCE | *and* OTHERS | FARRAR & RINEHART, Inc. [publisher's device] PUBLISHERS : NEW YORK

7 3/4 x 5 1/4. Pamphlet. 24 pages, including the cover. Copyrighted in 1933. Unbound; wire stapled. White paper cover with black lettering, as shown above. Table of contents on the inside back cover, p. [23].

Hemingway's tribute to Ezra Pound is on p. 13: [Number] x. | From ERNEST HEMINGWAY. Below the ten-line tribute is the date: 21 Nov. 1932.

NOTE: Reprinted in full on the back cover of the dust jacket of Pound's *A Draft of XXX Cantos*, New York: Farrar & Rinehart, 1933. The last sentence is also quoted on the front cover of the dust jacket. Reprinted, under the title "A Note on Ezra Pound," in *Ezra Pound: Perspectives: essays in honor of his eightieth birthday*, ed. Noel Stock, New York: Regnery, 1966, p. 151.

13 Active Anthology

ACTIVE | ANTHOLOGY | EDITED BY | EZRA | POUND | LONDON | FABER AND FABER LTD | 24 RUSSELL SQUARE

7 5/16 x 4 3/4. 256 pages. Published in October 1933, at 7s. 6d. Issued in red-brown cloth, stamped in blue on the backstrip. Backstrip: EZRA | POUND | ACTIVE ANTHOLOGY [title reading downward, enclosed in a double-ruled border] | FABER | FABER |. All edges trimmed; top edges stained blue. Yellow dust jacket printed in black and red.

Hemingway's poem "They All Made Peace—What Is Peace?" on pp. 185-186, is reprinted from the *Little Review*, IX (Spring 1923). Note: The words "young boys" were deleted from line five in the book.

NOTE: "1516 sets of sheets printed." [See Donald Gallup's *A Bibliography of Ezra Pound*, London: Hart-Davis, 1963, p. 162.]

14 Joan Miró: Paintings

Joan | Miro | Paintings—December 29th–January 18th, 1934 | Pierre Matisse Gallery | 51 East 57th Street Fuller Building New York City

4 11/16 x 6 13/16. Folder. 6 pages. Printed on a single sheet folded twice horizontally; white paper, lettered in black. The front cover, as shown above, serves as the title page; an excerpt from Hemingway's article on Miró's painting, The Farm, "to be published" in Cahiers d'Art, IX (1934), is on p. [2]; catalogue of nine PAINT-INGS ON WOOD and ten PAINTINGS ON CANVAS, on p. [3]; note by James Johnson Sweeney on p. [4]; pp. [5] and [6] are blank.

NOTE: Hemingway's article was published, in full, in Joan Miró by Clement Greenberg, New York, [1949], p. [5]. See (B45).

15 This Must Be the Place

THIS | MUST BE THE PLACE | MEMOIRS OF MONTPAR-NASSE | BY | JIMMIE THE BARMAN | (JAMES CHARTERS) | Edited by MORRILL CODY | With an Introduction by ERNEST HEM-INGWAY | Illustrated by | IVAN OPFFER and HILAIRE HILER | LON-DON | HERBERT JOSEPH LTD. 9 JOHN ST. ADELPHI

8 5/16 x 5 3/8. 304 pages. Published in July 1934, at 12s. 6d. Issued in blue cloth, stamped in red on the backstrip. Backstrip: THIS | MUST BE | THE PLACE | JIMMIE | CHARTERS | HERBERT JOSEPH |. All edges trimmed; top edges stained red. Hemingway's introduction, on pp. 11-13, is dated: Serengetti Plains, | Tanganyika. | December, 1933.

NOTE: References to Hemingway appear on pp. 98-99, 118, 131, 167, 222, 288, 292, 296.

NOTE: A revised edition, titled This Must Be the Place: Memoirs of Jimmie the Barman by James Charters, as told to Morrill Cody, was published by Lee Furman, Inc., New York, in October 1937, at $3.00. Issued in gray-blue cloth, stamped in silver on the backstrip. Top edges stained gray-blue. 320 pages. Hemingway's introduction appears on pp. [ix]-xii; no date of composition is given. Hemingway is mentioned on pp. 62-64, 104-111, 145, 311, 312. Ch. [VIII]: "The Sun Also Sinks," on pp. 104-111, discusses the characters in SAR. Note: Issued in a variant binding of orange cloth, stamped in gold on the black backstrip.

NOTE: The American version was reissued in a paperback edition, under the title Hemingway's Paris, by Tower Books (Macaulay Co.), New York, in 1965, at sixty cents. Hemingway's introduction appears on pp. 7-9.

₁₆ Luis Quintanilla Catalogue

QUINTANILLA | [drawing] | PIERRE MATISSE GALLERY | MADISON AVENUE AND 57 STREET | FULLER BUILDING, NEW YORK | NOVEMBER 20 TO DECEMBER 4

3 1/8 x 6 1/8. Folder. 6 pages. Published in 1934. Printed on a single sheet folded twice horizontally; white paper with lettering and drawing in black. The cover, as shown above, serves as the title page; Hemingway's appraisal of Luis Quintanilla's work is on pp. [2]-[3]; list of thirty-nine paintings on p. [4]; an appraisal of the artist's work by John Dos Passos is on p. [5]; the back cover, p. [6], is blank.

NOTE: Hemingway's article was reprinted, with minor changes, in *Esquire*, III (Feb. 1935).

₁₇ Gattorno

ERNEST HEMINGWAY | GATTORNO [red] | WITH 38 RE-PRODUCTIONS AND A FEW CRITICAL OPINIONS | CON 38 REPRODUCCIONES Y ALGUNAS OPINIONES CRITICAS | [publisher's device] | HABANA 1935 | [thick rule]

10 x 7 3/4. 96 pages. An edition of 460 numbered copies was published by Ucar, Garcia y Cia, in Havana, in April 1935. Issued in light gray paper covers, lettered in red over a brown drawing on the front cover. Cover: Gattorno [signature] | ERNEST HEMINGWAY. Backstrip, reading upward: A. GATTORNO [red].

Hemingway's commentary on the work of the Cuban artist Antonio Gattorno, on pp. 11-16, appears in English and Spanish in parallel columns.

NOTE: Hemingway's commentary was reprinted in *Esquire*, V (May 1936).

₁₈ American Big Game Fishing

AMERICAN BIG GAME FISHING [blue] | *BY* | Mrs. Oliver C. Grinnell | Frances H. Low [ornament] Herman P. Gray | Charles L. Lehmann [ornament] Lynn Bogue Hunt | Ernest Hemingway [ornament] Van Campen Heilner | George C. Thomas, III [ornament] David M. Newell | Otto J. Scheer [ornament] Francis H. Geer | S. Kip Farrington, Jr. | Thomas G. F. Aitken | Eugene V. Connett, *Editor* | *ILLUSTRATED BY* | Lynn Bogue Hunt | AND FROM PHOTOGRAPHS | DRAWINGS AND MAPS | [circular blue drawing of a fish] | NEW YORK : : THE DERRYDALE PRESS

12 1/4 x 9 1/2. xxiv + 252 pages. Published May 15, 1935. Issued in blue cloth, lettered and decorated in gold. Cover: American [in

script] | BIG GAME | FISHING [all enclosed in a narrow decorative border within a wide decorative border]. Backstrip: [wide decorative band] | AMERICAN | BIG | GAME | FISHING | [wide decorative band] | DERRYDALE | PRESS | [wide decorative band]. Bottom and fore edges untrimmed; top edges stained gold. Decorative blue and white endpapers.

Ch. II, "Marlin Off Cuba," on pp. 55-81, by Hemingway. Parts of this article first appeared, in slightly different form, in "Marlin Off the Morro," *Esquire*, I (Autumn 1933).

See also an extract of a letter from Hemingway, on pp. 49-51, describing the taking of the largest Atlantic sailfish, in the Spring of 1934. Photographs of Hemingway, opp. pp. 1, 75, 79.

NOTES: This book was designed by Eugene V. Connett as Volume 4 of The Derry Library of Sport. 850 copies of the regular edition, described above, were published at $25.00. 56 numbered copies of a deluxe edition were published at $75.00. An additional 100 copies of the regular edition were published by Hutchinson & Co. Ltd., London, in March 1936, at 105s., with their name on the title page.

19 So Red the Nose

[Drawing of a champagne glass] | SO RED THE NOSE [in a wavy line] | or | Breath | in the Afternoon | EDITED BY STERLING NORTH | AND CARL KROCH | ILLUSTRATED BY ROY C. NELSON | [star] | FARRAR & RINEHART | INCORPORATED | ON MURRAY HILL [dot] NEW YORK

7 9/16 x 5 1/4. 74 unnumbered pages. Published in December 1935, at $1.00. Issued in purple cloth, stamped in silver on the front cover only. [Drawing] | SO RED THE NOSE [in a wavy line].

This collection of cocktail recipes by thirty authors begins with Hemingway's "Death in the Afternoon Cocktail" and a short comment by him, on p. [9]. A brief biographical note appears on the same page. A caricature of Hemingway is on p. [8]. Reprinted from *Esquire*, IV (Dec. 1935).

NOTE: The publisher's device which appeared in all Farrar & Rinehart first editions was inadvertently omitted from this book.

20 The Third New Year

THE THIRD NEW YEAR [red] | *An* | *Etude in the Key of* | *Frankness* | *Esquire, Inc.* | *Chicago and New York* | MCMXXXV

7⅛ x 4⅝. 132 pages. Published in December 1935. Issued in dark blue leather, stamped in gold. Front and back covers: Three outer ruled borders and five inner ruled borders. Backstrip: [double-ruled oblong, with ornament in center] | THE | THIRD | NEW | YEAR [all in a single-ruled oblong] | [four double-ruled oblongs, with ornament in center of each] | [rule] | ESQUIRE | [rule]. All edges gilt. Mottled white endpapers.

Hemingway's "Notes on the Next War," on pp. 45-55, is reprinted from *Esquire*, IV (Sept. 1935).

COLOPHON ON P. [3]: This edition is limited to five hundred | numbered copies of which four hundred | and fifty copies are for distribution and | are inscribed by the editor of Esquire. | No. | For |. Note: These copies were inscribed by Arnold Gingrich.

NOTE: A second edition, so marked on the verso of the copyright page, was issued in dark red cloth, stamped in gold. The pagination is the same. The edges are unadorned. The colophon, on p. [3], states: This edition is limited to five hundred | and fifty numbered copies of which this | is Number |.

21 Portraits and Self-Portraits

PORTRAITS AND | SELF-PORTRAITS | COLLECTED AND ILLUS-TRATED BY | GEORGES SCHREIBER | 1936 | HOUGHTON MIFFLIN COMPANY BOSTON | The Riverside Press Cambridge [Gothic]

9 3/4 x 7. x + 182 pages. Published in December 1936, at $2.75. Issued in tan cloth, stamped in red and black on the front cover and the backstrip. Cover: Portraits | and Self- | Portraits [title in red] | Schreiber [signature in black, reading upward]. Backstrip: Portraits | and Self- | Portraits [title in black, horizontal] | Schreiber [signature in red, reading upward] | HOUGHTON | MIFFLIN CO. [horizontal, in black]. All edges trimmed. The red dust jacket is printed in brown and white.

Hemingway's autobiographical sketch, on p. 57, is dated: Key West, Florida. A drawing of Hemingway by Schreiber is on p. [56]. A short biographical note appears on p. 55.

22 American Points of View: 1936

[Long double rule] | AMERICAN | POINTS OF VIEW | 1936 | Edited By | WILLIAM H. CORDELL | and | KATHRYN COE CORDELL | [long rule] | [publisher's device] | [long rule] | Doubleday, Doran & Company, Inc. | GARDEN CITY 1937 NEW YORK | [long double rule]

7 3/4 x 5 3/8. x + 310 pages. Published in February 1937, at $2.00. Issued in black cloth with a design blind-stamped on the front cover. Lettered in black, on seven gold bands, on the backstrip:

CORDELL | [design blind-stamped] | AMERICAN | POINTS | OF | VIEW | 1936 | [design blind-stamped] | DOUBLEDAY | DORAN. All edges trimmed. Top edges stained orange.

"The Malady of Power," on pp. 184-191, is reprinted from *Esquire,* IV (Nov. 1935). A brief note on Hemingway's work precedes the article, on p. 184.

NOTE: A text edition was issued simultaneously, at $1.00, in blue cloth with a design stamped in gold on the front cover. Lettered in blue, on gold bands, on the backstrip. Same pagination.

23 All Good Americans

ALL GOOD | AMERICANS | *By* | JEROME BAHR | *With a Preface by Ernest Hemingway* | NEW YORK | CHARLES SCRIBNER'S SONS | 1937 [title page enclosed in a triple border, with a wavy center line between ruled lines]

7 3/8 x 5 1/16. xii + 274 pages. Published in March 1937, at $2.50. Issued in blue cloth with silver bands lettered in blue on the front cover and backstrip. Cover: ALL GOOD | AMERICANS | Jerome Bahr. Backstrip: ALL | GOOD | AMERICANS | [short rule] | BAHR | SCRIBNERS. Bottom edges trimmed, fore edges untrimmed; top edges stained blue. The dust jacket, designed by Waldo Peirce, is printed in red, black, and white.

Hemingway's preface, on pp. vii-viii, is not dated.

NOTE: This book of short stories was reissued in yellow cloth, in July 1939. Both impressions have Scribner's "A" on the copyright page.

24 The Best Short Stories 1937

THE | BEST SHORT STORIES | 1937 | AND THE | YEARBOOK OF THE AMERICAN | SHORT STORY | EDITED BY | EDWARD J. O'BRIEN | [publisher's device] | BOSTON AND NEW YORK | HOUGHTON MIFFLIN COMPANY | The Riverside Press Cambridge [Gothic] | 1937

8 x 5 1/2. xxiv + 456 pages. Published in May 1937, at $2.50. Issued in red cloth with a blind-stamped border around the front cover. Stamped in gold on the front cover and backstrip. Cover: THE | BEST SHORT STORIES | 1937 | *AND THE* | *YEARBOOK OF* | *THE AMERICAN* | *SHORT STORY* | [ornament] | EDITED BY | EDWARD J. O'BRIEN. Backstrip: THE BEST | SHORT | STORIES | 1937 | AND THE | YEARBOOK | OF THE | AMERICAN | SHORT | STORY | [ornament] | EDITED BY | EDWARD J. | O'BRIEN | HOUGHTON | MIFFLIN CO. All edges trimmed.

"The Snows of Kilimanjaro," on pp. 105-126, is reprinted from *Esquire*, VI (Aug. 1936), and contains the original reference to "poor Scott Fitzgerald" on p. 122, line 6. For revisions made in this story prior to publication in the *First 49*, see (A16a).

See also the editor's introduction, p. xviii, for commentary on this story.

25 Blow the Man Down

THE YACHTSMAN'S READER | *BLOW THE MAN* | *DOWN* | [drawing] | EDITED BY ERIC DEVINE | Doubleday, Doran & Company, Inc. | *Garden City* MCMXXXVII *New York* [title page enclosed in a double-ruled border]

9 x 6. xiv + 334 pages. Published in August 1937, at $3.00. Issued in light blue cloth with the design of a barometer stamped in black on the front cover. Lettered and decorated in gold, on a black background, on the backstrip: [double rule] | BLOW | THE MAN | DOWN | ERIC | DEVINE | [double rule] | [design of a barometer] | DOUBLEDAY | DORAN. Bottom and fore edges untrimmed; top edges stained blue. The blue dust jacket is printed in white, black, and gold.

"On the Blue Water," on pp. 304-311, is reprinted from *Esquire*, V (April 1936).

26 The Writer in a Changing World

The | WRITER | *in a* | CHANGING | WORLD | *Edited by* | HENRY HART | EQUINOX | COOPERATIVE | PRESS [title page enclosed in a black border with decorative vertical bands]

8 x 5 3/8. 256 pages. Published by the League of American Writers, in November 1937, at $2.00. Issued in beige cloth with the publisher's device in orange on the front cover. Stamped in green on the backstrip: [rule] | ARVIN | [rule] | BEALS | [rule] | BOTKIN | [rule] | BROWDER | [rule] | BURKE | [rule] | COWLEY | [rule] | FREEMAN | [decorative band] | *The* | WRITER | *in a* | CHANGING | WORLD | [rule] | *Equinox* | [decorative band] | GELHORN | [rule] | HART | [rule] | HEMINGWAY | [rule] | HICKS | [rule] | HOLMES | [rule] | MACLEISH | [rule] | SLOCHOWER | [rule] | STEWART | [rule] | WILLIAMS | [rule] | WINWAR | [rule]. All edges trimmed. Top edges stained red. The dust jacket is printed in red, white, and blue.

"The Writer and War" on pp. 69-73. This paper, which Hemingway delivered before the Second Writers' Congress, in New York, June 4, 1937, first appeared in *New Masses*, XXIII (June 22, 1937).

27 Atlantic Game Fishing

ATLANTIC | GAME FISHING | *by* | S. KIP FARRINGTON, JR. | *color illustrations by* | LYNN BOGUE HUNT | *introduction by* | ERNEST HEMINGWAY | [design of a fish] | NEW YORK [short wavy line] 1937 | KENNEDY BROS., INC., *Publishers of* YACHTING

11 1/4 x 8 1/2. xxii + 298 + 7 color plates and 68 pages of photographs. Published in December 1937, at $7.50. Issued in dark blue cloth with the design of a fish stamped in gold on the front cover. Lettered and ruled in gold on the backstrip: [rule] | ATLANTIC | GAME | FISHING | [dot] | FARRINGTON | [rule] | KENNEDY BROS. |. All edges trimmed. The endpapers, in two shades of green, depict a drawing of decorative fish by Lynn Bogue Hunt. Pictorial, blue dust jacket.

Hemingway's Introduction, on pp. xvii-xxii, is not dated.

References to Hemingway, mainly in regard to record fish taken near Key West and Bimini in the 1930s, appear on pp. 162-163, 190-191, 195, 212-213, 215, 216, 236, 238. 9 photographs of Hemingway are included.

NOTE: This book was designed by Goldthwait Jackson and printed by the Rumford Press, Concord, N.H.

NOTE: A "Deluxe Edition," 10 x 7 3/4, was published by the Garden City Publishing Co., Inc., New York, in 1939, at $2.95. Issued in dark blue buckram, with the design of a fish blind-stamped on the front cover. The backstrip and the endpapers are identical to the Kennedy edition. The top edges are stained dark blue. Same pagination.

28 Quintanilla: An Exhibition of Drawings of the War in Spain

[Drawing] | QUINTANILLA | AN EXHIBITION OF DRAWINGS OF THE WAR IN SPAIN | THE MUSEUM OF MODERN ART [dot] NEW YORK [dot] MARCH [dot] 1938

10 x 7 1/2. Folder. 4 pages. Printed on a single sheet folded once; cream paper with lettering and drawings in black. Cover, as shown above, serves as the title page; Hemingway's preface [not dated] on p. [2]; drawing by Quintanilla on p. [3]; CATALOG OF THE EXHIBITION and Acknowledgments, including mention of Hemingway's preface, on p. [4].

NOTE: Reprinted in *Among Friends*, 1 (Spring 1938). See (C278).

29 Writers Take Sides

WRITERS TAKE SIDES | Letters about the war in Spain [in script] | from 418 American authors [in script] | PUBLISHED BY | THE LEAGUE OF AMERICAN WRITERS | 381 FOURTH AVENUE, NEW YORK CITY

7 5/8 x 5 1/2. viii + 82 pages. Published in May 1938, at fifteen cents. Issued in stiff blue paper covers, lettered in black over an alphabetized list of the contributors names in small white letters. Cover: Writers | take Sides [all in script at an upward angle] | on the question: | Are you for, or are you against | Franco and fascism? | Are you for, or are you against | the legal government and the | people of Republican Spain?

A one-line statement by Hemingway, giving his view of fascism, is on p. 30.

A telegram received from Paris, April 1, [1938], appealing for contributions for ambulances, signed: ERNEST HEMINGWAY | VINCENT SHEEAN | LOUIS FISCHER, is on p. [viii].

30 Just What the Doctor Ordered

Fun in Bed—Series Four | ℞ Just What the | Doctor Ordered | *Edited by* FRANK SCULLY | *and an* | ALL-STAR CAST | *including* | ROBERT BENCHLEY, WOLCOTT GIBBS, FRED ALLEN, | OGDEN NASH, DONALD OGDEN STEWART, MARK | HELLINGER, KAY BOYLE, CEDRIC BELFRAGE, | HEYWOOD BROUN, WILLIAM SAROYAN, | JACK BENNY, STEWART EDWARD WHITE, | ERNEST HEMINGWAY, GEORGE E. SO- | KOLSKY, WILLIAM SHAKESPEARE | AND MANY, MANY MORE | *SIMON AND SCHUSTER, INC.* | New York 1938

10 x 6 3/4. x + 188 pages. Published in September 1938, at $2.00. Issued in orange cloth with dark blue lettering and drawing on the front cover and backstrip. Cover: "Just What the Doctor Ordered" [in script] | FUN IN BED | [drawing by O. Soglow]. Backstrip: FUN IN BED SERIES 4 FRANK | SCULLY [all reading downward] | SIMON AND | SCHUSTER [horizontal]. All edges trimmed. A loop of the same material as the binding is attached to the back cover to hold a pencil.

Two of Hemingway's *Esquire* articles, concerning amoebic dysentery, are *partially* reprinted under the general heading: "Running Story." [Part] 1. "A.D. in Africa," pp. 165-166, is reprinted from *Esquire*, 1 (April 1934), with a new last sentence added. [Part] 2.

"A.D. in America," pp. 166-168, is reprinted from *Esquire*, III (May 1935), with a new last sentence added.

NOTE: This book was reissued in 1943. Issued in light green cloth, stamped in dark blue. Same pagination.

31 An Exhibition of Sculpture

AN EXHIBITION | OF SCULPTURE | *by* | JO DAVIDSON | [star] | including | portraits of leading Spanish personalities | completed during the summer and autumn of 1938 in Spain | [star] | *for the benefit of the* | SPANISH CHILDREN'S MILK FUND | DOROTHY PARKER, *Chairman* | NOVEMBER 18TH | THROUGH | DECEMBER 3RD | ARDEN GALLERY | 460 PARK AVENUE

9 1/8 x 6 1/16. Catalogue. 24 pages. Published in New York, in 1938. The yellow paper cover, slightly larger than the leaves, is printed in purple.

Hemingway's article, "Milton Wolff," is on p. 22. It is listed, on p. 13, as: [Number] 10. MAJOR MILTON WOLFF (*of the Abraham Lincoln Brigade*) by ERNEST HEMINGWAY.

Reissued:

JO DAVIDSON | SPANISH | PORTRAITS | [graduated line] | Texts by | ERNEST HEMINGWAY | VINCENT SHEEAN | LAWRENCE A. FERNSWORTH | HERBERT L. MATTHEWS | EDGAR ANSEL MOWRER | DOROTHY PARKER | JOHN GUNTHER | LELAND STOWE | ELLIOT PAUL | WALDO FRANK | JAY ALLEN | [graduated line] | *ONE DOLLAR* [all enclosed in an irregularly ruled border]

11 1/8 x 8 9/16. 28 pages. The white paper cover lettered in black, as shown above, serves as the title page. Note on the back cover: Designed and Printed by The Georgian Press, Inc., New York, N.Y. No date is given. It was probably issued for the exhibition of Davidson's work at the Whyte Gallery, in Washington, D.C., January 5 through January 18, 1939.

Hemingway's article, "Milton Wolff," is on p. [25]. A photograph of Jo Davidson's bust of Milton Wolff appears on p. [24].

NOTE: This article was reprinted in *American Dialog*, I (Oct.-Nov. 1964).

32 Somebody Had to Do Something

SOMEBODY | HAD TO | DO SOMETHING | *A Memorial to* | JAMES PHILLIPS LARDNER | By Ernest Hemingway, | Ring Lardner, Jr., Jay Allen, | Don Jesus Hernandez, El Campesino, | Dolores Ibarruri, Vincent Sheean | and Drawings by Castelao |

THE JAMES LARDNER MEMORIAL FUND | 617 UNION LEAGUE BUILDING, LOS ANGELES | 1939

9 1/2 x 6 1/8. 2 leaves, x + 46 pages. An edition of 500 copies was printed at the Plantin Press, Los Angeles, California. Issued in brown paper covers slightly larger than the buff leaves. Lettered and a drawing in red on the cover only: SOMEBODY HAD TO DO SOMETHING | [circular drawing]. All edges trimmed.

Hemingway's article "On the American Dead in Spain," on pp. 3-5, is reprinted from *New Masses*, xxx (Feb. 14, 1939).

NOTE: Hemingway is listed as a sponsor of The James Phillips Lardner Memorial Fund on p. [iv].

33 Men in the Ranks

5c | [drawing] | MEN IN THE RANKS | THE STORY OF 12 AMERICANS IN SPAIN | [rule] | BY JOSEPH NORTH | [rule] | WITH A FOREWORD BY | [rule] | ERNEST HEMINGWAY

7 5/16 x 5. 48 pages, including paper cover, as shown above. Published by the Friends of the Abraham Lincoln Brigade, New York, in March 1939, for five cents. Wire stapled.

Hemingway's foreword, on pp. 3-4, is not dated. A photograph of Hemingway, "visiting the 15th International Brigade, December, 1937," appears on p. 3.

34 All the Brave

ALL THE BRAVE | *By* | LUIS QUINTANILLA | *Preface by* | ERNEST HEMINGWAY | *Text by* | ELLIOT PAUL and JAY ALLEN | MODERN AGE BOOKS NEW YORK

11 x 8. 29 + [91] pages. Published in April 1939, at $10.00, in a "Deluxe Edition" limited to 440 numbered copies. Issued in blue buckram with a white vellum backstrip and a line-drawing stamped in silver on the blue front cover. Stamped in silver on the backstrip: [double rule] | *All* | *The* | *Brave* | [short rule] | *modern age* | *books* | [double rule]. All edges trimmed. Plain gray endpapers. Issued in a red board slip-case with a cream paper label on the front, lettered in gray.

"Three Prefaces" by Hemingway, on pp. 7-11. Dated: March 10, 1938, Key West; April 18, 1938, Somewhere in Spain; May, 1938, Somewhere in Spain.

The frontispiece, on p. [2], is a drawing by Quintanilla of Jay Allen, Elliot Paul, Hemingway, and a self-portrait.

NOTE: This book was first announced under the title *Guns and Castanets*, to be published in June 1938.

NOTE: A trade edition was published simultaneously, at ninety-five cents, in stiff red paper covers printed in white. Same size; same pagination.

35 Five Kinds of Writing

FIVE KINDS OF | WRITING | *Selections from British and American* | *authors, old and new* | Edited by | THEODORE MORRISON | and the staff of | ENGLISH A | at Harvard University | [publisher's device] | *For a man to write well, there are required three necessities:* | *to read the best authors, observe the best speakers,* | *and much exercise his own style.* | —BEN JONSON | LITTLE, BROWN AND COMPANY [dot] BOSTON | 1939

8 1/2 x 5 5/8. xx + 660 pages. Published in September 1939, at $2.50. Issued in red cloth with a device blind-stamped on the front cover. Stamped in gold on the backstrip: [decorative band] | FIVE | KINDS | OF | WRITING | [ornament] | Edited by | THEODORE | MORRISON | and Others | LITTLE BROWN | [decorative band]. All edges trimmed.

Contains Hemingway's "Dispatches from Spain," on pp. 172-181, reprinted as follows: pp. 172-173: Barcelona, reprinted from the *New Republic*, xciv (April 27, 1938); pp. 173-174: Ebro Delta, reprinted from the *New Republic*, xcv (June 8, 1938); pp. 174-175: Lerida, *ibid.*; pp. 175-177: On the Guadalajara Front, reprinted from the *New Republic*, xc (May 5, 1937); pp. 177-180: Madrid, *ibid.*; pp. 180-181: Madrid, *ibid.*

"A Clean, Well-Lighted Place" is reprinted on pp. 543-547.

36 A Stricken Field

A Stricken Field [in script] | MARTHA GELLHORN | DUELL, SLOAN AND PEARCE | NEW YORK

8 x 5 3/8. viii + 304 pages. Published in March 1940, at $2.50. Issued in nubby beige cloth with dark red lettering on the front cover and backstrip. Cover: A Stricken Field [in script at an upward angle] | MARTHA | GELLHORN. Backstrip: A | Stricken | Field [all in script at an upward angle] | MARTHA | GELLHORN | DUELL, SLOAN | AND PEARCE. All edges trimmed, top edges stained dark red. The black dust jacket is printed in red and white.

The thirteen-line epigraph, *"from a Medieval Chronicle,"* on p. [vii], was written by Hemingway. Martha Gellhorn acknowledged to the bibliographer that: "Ernest did write that excerpt from a Medieval Chronicle. It came about this way: I thought I had seen the phrase, 'A Stricken Field' in the History of the Peninsular

Wars. . . . I was sure I had seen it, and knew exactly how I wanted to use it; the meaning is altogether clear. So I searched and searched and it was not there. Whereupon Ernest stepped in and said he'd write a quote to fit the phrase and did."

NOTE: On p. [v], the dedication of this novel reads: *For Ernest Hemingway.*

NOTE: This novel, which is laid in Prague during the period between Munich and the Nazi invasion of the city, is told from the point of view of an American newspaper woman. Her friend "John," who is mentioned several times but never actually appears in the book, may be assumed to be portrayed after Hemingway.

NOTE: Reprinted by Grosset & Dunlap, in 1941, at $1.00, in the Books of Distinction series. Published in England by Cape, in February 1942. The epigraph appears on p. [7], and is quoted on the blue dust jacket.

37 The Best Short Stories 1940

THE | *Best* [red] | SHORT STORIES | 1940 | [long decorative line] | *and The Yearbook of the American Short Story* | [long rule] | *Edited by* | EDWARD J. O'BRIEN | 19 [publisher's device, in red] 40 | [broken rule] | HOUGHTON MIFFLIN COMPANY [dot] BOSTON | The Riverside Press Cambridge [Gothic]

8 x 5 1/2. xviii + 526 pages. Published in June 1940, at $2.75. Issued in brown cloth, stamped in dark blue on the front cover and backstrip. Cover: THE | *Best* | SHORT STORIES | 1940 | [long decorative line] | *and The Yearbook of the American Short Story* | [long rule]. Backstrip: THE | *Best* | SHORT | STORIES | 1940 | [decorative line] | *O'Brien* | [rule] | HOUGHTON | MIFFLIN CO. All edges trimmed.

"Under the Ridge," on pp. 109-122, is reprinted from *Cosmopolitan*, CVII (Oct. 1939).

38 The Great Crusade

THE | GREAT CRUSADE | By | GUSTAV REGLER | With a Preface | By Ernest Hemingway | Translated by | Whittaker Chambers | and Barrows Mussey | LONGMANS, GREEN AND CO. | New York [dot] Toronto | 1940

8 x 5 1/2. xiv + 448 pages. Published in September 1940, at $2.50. Issued in red cloth, stamped in gold on the backstrip only. THE | GREAT | CRUSADE | GUSTAV | REGLER | LONGMANS. Top and bottom edges trimmed, fore edges untrimmed. The endpapers are printed in black and white with a map of Spain. The red dust jacket is printed in cream and gray.

Hemingway's preface to this novel of the Spanish Civil War is on pp. vii-xi and is dated: Camaguey, Cuba: 1940.

NOTE: The publishers issued a sixteen-page promotion leaflet, three months before book publication, which included Hemingway's preface in full, on pp. [5]–[9], numbered vii-xi, as in the book. The leaflet measures 8 x 6 1/8 and is enclosed in the dust jacket that was later issued with the book. The preface is briefly quoted on the back cover of the dust jacket.

39 Henrietta Hoopes Catalogue

[Drawing] | HENRIETTA HOOPES | *Knoedler Galleries* DE-CEMBER 18, 1940 [dot] JANUARY 4, 1941

8 5/8 x 6 1/8. Folder. 4 pages. Published in New York, in 1940. Printed on a single sheet folded once; stiff yellow paper, with lettering and drawing in red. The cover, as shown above, serves as the title page; appraisals of the artist's work by Ernest Hemingway, Harry A. Bull, and Roger Beirne appear on p. [2]; CATALOGUE of paintings, in four groupings: HORSES, PORTRAITS, TO-RERO SERIES, and STILL LIFE, on p. [3]; the back cover, p. [4], is blank.

40 Vogue's First Reader

Vogue's | First | Reader [all in script] | [long rule] | INTRODUC-TION BY FRANK CROWNINSHIELD | Julian Messner, Incorporated [star] 1942 [star] New York [last line in script]

10 x 6 3/4. xvi + 560 pages. Published in December 1942, at $3.50. Issued in beige buckram, stamped in black and pink on the front cover and backstrip. Cover: [three short pink bands] | [decorative black "V"] | [ten short pink bands]. Backstrip: [two pink bands] | VOGUE'S | FIRST | READER [all at an upward angle] | Julian Messner [in script, at an upward angle] | [eight pink bands]. Top and bottom edges trimmed, fore edges untrimmed. The white and lavender dust jacket is printed in black.

"The Clark's Fork Valley, Wyoming," on pp. 32-34, is reprinted from *Vogue*, XCIII (Feb. 1, 1939).

NOTE: A smaller edition, which measures 8 1/2 x 6, was issued simultaneously by The Literary Guild, New York. Same pagination and binding. Reprinted by Halcyon House, Garden City, N.Y., in 1944.

41 They Were There

THEY WERE THERE | THE STORY OF | WORLD WAR II
AND HOW IT CAME ABOUT | BY AMERICA'S FOREMOST
CORRESPONDENTS | EDITED BY CURT RIESS | G. P. PUT-
NAM'S SONS [publisher's device] NEW YORK
8 1/2 x 5 1/2. xliv + 670 pages. Published in July 1944, at $5.00.
Issued in dark red cloth, stamped in gold on the backstrip only.
[Double rule] | *THEY* | *WERE* | *THERE* | [double rule] | *Edited
by* | *CURT RIESS* | [double rule] | PUTNAM. All edges trimmed.
White endpapers printed in gray with the contributors names.
The white dust jacket is printed in black and red.
"The Loyalists," on pp. 97-101, consists of three of Hemingway's
Spanish Civil War dispatches: "On the Aragon Front," "Madrid,"
and "Loyalist Army Headquarters, Teruel Front," reprinted from
the *New Republic*, xciii (Jan. 12, 1938).
See the editor's introduction, p. xxxiv, and the biographical note
on p. 637.

42 Esquire's First Sports Reader

ESQUIRE'S | First | Sports | Reader | *Edited by* | HERBERT
GRAFFIS | [drawing] | NEW YORK | A. S. BARNES &
COMPANY
9 x 6. xii + 292 pages. Published in March 1945, at $2.75. Issued
in red cloth with a drawing in black stamped on the front cover.
Lettered in black on the backstrip, reading downward: ES-
QUIRE'S FIRST SPORTS READER GRAFFIS BARNES. All
edges trimmed; top edges stained black. The red dust jacket is
printed in black and white.
"Remembering Shooting-Flying," on pp. 76-81, is reprinted from
Esquire, iii (Feb. 1935).
"On the Blue Water," on pp. 63-70, was previously collected in
Blow the Man Down, ed. Eric Devine, New York, 1937.
NOTE: Reprinted in an Armed Services Edition, n.d., as No. 965.
Issued in stiff paper covers, measuring 6 1/2 x 4 1/2.

43 Studio: Europe

[On the left hand page:] Studio: [in script] | EUROPE [white, on
black block] | [drawing of a London air raid shelter]. [On right
hand page:] [Drawing of medics with a stretcher] | By John Groth
[in script] | ILLUSTRATED BY THE AUTHOR | WITH AN
INTRODUCTION | BY ERNEST HEMINGWAY | The Van-
guard Press [dot] New York [dot] 1945 [last line in script]

9 3/4 x 7. 284 pages. Published in October 1945, at $3.50. Issued in dark blue cloth with a drawing stamped in silver on the front cover. Lettered in silver on the backstrip, reading downward: GROTH [dot] STUDIO: EUROPE [dot] VANGUARD. All edges trimmed; top edges stained blue. The endpapers are white with blue drawings. The gray dust jacket is printed in blue and white. Hemingway's introduction, on pp. 7-9, is dated : *August 25, 1945 | San Francisco de Paula, Cuba.*

NOTE: The artist-author writes of Hemingway, during World War II, in Ch. xii: " 'Schloss' Hemingway," on pp. 202-220. A drawing of Hemingway autographing a book (according to the text, *THAHN*) for a soldier, appears on pp. [216]–[217]. The drawing is dated: Sept. 29, 1944.

44 Treasury for the Free World

[On the left hand page:] [Contributors' names alphabetized] | TREASURY F | [contributors' names alphabetized]. [On the right hand page:] OR THE FREE | WORLD | INTRODUCTION BY ERNEST HEMINGWAY | EDITED BY BEN RAEBURN | NEW YORK [publisher's device] ARCO PUBLISHING COMPANY

9 1/4 x 6 1/4. xxii + 418 pages. Published in February 1946, at $3.50. Issued in beige cloth, stamped in silver on the front cover and backstrip. Cover: TREASURY FOR | THE FREE WORLD. Backstrip, reading downward: TREASURY | FOR THE [two lines] FREE WORLD [one line] EDITED BY | BEN RAEBURN [two lines] ARCO [one line]. Bottom edges trimmed, fore edges untrimmed; top edges stained dark brown. The dust jacket is printed in red, yellow, black, and white. A brief quote from Hemingway's foreword appears on the back cover.

Hemingway's foreword, on pp. xiii-xv, is dated: *San Francisco de Paula, Cuba | September* 1945. It was reprinted in the *Free World*, xi (March 1946), under the title "The Sling and the Pebble."

45 Joan Miró

CLEMENT GREENBERG | JOAN MIRÓ [green-yellow] | [publisher's device] | THE QUADRANGLE PRESS | NEW YORK MCMXLVIII

11 x 8 1/2. iv + 134 pages, including 85 plates. Published in January 1949, at $10.00. Issued in yellow paper-covered boards, with a drawing stamped in black on the front cover. Lettered in black on the backstrip: CLEMENT | GREENBERG | MIRÓ | [publisher's device]. All edges trimmed.

Hemingway's account of his acquisition of Miró's canvas, "The

Farm," is reprinted, on p. [5], from *Cahiers d'Art*, IX (1934). A small reproduction of the painting appears on p. [4]. For a larger reproduction, see Plate X: THE FARM, 1921-22 | Oil on canvas, 58 x 52 | *Collection of Ernest Hemingway, Havana, Cuba.*

NOTE: An excerpt from Hemingway's article was printed in the catalogue *Joan Miró: Paintings*, New York, 1934. See (B14).

NOTE: An excerpt from the last chapter of *DIA*, in which Hemingway describes Miró's home at Montroig, is quoted in the footnote on p. 13.

NOTE: Reissued in 1950, with the same binding and the same title page as shown above. Same pagination. The heavier gray leaves, on which the color plates were pasted in the first edition, were changed to white leaves of the same weight as the leaves of the text.

46 A Treasury of Great Reporting

A TREASURY OF | GREAT [red] | REPORTING [red] | "Literature under Pressure" | from the Sixteenth Century | to Our Own Time | Edited by | Louis L. Snyder [red] | ASSOCIATE PROFESSOR OF HISTORY | THE COLLEGE OF THE CITY OF NEW YORK | AND | RICHARD B. Morris [red] | PROFESSOR OF HISTORY, COLUMBIA UNIVERSITY | 1949 [red] | SIMON AND SCHUSTER [dot] NEW YORK [title page enclosed in a single-ruled red border]

9 1/8 x 6. xlvi + 786 pages. Published in October 1949, at $5.00. Issued in black cloth with a cream cloth backstrip. Stamped in gold on the black front cover: A TREASURY OF | [ornament, three long rules, ornament] | GREAT REPORTING. Stamped in gold on the backstrip: [triple rule] | A TREASURY OF | GREAT | REPORTING | Edited by | Richard B. Morris | and Louis L. Snyder | [triple rule] [all on red background] | [ornament] | [triple rule] | [ornament] | [triple rule] | SIMON AND SCHUSTER. All edges trimmed; top edges stained red.

On pp. 524-528, under the heading "The author of *For Whom the Bell Tolls* interviews a countryman from Pennsylvania, 'where once we fought at Gettysburg,'" Hemingway's NANA dispatch is reprinted from the *N.Y. Times* (April 25, 1937). Dateline: Madrid, April 24.

See also commentary on pp. 524, 530; Hemingway's dispatch from the Lerida front, in May 1937, is briefly quoted.

47 Game Fish of the World

GAME FISH | OF | THE WORLD [title in blue] | Edited by | BRIAN VESEY-FITZGERALD, F.L.S. | and | FRANCESCA

LAMONTE, Secretary, I.G.F.A. | (*Associate Curator of Fishes, American Museum of Natural History*) | Illustrations by | A. FRASER-BRUNNER | [design of a seahorse] | NICHOLSON & WATSON | LONDON BRUSSELS
9 5/8 x 7 3/16. [xx] + 446 pages + 80 plates. Published in [November] 1949, at 63s., in a limited edition of 100 copies. Printed in Great Britain by Love & Malcomson, Ltd., Redhill. Issued in blue cloth, stamped in gold on the front and back covers. Lettered and decorated in gold on the backstrip: [two bands] | GAME | FISH | OF THE | WORLD | [two bands] | *Edited by* | BRIAN | VESEY-FITZGERALD, F.L.S. | *and* | FRANCESCA LAMONTE, | Secy. I.G.F.A. | [design of a fish] | NICHOLSON | *and* | WATSON. All edges trimmed; top edges gold. Blue and white pictorial endpapers.
Hemingway's article, "Cuban Fishing," on pp. 156-160, is not dated.
NOTE: Published in the United States by Harper & Brothers, Publishers, New York, in November 1949, at $15.00. Issued in greenish-blue cloth with the publisher's device blind-stamped on a green background on the front cover. Printed in Great Britain by Love & Malcomson, Ltd., Redhill. Same pagination as the English edition.

48 In Sicily

IN SICILY | [long rule] | BY | ELIO VITTORINI | [long rule] | TRANSLATED | BY WILFRID DAVID | INTRODUCTION | BY ERNEST HEMINGWAY | A NEW DIRECTIONS BOOK | [long rule]
7 3/4 x 5 1/4. 164 pages. Published in New York, in November 1949, at $2.50. Printed in England. Issued in bluish-green cloth, stamped in black on the backstrip only. Backstrip, reading downward: ELIO VITTORINI IN SICILY NEW DIRECTIONS. All edges trimmed. The dust jacket is printed in yellow, green, blue, orange, white, and black.
Hemingway's introduction, on pp. [7]–[8], is dated: Cortina D'Ampezzo, 1949. The introduction is briefly quoted on the front flap of the dust jacket, which was reproduced as the cover of a promotion leaflet prior to book publication.
NOTE: Translated from the Italian novel, *Conversazione in Sicilia*, published by Bompiani, Milan, in 1937.
NOTE: First published in English by Benn, London, in 1949, at 8s. 6d. The English edition was not examined by the bibliographer.
NOTE: Reissued by New Directions, date unknown. Issued in yellow cloth, stamped in red on the backstrip only. 8 x 5 1/4. 256

pages. Printed by the Haddon Craftsmen, Inc., Scranton, Pa. Hemingway's introduction is on pp. 7-9.

49 Ezra Pound: A Collection of Essays

EZRA POUND | *A collection of essays edited by* | *Peter Russell*
to be presented | *to Ezra Pound on his sixty-fifth* | *birthday* | PETER
NEVILL LIMITED | *London New York*

8 3/8 x 5 3/8. 268 pages. Published in October 1950, at 12s. 6d. Issued in beige cloth, stamped in gold on the backstrip. All edges trimmed, top edges stained brown. Note: Issued in a variant binding of green cloth, stamped in black; top edges unstained.
Contains Hemingway's "Homage to Ezra," on pp. 73-76, reprinted from *This Quarter*, 1 (Spring 1925).

NOTE: An American edition, titled *An Examination of Ezra Pound: A Collection of Essays*, was published by New Directions, Norfolk, Conn., October 30, 1950, at $3.75. Issued in beige cloth, stamped in gold and blue on the backstrip. Printed in Great Britain. Same pagination as the English edition.

50 Pourquoi ces Bêtes Sont-Elles Sauvages?

FRANÇOIS SOMMER | POURQUOI CES BÊTES | SONT-ELLES SAUVAGES | Préface de ERNEST HEMINGWAY | [Note regarding the photographs] | Les illustrations sont de LUCIEN BLANCOU, Inspecteur | Principal des Chasses en Afrique Equatoriale Française. | 1951 | NOUVELLES ÉDITIONS DE LA TOISON D'OR | 106bis, RUE DE RENNES | PARIS-VIe

9 7/8 x 7 1/2. 232 pages. An edition of 500 copies was published March 28, 1951. Issued in paper covers. Front cover: F. SOMMER | POURQUOI | CES BÊTES | SONT-ELLES | SAUVAGES? | NOUVELLES ÉDITIONS DE LA TOISON D'OR | 106bis, rue de Rennes, PARIS-VIe. The dust jacket is printed in yellow letters over a gray photograph of an elephant on the front cover.
Hemingway's preface, on pp. 9-11, is translated into French by Paule de Beaumont. Dated: Finca Vigia. | San Francisco de Paula. | Cuba. Février 1951.
First English edition:
MAN AND BEAST | IN AFRICA | *By* FRANÇOIS SOMMER | *With a Foreword by* | ERNEST HEMINGWAY | *Translated from the French by* | EDWARD FITZGERALD | LONDON : HERBERT JENKINS

9 1/4 x 6 1/8. 208 pages. Published in January 1953, at 30s. Issued in blue cloth, stamped in gold on the backstrip only. MAN | AND

|BEAST | IN | AFRICA | FRANÇOIS | SOMMER | HERBERT | JENKINS |. Publisher's device blind-stamped on the back cover. All edges trimmed; top edges stained blue.

Hemingway's foreword, on pp. 5-7, is not dated. For date, see the French edition.

NOTE: An American edition was published by Citadel Press, New York, in 1954, at $4.00. 208 pages. Hemingway's foreword is on pp. 5-7.

51 A Hemingway Check List

A | Hemingway | Check | List | [ornament] | LEE SAMUELS | Charles Scribner's Sons | NEW YORK [dot] 1951

9 x 6. 64 pages. Published in July 1951, at $2.50. The first and only printing consisted of 750 copies. Issued in dark blue cloth, lettered in gold on the front cover and the backstrip. Front cover: A HEMINGWAY CHECK LIST | LEE SAMUELS. Backstrip, reading downward: SAMUELS [dot] A HEMINGWAY CHECK LIST [dot] SCRIBNER'S. All edges trimmed. Plain endpapers. The white dust jacket is printed in blue and white.

Hemingway's preface, on pp. 5-6, is dated: *Finca Vigia | San Francisco de Paula | Cuba, 11/8/50.*

CONTENTS: The Books/The Short Stories, indicating first appearance in periodicals and/or books/Short Stories, which have not as yet been published in book form/Poetry/Contributions to Periodicals (other than stories) /First Appearance in Book Form, of some of the preceding articles/Prefaces and Introductions/Unclassified Work.

NOTE: An erratum slip is inserted between pp. 50–[51], noting that p. [51] should precede the description of "Marlin Off Cuba," which appears on p. 54.

52 Reginald Rowe Catalogue

[Drawing] | Reginald Rowe | FEBRUARY 18 TO MARCH 1, 1952 | HOURS 10-6 | FRIDAY to 8 P.M. | WELLONS GALLERY | 70 EAST 56 STREET, NEW YORK

5 x 7. Folder. 4 pages. Printed on a single sheet folded twice; cream paper with cover drawing and all lettering in green. The cover, as shown above, serves as the title page; list of fourteen paintings on p. [2]; Hemingway's appraisal of the artist's work, on p. [3], is dated: *Finca Vigia | San Francisco de Paula, Havana | January, 1952;* the back cover, p. [4], is blank.

NOTE: The artist was a neighbor of the Hemingways, in Cuba.

53 The Little Review Anthology

THE LITTLE REVIEW | ANTHOLOGY | *Edited by* MARGA-
RET ANDERSON | HERMITAGE HOUSE, INC. | New York,
1953

8 1/4 x 5 5/8. 384 pages. Published in January 1953, at $3.95. Is-
sued in gray cloth backstrip over gray-green boards. Decorative
black initials, "M A," stamped on lower right corner of the gray-
green front cover. Black and gray lettering on gray backstrip:
LITTLE | REVIEW | THE LITTLE REVIEW ANTHOLOGY
[title reading downward] | EDITED BY | MARGARET | AN-
DERSON [gray, on a black background] | HERMITAGE | 1953 |.
Top edges stained green; bottom edges trimmed, fore edges untrimmed. The white dust jacket is printed in green and black.

Hemingway's poem, "Valentine," on p. 367, is reprinted from the
final number of the *Little Review*, XII (May 1929). A short letter
from Hemingway, also reprinted from the final number, appears
on the same page.

"Mr. and Mrs. Elliot," on pp. 332-335, first appeared in the *Little
Review*, X (Autumn–Winter 1924–1925). Published in *IOT*.

54 Salt Water Fishing

SALT WATER | FISHING | VAN CAMPEN HEILNER | *Pref-
ace by Ernest Hemingway* | *Color paintings and line drawings by
W. Goadby Lawrence* | SECOND EDITION REVISED | [pub-
lisher's device] | ALFRED A. KNOPF : NEW YORK | 1953

9 3/8 x 6 1/4. xviii + 362 pages. Published in February 1953, at
$7.50. Issued in blue cloth backstrip over beige cloth. Beige front
cover plain. Design blind-stamped on blue front cover. Publisher's
device blind-stamped on blue back cover. Lettered and ruled in
gold on blue backstrip: [two sets of double rules] | SALT | WA-
TER | FISHING | [two sets of double rules] | HEILNER | [four
sets of double rules] | Knopf [in script] | [two sets of double rules].
Bottom edges trimmed, fore edges untrimmed; top edges stained
light green. The yellow dust jacket is printed in black and red,
with the painting of a fish in blue and green.

Hemingway's preface, on pp. vii-viii, is dated: *Finca Vigia* | *San
Francisco de Paula, Cuba* | *June 1951.*

NOTE: References to Hemingway appear in the text on pp. 131-
132, 146, 158, 203, 307-308.

NOTE: Hemingway's preface did not appear in the first edition,
which was published by the Penn Publishing Co., Philadelphia,
1937. The revised and enlarged second edition was reset and
printed from new plates.

55 Ezra Pound at Seventy

Ezra Pound [in script] | AT SEVENTY ——
4 3/4 x 3 1/2. 12 unnumbered pages. Published by New Directions,
Norfolk, Conn., in [1955]. Issued in paper covers of the same
weight as the leaves. Wire stapled. The cover portrait of Pound,
by La Martinelli, and all lettering throughout the pamphlet is in
brown.
Hemingway's tribute to Pound appears on p. [4]. No title or date
is given. It is preceded by his name in lower case letters.
NOTE: The publishers' note on the inside front cover states: "To
mark Ezra Pound's seventieth year New Directions wrote to a
number of persons and here publishes the statements they sent
about him, together with a list of his books in print so that the
reader of this pamphlet may be led to Pound's own writings. . . ."
The contributors are: W. H. Auden, e. e. cummings, T. S. Eliot,
Ernest Hemingway, Archibald MacLeish, Jose V. de Pina Martins, Marianne Moore, Norman H. Pearson, Stephen Spender, and
Dame Edith Sitwell.

56 Les Prix Nobel en 1954

LES PRIX NOBEL | EN 1954 | STOCKHOLM | IMPRIMERIE
ROYALE P. A. NORSTEDT & SÖNER | 1955
9 5/8 x 6 1/2. 136 pages. Published in November 1955, at 25
kronor. Issued in white paper covers, lettered in red. Cover: LES
PRIX NOBEL | EN 1954 |. Backstrip, reading downward: LES
PRIX NOBEL EN 1954. All edges trimmed.
Contains the citation to Hemingway (in French) on p. 6; the speech
by the Permanent Secretary of the Swedish Academy, Anders
Österling, "Nobelpriset i litteratur för År 1954" (in Swedish) on
pp. 43-46, and the English translation on pp. 47-50; Hemingway's
Nobel prize acceptance speech (in English) on pp. 54-55; a biographical sketch on pp. 74-75; and a photograph of Hemingway,
opp. p. 74.
NOTE: A special Laureates copy was issued in blue cloth, with gold
triple-ruled border and lettering on the front cover, gold ruling
and lettering on the backstrip, and a gold triple-ruled border on
the back cover. All edges are gilt. 132 copies were issued in this
binding.

57 Erlebtes Fliegenfischen

CHARLES C. RITZ | [long rule] | ERLEBTES | FLIEGEN-
FISCHEN | KUNST UND TECHNIK DES FLIEGENFISCH-

ENS | AUF ÄSCHEN, FORELLEN UND LACHSE | Mit einer Einführung von Ernest Hemingway, | einem Vorwort von L. de Boisset, | 35 Bildern im Text und 32 Kunstdrucktafeln | [publisher's device] | ALBERT MÜLLER VERLAG, AG., RÜSCH-LIKON-ZÜRICH

9 7/8 x 7 3/16. 232 pages + 32 plates. Published in 1956, in Zurich. Issued in blue cloth stamped in gold on the front cover and the backstrip. Cover: [author's signature]. Backstrip: [band] | [design] | [band] | Charles | C. Ritz | [star] | Erlebtes | Fliegen- | fischen [author's signature and title in blue, on gold block] | [band] | [design] | [band] | [design] | [band] | [design] | [band]. All edges trimmed. The white dust jacket is lettered in black and illustrated in color by Fredy Knorr.

"Zum Geleit" by Hemingway, on p. 9, is dated: An Bord der "Pilar," 12. Dezember 1954.

NOTE: A photograph of Hemingway and Charles Ritz is opposite p. [16].

NOTE: Hemingway's foreword did not appear in the original French edition, *Pris sur le Vif*, published by the Librairie des Champs-Élysées, Paris, in 1953.

ENGLISH TRANSLATION:

A | FLY FISHER'S | LIFE | by | CHARLES RITZ | [decorative line] | *With a Foreword by* | ERNEST HEMINGWAY | *and an Introduction by* | A. J. McCLANE | *Translated by* | HUMPHREY HARE | HENRY HOLT AND COMPANY | NEW YORK

9 11/16 x 6 7/8. 230 pages + 32 plates. Published in April 1960, at $8.50. Issued in light blue cloth, stamped in gold on the backstrip only. A | FLY | FISHER'S | LIFE | [short rule] | Charles | Ritz [all on a black block, enclosed in a ruled gold border] | HOLT. All edges trimmed; top edges stained blue.

Hemingway's foreword, on p. 11, is dated: On board the *Pilar* | December 12, 1954.

NOTE: A photograph of Hemingway and Charles Ritz appears opposite p. 16.

NOTE: A large paper edition of 250 numbered copies, signed by the author, was issued in blue leatherette, boxed.

58 The Armchair Esquire

THE ARMCHAIR | Esquire [in script] | *Edited by* ARNOLD GINGRICH | *and* L. RUST HILLS | INTRODUCTION BY *Granville Hicks* | [publisher's device] | G. P. PUTNAM'S SONS *New York*

8 3/8 x 5 1/8. 354 pages + 24-page Appendix. Published in October 1958, at $3.95. Issued in black cloth, stamped in red and silver on

the front cover and backstrip. Cover: THE ARMCHAIR [red] | [drawing in silver] Esquire [in script, in silver]. Backstrip: THE [red] | ARMCHAIR [red] | Esquire [in script, in silver] | Putnam [silver]. All edges trimmed.

"The Butterfly and the Tank," on pp. 136-144, is reprinted from *Esquire*, x (Dec. 1938). Prefatory note on p. 135, regarding the publication of Hemingway's stories and articles in *Esquire*. Also see the introduction, on pp. 10-11, for commentary on Hemingway.

NOTE: A checklist of Hemingway's work in *Esquire* appears on pp. 12-13 of the Appendix: "A Check-List of Contributions of Literary Import to *Esquire*, 1933-1958," compiled by E. R. Hagemann and James E. Marsh.

NOTE: Published simultaneously by Longmans, Green & Co., Toronto. An English edition was published by Heinemann, London, in 1959, at 18s.

59 Ernest Hemingway: Critiques of Four Major Novels

CARLOS BAKER | Princeton University | ERNEST HEMINGWAY: | Critiques of Four Major Novels | SRA CHARLES SCRIBNER'S SONS | New York

9 3/16 x 6 1/2. xx + 204 pages. Published in October 1962, at $2.25. Issued in green, stiff paper covers printed in black and white. "The Original Conclusion to *A Farewell to Arms*" appears on p. 75. The footnote states: ". . . Printed here for the first time and by permission of Mrs. Ernest Hemingway." In the introduction, on p. 1, Carlos Baker notes: "Students of the novel should find it instructive to compare this rejected conclusion with the one that was actually published."

NOTE: This Scribner Research Anthology includes critiques on *SAR, FTA, FWBT*, and *OMATS*. For a list of the contents, see (G28).

60 Masterpieces of War Reporting

Masterpieces | of | War Reporting | The Great Moments of World War II | Edited by | LOUIS L. SNYDER | [publisher's device] | Julian Messner, Inc. New York

9 1/4 x 6 1/8. xx + 556 pages. Published in November 1962, at $10.00. Issued in black cloth, stamped in gold on the backstrip only. SNYDER [horizontal] | Masterpieces of War Reporting | [short graduated line] | The Great Moments of World War II [in two rows, reading downward] | MESSNER [horizontal]. All edges

trimmed. The red dust jacket is printed in yellow, black, and white.

"London Fights the Robots," on pp. 361-367, is reprinted from *Collier's*, CXIV (Aug. 19, 1944). An introductory note, on p. 360, is titled "Second Battle of Britain: Ernest Hemingway Tells How London Fought Hitler's Vengeance Weapon # 1."

NOTE: Published simultaneously in Canada by Copp Clark Publishing Co. Ltd., Toronto.

61 Hemingway in Michigan

HEMINGWAY | IN MICHIGAN | by | Constance Cappel Montgomery | FLEET PUBLISHING CORPORATION | NEW YORK

9 x 6. 224 pages, including 24 pages of photographs. Published August 22, 1966, at $5.95. The first printing consisted of 5000 copies. Issued in brown paper-covered boards over a black cloth backstrip. Lettered in gold on the backstrip, reading downward: HEMINGWAY IN MICHIGAN | Montgomery [reading downward, on a second line] | FLEET [horizontal]. All edges trimmed. The gray dust jacket is lettered in white with a photograph on the cover, in brown tones, of Hemingway in 1920. The photograph also appears in the book, p. [152].

Contains three short stories which Hemingway wrote for the Oak Park High School literary magazine, *Tabula*. "Judgment of Manitou," on pp. 44-45, is reprinted from *Tabula*, XXII (Feb. 1916). "A Matter of Colour," on pp. 47-49, is reprinted from *Tabula*, XXII (April 1916). "Sepi Jingan," on pp. 50-52, is reprinted from *Tabula*, XXIII (Nov. 1916).

NOTE: Hemingway's long letter to his parents from the hospital in Milan after he was wounded in 1918, is reprinted from the Chicago *Evening Post* (Oct. 23, 1918), on pp. 111-114. See (F43).

62 The United States Navy in World War II

THE UNITED | STATES NAVY IN | WORLD WAR II | THE ONE-VOLUME HISTORY, FROM PEARL HARBOR | TO TOKYO BAY—BY MEN WHO FOUGHT IN THE | ATLANTIC AND THE PACIFIC AND BY DISTINGUISHED | NAVAL EXPERTS, AUTHORS AND NEWSPAPERMEN | *Selected and edited by S. E. Smith* | *With an Introduction by Rear Admiral* | *E. M. Eller, Director of Naval History* | [decorative line] | *William Morrow & Company, Inc. New York 1966*

9 1/4 x 6 1/4. xxiv + 1050 pages + plates. Published in November 1966, at $12.50. Issued in dark blue cloth with the seal of the United States Navy blind-stamped on the front cover. Lettered in white on the backstrip. All edges trimmed; top edges stained bright blue. Map endpapers. The black dust jacket is printed in red, white, and blue, with an illustration in color on the front cover.

"Voyage to Victory," on pp. 603-616, is reprinted from *Collier's,* cxiv (July 22, 1944).

NOTE: Hemingway's dispatch covering the invasion of Normandy, on June 6, 1944, was published in pamphlet form, as a promotion piece, by *Collier's* prior to magazine publication. See (A21).

SECTION C
CONTRIBUTIONS TO NEWSPAPERS AND PERIODICALS

This section comprises both first appearances and reprinted contributions to newspapers and periodicals. In 1930, Hemingway, in a letter to Louis Henry Cohn (see *Cohn's Bibliography*, p. 112), expressed his opposition to having his early newspaper work listed. However, this bibliographer believes that both the early journalism and Hemingway's high school *juvenilia*, are pertinent to a full understanding of his later work.

Unfortunately, there were no by-lined articles, nor is there any record of any credited articles, by Hemingway during the six months in 1917-1918 when he worked on the *Kansas City Star*.

With the exception of the December 1920 issue, the bibliographer was unable to locate any issues of the *Co-operative Commonwealth* for the winter of 1920-1921 when Hemingway was an assistant editor on the magazine.

The bibliographer gratefully acknowledges her debt to W. L. McGeary and William White for information regarding Hemingway's work on the *Toronto Daily Star* and the *Toronto Star Weekly* (abbreviated *TDS* and *TSW* in this work). A number of additions and corrections have been made to the list which appeared in Carlos Baker's *Hemingway: The Writer as Artist*, Princeton, 1963, Third edition, pp. 361-366. In the present work all *TSW* articles are in the Magazine Section unless otherwise noted.

Hemingway's North American Newspaper Alliance (NANA) dispatches on the Spanish Civil War were syndicated and the source given here is only one of numerous newspapers in which the dispatch appeared. All dispatches that appeared in the *N.Y. Times* are listed.

C1 Article. "Concert a Success," *Trapeze*, v, iv (Jan. 20, 1916), [2].

Review of a concert given by the Chicago Symphony Orchestra. Note: During the first half of the 1916 school year, Hemingway was listed under Reporters on the masthead of *Trapeze*, the weekly newspaper of the Oak Park and River Forest Township [Ill.] High School. Unless otherwise noted, by-line appeared as: Ernest M. Hemingway.

2 Article. "Hanna Club Tomorrow Night," *Trapeze*, v, v (Jan. 27, 1916), [4].

Subtitled: "Mr. David Goodwillie to Talk—Eats to Be a Surprise—Jokes and Good Fellowship Promised."

3 Short story. "Judgment of Manitou," *Tabula*, xxii, ii (Feb. 1916), 9-10.

Hemingway's first published story dealt with the murder of a friend by a vindictive trapper during a hunting expedition in northern Michigan. "Manitou" is an Indian word for "God." Reprinted in *Hemingway in Michigan*, pp. 44-45. See (B61). Note: *Tabula* was the Oak Park and River Forest Township High School literary magazine. For an appraisal of Hemingway's high school writing, see *The Apprenticeship of Ernest Hemingway* by Charles A. Fenton, New York, 1954, pp. 14-27.

4 Article. "Hanna Club Members Hear Practical Talk," *Trapeze*, v, vi (Feb. 3, 1916), [2].

Report of a guest speaker's talk on "the employer's side of the labor problem."

5 Article. "Practical Education VS. Theoretical," *Trapeze*, v, vii (Feb. 10, 1916), [1].

Subtitled: "Hanna Club, With Largest Attendance in Its History, Enthuse Over This Question." Report of a school club debate.

6 Article. "Mr. Quayle Rouses Hanna Club," *Trapeze*, v, viii (Feb. 17, 1916), [4].

A report of the guest speaker's talk on "business careers of the high school boys."

7 Article. "Problems of Boyhood Discussed at Hanna Club," *Trapeze*, v, xi (March 9, 1916), [4].

8 Article. "Big Hanna Club [M]eeting Hears Rousing Talk," *Trapeze*, v, xiii (March 23, 1916), [2].

9 Short story. "A Matter of Colour," *Tabula*, xxii, iii (April 1916), 16-17.

This story, told in the form of a monologue by a veteran prizefight manager, is about a crooked fight. Reprinted in *Hemingway in Michigan*, pp. 47-49. See (B61).

10 Short story. "Sepi Jingan," *Tabula*, xxiii, i (Nov. 1916) [8]-9.

This story of violence and revenge in northern Michigan is told by an Ojibway Indian. The title is taken from the name of his dog. Reprinted in *Hemingway in Michigan*, pp. 50-52. See (B61).

10₁ Poem. "How Ballad Writing Affects Our Seniors," *ibid.* p. 41.

A forty-eight-line ballad, which was written for a class assignment. The first stanza is reprinted in *The Apprenticeship of Ernest Hemingway* by Charles A. Fenton, New York, 1954, p. 19.

11 Article. "Athletic Association to | Organize Next Week," *Trapeze*, vi, ii (Nov. 3, 1916), [1].

Note: During his senior year Hemingway was one of the five Associate Editors who alternated weekly as Editor.

11₁ Article. "Stop Hellstrom," *ibid.*, [3]. Signed: E. H.
A report on a forthcoming football game. The title refers to a halfback on the rival team.

12 "Poem." Untitled, *Trapeze*, vi, iii (Nov. 10, 1916), [4].
A four-line "blank verse" consisting only of punctuation marks appears in the humor column, the Air Line. Signed: E. H.

13 Article. "Oak Park Victors | Over Waite High," *Trapeze*, vi, iv (Nov. 17, 1916), [1],[3].
A long account of a football game, which Oak Park won 35-19. Hemingway played right guard.

14 Article. "Midwayites Downed | By Oak Park Team," *Trapeze*, vi, v (Nov. 24, 1916), [1],[4].
An account of a football game.

14₁ Poem. Untitled, *ibid.*, [2]. Signed: E. H.
A four-line verse on football mayhem appears in the Air Line column, "Dedicated to F. W."

14₂ Column. "A 'Ring Lardner' On the Bloomington Game," *ibid.*, [3].
A Lardnerian account of a football game. Note: This is the first of six boxed columns which Hemingway wrote in the style of Ring Lardner. A facsimile of this column appears in *Hemingway* by Leo Lania, New York, 1961, p. 25.

14₃ Column. "Athletic Notes," *ibid.*, [4].
Eleven items relating to athletic events.

15 Article. "Basketball Season Opens | Poor Lightweight Prospects," *Trapeze*, vi, vi (Dec. 8, 1916), [1].
Note: Hemingway was Editor of this issue.

15₁ Column. "Our 'Ring Lardner' Jr. Breaks Into | Print with All-Cook County Eleven," *ibid.*, [3].
In his selections for an all-county football team, Hemingway lists himself as "Very fullback."

16 Column. "Athletic Notes," *Trapeze*, vi, viii (Dec. 22, 1916), [2].
Eighteen items on athletic events.

17 Column. "Personals," *Trapeze*, vi, x (Jan. 26, 1917), [3]. Signed: E. H. Eighteen items, including one about his trap-shooting club.

18 Article. "Gun Club Defeats Evanstons and Wil- | mette in Triangle Meet," *Trapeze*, vi, xi (Feb. 2, 1917), [1].

18₁ Article. "Interclass Meet Saturday," *ibid.*, [3]. An article about the high school track meet.

18₂ Column. "Athletic Notes," *ibid.*, [3]. Eight items on athletic events.

18₃ Column. " 'Ring Lardner Junior' Writes about Swim- | ming Meet. Oak Park Rivals Riverside," *ibid.*, [4].

This column is in the form of a letter to that week's editor, Earle Pashley. Reprinted in *My Brother, Ernest Hemingway* by Leicester Hemingway, Cleveland, 1962, pp. 38-40.

19 Editorial. "Support the Swimming Team," *Trapeze*, vi, xii (Feb. 9, 1917), [2]. Unsigned.

Note: Hemingway was Editor of this issue. He refers to this editorial in his column in *Trapeze*, vi (Feb. 16, 1917).

19₁ Column. "Athletic Notes, *ibid.*, [3]. Seven items regarding athletic events.

20 Column. "Ring Lardner, Jr., Discourses on Editorials," *Trapeze*, vi, xiii (Feb. 16, 1917), [3].

This column is in the form of a letter to that week's editor, Susan Lowrey. The letter is signed: Ernie Hemingway.

21 Article. "Who's Who in Beau Brummel?" *Trapeze*, vi, xiv (Feb. 23, 1917), [3]. By-line: By Roland Michael Kenney and Ernest Monahan Hemingway.

A humorous listing of the cast of the Senior Class play, "Beau Brummel," performed February 16, 1917. Hemingway played the part of Richard Brinsley Sheridan.

22 Poem. "The Worker," *Tabula*, xxiii, iii (March 1917), 22.

This twelve-line poem was reprinted in Frederic Babcock's column in the *Chicago Tribune* (May 24, 1959).

22₁ Poem. "Athletic Verse," *ibid.*, 39.

This free-verse was written in collaboration with a classmate, Fred Wilcoxen. It is in three parts: "The Tackle" (eleven lines), "The Punt" (eight lines), and "The Safety Man" (nine lines).

22₂ Poem. "The Inexpressible," *ibid.*, 46. Two verses of six lines each.

23 Article. "New Trier Tankers | Win From Locals," *Trapeze*, vi, xv (March 2, 1917), [1], [4]. An account of a water basketball game.

24 Article. "Oak Park Team Wins | From Main High," *Trapeze*, vi, xvi (March 9, 1917), [3]. By-line: Ernest Miller Hemingway. An account of a water basketball game.

25 Article. "O. P. Places Second | In Suburban Classic," *Trapeze*, vi, xvii (March 16, 1917), [1],[4]. An account of the interscholastic athletic meet.

26 Article. "Track Team Loses | to Culver," *Trapeze*, vi, xix (March 30, 1917), [1].

27 Article. "Oak Park Second In | Northwestern U," *Trapeze*, vi, xx (April 20, 1917), [1].

An account of the National Interscholastic meet. Note: A facsimile of this article appears in *Hemingway* by Leo Lania, New York, 1961, p. 22.

28 Article. "Win Two—Lose One," *Trapeze*, vi, xxii (May 4, 1917), [2]. An account of recent baseball games.

28₁ Column. "Ring Lardner Returns," *ibid.*, [3].

This column is in the form of a letter to his sister, Marcelline, who was editor of this issue. The letter is signed: Ernie.

29 Article. "Oak Park Athletes | Win Beloit Meet," *Trapeze*, xxv, xxiii (May 11, 1917), [3].

An account of an interscholastic track meet. Note: The volume number was unaccountably changed from vi to xxv beginning with this issue.

29₁ Column. "Some Space Filled by Ernest MacNamara Hemingway," *ibid.*, [3].

Subtitled: "Ring Lardner Has Objected to the Use of His Name." The column is in two parts. It contains a "Personal" item and an interview with "George Washington."

29₂ Article. "Shotgun Club News," *ibid.*, [3]. Signed: H. E. [*sic*].

30 Article. "High Lights and Low Lights," *Trapeze*, xxv, xxv (May 25, 1917), [4]. By-line: By Ernest Michaelowitch Hemingway, B.S.

Sixteen mock-social items concluding with a two-line verse. Signed: Ernest McDermott Hemingway. Note: Hemingway was Editor of this issue. A photograph of the *Trapeze* staff appears on p. [1].

31 Article. "Class Prophecy," *Senior Tabula* (June 1917) 57-62.

Reprinted in *Chicago*, 1 (Aug. 1954). A facsimile of the first page appears in *Hemingway* by Leo Lania, New York, 1961, p. 26. Note: The *Senior Tabula* was the Class Yearbook. Hemingway's photograph, and a photograph of his sister Marcelline, appear on p. 23; a photograph of Hemingway is included with the Class Day Speakers, p. [49]; and he appears in numerous group photographs, including the class photograph, opp. p. 48, the *Trapeze* staff, p. [91], Burke Club, p. [93], the football team, p. [119], the track team, p. [130], and the swimming team, p. [133].

32 Article. "Al Receives Another Letter," *Ciao* (June 1918), [2].

Excerpts from this Lardnerian article are reprinted in *The Ap-*

prenticeship of Ernest Hemingway by Charles A. Fenton, New York, 1954, pp. 59, 60. Note: *Ciao* was the monthly newspaper published by the American Red Cross ambulance unit, Section IV, in Vicenza, Italy. See also "Look Who's Here!" on p. [1], which lists Hemingway among the twenty-two new arrivals from the United States; and "Ye Sectione Gossippe," on p. [3], a column composed of a play on names.

33 Article. "Circulating Pictures a New | High-Art Idea in Toronto," *TSW* (Feb. 14, 1920), p. 7. Unsigned.

Note: All *Toronto Star Weekly* articles are in the Magazine Section unless otherwise noted.

34 Article. "Taking a Chance | For a Free Shave," *TSW* (March 6, 1920), p. 13.

This article about a Toronto barber school is the first with his by-line: Ernest M. Hemingway. Reprinted in *The Wild Years*, pp. 17-20. A facsimile of a section of the article is reproduced in *Hemingway* by Leo Lania, New York, 1961, p. 36.

35 Article. "Sporting Mayor | At Boxing Bouts," *TSW* (March 13, 1920), News section, p. 10. Reprinted in *The Wild Years*, pp. 29-31.

35₁ Article. "How to be Popular in Peace | Though a Slacker in War," *ibid.*, p. 11. Reprinted in *The Wild Years*, pp. 20-22.

36 Article. "Store Thieves | Use Three Tricks," *TSW* (April 3, 1920), pp. 9, 12. Reprinted in *The Wild Years*, pp. 60-62.

37 Article. "Are You All Set | for the Trout?" *TSW* (April 10, 1920), p. 11. Unsigned.

37₁ Article. "Toothpulling Not | a Cure-for-All," *ibid.*, p. 12.

37₂ Article. "Lieutenants' Mustaches the Only | Permanent Thing We Got Out of War," *ibid.*, p. 17.

38 Article. "Stores in the Wilds | Graveyards of Style," *TSW* (April 24, 1920), p. 11. Reprinted in *The Wild Years*, pp. 37-38.

38₁ Article. "Fishing for Trout | in a Sporting Way," *ibid.*, p. 13. Reprinted in *The Wild Years*, pp. 246-249.

39 Article. "Keeping Up with the Joneses | the Tragedy of the Other Half," *TSW* (May 1, 1920), p. 12.

40 Article. "Toronto Women Who Went to the Prize | Fights Applauded the Rough Stuff," *TSW* (May 15, 1920), p. 13.

41 Article. "Galloping Dominoes, alias African," *TSW* (May 22, 1920), Feature section, p. 21. Comparison of forms of crap-shooting.

42 Article. "Prices for 'Likenesses' Run From | 25 cents to $500 in Toronto," *TSW* (May 29, 1920), p. 13.

42₁ Article. "Canadian Fox-ranching Pays Since | the Wild-cats Let the Foxes Alone," *ibid.*, p. 32.

43 Article. "Canuck Whiskey | Pouring into U.S.," *TSW* (June 5, 1920), p. 1. Reprinted in *The Wild Years*, pp. 68-70.

44 Article. "It's Time to Bury the Hamilton Gag | Comedians Have Worked It to Death," *TSW* (June 12, 1920), p. 1.

45 Article. "When you Camp | Out Do It Right," *TSW* (June 26, 1920), p. 17. Reprinted in *The Wild Years*, pp. 264-268.

46 Article. "When You Go Camping Take Lots of | Skeeter Dope and Don't Ever Lose it," *TSW* (Aug. 7, 1920), p. 11. Reprinted in *The Wild Years*, pp. 268-270.

47 Article. "The Best Rainbow Trout Fishing in | the World is at the Canadian Soo," *TSW* (Aug. 28, 1920), p. 24. Reprinted in *The Wild Years*, pp. 243-246.

48 Article. "The Average Yank Divides Canadians | into Two Classes —Wild and Tame," *TSW* (Oct. 9, 1920), p. 13.

49 Article. "Carpentier Sure to Give | Dempsey Fight Worth While," *TSW* (Oct. 30, 1920), p. 8.

50 Article. "The Wild West Is | Now in Chicago," *TSW* (Nov. 6, 1920), p. 15.

50₁ Article. "No Danger of Commercial Tie-Up | Because Men Carry Too Much Money," *ibid.*, p. 11.

51 Article. "A Fight With a | 20-Pound Trout," *TSW* (Nov. 20, 1920), pp. 25, 26. Reprinted in *The Wild Years*, pp. 240-243.

52 Article. "Will You Let These Kiddies Miss Santa Claus?" *Co-operative Commonwealth*, II, iv (Dec. 1920), 27-28. By-line: Ernest M. Hemingway.
    A three-column article. Note: The *Co-operative Commonwealth* was a monthly magazine which was published in Chicago by the spurious Co-operative Society of America. Hemingway was an assistant editor on the magazine during the winter of 1920-1921, and was responsible for many of the human interest stories that made up the 50 to 60 page magazine. [See *The Apprenticeship of Ernest Hemingway* by Charles A. Fenton, New York, 1954, pp. 96-98, 106-109.]

53 Article. "Plain and Fancy | Killings, $400 Up," *TSW* (Dec. 11, 1920), pp. 25, 26. Dateline: Chicago, Dec. 9. Reprinted in *The Wild Years*, pp. 48-50.

54 Article. "Why Not Trade Other Public Entertainers Among | The Nations as the Big Leagues Do Baseball Players?" *TSW* (Feb. 19, 1921), p. 13.

55 Article. "Our Confidential Vacation Guide," *TSW* (May 21, 1921), p. 21. Reprinted in *The Wild Years*, pp. 38-41.

56 Article. "Gun-Men's Wild | Political War | On in Chicago," *TSW* (May 28, 1921), Feature section, pp. 21, 22. Reprinted in *The Wild Years*, pp. 46-48.

57 Article. "Chicago Never Wetter Than It Is To-day," *TSW* (July 2, 1921), p. 21. Reprinted in *The Wild Years*, pp. 71-73.

58 Article. "Condensing the Classics," *TSW* (Aug. 20, 1921), p. 22.

59 Article. "Cheap Nitrates Will | Mean Cheaper Bread," *TSW* (Nov. 12, 1921), p. 11.

60 Article. "On Weddynge Gyftes," *TSW* (Dec. 17, 1921), p. 15. Contains a five-line, free-verse poem. Reprinted in *The Wild Years*, pp. 41-43.

61 Article. "Tourists are Scarce | At the Swiss Resorts," *TSW* (Feb. 4, 1922), News section, p. 3. Dateline: Les Avants, Switzerland (By mail). Reprinted in *The Wild Years*, pp. 163-164.

61₁ Article. "A Canadian With One Thousand a Year Can Live | Very Comfortably in Paris," *ibid.*, p. 16. Dateline: Paris.

Hemingway describes the hotel in the Rue Jacob where he and his wife are living and comments on the low restaurant prices, *if* you seek the right restaurants.

62 Article. "Builder, Not Fighter, | Is What France Wants," *TDS* (Feb. 18, 1922), p. 7. Dateline: Paris. An article on Georges Clemenceau.

63 Article. "At Vigo, in Spain, is Where You Catch the | Silver and Blue Tuna, the King of All Fish," *TSW* (Feb. 18, 1922), p. 15. Dateline: Vigo, Spain. Reprinted in *The Wild Years*, pp. 257-259.

64 Article. "Influx of Russians | to All Parts of Paris," *TDS* (Feb. 25, 1922), p. 29. Dateline: Paris.

65 Article. "Exchange Pirates Hit | by German Export Tax," *TSW* (Feb. 25, 1922), p. 10. Dateline: Basle, Switzerland.

66 Article. "Try Bob-Sledding | If You Want Thrills," *TDS* (March 4, 1922), p. 9. Dateline: Les Avants, Switzerland.

57 Article. "Behind the Scenes | at Papal Election," *TSW* (March 4, 1922), News section, p. 3. Dateline: Paris (By mail).

71 Article. "Queer Mixture of Aristocrats, Profiteers, Sheep | And Wolves at the Hotels in Switzerland," *ibid.*, Feature section, p. 25. Dateline: Les Avants, Switzerland. Reprinted in *The Wild Years*, pp. 164-165.

68 Article. "Poincaré Making Good | on Election Promises," *TDS* (March 11, 1922), p. 13. Dateline: Paris.

69 Article. "Wives Buy Clothes | For French Husbands," *TSW* (March 11, 1922), News section, p. 12. Dateline: Paris (By mail). Reprinted in *The Wild Years*, pp. 84-85.

91 Article. "How'd You Like to Tip | Postman Every Time?" *ibid.*, p. 13. Dateline: Paris (By mail). Reprinted in *The Wild Years*, pp. 168-169.

70 Article. "Sparrow Hat Appears | On Paris Boulevards," *TSW* (March 18, 1922), p. 12. Dateline: Paris (By mail). Reprinted in *The Wild Years*, p. 85.

01 Article. "Flivver, Canoe, Pram and Taxi Combined is | The Luge, Joy of Everybody in Switzerland," *ibid.*, p. 15. Dateline: Chamby sur Montreux, Switzerland. Reprinted in *The Wild Years*, pp. 166-168.

71 Article. "The Mecca of Fakers | Is French Capital," *TDS* (March 25, 1922), p. 4. Dateline: Paris.

72 Article. "Prize-Winning Book | Is Centre of Storm," *TSW* (March 25, 1922), News section, p. 3. Dateline: Paris (By mail).
Review of *Batouala*, which won its author, René Maran, the Goncourt Academy Prize for 1921.

21 Article. "American Bohemians | in Paris a Weird Lot," *ibid.*, Magazine section, p. 15. Dateline: Paris. Reprinted in *The Wild Years*, pp. 77-79.

22 Article. "Wild Night Music of Paris Makes | Visitor Feel a Man of the World," *ibid.*, p. 22. Dateline: Paris. Reprinted in *The Wild Years*, pp. 79-81.

73 Article. "Much Feared Man | Is Monsieur Deibler," *TDS* (April 1, 1922), p. 7. Dateline: Paris.

31 Article. "95,000 Now Wearing | the Legion of Honour," *ibid.*, p. 7. Dateline: Paris.

74 Article. "Anti-Alcohol League | Is Active in France," *TDS* (April 8, 1922), p. 13. Dateline: Paris.

75 Article. "Tchitcherin Speaks," *TDS* (April 10, 1922), p. 1. Dateline: By cable from Genoa, Italy, April 9.
Regarding the Russian delegation at the World Economic Conference in Genoa. Reprinted in *The Wild Years*, pp. 176-177.

75₁ Article. "Must Work for Peace of Europe," *ibid.*, p. 1. Dateline: By cable from Genoa, April 9.

76 Article. "Tchitcherin At It Again, | Wants Jap Excluded," *TDS* (April 11, 1922), p. 1. Dateline: By cable from Genoa.

77 Article. "Picked Sharpshooters | Patrol Genoa Streets," *TDS* (April 13, 1922), p. 17. Dateline: Genoa, Italy, March 27. Reprinted in *The Wild Years*, pp. 183-185. Note: This dispatch was prefaced by a paragraph about Hemingway.

78 Article. "French Politeness," *TSW* (April 15, 1922), p. 29. Dateline: Paris. Reprinted in *The Wild Years*, pp. 81-84.

79 Article. "Regarded by Allies | as German Cunning," *TDS* (April 18, 1922), p. 1. Dateline: By cable from Genoa, April 18. A brief boxed dispatch regarding the signing of the treaty between Germany and Russia.

79₁ Article. "Barthou Refuses to Confer | with Russians and Germans," *ibid.*, p. 1. Dateline: By cable from Genoa, April 18. Unsigned.

80 Article. "Two Russian Girls | The Best Looking | At Genoa Parley," *TDS* (April 24, 1922), pp. 1, 2. Dateline: Genoa. Reprinted in *The Wild Years*, pp. 174-176.

80₁ Article. "Barthou, Like a Smith Brother, | Crosses Hissing Tchitcherin," *ibid.*, p. 2. Dateline: Genoa, April 10. Reprinted in *The Wild Years*, pp. 177-180.

81 Article. "Strongest Premier at Parley | Is Stambouliski of Bulgaria," *TDS* (April 25, 1922), p. 5. Dateline: Genoa.

82 Article. "Schober of Austria, at Genoa, | Looks Every Inch a Chancellor," *TDS* (April 26, 1922), p. 9. Dateline: Genoa.

83 Article. "Russian Delegates at Genoa | Appear Not to Be of This World," *TDS* (April 27, 1922), p. 9. Dateline: Genoa.

84 Article. "German Delegation at Genoa | Keeps Stinnes in Background," *TDS* (April 28, 1922), p. 9. Dateline: Genoa.

85 Fable. "A Divine Gesture," *Double Dealer*, III, xvii (May 1922), pp. 267-268.

A short account of an experience of The Lord God and Gabriel in the Garden of Eden. A facsimile of the first page appears in *The Little Magazine*, ed. Frederick J. Hoffman, *et al.*, Princeton, 1946, opp. p. 28. Note: The *Double Dealer*, which was published in New Orleans by Julius Weis Friend, was the first magazine in the United States to contain a contribution by Hemingway, other than his high school literary magazine, *Tabula*.

86 Article. "Getting a Hot Bath | an Adventure in Genoa," *TDS* (May 2, 1922), p. 5. Dateline: Genoa.

87 Article. "Russian Delegation | Well Guarded at Genoa," *TDS* (May 4, 1922), p. 10. Dateline: Genoa.

88 Article. "German Journalists | a Strange Collection," *TDS* (May 8, 1922), p. 3. Dateline: Genoa.

89 Article. "All Genoa Goes Crazy | Over New Betting Game," *TDS* (May 9, 1922), p. 2. Dateline: Genoa.

90 Article. "Lloyd George Gives | Magic to the Parley," *TDS* (May 13, 1922), p. 7. Dateline: Genoa.

91 Poem. "Ultimately," *Double Dealer*, III, xviii (June 1922), p. 337.
  Hemingway's quatrain appears on the same page with William Faulkner's "Portrait." It was reprinted on the back cover of *Salmagundi* by William Faulkner, Milwaukee, 1932. See (B11). Published in *The Collected Poems*.

92 Article. "There Are Great Fish | in the Rhone Canal," *TDS* (June 10, 1922), p. 5. Dateline: Geneva, May 22. Reprinted in *The Wild Years*, pp. 255-257.

93 Article. "Fascisti Party Now | Half-Million Strong," *TDS* (June 24, 1922), p. 16. Dateline: Milan. Interview with Benito Mussolini. Reprinted in *The Wild Years*, pp. 188-190.

94 Article. " 'Pot-Shot Patriots' | Unpopular in Italy," *TSW* (June 24, 1922), p. 5. Dateline: Milan. Reprinted in *The Wild Years*, pp. 186-188.

95 Article. "A Veteran Visits Old Front | Wishes He Had Stayed Away," *TDS* (July 22, 1922), p. 7. Dateline: Paris.

96 Article. "Expecting Too Much | in Old London Town," *TSW* (Aug. 5, 1922), p. 17. Dateline: Paris.

97 Article. "Did Poincaré Laugh | in Verdun Cemetery?" *TDS* (Aug. 12, 1922), p. 4. Dateline: Paris.

97₁ Article. "Rug Vendor Is Fixture | in Parisian Life," *ibid.*, p. 4. Dateline: Paris.

98 Article. "Latest Drink Scandal | Now Agitates Paris," *TSW* (Aug. 12, 1922), News section, p. 11. Dateline: Paris (By mail). Reprinted in *The Wild Years*, pp. 92-94.

99 Article. "Old Order Changeth | In Alsace-Lorraine," *TDS* (Aug. 26, 1922), p. 4. Dateline: Strasburg, France.

99₁ Article. "Takes to the Water | Solves Flat Problem," *ibid.*, p. 8. Dateline: Paris.

100 Article. "Germans Are Doggedly Sullen | Or Desperate Over the Mark," *TDS* (Sept. 1, 1922), p. 23. Dateline: Freiburg, Germany, Aug. 17. Reprinted in *The Wild Years*, pp. 113-115.

101 Article. "Once Over Permit Obstacle, | Fishing in Baden Perfect," *TDS* (Sept. 2, 1922), p. 28. Dateline: Triberg-in-Baden, Germany, Aug. 17. Reprinted in *The Wild Years*, pp. 119-123.

102 Article. "German Inn-Keepers Rough | Dealing with 'Auslanders'," *TDS* (Sept. 5, 1922), p. 9. Dateline: Oberprechtal-in-the-Black-Forest, Aug. 21. Reprinted in *The Wild Years*, pp. 105-109.

103 Article. "A Paris-to-Strasburg Flight | Shows Living Cubist Picture," *TDS* (Sept. 9, 1922), p. 8. Dateline: Strasburg, France, Aug. 23. Reprinted in *The Wild Years*, pp. 85-88.

104 Article. "Crossing to Germany | Is Way to Make Money," *TDS* (Sept. 19, 1922), p. 4. Dateline: Kehl, Germany (By mail). Reprinted in *The Wild Years*, pp. 116-119.

105 Article. "British Strong Enough | To Save Constantinople," *TDS* (Sept. 30, 1922), p. 1. Dateline: By cable from Constantinople, Sept. 30. Brief. Reprinted in *The Wild Years*, p. 194.

105₁ Article. "Hubby Dines First | Wifie Gets Crumbs!" *ibid.*, p. 9. Dateline: Cologne (By mail). Reprinted in *The Wild Years*, pp. 103-105.

106 Article. "Riots Are Frequent | Throughout Germany," *TSW* (Sept. 30, 1922), p. 16. Dateline: Cologne (By mail). Reprinted in *The Wild Years*, pp. 111-113.

107 Article. "Turk Red Crescent | Propaganda Agency," *TDS* (Oct. 4, 1922), p. 1. Dateline: By cable from Constantinople.

108 Article. "Hamid Bey Wears | Shirt Tucked In | When Seen By Star," *TDS* (Oct. 9, 1922), p. 1. Dateline: By cable from Constantinople, Oct. 9. Interview. Reprinted in *The Wild Years*, pp. 194-195.

109 Article. "Balkans Look Like Ontario, | A Picture of Peace, Not War," *TDS* (Oct. 16, 1922), p. 13. Dateline: Sofia.

10 Article. "Constantinople, Dirty White, | Not Glistening and Sinister," *TDS* (Oct. 18, 1922), p. 17. Dateline: Constantinople.

11 Article. "Constantinople Cut-Throats | Await Chance for an Orgy," *TDS* (Oct. 19, 1922), p. 4. Dateline: Constantinople.

12 Article. "A Silent, Ghastly | Procession Wends | Way from Thrace," *TDS* (Oct. 20, 1922), p. 17. Dateline: By cable from Adrianople. Reprinted in *The Wild Years*, pp. 199-200.

13 Article. "Russia to Spoil | The French Game | With Kemalists," *TDS* (Oct. 23, 1922), p. 13. Dateline: Constantinople, Oct. 4. Armistice talks at Mudania. Reprinted in *The Wild Years*, pp. 195-197.

14 Article. "Turks Beginning | To Show Distrust | Of Kemal Pasha," *TDS* (Oct. 24, 1922), p. 17. Dateline: Constantinople. Reprinted in *The Wild Years*, pp. 198-199.

15 Article. "Censor Too 'Thorough' | in Near East Crisis," *TDS* (Oct. 25, 1922), p. 7. Dateline: Constantinople.

16 Article. " 'Old Constan' | in True Light; | Is Tough Town," *TDS* (Oct. 28, 1922), p. 17. Dateline: Constantinople, Oct. 6. Reprinted in *The Wild Years*, pp. 169-171.

17 Article. "Kemal Has Afghans Ready | To Make Trouble for Britain," *TDS* (Oct. 31, 1922), p. 5. Dateline: Constantinople, Oct. 10. Reprinted in *The Wild Years*, pp. 207-209.

18 Article. "Betrayal Preceded Defeat, | Then Came Greek Revolt," *TDS* (Nov. 3, 1922), p. 10. Dateline: Muradii, Eastern Thrace, Oct. 14. Reprinted in *The Wild Years*, pp. 200-202.

19 Article. "Destroyers Were on Lookout | For Kemal's One Submarine," *TDS* (Nov. 10, 1922), p. 12. Dateline: Constantinople, Oct. 18.

20 Article. "Refugee Procession | Is Scene of Horror," *TDS* (Nov. 14, 1922), p. 7. Dateline: Sofia, Bulgaria, Oct. 23. Reprinted in *The Wild Years*, pp. 203-207.

21 Poems. "Wanderings," *Poetry, A Magazine of Verse*, XXI, iv (Jan. 1923), pp. 193-195.

Contains the following six poems: "Mitrailliatrice," "Oily Weather," "Roosevelt," "Riparto D'Assalto," "Champs d'Honneur," and "Chapter Heading." Published in *TSTP*. Also published in *The Collected Poems*. Note: A biographical note, on p. 231, refers to Hemingway as "a young Chicago poet now abroad, who will soon issue his first book of verse."

137

122 Article. "Mussolini, Europe's Prize Bluffer | More Like Bottomley than Napoleon," *TDS* (Jan. 27, 1923), p. 11. Dateline: Lausanne. Reprinted in *The Wild Years*, pp. 212-216.

123 Article. "Gaudy Uniform Is Tchitcherin's Weakness | A 'Chocolate Soldier' of the Soviet Army," *TDS* (Feb. 10, 1923), p. 2. Dateline: Lausanne, Jan. 25. Reprinted in *The Wild Years*, pp. 216-219.

124 Short stories. "In Our Time," *Little Review*, IX, iii (Spring 1923), pp. 3-5. Exiles' Number.

Reprinted with minor revisions as Chs. I to VI of *iot*. Ch. V is here titled "Mons" (Two). The other chapters are untitled. Note: This issue was edited by Margaret Anderson, jh [Jane Heap], and Ezra Pound.

124₁ Poem. "They All Made Peace—What Is Peace?" *ibid.*, pp. 20-21.

In a letter to Edmund Wilson, Hemingway described this poem as an effort to analyze the Lausanne Conference. [See Wilson's *The Shores of Light*, New York, 1952, p. 118.] Reprinted in the *Active Anthology*, ed. Ezra Pound, London, 1933, pp. 185-186. See (B13).

125 Article. "A Victory Without Peace Forced the French | to Undertake the Occupation of the Ruhr," *TDS* (April 14, 1923), p. 4. Dateline: Paris, April 3.

Reprinted in *The Wild Years*, pp. 136-139. Note: A prefatory note explains that this is the first of a series of articles on the Franco-German situation. The following nine articles, to *TDS* (May 16, 1923), are in the series.

126 Article. "French Royalist Party | Most Solidly Organized," *TDS* (April 18, 1923), pp. 1, 4. Dateline: Paris, April 6. Reprinted in *The Wild Years*, pp. 89-92.

127 Article. "Government Pays For | News in French Papers," *TDS* (April 21, 1923), pp. 1, 7. Dateline: Paris, April 10. Reprinted in *The Wild Years*, pp. 143-147.

128 Article. "Ruhr Commercial War | Question of Bankruptcy," *TDS* (April 25, 1923), pp. 1, 2. Dateline: Offenburg, Baden, April 12. Reprinted in *The Wild Years*, pp. 132-136.

129 Article. "A Brave Belgian Lady | Shuts Up German Hater," *TDS* (April 28, 1923), pp. 1, 2. Dateline: Frankfurt-on-Main, April. Reprinted in *The Wild Years*, pp. 123-127.

130 Article. "Getting into Germany | Quite a Job, Nowadays," *TDS* (May 2, 1923), p. 1, continued (May 1, 1923), p. 28. Dateline: Offenburg, Baden, April.

Reprinted in *The Wild Years*, pp. 97-102. Note: A prefatory note explains that *"The following article, one of a series on the Franco-German situation . . . was intended to be published before the one published* [April 25, 1923]."

31 Article. "Quite Easy To Spend | A Million, If In Marks," *TDS* (May 5, 1923), pp. 1, 35. Dateline: Mainz-Kassel, April 22. Article VII. [Note: The only article in the series to be so designated.] Reprinted in *The Wild Years*, pp. 127-130.

32 Article. "Amateur Starvers Keep | Out of View in Germany," *TDS* (May 9, 1923), p. 17. Dateline: Cologne, April 27. Reprinted in *The Wild Years*, pp. 109-111.

33 Article. "Hate in Occupied Zone | A Real, Concrete Thing," *TDS* (May 12, 1923), p. 19. Dateline: Dusseldorf, April 30. Reprinted in *The Wild Years*, pp. 140-143.

34 Article. "French Register Speed | When Movies Are on Job," *TDS* (May 16, 1923), p. 19. Dateline: Dusseldorf, May 5.
Vignettes of the Ruhr Occupation. Note: This is the tenth and final article in the series, which began in the *TDS* (April 14, 1923).

35 Article. "King Business in Europe Isn't What It Used to Be," *TSW* (Sept. 15, 1923), p. 15. Reprinted in *The Wild Years*, pp. 156-163. Note: This article was written in Toronto.

36 Article. "Search for Sudbury Coal a Gamble, | Driller Tells of What He Has Found," *TDS* (Sept. 25, 1923), p. 4. Dateline: Sudbury, [Ontario].

36₁ Article. "Anthraxolite, and Not Coal, | Declares Geologist Again," *ibid.*, p. 4. Unsigned.

36₂ Article. "Tossed About on Land Like Ships in a Storm," *ibid.*, p. 16. Unsigned.
An interview with two Canadian survivors of an earthquake in Yokohama, Japan. Reprinted in William White's article in *Journalism Quarterly*, XLIII (Autumn 1966). See (C427).

37 Article. "He's a Personality, No Doubt, | But a Much Maligned One," *TDS* (Oct. 4, 1923), p. 12. Unsigned. Interview with Lord Birkenhead.

38 Article. "Lloyd George Willing | To Address 10,000 Here," *TDS* (Oct. 5, 1923), p. 1. Dateline: New York, Oct. 3.

38₁ Article. "Lloyd George up Early | as Big Liner Arrives." *ibid.*, p. 14. Dateline: New York.

139 Article. "Little Welshman Lands | Anxious to Play Golf," *TDS* (Oct. 6, 1923), p. 3. Dateline: New York, Oct. 5.

139₁ Article. "Wonderful Voice | Is Chief Charm | of Lloyd George," *ibid.*, p. 17. Dateline: New York, Oct. 6.

139₂ Article. "Miss Megan George Makes Hit | 'A Wonder' Reporters Call Her," *ibid.*, p. 17. Dateline: New York, Oct. 5.

Note: According to Carlos Baker, this short article was prepared for Hemingway's signature by Miss Isabel Simmons of Oak Park, then a student in New York, at Hemingway's request.

140 Article. "Cope Denies Hearst | Paying Lloyd George," *TSW* (Oct. 6, 1923), News section, p. 1. Dateline: Special from Lloyd George's train traveling from New York to Montreal and Toronto, Oct. 6.

140₁ Article. "Lloyd George Attends | Theatre in New York," *ibid.*, p. 2. Dateline: New York, Oct. 6.

141 Article. " 'A Man of the People, | Will Fight for People,' " *TDS* (Oct. 8, 1923), p. 14. Dateline: Montreal, Oct. 8. Article on Lloyd George.

142 Article. "Hungarian Statesman | Delighted with Loan," *TDS* (Oct. 15, 1923), p. 21. Unsigned.

Note: This was Hemingway's last article for the *Toronto Daily Star*.

143 Article. "Bull Fighting Is Not a Sport—It Is a Tragedy," *TSW* (Oct. 20, 1923), p. 23.

Reprinted in *The Wild Years*, pp. 221-229. A facsimile of the article appears in *Hemingway* by Leo Lania, New York, 1961, p. 43. Note: This article was written in Toronto.

144 Article. "World's Series of Bull Fighting a Mad, Whirling Carnival," *TSW* (Oct. 27, 1923), p. 33.

This article about the fiesta at Pamplona was written in Toronto. Reprinted in *The Wild Years*, pp. 229-238.

145 Article. "More Game To Shoot in Crowded Europe Than in Ontario | Forests and Animals Are Really Protected Over There," *TSW* (Nov. 3, 1923), p. 20. Reprinted in *The Wild Years*, pp. 259-264.

146 Article. "Cheer Up! The Lakes Aren't Going Dry | High Up and Low Down Is Just Their Habit," *TSW* (Nov. 17, 1923), p. 18. By-line: John Hadley.

Note: This was the first time that Hemingway used this pseudonym, which is the name of his son, born in Toronto, in October 1923.

46₁ Article. "Trout Fishing All Across Europe | Spain Has the Best, Then Germany," *ibid.*, p. 19. Reprinted in the *Fisherman*, IX (Jan. 1958). Also in *The Wild Years*, pp. 249-254.

47 Vignette. "The Sport of Kings," *TSW* (Nov. 24, 1923), p. 17. By-line: Hem.
    The "story" of a sure-thing horse bet that loses.

47₁ Vignette. "The Big Dance | on the Hill," *ibid.*, p. 18.
    The "story" of an awkward moment at a party.

47₂ Article. "Wild Gastronomic Adventures of a Gourmet, Eating Sea Slugs, Snails, Octopus, etc. for Fun," *ibid.*, p. 18. By-line: Peter Jackson.
    Hemingway recounts how he ate poison ivy in Oak Park, sea slugs in Kansas City, snails in Dijon, porcupine in Canada, and octopus in Geneva. Note: This was the only time that Hemingway used this pseudonym.

47₃ Article. "General Wolfe's Diaries Saved for Canada," *ibid.*, p. 19.

47₄ Article. "Tancredo is Dead," *ibid.*, p. 20. By-line: E.M. Heminway [*sic*].
    An article about the performer, Tancredo, who originated an act in the bullring in which he stared down the bull as it was about to charge.

47₅ Article. "Learns to Commune With the Fairies, | Now Wins the $40,000 Nobel Prize," *ibid.*, p. 35. Unsigned. Article on William Butler Yeats.

48 Article. "Fifty-ton Doors Laugh at Robbers' Tools, | Bank Vaults Defy Scientific Cracksmen," *TSW* (Dec. 1, 1923), p. 33. Reprinted in *The Wild Years*, pp. 51-60.

49 Article. "German Marks Make Last Stand | As Real Money in Toronto's 'Ward,' " *TSW* (Dec. 8, 1923), p. 18. By-line: John Hadley. Reprinted in *The Wild Years*, pp. 25-29.

49₁ Article. "Lots of War Medals For Sale | But Nobody Will Buy Them," *ibid.*, p. 21. Reprinted in *The Wild Years*, pp. 22-25.

50 Article. "Night Life in Europe a Disease | Constantinople's Most Hectic," *TSW* (Dec. 15, 1923), p. 21. Reprinted in *The Wild Years*, pp. 149-156.

50₁ Article. "Dose Whole City's Water Supply to | Cure Goitre by Mass Medication," *ibid.*, pp. 33, 34. By-line: John Hadley.

51 Article. "The Blind Man's Christmas Eve," *TSW* (Dec. 22, 1923), p. 16. By-line: John Hadley.

141

151₁ Article. "Christmas on the Roof of the World," *ibid.*, p. 19.

A three-part autobiographical article: [Christmas in the Swiss Alps], "A North of Italy Christmas," and "Christmas in Paris." The last two parts are reprinted in *Two Christmas Tales*. See (A27).

151₂ Article. "Toronto 'Red' Children Don't Know Santa Claus," *ibid.*, p. 33. Unsigned.

151₃ Article. "W. B. Yeats A Night Hawk | Kept Toronto Host Up," *ibid.*, p. 35. Unsigned.

152 Article. "Toronto Is the Biggest Betting Place in North America | 10,000 People Bet $100,000 on Horses Every Day," *TSW* (Dec. 29, 1923), p. 17. Reprinted in *The Wild Years*, pp. 62-68.

152₁ Article. "Weird, Wild Adventures of Some | of Our Modern Amateur Impostors," *ibid.*, pp. 20, 21. Reprinted in *The Wild Years*, pp. 31-37.

152₂ Article. "Wild New Year's Eve Gone Forever | Only Ghost of 1914 Party Remains," *ibid.*, p. 20. By-line: John Hadley.

153 Article. "Ski-er's Only Escape From Alpine Avalanche is to Swim! Snow Slides Off Mountain as Fast as Off Roof of House," *TSW* (Jan. 12, 1924), p. 20. Reprinted in *The Wild Years*, pp. 270-277.

154 Article. "So This Is Chicago," *TSW* (Jan. 19, 1924), p. 19. Eleven short items of minor happenings in Chicago.

154₁ Article. "Must Wear Hats Like Other Folks If You Live in Toronto," *ibid.*, p. 33. By-line: John Hadley.

Note: The last two items presumably cleaned up all that Hemingway had written before going off the *Star* payroll on December 31, 1923.

155 Short story. "Work in Progress," *Transatlantic Review*, I, iv (April 1924), Literary Supplement, 230-234.

This story was titled "Indian Camp" and published in *IOT*. Note: The *Transatlantic Review* was edited in Paris by Ford Madox Ford. According to Louis Henry Cohn, the French, English, and American editions vary only as to the covers. The American edition for May 1924 was dated May–June 1924 and subsequently the American editions were dated one month later than the others. [See *Cohn's Bibliography*, p. 116.]

156 Article. "And to the United States," *Transatlantic Review*, I, v (May–June 1924), 355-357. Dateline: The Quarter. Early Spring.

This article is Part III under "Chroniques." It consists of sixteen short items regarding artists, writers, boxers, and bullfighters.

57 Article. "And Out of America," *Transatlantic Review*, II, i (Aug. 1924), 102-103.

Part III under "Chroniques." Regarding Cocteau's translations and the "snobbism of language," which leads up to the introduction of Ring Lardner's mock-translation "I Gaspari." Note: Hemingway edited the August and September issues. Ford Madox Ford commented: "During our absence . . . this Review has been ably edited by Mr. Ernest Hemingway, the admirable Young American prose writer. [With two exceptions] the present number [Sept. 1924] is entirely of Mr. Hemingway's getting together." [See *TR*, II (Sept. 1924), 213.]

58 Poem. "The Soul of Spain with Mc.Almon and Bird the Publishers" Part I, *Querschnitt*, IV, iv (Autumn 1924) , 229-230. In English.

Reprinted in *Das Querschnittbuch*, Berlin: Im Propyläen Verlag, 1924, pp. 229-230. An edition of 700 copies was printed. Also reprinted in *Der Querschnitt*, Vol. IV, 1924; same pagination as the monthly issues. Published in *The Collected Poems*. Part II of this poem appears in *Querschnitt*, IV (Nov. 1924). Note: *Der Querschnitt* was edited in Frankfurt-am-Main by H. v. Wedderkop.

58₁ Poem. "The Earnest Liberal's Lament," *ibid.*, p. 231. Reprinted in *Das Querschnittbuch*, Berlin, 1924, p. 231; in *Der Querschnitt*, Vol. IV, 1924, p. 231. Published in *The Collected Poems*.

59 Short story. "Mr. and Mrs. Elliot," *Little Review*, X, i (Autumn–Winter 1924–1925), 9-12. Juan Gris Number.

This story was published in *IOT* (1925) with numerous revisions. It was published in the 1930 Scribner's edition of *IOT* as it appears here.

60 Article. "Pamplona Letter," *Transatlantic Review*, II, iii (Oct. 1924), 300-302. Signed: E. H.

Part II under "Chroniques." Hemingway makes a reluctant attempt to write about Pamplona so that Ford can add "one more nice word to the cover." The article is followed by a long reply, in French, by the editor [Ford Madox Ford], on p. 302.

60₁ Article. [Part] III. [Appreciation of Conrad], *ibid.*, Joseph Conrad Supplement, pp. 341-342.

Shortly after Conrad's death, Ford Madox Ford asked a number of writers to do an article on Conrad's place in English letters. In Hemingway's article he states that he would grind T. S. Eliot into fine powder if the sprinkling of it on Conrad's grave would bring him back to life. For Ford's reply, see *Transatlantic Review*, II (Dec. 1924), 550.

161   Poem. "Part Two of The Soul of Spain with McAlmon and Bird the Publishers," *Querschnitt*, IV, v (Nov. 1924), 278.

Comprises Parts II–VI. Reprinted in *Das Querschnittbuch*, Berlin, 1924, p. 278; in *Der Querschnitt*, IV, 1924, 278. Published in *The Collected Poems*. For Part I, see *Querschnitt*, IV (Autumn 1924).

161₁   Poem. "The Lady Poets with Foot Notes," *ibid.*, p. 317. Reprinted in *Das Querschnittbuch*, Berlin, 1924, p. 317; in *Der Querschnitt*, IV, 1924, 317. Published in *The Collected Poems*.

162   Short story. "The Doctor and the Doctor's Wife," *Transatlantic Review*, II, v (Dec. 1924), 497-501. Published in *IOT*.

163   Short story. "Cross Country Snow," *Transatlantic Review*, II, vi (Jan. 1925), 633-638. Published in *IOT*.

164   Poem. "The Age Demanded," *Querschnitt*, v, ii (Feb. 1925), 111. Published in *The Collected Poems*.

165   Short story. "Big Two Hearted River," *This Quarter*, I, i (Spring [May] 1925), 110-128.

A brief biographical note appears on p. 262. A hyphen was added to Two-Hearted when this story was published in *IOT*. Note: *This Quarter* was edited in Paris by Ernest Walsh and Ethel Moorhead. This first issue contains an Art Supplement on Constantin Brancusi. The editors had six copies made on Dutch Hand Made Paper for the sculptor. This large paper edition measures 9 x 6 1/2, whereas the regular issues are 9 x 5 5/8.

165₁   Article. "Homage to Ezra," *ibid.*, pp. 221-225.

The first issue of *This Quarter* was dedicated to Ezra Pound. Hemingway's article was reprinted in *Ezra Pound*, ed. Peter Russell, London, 1950, pp. 73-76. See (B49). Note: See above note regarding the large paper edition.

166   Short story. "Stierkampf" [Part I], *Querschnitt*, v, vi (Summer 1925), 521-535. Two of the eight photographs, following p. 528, are credited to "Hemmingway" (*sic*). First appearance of "The Undefeated," translated into German by B. Bessmertny. See entry below for Part II.

167   Short Story. "Stierkampf" [Part] II, *Querschnitt*, v, vii (July 1925), 624-633. See above entry for Part I.

168   Short story. "The Undefeated," *This Quarter*, I, ii (Autumn–Winter 1925–1926), 203-232.

This is the first appearance in English of this story. Published in *MWW*. Note: This issue was edited in Milan.

69 Short story. "L'invincible," *Navire d'Argent*, ii (March 1926), 161-194.

"The Undefeated," translated into French by Georges Duplaix. Short biographical sketch on p. 194. Note: This magazine was edited in Paris by Adrienne Monnier.

70 Short story. "Banal Story," *Little Review*, xii, i (Spring–Summer 1926), 22-23. Published in *MWW*.

71 Parody. "My Own Life" [After reading the second volume of Frank Harris' "My Life,"] *New Yorker*, ii, lii (Feb. 12, 1927), 23-24. Reprinted in *The New Yorker Scrapbook*, New York, 1931, pp. 154-158. See (B10).

72 Short story. "The Killers," *Scribner's Magazine*, lxxxi, iii (March 1927), 227-233.

See Behind the Scenes, p. 2, which states that this is "the first short story by Ernest Hemingway ever to be published in an American magazine." A letter from Hemingway to his editor [Maxwell E. Perkins] is quoted on p. 4. See (F67). Photograph of Hemingway on p. 3. Published in *MWW*.

73 Letter. "A Protest Against Pirating 'Ulysses,'" *N.Y. Herald Tribune Books* (March 6, 1927), p. 21.

Hemingway was one of 162 signers of a letter To the Editor, dated Paris, February 2, 1927, protesting publication of *Ulysses* in an American magazine, for which James Joyce would receive no royalties. Reprinted in *James Joyce* by Richard Ellmann, New York, 1959, p. 598.

74 Poem. "Nothoemist Poem," *Exile*, No. 1 (Spring 1927), p. 21.

This was a misprint for "Neo-Thomist Poem." Ezra Pound's editorial comment appears on p. 91. In a letter to Louis Henry Cohn, Hemingway explained that the title "refers to temporary embracing of church by literary gents." [See *Cohn's Bibliography*, p. 89.] This explanation is used as a footnote to the poem in *The Collected Poems*. The poem was first reprinted in *Back to Montparnasse* by Sisley Huddleston, Philadelphia, 1931, p. 106.

75 Short story. "In Another Country," *Scribner's Magazine*, lxxxi, iv (April 1927), 355-357.

Published in *MWW*. Note: This short story and the one following are printed under the heading "Two Stories."

75₁ Short story. "A Canary for One," *ibid.*, pp. 358-360. Published in *MWW*.

176 Short story. "Indianisches Lager," *Frankfurter Zeitung* (April 10, 1927), p. 1. German translation of "Indian Camp."

177 Short story. "Der Boxer," *Frankfurter Zeitung* (April 17, 1927), p. 1. German translation of "The Battler."

178 Article. "Italy—1927," *New Republic*, L (May 18, 1927), 350-353.
Retitled as a short story "Che Ti Dice La Patria?" in *MWW*. Rough translation: What do you hear from home? A true account of a motor trip Hemingway made through Fascist Italy with his friend Guy Hickok, the *Brooklyn Daily Eagle's* European correspondent. [See *Baker*, p. 201.] Reprinted in *NR*, CXXXI (Nov. 22, 1954).

179 Short story. "Das Ende von Etwas," *Frankfurter Zeitung* (May 22, 1927), p. 3. German translation of "The End of Something."

180 Short story. "Fifty Grand," *Atlantic*, CXL, i (July 1927), [1]-15.
The title in the table of contents on the cover is subtitled "A Story of the Prize Ring." See the Contributor's Column, on p. 140, for a short note on Hemingway. Published in *MWW*.

181 Short story. "Hills Like White Elephants," *transition*, No. 5 (Aug. 1927), pp. 9-14. Published in *MWW*.

182 Short story. "Cinquante mille dollars," *Nouvelle Revue Française*, XXIX (Aug. 1, 1927), 161-191.
"Fifty Grand" translated into French by Ott de Weymer (pseudonym for Georges Duplaix).

183 Article. "The Real Spaniard," *Boulevardier*, I, viii (Oct. 1927), 6.
According to Hemingway, this article was "re-written" by the editor, Arthur Moss. [See *Cohn's Bibliography*, p. 83.] Note: Although it appears on pp. 52-53 of the galleys of *Hemingway: An Old Friend Remembers* by Jed Kiley, who was also an editor of *Boulevardier*, the article did not appear in the book.

184 Short story. "Le village indien," *Nouvelle Revue Française*, XXX (June 1, 1928), 736-741. "Indian Camp" translated into French by Ott de Weymer.

185 Short story. "Le Batailleur," *Revue Européenne*, 1-2 (Jan.–Feb. 1928), 111-124. "The Battler" translated into French by Jean Georges Auriol.

186 Short story. "Soldaten zuhause," *Europäische Revue*, IV, ix (Dec. 1928), 663-669. "Soldier's Home" translated into German by Annemarie Horschitz.

87 Poem. "Valentine," *Little Review*, XII, Final Number (May 1929), 42. Photograph of Hemingway by Helen Breaker.

This poem is addressed "For a Mr. Lee Wilson Dodd and Any of His Friends who Want it." Dodd wrote a review of *MWW*, titled "Simple Annals of the Callous," in *SRL*, IV (Nov. 19, 1927). Published in *The Collected Poems*. Reprinted in *The Little Review Anthology*, ed. Margaret Anderson, New York, 1953, p. 367. See (B53).

87₁ Letter. *Ibid.*, p. 41. Undated. Signed: HEM.

A short letter in which Hemingway jocularly asks for acknowledgment of the above poem. See (F71).

88 Novel. *A Farewell to Arms, Scribner's Magazine*, LXXXV, v (May 1929), 493-504, 597-610; vi (June 1929), 649-660, 723-728; LXXXVI, i (July 1929), 20-32, 109-118; ii (Aug. 1929), 169-181, 229-236; iii (Sept. 1929), 272-284, 343-354; iv (Oct. 1929), 373-385, 460-472.

Serialized in six installments. See Behind the Scenes, on pp. 43-44, and the photograph of Hemingway by Helen Breaker, p. [492], in the May issue; small photograph, on p. 41, and biographical note, on p. 42, in the June issue; What You Think About It, on p. 27, which includes a letter from Owen Wister praising *FTA*, and What the Papers Say, on pp. 27, 30, in the July issue; editorial comment from various newspapers on the barring of the June and July issues of *Scribner's Magazine* from Boston newsstands, on pp. 31, 34, in the August issue; What You Think About It, on pp. 52-53, in the September issue; and photograph of Hemingway in Gstaad, Switzerland, p. [372], in the October issue. Note: One or more dashes are used to denote deletions. For revisions made prior to book publication, see (A8a).

89 Short story. "Les Collines sont comme des elephants blancs," *Bifur*, No. 3 (Sept. 30, 1929), pp. 54-60.

"Hills Like White Elephants" translated into French by Alice Turpin. Note: 200 copies were published in a large paper edition and 3000 copies in a regular edition.

90 Short story. "Drei Tage Sturm," *Europäische Revue*, v, viii (Nov. 1929), 556-563. "The Three-Day Blow" translated into German by Annemarie Horschitz.

91 Short story. "Je vous salue marie," *Revue Européenne*, No. 1 (Jan. 1, 1930), pp. 76-86. "Now I Lay Me" translated into French by Victor Llona.

92 Article. "Bullfighting, Sport and Industry," *Fortune*, I, ii (March 1930), 83-88, 139-146, 150. Illustrated with color reproductions of

paintings by Goya, Manet, and Zuloaga; and etchings in black and white by Goya.

This article, dealing with the economics of the bullfight business in Spain, has not been reprinted. An "Appendix: Notes on bullfights" appears on p. 150.

193 Novel. *Schluss damit. Adieu Krieg! Frankfurter Zeitung* (May 8– July 16, 1930). *FTA* serialized. Translated into German by Annemarie Horschitz. Note: Published under the title: *In einem andern Land.*

194 Short story. "Abenteuer im Sommer," *Berliner Tageblatt* (June 8, 1930). "My Old Man" translated into German.

195 Short story. "Wine of Wyoming," *Scribner's Magazine,* LXXXVIII, ii (Aug. 1930), 195-204.

Published in *WTN.* A prefatory note states that this is Hemingway's first short story since *FTA.* See also the biographical note in Behind the Scenes on p. 26.

196 Excerpt. *Omnibus: Almanach auf das Jahr 1931.* Berlin & Dusseldorf: Verlag der Galerie Flechtheim, 1931, pp. 73-74.

The first chapter of *FTA* is reprinted, in English. Note: A photograph of Hemingway by Helen Breaker and a painting by Paul Klee, from Hemingway's collection, appear on p. 73.

197 Poem reprinted. "They All Made Peace—What Is Peace?" *Poetry, A Magazine of Verse,* XXXVII (Feb. 1931), 270-271. Reprinted in an article by Louis Zukofsky. The poem first appeared in the *Little Review,* IX (Spring 1923).

198 Short story. "The Sea Change," *This Quarter,* IV, ii (Dec. 1931), 247-251. Published in *WTN.* Note: This issue was edited and published in Paris by Edward W. Titus.

199 Poem. "Advice to a Son," *Omnibus: Almanach auf das Jahr 1932.* Berlin & Dusseldorf: Verlag der Galerie Flechtheim, 1932, p. 80.

A twenty-line poem; dated: *Berlin,* September 1931. Note: A photograph of Hemingway in Dry Tortugas Island, in March 1931, accompanies the poem.

200 Short story. "Mord på bestallning," *Bonniers Litterära Magasin,* I (April 1932), 52-58. "The Killers" translated into Swedish. A note on Hemingway appears on p. 58.

201 Short story. "After the Storm," *Cosmopolitan,* XCII, v (May 1932), 38-41, 155. Published in *WTN.*

202 Advertisement. *Contact,* I, iii (Oct. 1932), [4].

The publisher's advertisement for John Herrmann's novel *Sum-*

mer is Ended [New York: Covici-Friede, 1932] contains a laudatory quote from Hemingway.

03 Letter to the editor. *Hound & Horn*, VI, i (Oct.–Dec. 1932), 135.

Hemingway's letter is in rebuttal to Lawrence Leighton's article in *Hound & Horn*, V (July-Sept. 1932). See (F84).

04 Letter. *New Yorker*, VIII, xxxviii (Nov. 5, 1932), 86-87.

Robert M. Coates's column on books contains a letter from Hemingway objecting to a remark in Coates's review of *DIA*, in the *New Yorker*, VIII (Oct. 1, 1932). Hemingway denied that he had made any petulant jibes against William Faulkner in his book. See (F85).

05 Short story. "A Clean, Well-Lighted Place," *Scribner's Magazine*, XCIII, iii (March 1933), 149-150. Published in *WTN*.

06 Short story. "Homage to Switzerland," *Scribner's Magazine*, XCIII, iv (April 1933), 204-208.

A three-part story: Part I Portrait of Mr. Wheeler in Montreux/ Part II Mr. Johnson Talks About It at Vevey/Part III The Son of a Fellow Member at Territet. Brief biographical note on p. 14. Published in *WTN*.

07 Short story. "Ein sauberes, gut beleuchtetes Café," *Neue Rundschau*, XLIV (May 1933), 648-652.

"A Clean, Well-Lighted Place" translated into German by Annemarie Horschitz.

08 Short story. "Give Us a Prescription, Doctor," *Scribner's Magazine*, XCIII, v (May 1933), 272-278. Retitled "The Gambler, the Nun, and the Radio" and published in *WTN*. For revisions and additions in the book publication, see (A12a).

09 Article. "Marlin Off the Morro: A Cuban Letter," *Esquire*, I, i (Autumn 1933), 8, 39, 97. Photographs.

Parts of this article were reprinted, in slightly different form, in *American Big Game Fishing*, ed. Eugene V. Connett, New York, 1935, pp. 55-81. See (B18). Note: This first issue of *Esquire* was the only quarterly number issued.

10 Short story. "I coniugi Elliot," *Occidente*, v (Oct.–Dec. 1933), 114-116. "Mr. and Mrs. Elliot" translated into Italian by Achille Danieli.

11 Short story reprinted. "The Killers," *Golden Book Magazine*, XVIII (Dec. 1933), 481-487. Subheading: "Can Such Things Be? This Story Answers: Such Things Are!"

12 Short story reprinted. "After the Storm," *Lovat Dickson's Maga-*

zine, I, ii (Dec. 1933), 7-13. A brief note on Hemingway appears on p. 142.

213 Article. "The Farm," *Cahiers d'Art*, IX, No. 1-4 (1934), 28-29.

Hemingway's article regarding his purchase of Miró's painting, "The Farm," is reprinted in *Joan Miró* by Clement Greenberg, New York, [1949], p. [5]. See (B45). An excerpt was first printed in the leaflet *Joan Miró: Paintings*, New York, 1933. See (B14). Note: Hemingway owned this painting until his death.

214 Short story. "Ubitsy," *Internatsionalnaya Literatura*, No. 1 (Jan. 1934), pp. 52-56. "The Killers" translated into Russian by "G. K. Kh."

215 Article. "The Friend of Spain: A Spanish Letter," *Esquire*, I, ii (Jan. 1934), 26, 136.

216 Article. "A Paris Letter," *Esquire*, I, iii (Feb. 1934), 22, 156.

217 Short story. "One Trip Across," *Cosmopolitan*, XCVI, iv (April 1934), 20-23, 108-122.

This "Complete Short Novel" became Part 1 of *THAHN*, with only minor revisions.

218 Article. "a.d. in Africa: A Tanganyika Letter," *Esquire*, I, v (April 1934), 19, 146.

This article, concerning amoebic dysentery, was partially reprinted in *Just What the Doctor Ordered*, ed. Frank Scully, New York, 1938, pp. 165-166. See (B30).

219 Article. "Shootism vs. Sport: The Second Tanganyika Letter," *Esquire*, II, i (June 1934), 19, 150. Photographs.

220 Article. "Notes on Dangerous Game: The Third Tanganyika Letter," *Esquire*, II, ii (July 1934), 19, 94. Photographs.

221 Article. "Out in the Stream: A Cuban Letter," *Esquire*, II, iii (Aug. 1934), 19, 156, 158.

222 Article. "Defense of Dirty Words: A Cuban Letter," *Esquire*, II, iv (Sept. 1934), 19, 158 b, 158 d.

223 Article. "Genio after Josie: A Havana Letter," *Esquire*, II, v (Oct. 1934), 21-22. Photographs.

224 Article. "Old Newsman Writes: A Letter from Cuba," *Esquire*, II, vii (Dec. 1934), 25-26.

225 Short story reprinted. "My Old Man," *Golden Book Magazine*, XX (Dec. 1934), 655-663.

226 Article. "Notes on Life and Letters: Or a manuscript found in a bottle," *Esquire*, III, i (Jan. 1935), 21, 159.

227 Article. "Remembering Shooting-Flying: A Key West Letter," *Esquire*, III, ii (Feb. 1935), 21, 152.

Recollections of hunting in Illinois, in the Vorarlberg, in Clark's Fork, Wyoming, and elsewhere. Reprinted in *Esquire's First Sports Reader*, ed. Herbert Graffis, New York, 1945, pp. 76-81. See (B42).

271 Article. [Program Notes], *ibid.*, pp. 26-27.

Hemingway's appraisal of Luis Quintanilla's etchings, reprinted, with a few excisions, from the Pierre Matisse Gallery catalogue, *Quintanilla*, New York, 1934. (See B16).

228 Article. "Sailfish Off Mombasa: A Key West Letter," *Esquire*, III, iii (March 1935), 21, 156.

229 Article. "The Sights of Whitehead Street: A Key West Letter," *Esquire*, III, iv (April 1935), 25, 156.

230 Article. "a.d. Southern Style: A Key West Letter," *Esquire*, III, v (May 1935), 25, 156.

This article, concerning amoebic dysentery, was partially reprinted in *Just What the Doctor Ordered*, ed. Frank Scully, New York, 1938, pp. 166-168. See (B30).

231 Novel. *Green Hills of Africa*, *Scribner's Magazine*, XCVII, v (May 1935), 257-268; vi (June 1935), 334-344; XCVIII, i (July 1935), 14-21; ii (Aug. 1935), 74-83; iii (Sept. 1935), 157-165; iv (Oct. 1935), 200-206; v (Nov. 1935), 262-273. Decorations by Edward Shenton.

Serialized in seven installments. See the Foreword, on p. 257, The People in the Book, on p. 259, and Behind the Scenes, on p. 319, in the May issue; Behind the Scenes, on p. 127, in the August issue; and the same column, on p. 319, in the November issue.

232 Article. "On Being Shot Again: A Gulf Stream Letter," *Esquire*, III, vi (June 1935), 25, 156.

Hemingway recounts how he shot himself in the calves of both legs while gaffing a shark.

233 Article. "The President Vanquishes: A Bimini Letter," *Esquire*, IV, i (July 1935), 23, 167. Photographs. Note: Henry Strater, the artist, is the "President."

234 Article. "He Who Gets Slap Happy: A Bimini Letter," *Esquire*, IV, ii (Aug. 1935), 19, 182. Photographs.

235 Article. "Notes on the Next War: A Serious Topical Letter," *Esquire*, IV, iii (Sept. 1935), 19, 156.

Reprinted in *The Third New Year*, Chicago, 1935, pp. 45-55. See (B20). For Hemingway's award of first prize for this article, see *American Points of View: A Reader's Guide, 1935*, ed. William H. Cordell and Kathryn Coe Cordell, New York, 1936, p. xii.

236 Article. "Who Murdered the Vets?" *New Masses*, XVI, xii (Sept. 17, 1935), 9-10. Dateline: Key West, Florida.

A report on the Florida hurricane, which destroyed the C.C.C. work-camp and killed 458 veterans. Note: The title was written by the editors. Translated into Russian, "Kto ubil veteranov voiny vo Floride?" in *Internatsionalnaya Literatura*, No. 12 (Dec. 1935), p. 56. For the English translation of the editorial footnote which accompanied it, see *Soviet Attitudes toward American Writing* by Deming Brown, Princeton, 1962, p. 307.

237 Article. "Monologue to the Maestro: A High Seas Letter," *Esquire*, IV, iv (Oct. 1935), 21, 174 a, 174 b.

Hemingway answers the questions put to him by a young writer. Note: The "Maestro" was Arnold Samuelson. See Leicester Hemingway's *My Brother, Ernest Hemingway*, Cleveland, 1962, p. 173.

238 Article. "The Malady of Power: A Second Serious Letter," *Esquire*, IV, v (Nov. 1935), 31, 198.

Regarding the days when Hemingway was a "working newspaper man." Reprinted in *American Points of View: 1936*, ed. William H. Cordell and Kathryn Coe Cordell, New York, 1937, pp. 184-191. See (B22).

239 Article. "Million Dollar Fright: A New York Letter," *Esquire*, IV, vi (Dec. 1935), 35, 190 b.

An account of the Joe Louis-Max Baer prizefight, on September 24, 1935, in New York.

239₁ Recipe and comment. *Ibid.*, p. 55. Caricature by Roy Nelson.

Hemingway's "Death in the Afternoon Cocktail" and a short comment by him are followed by a brief biographical note. Reprinted in *So Red the Nose* by Sterling North and Carl Kroch, New York, 1935, p. [9]. See (B19).

240 Article. "Wings Always Over Africa: An ornithological letter," *Esquire*, v, i (Jan. 1936), 31, 174-175.

Regarding Mussolini's attack on Ethiopia.

241 Short story. "The Tradesman's Return," *Esquire*, v, ii (Feb. 1936), 27, 193-196.

This "short story" became Part II of *THAHN*. Deletions are indicated by a series of dots. For the numerous revisions prior to book publication, see (A14a).

42 Excerpt from article. "Wings Always Over Africa," *Reader's Digest,* xxviii (Feb. 1936), 42. Reprinted from *Esquire,* v (Jan. 1936).

43 Article. "On the Blue Water: A Gulf Stream Letter," *Esquire,* v iv (April 1936), 31, 184-185.

Note: The nucleus of *OMATS* appears in a long paragraph on p. 184. Reprinted in *Blow the Man Down,* ed. Eric Devine, New York, 1937, pp. 304-311. See (B25).

44 Article. "There She Breaches! or Moby Dick off the Morro," *Esquire,* v, v (May 1936), 35, 203-205.

About whales sighted off the coast of Cuba, in October 1934.

44₁ Article. "Gattorno: Program Note," *ibid.,* 111, 141.

Hemingway's article on the paintings of Antonio Gattorno was reprinted from *Gattorno,* Havana, 1935. See (B17).

45 Excerpt from article. "Notes on the Next War," *Reader's Digest,* xxviii (May 1936), 17-18. Reprinted from *Esquire,* iv (Sept. 1935).

46 Short story. "The Horns of the Bull," *Esquire,* v, vi (June 1936), 31, 190-193. Retitled "The Capital of the World" and published in the *First 49.*

47 Letter. "Hemingway on Mutilated Fish," *Outdoor Life,* lxxvii (June 1936), 70-72. Photograph.

A letter from Hemingway, in reply to a questionnaire on mutilated fish, is printed in Thomas Aitken's column, Big Game Fishing.

48 Excerpt. "The Man with the Tyrolese Hat," *Querschnitt,* xvi (June 1936), 355-356.

Excerpt, in English, from the first chapter of *GHOA,* regarding Hemingway's encounter with Kandisky.

49 Short story. "The Snows of Kilimanjaro," *Esquire,* vi, ii (Aug. 1936), 27, 194-201. Subheading: "A Long Story."

See Backstage with *Esquire,* on p. 24, regarding the fact that this story, which is "almost 9,000 words long," is nearly a third again as long as any previous *Esquire* feature. For editorial comment on this story in *Esquire,* xxxii (Sept. 1949), see (C353). Note: Reprinted, as it appeared here, in *The Best Short Stories 1937,* ed. Edward J. O'Brien, Boston, 1937, pp. 105-126. See (B24). For revisions prior to publication in the *First 49,* see (A16a). In the original manuscript, which is among the holdings of the University of Texas, the main character was given the surname "Walden"; however, he is referred to only as "Harry" in the published story.

50 Short story. "The Short Happy Life of Francis Macomber," *Cosmopolitan,* ci, iii (Sept. 1936), 30-33, 166-172. Published in the *First*

49. For editorial comment on this story in *Esquire,* XXXII (Sept. 1949), see (C353).

251 Greetings. "Greetings on Our Twenty-Fifth Anniversary," *New Masses,* XXI, x (Dec. 1, 1936), 21. Telegram from Hemingway quoted.

252 Short story reprinted. "The Killers," *Scribner's Magazine,* CI (Jan. 1937), 83-86. Fiftieth Anniversary Issue.

This story first appeared in *Scribner's Magazine,* LXXXI (March 1927).

253 NANA dispatch. "Hemingway Wants a Bullfighter to Toss Spain News!" *San Francisco Chronicle* (March 13, 1937), p. 2. Dateline: Paris, March 12.

Hemingway reported that the U.S. State Department had denied Sidney Franklin a passport to enter Spain. The State Department claimed that too many Americans were trying to enter Spain by representing themselves as newspaper correspondents. Note: This is the first of twenty-eight dispatches which Hemingway filed with the North American Newspaper Alliance (NANA) between March 12, 1937, and May 12, 1938.

254 NANA dispatch. "Hemingway Finds France is Neutral," *N.Y. Times* (March 17, 1937), p. 12. Dateline: Toulouse, France, March 16.

255 NANA dispatch. "Gay On Their Last Ride," *K.C. Times* (March 19, 1937), p. 12. Dateline: Valencia, Spain, March 18.

256 NANA dispatch. "Italians in a Trap," *K.C. Times* (March 24, 1937), p. 1. Dateline: On the Guadalajara Front, March 23.

257 NANA dispatch. "Brihuega Likened by Hemingway to Victory on World War Scale," *N.Y. Times* (March 29, 1937), p. 8. Dateline: Madrid, March 28.

258 Short story. "En Espagne, un endroit propre, bien éclairé," *Nouvelles Littéraires* (April 3, 1937), p. 9.

"A Clean, Well-Lighted Place" translated into French by Jeanine Delpech.

259 NANA dispatch. "Heavy Shell-Fire in Madrid Advance," *N.Y. Times* (April 10, 1937), p. 9. Dateline: Madrid, April 9.

260 NANA dispatch. "A 'New Kind of War,' " [Source not located]. Dateline: Madrid, April 14, [1937].

261 NANA dispatch. "War Is Reflected Vividly in Madrid," *N.Y. Times* (April 25, 1937), p. 28. Dateline: Madrid, April 24. Re-

printed in *A Treasury of Great Reporting*, Louis L. Snyder, ed., New York, 1949, pp. 524-528. See (B46).

262 NANA dispatch. "Egging Madrid to Fight," *K.C. Star* (May 3, 1937), p. 5. Dateline: Madrid, May 3.

263 Dispatches reprinted. "Hemingway Reports Spain," *New Republic*, xc (May 5, 1937) 376-379.

Selected passages from Hemingway's NANA dispatches covering the period from March 18th to April 11, 1937. Datelines: Valencia, Spain; On the Guadalajara Front; Madrid; Madrid. The last three are reprinted in *Five Kinds of Writing*, ed. Theodore Morrison, Boston, 1939, pp. 175-181. See (B35). See also (C276), (C290), (C298).

264 NANA dispatch. "The Chauffeurs of Madrid," *N.Y. Times* (May 23, 1937), II, 3. Reprinted in *Men at War*, pp. 993-997. Note: This dispatch was written in New York.

265 Speech. "Fascism Is a Lie," *New Masses*, XXIII, xiii (June 22, 1937), 4.

Hemingway delivered this paper before the Second Writers' Congress, in New York, on June 4, 1937. Reprinted in *The Writer in a Changing World*, ed. Henry Hart, New York, 1937, pp. 69-73. See (B26).

266 Captions. "The War in Spain Makes a Movie With Captions by Ernest Hemingway," *Life*, III, ii (July 12, 1937), 20-23.

Photographs from the film "The Spanish Earth," with fourteen brief captions by Hemingway.

267 Excerpt. "Une belle chasse," *Nouvelles Littéraires*, No. 770 (July 17, 1937), p. 6. Excerpt from Ch. III of *GHOA* translated into French by [Jeanine Delpech].

268 NANA dispatch. "Americans in Spain Veteran Soldiers," *N.Y. Times* (Sept. 14, 1937), p. 10. Dateline: On the Aragon Front, Sept. 13.

269 NANA dispatch. "Loyalists Capture Key Centers in Aragon Drive," *Los Angeles Times* (Sept. 15, 1937), p. 2. Dateline: On the Aragon Front, via Valencia, Sept. 14.

270 NANA dispatch. "Hemingway Doubts Teruel Drive Near," *San Francisco Chronicle* (Sept. 24, 1937), p. 2. Dateline: On the Teruel Front, via Madrid, Sept. 23.

271 NANA dispatch. "Life Goes On in Madrid," *K.C. Times* (Oct. 1, 1937), p. 3. Dateline: Madrid, Sept. 30.

272 NANA dispatch. "Loyalists' Drive Seen Progressing as Planned," [Source not located]. Dateline: Madrid, Oct. 7, [1937].

273 Short story. "Los cuernos del toro," *Hoy*, VI (Nov. 4, 1937), 83-86.
"The Horns of the Bull" [retitled "The Capital of the World" in the *First 49*] translated into Spanish. See also (H341).

274 NANA dispatch. "Fight in Blizzard," *K.C. Times* (Dec. 20, 1937), p. 6. Dateline: Army Headquarters, Teruel Front in Spain, Dec. 19.

275 NANA dispatch. "With Army Into Teruel," *K.C. Star* (Dec. 24, 1937), p. 5. Dateline: Loyalist Army Headquarters, Teruel Front, Dec. 24.

276 Dispatches reprinted. "Hemingway Reports Spain," *New Republic*, XCIII (Jan. 12, 1938), 273-276.
Selected passages from Hemingway's NANA dispatches covering the period from September 13th to December 21, 1937. Dateline: On the Aragon Front; On the Teruel Front; Madrid; Loyalist Army Headquarters, Teruel Front; Loyalist Army Headquarters, Teruel Front. Three of the five parts are reprinted in *They Were There*, ed. Curt Riess, New York, 1944, pp. 97-101. See (B41). See also (C263), (C290), (C298).

277 Ad. *N.Y. Times Book Review* (Jan. 30, 1938), p. 28.
The publisher's advertisement for Herbert L. Matthews' book *Two Wars and More to Come* (New York: Carrick & Evans, 1938) contains a laudatory cable from Hemingway, from Paris. Note: Facsimiles of Hemingway's cable were issued as a promotion piece. See (F161).

278 Preface reprinted. "Luis Quintanilla: Artist and Soldier," *Among Friends*, I, ii (Spring 1938), 7.
Hemingway's preface is reprinted from the catalogue *Quintanilla: An Exhibition of Drawings of the War in Spain*, New York, 1938, p. [2]. Note: *Among Friends* was issued quarterly by the Friends of the Abraham Lincoln Brigade, in New York.

279 Article. "The Heat and the Cold," *Verve*, I, ii (Spring 1938), 46. In English.
An article about the filming of "The Spanish Earth," and some of the people involved. Reprinted in *The Spanish Earth*, pp. 55-60. A French translation, "Chaud et froid," appears in *Hemingway*, ed. John Brown, Paris, 1961, pp. 224-227.

280 NANA dispatch. "Beauty of Spanish Spring Is Chilled by the Menace of Death," *K.C. Star* (April 4, 1938), p. 7. Dateline: Barcelona, April 4.

281 NANA dispatch. "Hemingway Tells Rebel Rout of Yanks in Spanish Army," *Chicago Daily News* (April 5, 1938), pp. 1, 4. Dateline: Barcelona, April 5.

282 NANA dispatch. "Spanish War Not Over By a Long Shot, Hemingway Reports," *K.C. Times* (April 7, 1938), p. 6. Dateline: Tortosa, Spain, April 6.

283 Article. "The Time Now, The Place Spain," *Ken*, i, i (April 7, 1938), 36-37.

Hemingway argues that a world war can be averted if Mussolini and fascism are beaten in Spain. Note: This is the first of thirteen articles (and the short story "The Old Man at the Bridge") which Hemingway contributed to *Ken*. A small promotion leaflet was issued prior to publication of the first issue. A drawing of Hemingway appears on p. [2], and it states, on p. [3], that "one of KEN's editors will be Ernest Hemingway." However, a boxed notice on p. 37 of the first issue states: "Ernest Hemingway has been in Spain since KEN was first projected. Although contracted and announced as an editor he has taken no part in the editing of the magazine nor in the formation of its policies. If he sees eye to eye with us on KEN we would like to have him as an editor. If not, he will remain as a contributor until he is fired or quits." This boxed notice was taken directly from a telegram which Hemingway sent to Arnold Gingrich, the editor, from Key West, on February 26, 1938. The only change was the insertion of the words "contracted and" in the second sentence.

284 NANA dispatch. "Main Rebel Threat Is Deemed in North," *N.Y. Times* (April 11, 1938), p. 2. Dateline: Tortosa, Spain, April 10.

285 NANA dispatch. "Infantry in a New Role," *K.C. Times* (April 14, 1938), p. 3. Dateline: Tarragona, Spain, April 13.

286 NANA dispatch. "Planes Wreck Tortosa Bridge; Hemingway Witnesses Action in Rebels' Drive to the Sea," *Chicago Daily News* (April 16, 1938), p. 2. Dateline: Tortosa, Spain, April 15.

287 NANA dispatch. "Loyalists Await Tortosa Assault," *N.Y. Times* (April 19, 1938), p. 12. Dateline: Ebro Delta, Spain, April 18.

288 Article. "Dying, Well or Badly," *Ken*, i, ii (April 21, 1938), 68.

Hemingway writes of the dead soldiers shown in the photographs on the pages following the article. Note: Hemingway is credited with photographs on pp. 69, 70, 71.

289 NANA dispatch. "Young Lardner Is Fighting for Loyalist Spain," *Chicago Daily News* (April 26, 1938), p. 2. Dateline: Barcelona, April 26.

Regarding war correspondent James Phillips Lardner.

290 Dispatches reprinted. "Hemingway Reports Spain," *New Republic*, xCIV (April 27, 1938), 350-351.

Selected passages from Hemingway's NANA dispatches covering the period from April 4 to April 6. Datelines: Barcelona; Barcelona; Tortosa. See also (C263), (C276), (C298).

291 NANA dispatch. "Lerida Is Divided By Warring Forces," *N.Y. Times* (April 30, 1938), p. 5. Dateline: Lerida, Spain, April 29.

292 Reply to questionnaire. *Transition*, No. 27 (April–May 1938), p. 237. Tenth Anniversary issue.

Hemingway's reply to editor Eugène Jolas's "Inquiry Into the Spirit and Language of Night," is quoted.

293 Article. "The Cardinal Picks a Winner," *Ken*, I, iii (May 5, 1938), 38.

This article is accompanied by two photographs, on p. 39. The top one of the dead children, whom, Hemingway reports, the Cardinal does not believe Franco would bomb, is credited to Hemingway.

294 NANA dispatch. "Leftists at Castellon Heavily Entrenched," *St. Louis Globe-Democrat* (May 9, 1938), p. 8 B. Dateline: Castellon, via Courier to Madrid, May 8.

295 NANA dispatch. "Hemingway Sees Year of War; Madrid Army Strong, Active; 'Moles' Peril Rebel Position," *Chicago Daily News* (May 12, 1938), p. 2. Dateline: Madrid, May 12 (by wireless).

296 Short story. "The Old Man at the Bridge," *Ken*, I, iv (May 19, 1938), 36.

"The" was omitted from the title when this story was published in the *First 49*. In his preface to the *First 49*, Hemingway mentions that this story was "cabled from Barcelona in April 1938." Note: Hemingway is credited with the photograph on p. 36.

297 Article. "United We Fall Upon *Ken*," *Ken*, I, v (June 2, 1938), 38.

Hemingway comments on the letters which he had received urging him to discontinue writing for *Ken*.

298 Dispatches reprinted. "Hemingway Reports Spain," *New Republic*, xCV (June 8, 1938), 124-126.

This is the fourth, and last, of a series drawn from Hemingway's NANA dispatches; covering the period from April 13 to May 10 1938. Datelines: Tarragona; Tortosa; Ebro Delta; Lerida; Castellon; Madrid. See also (C263), (C276), (C290).

299 Article. "H. M.'s Loyal State Department," *Ken*, I, vi (June 16, 1938), 36.

Hemingway accuses the fascists in the U.S. State Department of "doing the dirty work of a very temporary British policy."

300 Article. "Treachery in Aragon," *Ken*, I, vii (June 30, 1938), 26.
An article on a story "that cannot be written as yet," on how the German Gestapo arranged the treachery which led to the break-through on the Aragon front in March 1938.

301 Article. "Call for Greatness," *Ken*, II, i (July 14, 1938), 23.
Hemingway calls upon President Roosevelt to intervene in Spain.

302 Article. "My Pal the Gorilla Gargantua," *Ken*, II, ii (July 28, 1938), 26.
Regarding the Joe Louis-Max Schmeling prize fight, which Hemingway attended in New York, on June 22, 1938.

303 Article. "A Program for U.S. Realism," *Ken*, II, iii (Aug. 11, 1938), 26.
Hemingway predicted war in Europe within a year. In question and answer form, he quotes Karl von Clausewitz on war.

304 Article. "Good Generals Hug the Line," *Ken*, II, iv (Aug. 25, 1938), 28.

305 Article. "False News to the President," *Ken*, II, v (Sept. 8, 1938), 17-18.
Hemingway questions the reports which the President receives from the U.S. State Department.

306 Article. "Fresh Air on an Inside Story," *Ken*, II, vi (Sept. 22, 1938), 28.
Hemingway tells how he scuttled the plans of an unnamed journalist who tried to send his newspaper a false report of the "terror" which he claimed existed in Madrid.

307 Short story. "The Denunciation," *Esquire*, x, v (Nov. 1938), 39, 111-114.
Subheading: "First of a series of three short stories using a bar in Madrid as a background." The other two stories in this series are "The Butterfly and the Tank," *Esquire*, x (Dec. 1938), and "Night Before Battle," *Esquire*, xi (Feb. 1939).

308 Short story. "The Butterfly and the Tank," *Esquire*, x, vi (Dec. 1938), 51, 186, 188, 190.
Regarding an incident in Chicote's bar in Madrid, in which a man with a flit gun is killed. Reprinted in *The Armchair Esquire*, ed. Arnold Gingrich and L. Rust Hills, New York, 1958, pp. 136-144. See (B58).

159

309 Introduction. "Pyataya kolonna," *Internatsionalnaya Literatura,*
No. 1 (Jan. 1939), 99-100.
Introduction to *The Fifth Column* translated into Russian.

310 Article. "The Next Outbreak of Peace," *Ken,* III, i (Jan. 12, 1939),
12-13.
Regarding Neville Chamberlain's policy of appeasement.

311 Short story. "Night Before Battle," *Esquire,* XI, ii (Feb. 1939), 27-
29, 91-92, 95, 97.
The last story in a series using Chicote's bar in Madrid as a background.

312 Article. "The Clark's Fork Valley, Wyoming," *Vogue,* XCIII, iii
(Feb. 1, 1939), 68, 157.
Reprinted in *Vogue's First Reader,* New York, 1942, pp. 32-34.
See (B40). Also reprinted in *The World in Vogue,* ed. Bryan Holme
et al., New York, 1963, p. 153.

313 Article. "On the American Dead in Spain," *New Masses,* XXX, viii
(Feb. 14, 1939), 3. Anniversary issue on the Popular Front Victory
of 1936.
A photo of Hemingway and contributor's note, quoting Hemingway, appear on p. 2. This article was reprinted in the autobiography of the editor, Joseph North, *No Men Are Strangers,* New
York, 1958, pp. 146-147.

314 Short story. "Nobody Ever Dies!" *Cosmopolitan,* CVI, iii (March
1939), 28-31, 74-76.
A story about a returned Spanish Civil War veteran, who is
hunted down and killed in Havana.

315 Article. "The Writer as a Writer," *Direction,* II, iii (May–June
1939), 3.
Note: This issue was the official program for the Third American Writers' Congress.

316 Excerpt. "The Fifth Column," *Now and Then,* No. 63 (Summer
1939), 30-31.
The first nine paragraphs, concerning the play, are reprinted
from Hemingway's introduction to *TFC & First 49.*

317 Short story. "Under the Ridge," *Cosmopolitan,* CVII, iv (Oct. 1939),
34-35, 102-106.
A story of the Spanish Civil War, showing the Spanish hatred of
foreign interlopers. Reprinted in *The Best Short Stories 1940,* ed.
Edward J. O'Brien, Boston, 1940, pp. 109-122. See (B37).

318 Letter. "War Writers on Democracy," *Life,* VIII, xxvi (June 24,
1940), 8.

The editors of *Life* requested a comment on Archibald Mac-Leish's statement criticizing writers of his own generation for not fighting fascism. Reprinted in *Time*, xxxv (June 24, 1940), 92.

319 Article. "Man, What a Sport!" *Rotarian*, LVI (May 1940), 19, 21. Photograph.

Hemingway gives advice on fishing the Gulf Stream to convening Rotarians. Note: Cover painting of Hemingway's boat, the *Pilar*, by Lynn Bogue Hunt.

320 Dispatch. "Ernest Hemingway Says Russo-Jap Pact Hasn't Kept Soviet From Sending Aid to China," *PM* (June 10, 1941), pp. 4-5. Photographs. Dateline: Hong Kong.

Note: This is the first of seven dispatches which Hemingway wrote on the situation in the Far East for the New York daily newspaper *PM*. An interview, which Hemingway edited, appeared in *PM* (June 9, 1941). See (H481).

321 Dispatch. "Ernest Hemingway Says We Can't Let Japan Grab Our Rubber Supplies in Dutch East Indies," *PM* (June 11, 1941), p. 6. Dateline: Rangoon.

322 Dispatch. "Ernest Hemingway Says Japan Must Conquer China Or Satisfy USSR Before Moving South," *PM* (June 13, 1941), p. 6. Dateline: Rangoon.

323 Dispatch. "Ernest Hemingway Says Aid to China Gives U.S. Two-Ocean Navy Security for Price of One Battleship," *PM* (June 15, 1941), p. 6. Dateline: Rangoon.

324 Dispatch. "After Four Years of War in China Japs Have Conquered Only Flat Lands," *PM* (June 16, 1941), pp. 6-9. Dateline: Rangoon.

325 Dispatch. "Ernest Hemingway Says China Needs Pilots as Well as Planes to Beat Japanese in the Air," *PM* (June 17, 1941), p. 5. Dateline: Rangoon.

326 Dispatch. "Ernest Hemingway Tells How 100,000 Chinese Labored Night and Day to Build Huge Landing Field for Bombers," *PM* (June 18, 1941), pp. 16-17. Dateline: Manila.

327 Short story. "Varldens huvudstad," *Bonniers Litterära Magasin*, XI (Jan. 1942), 14-21. "The Capital of the World" translated into Swedish by Thorsten Jonsson.

328 Excerpt. "Un Pont dans la Montagne," *Choix*, I, i [1944], 118-128. Excerpt from *FWBT* translated into French.

329 Note. [Note on Martha Gellhorn], *Collier's*, CXIII, x (March 4, 1944), 43.

Hemingway wrote a short biographical note on his wife, Martha Gellhorn, for the column This Week's Work.

330 Dispatch. "Voyage to Victory," *Collier's*, CXIV, iv (July 22, 1944), 11-13, 56-57. Radioed from London. Radiophoto of Hemingway by Joe Dearing.

A brief cabled comment from Hemingway is boxed at the end of his dispatch covering the invasion of Normandy, on June 6, 1944. This article was published separately, as a promotion piece, by *Collier's*, prior to the magazine publication. See (A21). Note: This is the first of six dispatches which Hemingway sent from England and France during World War II. His name appeared on the *Collier's* masthead, as a staff correspondent, from July 8, 1944 to May 12, 1945. Note: Reprinted in *The United States Navy in World War II*, ed. S. E. Smith, New York, 1966, pp. 603-616. See (B62).

331 Dispatch. "London Fights the Robots," *Collier's*, CXIV, viii (Aug. 19, 1944), 17, 80-81. Radioed from London. Reprinted in *Masterpieces of War Reporting*, ed. Louis L. Snyder, New York, 1962, pp. 361-367. See (B60).

332 Dispatch. "Battle for Paris," *Collier's*, CXIV, xiv (Sept. 30, 1944) 11, 83-85. Cabled from Paris.

333 Short story. "C'est aujourd'hui vendredi," *Arbalete*, No. 9 (Autumn 1944), pp. 85-92. "Today Is Friday" translated into French by Marcel Duhamel.

334 Dispatch. "How We Came to Paris," *Collier's*, CXIV, xv (Oct. 7, 1944), 14, 65-66. Radioed from Paris.

335 Dispatch. "The G. I. and the General," *Collier's*, CXIV, xix (Nov. 4, 1944), 11, 46-47. By cable from France.

336 Dispatch. "War in the Siegfried Line," *Collier's*, CXIV, xxi (Nov. 18, 1944), 18, 70-73. By radio via Paris.

337 Greetings. "Golden Jubilee Greetings," *Program of the Cincinnati Symphony Orchestra* (March 23 and 24, 1945), p. 618.

Hemingway's brief "felicitations" was "the seventeenth of a series of messages received from distinguished representatives of the other arts."

338 Excerpt. "Att ha och inte ha," *AVB*, No. 7 (Sept. 1945), pp. 49-61. Ch. 1 of *THAHN* translated into Swedish by Thorsten Jonsson.

339 Novel. "L'homme qui croyait à la chance," *Paris-Matin* (Oct. 2– Nov. 11-12, 1945), p. 2. *THAHN* translated by Marcel Duhamel and serialized.

340 Short story. *Marginales,* 1 (Dec. 1945). "After the Storm" translated into French.

341 Article. "The Sling and the Pebble," *Free World*, XI, iii (March 1946), 16-17. Photograph.

This article was written as the foreword to *Treasury for the Free World*, ed. Ben Raeburn, New York, 1946, pp. xiii-xv. See (B44).

342 Short story. "Kanariefågel för em emsam," *AVB* (July 1946), pp. 75-79. "A Canary for One" translated into Swedish by Thorsten Jonsson.

343 Quote. "Quotes on Inflation," *N.Y. Times Magazine* (Aug. 4, 1946), p. 53.

Includes a brief quotation from Hemingway's article "Notes on the Next War," *Esquire*, IV (Sept. 1935), 19.

344 Speech. "Rede an das deutsche Volk" (1938), *Weltbühne*, I, v (Aug. 25, 1946), 135-136.

An excerpt from Hemingway's "Appeal to the German People." According to a prefatory note, Hemingway delivered this speech over short wave to the German Freedom Broadcasting Station, in November 1938. Partially reprinted under the title "An das Wirkliche Deutschland" (Geschrieben in Spanien 1937) in *Neue Deutsche Literatur*, IV (July 1956), 32.

345 Short story reprinted. "The Killers," *Life*, XXI, x (Sept. 2, 1946), 62, 67-69. Photographs. Reprinted with a pictorial review of the film.

346 Questionnaire. "Hemingway in the Afternoon," *Time*, L (Aug. 4, 1947), 80.

Hemingway answers *Time's* questions "on the state of U.S. writing."

347 Short story reprinted. "The Short Happy Life of Francis Macomber," *Cosmopolitan*, CXXIII (Oct. 1947), 203-212. First appeared in *Cosmopolitan*, CI (Sept. 1936).

348 Ad. "In the Hand of Ernest Hemingway Who is Writing a New Novel of Our Times," *Life*, XXIV, iv (Jan. 26, 1948), inside front cover. Photograph.

Parker Pen advertisement. Facsimile of a commentary on war, from Hemingway's foreword to *Treasury for the Free World*, ed. Ben Raeburn, New York, 1946, p. xv.

349 Greetings. *La Casa Belga*, No. 76 (March 27, 1948), p. 3.

Facsimile of Hemingway's greetings on the twentieth anniversary of the Havana book-shop.

350 Excerpt. "Abendessen im Hotel Gaylord," *Monat*, I (Nov. 1948), 30-41. Excerpt from Ch. XVIII of *FWBT* translated into German.

351 Article. "The Great Blue River," *Holiday*, VI, i (July 1949), 60-63, 95-97. Photographs by George Leavens.
    Article about fishing in the Gulf Stream, with a list of tackle specifications appended. See also " 'Papa' Hemingway tackles big fish, big wars and big books," on p. 32. This article was reprinted in *True*, XXXV (April 1955), 21-30.

352 Letter. "The Position of Ernest Hemingway," *N.Y. Times Book Review* (July 31, 1949), p. 1. Photograph.
    Part I: "Notes from a Novelist on His System of Work—a Letter from Hemingway." Part II: "Notes from a Critic on a Novelist's Work," by Maxwell Geismar. Translated into German in *Amerikanische Rundschau*, V (Oct.–Nov. 1949), 118-119.

353 Short story reprinted. "The Snows of Kilimanjaro," *Esquire*, XXXII, iii (Sept. 1949), 37, 106-109. Color photograph of Hemingway, on p. 36, by William Stone.
    This story first appeared in *Esquire*, VI (Aug. 1936). See the editorial remarks, on p. 6, reminiscing back to 1936 when Hemingway cabled that he owed *Cosmopolitan* a story and since their deadline came first, he was sending the story he had written for *Esquire* and would write them another. He sent *Cosmopolitan* "The Short Happy Life of Francis Macomber" and subsequently made his *Esquire* deadline with "The Snows of Kilimanjaro."

354 Letter. *Book Find News*, No. 85 (Jan. 1950), p. 5.
    Letter from Hemingway lauding Nelson Algren's novel *The Man With the Golden Arm* (New York: Doubleday, 1949).

355 Novel. *Across the River and Into the Trees, Cosmopolitan*, CXXVIII, ii (Feb. 1950), 31-33, 156-167; iii (March 1950), 34-35, 79-91; iv (April 1950), 58-59, 119-129; v (May 1950), 50-51, 130-139; vi (June 1950), 56-57, 79-83.
    Serialized in five installments. See the photograph of Hemingway in Venice and What Goes On at *Cosmopolitan*, on p. 4, in the February issue; and the same column, on p. 4, in the March issue, in which "J. O'C." [John J. O'Connell] notes: "The book will represent a somewhat longer version of the novel than appears on our pages, and the actual words, phrases, and passages written by Mr. Hemingway will be used instead of the ' (deletion)' device adapted by us for magazine purposes. . . ." Note: For the numerous additions and revisions in book form, see (A23a).

164

356 Cable. " 'Hemingway Is Bitter About Nobody'—But His Colonel Is," *Time*, LVI (Sept. 11, 1950), 110.
A long reply, cabled from Cuba, to questions regarding *ARIT*.

357 Autobiographical note. *N.Y. Herald Tribune Book Review* (Oct. 8, 1950), p. 4. Half-cover photograph of the Hemingways in Venice. General title: "Important Authors of the Fall Speaking For Themselves." An Italian translation, "Le abitudini di Hemingway," appeared in *Fiera Letteraria* (Jan. 14, 1951), p. 2.

358 Article. "Ezra Pound," *Fiera Letteraria* (Nov. 19, 1950), p. 3. Hemingway's "Homage to Ezra" translated into Italian from *Ezra Pound*, ed. Peter Russell, London, 1950, pp. 73-76.

359 Note. *N.Y. Times Book Review* (Dec. 3, 1950), p. 58.
Hemingway discusses *ARIT* in an article titled "Success, It's Wonderful," ed. Harvey Breit.

360 Note. "Books I Have Liked," *N.Y. Herald Tribune Book Review* (Dec. 3, 1950), p. 6.
Hemingway lists his three choices for 1950.

361 Cable. "Hemingway Rates Charles for *Gazette*," *National Police Gazette*, CLVI, i (Jan. 1951), 16. Photograph.
Quotes Hemingway's cable, from San Francisco de Paula, Cuba, to H. H. Roswell, the publisher, in regard to Ezzard Charles, who defeated Joe Louis on September 27, 1950, for the world's heavyweight championship. Note: See Jack Dempsey's reply to Hemingway in the *National Police Gazette*, CLVI (Feb. 1951).

362 Fable. "The Good Lion," *Holiday*, IX, iii (March 1951), 50-51. Illustrated by Adriana Ivancich. Published in *The Hemingway Reader*.

62₁ Fable. "The Faithful Bull," *ibid.*, p. 51.
For German translation of both fables, see (D99); for Polish translation, see (C416).

363 Article. "The Shot," *True*, XXVIII (April 1951), 25-28. Photographs.
An account of an antelope hunt in Idaho, with his friend Taylor Williams.

364 Ad. *Life*, XXXI, xix (Nov. 5, 1951), 90-91. Photograph of Hemingway at Finca Vigia, on p. 90.
A four-paragraph endorsement of Ballantine's ale. Repeated in *Life*, XXXIII (Sept. 8, 1952), 56-57, with the omission of one line in the second paragraph.

365 Letter. *N.Y. Herald Tribune Book Review* (Dec. 9, 1951), p. 3.
A letter from Hemingway about the books he liked in 1951, and

ones that he would have enjoyed but which have not been written, is included in John K. Hutchens' column On the Books.

366 Short story. "Ingen dor forgjeves," *Vinduet*, vi, i (1952), 63-71. "Nobody Ever Dies!" translated into Norwegian by Gunnar Larsen.

367 Article. "A Tribute to Mamma from Papa Hemingway," *Life*, xxxiii, vii (Aug. 18, 1952), 92-93.
Commentary on Marlene Dietrich.

368 Letter. "From Ernest Hemingway To the Editors of *Life*," *Life*, xxxiii, viii (Aug. 25, 1952), 124.
Regarding the writing of *OMATS* and its publication in *Life*, xxxiii (Sept. 1, 1952).

369 Letter. "A Letter from Ernest Hemingway," *N.Y. Post* (Aug. 31, 1952), 8 M.
Earl Wilson's column. Hemingway's letter explains why he lives in Cuba and mentions the different places where he wrote various books. See (F125).

370 Novel. *The Old Man and the Sea*, *Life*, xxxiii, ix (Sept. 1, 1952), 35-54. Illustrated with drawings by Noel Sickles. Cover photograph and color photograph, on p. 34, by Alfred Eisenstaedt.
See also the editorial, "A Great American Storyteller," on p. 20.
Note: *Life* circulation in September 1952 was 5,449,833. Prior to magazine publication, *Life* distributed 5000 sets of advance galley proofs of the story for promotional purposes.

371 Letter. "A Letter from Hemingway," *Saturday Review*, xxxv, xxxvi (Sept. 6, 1952), 11. Cover drawing of Hemingway.
Letter to Bernard Kalb, from Cuba, in lieu of an interview. See (F126).

372 Novel. *Le vieil Homme et la Mer*, *Paris-Presse-l'Intransigeant* (Dec. 2–Dec. 14-15, 1952), p. 2. *The Old Man and the Sea* translated into French by Jean Dutourd and serialized.

373 Note. *N.Y. Herald Tribune Book Review* (Dec. 7, 1952), p. 9. Hemingway lists the three books he liked best in 1952.

374 Novel. *Il vecchio e il mare*, *Epoca*, iii (Dec. 20, 1952), 77-94. *OMATS* translated into Italian by Fernanda Pivano.
See also "In Italia Mister Papa arriva sempre in autunno" by Alberto Cavalleri on pp. 73-75.

375 Essay. "The Circus," *Ringling Bros. and Barnum & Bailey Circus Magazine & Program* (1953), pp. 7, 51. Photographs on pp. 6-7. See also the boxed note, on p. 7, by John Ringling North.

76 Novel. *El viejo y el mar, Bohemia,* XLV, xi (March 15, 1953), 67-97. Cover drawing of Hemingway. *OMATS* translated into Spanish by Lino Novás Calvo.

77 Greetings. *La Casa Belga,* No. 92 (March 30, 1953), p. 5.
Facsimile of Hemingway's greetings to the Havana book shop on its twenty-fifth anniversary.

78 Novel. *El viejo y el mar, Life,* en Español, I, vii (March 30, 1953), 27-46. *OMATS* translated into Spanish.

79 Article. "Safari," *Look,* XVIII, ii (Jan. 26, 1954), 19-34. Cover and photographs by Earl Theisen.
Hemingway describes the early weeks in southern Kenya of a proposed five months' safari through East Africa [which was cut short by the two plane crashes]. See also Behind the Scenes, on p. 7.

80 Letter. *Library Journal,* LXXIX (Feb. 15, 1954), 292.
Letter from Hemingway to the Oak Park, Ill., Public Library, on the occasion of the library's fiftieth anniversary. See (F132). Reprinted in the *Wilson Library Bulletin,* XXVIII (March 1954), 542.

81 Article. "The Christmas Gift," *Look,* XVIII, viii (April 20, 1954), 29-37, Part I; ix (May 4, 1954), 79-89, Part II. Cover and photographs by Earl Theisen.
A two-part article describing the two African airplane crashes in January 1954.

82 Short story. "Efter stormen," *AVB* (May 1954), pp. 403-408. "After the Storm" translated into Swedish by Thorsten Jonsson.

83 Short story reprinted. "Big Two-Hearted River," *Field & Stream,* LIX (May 1954), 45-48, 96-105.

84 Excerpts. *Green Hills of Africa, Argosy,* CCCXXXVIII, vi (June 1954), 18-19, 62-72. Ch. IV and Ch. V are reprinted.

85 Cable. *Life,* XXXVI, xxiii (June 7, 1954), 25.
The editorial on Robert Capa's death quotes a cable from Hemingway, from Madrid.

86 Short story. "En kort tid av lycka för Francis Macomber," *AVB* (Oct. 1954), pp. 934-958. "The Short Happy Life of Francis Macomber" translated into Swedish by Thorsten Jonsson.

87 Short story. "Vindkantring," *Dagens Nyheter* (Oct. 31, 1954), p. 3. "The Sea Change" translated into Swedish by Mårten Edlund.

88 Short story. "Sno over laudet," *BLM,* XXIII (Dec. 1954), 796-799. "Cross-Country Snow" translated into Swedish by Mårten Edlund.

389 Short story. "Dödsäsong," *Vi*, No. 2 (Jan. 14, 1955), pp. 16-17. "Out of Season" translated into Swedish by Mårten Edlund.

390 Short story. "En mycket kort historia," *Vi*, No. 7 (Feb. 18, 1955), p. 2. "A Very Short Story" translated into Swedish.

391 Excerpt. "Africa: Happy is the dream . . . ," *Look*, XIX, xxiii (Nov. 15, 1955), 38-39. Photograph. Short excerpts from *GHOA*.

392 Recipe. "Ernest Hemingway's Fillet of Lion," *Sports Illustrated*, III, xxvi (Dec. 26, 1955), 40-42.

Included, with commentary by Hemingway, in the article "A Christmas Choice of Fair and Fancy Game," collected by Reginald Wells, pp. 40-43.

393 Ad. *Holiday*, XIX, ii (Feb. 1956), 60. Photograph of Hemingway by A. E. Hotchner.

Testimonial for Pan American Airline. Dated: Finca Vigia, Cuba. Dec. 1, 1955. Note: This advertisement also appeared in the *National Geographic Magazine*, CIX (Feb. 1956), [4]–[5].

394 Excerpt. "Der alte Mann und das Meer," *Aufbau*, XII, iii (March 1956), 247-258.

A long excerpt from *OMATS* translated into German by Annemarie Horschitz-Horst.

395 Article. "A Visit With Hemingway: A Situation Report," *Look*, XX, xviii (Sept. 4, 1956), 23-31. Dateline: Havana. Photographs by Earl Theisen. Color photograph, on p. 27, by Mary Hemingway.

Text and captions by Hemingway, regarding his life in Cuba. See also Behind the Scenes: "at the Hemingways," p. 20.

396 Article. "My Life and the Woman I Love," *Daily Express*, London (Sept. 10, 1956), pp. 4, 5. Dateline: Havana. Photographs by Earl Theisen. "A Photo News Special."

The text and captions are by Hemingway. Part I: "A Situation Report." Part II: "Miss Mary, My Wife." Part III: "This Fishing is Punishing Work." See also the *Daily Express* (Sept. 11, 1956). Note: This is not a reprint of the above entry.

397 Article. "Hemingway on the Town," *Daily Express*, London (Sept. 11, 1956), p. 4. Photographs by Earl Theisen.

Hemingway describes a night at the Floridita Bar in Havana. See also the *Daily Express* (Sept. 10, 1956).

398 Short story. "A Man of the World," *Atlantic*, CC, v (Nov. 1957), 64-66. 100th Anniversary Issue.

This short story, which takes place in a western saloon, concerns a man who had been blinded in a brawl. Note: This story and the following entry appear under the heading: "Two Tales of Darkness."

398₁ Short story. "Get a Seeing-Eyed Dog," *ibid.*, pp. 66-68.
A story about a writer, who recently had become blind, and his wife, in Italy. See note in above entry.

399 Short story. "Herrskapet Elliot," *Folket i Bild*, No. 21, [1958], pp. 15, 36. "Mr. and Mrs. Elliot" translated into Swedish by Helge Åkerhielm.

400 Article reprinted. *Fisherman*, IX, i (Jan. 1958), 80-82.
Hemingway's article on trout fishing in Europe is reprinted from the *Toronto Star Weekly* (Nov. 17, 1923). See also (H1058).

401 Excerpts. "From the Wisdom of Ernest Hemingway," *Wisdom*, III, xxvi (June 1958), 18-20.
Short excerpts on writing and books, taken from Hemingway's various works. [The sources are not cited.] See also (H1071). Partially reprinted in *Wisdom*, No. 38 (1962), [34]. Limited edition. A facsimile of a manuscript page from "The Dangerous Summer" is reproduced.

402 Short story reprinted. "Nobody Ever Dies!" *Cosmopolitan*, CXLVI (April 1959), 78-83.
First appeared in *Cosmopolitan*, CVI (March 1939).

403 Poem reprinted. "The Worker," *Chicago Tribune* (May 24, 1959), Magazine of Books, p. 8.
Hemingway's poem is reprinted in Frederic Babcock's column Among the Authors, from *Tabula*, XXIII (March 1917). Reprinted in *Newsweek*, LIV (Aug. 3, 1959), 43.

404 Article. "A Matter of Wind," *Sports Illustrated*, XI, vii (Aug. 17, 1959), 43.
Short article on the mano a mano between Antonio Ordoñez and Luis Miguel Dominguín, in July 1959. See also (H1143).

405 Short story. "Berg som vita elefanter," *Folket i Bild*, No. 3, [1960], pp. 12-13, 31. "Hills Like White Elephants" translated into Swedish by Thorsten Jonsson.

406 Novel. *Moskva*, No. 7 (July 1960), pp. 101-145; No. 8 (Aug. 1960), pp. 88-132; No. 9 (Sept. 1960), pp. 124-166.
ARIT translated into Russian by E. Golysheva and B. Izakov. See also the introduction, "Sud'ba polkovnika Kantuella," by E. Litoshko, on pp. 98-100, in the July issue.

407 Article. "The Dangerous Summer," *Life*, XLIX, x (Sept. 5, 1960), 78-109, Part I; xi (Sept. 12, 1960), 60-82, Part II: "The Pride of the

Devil"; xii (Sept. 19, 1960), 74-96, Part III: "An Appointment with Disaster." Photographs and facsimile of manuscript page.

A three-part article on Hemingway's return to Spain and the rivalry between the two bullfighters, Antonio Ordoñez and Luis Miguel Dominguín. See the editor's letter, "Two Prideful Rivals and a Prideful *Life*," on p. 2, of the first issue. See also "One Year Later, A Cable to *Life*," on p. 96, at the end of Part III, in which Hemingway brings the careers of the two bullfighters up to date. Note: For Korean translation in book form, see (D226).

408 Article. "El Verano Sangriento," *Life*, en Español, XVI, ix (Oct. 31, 1960), 44, 51-66; x (Nov. 14, 1960), 68-82; xi (Nov. 28, 1960), 66-81. Photographs.

"The Dangerous Summer" translated into Spanish by Angel Bonomini. See also "Rivalidad de diestros, triunfo literario," on p. 2, of the first issue.

409 Excerpts. "Hemingway Speaks His Mind," *Playboy*, VIII, i (Jan. 1961), 55, 95-97.

A compilation, by William F. Nolan, of excerpts on "life, love and related matters" as expressed by Hemingway in interviews, articles, and books. Note: The sources are not cited.

410 Excerpts. "Pamplona!" *True*, XLII (Feb. 1961), 41-45. Twenty-fifth Anniversary Issue. Short excerpts from Ch. xv and Ch. xvii of *SAR*.

411 Short story reprinted. "After the Storm," *Cosmopolitan*, CL (March 1961), 81-83. Diamond Jubilee Issue. Drawing of Hemingway by Saul Lambert, on p. 80. First appeared in *Cosmopolitan*, XCII (May 1932).

412 Excerpt. "Caccia nell' erba alta," *Epoca*, XII (July 16, 1961), 44-57. Long excerpt from *GHOA*, translated into Italian by Attilio Bertolucci and Alberto Rossi. See also (H1280).

413 Short story. "Ett snyggt ställe med god belysning," *Vi*, No. 29-30 (July 22-29, 1961), pp. 12-13. "A Clean, Well-Lighted Place" translated into Swedish by Thorsten Jonsson.

414 Letter. "Letter to a Young Writer," *Mark Twain Journal*, XI (Summer 1962), 10. Hemingway Memorial Number. See (H1398).

Letter to [Jack Hirschman], written in 1953. Previously published in the *N.Y. Times* [City Edition] (July 3, 1961). See (F131).

414₁ Speech. "The Nobel Prize Speech," *ibid.*, p. 14.

Hemingway's Nobel prize acceptance speech, which was read by the American Ambassador, John Moors Cabot, at the award ceremonies in Stockholm, on December 10, 1954.

15 Aphorisms. "A Man's Credo," *Playboy*, x, i (Jan. 1963), 120, 124, 175. Two-sided cut photograph of Hemingway by Andrew St. George, on pp. 121-122.

"A series of previously unpublished observations on life and art, love and death by Ernest Hemingway, who gave them shortly before his death to California's nonprofit Wisdom Foundation." Quoted from Playbill, on p. 5. Another selection of aphorisms was published in *Playboy*, xi (Jan. 1964).

16 Two fables. "O dobrym lwie" and "O wiernym byku," *Ameryka*, No. 49, [Feb. 1963], p. 6. "The Good Lion" and "The Faithful Bull" translated into Polish. See also (H1441).

17 Letters. "Dear Seelviah," *Mercure de France*, No. 1198-99 (Aug.–Sept. 1963), pp. 105-110. Sylvia Beach Memorial Number.

Two letters from Hemingway to Sylvia Beach, written in the early 1920s, are printed in English and French. See (F46), (F56).

18 Short story reprinted. "The Capital of the World," *Toros*, [1964], pp. 15-20. Photograph of Hemingway at the St. Isidro Fair, in 1959, by Alvara Delgado. See also "Don Ernesto at the Bullfights," on p. 20.

19 Aphorisms. "Advice to a Young Man," *Playboy*, xi, i (Jan. 1964), 153, 225-227.

"Unpublished observations . . . from interviews given to California's nonprofit Wisdom Foundation just before his death." Quoted from Playbill, on p. [2]. Another selection appeared in *Playboy*, x (Jan. 1963).

20 Excerpts. "Paris," *Life*, LVI, xv (April 10, 1964), 60-80, 83-84, 88 A-92. Photographs.

Selected passages from eleven of the sketches in *AMF*: "A Good Café on the Place St.-Michel," " 'Une Génération Perdue,' " "Miss Stein Instructs," "Ford Madox Ford," "Ezra Pound," "An Agent of Evil," "Hunger Was Good Discipline," "People of the Seine," "A False Spring," "Scott Fitzgerald," and "Hawks Do Not Share." See also the editor's note, "How Hemingway Wrote *A Moveable Feast*," on p. 1.

21 Excerpts. "My Paris Memoirs," *Observer* (May 10, 1964), pp. 21, 29; (May 17, 1964), pp. 21, 22; (May 24, 1964), p. 23. Photographs. Excerpts from *AMF*.

22 Excerpts. "Paris . . . est une fête," *Elle*, No. 960 (May 15, 1964); No. 961 (May 22, 1964); No. 962 (May 29, 1964); No. 963 (June 5, 1964); No. 964 (June 12, 1964). Excerpts from *AMF* translated into French by Marc Saporta.

423 Excerpts. "Parigi è una festa," *Epoca*, xv (May 17, 1964), 54-70, Part I; (May 24, 1964), 56-72, Part II: "I folli di Montparnasse." Photographs. Cover photograph on Part I. Excerpts from *AMF* translated into Italian by Vincenzo Mantovani. See also the editor's note, on p. 3, in Part I.

424 Article reprinted. "The Last Commander," *American Dialog*, I, ii (Oct.–Nov. 1964) 10.

Hemingway's tribute to Milton Wolff, Commander of the Abraham Lincoln Battalion during the Spanish Civil War, is reprinted from *An Exhibition of Sculpture* by Jo Davidson, New York, 1938, p. 22. Note: The first reference to Wolff's age was changed to "45 years old," but the second reference was left as "twenty-three."

424₁ Letters. "Unpublished Letters of Ernest Hemingway," *ibid.*, pp. 11-13.

Seven letters from Hemingway to Milton Wolff are printed with one name changed and "the more anatomical expressions" deleted. See (F97), (F98), (F99), (F100), (F103), (F113), (F145). For background on these letters, see Wolff's article in the same issue, pp. 8-9.

425 Novel. *Au-delà du fleuve et sous les arbres*, *Figaro Littéraire* (May 6-12, 1965), pp. 1, 6-7; (May 13-19, 1965), p. 7; (May 20-26, 1965), p. 8. Illustrated by Carzou. Excerpts from *ARIT* translated into French by Paule de Beaumont and Jean Périer.

426 Poems. "Two Love Poems," *Atlantic*, CCXVI, ii (Aug. 1965), 94-100. Cover portrait of Hemingway by Laurence Channing.

"To Mary in London," on pp. 94-95, dated May 1944. "Second Poem to Mary," on pp. 96-100, dated September 1944. In a note, on p. 96, Mary Hemingway explains the circumstances in which the poems were written. Note: The second poem is read by Hemingway on "Ernest Hemingway Reading" (Caedmon, TC 1185). See (F154).

427 Article reprinted. "Tossed About on Land Like Ships in a Storm," *Journalism Quarterly*, XLIII, iii (Autumn 1966), 538-542.

Reprinted, from the *Toronto Daily Star* (Sept. 25, 1923), in William White's article "Hemingway as Reporter: an Unknown News Story." For White's authentication of this unsigned Hemingway article, see p. 542.

SECTION D
TRANSLATIONS

This section was largely compiled from the *Index translationum* (the International Bibliography of Translations which is published annually in Paris by UNESCO), and supplemented by Hans W. Bentz's *Ernest Hemingway in Übersetzungen* (G41), collectors' copies, library copies, and other sources. Various reissued editions by the same translator are listed together.

AFRIKAANS

D1　*Die ou man en die see (OMATS)*. Stellenbosch and Grahamstad: Universiteits-Uitgewers, 1964. 86 pages. Translated by M. S. Taljaard.

ALBANIAN

2　*Plaku e deti, dhe novela tjera* (*OMATS* and six short stories). Prishtinë, Yugoslavia: Milladin Popoviq, 1957. 189 pages. Translated by Masar Murtezai and Ramiz Kelmendi. Afterword: "Hemingveji edhe diçka tjetër" on pp. 179-187.

3　*Lamtumirë, armë! (FTA)*. Tiranë: N.Sh.B., [1961], [Naim Frasheri]. 301 pages. Translated by Vedat Kokona.

ARABIC

4　*Moghamarat fi Afrikia (GHOA)*. Cairo: Maktabat Misr., 1956. Translated by Abd El Aziz Abdul Megid and Farouk Khourshed.

5　*Mukhtārāt (FTA, THAHN, FWBT)*. Baghdad: Al-Alāhi Press, [1957]. Translated by Abdul Majīd Al-Wandawi.

6　*Liman taduq al-ajrās (FTA)*. 2 volumes. Cairo: Dār al-Qalaml el Tibā 'ah wa al-Nashr, 1959. Translated by Majdī al-Din Nasif.

7　*Al-Muharribūn (THAHN)*. al-Qāhirah: Dār al-Hilāl, [1962]. 162 pages. Translated by Nūr-il-Dīn Muṣṭafā.

8　*Qiṣaṣ min al-gharb* (short stories). al-Qāhirah: al-Dār al-Qawmiyyah, [1962]. 94 pages. Translated by al-Rabbāt.

9　*Sawfa tashruq al-shams (SAR)*. al-Qāhirah: Dār al-Hilāl, [1962]. 161 pages.

BULGARIAN

10　*Staretsŭt i moreto (OMATS)*. Sofia: Nar. Kultura, 1957. 103 pages. Translated by Teodora Atanasova and Bojan Atanasova. Afterword on pp. [102]–[103].

11　*Da imash i da niamash (THAHN)*. Sofia. NS OF, 1960. Translated by Marija Cvetkova.

BURMESE

12 *Way powh way powh* *(FTA)*. Rangoon: Guide Daily, 1957. Translated by Than Swe.

CHINESE

13 *Lao jên yü ta hai* *(OMATS)*. Hong Kong: Chung Yih, 1952. 105 pages. Translated by Chen-ling Hsieh. Preface on pp. [iii]–[iv]. Reissued: Taipei: Hsin Lu Book Co., 1958.

14 *Chan ti chung shêng* *(FWBT)*. Taipei: Ta Chung Kuo, 1953. Translated by Peng Sze-yen.

15 *Hai shang yü wêng* *(OMATS)*. Kao Hsiung: Shih-Sui, 1953. Translated by Hsin Yuan.

16 *Hsüeh shan mêng* ("The Snows of Kilimanjaro"). Taipei: Tung Fang, 1953. Translated by Peng Sze-yen. Reissued: Taipei: Ming Hwa, 1956.

17 *Chan ti ch'un mêng* *(FTA)*. Taipei: Nan I Press, 1958. Translated by Huang-min.

18 *Hsü jih ch'u shêng (SAR)*. Taipei: Po Hsing Book Co., 1958. Translated by Peng Sze-yen.

19 *Jin ch'u* *(SAR)*. Taipei: Hsin Lu Book Co., 1960. Translated by Peng Sze-yen.

CZECH

20 *Pĕt Stováků* (short stories). Prague: Adolf Synek, 1933. Translated by Staša Jílovská.

21 *Komu zvoní hrana (FWBT)*. Prague: Fr. Borový, 1947. 513 pages. Translated by A. Sonková and Z. Zinková.

22 *Stařec a moře (OMATS)*. Prague: Státní nakladatelství krásné literatury a uměni, 1956. 114 pages. Illustrated by C. F. Tunnicliffe and Raymond Sheppard. Translated by František Vrba. Afterword by the translator on pp. 109-114. Same: Prague: Československý spisovatel', 1957.

23 *Sbohem, armádo!* *(FTA)*. Prague: Státní nakladatelství krásné literatury a umění, 1958. 299 pages. [Klub Čtenářů, 82.] Translated by Josef Škvorecký. Afterword: "Poznámka o autorovi" by the translator on pp. 293-296. Glossary on pp. 297-299. Reissued: Prague: Odeon, [1965]. 292 pages. Illustrated by Arnost Paderlik.

24 *Komu zvoní hrana (FWBT)*. Prague: Naše Vojsko, 1958. [Knihovna Vojaka, 116.] Translated by Alois Humplík and Jaroslav Schejbal.

25 *Přes řeku a do lesů (ARIT).* Prague: Mladá fronta, 1958. 222 pages. Translated by Zorka Dostálová-Dandová. Glossary on pp. 220-222.

26 *49 poviedok* (short stories). Bratislava: Slovenské Vydavateľstvo Krásné Literatúry, 1961. 463 pages. [Prameň, 55.] Translated by Jozef Olexa. Afterword by Julius Pašteka.

27 *Komu zvoní hrana (FWBT).* Prague: Mladá fronta, [1962]. 453 pages. Translated by Jiři Valja.

28 *Pátá kolona (TFC).* Prague Orbis, 1964.

29 *Zelené pahorky africké (GHOA).* Prague: Státní nakladatelství krásné literatury a umění, 1965.

DANISH

30 *Farvel til våbnene (FTA).* Copenhagen: J. H. Schultz, 1936. Translated by Ole Restrup.

31 *At have og ikke have (THAHN).* Copenhagen: J. H. Schultz, 1937. 284 pages. Translated by Ole Restrup. Same: Copenhagen: Aschehoug, 1946. [Levende Litteratur, 2.]

32 *Og solen går sin gang (SAR).* Copenhagen: J. H. Schultz, 1941. 245 pages. Translated by Ole Restrup.

33 *Lys og mørk latter (TOS).* Copenhagen: Thaning & Appels Forlag, 1941. Translated by Flemming Helweg-Larsen. Foreword by Sven Møller Kristensen, on pp. 7-13.

34 *Efter stormen* ("After the Storm" and fifteen other short stories). Copenhagen: J. H. Schultz, 1942. 243 pages. Translated by Sigvard Lund. Introduction by Niels Kaas Johansen.

35 *De ubesejrede* ("The Undefeated" and thirteen other short stories). Copenhagen: J. H. Schultz, 1942. 250 pages. Translated by Sigvard Lund.

36 *Kilimanjaros sne* ("The Snows of Kilimanjaro"). Copenhagen: J. H. Schultz, 1943. Illustrated by Povl Christensen.

37 Numbered, six-volume set: 1. *Efter stormen: noveller.* 2. *De ubesejrede: noveller.* 3. *Og solen går sin gang.* 4. *Farvel til våbnene.* 5. *At have og ikke have.* 6. *Hvem ringer klokkerne for?* Copenhagen: J. H. Schultz, 1944.

38 *Hvem ringer klokkerne for? (FWBT).* 2 volumes. Copenhagen: J. H. Schultz, 1945. Translated by Ole Restrup. Reissued: 1947, 1 volume, 533 pages.

39 *Afrikas grønne bjerge* *(GHOA)*. Copenhagen: J. H. Schultz, 1945. 235 pages. Translated by Ole Restrup. Reissued: 1956, 212 pages.

40 *Min gamle* ("My Old Man"). Copenhagen: Grafisk Cirkel, 1950. [No. 77.] 29 pages. Illustrated by Palle Pio. Translated by Henry Theils. Limited edition of 200 copies. Published for the members of the graphical association, Grafisk Cirkel. [14 3/4 x 10.]

41 *Over floden—ind i skovene* *(ARIT)*. Copenhagen: J. H. Schultz, 1951. Translated by Georg Gjedde.

42 *Den gamle mand og havet (OMATS)*. Copenhagen: J. H. Schultz, 1952. 104 pages. Translated by Ole Restrup.

43 *Sov sødt, mine herrer* ("God Rest You, Merry Gentlemen" and thirteen other short stories). Copenhagen: J. H. Schultz, 1955. Translated by Ole Restrup.

44 *Døden kommer om eftermiddagen (DIA)*. Copenhagen: Hasselbalch, 1961. 327 pages. Illustrated with photographs. Translated by Michael Tejn.

45 *Der er ingen ende på Paris* *(AMF)*. Copenhagen: J. H. Schultz, 1964. 159 pages. Translated by Michael Tejn.

DUTCH

46 *Voor wien de klok luidt (FWBT)*. Amsterdam: van Holkema & Warendorf: 1945. 528 pages. Translated by J.N.C. van Dietsch. Same: Antwerp: De Magneet, 1946. 431 pages.

47 *De groene heuvelen van Africa (GHOA)*. Amsterdam: Republiek der Letteren, 1946. Translated by J. F. Kliphuis.

48 *Paupers en prinsen* *(THAHN)*. Amsterdam: Elmar, 1947. 268 pages. Translated by David Koning.

49 *De laatste etappe (FTA)*. Antwerp: De Magneet, 1947. 287 pages. Translated by Nico Rost and Margo van Rees. Same: Amsterdam: Nederlandsche Keurboekerij, [1947].

50 *Ook rijst de zon op (SAR)*. Amsterdam: van Holkema & Warendorf, 1949. Translated by W. A. Fick-Lugten.

51 *Over de rivier en onder de bomen (ARIT)*. Amsterdam: A.J.G. Strengholt, 1952. Translated by E. Veegens-Latorf.

52 *De oude man en de zee (OMATS)*. Amsterdam: A.J.G. Strengholt, 1953. 152 pages. Illustrated by Noël Sickles. Translated by E. Veegens-Latorf and J.W.F. Werumeus Buning. Foreword by J.W.F. Werumeus Buning, on pp. 5-7.

53 *Afscheid van de wapenen (FTA).* Amsterdam and Antwerp: Uitgeverij Contact, 1958. 272 pages. Translated by Katja Vranken.

54 *Amerikaan in Parijs (AMF).* Amsterdam: A.J.G. Strengholt, 1964. Translated by John Vandenbergh.

ESTONIAN

55 *Jumalaga, relvad! (FTA).* Toronto, Canada: Orto, 1955. Translated by Tolkinud Valve Ristok.

56 *Vanamees ja meri (OMATS).* Tallin: Éstgosizdat, 1957. Translated by Ellen Laane.

57 *Mehed ilma naisteta (MWW).* Tallin: Gaz. -Zurn, 1959. Translated by J. Seppik.

58 *Ja päike tõuseb (SAR).* Tallin: Éstgosizdat, 1961. 213 pages. Translated by V. Raud.

FINNISH

59 *Kenelle kellot soivat (FWBT).* Helsinki: Tammi, 1944. Translated by Tauno Tainio.

60 *Kirjava satama (THAHN).* Helsinki: Tammi, 1945. 276 pages. Translated by Toini Aaltonen.

61 *Jäähyväiset aseille (FTA).* Helsinki: Tammi, 1946. 336 pages. Translated by Hugo L. Mäkinen.

62 *Joen yli puiden siimekseen (ARIT).* Helsinki: Tammi, 1951. 284 pages. Translated by Tauno Tainio.

63 *Vanhus ja meri (OMATS).* Helsinki: Tammi, 1952. 154 pages. Translated by Tauno Tainio.

64 *Ja aurinko nousee (SAR).* Helsinki: Tammi, 1954. Translated by Jouko Linturi.

65 *Kilimandšaron lumet* ("The Snows of Kilimanjaro" and twenty other short stories). Helsinki: Tammi, 1958. 274 pages. Translated by Kristiina Kivivuorija and Jouko Linturi.

66 *Afrikan vihreät kunnaat (GHOA).* Helsinki: Tammi, [1960]. 247 pages. Translated by Tauno Tainio.

67 *Kuolema iltapäivällä (DIA).* Helsinki: Tammi, 1962. 264 pages. Translated by Tauno Tainio.

68 *Nuoruuteni Pariisi (AMF).* Helsinki: Tammi, 1964. Translated by Jouko Linturi.

FRENCH

69 *Cinquante mille dollars* ("Fifty Grand" and five other short stories). Paris: Éditions de la Nouvelle Revue Française, 1928. 226 pages. Translated by Ott de Weymer (pseudonym of Georges Duplaix). Issued in a large paper edition of 110 numbered copies. Reissued: Paris: Gallimard, 1928. Small paper edition of 796 copies. Reissued in a regular edition, 1928. Reissued: Paris: Club du Meilleur Livre, 1958. 212 pages. Reissued: Neuchâtel: Nouvelle Bibliothèque, 1959. Reissued: Paris: Livre de Poche (Hachette), 1962. [No. 333.]

70 *L'adieu aux armes (FTA)*. Paris: Gallimard, 1932. [Du Monde Entier, No. 2.] Translated by Maurice-Edgar Coindreau. Preface by Drieu la Rochelle. Note: Hemingway filled in the deletions in the Scribner edition for this translation. [See James B. Meriwether's "The Dashes in Hemingway's *A Farewell to Arms*," *Papers of the Bibliographical Society of America*, LVIII (Oct.–Dec. 1964).] Reissued: Paris: Club du Meilleur Livre, 1953. Reissued: Paris: Livre de Poche, 1953. [No. 16.] Reissued: Paris: Collection Pourpre (Hachette), 1955. Reissued: Paris: Éditions Soleil, 1959. [No. 34.]

71 *Le soleil se lève aussi (SAR)*. Paris: Gallimard, 1933. [Du Monde Entier.] 244 pages. Translated by Maurice-Edgar Coindreau. Preface by Jean Prévost, on pp. 7-11. Reissued: 1949. 252 pages. Reissued: Paris: Livre de Poche (Hachette), 1957. [No. 220.] Reissued: Paris: Collection Pourpre (Hachette), 1958. Illustrated by M. Prassinos.

72 *Les vertes collines d'Afrique (GHOA)*. Paris: Gallimard, 1937. [Du Monde Entier.] Translated by Jeanine Delpech. Reissued: 1949. 238 pages. Reissued: 1957.

73 *Mort dans l'après-midi (DIA)*. Paris: Gallimard, 1938. [Du Monde Entier.] 304 pages. Translated by René Daumal. Reissued: 1949. 304 pages. Reissued: Paris: Club des Libraires de France, 1958. [Destins de l'art, 8.] 228 pages. Illustrated limited edition of 4,150 copies. (Oblong. 7⅝ x 9¼.)

74 *Pour qui sonne le glas (FWBT)*. London: Heinemann & Zsolnay, 1944. 306 pages. Translated by Denise V. Ayme. Reissued: Paris: Heinemann & Zsolnay, 1948. Revised translation by Denise Van Moppès. Reissued: Paris: Gallimard, 1950. Reissued: Paris: Club Français du Livre, 1955. Reissued: Paris: Club du Livre du Mois, 1955. 2 volumes. Reissued: Paris: Livre de Poche (Hachette), 1956. [No. 28 and 29.] Paris: Éditions Soleil, 1961. [No. 77.] 499 pages.

75 *En avoir ou pas (THAHN)*. Paris: Gallimard, 1945. [Du Monde

Entier, No. 45.] 256 pages. Translated by Marcel Duhamel. First edition of 110 copies. [Numbered I to C, and lettered A to J.] Note: The title page gives the translator's name as "Maurice" Duhamel. An erratum slip was laid in correcting this error.

76 *Dix indiens* ("Ten Indians" and eleven other short stories). Paris: Gallimard, 1946. [Du Monde Entier, No. 50.] 245 pages. Translated by Marcel Duhamel. First edition of 100 copies. Reissued: Lausanne: Abbaye du Livre, 1947. [Amica America, No. 1.] Reissued: Lausanne: Éditions Rencontres, 1957.

77 *Paradis perdu* suivi de *La cinquième colonne* (thirty-one short stories and *TFC*). Paris: Gallimard, 1949. [Du Monde Entier, No. 87.] 398 pages. Translated by Henri Robillot and Marcel Duhamel. Note: The title story is a translation of "Hills Like White Elephants." Reissued: Paris: Livre de Poche (Hachette), n.d. [No. 380 and 381.]

78 *Le vieil homme et la mer* (*OMATS*). Paris: Gallimard, 1952. [Du Monde Entier.] 189 pages. Translated by Jean Dutourd. Reissued: Paris: Bibliothèque Verte (Hachette), 1955. Reissued: Paris: Club du Meilleur Livre, 1955. Reissued: Paris: Gallimard, 1961. 128 pages. Illustrated by Fernando Puig Rosado. Reissued: Paris: Éditions Soleil, 1961. [No. 62.] Reissued: Paris: Livre de Poche, 1964. [No. 946.]

79 *L'adieu aux armes* (*FTA*). Monte Carlo: Sauret, 1956. 365 pages. Translated by Maurice-Edgar Coindreau. Preface by Roland Dorgelès. Illustrated by Pierre-Yves Trémois.

80 *Les neiges du Kilimandjaro et autres nouvelles* (The Snows and other short stories). Paris: Club du Meilleur Livre, 1957. Translated by Marcel Duhamel. Reissued: Paris: Gallimard, 1957. [Du Monde Entier.] Reissued: Paris: Livre de Poche (Hachette), 1958. [No. 301.]

81 *Romans.* Paris: Gallimard, 1957. 876 pages. Contents: *Le soleil se lève aussi.* Translated by Maurice-Edgar Coindreau. Illustrated by Édy Legrand. *L'adieu aux armes.* Translated by Maurice-Edgar Coindreau. Illustrated by Chapelain-Midy. *En avoir ou pas.* Translated by Marcel Duhamel. Illustrated by Robert Naly. *Pour qui sonne le glas.* Translated by Denise Van Moppès. Illustrated by Yves Brayer. *Le vieil homme et la mer.* Translated by Jean Dutourd. Illustrated by Pierre-Yves Trémois. [Frontispiece: Portrait of Hemingway by Pierre-Yves Trémois, dated: 1957.]

82 *Le vieil homme et la mer* (*OMATS*). Paris (aux dépens de l'artiste), 1958. Illustrated with "gravures a la manière noire" by Robert

Naly. 144 pages. (12 1/2 x 10.) Unbound. Enclosed in a cork box. 115 numbered copies.

83 *Nouvelles et Récits (First 49, GHOA, DIA, TFC)*. Paris: Gallimard, 1963. 828 pages. With 32 illustrations by M. Ciry, L. Coutard, H. Erni, and A. Masson.

84 *Oeuvres Complètes*. Paris: Gallimard, 1964. Illustrated eight-volume edition, under the editorship of André Sauret.

> *Le vieil homme et la mer, En avoir ou pas (OMATS, THAHN)*. 343 pages. Introduction by Jean Dutourd. Translated by Jean Dutourd and Marcel Duhamel. Lithographs by André Masson.
> *Le soleil se lève aussi (SAR)*. 277 pages. Translated by Maurice-Edgar Coindreau. Lithographs by Garbell.
> *L'adieu aux armes (FTA)*. 349 pages. Translated by Maurice-Edgar Coindreau. Lithographs by Carzou.
> *Mort dans l'après-midi (DIA)*. 378 pages. Translated by René Daumal. Lithographs by Pelayo.
> *Les vertes collines d'Afrique (GHOA)*. 262 pages. Translated by Jeanine Delpech. Lithographs by Luc Simon.
> *Paradis perdu et autres nouvelles* (thirty short stories). 397 pages. Translated by Henri Robillot. Lithographs by Guiramand.
> *Les neiges du Kilimandjaro et autres nouvelles* (eighteen short stories). 312 pages. Translated by Marcel Duhamel. Lithographs by Commère.
> *Pour qui sonne le glas (FWBT)*. 525 pages. Translated by Denise Van Moppès. Lithographs by Fontanarosa.

85 *Paris est une fête (AMF)*. Paris: Gallimard, 1964. [Du Monde Entier, No. 354.] 216 pages. Translated by Marc Saporta. Preface by Hemingway on p. 5. First edition of 112 numbered copies.

86 *Au-delà du fleuve et sous les arbres (ARIT)*. Paris: Gallimard, 1965. 253 pages. Translated by Paule de Beaumont.

GERMAN

87 *Fiesta (SAR)*. Berlin: Rowohlt, 1928. 312 pages. Translated by Annemarie Horschitz. Reissued: Hamburg: Rowohlt, 1950. [Rororo, 5.] 181 pages. Same: Gütersloh: Bertelsmann Lesering, 1960. 318 pages.

88 *Männer (MWW)*. Berlin: Rowohlt, 1929. 256 pages. Translated by Annemarie Horschitz.

89 *In einem andern Land (FTA)*. Berlin: Ernst Rowohlt, 1930. 368 pages. Translated by Annemarie Horschitz. Note: The title for the German edition is taken from the epigraph quoted on p. [6]:

Barnardine: Thou hast committed— | *Barabas*: Fornication: but that was | in another country; and besides | the wench is dead. | CHRISTOPHER MARLOWE: | THE JEW OF MALTA. Reissued: Hamburg: Rowohlt, 1951. [Rororo, 216.] Same: Zurich: Steinberg-Verlag, 1948. 360 pages. Berlin: Volksverband der Bücherfreunde, 1949. Berlin: Deutsche Buch-Gemeinschaft, 1952. Berlin: Aufbau-Verlag, 1957. Zurich: Buchclub Ex Libris, 1957. Stuttgart: Deutscher Bücherbund, 1963.

90 *In unserer Zeit (IOT)*. Berlin: Rowohlt, 1932. 184 pages. Translated by Annemarie Horschitz. Reissued: Hamburg: Rowohlt, 1958. [Rororo, 278.] 141 pages. Biographical note on Hemingway on p. [2].

91 *Wem die Stunde schlägt (FWBT)*. Stockholm: Bermann-Fischer, 1941. 560 pages. Translated by Paul Baudisch. Same: Vienna: Bermann-Fischer, 1948. 550 pages. Berlin: Suhrkamp, 1948. 544 pages. Zurich: Büchergilde Gutenberg, 1949. Frankfurt a.M.: S. Fischer, 1951. Berlin: G. B. Fischer, 1958. 582 pages. Vienna: Deutsche Buch-Gemeinschaft, 1959. Frankfurt a.M.: Fischer-Bücherei, 1961.

92 *Der Schnee vom Kilimandscharo und andere Erzählungen* ("The Snows of Kilimanjaro" and three other short stories). Stuttgart: Rowohlt, 1949. 144 pages. Illustrated. Translated by Annemarie Horschitz-Horst. Same: Zurich: Steinberg-Verlag, 1949. 200 pages.

93 *49 Stories (First 49)*. Hamburg: Rowohlt, 1950. 468 pages. Translated by Annemarie Horschitz-Horst. Preface by Hemingway, on pp. 5-6, translated from the *First 49*.

94 *Haben und Nichthaben (THAHN)*. Hamburg: Rowohlt, 1951. 279 pages. Translated by Annemarie Horschitz-Horst. Reissued: 1964. [Rororo, 605.] Same: Frankfurt a.M.: Büchergilde Gutenberg, 1957. Zurich: Buchclub Ex Libris, 1958. Düsseldorf: Deutscher Bücherbund, 1960.

95 *Über den Fluss und in die Wälder (ARIT)*. Hamburg: Rowohlt, 1951. 340 pages. Translated by Annemarie Horschitz-Horst. Same: Zurich: Steinberg-Verlag, 1952. 282 pages. Berlin: Aufbau-Verlag, 1957. Stuttgart: Stuttgarter Hausbücherei, 1958. Zurich: Buchclub Ex Libris, 1959. Hamburg: Deutsche Hausbücherei, 1960. Berlin: Deutsche Buch-Gemeinschaft, 1964. 282 pages.

96 *Das Ende von Etwas und andere Kurzgeschichten* ("The End of Something" and five other short stories). Stuttgart: Reclam, 1951. 77 pages. Translated by Annemarie Horschitz-Horst. Afterword by Kurt W. Marek, on pp. 74-77.

97 *Der alte Mann und das Meer (OMATS)*. Hamburg: Rowohlt, 1952.

[Rororo, 328.] 128 pages. Translated by Annemarie Horschitz-Horst. Same: Zurich: Steinberg-Verlag, 1954. 126 pages. Stuttgart: Europäischer Buchklub, 1955. Berlin: Deutsche Buch-Gemeinschaft, 1956. Hamburg: Asmus Verlag, [1961]. 160 pages. Illustrated by Frans Masereel. Berlin: Aufbau-Verlag, [1962].

98 *Der Unbesiegte: 2 Erzählungen* ("The Undefeated" and "The Short Happy Life of Francis Macomber"). Munich: R. Piper, 1952. [Piper-Bücherei, 52.] Translated by Annemarie Horschitz-Horst.

99 *Der gute Löwe—Der treue Stier* ("The Good Lion," "The Faithful Bull"). Hamburg: Rowohlt, 1953. 16 pages. Translated by Annemarie Horschitz-Horst. Note: This is a Christmas edition of the two fables which were first published in *Holiday,* IX (March 1951).

100 *Schnee auf dem Kilimandscharo* ("The Snows of Kilimanjaro"). Hamburg: Rowohlt, 1952. 56 pages. Translated by Annemarie Horschitz-Horst. Biographical note on Hemingway on p. [ii].

101 *Erzählungen (TFC* and *First 49).* Berlin: Deutsche Buch-Gemeinschaft, 1954. 375 pages. Translated by Annemarie Horschitz-Horst.

102 *Die grünen Hügel Afrikas (GHOA).* Hamburg: Rowohlt, 1954. 249 pages. [Rororo, 47.] Translated by Annemarie Horschitz-Horst. Same: Gütersloh: Bertelsmann Lesering, 1962.

103 *Die Haupstadt der Welt* ("The Capital of the World" and three other short stories). Munich: Langen-Müller, 1955. [Langen-Müllers kleine Geschenkbücher, 27.] 67 pages. Translated by Annemarie Horschitz-Horst.

104 *Die Sturmfluten des Frühlings (TOS).* Hamburg: Rowohlt, 1957. 136 pages. Translated by Annemarie Horschitz-Horst. Same: Zurich: Steinberg-Verlag, 1957.

105 *Tod am Nachmittag (DIA).* Hamburg: Rowohlt, 1957. 376 pages, including 81 illustrations. Translated by Annemarie Horschitz-Horst.

106 *Männer ohne Frauen (MWW).* Hamburg: Rowohlt, 1958. [Rororo, 279.] 142 pages. Translated by Annemarie Horschitz-Horst.

107 *Der Sieger geht leer aus (WTN).* Hamburg: Rowohlt, 1958. [Rororo, 280.] Translated by Annemarie Horschitz-Horst.

108 *Um eine Viertelmillion—Die Killer* ("Fifty Grand," "The Killers"). Freiburg im Breisgau: Hyperion-Verlag, 1958. Translated by Annemarie Horschitz-Horst.

109 *Der Unbesiegte* ("The Undefeated"). Hannover: Fackelträger-Verlag, 1959. [60] pages. Illustrated with 28 black-and-white draw-

ings by Picasso. Translated by Annemarie Horschitz-Horst. [Oblong. 5 11/16 x 7 7/8.] Same: Gütersloh: Bertelsmann Lesering, 1962. [Kleine Lesering, Bibliothek, 63.]

110 *Das kurze glückliche Leben des Francis Macomber* ("The Short Happy Life of Francis Macomber"). Gütersloh: Bertelsmann Lesering, 1961. [Kleine Lesering, Bibliothek, 2.] Translated by Annemarie Horschitz-Horst.

111 *Schnee auf dem Kilimandscharo* ("The Snows of Kilimanjaro" and five other short stories). Hamburg: Rowohlt, 1961. [Rororo, 413.] 148 pages. Translated by Annemarie Horschitz-Horst.

112 *Paris—ein Fest fürs Leben* (*AMF*). Hamburg: Rowohlt, 1965. 256 pages. Translated by Annemarie Horschitz-Horst. Foreword by Hemingway on pp. 5-6.

113 *Sämtliche Erzählungen* (collected stories and *OMATS*). Hamburg: Rowohlt, 1966. 480 pages. Translated by Annemarie Horschitz-Horst.

GREEK

114 *Gia poion chtypa ē kampana* (*FWBT*). Athens: I Phili tou Vivliou, 1946. Translated by N. Simiriotis.

115 *Hè Súntomè eutuchisménè zoè toú Makómper* ("The Short Happy Life of Francis Macomber"). Athens: Logotechniki Gonia, 1949. Translated by K. Poziopoulou.

116 *Nakheis kai na mēn ekheis* (*THAHN*). Athens: Marēs, 1952. Translated by Minas Zōgraphou-Meranaiou.

117 *O apochairetismos ton oplon* (*FTA*). Athens: Synchroni Loghotechnie [1953]. Translated by D. Constantinidis.

118 *O ilios anatellei panta* (*SAR*). Athens: O cosmos, 1953. Translated by S. Tsampiras.

119 *O jeros kai i Thalassa* (*OMATS*). Athens: Icaros, [1954]. Translated by D. Berachas.

120 *Ghia poion chtypa i cambana* (*FWBT*). Athens: Homiros, 1955. Translated by J. Kouchtsoghlou.

121 *Oi prassinoi lofoi tis Afrikis* (*GHOA*). Athens: M.B., 1955. 215 pages. Translated by Ph. Antreou.

22 *Gia poion chtypa ē kampana* (*FWBT*). Athens: Daremas, 1958. Translated by S. Vourdoumba.

23 *Apochairetismos sta opla* (*FTA*). Athens: Delta, 1961. 216 pages. Translated by Othon Argyropoulos.

124 *Pera apo to potami* (*ARIT*). Athens: Phexēs, 1964. Translated by Petros Anagnōstopoulos.

HEBREW

125 *Le-mi zilzelu ha-pa'amonim* (*FWBT*). Merhaviah, Palestine, 1947. 479 pages. Translated by Menashe Lewin. Reissued: Tel Aviv: Idit, 1954.

126 *Ha-zaken weha-yam* (*OMATS*). Tel Aviv: Am Oved Prutoth, 1953. Illustrated. Translated by Ehud Rabin.

127 *Ha-gevaot ha-yerukot shel Afrika* (*GHOA*). Jerusalem: Karni, 1954. Translated by Aharon Amir.

128 *Der alter un der yam* (*OMATS*). New York: Der Kval, 1958. Illustrated by Leonard Baskin. Translated into Yiddish by M. Shtiker.

129 *Wezarah hashemesh* (*SAR*). Tel Aviv: Am Oved, 1962. 208 pages. Translated by Wera Israelit.

HUNGARIAN

130 *Különös tarsaság* (*SAR*). Budapest: Pantheon, 1937. Translated by Andor Németh.

131 *Akiért a harang szól* (*FWBT*). 2 volumes. Budapest: Révai, 1947. Translated by Sőtér István. Same: Budapest: Zrinyi Kiadó, 1957. Same: Szépirodalmi Könyvkiadó, 1964. 3 volumes. 239 pages; 219 pages; 236 pages. Afterword by Vajda Miklós in Vol. III, on pp. 237-[240].

132 *Gazdagok és szegények* (*THAHN*). Budapest: Révai, [1948].

133 *Az öreg halász és a tenger* (*OMATS*). Budapest: Uj Magyar Kiadó, 1956. Translated by Ottlik Géza. Same: Budapest: Helikon, 1962. 199 pages. Illustrated.

134 *A bérgyilkosok* ("The Killers"). Budapest: Terra, 1958. Translated by Elek Máthé.

135 *Búcsú a fegyverektől* (*FTA*). Budapest: Európa Könyvkiadó, 1958. 305 pages. Translated by Örkény István. Same: 1963, 344 pages. Afterword by Szász Imre, on pp. 341-[344].

136 *A folyón át, a fák közé* (*ARIT*). Budapest: Magvetö, 1958. Translated by Elek Máthé.

137 *Novellák* (thirty-six short stories). Budapest: Európa Könyvkiadó, 1960. 410 pages. Translated by ten translators. Same: 1963, 576 pages. Foreword by Szász Imre, on pp. i-xxii. Glossary on pp. 571-574.

138 *A Kilimandzsáro hava: elbeszélések* ("The Snows of Kilimanjaro" and other short stories). Budapest: Szépirodalmi Könyvkiadó, 1960. 319 pages. Translated by László András *et al.*

139 *Afrikai vadásznapló (GHOA).* Budapest: Európa Könyvkiadó, 1961. 236 pages. Illustrated by Kondor Lajos. Translated by Szász Imre. Letter to "Mr. J. P." from Hemingway, on p. [5]. See the 1st English edition (A39a).

140 *Fiesta | A nap is felkel (SAR).* Budapest: Európa Könyvkiadó, 1962. 250 pages. Translated by Déry Tibor.

ICELANDIC

141 *Klukkan kallar (FWBT).* Reykjavik: Helgafell, 1951. 454 pages. Translated by Stefán Bjarman. Foreword by the translator on pp. 7-8.

142 *Gamli madurinn og hafid (OMATS).* Reykjavik: Bókaforlag Odds Björnssonar, 1954. 150 pages. Translated by Björn O. Björnsson. Afterword by the translator on pp. 149-150. Reissued: 1955. 150 pages.

REGIONAL LANGUAGES OF INDIA

143 *Aparajita (OMATS).* Cuttack: Praphullachandra Dasa, 1955. Translated into Oriya by Subhadranandan.

144 *Budo o sagar (OMATS).* Calcutta: Manamohan, 1955. Translated into Bengali by Lila Majumdar.

145 *Kizhavanum Katalum (OMATS).* Kadambanad: N. G. Thomas, 1956. Translated into Malayalam by Xavier Paul. Same: Quilon: M. S. Book Depot, [1961].

146 *Shastrasannyas (FTA).* Bombay: Pearl Publications, 1957. Translated into Marathi by V. V. Dalavi.

147 *Shastrasannyas (FTA).* Bombay: Pearl Publications, 1957. Translated into Gujarati by Vrajalal Parekh.

148 *Shastra-viday (FTA).* Bombay: Pearl Publications, 1957. Translated into Hindi by Purushottam Dube.

149 *Kaṭalum kilavanum (OMATS).* Madras: A. K. Gopolan, 1957. Translated into Tamil by S.D.S. Yōgi.

150 *He yuddha, Vidāy (FTA).* Bombay: Pearl Publications, 1958. Translated into Bengali by Dipali Mukherji.

151 *Pōrē, nipo (FTA).* Bombay: Pearl Publications, 1958. Translated into Tamil by M. S. Sivasvāmi.

¹⁵² *Sagar aur manushya (OMATS)*. Delhi: Rajpal & Sons, 1959. Translated into Hindi by Anandprakash Jain. Same: Delhi: Hind Pocket Books, [1960]. 119 pages.

ITALIAN

¹⁵³ *L'invincibile* ("The Undefeated" and five other short stories). Milan: Jandi-Sapi, 1944. [Universale Jandi, 14.] 159 pages. Foreword by Sandro Surace.

¹⁵⁴ *E il sole sorge ancora (SAR)*. Milan: Jandi-Sapi, 1944. [Le Najadi, Collezione di grandi narratori, 3.] 290 pages. Translated by Rosetta Dandolo.

¹⁵⁵ *Chi ha e chi non ha (THAHN)*. Milan: Jandi-Sapi, 1945. [Le Najadi, Collezione di grandi narratori, 15.] 213 pages. Translated by Bruno Fonzi.

¹⁵⁶ *Un addio alle armi (FTA)*. Milan: Jandi-Sapi, 1945. [Le Najadi, Collezione di grandi narratori, 16.] 273 pages. Translated by Bruno Fonzi.

¹⁵⁷ *Addio alle armi (FTA)*. Milan: Mondadori, 1946. 417 pages. Illustrated by Renato Guttuso. Translated by Giansiro Ferrata, Puccio Russo, and Dante Isella. Foreword by Giansiro Ferrata, on pp. [9]-24. Same: Lugano: Ghilde del Libro, 1946.

¹⁵⁸ *Per chi suona la campana (FWBT)*. Milan: Mondadori, 1946. [Medusa, i grandi narratori d'ogni paese, 166.] 479 pages. Translated by Maria Napolitano Martone. Reissued: 1965. 2 volumes. [Libri del Pavone, 8/9.]

¹⁵⁹ *Per chi suona la campana (FWBT)*. Lugano: Ghilde del Libro, 1946. Translated by Luciano Foa and Alberto Zevi.

¹⁶⁰ *La quinta colonna (TFC)*. Turin: Einaudi, 1946. [Politecnico, biblioteca, 4.] 90 pages. Translated by Giuseppe Trevisani.

¹⁶¹ *Verdi colline d'Africa (GHOA)*. Milan: Jandi-Sapi, 1946. [Le Najadi, Collezione di grandi narratori, 19.] 222 pages. Translated by Gaetano Carancini.

¹⁶² *Avere e non avere (THAHN)*. Turin: Einaudi, 1946. [Narratori contemporanei, 19.] 276 pages. Translated by Giorgio Monicelli. Reissued: Milan: Mondadori, [1961]. [Il Bosco, 26.]

¹⁶³ *Fiesta (SAR)*. Turin: Einaudi, 1946. [Narratori contemporanei, 16.] 334 pages. Translated by Giuseppe Trevisani. Reissued: Milan: Mondadori, 1957. [Il Bosco, 15.]

164 *I quarantanove racconti (First 49)*. Turin: Einaudi, 1946. [I Millenni, 1.] 494 pages. Translated by Giuseppe Trevisani. Preface by Hemingway, on pp. v-vi, translated from *First 49*. Reissued: Milan: Mondadori, [1961]. 2 volumes. [Libri del Pavone, 184/185, 186/187.]

165 *Uomini senza donne (MWW)*. Rome: Elios, 1946. [Le Streghe, 19.] 235 pages. Translated by Angela Salomone.

166 *Morte nel pomeriggio (DIA)*. [Turin]: Einaudi, 1947. [Saggi, 88.] 418 pages. Illustrated. Translated by Fernanda Pivano. Foreword by the translator on pp. 9-17. Biographical note on pp. 17-19. Reissued: Milan: Mondadori, [1962]. [Il Bosco, 78.] Foreword by the translator on pp. 7-14.

167 *Verdi colline d'Africa (GHOA)*. Turin: Einaudi, 1948. [I Coralli, 14.] 281 pages. Translated by Attilio Bertolucci and Alberto Rossi. Prefatory note by Hemingway on p. 7, translated from the 1935 Scribner edition. Letter to "Signor J. P.," signed: E. H., on p. 11. See first English edition (A39a). Reissued: Milan: Mondadori, 1961. [Il Bosco, 94.] 155 pages.

168 *Addio alle armi (FTA)*. Milan: Mondadori, 1949. [Medusa, 234.] 327 pages. Translated by Fernanda Pivano. Introduction by Hemingway on pp. [9]-11, translated from the 1948 Scribner edition.

169 *Torrenti di primavera (TOS)*. Turin: Einaudi, 1951. 116 pages. Translated by Bruno Fonzi.

170 *Il vecchio e il mare (OMATS)*. Milan: Mondadori, 1952. [Medusa, 306.] 169 pages. Illustrated by Ugo Marantonio. Translated by Fernanda Pivano.

171 *I quarantanove racconti—La quinta colonna (First 49, TFC)*. Turin: Einaudi, 1961. 540 pages. Translated by Giuseppe Trevisani.

172 *Fiesta—Avere e non avere—Verdi colline d'Africa (SAR, THAHN, GHOA)*. Turin: Einaudi, 1961. 575 pages. Translated by Giuseppe Trevisani, Giorgio Monicelli *et al*.

173 *Fiesta—Addio alle armi—Avere e non avere—I quarantanove racconti—Il vecchio e il mare (SAR, FTA, THAHN, First 49, OMATS)*. Vol. II. Milan: Mondadori, 1962. Translated by Giuseppe Trevisani, Attilio Bertolucci, Maria Napolitano Martone, Fernanda Pivano, and Alberto Rossi.

174 *Verdi colline d'Africa—Morte nel pomeriggio—Per chi suona la campana—La quinta colonna (GHOA, DIA, FWBT, TFC)*. Vol. III. Milan: Mondadori, 1962. Translated by Attilio Bertolucci,

Fernanda Pivano, Maria Napolitano Martone, and Giuseppe Trevisani.

175 *Festa mobile (AMF)*. Verona: Mondadori, 1964. [Medusa, 484.] 218 pages. Translated by Vincenzo Mantovani. Preface by Hemingway on pp. [9]-10, translated from the Scribner edition.

176 *Di là dal fiume e tra gli alberi (ARIT)*. Verona: Mondadori, 1965. [Medusa, 492.]

JAPANESE

177 *Bu-ki yo, saraba (FTA)*. Tokyo: Tenzhin-sha, 1930. 583 pages. Translated by Oda Ritsu.

178 *Tare ga tame ni kane wa naru (FWBT)*. 2 volumes. Tokyo: Seinen Shobo, [1941]. Translated by Oi Shigeo.

179 *Otoko dake no sekai—Shôsa niwa nani mo yaru na (MWW, WTN* and "The Short Happy Life of Francis Macomber"). Tokyo: Mikasa Shobo, 1955. [Zenshu, 1.] Translated by Rikuo Taniguchi *et al.*

180 *Warera no jidai ni—Haru no honryû—Dai-go retsu (IOT, TOS, TFC* and short stories). Tokyo: Mikasa Shobo, 1956. [Zenshu, 2.]

181 *Hi wa mata noboru—Kirimanjaro no yuki—Sekai no shuto—Hashi ni ita rōjin (SAR,* "The Snows of Kilimanjaro," "The Capital of the World," "Old Man at the Bridge"). Tokyo: Mikasa Shobo, 1955. [Zenshu, 3.] Translated by Katsuji Takamura and Rikutarô Fukuda.

182 *Buki yo saraba (FTA)*. Tokyo: Mikasa Shobo, [1958]. [Zenshu, 4.] Translated by Michinosuke Takeuchi.

183 *Afurika no midori no oka (GHOA)*. Tokyo: Mikasa Shobo, 1956. [Zenshu, 5.] Translated by Kôji Nishimura.

184 *Ta ga tame ni kane wa naru (FWBT)*. 2 volumes. Tokyo: Mikasa Shobo, 1951. [Zenshu, 7/8.] Illustrated. Translated by Yasuo Ôkubo. Reissued: 1955.

185 *Kawa o watatte kodachi no naka e (ARIT)*. Tokyo: Mikasa Shobo, 1952. [Zenshu, 9.] Translated by Yasuo Ôkubo. Reissued: 1956.

186 *Rôjin to umi (OMATS)*. Tokyo: Mikasa Shobo, 1956. [Zenshu, 10.] Translated by Tsuneari Fukuda.

187 *Buki yo saraba (FTA)*. Tokyo: Hibiya shuppan-sha, 1951. Translated by Yasuo Ôkubo. Same: Shincho-Sha, 1955.

188 *Kirimanjaro no yuki* ("The Snows of Kilimanjaro"). Tokyo: Mikasa Shobo, 1952. Translated by Yasuo Ôkubo.

189 *Kirimanjaro no yuki* ("The Snows of Kilimanjaro"). Tokyo: Kadokawa shoten, 1953. Translated by Naotarô Tatsunokuchi.

190 *Satsujin-sha* ("The Killers"). Tokyo: Mikasa Shobo, 1953. Translated by Yasuo Ôkubo.

191 *Buki yo saraba* (*FTA*). Tokyo: Sogen-sha, 1953. [Zenshu, 2.] Translated by Minoru Fukuda.

192 *Rôjin to umi* (*OMATS*). Tokyo: Charles E. Tuttle, 1953. 198 pages. Translated by Tsuneari Fukuda.

193 *Hi wa mata noboru* (*SAR*). Tokyo: Mikasa Shobo, 1954. Translated by Yasuo Ôkubo. Same: Tokyo: Shincho-Sha, 1955.

194 *Motsukoto to motazarukoto* (*THAHN*). Tokyo: Kôchi shuppan-sha, 1954. Translated by Kôji Nakata. Same: Tokyo: Arechi shuppan-sha, 1955.

195 *Haru no honryû* (*TOS*). Tokyo: Kawade Shobo, 1955. Translated by Kôji Nakata.

196 *Tampen-shû* (twelve short stories). Tokyo: Arechi shuppan-sha, 1955. Translated by Kôji Nakata and Tarô Kitamura.

197 *Buki yo saraba* (*FTA*). Tokyo: Shin Hyoron-sha, 1955. [Zenshu, 1.] Translated by Katsuji Takamura. Same: Tokyo: Tarumi Shobo, [1960].

198 *Buki yo saraba* (*FTA*). Tokyo: Kawade Shobo, 1955. Translated by Katsuji Takamura. Together with *Ikari no budo*, *The Grapes of Wrath* by John Steinbeck, translated by Ichiro Ishi.

199 *Shiroi zô no yôna yamayama* ("Big Two-Hearted River" and "Hills Like White Elephants"). Tokyo: Eiho-sha, 1956. Translated by Minoru Fukuda and Kazuhiko Yoneda.

200 *Moterumono motazarumono* (*THAHN*). Tokyo: Kawade Shobo, 1956. Translated by Kôji Nakata.

201 *Motsu to motanu to* (*THAHN*). Tokyo: Mikasa Shobo, 1956. Translated by Shôichi Saeki.

202 *Tampen-shû* (short stories). Tokyo: Kenkyu-sha, 1957. Translated by Rikuo Taniguchi.

203 *Hi wa mata noboru* (*SAR*). Tokyo: Kadokawa Shoten, 1957. Translated by Susumu Oikawa.

204 *Hi wa mata noboru (SAR)*. Tokyo: Mikasa Shobo, 1957. Translated by Katsuji Takamura.

205 *Buki yo saraba—Warera no jidai ni—Onna no Inai otokotachi (FTA, IOT, MWW)*. Tokyo: Arechi shuppan-sha, 1957. [Gendai Amerika Bungaku Zenshu, 7.] Translated by Katsuji Takamura *et al.*

206 *Buki yo saraba (FTA)*. 2 volumes. Tokyo: Iwanami Shoten, 1957. Translated by Rikuo Taniguchi.

207 *Ta ga tame ni kane wa naru (FWBT, "The Killers," "The Short Happy Life of Francis Macomber," "The Snows of Kilimanjaro")*. Tokyo: Kawade Shobo, 1957. [Sekai Bungaku Zenshu, 23.] Translated by Yasuo Ôkubo.

208 *Hi wa mata noboru (SAR)*. Tokyo: Iwanami Shoten, 1958. Translated by Rikuo Taniguchi.

209 *Buki yo saraba (FTA)*. 2 volumes. Tokyo: Kadokawa Shoten, [1958]. Translated by Ichiro Ishi. Same: Tokyo: Chikuma-Shobo, 1959.

210 *Kirimanjaro no yuki—Futatsu no kokoro no kawa ("The Snows of Kilimanjaro" and "Big Two-Hearted River")*. Tokyo: Nan'undo, 1959. Translated by Ichiro Ishi and Yuti Ejima.

211 *Buki yo saraba (FTA)*. Tokyo, 1959. 435 pages. Translated by Sakai and Ohashi. Together with *As I Lay Dying* and *Pylon* by William Faulkner. Afterword, with photographs.

212 *Buki yo saraba—Rōjin to umi—Tampen 6 hen (FTA, OMATS* and six short stories). Tokyo: Charles E. Tuttle, 1964. [A Treasury of World Literature, 44.] 519 pages. Afterword, with photographs, on pp. 496-519.

213 *Buki yo saraba—Rōjin to umi (FTA, OMATS* and short stories). Tokyo: Kawade-Shobo, 1964. [Sekai Bungaku Zenshu, 18.] 450 pages. Photographs.

214 *Hemingway Zenshu*. 8 volumes. Tokyo: Mikasa-Shobo, 1963-1965. Photographs.
> Vol. 1: *The Complete Short Stories*. 1963. 457 pages. Frontispiece.
> Vol. 2: *SAR* and *GHOA*. 1964. 446 pages. Frontispiece.
> Vol. 3: *FTA, TOS* and *TFC*. 1964. 464 pages. Frontispiece.
> Vol. 4: *DIA*. 1964. 337 pages. Frontispiece and 16 pages of bullfight photographs.
> Vol. 5: *FWBT*. Part I. 1963. 349 pages. Frontispiece.
> Vol. 6: *FWBT*. Part II. *THAHN*. 1964. 364 pages. Frontispiece.
> Vol. 7: *ARIT, OMATS* and Poems. 1964. 356 pages. Frontispiece.
> Note: The poems are translated from *The Collected Poems.*

Vol. 8: *AMF*. 1965. 318 pages. 8 pages of photographs. Note: The endpapers in this volume are street maps of Paris in gray and white.

KOREAN

15 *Bada wa Noin (OMATS)*. [Seoul]: Jang Won Sa, 1957. 175 pages. Translated by Bong-Hwa Chung. Afterword on pp. 170-175.

16 *Mugiyeo jal itgeora (FTA)*. Seoul: Lee In Seok & Choe Ki Seon, 1958. Translated by Beo-Mun Gak.

17 *Bada wa Noin (OMATS)*. [Seoul]: Shin Yang Sa, 1958. 140 pages. Translated by Hwang Chan Ho.

18 *Mugiyeo jal itgeora (FTA)*. Seoul: Tong-a Sa, 1959. [World Masterpieces, 12.] 512 pages. Translated by Byung-Chul Kim. In the same volume: *Sanctuary* and *Red Leaves* by William Faulkner, translated by Koh Sukkoo.

19 *Mu'gi'yeo jal'it'geo'ra (FTA)*. Seoul: Mun Ho Sa, 1959. Translated by Byung-Chul Kim.

20 *Kilimanjaro eui nun* ("The Snows of Kilimanjaro" and eight other short stories). Seoul: Yang Mun Sa, 1959. 197 pages. Translated by Byung-Chul Kim.

21 *Gang'geon'neo sub'sog'eu'ro (ARIT)*. Seoul, 1959. Translated by Kwang-Mug Jo.

22 *Hemingway dan'pyon'jib (TFC & First 49)*. Seoul: Yeo Weon Sa, 1959. Translated by Chul-Mo Lee.

23 *Hae neun ddo dasi ddeo oreunda (SAR)*. Seoul: Yang Mun Sa, 1960. 259 pages. Translated by Byung-Chul Kim.

24 *Mugiyeo jal itgeora (FTA)*. Seoul: Bum Mun Sa, 1960. 302 pages. Translated by Gim Hae-dong.

25 *Nugureul wihayeo jongeun ulina (FWBT)*. Seoul: Chung Um Sa, 1962. [World Masterpieces, 28.] 482 pages. Translated by Bong-Hwa Chung.

26 *Wiheomhan Yeoreum* ("The Dangerous Summer"). Seoul: Sin Gum Un Hwa Sa, [1962]. 230 pages. Translated by Se-il Sen.

27 *Yeoja-eobsnun Segye (MWW)*. Seoul: Yeongmun-gag, [1962]. 226 pages. Translated by Sag Lee.

28 *Bada wa Noin (OMATS)*. Seoul: Cheong San Mun-Hwa Sa, [1963]. 105 pages. Translated by Jae-myeong Gim.

LATVIAN

29 *Ardievas ieročiem (FTA)*. Örebro, Sweden: Parnass, 1949. 280 pages.

Same: Stockholm, Sweden: Wegastift, 1949. [Parnasa Pasaules rakstnieku sefyá, 6.] Same: Riga: Latgosizdat, 1958.

230 *Vecais vīrs un jūra (OMATS)*. London: Latvju Biedrības Lielbritānijā, 1957. 93 pages. Translated by Jānis Andrups.

MALAYAN

231 *Orang Tua děngan Laut (OMATS)*. Kuala Lumpur: Oxford University Press, 1961. 127 pages. Translated by Abdullah Hussain. Foreword by the translator, on pp. v-xi.

NORWEGIAN

232 *Og solen går sin gang (SAR)*. Oslo: Gyldendal, 1929. 249 pages. Translated by Gunnar Larsen. Foreword by Sigurd Hoel, on pp. 5-8.

233 *Farvel til våpnene (FTA)*. Oslo: Gyldendal, 1930. 348 pages. Translated by Herman Wildenvey. Foreword by Sigurd Hoel, on pp. 5-8. Reissued: 1955, 320 pages. [Gyldendals Gyldne Bibliotek, 86.]

234 *Den ene mot de mange (THAHN)*. Oslo: Gyldendal, 1938. Translated by Gunnar Larsen. Foreword by Sigurd Hoel. Reissued: 1952, 208 pages. (No foreword.)

235 *Klokkene ringer for deg (FWBT)*. Oslo: Gyldendal, 1946. 706 pages. Translated by Paul Gauguin. Foreword by Sigurd Hoel, on pp. 1-6. Reissued: 1958, 2 volumes; 231 pages, 255 pages. (No foreword.)

236 *Samlede noveller (First 49)*. Oslo: Gyldendal, 1947. 410 pages. Translated by Gunnar Larsen. Foreword by the translator, on pp. [3]-[4].

237 *Over floden og inn i skogene (ARIT)*. Oslo: Gyldendal, 1951. 212 pages. Translated by Gunnar Larsen.

238 *Den gamle mannen og havet (OMATS)*. Oslo: Gyldendal, 1952. 142 pages. Translated by Leo Strom.

239 *Samlede romaner og fortellinger*. Eight-volume set. Oslo: Gyldendal, 1951-1952.

240 *Noveller (First 49)*. 2 volumes. Oslo: Gyldendal, 1952. Translated by Paul Gauguin.

241 *Sneen på Kilimanjaro og andre noveller* ("The Snows of Kilimanjaro" and fifteen other short stories). Oslo: Gyldendal, 1953. [Gyldendals Gyldne Bibliotek, 21.] 238 pages. Translated by Gunnar Larsen.

242 *Afrikas grönne fjell (GHOA)*. Oslo: Gyldendal, 1955. 228 pages. Illustrated. Translated by Nils Lie.

243 *Döden om ettermiddagen (DIA)*. Oslo: Gyldendal, 1963. Translated by Nils Lie.

244 *En varig fest: Unge dager i Paris (AMF)*. Oslo: Gyldendal, 1964. 179 pages. Translated by Nils Lie.

PERSIAN

245 *Vedā'bā aslaḥe (FTA)*. Teheran: Sāzmān-e Ketābhā-ye Jībī, 1961. 276 pages. Translated by Najaf-e Daryā-bandarī.

246 *Be rāh-e xarābāt dar čub-f tāk (ARIT)*. Teheran: Pocket Books, [1961]. 232 pages. Translated by Parviz Dāryuš.

247 *Xoršid hamcŏnān midaraxšad (SAR)*. Teheran: Pocket Books, [1961]. 263 pages. Translated by Rezā Moqaddam.

248 *Dāštan o nadāštan (THAHN)*. Teheran: Pocket Books, 1961. 206 pages. Translated by Parviz Dāryuš.

249 *Mard-e pir o daryā (OMATS)*. Teheran: Ma'refat, 1961. Translated by M. X. Yahyavi.

250 *Az pā nayoftāde va do dāstān-e digar* ("The Undefeated" and two other short stories). Teheran: Morvārid, 1963. 118 pages. Translated by Sirus Tāhbāz.

POLISH

251 *Pożegnanie z bronią (FTA)*. Warsaw: Roj, 1931. Translated by Zbigniew Grabowski.

252 *Statek śmierci (THAHN)*. Warsaw: "Plan," 1938. Translated by Teresa Rogala-Zawadska. Reissued as *Biedni i bogaci*. Warsaw: S. Cukrowski, 1948.

253 *Stary czlowiek i morze (OMATS)*. Warsaw: Państwowy Instytut Wydawniczy, 1955. 88 pages. Translated by Bronislaw Zieliński. Foreword: "Baśń Hemingwaya" by Andrzej Kijowski, on pp. 5-8. Reissued: 1962, 98 pages. (No foreword.)

254 *Śniegi Kilimandżaro i inne opowiadania* ("The Snows of Kilimanjaro" and twenty-two other short stories). Warsaw: Państwowy Instytut Wydawniczy, 1956. 349 pages. Translated by Mira Michalowska, Jan Zakrzewski, and Bronislaw Zieliński. Foreword by Bronislaw Zieliński, on pp. 5-[10].

255 *Pożegnanie z bronią (FTA)*. Warsaw: Państwowy Instytut Wydawniczy, 1957. 349 pages. Translated by Bronislaw Zieliński.

256 *Komu bije dzwon* *(FWBT)*. Warsaw: Czytelnik, 1957. 579 pages. Translated by Bronislaw Zieliński. Reissued: 1961. 2 volumes. [Biblioteka Powszechna, 53 and 54.] 344 pages, 239 pages.

257 *Słońce też wschodzi (SAR)*. Warsaw: Państwowy Instytut Wydawniczy, 1957. 275 pages. Translated by Bronislaw Zieliński.

258 *Mieć i nie mieć (THAHN)*. Warsaw: Czytelnik, 1958. Translated by Krystyna Tarnowska.

259 *Zielone wzgórza Afryki (GHOA)*. Warsaw: Iskry, 1959. 250 pages. Illustrated. Translated by Bronislaw Zieliński.

260 *Za rzekę w cień drzew (ARIT)*. Warsaw: Państwowy Instytut Wydawniczy, 1961. 274 pages. [Klub interesującej Książki, 4.] Translated by Bronislaw Zieliński.

261 *Rogi byka i inne opowiadania* ("The Capital of the World" and twenty-four other short stories). Warsaw: Państwowy Instytut Wydawniczy, 1961. 220 pages. Translated by Bronislaw Zieliński. Preface by Hemingway, translated from the *First 49*, on pp. 5-[6].

262 *Rzeka dwóch serc, i inne opowiadania* ("Big Two-Hearted River" and eleven other short stories). Warsaw: Państwowy Instytut Wydawniczy, 1962. 183 pages. Translated by Mira Michalowska, Jan Zakrzewski and Bronislaw Zieliński. Foreword by Jerzy R. Krzyżanowski, on pp. 5-[14].

263 *Ruchome święto (AMF)*. Warsaw: Czytelnik, 1966. 162 pages. Illustrated. Translated by Bronislaw Zieliński.

PORTUGUESE

264 *Adeus às armas (FTA)*. São Paulo: Editora Nacional, 1942. 247 pages. Translated by Monteiro Lobato.

265 *Por quem os sinos dobram (FWBT)*. São Paulo: Editora Nacional, [1944]. 417 pages. Translated by Monteiro Lobato.

266 *Uma aventura na Martinica (THAHN)*. São Paulo: Editora Cúpolo, 1945. [Coleção Seculo, 20.] 214 pages. Translated by Aidano Arruda.

267 *O sol também se levanta (SAR)*. Rio de Janeiro: Cruzeiro, 1946. 253 pages. Translated by Luiz Alípio de Barros.

268 *Os melhores contos* (eleven short stories). Lisbon: Editorial Hélio, 1947. [Coleção Antologia, 9.] 222 pages. Translated and edited with notes by Elisio Correia Ribeiro.

269 *Do outro lado do rio, entre as árvores (ARIT)*. Rio de Janeiro: Mérito, 1951. 342 pages. Translated by José Geraldo Vieira.

70 *Fiesta (SAR)*. Lisbon: Editora Ulisseia, 1954. 253 pages. Translated by Jorge de Sena. Foreword by the translator, on pp. 7-17.

71 *O Adeus às Armas (FTA)*. Lisbon: Editora Ulisseia, 1954. 354 pages. Translated by Adolfo Casais Monteiro. Foreword by the translator, on pp. [7]-[14].

72 *As neves de Kilimanjaro* ("The Snows of Kilimanjaro"). Lisbon: Livros do Brasil, 1954. [Miniatura, 46.] 135 pages. Translated by José Correia Ribeiro.

73 *O velho e o mar (OMATS)*. Lisbon: Livros do Brasil, 1954. [Miniatura, 41.] 123 pages. Translated by Fernando de Castro Ferro.

74 *Ter e não ter (THAHN)*. Lisbon: Livros do Brasil, 1955. [Miniatura, 53.] Translated by Jorge de Sena.

75 *Por quem os sinos dobram (FWBT)*. Lisbon: Livros do Brasil, 1955. [Dois Mundos, 24.] Translated by Monteiro Lobato and Alfredo Margarido.

76 *O velho e o mar (OMATS)*. Rio de Janeiro: Civilização Brasileira, 1956. Translated by Fernando de Castro Ferro.

77 *Cinquenta mil dólares* ("Fifty Grand"). Lisbon: Fomento de Publicações, [1958]. [Mosaico, 34.]

78 *A Capital do mundo e outras historias* ("The Capital of the World" and four other short stories). Lisbon: Livros do Brasil, 1959. [Miniatura, 101.] Translated by Virgínia Motta and Alexandre Pinheiro Torres.

79 *As verdes Colinas de Africa (GHOA)*. Lisbon: Livros do Brasil, [1960]. [Dois Mundos, 54.] 278 pages. Translated by Guilherme de Castilho.

80 *Um gata à chuva* ("Cat in the Rain"). Lisbon: Livros do Brasil, [1960]. Translated by Alexandre Pinheiro Torres.

81 *Na outra margem entre as árvores (ARIT)*. Lisbon: Livros do Brasil, [1962]. Translated by João Palma Ferreira.

82 *Paris é uma Festa (AMF)*. Lisbon: Livros do Brasil, 1966. [Dois Mundos, 90.]

RUMANIAN

83 *Nuvele* (four short stories). Bucharest: Editura de Stat Pentru Literatură şi Arta, 1958. 133 pages. Translated by I. Buieş. Foreword by Dan Grigorescu, on pp. 3-14.

84 *Coloana a cincea (TFC)*. Bucharest: Lit. Tip. Inv., 1960. 96 pages. Illustrated. Translated by Mircea Alexandrescu.

285 *Bătrînul și marea (OMATS)*. Bucharest: Editura Tineretului, 1960. 88 pages. Translated by Mircea Alexandrescu and Costache Popa.

286 *Adio, arme—A avea și a nuavéa (FTA, THAHN)*. Bucharest: Editura Pentru Literatură Universală, 1961. 568 pages. Translated by Radu Lupan.

RUSSIAN AND OTHER SLAVIC TRANSLATIONS

287 *Smert' Posle Poludnya* (selections from *DIA* and three other books). Edited and with an Introduction by Ivan Kashkin. Moscow: Goslitizdat, 1934.

288 *Fiyesta (SAR)*. Moscow: Goslitizdat, 1935. Translated by V. Toper. Afterword by N. Gorin, on pp. 222-[224].

289 *Proshchai oruzhiye (FTA)*. Moscow: Goslitizdat, 1936. Translated by E. Kalašhnikova. Foreword by Serge Dinamov.

290 *Imet' i Ne Imet' (THAHN)*. Moscow: Goslitizdat, 1938. Translated by E. Kalašhnikova. Foreword by I. Anisimov.

291 *Pjataja kolonna i Pervye Tridcat' Vosem' Rasskazov (TFC* and thirty-eight stories). Moscow: Goslitizdat, 1939.

292 *Starik i more (OMATS)*. Moscow: Gos. izd-vo detskoi lit-ry, 1956. 95 pages. Frontispiece. Translated by E. Golyseva and B. Izakova. Foreword on p. [3]. Reissued: Moscow: Pravda, 1956. Kiev: Goslitizdat Ukrainy, 1956.

293 *P'jata kolona (TFC)*. Kiev: Goslitizdat Ukrainy, 1957. 125 pages. Translated into Ukrainian by N. Kalacevskaja.

294 *Starik i more (OMATS)*. Erevan: Aipetrat, 1957. Translated into Armenian by V. Mikaeljan.

295 *Bétrynul ši marja (OMATS)*. Kishinev: Goslitizdat Moldavii, 1958. Translated into Moldavian by M. Aleksandresku and I. Toma.

296 *Izbrannye proizvedenija*. 2 volumes. (*SAR, FTA, THAHN, OMATS, TFC, TSE*, the 49 short stories, excerpts from *DIA, GHOA*, and a selection of Hemingway's articles). Moscow: Goslitizdat, 1959. 734 pages. By various translators. Edited and with an Introduction by Ivan Kashkin, on pp. 3-38.

297 *Zelenye kholmy Afriki (GHOA)*. Moscow: Geografgiz, 1959. Translated by V. A. Khinkis.

298 *Godža vä däniz (OMATS)*. Baku: Azernešr, 1959. Translated into Azerbaijan by Dž. Mämädzaoá.

299 *Godža ve den'iz (OMATS)*. Ashkhabad: Turkmengosizdat, 1959. Translated into Turkmenian by Hadzy Nyjazov.

00 *Proshchai oruzhie!* *(FTA)*. Moscow: 1961. 285 pages. Translated by M. Urnova. Foreword on pp. 5-15.

01 *Za rekoĭ, v teni derev'ev (ARIT)*. Moscow: Izd. inostrannaya literatura, 1961. 214 pages. Translated by E. Golysheva and B. Izakova.

02 *Älvida, silah!* *(FTA)*. Baku: Detjunizdat, 1961. 346 pages. Translated into Azerbaijan by Hadžy Hadžyjev.

03 *Atsisveikinimas su ginklais (FTA)*. Vilna: Goslitizdat, [1961]. 363 pages. Translated into Lithuanian by G. Bekerytė and R. Lankauskas.

04 *Za rikoju, v zatinku derev (ARIT)*. Kiev: Rad. pis'mennik, 1961. 258 pages. Translated by K. Suhenko and N. Tarasenko.

SLOVAK

05 *Sbohom, Armáda!* *(FTA)*. Bratislava: J. Tokárová-Menyhartová, 1948. Translated by Pal'o Orth.

06 *Starec a more (OMATS)*. Bratislava: Slovenský Spisovateľ, 1956. 111 pages. Translated by Peter Javor. Glossary on p. 111.

07 *Starec a more (OMATS)*. Bratislava: Slovenské Vydavateľstvo Krásná Literatúry, [1957]. [Malá Svetová Knižnica, 15.] Translated by Peter Ždán.

08 *Komu zvonia do hrobu (FWBT)*. Bratislava: Slovenský Spisovateľ, 1959. 496 pages. Translated by Alfonz Bednár. Afterword: "Ernest Hemingway a jeho hrdina" by Jaroslav Schejbal on pp. 485-496.

09 *Mať a nemať (THAHN)*. Bratislava: Slovenské Vydavateľstvo Krásná Literatúry, 1962. 194 pages. Translated by Miloš Ruppeldt. Afterword by the translator on pp. 191–[194].

10 *Poviedky* (short stories). Bratislava: Krásná literatura, 1962.

11 *Zbohom zbraniam (FTA)*. Bratislava: Slovenský Spisovateľ, 1964. 269 pages. Translated by Alfonz Bednár. Afterword by Josef Kot on pp. 265-269.

SPANISH

12 *Adiós a las armas (FTA)*. Buenos Aires: Kraft, 1940. 310 pages. Translated by Héctor Pedro Blomberg. Reissued: Buenos Aires: Editorial Claridad, 1955. 286 pages. Foreword: "Tiempo y ambiente de Hemingway" by Alfredo Casey on pp. 5-24.

13 *Por quien doblan las campanas (FWBT)*. Buenos Aires: S.A.D.E., 1942. 454 pages. Illustrated. Translated by Eduardo Johnson Seguí.

314 *Por quien doblan las campanas* (*FWBT*). Buenos Aires: Editorial Claridad, 1944. 500 pages. Translated by Olga Sanz. Same: Mexico City: Editorial Diana, 1948.

315 *Fiesta* (*SAR*). Buenos Aires: Santiago Rueda, 1944. 267 pages. Translated by José Mora Guarnido and John E. Hausner. Same: Barcelona: Janés, 1948. 350 pages. Reissued: Barcelona: El Club de los Lectores, 1955.

316 *Tener y no tener* (*THAHN*). Buenos Aires: Editorial Sudamericana, 1945. 282 pages. Translated by Pedro Ibarzábal.

317 *Torrentes de primavera* (*TOS*). Barcelona: Ediciones Albón, 1946. 160 pages. Translated by Enrique Romero. Also contains "El torero" ("The Undefeated") on pp. 119-160.

318 *La vida feliz de Francis Macomber* ("The Short Happy Life of Francis Macomber" and other short stories). Buenos Aires: Santiago Rueda, 1948. 287 pages. Translated by Francisco Brumat.

319 *La quinta columna* (*TFC* and twenty-six short stories). Buenos Aires: Santiago Rueda, 1950. 329 pages. Translated by Carlos Foresti.

320 *Al otro lado del río y entre los árboles* (*ARIT*). Buenos Aires: G. Kraft, 1952. 322 pages. [Colección Vertice.] Translated by Manuel Gurrea.

321 *El viejo y el mar (OMATS*). Buenos Aires: G. Kraft, 1954. 168 pages. Translated by Lino Novás Calvo.

322 *Adiós a las armas* (*FTA*). Barcelona: Luis de Caralt, 1955. 318 pages. Translated by Joaquim Horta. Reissued: 1957. 334 pages. [Colección Gigante.] Reissued: 1964. 315 pages.

323 *Las nieves del Kilimanjaro* ("The Snows of Kilimanjaro" and fourteen other short stories). Barcelona: Luis de Caralt, 1955. 180 pages. Translated by José María Cañas. Reissued: 1963. 155 pages.

324 *Fiesta (SAR)*. Barcelona: Luis de Caralt, 1956. Translated by José Mora Guarnido and John E. Hausner. Reissued: 1962. 208 pages.

325 *Los asesinos* ("The Killers" and eighteen other short stories). Barcelona: Luis de Caralt, 1956. Reissued: 1965. 159 pages.

326 *Relatos* (thirty-two short stories). Barcelona: Luis de Caralt, 1957. [Colección Gigante.] Reissued: 1965. 440 pages.

327 *Ahora brilla el sol (SAR*). Buenos Aires: Mariel, 1958. Translated by José Mora Guarnido and John E. Hausner.

8 *Agurea ta Itxasoa (OMATS)*. Zarautz, Guipúzcoa: Editorial Icharopena, 1962. [Kuliska Sorta, 52.] 118 pages. Translated into Basque by P. Angel Goenaga. Foreword by José de Arteche on pp. 5-10.

SWEDISH

9 *Och solen går sin gång (SAR)*. Stockholm: Holger Schildt, 1929. Translated by Bertel Gripenberg.

0 *Farväl till vapnen (FTA)*. Stockholm: Bonnier, 1932. 361 pages. Translated by Louis Renner. Foreword by Sten Selander. Reissued: Stockholm: Åhlén & Åkerlund, 1941. Stockholm: Forum, 1947. [Forum-Bibliotek, 25.]

1 *Att ha och inte ha (THAHN)*. Stockholm: Bonnier, 1939. 252 pages. Translated by Thorsten Jonsson. Reissued: Stockholm: Svalan (Bonnier), 1952. Stockholm: Bonnier, 1958. [Bonniers Folkbibliotek.]

2 *Klockan klämtar för dig (FWBT)*. Stockholm: Bonnier, 1941. 486 pages. Translated by Thorsten Jonsson. Foreword by Anders Österling, on pp. 5-6. Reissued: Stockholm: Forum, 1949. Helsingfors: Söderström, [1957].

3 *Snön på Kilimandjaro och andra noveller* ("The Snows of Kilimanjaro" and other short stories). Stockholm: Bonnier, 1942. Translated by Thorsten Jonsson.

4 *Och solen har sin gång (SAR)*. Stockholm: Bonnier, 1947. Translated by Olov Jonason. Reissued: Stockholm: Aldus/Bonnier, 1961. [Delfinböckerna, 3.]

5 *Över floden in bland träden (ARIT)*. Stockholm: Bonnier, 1951. 278 pages. Translated by Mårten Edlund. Reissued: Stockholm: Svalan (Bonnier), 1954.

6 *Den gamle och havet (OMATS)*. Stockholm: Bonnier, 1952. 124 pages. Translated by Mårten Edlund. Reissued: 1963. 96 pages. Illustrated by C. F. Tunnicliffe and Raymond Sheppard.

7 *Den gamle och havet—Fyra noveller ur Snön på Kilimandjaro* (*OMATS* and "The Snows of Kilimanjaro"). Stockholm: Bonnier, 1954. Translated by Mårten Edlund.

8 *Afrikas gröna berg (GHOA)*. Stockholm: Bonnier, 1954. Illustrated by Erik Palmquist. Translated by Mårten Edlund. Reissued: Stockholm: Aldus/Bonnier, 1962. [Delfinböckerna, 65.] 193 pages.

9 *Noveller (First 49)*. Stockholm: Bonnier, 1955. 372 pages. Translated by Mårten Edlund and Thorsten Jonsson. Preface by Hem-

ingway, on pp. 9-[10], translated from the *First 49* by Mårten Edlund.

340 *Döden på eftermiddagen (DIA)*. Stockholm: Bonnier, 1958. 387 pages. Illustrated. Translated by Arne Häggqvist.

341 *Vårflod (TOS)*. Stockholm: Bonnier, 1962. 156 pages. Translated by Olov Jonason. Same: Helsingfors: Schildt, 1962.

342 *En fest för livet (AMF)*. Stockholm: Bonnier, 1964. 201 pages. Translated by Pelle Fritz-Crone.

TURKISH

343 *Asla vedalaşmıyacağiz (ARIT)*. Istanbul: M. Sıralar, 1951. Translated by Semih Yazıcıoğlu. Reissued: Istanbul: Bolat Kitabevi, 1956.

344 *İhtıyar balıkçı (OMATS)*. Istanbul: Varlık Yayınevi, 1953. Translated by Orhan Azizoğlu.

345 *Elli bin dolar* ("Fifty Grand" and other short stories). Istanbul: Varlık Yayınevi, 1953. Translated by Türköz Taga and Mustafa Yurdakul.

346 *Silâhlara veda (FTA)*. Istanbul: Ekicigil Basımevi, 1954. Translated by Erçetin Tümay.

347 *Vatan sana ne der?* ("Che Ti Dice La Patria?" and other short stories). Istanbul: Varlık Yayınevi, 1954. Translated by Tunç Yalman, Vahdet Gültekin, and Mustafa Yurdakul.

348 *Denizin değistirdiği* ("The Sea Change"). Istanbul: Kutulmuş Basımevi, 1954. Translated by Mehmet Fuat.

349 *Güneş de doğar (SAR)*. Istanbul: Varlık Yayınevi, 1955. Translated by Filiz Karabey.

350 *İspanya geceleri (SAR)*. Istanbul: Çağlayan Yayınevi, 1955. Translated by Nil Serdar.

351 *Afrıka'nın yeşil tepeleri (GHOA)*. Istanbul: Varlık Yayınevi, 1955. Translated by Filiz Karabey.

352 *Kilimanjaro'nun karları* ("The Snows of Kilimanjaro" and other stories). Istanbul: Varlık Yayınevi, 1956. Translated by M. Zeki Gülsoy.

353 *Yine sabah oldu (SAR)*. Istanbul: Arif Bolat Kitabevi, [1957]. Translated by Vahdet Gültekin.

354 *Silâhlara veda (FTA)*. Istanbul: Güven Yayınevi, 1958. 368 pages. Translated by Vahdet Gültekin.

5 *Ya hep ya hiç (THAHN)*. Istanbul: Varlık Yayınevi, 1960. 166 pages. Translated by Tarık Dursun Kakınç.

6 *Kadınsız erkekler (MWW)*. Istanbul: Ar-El Matbaası, 1960. Translated by Vahdet Gültekin.

7 *Çanlar kimin için çalıyor (FWBT)*. Istanbul: Türkiye Basımevi, [1960]. Fourth edition. 332 pages. Translated by Vahdet Gültekin.

YUGOSLAV

8 *Komu zvoni (FWBT)*. Ljubljana: Cankarjeva Založba, 1950. 528 pages. Translated into Slovenian by Janez Gradišnik. Afterword by the translator on pp. 525-527.

9 *Kome zvono zvoni (FWBT)*. Zagreb: Zora, 1952. 482 pages. Translated into Croatian by Šime Balen. Reissued: 1954. Frontispiece. Afterword by the translator on pp. 473-478.

10 *Prestonica sveta* (short stories). Novi Sad: Matica Srpska, 1952. [Mozaik, 10.] Translated into Serbian by Vera Ilić and Aleksandar Nejgebauer.

11 *Zbogom oružje (FTA)*. Zagreb: Mladost, 1952. Translated into Croatian by Branko Kojić.

12 *Starac i more (OMATS)*. Zagreb: Seljačka Sloga, 1952. Translated into Croatian by Barbara Lojen.

13 *Starac i more (OMATS)*. Belgrade: Duga, 1952. Translated into Serbian by Karlo Ostojić.

14 *Za kim zvono zvoni (FWBT)*. Novi Sad: Bratstvo-Jedinstvo, 1952. 468 pages. Translated into Serbian by Svetozar Brkič. Afterword on pp. 459-468. Same: Belgrade: Kultura, 1961. 451 pages.

15 *Snegovi Kilimandžara, i druge pripovetke* ("The Snows of Kilimanjaro" and other short stories). Belgrade: Novo Pokolenje, 1953. Translated into Serbian by Vera Ilić.

16 *Sunce se ponovo radja (SAR)*. Belgrade: Novo Pokolenje, 1953. Translated into Serbian by Radmila Todorović.

17 *Imati i nemati (THAHN)*. Belgrade: Omladina, 1954. [Biblioteka Plava knjija, 2.] 260 pages. Frontispiece. Translated into Serbian by Ljubica Vuković and Jelena Stojanović. Afterword on pp. 247-259.

18 *Sunce se ponovo radja—Starac i more (SAR, OMATS)*. Belgrade: Omladina, 1954. 424 pages. Translated into Serbian by Kaliopa Nikolajević and Karlo Ostojić. Afterword on pp. 419-423.

369 *Starec in morje* (*OMATS*). Ljubljana: Državna Založba Slovenije, 1955. Translated into Slovenian by Janez Gradišnik. New edition: Ljubljana: Mladinska Knjiga, 1959. 102 pages. Illustrated by Marij Pregelj. Afterword: "O ideji in kompoziciji Hemingwayeve novele *Starec in morje*" by Dusan Pirjevec, on pp. 87-98. Brief biography and a glossary by the translator on pp. 99-102.

370 *Preko reke i u šumu* (*ARIT*). Subotica: Minerva, 1956. [Biblioteka Minerva, 22.] 256 pages. Translated into Croatian by Predrag Milojević.

371 *Zbogom oružhje* (*FTA*). Belgrade: Narodna Knjiga, 1957. Translated into Serbian by Radojitsa V. Ćirović.

372 *Novele* (short stories). Zagreb: Seljačka Sloga, 1957. 284 pages. Translated into Croatian by Barbara Lojen, Ivan Slamnig, and Antun Šoljan. Afterword by Antun Šoljan on pp. 273-281.

373 *Fiesta* (*SAR*). Zagreb: Znanje, 1959. 230 pages. Translated into Croatian by Stanislav Simić.

374 *Zbogum na oružjeto* (*FTA*). Skoplje: Kultura, 1959. 326 pages. Translated into Macedonian by Gane Todorovski. Foreword by the translator, on pp. i-viii.

375 *Starac i more—Snegovi Kilimandžara* (*OMATS* and "The Snows of Kilimanjaro"). Belgrade: Narodna Knjiga, 1959. Translated into Serbian by Karlo Ostojić and Vera Ilić.

376 *Starecot i moreto* (*OMATS*). Skoplje: Kultura, 1960. 79 pages. Translated into Macedonian by Dušan Crvenkovski.

377 *Zbogom orožje* (*FTA*). Maribor: Založba Obzorja, 1960. 372 pages. Translated into Slovenian by Uroš Vagaja. Foreword by Hemingway, on pp. 7-11, translated from the 1948 Scribner edition. Afterword: "Pričevanje Ernesta Hemingwaya" by Rado Bordon, on pp. 343-364. Glossary on pp. 365-372. Reissued: 1964, 380 pages. Revised afterword on pp. 339-368.

378 *Proletnje bujice* (*TOS*). Belgrade: Mlado Pọkolenje, 1961. [Biblioteka Apolo, 5.] 148 pages. Translated into Serbian by Saša Petrović. Afterword by Aleksander I. Spasić on pp. 119-[148].

379 *Priče o Niku* ("Tales of Nick"). Belgrade: Mlado Pọkolenje, 1961. 144 pages. Translated into Serbian by Vera Ilić.

380 *Starac i more* (*OMATS*). Belgrade: Branko Donović, 1963. [Knjiga za svakoga, 47.] 154 pages. Translated into Croatian by Živojin Simić. Foreword: "Ernest Hemingvej ili čovek u borbi sa sudbinom" by Dragan M. Jeremić on pp. 7-75.

1 *Sonce vzhaja in zahaja (SAR)*. Maribor: Založba Obzorja, 1964. 247 pages. Translated into Slovenian by Bruno Hartman and Uroš Vagaja.

2 *Pokretni praznik (AMF)*. Belgrade: Prosveta, 1964. 236 pages. Translated into Serbian by Aleksandar V. Stefanovic. Foreword by Hemingway on p. 11, translated from the Scribner edition. Afterword by the translator, on pp. 229-236.

SECTION E

ANTHOLOGIES

This section is listed chronologically, and is alphabetized within each year by the editor's name or, if no editor is given, by the title of the collection. Various editions are listed and any changes in the pagination or title of the collection are noted. A change in the selection of the story is also noted. In some cases this change was necessary to conform with Scribner's permissions' policy. Since 1958, Hemingway's publishers have limited the inclusion of his short stories to one selection in an anthology.

The nucleus of this list was drawn from the *Short Story Index*, compiled by Dorothy E. Cook and Isabel S. Munro, New York: H. W. Wilson, 1953.

E1 *The Best Short Stories of 1923 and the Yearbook of the American Short Story*. Edited by Edward J. O'Brien. Boston: Small, Maynard, 1924.
Contains "My Old Man." For description, see (B1).

2 *The Best Poems of 1923*. Edited by L. A. G. Strong. Boston: Small, Maynard, 1924.
Contains "Chapter Heading." For description, see (B2).

3 *Contact Collection of Contemporary Writers*. Paris: Three Mountains Press, 1925.
First book appearance of "Soldier's Home." See (B3).

4 *Transatlantic Stories: Selected from the Transatlantic Review*. With an Introduction by Ford Madox Ford. London: Duckworth, 1926. [New York: Dial Press, 1926.]
pp. 213-219: "The Doctor and the Doctor's Wife," which first appeared in the *Transatlantic Review*, II (Dec. 1924), is titled here "A Story."

5 *The Best Short Stories of 1926 and the Yearbook of the American Short Story*. Edited by Edward J. O'Brien. New York: Dodd, Mead, 1926.
First book appearance of "The Undefeated." See (B4).

6 *The American Caravan: A Yearbook of American Literature*. Edited by Van Wyck Brooks, Lewis Mumford, Alfred Kreymborg, and Paul Rosenfeld. New York: Macaulay, 1927.
First book appearance of "An Alpine Idyll." See (B5).

7 *Contemporary Short Stories*. Edited by Gordon Hall Gerould and Charles Bayly, Jr. New York and London: Harper, 1927.
p. 234: Ch. VIII of *iot*, titled here "A Separate Peace." Note: The school edition, titled *Contemporary Types of the Short Story*, has the same pagination.

8 *The Best Short Stories of 1927 and the Yearbook of the American Short Story.* Edited by Edward J. O'Brien. New York: Dodd, Mead, 1927.
pp. 40-49: "The Killers." Comments by the editor on pp. ix and x of the Introduction.

9 *Samples: A Collection of Short Stories.* Compiled for the Community Workers of the New York Guild for the Jewish Blind by Lillie Ryttenberg and Beatrice Lang. New York: Boni & Liveright, 1927.
pp. 280-297: "My Old Man."

10 *Prose Models: For Use with Classes in English Composition.* Edited by Edwin Long Beck and William Lucius Graves. Boston: D. C. Heath, 1928.
pp. 101-109: Part I of "Big Two-Hearted River."

11 *Anthologie de la nouvelle poésie américaine.* By Eugène Jolas. Paris: Simon Kra, 1928.
pp. 102-103: Hemingway's poem "Montparnasse" translated into French. Biographical note on p. 102. Note: First edition of 100 numbered copies.

12 *Short Story Writing.* Edited by Mary Burchard Orvis. New York: Ronald Press, 1928.
pp. 173-184: "The Killers."

13 *A Book of Modern Short Stories.* Edited by Dorothy Brewster. New York: Macmillan, 1928.
pp. 393-403: "The Killers."

14 *O. Henry Memorial Award Prize Stories of 1927.* Chosen by the Society of Arts and Sciences, with an Introduction by Blanche Colton Williams. Garden City, N.Y.: Doubleday, Doran, 1928. [Also issued, as Vol. IV, in a paperbound series.]
pp. 15-24: "The Killers." Note: Hemingway was awarded second prize for this story. See (H91).

15 *Modern American and British Short Stories.* Edited by Leonard Brown. New York: Harcourt, Brace, 1929.
pp. 310-322: "The Killers." Editor's Note on p. 310. Note: Reissued in 1937 under the title *Modern Short Stories*; same pagination.

16 *Creating the Short Story: A Symposium-Anthology.* Edited by Henry Goodman. New York: Harcourt, Brace, 1929.
pp. 121-134: "The Killers." For description, see (B6).

7 *Significant Contemporary Stories.* Edited by Edith Mirrielees. Garden City, N.Y.: Doubleday, Doran, 1929.

pp. 140-151: "The Killers."

8 *The Dance of the Machines: The American Short Story and the Industrial Age.* Edited by Edward J. O'Brien. New York: Macaulay, 1929.

pp. 240-241: Ch. vi and Ch. viii of *iot*, and commentary by the editor.

9 *Present-Day American Stories.* New York: Scribner's, 1929.

pp. 221-277: "The Undefeated."

20 *Great Short Stories of the War: England, France, Germany, America.* Introduction by Edmund Blunden. London: Eyre & Spottiswoode, 1930.

pp. 907-913: "In Another Country." Note: The large paper first edition was limited to 250 numbered copies on India paper, signed by Edmund Blunden.

1 *Armageddon: The World War in Literature.* Edited by Eugene Löhrke. New York and London: Jonathan Cape and Harrison Smith, 1930.

pp. 332-347: Ch. xxx of *FTA*, titled here "The Retreat from the Isonzo."

2 *Great Modern Short Stories.* Edited by Grant Overton. New York: Modern Library, 1930. [No. 168.]

p. 113: Ch. iv of *iot* serves as chapter heading for "The Three-Day Blow," on pp. 113-124.

3 *Modern Writers at Work.* Edited by Josephine K. Piercy. New York: Macmillan, 1930.

pp. 491-494: "Cat in the Rain." For description, see (B8).

4 *Great American Short Stories.* Edited by Stephen Graham. London: Ernest Benn, 1931.

pp. 913-940: "Fifty Grand." pp. 940-955: "My Old Man."

5 *Les Romanciers américains.* Edited by Victor Llona. Paris: Denoël et Steele, 1931.

pp. 198-214: "Je vous salue marie." "Now I Lay Me" translated into French by the editor.

6 *The Twenty-five Finest Short Stories.* Edited by Edward J. O'Brien. New York: Richard R. Smith, 1931. [Also published in a School Edition.]

pp. 177-190: "My Old Man."

7 *Best Short Stories of the War: An Anthology.* With an Introduc-

tion by H. M. Tomlinson. New York and London: Harper, 1931. pp. 761-766: "In Another Country."

28 *20 Best Short Stories in 20 Years as an Editor*. Edited by Ray Long. New York: Long & Smith, 1932.

pp. 4-34: "Fifty Grand." For commentary concerning the editor's rejection of this story when Hemingway submitted it to *Cosmopolitan*, see pp. 1-3. A letter from Hemingway is briefly quoted on p. 3. See (F81).

29 *Americans Abroad: An Anthology*. Edited by Peter Neagoe. The Hague, Holland: Servire Press, 1932. [London: Faber & Faber, 1932.]

pp. 184-201: "Big Two-Hearted River." Biographical note on p. 183.

30 *Modern American Short Stories*. Edited by Edward J. O'Brien. New York: Dodd, Mead, 1932. [London: Cape, 1932.]

pp. 284-313: "The Undefeated."

31 *Profile: An Anthology Collected in MCMXXXI*. Edited by Ezra Pound. Milan: Scheiwiller, 1932.

p. 80: "Neothomist Poem." First published in *Exile*, No. 1 (Spring 1927). The editor comments, on p. 80, that "*Exile* was privileged to contain his cryptic, prophetic and allusional Neothomist Poem." Note: 250 copies were printed.

32 *The Omnibus of Sport*. Edited by Grantland Rice and Harford Powel. New York: Harper, 1932.

pp. 584-611: "The Undefeated."

33 *Twentieth Century Short Stories*. Edited by Sylvia Chatfield Bates. Boston: Houghton Mifflin, 1933.

pp. 55-87: "The Undefeated." Biographical note on pp. 53-54.

34 *Capajon: Fifty-four Short Stories*. [Published 1921-1933 by Jonathan Cape.] Introduction by Edward Garnett. London: Cape, 1933.

pp. 189-194: "Hills Like White Elephants." pp. 194-204: "The Killers." pp. 205-214: "The Battler." See also the Introduction, pp. 16-17. Note: The title is the telegraphic and cable address of the publisher.

35 *Great American Short Stories: O. Henry Memorial Prize Stories, 1919-1932*. With an Introduction by Blanche Colton Williams. Garden City, N.Y.: Doubleday, Doran, 1933.

pp. 453-462: "The Killers."

36 *Creative America: An Anthology*. Chosen and edited by Ludwig Lewisohn. New York: Harper, 1933.

pp. 627-633: An excerpt from Ch. xxxvii of *FTA*, titled here "Escape."

37 *The Active Anthology*. Edited by Ezra Pound. London: Faber & Faber, 1933.
First book appearance of "They All Made Peace—What Is Peace?" See (B13).

38 *American Omnibus*. Introduction by Carl Van Doren. New York: Doubleday, Doran, 1933. [New York: Literary Guild, 1933.]
pp. 453-462: "The Killers."

39 *International Short Stories*. Edited by Virginia W. F. Church. Dallas & Chicago: Lyons & Carnahan, 1934.
pp. 387-391: "Cat in the Rain." Introductory note on p. 386.

40 *A Book of the Short Story*. Edited by Ethan Allen Cross. New York: American Book, 1934.
pp. 986-1005: "Fifty Grand." Study Notes on p. 1098.

41 *Editor's Choice*. Edited by Alfred Dashiell. New York: Putnam, 1934.
pp. 113-131: "The Gambler, the Nun, and the Radio." Dashiell was editor of *Scribner's Magazine*, where this story first appeared. See Introduction, pp. 13, 16, and commentary following the story, pp. 131-132.

42 *Amerikanskaya novella XX veka*. Edited by A. Gavrilov, I. Kashkin, N. Eishiskina, and A. Yelistratova. Moscow: Goslitizdat, 1934.
This anthology of the American Short Story of the 20th Century contains "Alpiskaya idilliya," the Russian translation of "An Alpine Idyll."

43 *Modern English Readings*. Edited by Roger S. Loomis, Donald L. Clark, and John H. Middendorf. New York: Rinehart, 1934.
pp. 700-703: "The End of Something." [Fourth edition, revised, 1942, pp. 625-628.]

44 *Modern American Prose*. Edited by Carl Van Doren. New York: Harcourt, Brace, 1934.
pp. 616-624: "The Killers."

45 *A Quarto of Modern Literature*. Edited by Leonard Brown and Porter G. Perrin. New York: Scribner's, 1935.
pp. 263-265: "After the Storm." Biographical note on p. 263. [Second edition, revised, 1940. pp. 267-269: "After the Storm." pp. 485-499: Ch. xxvii through Ch. xxxii of *FTA*, titled here "Retreat from Caporetto." Third edition, revised, 1950. pp. 81-94: "The Short Happy Life of Francis Macomber." Fourth edition, revised,

1957. pp. 97-110: "Macomber." Fifth edition, revised, 1964. pp. 85-98: "Macomber."]

46 *Study of the Short Story.* By Henry Seidel Canby and Alfred Dashiell. New York: Holt, 1935. Revised edition.

    pp. 320-332: "The Killers." See also the editors' commentary on pp. 82-83.

47 *The Great American Parade.* Garden City, N.Y.: Doubleday, 1935.

    pp. 270-280: "The Killers."

48 *Short Stories for English Courses.* Edited, with Introduction and Notes, by Rosa M. R. Mikels. New York: Scribner's, 1935. Third edition, revised.

    pp. 457-460: "A Day's Wait." Biographical note on p. 456.

49 *The Short Story Case Book.* Edited by Edward J. O'Brien. New York: Farrar & Rinehart, 1935.

    pp. 262-323: "The Undefeated." Running commentary by the editor on each page.

50 *The Third New Year: An Etude in the Key of Frankness.* Chicago: Esquire, Inc., 1935.

    First book appearance of "Notes on the Next War." See (B20).

51 *Great American Short Stories: O. Henry Memorial Prize Winning Stories, 1919–1934.* Introduction by Blanche Colton Williams. Garden City, N.Y.: Doubleday, Doran, 1935.

    pp. 453-462: "The Killers."

52 *An Approach to Literature.* Edited by Cleanth Brooks, John T. Purser, and Robert Penn Warren. New York: Appleton-Century-Crofts, 1936.

    pp. 101-104: "In Another Country." pp. 104-106: Discussion. pp. 106-111: "The Killers." [Second edition, revised, 1939. pp. 46-50: "The Killers." Questions on p. 50. Fourth edition, revised, 1964. pp. 132-135: "In Another Country." pp. 137-142: "The Killers." Discussion and Exercises on pp. 135-137, 142-143.]

53 *An Anthology of Famous American Stories.* Edited by Angus Burrell and Bennett Cerf. New York: Modern Library, 1936. [Modern Library Giant, G 77.]

    pp. 1089-97: "The Killers." pp. 1098-1112: "The Gambler, the Nun, and the Radio."

54 *American Points of View: A Reader's Guide, 1935.* Edited by William H. Cordell and Kathryn Coe Cordell. Garden City, N.Y.: Doubleday, Doran, 1936. [Text edition, 1936.]

    pp. 1-8: "Notes on the Next War." This article first appeared in

Esquire, IV (Sept. 1935). It was awarded first prize, of $200, for the best article or essay in 1935. The judges, Erskine Caldwell, Burton Rascoe, and John Gould Fletcher, give their reasons for selection on pp. xii-xiv.

55 *Stories For Men*. Edited by Charles Grayson. Boston: Little, Brown, 1936. [New York: Garden City Publishing Co., 1944.]
   pp. 250-277: "The Undefeated."

56 *American Points of View: 1936*. Edited by William H. Cordell and Kathryn Coe Cordell. Garden City, N.Y.: Doubleday, Doran, 1937.
   First book appearance of "The Malady of Power." See (B22).

57 *Blow the Man Down: The Yachtsman's Reader*. Edited by Eric Devine. Garden City, N.Y.: Doubleday, Doran, 1937.
   First book appearance of "On the Blue Water." See (B25).

58 *The Best Short Stories 1937 and the Yearbook of the American Short Story*. Edited by Edward J. O'Brien. Boston: Houghton Mifflin, 1937.
   First book appearance of "The Snows of Kilimanjaro." See (B24).

59 *The American Mind: Selections from the Literature of the United States*. Edited by Harry R. Warfel, Ralph H. Gabriel, and Stanley T. Williams. New York: American Book, 1937.
   pp. 1437-42: "The Killers." Introductory note on p. 1437. [Second edition, 1963. Vol. II. pp. 1463-68.]

60 *Woollcott's Second Reader*. Edited by Alexander Woollcott. New York: Viking Press, 1937.
   pp. 639-657: "Big Two-Hearted River." Afterword on pp. 658-659. Note: Large paper first edition, not exceeding 1500 copies.

61 *The Oxford Anthology of American Literature*. Vol. II. Chosen and edited by William Rose Benét and Norman Holmes Pearson. New York: Oxford Univ. Press, 1938.
   pp. 1460-74: "The Undefeated." Biographical and critical commentary on pp. 1633-34.

62 *War or Peace*. Edited by Alfred Brant and Frederick H. Law. New York: Harper, 1938.
   pp. 171-178: Excerpt from Ch. xxx of *FTA*, titled here "Retreat."

63 *Interpretative Reporting*. By Curtis D. MacDougall. New York: Macmillan, 1938.
   pp. 254-255: Hemingway's NANA dispatch, from Madrid, April 24, 1937, is partially reprinted. It appeared in the *N.Y. Times* (April 25, 1937).

64 *The Literature of America: An Anthology of Prose and Verse.* Vol. II: *From the Civil War to the Present.* Edited by Arthur Hobson Quinn, Albert Croll Baugh, and Will David Howe. New York: Scribner's, 1938.

pp. 1335-39: "The Killers." Biographical note, N 57.

65 *The Story Workshop.* By Wilbur L. Schramm. Boston: Little, Brown, 1938.

pp. 135-147: "The Killers." Brief commentary on each page. Introductory note on p. 135.

66 *This Generation: A Selection of British and American Literature from 1914 to the Present.* Edited by George K. Anderson and Eda Lou Walton. Chicago: Scott, Foresman, 1939.

pp. 448-453: "The Killers." Commentary on pp. 447-448.

67 *The Story Survey.* Edited by Harold W. Blodgett. Philadelphia: Lippincott, 1939. [Revised edition, 1953.]

pp. 215-219: "After the Storm." Commentary on p. 214.

68 *The Bedside Book of Famous American Stories.* Edited by John A. Burrell and Bennett A. Cerf. New York: Random House, 1939.

pp. 1130-38: "The Killers." pp. 1139-53: "The Gambler, the Nun, and the Radio." Biographical note on pp. 1270-71.

69 *Poeti Ameriki XX veka.* Selected and translated by Ivan Kashkeen and Michael Zenkevitch. Introduction by Ivan Kashkeen. Moscow: Goslitizdat, 1939. Photograph.

p. 219: Hemingway's poem "Montparnasse," translated into Russian, is included in this anthology of American Poets of the 20th Century. Two chapters of *iot* are reprinted, on pp. 217-218.

70 *Short Stories.* Edited by William Thomson Hastings and Benjamin Crocker Clough. Boston: Houghton Mifflin, 1939. Revised edition.

pp. 388-401: "My Old Man."

71 *Tellers of Tales: One Hundred Short Stories from the United States, England, France, Russia, and Germany.* Selected and with an Introduction by W. Somerset Maugham. New York: Doubleday, Doran, 1939.

pp. 1170-78: "The Killers."

72 *Five Kinds of Writing.* Edited by Theodore Morrison *et al.* Boston: Little, Brown, 1939.

pp. 172-181: "Dispatches from Spain." For list of dispatches and description of this book, see (B35). pp. 543-547: "A Clean, Well-Lighted Place."

73 *50 Best American Short Stories: 1915–1939.* Edited by Edward J.

O'Brien. Boston: Houghton Mifflin, 1939. [New York: Literary Guild, 1939.]

pp. 175-190: "My Old Man." Biographical note appears on p. 856. Note: Also published in a text edition, with study guides by Wilbur L. Schramm.

74 *The Sixth New Year: A Resolution.* Chicago and New York: Esquire, 1939.

pp. 73-96: "The Snows of Kilimanjaro." Note: Limited edition.

75 *Patterns for Living.* Part ii. Edited by Oscar J. Campbell, Justine Van Gundy, and Caroline Shrodes. New York: Macmillan, 1940.

pp. 1078-79: "Old Man at the Bridge." [Third edition, 1949, pp. 758-759. Also, an excerpt from the final chapter of *FWBT*, titled "The Decision," on pp. 760-767.]

76 *A College Book of American Literature.* Vol. ii. Edited by Milton Ellis, Louise Pound, and George Weida Spohn. New York: American Book, 1940.

pp. 1047-50: "A Canary for One." An Introductory Note, including selected bibliography, appears on pp. 1046-47. [Second edition, 1954. Edited also by Frederick J. Hoffman. pp. 962-967: "The Killers." pp. 967-969: "In Another Country." Introductory note on pp. 959-962.]

77 *The Bedside Esquire.* Edited by Arnold Gingrich. New York: McBride, 1940. [New York: Tudor (1944).]

pp. 253-274: "The Snows of Kilimanjaro." pp. 473-480: "On the Blue Water."

78 *The Short Story Parade.* Edited by Mabel Holman. New York: Harcourt, Brace, 1940.

pp. 437-441: "A Day's Wait." Biographical note on p. 436.

79 *The Best Short Stories 1940 and the Yearbook of the American Short Story.* Edited by Edward J. O'Brien. Boston: Houghton Mifflin, 1940.

First book appearance of "Under the Ridge." See (B37).

80 *Prose Pieces: Descriptive, Narrative, Expository.* Edited by Richard H. Barker, Margaret M. Bryant, and Catherine Tully Ernst. New York: F. S. Crofts, 1941.

pp. 125-132: Excerpt from Ch. xvii of *SAR*, titled here "The Bull-Fight."

81 *Reading I've Liked.* A personal selection drawn from two decades of reading and reviewing presented with an informal prologue and various commentaries by Clifton Fadiman. New York: Simon & Schuster, 1941.

pp. 435-458: "The Snows of Kilimanjaro." The Commentary, on pp. 426-434, includes a condensed version of Fadiman's essay from the *Nation*, cxxxvi (Jan. 18, 1933), and his review of *FWBT* from the *New Yorker*, xvi (Oct. 26, 1940).

82 *Present-Day Stories.* Selected by John T. Frederick. New York: Scribner's, 1941.
   pp. 160-194: "The Undefeated." Introductory note on p. 159. Note: The cover title is: *Thirty-four Present-Day Stories.*

83 *A Book of Short Stories.* Edited by Cynthia Ann Pugh. New York: Macmillan, 1941. Revised edition.
   pp. 553-566: "Under the Ridge." Biographical note on pp. 592-593.

84 *Reading the Short Story.* Edited by Harry Shaw and Douglas Bement. New York: Harper, 1941.
   pp. 360-366: "In Another Country."

85 *Short Stories for Study: An Anthology.* Edited by Raymond W. Short and Richard B. Sewall. New York: Henry Holt, 1941.
   pp. 183-189: "In Another Country." pp. 190-201: "The Killers." A Note on the Author on pp. 516-517. [Second edition, revised, 1950. pp. 146-152: "In Another Country." pp. 153-164: "The Killers." Note on the Author on p. 596. *A Manual of Suggestions for Teachers Using "Short Stories for Study,"* 1950 edition, pp. 22-26. Third edition, revised, 1956. pp. 42-48: "In Another Country."]

86 *The American Reader.* Edited by Claude M. Simpson and Allan Nevins. Boston: D. C. Heath, 1941.
   pp. 703-710: "The Three-Day Blow." Biographical note on pp. 862-863.

87 *American Issues.* Vol. ii: *The Literary Record.* Edited by Willard Thorp, Merle Curti, and Carlos Baker. Philadelphia: Lippincott, 1941.
   pp. 844-849: "The Killers." Introductory note on pp. 843-844.

88 *Readings for Our Times.* Vol. ii. Edited by Harold Blodgett and Burges Johnson. Boston: Ginn, 1942.
   pp. 218-232: "The Gambler, the Nun, and the Radio." Introductory note on p. 218.

89 America's 93 Greatest Living Authors Present *This Is My Best.* Edited by Whit Burnett. New York: Dial Press, 1942.
   pp. 22-52: "The Short Happy Life of Francis Macomber." A short letter from Hemingway is quoted on p. 22. See (F101).

90 *Great Modern Short Stories: An Anthology of 12 Famous Stories*

and Novelettes. Edited by Bennett A. Cerf. New York: Modern Library, 1942.

pp. 263-289: "The Snows of Kilimanjaro." Biographical note on p. 474.

91 *Vogue's First Reader.* Introduction by Frank Crowninshield. New York: Julian Messner, 1942.

First book appearance of "The Clark's Fork Valley, Wyoming." See (B40).

92 *Readings for Composition: From Prose Models.* Selected and Edited by Donald Davidson and Sidney Erwin Glenn. New York: Scribner's, 1942. [Revised edition, 1957.]

pp. 315-318: Excerpt from Ch. xxiii of *FWBT*, titled here "The Cavalry Patrol." Study suggestions on p. 318.

93 *Great Modern Catholic Short Stories.* Edited by Sister Mariella Gable, O.S.B. New York: Sheed & Ward, 1942.

pp. 99-120: "The Gambler, the Nun, and the Radio." Commentary on p. 99. [Published under the title *They Are People: Modern Short Stories of Nuns, Monks and Priests.* London: Sheed & Ward, 1943.]

94 *Writers of the Western World.* Edited by Clarence A. Hibbard. Boston: Houghton Mifflin, 1942.

pp. 884-896: "The Undefeated." Introductory note on pp. 883-884. [Second edition, 1954. Edited by Horst Frenz. pp. 1062-75.]

95 *WORLD'S Great Short Stories: Masterpieces of American, English and Continental Literature.* Edited and with an Introduction by M. E. Speare. Cleveland: World, 1942.

pp. 55-67: "My Old Man."

96 *American Harvest: Twenty Years of Creative Writing in the United States.* Edited by Allen Tate and John Peale Bishop. New York: L. B. Fischer, 1942.

pp. 15-47: "The Undefeated." [Translated into Spanish, *Antología de escritores contemporáneos de los Estados Unidos,* Vol. I. Santiago, Chile: Editorial Nascimento, 1944. pp. 3-38: "El Invencible."]

97 *Understanding Fiction.* Edited by Cleanth Brooks and Robert Penn Warren. New York: F. S. Crofts, 1943.

pp. 306-315: "The Killers." The Interpretation, on pp. 316-324, first appeared in slightly different form in *American Prefaces,* vii (Spring 1942). [Second edition, Appleton-Century-Crofts, 1959. pp. 296-303: "The Killers." The Interpretation, on pp. 303-312, is reprinted in *Weeks collection,* pp. 114-117.]

98 *Deti Ameriki.* Moscow: Detizdat, 1943.

Russian translation of "Big Two-Hearted River" in an anthology on Children of America.

99 W. Somerset Maugham's *Introduction to Modern English and American Literature.* New York: New Home Library, 1943.

pp. 176-203: "The Short Happy Life of Francis Macomber."

100 *Literature and Life in America.* Book 3. Edited by Dudley Miles and Robert C. Pooley. Chicago: Scott, Foresman, 1943. Photograph.

pp. 524-526: "Old Man at the Bridge." pp. 526-528: "Cat in the Rain." Class Discussion on p. 528. Biographical and critical commentary on pp. 490-491. [Revised edition, 1948. pp. 527-529: "Old Man at the Bridge." pp. 529-531: "Cat in the Rain." Class Discussion on p. 531.]

101 *The Pocket Book of Modern American Short Stories.* Edited and with an Introduction by Philip Van Doren Stern. New York: Pocket Books, 1943. Paperback.

pp. 52-77: "The Snows of Kilimanjaro." [New York: Washington Square Press, 1963. Twenty-first printing.]

102 *As You Were: Viking Portable of American Prose and Poetry.* Edited by Alexander Woollcott. New York: Viking Press, 1943.

pp. 315-345: "Fifty Grand."

103 *The American Looks at the World.* Edited by Carlos Baker. New York: Harcourt, Brace, 1944.

pp. 54-81: "The Undefeated." Introductory note on p. 54.

104 *The Seas of God: Great Stories of the Human Spirit.* Edited by Whit Burnett. Philadelphia: Lippincott, 1944.

pp. 295-316: "The Snows of Kilimanjaro."

105 *For Men Only.* Edited and with an Introduction by James M. Cain. Cleveland: World, 1944.

pp. 13-44: "The Undefeated."

106 *Twelve Great Modern Stories: A New Collection.* New York: Avon Book, 1944. Paperback.

pp. 11-37: "The Short Happy Life of Francis Macomber."

107 *La Table Ronde.* No. 1. Paris: Éditions du Centre, 1944.

pp. 65-82: "Hommage à la Suisse." "Homage to Switzerland" translated into French by Marcel Duhamel.

108 *Out of the Midwest: A Collection of Present-Day Writing.* Edited by John T. Frederick. New York: Whittlesey House, 1944.

pp. 154-158: "Indian Camp."

109 *Bachelor's Quarters: Stories from Two Worlds.* Edited by Norman Lockridge. New York: Biltmore, 1944.
pp. 20-23: "The Doctor and the Doctor's Wife."

110 *They Were There: The story of World War II and how it came about by America's foremost correspondents.* Edited by Curt Riess. New York: Putnam, 1944.
First book appearance of Hemingway's NANA dispatch "The Loyalists." See (B41).

111 *Great Tales of Terror and the Supernatural.* Edited by Herbert A. Wise and Phyllis M. Fraser. New York: Random House, 1944.
pp. 242-252: "The Killers."

112 *The Bedside Tales: A Gay Collection.* Introduction by Peter Arno. New York: William Penn, 1945.
pp. 216-244: "The Short Happy Life of Francis Macomber."

113 *Time to be Young: Great Stories of the Growing Years.* Edited by Whit Burnett. Philadelphia: Lippincott, 1945.
pp. 87-89: "A Day's Wait."

114 *Modern American Short Stories.* Edited, with an Introduction and critical and biographical notes, by Bennett A. Cerf. Cleveland: World, 1945.
pp. 203-231: "The Short Happy Life of Francis Macomber." Editor's notes on pp. 201-202.

115 *Esquire's First Sports Reader.* Edited by Herbert Graffis. New York: A. S. Barnes, 1945.
pp. 63-70: "On the Blue Water." First book appearance of "Remembering Shooting-Flying." See (B42).

116 *Half-a-Hundred: Tales by Great American Writers.* Edited by Charles Grayson. Philadelphia: Blakiston, 1945.
pp. 148-159: "The Capital of the World."

117 *Masters of the Modern Short Story.* Edited by Walter Havighurst. New York: Harcourt, Brace, 1945.
pp. 470-486: "My Old Man." Biographical note on p. 470. [Revised edition, 1955. pp. 171-200: "The Undefeated." Biographical note on p. 171. See also *Instructor's Manual: "Masters of the Modern Short Story,"* 1955 edition, pp. 17-18.]

118 *Major American Writers.* Edited by Howard Mumford Jones and Ernest E. Leisy. New York: Harcourt, Brace, 1945. Revised and enlarged edition.
pp. 1787-97: "My Old Man." pp. 1797-1818: "The Undefeated." Biographical notes and bibliography on pp. 1785-87. [Third edi-

tion, revised, 1952. Edited also by Richard M. Ludwig. pp. 1887-97: "My Old Man." pp. 1897-1916: "The Undefeated." Notes on pp. 1885-87.]

119 *North, East, South, West: A Regional Anthology of American Writing.* Edited by Charles Lee. New York: Howell, Soskins, 1945.
pp. 412-415: "The End of Something."

120 *Ten Great Stories: A New Anthology.* New York: Avon Book, 1945. Paperback.
pp. 49-58: "The Capital of the World."

121 *18 Great Modern Stories.* New York: Avon Book, 1945. Paperback.
pp. 174-197: "The Undefeated."

122 *A Treasury of Doctor Stories.* Compiled by Noah D. Fabricant and Heinz Werner. New York: Frederick Fell, 1946.
pp. 181-185: "Indian Camp." pp. 470-473: "A Day's Wait."

123 *Here Let Us Feast: A Book of Banquets.* By M.F.K. Fisher. New York: Viking Press, 1946.
pp. 473-480: Excerpt from "The Short Happy Life of Francis Macomber." pp. 480-485: Two excerpts from Ch. VIII and Ch. XXIV of *FWBT*.

124 *Esquire's 2nd Sports Reader.* Edited and with an Introduction by Arnold Gingrich. New York: A. S. Barnes, 1946.
pp. 23-33: "The Horns of the Bull." This was the original title of "The Capital of the World" when it appeared in *Esquire*, V (June 1936).

125 *Great Fishing Stories.* Compiled and with a Foreword by Edwin Valentine Mitchell. Garden City, N.Y.: Doubleday, 1946.
pp. 15-44: "Big Two-Hearted River."

126 *Taken at the Flood: The Human Drama as Seen by Modern American Novelists.* Collected and Arranged by Ann Watkins. New York: Harper, 1946.
pp. 192-210: Excerpt from the last chapter of *FWBT*, titled here "Death of Robert Jordan."

127 *The Bathroom Reader.* Introduction by Earl Wilson. New York: Penn, 1946.
pp. 69-73: "Mr. and Mrs. Elliot." See Introduction, p. 12.

128 *The Literature of the United States: An Anthology and a History.* Vol. II: *From the Civil War to the Present.* Edited by Walter Blair, Theodore Hornberger, and Randall Stewart. Chicago: Scott, Foresman, 1947.
pp. 989-993: "The Killers." pp. 994-996: "In Another Country."

Introductory note by Walter Blair, on pp. 987-989. [Third edition, revised, 1966. pp. 1251-54: "In Another Country." Biographical note on pp. 1249-50.]

129 *Readings from the Americas: An Introduction to Democratic Thought.* Edited by Guy A. Cardwell. New York: Ronald Press, 1947.

pp. 591-598: "Soldier's Home." Biographical note on pp. 932-933.

130 *The Golden Argosy: A Collection of the Most Celebrated Short Stories in the English Language.* Edited by Van H. Cartmell and Charles Grayson. Garden City, N.Y.: Garden City Publishing Co., 1947. [Revised edition, Dial Press, 1955.]

pp. 265-273: "The Killers."

131 *Prosateurs américains du XXᵉ Siècle.* Edited by Albert-J. Guérard. Paris: Robert Laffont, 1947. Photograph.

pp. 271-281: "Dépêches d'Espagne." Three dispatches are translated into French by Georges Belmont: "Le delta de l'Èbre," from the *New Republic,* xcv (June 8, 1938); "Sur le front de Guadalajara," and "Madrid," from the *New Republic,* xc (May 5, 1937). Introductory essay on pp. 265-269.

132 *A World of Great Stories.* Edited by Hiram Haydn and John Cournos. New York: Crown, 1947.

pp. 33-37: "Ten Indians."

133 *The Process of Creative Writing.* By Pearl Hogrefe. New York: Harper, 1947.

pp. 138-142: Hemingway's "A Clean, Well-Lighted Place."

134 *A Treasury of Short Stories.* Edited by Bernardine Kielty. New York: Simon & Schuster, 1947.

pp. 670-685: "The Snows of Kilimanjaro." Biographical note on p. 669.

135 *Discovery of Europe: The Story of American Experience in the Old World.* Edited by Philip Rahv. Boston: Houghton Mifflin, 1947.

pp. 678-701: Ch. xviii of *FWBT,* titled here "An American in Spain." Commentary on pp. 677-678.

136 *Atlantic Harvest: Memoirs of the Atlantic.* Compiled by Ellery Sedgwick. Boston: Little, Brown, 1947.

pp. 580-602: "Fifty Grand." First published in the *Atlantic,* cxl (July 1927). Commentary on pp. 579-580.

137 *Americana: Raccolta di Narratori dalle origini ai nostri giorni.* Edited by Elio Vittorini. Introduction by Emilio Cecchi. Milan: Bompiani, 1947.

pp. 793-801: "Il ritorno del soldato Krebs." "Soldier's Home" translated by Carlo Linati. pp. 802-819: "Monaca e messicani, la radio." "The Gambler, the Nun, and the Radio" translated by Elio Vittorini. pp. 820-848: "Vita felice di Francis Macomber, per poco." "The Short Happy Life of Francis Macomber" translated by Elio Vittorini. See the Introduction, pp. xvi-xviii.

138 *Literature for Our Time: An Anthology for College Students.* Edited by Harlow O. Waite and Benjamin P. Atkinson. New York: Henry Holt, 1947.

pp. 307-321: "The Snows of Kilimanjaro."

139 *Better Reading II: Literature.* Edited by Walter Blair and John Gerber. Chicago: Scott, Foresman, 1948.

pp. 81-84: Excerpt from *THAHN* analyzed. pp. 386-394: "The Killers." [Reprinted, 1949, under the title *The College Anthology;* same pagination. Third edition, 1959, with original title. pp. 75-78: Excerpt from *THAHN* analyzed. pp. 401-409: "The Killers." Excerpts of reviews of *OMATS* reprinted from the *Book Review Digest* (1952) on pp. 205-207.]

140 *A Collection of Travel in America: By Various Hands.* Edited by George Bradshaw. New York: Farrar, Straus, 1948.

pp. 290-310: "Big Two-Hearted River."

141 *Mainstream of English and American Literature.* Vol. II. Edited by P. H. Breitenstein and H. A. Vermeer. Amsterdam: J. M. Meulenhoff, 1948. Text in English. Photograph.

pp. 150-156: Two excerpts from Ch. xxx of *FTA*, on the retreat from Caporetto. pp. 156-160: Excerpt from the last chapter of *FWBT*. Introductory note on p. 150.

142 *The Book of the Short Story.* Edited by Henry Seidel Canby and Robeson Bailey. New York: Appleton-Century-Crofts, 1948. New and enlarged edition.

pp. 354-362: "The Killers." Editor's note on p. 354. Commentary on p. 24.

143 *Readings for Liberal Education.* Vol. II: *Introduction to Literature.* Edited by Louis G. Locke, William M. Gibson, and George W. Arms. New York: Rinehart, 1948.

pp. 231-254: "The Short Happy Life of Francis Macomber." [Second edition, revised, 1952. pp. 455-478: "Macomber." See also pp. 479-481, "On Hemingway's 'The Short Happy Life of Francis Macomber'" by Ray B. West, Jr. Reprinted from *College English,* XII (Jan. 1951). Enlarged third edition, 1957. pp. 447-470: "Macomber." See also pp. 470-479, "Observations on a Story by Hemingway" by Ronald S. Crane. An essay on "Macomber," reprinted from *English "A" Analyst*, No. 16, "with some changes." Fourth edition, published by Holt, Rinehart & Winston, 1962. pp. 452-475: "Macomber." Crane's essay on pp. 476-484.]

144 *Courtes Histoires Américaines.* Edited by Nicholas Moore. [Paris]: Corrêa, [1948].

pp. 305-314: "La lumière du monde." "The Light of the World" translated into French by Marcel Duhamel. Biographical note on p. 305.

145 *The Short Story.* Edited by Sean O'Faolain. London: Collins, 1948.

pp. 314-320: "The Light of the World."

146 *Craft of the Short Story.* By Richard Summers. New York: Rinehart, 1948.

pp. 168-190: "Fifty Grand." Analysis on pp. 190-191. Biographical note on pp. 191-192.

147 *Antologia Einaudi: 1948.* Turin: Einaudi, 1949. Photograph.

pp. 14-17: "Breve la vita felice di Francis Macomber." "The Short Happy Life of Francis Macomber" translated into Italian by Guiseppe Trevisani.

148 *American Literature: An Anthology and Critical Survey.* Edited by Joe Lee Davis, John T. Frederick, and Frank Luther Mott. New York: Scribner's, 1949.

pp. 732-742: "Big Two-Hearted River." pp. 743-744: "A Day's Wait." pp. 744-753: Ch. xxvii from *FWBT.* Introductory note on pp. 731-732.

149 *The Critical Reader.* Compiled and Edited by Wallace Douglas, Roy Lamson, and Hallett Smith. New York: Norton, 1949.

pp. 208-242: "The Short Happy Life of Francis Macomber." pp. 554-564: Ch. xvi from *DIA*, titled here "The Picador." [Revised edition, 1962. Edited also by Hugh N. MacLean. pp. 101-109: Ch. xvi from *DIA*. pp. 109-111: Suggestions for Study. pp. 391-425: "The Short Happy Life of Francis Macomber."]

150 *United States Stories: Regional Stories from the Forty-eight States.* Selected with a Foreword by Martha Foley and Abraham Rothberg. New York: Farrar, Straus, 1949.

pp. 595-609: "Wine of Wyoming." Biographical note on pp. 671-672.

151 *Short Stories: Tradition and Direction.* Edited by James Hall, William M. Sale, Jr., and Martin Steinmann, Jr. Norfolk, Conn.: New Directions, 1949.

pp. 262-295: "The Short Happy Life of Francis Macomber." Biographical note on p. 261. See also *Critical Discussions for Teachers Using "Short Stories: Tradition and Direction,"* pp. 40-44.

152 *Panorama della letteratura inglese e americana: lineamenti di storia letteraria e antologia commentata.* Edited by Mario Hazon. Milan: Garzanti Editore, 1949. Text in English.

pp. 520-521: Short excerpt from Ch. xxii of *FTA*, titled here "Jaundice." Biographical note on pp. 519-520.

153 *American Life in Literature.* Vol. ii. Edited by Jay B. Hubbell. New York: Harper, 1949. Revised edition.

pp. 823-842: Ch. xxvii through Ch. xxxii from *FTA*, titled here "The Retreat from Caporetto." pp. 842-853: "The Snows of Kilimanjaro." Biographical note on pp. 822-823.

154 *Studies in the Short Story.* Edited by Adrian H. Jaffe and Virgil Scott. New York: Sloane, 1949.

pp. 199-207: "The Killers." Analysis and Study on pp. 208-213. [Revised edition: New York: Holt, Rinehart & Winston, 1960, pp. 382-392.]

155 *Transition Workshop.* Edited by Eugène Jolas. New York: Vanguard Press, 1949.

pp. 81-85: "Hills Like White Elephants." First published in *transition,* v (Aug. 1927).

156 *Modern Minds: An anthology of ideas.* Compiled by Howard Mumford Jones, Richard M. Ludwig, and Marvin B. Perry, Jr. Boston: D. C. Heath, 1949.

pp. 546-553: "The Battler." Biographical note on p. 546. Interpreting Your Reading on p. 553. [Revised edition, 1954, pp. 612-619.]

157 *The Great Horse Omnibus: From Homer to Hemingway.* Edited by Thurston Macauley. Chicago: Ziff-Davis, 1949.

pp. 95-97: Excerpt from Ch. i of *DIA*, on the use of horses in the bullring. pp. 244-247: Excerpt from "My Old Man," titled here "A Great Jock."

158 *A Little Treasury of American Prose: 1620 to Today.* Edited and with an Introduction by George Mayberry. New York: Scribner's, 1949. Photograph.

pp. 712-722: "A Natural History of the Dead." pp. 722-735: "The Capital of the World."

159 *100 Modern Poems.* Selected and with an Introduction by Selden Rodman. New York: Pellegrini & Cudahy, 1949.

pp. 66-67: An excerpt from Ch. xx of *DIA*, titled here "Miró's Spain."

160 *American Life and Literature: An Anthology.* Edited by Anton Sieberer and Norbert Krejcik. Vienna: Verlag Neue Welt, 1949. Text in English with German footnotes.

pp. 277-280: An excerpt from Ch. xxx and Ch. xxxi of *FTA*, titled here "A Narrow Escape." Biographical note on p. 413.

161 *A Treasury of Great Reporting: "literature under pressure" from the sixteenth century to our own time.* Edited by Louis L. Snyder and Richard B. Morris. New York: Simon & Schuster, 1949.

First book appearance of Hemingway's NANA dispatch from Madrid, April 24, 1937. See (B46).

162 *The Art of Modern Fiction.* Edited by Ray B. West, Jr. and Robert W. Stallman. New York: Rinehart, 1949.

pp. 235-259: "The Short Happy Life of Francis Macomber." Analysis on pp. 259-262.

163 *15 Stories.* Edited by Herbert Barrows. Boston: D. C. Heath, 1950.

pp. 42-51: "Now I Lay Me." See also *Suggestions for Teaching "Fifteen Stories,"* pp. 7-9.

164 105 Greatest Living Authors Present *The World's Best.* Edited by Whit Burnett. New York: Dial Press, 1950.

pp. 16-37: "The Snows of Kilimanjaro." A brief letter from Hemingway is quoted on p. 16. See also commentary on the editor's survey of "the fifty greatest living writers," on p. xv, in which Hemingway ranked fourth.

165 *The House of Fiction: An Anthology of the Short Story.* With Commentary by Caroline Gordon and Allen Tate. New York: Scribner's, 1950.

pp. 402-419: "The Snows of Kilimanjaro." Commentary on pp. 419-423. [Paperback edition, revised, 1960. pp. 394-401: "The Killers." Biographical note on pp. 464-465.]

166 *Modern Short Stories: A Critical Anthology.* Edited by Robert B. Heilman. New York: Harcourt, Brace, 1950.

pp. 386-390: "A Clean, Well-Lighted Place." Critical commentary on pp. 390-392.

167 *Reading Fiction: A Method of Analysis with Selections for Study.* By Fred B. Millett. New York: Harper, 1950.

pp. 104-114: "The Three-Day Blow." Analysis and Questions on pp. 114-116.

168 *Great Short Stories: from the World's Literature.* Edited by Charles Neider. New York: Rinehart, 1950.

pp. 128-151: "The Snows of Kilimanjaro."

169 *The Literature of Crime.* Edited by Ellery Queen. Boston: Little, Brown, 1950.
pp. 165-174: "The Killers." Introductory note on p. 165.

170 *The Story: A Critical Anthology.* Edited by Mark Schorer. New York: Prentice-Hall, 1950.
pp. 420-425: "A Clean, Well-Lighted Place." Critical comment on pp. 425-428.

171 *Great Short Stories.* Edited by Wilbur Schramm. New York: Harcourt, Brace, 1950.
pp. 228-235: "Now I Lay Me." Introductory note on pp. 227-228. See also "Reading with insight," pp. 235-236.

172 *Modern American Literature.* Edited by Bernard J. Duffey. New York: Rinehart, 1951.
pp. 86-111: "The Snows of Kilimanjaro." Biographical note on p. 360.

173 *50 Great Short Stories.* Edited by Milton Crane. New York: Bantam, 1952. Original paperback edition.
pp. 14-22: "The Three-Day Blow."

174 *The Best of the Best American Short Stories: 1915–1950.* Edited by Martha Foley. Boston: Houghton Mifflin, 1952.
pp. 148-161: "My Old Man."

175 *The American Twenties: A Literary Panorama.* Edited by John K. Hutchens. Philadelphia: Lippincott, 1952.
pp. 72-101: "The Undefeated."

176 *Reading Modern Fiction: 30 Stories with Study Aids.* Edited by Winifred Lynskey. New York: Scribner's, 1952.
pp. 247-266: "The Snows of Kilimanjaro." Comment and Questions on pp. 266-267. "An Analysis of the Scene in the Airplane" on pp. 267-268. [Second edition, revised, 1957. *Reading Modern Fiction: 29 Stories with Study Aids.* Third edition, revised, 1962. *Reading Modern Fiction: 31 Stories with Critical Aids.* Same pagination.]

177 *The World's Greatest Boxing Stories.* Edited by Harold U. Ribalow. New York: Twayne, 1952.
pp. 113-136: "Fifty Grand."

178 *Reading Prose: An Introduction to Critical Study.* By Wright Thomas and Stuart Gerry Brown. New York: Oxford Press, 1952.
pp. 613-619: "The Killers." Critical note and questions for study on p. 684.

179 *College English: The First Year.* Edited by J. Hooper Wise, J. E.

Congleton, Alton C. Morris, and John C. Hodges. New York: Harcourt, Brace, 1952. [Revised edition, 1956.]

pp. 358-360: "A Clean, Well-Lighted Place." Introductory note on p. 358. Note: See also 1964 edition (E341).

180 *The New Treasure Chest: An Anthology of Reflective Prose.* Edited by J. Donald Adams. New York: Dutton, 1953.

pp. 354-355: Excerpt from *OMATS*, titled here "Birds and the Sea." pp. 356-357: Two excerpts from Hemingway's Introduction to *Men at War*, titled here "The Idea of Death" and "Honesty in Writing."

181 *The Little Review Anthology.* Edited by Margaret Anderson. New York: Hermitage House, 1953.

pp. 332-335: "Mr. and Mrs. Elliot." Also, first book appearance of Hemingway's poem, "Valentine." See (B53).

182 *Eyes of Boyhood.* Edited by Clyde Brion Davis. Philadelphia: Lippincott, 1953.

pp. 45-48: "A Day's Wait."

183 *Ten Modern Masters: An Anthology of the Short Story.* Edited by Robert Gorham Davis. New York: Harcourt, Brace, 1953.

pp. 65-77: "My Old Man." pp. 77-82: "In Another Country." pp. 82-111: "The Short Happy Life of Francis Macomber." pp. 497-498: Excerpt from Ch. 1 of *DIA*, titled here "How to Look at Violence." Introductory note on pp. 63-65. See also *Instructor's Manual for Ten Modern Masters*, pp. 25-29. [Second edition, 1959. pp. 527-532: "In Another Country." pp. 552-553: Excerpt from Ch. 1 of *DIA*.]

184 *The Esquire Treasury: The Best of Twenty Years of Esquire.* Edited by Arnold Gingrich. New York: Simon & Schuster, 1953.

pp. 89-98: "The Tradesman's Return." Reprinted as it originally appeared in *Esquire*, v (Feb. 1936). For revisions made prior to publication as Part II of *THAHN*, see (A14a). Prefatory note on pp. 86-87.

185 *The Fourth Round: Stories for Men.* Edited by Charles Grayson. New York: Holt, 1953.

pp. 1-5: "After the Storm."

186 *Stories: British and American.* Edited by Jack Barry Ludwig and W. Richard Poirier. Boston: Houghton Mifflin, 1953.

pp. 103-108: "In Another Country." Brief note on Hemingway on p. 500. See also *Instructor's Manual to Accompany "Stories: British and American,"* pp. 12-13.

229

187 *Short Stories in Context.* Edited by Woodburn O. Ross and A. Dayle Wallace. New York: American Book, 1953.

pp. 279-309: "The Short Happy Life of Francis Macomber." Critical commentary on pp. 310-314.

188 *Symposium.* Edited by George Arms and Louis Locke. New York: Rinehart, 1954. [An anthology for first-year college English students.]

pp. 584-603: "The Snows of Kilimanjaro."

189 *Contemporary Short Stories: Representative Selections.* Vol. II. Edited by Maurice Baudin, Jr. New York: Liberal Arts Press, 1954. [Paperback edition: Indianapolis: Bobbs-Merrill, 1954. (American Heritage Series, No. 13.)]

pp. 141-171: "The Undefeated." Introductory note on p. 141.

190 *Panorama de la Littérature contemporaine aux États-Unis.* By John Brown. Paris: Gallimard, [1954]. Photographs.

pp. 352-356: Excerpt from Ch. XIX of *SAR*, titled here "Une femme qui ne veut pas être une garce." pp. 356-360: Excerpt from *FWBT*, titled here "Une alliance contre la mort." pp. 360-362: Excerpt from *OMATS*. Discussion on Hemingway's work on pp. 111-129. Bibliography on p. 363. See also (G66).

191 *Reader and Writer.* Edited by Harrison Hayford and Howard P. Vincent. Boston: Houghton Mifflin, 1954.

pp. 119-121: Excerpt from Ch. I of *DIA*, titled here "Why I Wrote About Bullfights." Introductory note on p. 119. [Second edition, revised, 1959, pp. 141-143.]

192 *The Family Book of Best Loved Short Stories.* Edited by Leland W. Lawrence. [Lawrence Lamb.] Garden City, N.Y.: Hanover House, 1954.

pp. 474-483: "The Killers."

193 *Man Against Nature: Tales of Adventure and Exploration.* Collected and edited by Charles Neider. New York: Harper, 1954.

pp. 239-246: Ch. II of *DIA.*

194 *The Creative Reader: An Anthology of Fiction, Drama, and Poetry.* Edited by R. W. Stallman and R. E. Watters. New York: Ronald Press, 1954.

pp. 54-57: "A Clean, Well-Lighted Place." Notes and Questions on p. 328.

195 *Living Masterpieces of American Literature.* Book III: *Modern American Narratives.* Edited by Randall Stewart and Dorothy Bethurum. Chicago: Scott, Foresman, 1954.

pp. 71-78: "The Battler." pp. 78-98: "The Undefeated." pp. 98-

101: "A Clean, Well-Lighted Place." Introductory notes on pp. 65-71.

96 *Short Story Masterpieces.* Edited by Robert Penn Warren and Albert Erskine. New York: Dell Books, 1954. Paperback.

pp. 207-215: "Soldier's Home."

97 *Texte und Zeichen: Eine literarische Zeitschrift.* Edited by Alfred Andersch. Berlin: Luchterhand, 1955.

pp. 111-112: "Der treue Stier." "The Faithful Bull" translated into German by Annemarie Horschitz-Horst.

98 *Best-in-Books.* Garden City, N.Y.: Doubleday, 1955.

pp. 517-541: Part I of *GHOA*, "Pursuit and Conversation."

99 *The Types of Literature.* Edited by Francis Connolly. New York: Harcourt, Brace, 1955.

pp. 148-150: "After the Storm."

00 *A Book of Stories.* Edited by Royal A. Gettmann and Bruce Harkness. New York: Rinehart, 1955.

pp. 188-195: "Now I Lay Me." See also *Teacher's Manual for "A Book of Stories,"* pp. 34-36.

01 *America's Literature.* Edited by James D. Hart and Clarence Gohdes. New York: Dryden Press, 1955.

pp. 907-909: "In Another Country." pp. 909-911: "A Clean, Well-Lighted Place." Introductory note on pp. 905-906.

02 *Selection: A Reader for College Writing.* Edited by Walter Havighurst, Robert F. Almy, Gordon D. Wilson, and L. Ruth Middlebrook. New York: Dryden Press, 1955.

pp. 482-488: "My Old Man." Biographical note on p. 481. Suggestions for Study and for Writing on p. 488.

03 *American Heritage: An Anthology and Interpretive Survey of Our Literature.* Vol. II. Edited by Leon Howard, Louis B. Wright, and Carl Bode. Boston: D. C. Heath, 1955.

pp. 664-666: "In Another Country." p. 743: "Old Man at the Bridge." Headnote on Hemingway on pp. 663-664.

04 *A Hundred Years of Sea Stories: From Melville to Hemingway.* Edited by Peter K. Kemp. London: Cassell, 1955.

pp. 185-189: "After the Storm."

05 *Reading Modern Short Stories.* Edited by Jarvis A. Thurston. Chicago: Scott, Foresman, 1955.

pp. 167-171: "Ten Indians." Analysis on pp. 171-176. pp. 176-186: "The Capital of the World."

206 *Theme and Form: An Introduction to Literature.* Edited by Monroe Beardsley, Robert Daniel, and Glenn Leggett. Englewood Cliffs, N.J.: Prentice-Hall, 1956.
   pp. 590-604: "The Undefeated." [Revised edition, 1962, pp. 571-585.]

207 *Eine Prosaschule.* Stuttgart: Reclam, 1956.
   Contains "Katze im Regen." "Cat in the Rain" translated into German.

208 *The Short Story.* Edited by James B. Hall and Joseph Langland. New York: Macmillan, 1956.
   pp. 451-456: "In Another Country." Commentary on pp. 456-457.

209 *A College Treasury: Prose, Fiction, Drama, Poetry.* Edited by Paul A. Jorgensen and Frederick B. Shroyer. New York: Scribner's, 1956.
   pp. 148-166: "The Short Happy Life of Francis Macomber." [Second edition, 1962. Vol. II. Same pagination.]

210 *Uden for Saesonen.* Edited by Sven Moeller Kristensen. Copenhagen: Carit Andersens Forlag, 1955.
   Contains "Old Man at the Bridge," "The Revolutionist," "Out of Season," and "A Simple Enquiry." Translated into Danish by Ole Restrup.

211 *Dealer's Choice: A Collection of the World's Great Poker Stories.* Edited by Jerry D. Lewis. New York: Barnes, 1955.
   pp. 133-151: "The Gambler, the Nun, and the Radio." Biographical note on p. 132.

212 *Literatur-kalender 1955.* Stuttgart: Reclam, 1955.
   Contains "Der Kämpfer." "The Battler" translated into German.

213 *Los Premios Nobel de Literatura.* Vol. II. Barcelona: José Janés, 1955.
   pp. 1913-78: *El viejo y el mar. OMATS* translated into Spanish by Fernando Gutiérrez. See also the "Prólogo" by Antonio Rabinad.

214 *A szentelt berek.* By Vajay Szabolcs. [Budapest]: Amerikai Magyar Kiadó, 1955.
   pp. 155-161: Excerpt from *OMATS*, "Az öreg és a tenger." Introductory essay, "Játék a halállal: Ernest Hemingway," on pp. 151-154.

215 *Cuentos Norteamericanos: (Para estudiantes de inglés).* Edited by Jacob Canter. New York: Crowell, 1956. Text in English.
   pp. 38-42: "A Day's Wait." Notes on pp. 59-60. Exercises on pp. 73-74.

16 *Humor fra Amerika.* Edited by Mogens Knudsen and Orla Lundbo. Copenhagen: Carit Andersens Forlag, 1956.
   pp. 227-231: "Hr. og fru Elliot." "Mr. and Mrs. Elliot" translated into Danish by Sigvard Lund.

17 *Nobelpristagere.* Edited by Orla Lundbo. Copenhagen: Carit Andersens Forlag, 1956.
   Contains "The Killers" translated into Danish by Sigvard Lund.

18 *Essays of the Masters.* Edited by Charles Neider. New York: Rinehart, 1956.
   pp. 165-173: Ch. II of *DIA*.

19 *Lob des Bettes: Eine klinophile Anthologie.* Edited by Hans Ohl. Hamburg: Rowohlt, 1956.
   pp. 71-73: Excerpt from *FWBT* translated into German.

20 *Treasury of World Literature.* Edited by Dagobert D. Runes. New York: Philosophical Library, 1956.
   pp. 570-575: "Ten Indians."

21 *En silverantologi: Ur Bonniers Litterära Magasin under 25 år.* Edited by Georg Svensson. Stockholm: Bonniers, 1956.
   pp. 224-234: "Världens huvudstad." "The Capital of the World" translated into Swedish by Thorsten Jonsson. This story appeared in *BLM*, XI (Jan. 1942).

22 *Les vingt meilleures nouvelles américaines.* Selected and Edited by Alain Bosquet. [Paris]: Éditions Seghers, [1957].
   pp. 377-404: "Les neiges du Kilimandjaro" translated by Marcel Duhamel. Introductory note on p. 376.

23 *The American Tradition in Literature.* Vol. II: *Whitman to the Present.* Edited by Sculley Bradley, Richmond Croom Beatty, and E. Hudson Long. New York: W. W. Norton, 1957.
   pp. 1079-1105: "The Short Happy Life of Francis Macomber."
   pp. 1105-16: "A Way You'll Never Be." Explanatory footnotes by the editors. Biographical and critical note on pp. 1077-79.

24 *Reading for Pleasure.* Chosen, with Introduction and Comment, by Bennett Cerf. New York: Harper, 1957.
   pp. 454-457: "The Sea Change."

25 *Amerikanische Erzähler von Washington Irving bis Dorothy Parker.* Zurich: Manesse Verlag, 1957.
   Contains "Ein sauberes, gut beleuchtetes Café." "A Clean, Well-Lighted Place" translated into German.

26 *Stories.* Edited by Frank G. Jennings and Charles J. Calitri. New York: Harcourt, Brace, 1957.

pp. 68-90: "The Undefeated." See also *Teacher's Guide,* pp. 17-18.

227 *Kriegsblinden-Jahrbuch 1957.* Wiesbaden: Bund der Kriegsblinden, 1957.
Contains "Alter Mann an der Brücke." "Old Man at the Bridge" translated into German.

228 *Maravilhas do Conto Norte-Americano.* São Paulo: Cultrix, 1957.
Contains "A curta e feliz existenzia de Francis Macomber" translated into Portuguese by Becker Taliaferro Washington.

229 *Masters and Masterpieces of the Short Story.* Compiled by Joshua McClennen. New York: Holt, 1957. Quarto, paperback.
pp. 24-28: "The Capital of the World." [Second Series, 1960. Holt, Rinehart & Winston. Quarto, paperback. pp. 266-276: "My Old Man."]

230 *Das Meer.* Munich: Kindler Verlag, 1957.
Contains an excerpt from *OMATS* translated into German.

231 *Sportgeschichten aus aller Welt.* Berlin: Sportverlag, 1957.
Contains "Un eine Viertelmillion." "Fifty Grand" translated into German.

232 *Writing from Experience.* Edited by Raymond C. Palmer, James A. Lowrie, and John F. Speer. Ames: Iowa State College Press, 1957.
pp. 247-251: "Ten Indians." Questions for discussion on p. 252. [Reissued under the title *Experiences and Expression.* New York: Scribner's, 1962, pp. 240-245.]

233 *Biography of the Bulls: An Anthology of Spanish Bullfighting.* Edited by Rex Smith. New York: Rinehart, 1957.
pp. 98-108: "The Capital of the World." Biographical note on pp. 95-98. See also (G379).

234 *Jubilee: One Hundred Years of the Atlantic.* Selected and Edited by Edward Weeks and Emily Flint. Boston: Atlantic–Little, Brown, 1957.
pp. 511-532: "Fifty Grand." Commentary on pp. 509-510. This story appeared in the *Atlantic,* CXL (July 1927).

235 *Men at War.* Edited by Fred Urquhart. London: Arco, 1957.
pp. 472-502: Ch. x of *FWBT,* titled here "The Killing of the Fascists."

236 *Der Wald.* Munich: Kindler Verlag, 1957.
Contains an excerpt from *GHOA* translated into German.

237 *Amerikaanse Verhalen.* Amsterdam and Antwerp: Spectrum, [1958]. [Prisma-Boeken, 51.]

Contains "Onverslagen." "The Undefeated" translated into Dutch by André Noorbek.

38 *Im Bann-e des Abenteuers: die spannendsten Geschichten der Welt.* Foreword by Walter Bauer. Vienna: Kurt Desch, 1958.

pp. 854-861: "Der Kämpfer." "The Battler" translated into German by Annemarie Horschitz-Horst. Biographical note on pp. 870-871.

39 *More Stories to Remember.* Vol. 1. Selected by Thomas B. Costain and John Beecroft. Garden City, N.Y.: Doubleday, 1958.

pp. 193-194: "Old Man at the Bridge."

40 *Im Netz der Fische: fünf Dutzend Anglergeschichten.* Edited by Albert Drexler. Munich: Ehrenwirth, 1958.

pp. 65-77: "Grosser doppelherziger Strom." "Big Two-Hearted River" translated into German. pp. 115-119: Excerpt from Ch. XII of *SAR*, titled here "Rio de la Fabrica."

41 *Adventures in American Literature.* Edited by John Gehlmann and Mary Rives Bowman. New York: Harcourt, Brace, 1958.

pp. 105-107: "Old Man at the Bridge." Biographical articles on pp. 106, 108. pp. 208-209: "Hemingway at His Best," by Edward Weeks. Review of *OMATS*, reprinted from the *Atlantic*, CXC (Sept. 1952).

42 *The Armchair Esquire.* Edited by Arnold Gingrich and L. Rust Hills. New York: Putnam, 1958.

First book appearance of "The Butterfly and the Tank." See (B58).

43 *Inquiry and Expression: A College Reader.* Edited by Harold C. Martin and Richard M. Ohmann. New York: Holt, Rinehart & Winston, 1958.

pp. 492-496: Ch. II of *GHOA*, titled here "The Lion." [Second edition, revised, 1963, pp. 546-550.]

44 *Pavannes and Divagations.* By Ezra Pound. Norfolk, Conn.: New Directions, 1958. [London: Peter Owen, 1960.]

p. 236: "Neothomist Poem." Hemingway's poem appears in the Appendix: "Poems by 5 Friends: A Brief Anthology."

45 *Great Stories from the World of Sport.* Vol. 1. Edited by Peter Schwed and Herbert W. Wind. New York: Simon & Schuster, 1958.

pp. 154-174: "Fifty Grand."

46 *Literaturkalender: 1958.* Ebenhausen: Langewiesche-Brandt, 1958.

Contains an excerpt from *DIA* translated into German.

247 *Amerika erzählt.* Edited by Heinrich Politzer. Frankfurt: Fischer Bücherei, 1958.
    pp. 17-25: "Die Killer." "The Killers" translated into German by Annemarie Horschitz-Horst.

248 *Textsammlung moderner Kurzgeschichten.* Frankfurt: Diesterweg Verlag, 1958.
    Contains "Das Ende von Etwas." "The End of Something" translated into German.

249 *Literature as Experience.* By Wallace A. Bacon and Robert S. Breen. New York: McGraw-Hill, 1959.
    pp. 242-246: "A Clean, Well-Lighted Place." Analysis on pp. 246-251.

250 *An Introduction to Literature.* Edited by Herbert Barrows, Hubert Heffner, John Ciardi, and Wallace Douglas. Boston: Houghton Mifflin, 1959.
    pp. 223-232: "The Capital of the World." Commentary on pp. 221-223.

251 *Blühendes Leben.* Munich: Südwest-Verlag, 1959.
    Contains "Katze im Regen." "Cat in the Rain" translated into German.

252 *The Fireside Book of Fishing.* Edited by Raymond R. Camp. New York: Simon & Schuster, 1959.
    pp. 233-248: "Big Two-Hearted River."

253 *Readings for Enjoyment.* Edited by Earle Davis and William C. Hummel. Englewood Cliffs, N.J.: Prentice-Hall, 1959.
    pp. 444-447: "An Alpine Idyll." Biographical note on p. 444. Questions for Study on p. 447.

254 *Dein Weg in die Welt.* Gütersloh: Rufer Verlag, 1959.
    Contains an excerpt from *OMATS* translated into German.

255 *Short Fiction: A Critical Collection.* Edited by James R. Frakes and Isadore Traschen. Englewood Cliffs, N.J.: Prentice-Hall, 1959. Paperback.
    pp. 384-387: "A Clean, Well-Lighted Place."

256 *Jagdgeschichten.* Lübeck: Matthiesen Verlag, 1959.
    Contains "Alter Mann an der Brücke." "Old Man at the Bridge" translated into German. Also, an excerpt from *GHOA.*

257 *Der goldene Schnitt: Gross Erzähler der Neuen Rundschau, 1890-1960.* Edited by Christoph Schwerin. Frankfurt: Fischer Verlag, 1959.
    pp. 543-546: "Ein sauberes, gut beleuchtetes Café." "A Clean,

Well-Lighted Place" translated into German by Annemarie Horschitz. Reprinted from *Neue Rundschau*, XLIV (May 1933).

58 *A Complete Course in Freshman English*. By Harry Shaw. New York: Harper, 1959.

pp. 1069-72: "In Another Country." Introductory note on p. 1069. Questions on p. 1073.

59 *American Short Stories*. Edited by Ray B. West, Jr. New York: Crowell, 1959. [Reader's Bookshelf of American Literature series.]

pp. 179-186: "The Capital of the World."

50 *Reading and Writing*. Edited by W. F. Belcher, E. S. Clifton, R. R. Male, Jr., W. J. Olive, and M. S. Shockley. New York: Holt, Rinehart & Winston, 1960.

pp. 352-354: "A Clean, Well-Lighted Place." Comprehension on p. 355. Discussion and Composition on pp. 357-358.

51 *Fifty Modern Stories*. Edited by Thomas M. H. Blair. Evanston, Ill.: Row, Peterson, 1960.

pp. 498-504: "Soldier's Home." Brief biographical note on p. 707.

52 *31 Stories*. Edited by Michael R. Booth and Clinton S. Burhans, Jr. Englewood Cliffs, N.J.: Prentice-Hall, 1960. Paperback.

pp. 154-156: "Cat in the Rain."

53 *The Scope of Fiction*. Edited by Cleanth Brooks and Robert Penn Warren. New York: Appleton-Century-Crofts, 1960.

pp. 258-266: "The Killers." Interpretation on pp. 266-274.

54 *Das Gesetz des Lebens*. Braunschweig: Westermann-Verlag, 1960.

Contains "Alter Mann an der Brücke" and "Ein Tag warten." "Old Man at the Bridge" and "A Day's Wait" translated into German.

55 *Introduction to Imaginative Literature*. Edited by Bernard Grebanier and Seymour Reiter. New York: Crowell, 1960.

pp. 693-698: "The Capital of the World."

56 *Nye Historier fra de Syv Have*. Edited by Mogens Knudsen. Copenhagen: Carit Andersens Forlag, 1960.

Contains "After the Storm" translated into Danish by Sigvard Lund.

57 *Thought and Statement*. By William G. Leary and James Steel Smith. New York: Harcourt, Brace & World, 1960. Second edition.

pp. 296-298: "A Day's Wait." Exercises in Thought and Statement on pp. 298-299.

58 *Literary Types and Themes*. Edited by Maurice B. McNamee,

James E. Cronin, and Joseph A. Rogers. New York: Rinehart, 1960. pp. 55-59: "The Killers."

269 *Rendezvous: A Prose Reader.* Edited by John J. McShea, O.S.A. and Joseph W. Ratigan. New York: Scribner's, 1960.
pp. 403-407: "In Another Country." Biographical note on p. 425. Essay on *OMATS* by J. Donald Adams, reprinted from the *N.Y. Times Book Review* (Sept. 21, 1952), on pp. 216-218.

270 *Nagyvilág: mai kulfoldi elbeszelok.* Budapest: Magyar Helikon, 1960.
pp. 111-117: "Vihar utan." "After the Storm" translated into Hungarian by Örkény Istvan.

271 *Twenty-nine Stories.* Edited by William Peden. Boston: Houghton Mifflin, 1960.
pp. 283-287: "Indian Camp." Biographical note and Questions on pp. 287-288.

272 *The Arts of Reading.* Edited by Ralph Ross, John Berryman, and Allen Tate. New York: Crowell, 1960.
pp. 226-230: "A Clean, Well-Lighted Place." Critical commentary on pp. 231-236.

273 *The Short Story and the Reader.* Edited by Robert Stanton. New York: Henry Holt, 1960.
pp. 74-99: "The Undefeated." Questions on p. 99.

274 *Literature: An Introduction.* Edited by Hollis Summers and Edgar Whan. New York: McGraw-Hill, 1960.
pp. 64-70: "The Capital of the World."

275 *Great Reading from Life: A Treasury of the Best Stories and Articles.* Chosen by the Editors of *Life.* Introduction by Edward K. Thompson. New York: Harper, 1960.
pp. 3-48: A long excerpt from *OMATS.*

276 *Short Stories from America.* Compiled by Jeffery Tillett. London: Hutchinson Educational, 1960.
Contains "After the Storm."

277 *The Britannica Library of Great American Writing.* Vol. II. Edited and with Historical Notes and a Running Commentary by Louis Untermeyer. Chicago: Britannica Press, 1960.
pp. 1589-1613: "The Undefeated." Commentary on pp. 1585-89.

278 *Wir—heute und morgen.* Gelnhausen: Burckhardthaus Verlag, 1960.
Contains "Das ende von etwas." "The End of Something" translated into German.

79 *Wohin die Wolken ziehen.* Stuttgart: Union Verlag, 1960.
Contains "Das Ende von etwas." "The End of Something" translated into German.

80 *Modern American Short Stories.* Preface and Notes in Russian by
I. Zasurskii. Moscow: Foreign Languages Publishing House, 1960.
Text in English.
pp. 226-248: "The Snows of Kilimanjaro." pp. 249-251: "Old
Man at the Bridge." pp. 252-256: "Indian Camp." pp. 257-260: "Cat
in the Rain." pp. 261-266: "In Another Country." pp. 267-276:
"The Killers." Notes and glossary on Hemingway's work on pp.
532-536.

81 *An Introduction to Literature: Fiction, Poetry, Drama.* Edited by
Sylvan Barnet, Morton Berman, and William Burto. Boston: Little, Brown, 1961.
pp. 203-207: "Ten Indians." Brief explication on p. 40.

82 *The Complete Reader.* Edited by Richard S. Beal and Jacob Korg.
Englewood Cliffs, N.J.: Prentice-Hall, 1961.
pp. 261-265: "In Another Country."

83 *Best-in-Books.* Garden City, N.Y.: Nelson Doubleday, 1961.
pp. 299-306: "The Battler."

84 *Best Gambling Stories.* Edited by John Welcome [Brennan]. London: Faber & Faber, 1961.
pp. 13-37: "Fifty Grand."

85 *American Literature: A College Survey.* Edited by Clarence A.
Brown and John T. Flanagan. New York: McGraw-Hill, 1961.
pp. 747-757: "Fifty Grand." Biographical note on p. 746. Evaluative commentary on p. 747.

86 *Modern American Prose.* Edited by Brother Anthony Cyril, F.S.C.
New York: Macmillan, 1961. [Pageant of Literature series, Vol. v.]
[Revised edition, 1966.]
pp. 170-176: "In Another Country." Introductory note on p. 170.
Study questions on p. 176.

87 *Reading in English: for students of English as a second language.*
Edited by Dorothy Danielson and Rebecca Hayden. Englewood
Cliffs, N.J.: Prentice-Hall, 1961.
pp. 60-64: "A Day's Wait." With explanatory footnotes. Comprehension questions on pp. 185-186.

88 *Stories of Modern America.* Edited by Herbert Gold and David L.
Stevenson. New York: St Martin's Press, 1961.
pp. 228-236: "The Battler." Introductory note on p. 228. Editor's analysis on p. 236. Questions on p. 237.

289 *Sportshistorier*. Edited by Vagn Groesen. Copenhagen: Carit Andersens Forlag, 1961.
Contains "Fifty Grand" translated into Danish by Sigvard Lund.

290 *The Fireside Book of Boxing*. Edited by W. C. Heinz. New York: Simon & Schuster, 1961.
pp. 187-197: "Fifty Grand."

291 *Our Living Language*. Edited by Kellogg W. Hunt and Paul Stoakes. Boston: Houghton Mifflin, 1961.
pp. 315-319: "A Clean, Well-Lighted Place."

292 *Im weiten Revier*. Hamburg: Verlag der Freizeit-Bibliothek, 1961.
Contains "Das kurze glückliche Leben des Francis Macomber" translated into German.

293 *Das Jahr-Kalendarium für junge Leute*. Munich: List Verlag, 1961.
Contains an excerpt from *FTA* translated into German.

294 *Kindheit*. Munich: Droemersche Verlagsanstalt, 1961.
Contains "Väter und Söhne." "Fathers and Sons" translated into German.

295 *Using Prose: Readings for College Composition*. By Donald W. Lee and William T. Moynihan. New York: Dodd, Mead, 1961.
p. 22: Short excerpt from Ch. xi of *SAR*, titled here "Bus Ride." Exercises and questions on p. 23.

296 *Twelve Short Stories*. Edited by Marvin Magalaner and Edmond L. Volpe. New York: Macmillan, 1961. Paperback.
pp. 93-101: "The Battler." Introductory note on pp. 87-92.

297 *Melodie der Welt*. Freiburg: Herder Verlag, 1961.
Contains "Die Killer." "The Killers" translated into German.

298 *Short Stories: A Study in Pleasure*. Edited by Sean O'Faolain. Boston: Little, Brown, 1961.
pp. 72-76: "A Clean, Well-Lighted Place." The critical commentary, on pp. 76-79, was reprinted in *Weeks collection*, pp. 112-113.

299 *Panik*. Zurich: Diogenes Verlag, 1961.
Contains "Die Killer." "The Killers" translated into German.

300 *75 Prose Pieces*. Edited by Robert C. Rathburn and Martin Steinmann, Jr. New York: Scribner's, 1961. Paperback.
p. 37: Short excerpt from Ch. xxvii of *FTA*, titled here "Abstract and Concrete Words."

301 *A College Book of Modern Fiction*. Edited by Walter B. Rideout and James K. Robinson. Evanston, Ill.: Row, Peterson, 1961.

pp. 150-154: "In Another Country." Notes, including bibliography, on pp. 649-651. See also (G334).

02 *The Idea of an American Novel.* Edited by Louis D. Rubin, Jr. and John Rees Moore. New York: Crowell, 1961.

pp. 312-316: Hemingway's "lecture" on American writers from Ch. I of *GHOA*.

03 *American Literature: Readings and Critiques.* Edited by Robert W. Stallman and Arthur Waldhorn. New York: Putnam, 1961.

pp. 784-786: "A Clean, Well-Lighted Place." Commentary by Robert B. Heilman on pp. 786-787.

04 *The American Literary Record.* Edited by Willard Thorp, Carlos Baker, James K. Folsom, and Merle Curti. Philadelphia: Lippincott, 1961.

pp. 877-881: "The Killers." Introductory note on pp. 876-877.

05 *American Satire: In Prose and Verse.* Edited by Henry C. Carlisle, Jr. New York: Random House, 1962.

pp. 407-410: "Mr. and Mrs. Elliot." Introductory note on p. 407.

06 *Essays.* Edited by Leonard F. Dean. New York: Harcourt, Brace & World, 1962. Third edition.

pp. 182-186: "In Another Country." Introductory note on pp. 181-182.

07 *Erde, Stern des Menschen.* Munich: Prestel Verlag, 1962.

Contains an excerpt from *GHOA* translated into German.

08 *The Forms of Fiction.* Edited by John Gardner and Lennis Dunlap. New York: Random House, 1962.

pp. 43-48: "After the Storm." Analysis on pp. 48-50.

09 *Angles of Vision: Readings in Thought and Opinion.* Edited by Edward Huberman and Robert R. Raymo. Boston: Houghton Mifflin, 1962.

pp. 234-241: "The Three-Day Blow." Questions on p. 305.

10 *Kleine Texte zum Spielen.* Wuppertal: Jugenddienst Verlag, 1962.

Contains "Heute ist Freitag." "Today Is Friday" translated into German.

11 *Modern Short Stories: the fiction of experience.* Edited by M. X. Lesser and John N. Morris. New York: McGraw-Hill, 1962.

pp. 218-228: "The Capital of the World." Biographical note on p. 217.

12 *Major Writers of America.* Vol. II. General Editor: Perry Miller. New York: Harcourt, Brace & World, 1962.

pp. 744-752: "Big Two-Hearted River." pp. 752-757: Two excerpts from Ch. 1 of *GHOA*. Introductory essay by Mark Schorer, on pp. 675-677. Annotated reading suggestions on p. 684.

313 *Modern Short Stories: The Uses of Imagination.* Edited by Arthur Mizener. New York: Norton, 1962.

pp. 299-316: "The Gambler, the Nun, and the Radio." See the Introduction, pp. 153-155.

314 *Los Premios Pulitzer de Novela.* Vol. IV. Barcelona: José Janés, 1962.

pp. 947-1010: *El viejo y el mar. OMATS* translated into Spanish by Fernando Gutiérrez.

315 *Reading for Rhetoric: Applications to Writing.* Edited by Caroline Shrodes, Clifford Josephson, and James R. Wilson. New York: Macmillan, 1962.

pp. 191-208: "Big Two-Hearted River." Purpose and structure on pp. 208-209. Diction and tone on p. 209. Applications to writing on pp. 209-210.

316 *Two and Twenty.* Edited by Ralph H. Singleton. New York: St Martin's Press, 1962.

pp. 122-136: "My Old Man." Biographical note on pp. 118-121.

317 *Noveller av Nobelprisvinnere.* Edited and with a Foreword by Ragnvald Skrede. Oslo: Aschehoug, 1962.

pp. 212-216: "Fjell som hvite elefanter." "Hills Like White Elephants" translated into Norwegian by Gunnar Larsen. Brief biographical note on p. 249.

318 *Masterpieces of War Reporting: The Great Moments of World War II.* Edited by Louis L. Snyder. New York: Messner, 1962.

First book appearance of "London Fights the Robots." See (B60).

319 *An Anthology of American Humor.* Edited by Brom Weber. New York: Crowell, 1962.

pp. 545-550: "The Light of the World." Introductory note on pp. 544-545. See also (G444).

320 *Introduction to Literature: Stories.* Edited and with a Handbook for the Study of Fiction by Lynn Altenbernd and Leslie L. Lewis. New York: Macmillan, 1963.

pp. 345-356: "Big Two-Hearted River."

321 *Many Minds: An Anthology of Prose for Senior Students.* Book 2. Edited by Bert Case Diltz and Ronald Joseph McMaster. Toronto: McClelland & Stewart, 1963.

pp. 296-298: "Old Man at the Bridge." Questions on pp. 431-432. Biographical note on pp. 448-449.

322 *Adventures in American Literature.* Edited by Edmund Fuller and B. Jo Kinnick. New York: Harcourt, Brace & World, 1963. Photographs.

pp. 27-28: "Old Man at the Bridge." Questions for discussion and biographical note on p. 28.

323 *Short Fiction of the Masters.* Edited by Leo Hamalian and Frederick R. Karl. New York: Putnam, 1963.

pp. 370-374: "A Clean, Well-Lighted Place." Introductory note on p. 370. Questions on pp. 374-375.

324 *The World in Vogue.* Edited by Bryan Holme, Katharine Tweed, Jessica Daves, and Alexander Liberman. New York: Viking Press, 1963.

p. 153: "The Clark's Fork Valley, Wyoming." Reprinted from *Vogue*, XCIII (Feb. 1, 1939).

325 *23 Modern Stories.* Edited by Barbara Howes. New York: Vintage, 1963. Original paperback edition.

pp. 103-110: "The Light of the World."

326 *Literature of the World.* Edited by Thelma G. James, Walter R. Northcott, Marquis E. Shattuck, and Frederick G. Kiley. New York: McGraw-Hill, 1963.

pp. 430-433: Excerpt from Ch. XII of *GHOA*, titled here "African Encounter." Biographical note on p. 432.

327 *Karussell der Kindheit.* Hamburg: Mosaik Verlag, 1963.

Contains "Mein Alter." "My Old Man" translated into German.

328 *Amerikanske Fortaellere.* Edited by Tom Kristensen and Tage la Cour. Copenhagen: Carit Andersens Forlag, 1963.

Contains "The Killers" translated into Danish by Sigvard Lund.

329 *Portrait of Spain: British and American Accounts of Spain in the Nineteenth and Twentieth Centuries.* Selected by Thomas F. McGann. New York: Knopf, 1963.

pp. 373-387: Two excerpts from Ch. VII and Ch. XVIII of *DIA*. Introductory note on bullfighting, on pp. 372-373.

330 *Readings for Progress in Writing: From Paragraph to Essay.* Edited by Woodrow Ohlsen and Frank L. Hammond. New York: Scribner's, 1963. Paperbound.

pp. 267-270: "Old Man at the Bridge." Exercises on pp. 270-271.

331 *The Story at Work: An Anthology.* Edited by Jessie Rehder. New York: Odyssey Press, 1963.

pp. 1-5: "Indian Camp." Explication on pp. 5-6.

332 *Contemporary American Prose.* Edited by Clarence W. Wachner,

Frank E. Ross, and Eva Marie Van Houten. New York: Macmillan, 1963.

pp. 134-139: "In Another Country." Questions on pp. 139-140. Biographical note on pp. 360-361.

333 *Short Stories: An Anthology for Secondary Schools.* Edited by Edwin H. Sauer and Howard Mumford Jones. New York: Holt, Rinehart & Winston, 1963.

pp. 33-59: "The Undefeated." Introductory note on pp. 32-33. Study questions on pp. 59-60.

334 *Auf leisen Pfoten.* Hamburg: Verlag der Freizeit-Bibliothek, 1964.

Contains "Katze im Regen." "Cat in the Rain" translated into German.

335 *Literature in English.* Book Six. Edited by Luella B. Cook. New York: McGraw-Hill, 1964. [English for Today series by the National Council of Teachers of English.] Paperback.

pp. 26-30: "A Clean, Well-Lighted Place." Brief explication on p. 26. Questions on p. 31. See also *Teacher's Text*, pp. 10-11.

336 *Concise American Composition and Rhetoric.* Edited by Donald Davidson. New York: Scribner's, 1964.

pp. 362-365: An excerpt from Ch. xxx of *FTA*, titled here "The Lieutenant Escapes." Introductory note on pp. 361-362.

337 *The Critical Question: An Approach to the Problems of Critical Reading and Critical Writing.* Edited by Robert W. Frank and Harrison T. Meserole. Boston: Allyn & Bacon, 1964.

pp. 39-41: "Old Man at the Bridge." Questions on pp. 41-42.

338 *Quaranta storie americane di guerra: Da Fort Sumter a Hiroshima.* Edited by Carlo Fruttero and Franco Lucentini. Milan: Mondadori, 1964.

Contains Ch. xxx, regarding the retreat from Caporetto, from *FTA*. Also, the poem "Riparto d'Assalto" from *TSTP*.

339 *The Modern Talent: An Anthology of Short Stories.* By John Edward Hardy. New York: Holt, Rinehart & Winston, 1964.

pp. 23-32: "The Battler." pp. 32-36: "Ernest Hemingway's 'The Battler'" by John Edward Hardy. Reprinted from *Commentaries on Five Modern American Short Stories.* (Frankfurt a.M.: Verlag Moritz Diesterweg, 1962.) Study questions on pp. 471-472. Biographical note on p. 494.

340 *Writing Prose: Techniques and Purposes.* By Thomas S. Kane and Leonard J. Peters. New York: Oxford Univ. Press, 1964. Second edition.

pp. 375-381: Ch. III from *DIA*, titled here "The Bullfight." Questions on pp. 381-383.

341 *College English: The First Year.* Edited by Alton C. Morris, Biron Walker, Philip Bradshaw, John C. Hodges, and Mary E. Whitten. New York: Harcourt, Brace & World, 1964.
pp. 451-454: "After the Storm." Introductory note on p. 451. Note: See also 1952 edition (E179).

342 *Studies in Fiction.* Edited by Blaze O. Bonazza and Emil Roy. New York: Harper & Row, 1965.
pp. 119-128: "The Killers." Questions for discussion on p. 128.

343 *Read With Me.* Selected by Thomas B. Costain. Garden City, N.Y.: Doubleday, 1965.
pp. 267-271: "In Another Country." Introductory note on p. 265.

344 *Fifty Best American Short Stories, 1915–1965.* Edited by Martha Foley. Boston: Houghton Mifflin, 1965.
pp. 49-60: "My Old Man." The introductory note, on p. 49, states that this story, which first appeared in *The Best Short Stories of 1923* (B1), is "the only story in the entire series which did not first appear in a magazine."

345 *American Short Stories.* Selected by Douglas Grant. London: Oxford Univ. Press, 1965.
pp. 359-398: "The Short Happy Life of Francis Macomber."

346 *The Realm of Fiction: 61 Short Stories.* Edited by James B. Hall. New York: McGraw-Hill, 1965.
pp. 341-344: "A Clean, Well-Lighted Place." Brief biographical note on p. 341.

347 *The Art of Prose.* Edited by Paul A. Jorgensen and Frederick B. Shroyer. New York: Scribner's, 1965.
pp. 435-443: "On the Blue Water: A Gulf Stream Letter." Introductory note on p. 435. Study questions on pp. 443-444. Theme assignment on p. 444.

348 *Literature for Composition.* By James R. Kreuzer and Lee Cogan. New York: Holt, Rinehart & Winston, 1965.
pp. 200-203: "Cat in the Rain." Questions on p. 203.

349 *Short Story: A Thematic Anthology.* Edited by Dorothy Parker and Frederick B. Shroyer. New York: Scribner's, 1965.
pp. 193-196: "Indian Camp." Biographical note on p. 455.

350 *Short Stories for Discussion.* Edited by Albert K. Ridout and Jesse Stuart. New York: Scribner's, 1965.

245

pp. 182-189: "In Another Country." Introductory note on p. 182. Questions on pp. 189-190.

351 *Twentieth Century American Writing.* Edited by William T. Stafford. New York: Odyssey Press, 1965.

pp. 209-216: Two excerpts from Ch. 1 and Ch. iv of *GHOA*. pp. 216-230: "Big Two-Hearted River." Chronology and bibliography on pp. 208-209.

SECTION F

LIBRARY HOLDINGS

OF MANUSCRIPTS

AND LETTERS;

FACSIMILES

OF MANUSCRIPTS;

PUBLISHED LETTERS;

AND EPHEMERA

This section comprises library holdings of Hemingway manuscripts and letters. It makes no pretense of completeness. The bibliographer made a limited survey of fifty-five university and public libraries in 1964 and in 1966 followed up on the survey to many of the libraries which had earlier reported Hemingway holdings. The collecting of Hemingway manuscripts and letters by institutions is, as it is for any twentieth-century author, still in its infancy. Many items that are now in private collections will, of course, eventually be donated to public institutions. An important collection, not yet listed, will be the Hemingway papers, including manuscripts, letters and copies of replies, and memorabilia, which Mary Hemingway is presenting to the John F. Kennedy Library in Cambridge. No attempt was made by the bibliographer to list private collections, since they would rarely be available to the student or scholar for research.

LIBRARY HOLDINGS OF MANUSCRIPTS

F1 The Baker Memorial Library, Dartmouth College, Hanover, N.H.

A. "Havana Letter." Typescript with holograph corrections. 10 pages. Published under the title "Defense of Dirty Words: A Cuban Letter," in *Esquire*, II (Sept. 1934).

2 The Clifton Waller Barrett Library, University of Virginia, Charlottesville.

A. *The Green Hills of Africa*. Holograph manuscript. Ca. 491 pages.

3 The Library of Congress, Washington, D.C.

A. Untitled holograph manuscript. 15 pages. [July 1937.] A commentary to accompany the documentary film of the Spanish Civil War, "The Spanish Earth." See the *Library of Congress Information Bulletin*, XXII (Oct. 7, 1963), 533-534.

4 The Houghton Library, Harvard University, Cambridge, Mass.

A. "After the Storm." 28 pages.

B. "The Killers." First carbon of typescript. 14 pages. [Paris, 1926.]

5 The Lilly Library, Indiana University, Bloomington.

A. "The Sea Change." Typescript with holograph corrections, signed. 5 pages. Dated: September 22, 1931.

B. "Homage to Ezra." Holograph manuscript, signed. 6 pages.

C. "Second Tanganyika Letter." Typescript with holograph corrections. 6 pages. Published under the title "Shootism vs. Sport: The Second Tanganyika Letter," in *Esquire*, II (June 1934).

D. "Third Tanganyika Letter." Typescript with holograph additions. 6 pages. Published under the title "Notes on Dangerous Game: The Third Tanganyika Letter," in *Esquire*, II (July 1934). Appended is a long note to "Mr. G" [Arnold Gingrich], regarding future letters, dated: March 17.

E. "Key West Letter." Typescript with holograph corrections. 7 pages. Published under the title "The Sights of Whitehead Street: A Key West Letter," in *Esquire*, III (April 1935).

F. "Gulf Stream Letter." Typescript with holograph corrections. 7 pages. Published under the title "On Being Shot Again: A Gulf Stream Letter," in *Esquire*, III (June 1935).

6 The Morris Library, Southern Illinois University, Carbondale.

A. "The Short Happy Life of Francis Macomber." Corrected typescript, signed. 39 pages.

B. "After the Storm." Corrected typescript, signed. 7 pages.

C. "A Natural History of the Dead." Page one of original typescript, with carbon copy of same.

D. Untitled manuscript, signed. 6 pages. Dated: Nairobi, January 18, 1934. Published under the title "a.d. in Africa: A Tanganyika Letter," in *Esquire*, I (April 1934).

7 Firestone Library, Princeton University, Princeton, N.J.

A. Carbon of a typescript of *The Torrents of Spring*. Inscribed: "To Scott and Zelda with love from Ernest." 101 pages.

B. Corrected typescript of "War Poem," published as "Second Poem to Mary," *Atlantic*, CCXVI (Aug. 1965).

8 The Academic Center Library, University of Texas, Austin.

A. *Death in the Afternoon*. Corrected typescript and holograph manuscript. 311 pages. An "early draft, apparently the first." See Max Westbrook's article "Necessary Performance: the Hemingway Collection at Texas," in the *Library Chronicle of the University of Texas*, VII (Spring 1964), 26-31.

B. "The Snows of Kilimanjaro." Typescript with holograph revisions. 28 pages.

C. "Big Two-Hearted River." Carbon copy of typescript, signed. 32 pages.

D. *To Have and Have Not*. Chapters I-V. Carbon copy of typescript with holograph corrections, signed. 55 pages.

E. "Under the Ridge." Corrected typescript and holograph manuscript, signed. 23 pages.

9 The Yale University Library, New Haven, Conn.

A. "The Age Demanded." Carbon copy of typescript. 1 page. Gertrude Stein Collection.

B. "Quick Assets and Dead." Typescript. 3 pages. Published under the title "Why Not Trade Other Public Entertainers Among the Nations as the Big Leagues Do Baseball Players?" in the *Toronto Star Weekly* (Feb. 19, 1921). Gertrude Stein Collection.

C. "Today Is Friday." Typescript with corrections. 5 pages.

9-A The New York Public Library, Rare Book Division.

A. *The Old Man and the Sea.* Typescript with corrections. 101 pages. Also, corrected galley proofs and page proofs.

B. Nobel prize acceptance speech. First draft, written on two blank pages in the back of John P. Marquand's *Thirty Years.* The book is inscribed to Lee Samuels, with reference to the first draft of the speech.

C. Untitled. Corrected typescript. 8 pages. Published as "Safari" in *Look*, XVIII (Jan. 26, 1954).

D. Untitled. Corrected typescript, 47 pages; holograph manuscript, 7 pages. Dated: Nairobi | 20/2/54. Published as "The Christmas Gift" in *Look*, XVIII (April 20, 1954) and (May 4, 1954).

Note: The above items were presented to the New York Public Library by Lee Samuels.

LIBRARY HOLDINGS OF LETTERS

10 The Baker Memorial Library, Dartmouth College, Hanover, N.H.

A. Photostat of letter to Messrs. Sklar, Margulies, Denneman, and Fearing, regarding writing and *SAR.* 1 page. n.d. Finca Vigia, San Francisco de Paula.

11 The Bancroft Library, University of California, Berkeley.

A. 5 ALS to George S. Albee. May 1, [1931]–Jan. 31, 1934. Key West and the S. S. Volendam (en route to Spain). In the Albee Papers.

12 The Clifton Waller Barrett Library, University of Virginia, Charlottesville.

A. 5 ALS and 8 TLS to Ernest Walsh and Ethel Moorhead. March 27, [1925]–Feb. 1, [1926].

B. Carbon copies of 5 TLS to Horace Liveright. March 31, 1925–Dec. 30, 1925.

C. ALS to [Herbert] Gorman. 2 pages. April 4, 1926.

D. TLS, with holograph additions, to Georgia Lingafelt. 1 page. Oct. 3, 1927.

E. ALS to Charles T. Scott. 2 pages. Jan. 23, 1929.

F. ALS to "Mr. Gud." 1 page. Oct. 28, 1929.

G. ALS to [Samuel] Putnam. 2 pages. June 9, [1932?]. [Havana]. See (F83).

H. TLS to [Ralph Ingersoll]. 1 page. May 20, 1939.

I. ALS to [Merle] Armitage. 2 pages. n.d.

J. ALS to "Mr. Vance." 1 page. n.d.

K. Photostat of TLS to [Robert W.] Stallman. 1 page. Jan. 17, 1951.

L. ALS to Harry M. Meacham. 1 page. Oct. 12, 1957. In the Harry M. Meacham Collection.

13 The Berg Collection, New York Public Library, New York.

A. 2 ALS and 2 TLS to [Sir Hugh] Walpole. April 14, 1927-Dec. 10, [1929]. Paris.

B. 1 ALS, 2 TLS, and 2 telegrams to the firm of James B. Pinker & Son, literary agents, in London. Sept. 13, 1927–Oct. 10, 1927. Paris, etc.

14 The University of Chicago Library, Chicago, Ill.

A. 2 letters to Harriet Monroe. July 16, 1922, and Nov. 16, 1922. In the Monroe Collection.

15 The Columbia University Library, New York.

A. TLS to Roger Chase. 1 page. Feb. 11, 1936. Key West.

B. TLS to Ella Winter. 1 page. Oct. 25, 1936. Cooke City, Montana.

C. 5 telegrams and 1 cablegram to Roger Chase and others. Dec. 1936–April 1939. Key West and Havana.

16 The Library of Congress, Washington, D.C.

A. 27 letters (typescript and holograph), signed, and 1 telegram to Archibald MacLeish. 1927-1954 and undated. (Restricted.) In the Archibald MacLeish Papers.

B. ALS to General Curtis LeMay. 6 pages. Sept. 19, 1954. 2 TLS to General LeMay. 1 page each. Oct. 9, 1954, and April 14, 1955. (Restricted.) In the Curtis LeMay Papers.

C. Telegram to *Harper's Magazine*, declining inquiry concerning serial publication of some of his reminiscences. Oct. 10, 1960. In the *Harper's Magazine* Collection.

17 The Cornell University Library, Ithaca, N.Y.

A. 2 ALS to Wyndham Lewis. The dated one being Oct. 24, 1927. See (F70).

18 The University of Florida Library, Gainesville.

A. TLS to Marjorie Kinnan Rawlings. 1 1/4 pages. Aug. 16, 1936. Cooke City, Mont.

19 The Lilly Library, Indiana University, Bloomington.

A. ALS to Edward W. Titus. 1 page. n.d. Paris.

B. ALS to Josephine Ketcham Piercy. 5 pages. [1930.] Key West. See (F73).

c. TLS, with holograph postscript, to Jack Hirschman. 1 page. Jan. 9, 1953. Finca Vigia, San Francisco de Paula, Cuba. See (F131).

D. ALS to [Christopher G.] Janus. 2 pages. Oct. 21, 1958. Ketchum, Idaho.

20 The Lockwood Memorial Library, State University of New York at Buffalo.

A. ALS to [James] Joyce. 2 pages. Jan. 30, 1928. Hotel Rossli, Gstaad, Switzerland.

21 The Morris Library, Southern Illinois University, Carbondale.

A. ALS to Harry Crosby. 1 page. [1927.] Paris.

B. ALS to Jewell F. Stevens. 1 page. Dec. 1, 1929. Paris.

c. ALS to Ray Long. 2 pages. Oct. 29, 1930. Cooke City, Mont.

D. 5 ALS to William C. Lengel. The dated one being Jan. 21, 1931. Havana, Key West, and Cooke City, Mont.

E. 7 ALS, 1 telegram, and 1 cablegram to Caresse Crosby. July 22, [1931]–March 1, [1933]. Key West, Paris, Kansas City, etc.

F. ALS to Harvey Breit. 1 page. Aug. 17, 1957. Finca Vigia, Cuba.

G. ALS to John Wain. 1 1/2 pages. Aug. 17, 1957. Finca Vigia, Cuba.

22 The Newberry Library, Chicago, Ill.

A. 6 TLS to Sherwood Anderson. [1921]–1926. Paris, etc. In the Sherwood Anderson Collection.

23 The Northwestern University Library, Evanston, Ill.

A. Brief letter to Jon Webb, New Orleans publisher, declining a request for a story. Dec. 15, 1934. Key West.

24 The Oak Park Public Library, Oak Park, Ill.

A. TLS to Fred Wezeman. 1 page. June 10, 1953. Finca Vigia, San Francisco de Paula, Cuba. See (F132).

25 The Pennsylvania State University Library, University Park.

A. ALS to "Mr. Devoe." 1 page. Dec. 30, 1929. On the stationery of the Palace-Hôtel, Montana-Vermala (Suisse).

26 The University of Pennsylvania Library, Philadelphia.

A. ALS to Struthers Burt. Nov. 30, [1938?]. Paris.

27 The Library of the College of Physicians of Philadelphia, Philadelphia.

A. ALS to Dr. Israel Bram, in reply to a questionnaire on sleeping habits submitted by Dr. Bram to a considerable number of the persons listed in *Who's Who in America*. 1 page. Dec. 9, [1931?]. Kansas City, Mo.

28 Firestone Library, Princeton University, Princeton, N.J.

A. In the Sylvia Beach Papers, there are nine letters and two postcards to Sylvia Beach, dated 1923-1929, and one without date, [1930?]

B. In the papers given to the Library by Harold Loeb, there are five letters to Harold Loeb, the dated ones being 1924-1925.

C. Forty-seven letters to Henry Strater. The dated ones extend from 1924-1936.

D. In the F. Scott Fitzgerald Papers, there are twenty-nine letters to Fitzgerald, 1926-1934.

E. One letter to George Slocombe, Nov. 26 [1929].

F. In the collection given to the Library by Major General Charles T. Lanham, there are 129 letters to General Lanham, 1940-1961. In addition, there is one letter to Mrs. C. T. Lanham, June 30, 1945; and one letter to Maxwell Perkins, April 28, 1947.

G. In the Files of *Story*, edited by Whit and Hallie Burnett, there is one letter to Whit Burnett, [Sept. 1947].

H. Five letters to Juanito Quintana, 1954-1960. One without date.

I. In the papers of Samuel Putnam, editor of *Broom*, there is one letter without date.

Note: All letters are restricted at present.

29 The Academic Center Library, University of Texas, Austin.

A. 3 ALS and 1 TLS to Howell G. Jenkins. March 20, 1922–[1925].

B. TLS, with holograph additions, to David Garnett. 2 pages. [1938.] Paris.

C. Telegram to Jasper Wood. 2 pages. July 19, 1938. Key West. ALS to Jasper Wood. Aug. 20, 1938. Key West. Regarding publication of *The Spanish Earth*. See (A15).

D. 1 ALS and 5 TLS to Robert Morgan Brown. July 14, 1954–Aug. 8, 1956. Cuba.

E. Letters to Lee Samuels. (Restricted until 1989, which is twenty-five years from the date of their arrival at the Library.)

30 The Louis Round Wilson Library, University of North Carolina, Chapel Hill.

A. 2 letters to Burton Emmett. Oct. 15, 1927, and March 16, 1928. In the Burton Emmett Papers.

31 The Yale University Library, New Haven, Conn.

A. 5 ALS and 5 TLS to Grace Quinlan (later Mrs. Joseph Otis). Jan. 1, 1920–[Aug. 19, 1921]. Oak Park, Chicago, etc.

B. 31 letters, notes, and cards to Gertrude Stein. June 11, 1922–Aug. 20, [1925]. Paris, etc.

C. 5 ALS and 2 TLS to Edmund Wilson. 1923-1951.

D. TLS to "Miss Finch." Aug. 18, 1926. Paris.

E. TLS to James T. Babb. April 24, [1930]. Key West.

F. 2 ALS and 1 TLS to Thornton Wilder. May 6, 1931–July 18, [n.y.].

G. ALS to F. B. Millett. July 28, 1937. Bimini, B.W.I. (Written at bottom of TLS to Hemingway from Millett, July 3, 1937.)

H. TLS to Sinclair Lewis. Nov. 15, 1941. Sun Valley, Idaho.

PUBLISHED FACSIMILES
OF HEMINGWAY'S MANUSCRIPTS

32 *Modern Writers at Work* by Josephine K. Piercy. New York: Macmillan, 1930. p. [489]. Facsimile of a holograph manuscript page from chapter one of *FTA*, "showing how he revises a sentence." See (B8).

33 *A Bibliography of the Works of Ernest Hemingway* by Louis Henry Cohn. New York: Random House, 1931. Frontispiece. Facsimile of a holograph manuscript page from an unpublished work, titled "Death of the Standard Oil Man." See (B9).

34 *Paris Review*, No. 18 (Spring 1958), p. [60]. Facsimile of a holograph manuscript page from "The Battler." See (H1066). Also reproduced in *Writers at Work: The Paris Review Interviews*. Second series. New York: Viking Press, 1963. p. 216. See (G319).

35 *The Library of Dr. Don Carlos Guffey*. New York: Parke-Bernet Galleries, 1958. Catalogue. Frontispiece. Facsimile of the first manuscript page of *DIA*, with holograph corrections. See (G174). Also reproduced in *American Book Collector*, IX (March 1959), 4. See (H1110). Also reproduced in *A Creative Century: Collections at the University of Texas*. Austin: Univ. of Texas, 1964. p. 30. See (G414).

35₁ *Ibid.*, p. [27]. Facsimile of a holograph manuscript page from chapter three of *DIA*.

36 *Life*, XLIX (Sept. 5, 1960), 88. A facsimile of a holograph manuscript page from "The Dangerous Summer" accompanies the first installment. See (C407). Partially reproduced in *Wisdom*, No. 38 (1962), p. [34]. See (C401).

37 *Library Chronicle of the University of Texas*, VII (Spring 1964), [26]. Facsimile of a manuscript page from *DIA*, from the collection of the University of Texas Library. See (H1505).

38 *Texas Quarterly*, VII (Summer 1964), [6]. Facsimile of a holograph manuscript page from chapter nineteen of *DIA*, from the collection of the University of Texas Library. See (H1538).

This section comprises a list of letters by Hemingway which have been published in full or partially quoted. Briefly quoted letters have only been included when the content was of sufficient interest to merit inclusion. In a number of instances during his later years Hemingway requested that a letter or statement of his be quoted "only in entirety and exactly as written."

Hemingway's wishes regarding publication of his letters were placed in the safe at Finca Vigía, in a sealed envelope marked: "Important. To be Opened in case of my Death. Ernest Hemingway. May 24, 1958." The paper inside, which was dated May 20, 1958, read: "To my Executors: It is my wish that none of the letters written by me during my lifetime shall be published. Accordingly, I hereby request and direct you not to publish or consent to the publication by others, of any such letters." [Quoted by permission of Mary Hemingway.]

PUBLISHED LETTERS

39 [June 1909]. From Oak Park, to his sister Marcelline, who was in Nantucket. Quoted in *At the Hemingways* by Marcelline Hemingway Sanford, Boston, 1962, pp. 114-115.

40 May 5, 1915. From Oak Park, to his sister Marcelline. Regarding the high school Story Club. Quoted in *At the Hemingways* by Marcelline Hemingway Sanford, Boston, 1962, p. 136.

41 [June 1918]. From Milan, Italy, to friends on the *Kansas City Star.* Extracts from postcards quoted in the *K.C. Star* (July 14, 1918), 5 A. Reprinted in *The Apprenticeship of Ernest Hemingway* by Charles A. Fenton, New York, 1954, pp. 57, 58.

42 [July 1918]. From the American Red Cross Hospital in Milan. Postscript to Theodore Brumback's letter to Ernest's parents. Printed in *Oak Leaves* (Aug. 10, 1918), p. 56. Reprinted in *At the Hemingways* by Marcelline Hemingway Sanford, Boston, 1962, p. 163.

43 [Sept. 1918]. From the hospital in Italy, to his parents. Long letter printed in *Oak Leaves* (Oct. 5, 1918), pp. 12-13. Reprinted in *My Brother, Ernest Hemingway* by Leicester Hemingway, Cleveland, 1962, pp. 47-50; in *At the Hemingways* by Marcelline Hemingway Sanford, Boston, 1962, pp. 166-169; in *Hemingway in Michigan* by Constance Cappel Montgomery, New York, 1966, pp. 111-114.

44 March 9, 1922. To Sherwood Anderson, about *Ulysses.* Quoted in *James Joyce* by Richard Ellmann, New York, 1959, p. 543. The

original letter is in the Anderson Collection in the Newberry Library.

45 [1923?] To Edward J. O'Brien. Stating what he tries to do in his writing. Two extracts are quoted in O'Brien's *The Advance of the American Short Story*, New York, 1931, p. 270.

46 Nov. 6, 1923. From Toronto, to Sylvia Beach. Printed in *Mercure de France*, No. 1198-99 (Aug.–Sept. 1963), pp. 105-106. French translation on pp. 107-108.

47 Nov. 11, 1923. From 1599 Bathurst Street, Toronto, to Edmund Wilson. Regarding an item in Burton Rascoe's column in the *N.Y. Tribune*, which mentioned that Wilson had called Rascoe's attention to Hemingway's work in the *Little Review*. Printed in Wilson's *The Shores of Light*, New York, 1952, pp. 115-116. Reprinted in *Baker anthology*, pp. 55-56.

48 Nov. 25 [1923]. From 1599 Bathurst Street, Toronto, to Edmund Wilson. A reply to Wilson's proposal to review *TSTP* in the *Dial*. Printed in Wilson's *The Shores of Light*, New York, 1952, pp. 116-118. Reprinted in *Baker anthology*, pp. 56-57.

49 Feb. 17, 1924. From 113, rue Notre Dame des Champs, Paris, to Gertrude Stein. Regarding publication of her book, *The Making of Americans*, in the *Transatlantic Review*. Facsimile of holograph letter reproduced in *New Colophon*, III (1950), [65]. Also quoted on p. 59. Printed in *The Flowers of Friendship: Letters to Gertrude Stein*, ed. Donald C. Gallup, New York, 1953, p. 159. The original letters in this volume are in the Collection of Gertrude Stein's Papers at the Yale University Library.

50 [April 1924]. To Gertrude Stein, regarding Liveright's rejection of *The Making of Americans*. Quoted in *New Colophon*, III (1950), 60.

51 Aug. 9, 1924. From Paris, to Gertrude Stein. Regarding the *Transatlantic Review's* financial difficulties. Quoted in *New Colophon*, III (1950), 61. Printed in *The Flowers of Friendship: Letters to Gertrude Stein*, ed. Donald C. Gallup, New York, 1953, pp. 163-164.

52 Aug. 15 [1924]. From Paris, to Gertrude Stein. Regarding his work in progress. Printed in *The Flowers of Friendship: Letters to Gertrude Stein*, ed. Donald C. Gallup, New York, 1953. pp. 164-165.

53 Sept. 14, 1924. To Gertrude Stein, regarding payment for serializing *The Making of Americans* in the *Transatlantic Review*. Quoted in *New Colophon*, III (1950), 61-62.

54 Oct. 10 [1924]. From Paris, to Gertrude Stein. Regarding *Transatlantic Review* difficulties. Quoted in *New Colophon*, III (1950),

62-63. Printed in *The Flowers of Friendship: Letters to Gertrude Stein*, ed. Donald C. Gallup, New York, 1953, pp. 166-167.

55 Oct. 18, 1924. From 113, rue Notre Dame des Champs, Paris VII, to Edmund Wilson. Regarding Wilson's review of *TSTP* and *iot* in the *Dial*, LXXVII (Oct. 1924). Printed in Wilson's *The Shores of Light*, New York, 1952, pp. 122-124. Reprinted in *Baker anthology*, pp. 59-60.

56 [1925]. From the Hotel Taube, Schruns, Vorarlberg, Austria, to Sylvia Beach. Printed in *Mercure de France*, No. 1198-99 (Aug.–Sept. 1963), pp. 109-110. French translation on p. 110.

57 Jan. 29, 1925. From Austria, to Ernest Walsh and Ethel Moorhead, coeditors of *This Quarter*. Regarding negotiations with Boni & Liveright for *IOT*. Extract quoted in the catalogue of the *Ulysses Book Shop*, London, No. 1 (March 1930), p. 5. Note: See *Cohn's Bibliography*, pp. 73-74, stating that the extracts in this catalogue are not accurate transcriptions of the original letters.

58 Feb. 2, 1925. From the Hotel Taube, Schruns, Austria, to [Howell G. Jenkins]. Regarding the skiing and Hemingway's plans to go to Italy. Quoted in the introduction to the *Baker anthology*, p. 3. The original letter is in the Princeton University Library.

59 Feb. 28, 1925. From Austria, to Ernest Walsh and Ethel Moorhead. Autobiographical. Extract quoted in the catalogue of the *Ulysses Book Shop*, London, No. 1 (March 1930), p. 5. [See note under the Jan. 29, 1925 entry.]

60 July 1, 1925. To F. Scott Fitzgerald. Briefly quoted in *The Far Side of Paradise* by Arthur Mizener, Boston, 1949, p. 152. [Second edition, p. 165.]

61 July 20, 1925. From Madrid, to Ernest Walsh and Ethel Moorhead. Extract quoted in the catalogue of the *Ulysses Book Shop*, London, No. 1 (March 1930), p. 5. [See note under the Jan. 29, 1925 entry.]

62 Aug. 15 [1925]. To "Dear Old Carper" [Howell G. Jenkins]. Regarding a trip to Spain and the bullfights. Quoted in *A Creative Century: Collections at the University of Texas*, Austin, 1964, p. 29.

63 Dec. 31, 1925. To F. Scott Fitzgerald. Regarding *TOS*. Briefly quoted in *The Far Side of Paradise* by Arthur Mizener, Boston, 1949, p. 196. [Second edition, p. 216.]

64 Jan. 2, 1926. From Madrid, to Ernest Walsh and Ethel Moorhead. Extract quoted in the catalogue of the *Ulysses Book Shop*, London, No. 1 (March 1930), p. 6. [See note under the Jan. 29, 1925, entry.]

65 [April 1926]. To F. Scott Fitzgerald, regarding *SAR*. Quoted in *The Far Side of Paradise* by Arthur Mizener, Boston, 1949, p. 197. [Second edition, p. 217.]

66 May 4 [1926]. From Paris, to F. Scott Fitzgerald. Regarding publication of *SAR* and his plans to go to Spain. Quoted in the *Princeton University Library Chronicle*, XVII (Summer 1956), 248. The original letter is in the Fitzgerald Papers at Princeton University Library.

67 [Dec. 7, 1926]. To [Maxwell E. Perkins]. Regarding his philosophy about people and about his writing. Paragraph quoted in *Scribner's Magazine*, LXXXI (March 1927), 4. Reprinted, with a long dash indicating the deletion of "some writers," in *Scribner's Magazine*, LXXXVI (July 1929), 25. Reprinted in *Cohn's Bibliography*, p. 88.

68 Jan. 20, 1927. From Paris, to Maxwell E. Perkins. Regarding Sherwood Anderson. Briefly quoted in a footnote in *Baker*, p. 44.

69 [Spring 1927]. A reply to questions regarding various editions of his books. Excerpts quoted in the catalogue of the *Walden Bookshop*, Chicago (1930), pp. 2-3.

70 Oct. 24, 1927. To Wyndham Lewis. A reply to a letter of congratulations on *TOS*; also regarding Sherwood Anderson. Quoted in Lewis's *Rude Assignment*, London, [1950], p. 203.

71 [1929]. To Margaret C. Anderson. Regarding his contribution to the final number of the *Little Review*. Printed in the *Little Review*, XII (May 1929), 41. Reprinted in *The Little Review Anthology* edited by Margaret C. Anderson, New York, 1953, p. 367.

72 [July 1929]. From the Hotel Eskcalduna, Hendaye, France, to Caresse Crosby. Regarding the Hemingways' passports, which had been inadvertently left in her car. Facsimile of holograph letter reproduced in *The Passionate Years* by Caresse Crosby, London, 1955, p. [354]. Note: This letter was not reproduced in the American edition.

73 [1930]. From [Box 323, Key West, Fla.], to Josephine K. Piercy. A reply to her inquiry regarding his writing. Long extract printed in *Modern Writers at Work*, edited by Josephine K. Piercy, New York, 1930, pp. 488, 490. The original letter is in the Lilly Library at Indiana University.

74 April 6, 1930. From Box 396, Key West, Fla., to Mr. [Cyril] Clemens. Regarding his acceptance of an Honorary Vice-presidency in the Mark Twain Society. Facsimile of holograph letter reproduced on the cover of the *Mark Twain Journal*, XI (Summer 1962).

75 [1931]. To Capt. [Louis Henry] Cohn. Short note typed at the top of manuscript page, which was reproduced as the frontispiece in *Cohn's Bibliography*.

76 [1931]. To Louis Henry Cohn. Stating his opinion on bibliographies of living authors. Quoted in *Cohn's Bibliography*, pp. 10-11.

77 [1931]. To Louis Henry Cohn. Regarding his views on the listing of his early newspaper work. Quoted in *Cohn's Bibliography*, p. 112.

78 April 12, 1931. From Key West, Fla., to Dr. Guffey. Extract quoted in the catalogue of *The Library of Dr. Don Carlos Guffey* (Parke-Bernet Galleries), New York, 1958, p. 28.

79 April 27, 1931. From Key West, Fla., to Dr. Guffey. Extract quoted in the catalogue of *The Library of Dr. Don Carlos Guffey* (Parke-Bernet Galleries), New York, 1958, p. 28.

80 [May 1931?] From [Paris?], to Dr. Guffey. Long inscription, in letter form, in a copy of *iot*. Concerning the delay in the publication of *iot*. Facsimile of holograph inscription reproduced in the catalogue of *The Library of Dr. Don Carlos Guffey* (Parke-Bernet Galleries), New York, 1958, p. 31. Also quoted in full on p. 32. Reprinted in *Ezra Pound* by Charles Norman, New York, 1960, p. 256.

81 [Fall 1931?] To Ray Long. Regarding quail shooting in Arkansas. Paragraph quoted in the editor's comments in *20 Best Short Stories in 20 Years as an Editor*, New York, 1932, p. 3.

82 Feb. 11 [1932]. From Key West, Fla., to William C. Lengel, editor of *Cosmopolitan*. Regarding his short story "After the Storm." Extract quoted in *Guide to a Memorial Exhibition* by William White, Detroit, 1961, p. [7].

83 June 9 [1932?] From [Havana], to Samuel Putnam. Hemingway agrees to serve on a jury and lists three outstanding books of 1932. Extract quoted in Putnam's *Paris Was Our Mistress*, New York, 1947, p. 134. The original letter is in the Barrett Library at the University of Virginia.

84 Aug. 27, 1932. From Cooke City, Mont., to the editors of *Hound & Horn*. A reply to Lawrence Leighton's article in *H&H*, v (July-Sept. 1932). Printed in *Hound & Horn*, vi (Oct.-Dec. 1932), 135.

85 Oct. 5, 1932. From Cooke City, Mont., to Bob [Robert M. Coates]. Regarding Coates's review of *DIA* in the *New Yorker*, viii (Oct. 1, 1932). Printed in the *New Yorker*, viii (Nov. 5, 1932), 86-87.

86 [1933?] To Morrill Cody. Presumably regarding his willingness to write an introduction to James Charters' (and Morrill Cody's) book

This Must Be the Place. Facsimile of last page of holograph letter reproduced in *Hemingway, par lui-même* by G.-A. Astre, Paris, 1959, p. 131.

7 [June 1933]. From Havana, to the editors of the *New Republic.* Regarding Max Eastman's essay in the *NR,* LXXV (June 7, 1933). Printed in *Great Companions* by Max Eastman, New York, 1959, p. 57. Reprinted in the *Saturday Review,* XLII (April 4, 1959), 14.

8 [1934]. Long extract from a letter, describing the taking of the largest Atlantic sailfish, on May 23, 1934. Quoted in *American Big Game Fishing,* ed. Eugene V. Connett, New York, 1935, pp. 49-51.

9 May 28, 1934. To F. Scott Fitzgerald. Regarding Fitzgerald's sense of "personal tragedy." Quoted in *The Far Side of Paradise* by Arthur Mizener, Boston, 1949, pp. 238-239. [Second edition, p. 264.]

0 Aug. 19, 1935. From Key West, to Ivan Kashkeen. Letter and two postscripts printed (in English) in *Soviet Literature,* No. 11 (Nov. 1962), pp. 160-163.

1 Dec. 21, 1935. To F. Scott Fitzgerald. Two extracts quoted in *The Far Side of Paradise* by Arthur Mizener, Boston, 1949, pp. 69, 239-240. [Second edition, pp. 73, 265.]

2 [1936]. To Thomas Aitken, editor of *Outdoor Life.* A reply to a questionnaire regarding mutilated fish. Printed in *Outdoor Life,* LXXVII (June 1936), 70-72.

3 March 17, 1936. From Key West, Fla., to T. [Thomas] Aitken. Regarding good sportsmanship in fishing. Quoted in the catalogue of *Charles Hamilton Autographs, Inc.,* No. 4 (May 21, 1964), pp. 15-16. Also, a facsimile of the holograph closing lines is reproduced on p. 16.

4 [Nov. 1936]. To the editors of *New Masses,* congratulating them on their twenty-fifth anniversary. Telegram quoted in *New Masses,* XXI (Dec. 1, 1936), 21.

5 March 23, 1939. From Key West, Fla., to Ivan Kashkeen. Letter printed (in English) in *Soviet Literature,* No. 11 (Nov. 1962), pp. 163-164.

6 [1940]. To *Life,* regarding war writers on democracy. Printed in *Life,* VIII (June 24, 1940), 8. Reprinted in *Time,* XXXV (June 24, 1940), 92.

7 [Jan. 1941]. To Milton Wolff, regarding *FWBT.* Printed in *American Dialog,* I (Oct.–Nov. 1964), 11.

98 [1941]. From The Lombardy, 111 East 56 Street, New York, to Milton Wolff. Regarding the above letter. Printed in *American Dialog*, 1 (Oct.–Nov. 1964), 11.

99 Aug. 25, 1941. From Finca Vigia, San Francisco de Paula, Cuba, to Milton Wolff. Regarding the terms of a loan to Wolff. Printed in *American Dialog*, 1 (Oct.–Nov. 1964), 11.

100 Sept. 12, 1941. From Finca Vigia, San Francisco de Paula, Cuba, to Milton Wolff. Regarding his loan to Wolff. Printed in *American Dialog*, 1 (Oct.–Nov. 1964), 12.

101 May 12, 1942. From Cuba, to Whit Burnett. Regarding the inclusion of "The Short Happy Life of Francis Macomber" in Burnett's anthology. Quoted in *This Is My Best*, New York, 1942, p. 22. Note: The editor dates the letter as May 12, 1942; however, the date "June 1942" appears below it.

102 June 20, 1946. From Finca Vigia, San Francisco de Paula, Cuba, to Konstantin Simonov. Printed (in English) in *Soviet Literature*, No. 11 (Nov. 1962), pp. 165-167.

103 July 26, 1946. From Finca Vigia, to Milton Wolff. Regarding his reasons for refusing the chairmanship of an Abraham Lincoln Brigade rally. Printed in *American Dialog*, 1 (Oct.–Nov. 1964), 12-13.

104 Dec. 18, 1946. To Ernst Rowohlt, regarding the resumption of Rowohlt's publishing his work in German. Printed (in English) in *Rowohlts Rotblonder Roman*, [Hamburg, 1947], p. 44.

105 [1948]. To [René de Smedt], owner of La Casa Belga, a Havana book shop. Facsimile of a holograph congratulatory note on the book shop's twentieth anniversary, reproduced in the catalogue of *Casa Belga*, No. 76 (March 27, 1948), p. 3.

106 Jan. 18, 1949. From Villa Aprile, Italy, to W. J. Weatherby. Regarding bullfighting and *SAR*. Quoted in the catalogue of *Charles Hamilton Autographs, Inc.*, No. 6 (Jan. 14, 1965), p. 20.

107 July 6, 1949. To Arthur Mizener, regarding F. Scott Fitzgerald. Quoted in Mizener's *The Far Side of Paradise*, Boston, 1949, p. 342 (n. 3). [Second edition, p. 390 (n. 3).]

108 Oct. 4, 1949. To Arnoldo Mondadori. Printed (in Italian) in *Il Cinquantennio Editoriale di Arnoldo Mondadori, 1907–1957*, Verona, 1957, p. 219.

109 [1950]. Letter praising Nelson Algren's novel *The Man With the Golden Arm*. Printed in the *Book Find News*, No. 85 (Jan. 1950), p. 5.

110 [March 1950]. To Leonard Lyons. Regarding skiing in Cortina d'Ampezzo and his five "home towns." Quoted in Lyons' column in the *N.Y. Post* (March 30, 1950), p. 30. Partially reprinted in *Time*, LV (April 10, 1950), 36.

111 June 18, 1950. To Clara H. Franklin, sending his autograph and commenting on fishing. Briefly quoted in the catalogue of *Charles Hamilton Autographs, Inc.*, No. 9 (Sept. 30, 1965), p. 22.

112 July 5, 1950. To Arnoldo Mondadori, giving his views of three Italian novels. Printed (in Italian) in *Il Cinquantennio Editoriale di Arnoldo Mondadori, 1907–1957*, Verona, 1957, p. 228.

113 July 5, 1950. From Finca Vigia, to Milton Wolff. Regarding members of the Abraham Lincoln Battalion; and an accident aboard the *Pilar*. Printed in *American Dialog*, 1 (Oct.–Nov. 1964), 13.

114 [1951]. From Cuba, [presumably to Eric Edward Dorman-Smith]. Regarding the critics reception to *ARIT*. Quoted in Elise Morrow's column in the *St. Louis Post-Dispatch* (Jan. 15, 1951), 1 C.

115 [1951]. To Carlos Baker, regarding his first trip back to Italy after World War II. Quoted in *Baker anthology*, p. 8.

116 Feb. 17, 1951. From Cuba, to Carlos Baker. Regarding the number of words he had completed in the previous month. Quoted in *Baker anthology*, p. 10.

117 [March 1951]. From Havana, to Adriana Ivancich. Quoted (in Italian) in *Epoca*, LX (July 25, 1965), 75. Translated into English in *Parade* (Oct. 10, 1965), p. 12.

118 [March 25] 1951. To Carlos Baker. Regarding the "lost generation." Quoted in *Baker*, pp. 80-81.

119 April 1, 1951. To Carlos Baker. Regarding the political implications of the Spanish Civil War. Quoted in *Baker*, p. 228.

120 Sept. 30, 1951. To Fraser Drew. Concerning the importance of the reader knowing the places which a writer describes. Quoted in the *Mark Twain Journal*, XI (Summer 1962), 19.

121 [Nov. 1951]. From Cuba, to the editor of the *N.Y. Herald Tribune Book Review*. Regarding the three books he liked in 1951. Also, Hemingway listed six imaginary books which he would have enjoyed reading. Printed in John K. Hutchens' column in the *N.Y. Herald Tribune Book Review* (Dec. 9, 1951), p. 3.

122 April 12, 1952. To Adriana Ivancich, regarding *OMATS*. Quoted (in Italian) in *Epoca*, LX (July 25, 1965), 72.

123 [June 1952]. To a correspondent on the *N.Y. Herald Tribune*. Regarding the "luck" he had writing *OMATS*. Quoted in the *N.Y. Herald Tribune Book Review* (June 22, 1952), p. 2.

124 [July 1952]. To the editors of *Life*, regarding the publication of *OMATS* in *Life*. Four paragraphs quoted in *Life*, XXXIII (Aug. 25, 1952), 124. Partially quoted in *Time*, LX (Sept. 1, 1952), 48. First paragraph reprinted in *Life*, XXXIV (May 11, 1953), 25.

125 July 11, 1952. From Finca Vigia, to Earl Wilson. A reply to Wilson's query as to why he lives in Cuba. Printed in Wilson's column in the *N.Y. Post* (Aug. 31, 1952), p. 8 M. Partially reprinted in his column in the *N.Y. Post* (July 5, 1961), p. 14.

126 Aug. 17, 1952. From Cuba, to Bernard Kalb. A reply to questions about his writing, how the "big book" is coming, and about the fishing. Printed in the *Saturday Review*, XXXV (Sept. 6, 1952), 11.

127 Oct. 1, 1952. To Adriana Ivancich, regarding her book of poetry. Briefly quoted (in Italian) in *Epoca*, LX (July 25, 1965), 73.

128 Nov. 7, 1952. To Arnoldo Mondadori, regarding the Italian translation of *OMATS*. Printed (in Italian) in *Il Cinquantennio Editoriale di Arnoldo Mondadori, 1907–1957*, Verona, 1957, p. 239.

129 [1953]. To [René de Smedt], owner of La Casa Belga, a Havana book shop. Facsimile of a holograph congratulatory note on the book shop's twenty-fifth anniversary, reproduced in the catalogue of *Casa Belga*, No. 92 (March 30, 1953), p. 5.

130 [1953]. From Cuba, to twenty-three junior high school students in Louisville, Kentucky, thanking them for their letter about *OMATS*. Quoted in *Time*, LXI (March 2, 1953), 33.

131 Jan. 9, 1953. From Finca Vigia, San Francisco de Paula, Cuba, to Jack Hirschman. Advises a young writer who had sent him a story to read and criticize. Printed in the *N.Y. Times* [City Edition] (July 3, 1961), p. 6. Reprinted in the *Wolf Magazine of Letters*, Detroit, XXVII (Oct. 1961), 11-12. Reprinted under the title "Letter to a Young Man," without the recipient's name, in the *Mark Twain Journal*, XI (Summer 1962), 10. The original letter is in the Lilly Library at Indiana University.

132 [June 10, 1953]. From Cuba, to Frederick Wezeman, Chief Librarian of the Oak Park, Illinois, Public Library, on the occasion of the library's fiftieth anniversary. Printed in the *Library Journal*, LXXIX (Feb. 15, 1954), 292. Reprinted in *Wilson Library Bulletin*, XXVIII (March 1954), 542.

33 [1954?] To Juanito [Quintana]. Facsimile of a portion of a holograph letter reproduced as the frontispiece in *Hemingway, par lui-même* by G.-A. Astre, Paris, 1959. Also reproduced, in part, on the back cover of the German translation, *Hemingway in Selbstzeugnissen und Bilddokumenten*, Hamburg, 1961.

34 [May 1954]. From Madrid. Cable to *Life*, regarding Robert Capa's death. Quoted in *Life*, XXXVI (June 7, 1954), 25.

35 [Feb. 1955]. To Harvey Breit, regarding the number of words he had recently completed. Briefly quoted in *Encounter*, XVIII (April 1962), 93.

36 March 31, 1955. From Cuba, to Adriana Ivancich. Regarding Finca Vigia. Quoted (in Italian) in *Epoca*, LX (July 25, 1965), 72.

37 July 29, 1956. From San Francisco de Paula, Cuba, to "Mr. Rider." Regarding his views of William Faulkner's work. Facsimile of holograph letter reproduced in the catalogue of *Charles Hamilton Autographs, Inc.*, No. 5 (Oct. 8, 1964), 27. Also quoted on pp. 27-28.

38 [Fall 1956]. To the students of the University of Glasgow who had nominated him for the honorary job of university Lord Rector. Quoted in *Newsweek*, XLVIII (Oct. 29, 1956), 57.

39 Aug. 24, 1958. From San Francisco de Paula, Cuba, to Peter Briggs. Regarding wines. Briefly quoted in the catalogue of *Charles Hamilton Autographs, Inc.*, No. 9 (Sept. 30, 1965), p. 22.

40 [1959]. To Scribner's, regarding his work on an appendix to *DIA*. Briefly quoted by Lewis Nichols in the *N.Y. Times Book Review* (Oct. 4, 1959), p. 8.

41 [1960]. To Will Lang, correspondent for *Life*. Regarding the length of "The Dangerous Summer." Quoted in *Life*, XLIX (Sept. 5, 1960), 2.

42 Sept. 6, 1960. From Malaga, Spain. A cable to *Life*, regarding the mano a mano reported in "The Dangerous Summer." Printed in *Life*, XLIX (Sept. 19, 1960), 96.

43 [Jan. 1961]. From Mayo Clinic, Rochester, Minn. Regarding the inauguration of President John F. Kennedy. Quoted in *A Thousand Days* by Arthur M. Schlesinger, Jr., Boston, 1965, p. 372.

44 Jan. 13, 1961. From Rochester, Minn., to Mel Evans, Jr. Mentions being an honorary game warden of the Kenya Game Department. Facsimile of holograph closing sentences reproduced in the catalogue of *Charles Hamilton Autographs, Inc.*, No. 2 (Oct. 17, 1963), p. 37.

145 Jan. 18, 1961. From St. Mary's Hospital, Rochester, Minn., to the Milton Wolffs. Thanking them for their letter. Printed in *American Dialog*, 1 (Oct.–Nov. 1964), 13.

146 Jan. 19, 1961. From St. Mary's Hospital, Rochester, Minn., to Peter Briggs. Regarding his health. Briefly quoted in the catalogue of *Charles Hamilton Autographs, Inc.*, No. 9 (Sept. 30, 1965), p. 22.

147 June 15, 1961. From St. Mary's Hospital, Rochester, Minn., to Fritz Saviers, a nine-year-old friend in Ketchum, Idaho. Facsimile of two-page holograph letter reproduced in *Life*, LI (Aug. 25, 1961), 7.

148 [No date]. To Keith Hanson. A one-line letter verifying his date of birth as: July 21, 1899. Printed in the *Saturday Review*, XLIV (Sept. 2, 1961), 23.

EPHEMERA

149 GALLEY PROOFS OF FOUR POEMS

FOUR POEMS | *By* | ERNEST HEMINGWAY | [decorative line] | *On* August 31, 1930 *There were printed privately* | *for the prevention of piracy* 12 *copies of* Four Poems, | *for* E. H. *by* L.H.C. *This is Number* |

25 x 9. Galley proofs. Printed in black on a single sheet of glossy cream-colored paper.

CONTENTS: "The Age Demanded," "The Earnest Liberal's Lament," "The Lady Poets with Foot Notes," and "The Soul of Spain with McAlmon and Bird the Publisher [*sic*]."

NOTE: Louis Henry Cohn had planned to publish the poems in a six-page pamphlet, with the text on pp. [1]–[5]. However, he was advised by John S. Sumner, who was at that time Executive Secretary of the New York Society for the Suppression of Vice, that a copyright would be refused due to certain words that Hemingway had used in the poems.

150 Bastard note. 10 1/2 x 8 1/2. 1 page. Issued in December 1931 by Louis Henry Cohn. Facsimile of the proof sheet of the legal disclaimer, on p. [x], of the second printing of *A Farewell to Arms*, in 1929. Enclosed in a black dead metal border. Signed by Hemingway, with a humorous comment about using "bastard" rather than "illegitimate child," in the right-hand margin. A note in the lower left-hand corner states: OF THIS FACSIMILE FOUNDRY PROOF, | 93 COPIES HAVE BEEN PRIVATELY | PRINTED AND THE PLATE DESTROYED | *This is number* | L.H.C.

151 Circular letter. 10 1/2 x 7 1/2. 1 page. Letterhead: 79 Fifth Avenue | New York, N.Y. Dated: Jan. 16, 1940. A fund raising appeal

for the work of the Committee of 100 Sponsors for the Fourth Annual Conference of the American Committee for Protection of Foreign Born. Signed by Hemingway, who was a co-chairman of the committee. A footnote states that checks could be made payable to
Hemingway.

52 *Cuba: Isla de las Maravillas* by Ernesto T. Brivio. Havana [1953].
Printed by the Empresa Editora de Publicaciones, S.A., in Havana.
("Year of the Centenary of José Marti.") 332 pages. Text in Spanish, English, and French.
A short laudatory appraisal of the book by Hemingway appears on
p. [1]. A facsimile of his holograph statement, which is signed and
dated: Finca Vigia, San Francisco de Paula, is followed by the Spanish and French translation.

53 THE | SECRET AGENT'S | BADGE | OF COURAGE | Ernest
Hemingway | [publisher's device: B B encircled by: BELMONT ·
BOOKS ·]
7 1/16 x 4 1/4. Published by Belmont Productions, Inc., New
York, in 1961, at fifty cents, as No. L 506. Issued in black stiff paper
covers. Front cover: HEMINGWAY [in large white letters] | L 506 |
[publisher's device] | 50¢ [all in blue, in the upper left-hand corner]
| THE [purple] | SECRET AGENT'S [white] | BADGE OF [blue] |
COURAGE [orange] | [illustrative scene] | The world's greatest spy
stories | edited by Kurt Singer | with Eric Ambler, Pearl Buck, |
Joseph Conrad and others [all in blue]. Backstrip, reading down-
ward: L 506 [horizontal] | HEMINGWAY [white] The Secret
Agent's Badge of Courage [red] | [publisher's device] | 50¢. All edges
stained yellow.
"The Secret Agent's Badge of Courage" "by Ernest Hemingway,"
on p. 158, is listed under the acknowledgments, on p. 4, as being reprinted from *Men at War*, which is correct. However, the first two
paragraphs are reprinted from a quotation by General Karl von
Clausewitz, on p. 428, and the remaining three paragraphs are from
another quotation by General von Clausewitz, on p. 120. The brief
quotation, on p. [1], under the caption: ERNEST HEMINGWAY |
DEFINES COURAGE is also from General von Clausewitz's quotation on p. 120.
NOTE: For commentary on this book, which contains nothing by
Hemingway, see William White's "Some Thoughts on the Hemingway Racket," *New Republic*, CXLVI (March 26, 1962), 24-25.

54 Ernest Hemingway Reading. A long-playing 33 1/3 r.p.m. mi-
crogroove record. Released by Caedmon Records, Inc., in New
York, in July 1965, as *Caedmon* TC 1185, at $5.95. Recorded at
Finca Vigia, San Francisco de Paula, Cuba, 1948-1961.

CONTENTS: Side 1: The Nobel Prize Acceptance Speech/Second Poem to Mary/In Harry's Bar in Venice. Side 2: The Fifth Column /Work in Progress/Saturday Night at the Whorehouse in Billings, Montana.

NOTE: Three of the readings are from unpublished work: In Harry's Bar in Venice, an improvised parody of *ARIT*; Work in Progress, an excerpt from an unpublished novel about the sea, a chapter of which was read at a White House gathering in 1962 [see the *N.Y. Times* (April 30, 1962)]; and Saturday Night at the Whorehouse in Billings, Montana.

NOTE: Second Poem to Mary was published in the *Atlantic*, CCXVI (Aug. 1965). There are a number of minor additions and omissions in the reading.

NOTE: The Fifth Column is from Hemingway's preface to the *First 49*. Except for the omission of the fourth paragraph, regarding the difficulties in finding someone to produce the play, the preface is read to the line: "Some other places were not so good but maybe we were not so good when we were in them."

NOTE: The "Notes" by Mary Hemingway and A. E. Hotchner on the inside front cover and the back cover of the record jacket give the circumstances in which the original tapes were made. A photograph of Hemingway by Mary Hemingway appears on the jacket cover. A photograph of the Hemingways in 1953 at the bullfight in Pamplona appears on the inside back cover.

155   A Keepsake | from | The Fales Library | NEW YORK UNIVER-SITY | [design] | ON THE OCCASION OF A PRESENTATION | OF A GIFT OF BOOKS AND MANUSCRIPTS | BY DE COURSEY FALES, ESQ. | 18 JANUARY 1966

9 x 6. Folder. 4 pages. Printed on a single sheet folded once; cream-colored paper, printed in black. The cover, as shown above, serves as the title page; a statement at the bottom of p. [2] reads: A drawing and inscription by Ernest Hemingway done | on the fly-leaf of a copy of *Torrents of Spring* (1926); the drawing and inscription, enclosed in a ruled border, is on p. [3]; the back cover, p. [4], is blank. 200 copies were printed.

BOOK BLURBS BY HEMINGWAY

156   Pamphlet. *Time for Laughter* by Robert Whitcomb. Brooklyn, N.Y. (published by the author), 1931. A New Capricornus Social Experimental Story. First edition of 1000 copies. 7 3/4 x 5 7/8. A two-line quotation by Hemingway appears on the front paper cover.

157   Book band. *Conquistador* by Archibald MacLeish. Boston: Houghton Mifflin, 1932. Issued in March 1932. Orange paper band,

printed in black. 3 1/4 x 20. Reads: ERNEST HEMINGWAY says: "If it is of any interest to you to read great poetry as it is published before it becomes classic and compulsory, I advise you to read 'Conquistador.' " Note: A blurb by Stephen Vincent Benét also appears on the band. [Used by permission of Houghton Mifflin Company.]

58   Advertisement. *Summer is Ended* by John Herrmann. New York: Covici-Friede, 1932. The publishers' advertisement in *Contact*, i, iii (Oct. 1932) 4, includes an appraisal by Hemingway.

59   Dust jacket. *My Life and Hard Times* by James Thurber. New York: Harper, 1933. Boxed blurb on the front cover reads: ERNEST HEMINGWAY says: "I find it far | superior to the auto- | biography of Henry Adams. Even in the | earliest days when | Thurber was writing under the name of | Alice B. Toklas we | knew he had it in him | if he could get it out." [Used by permission of Harper & Row, Publishers.]

60   Dust jacket. *The Chink in the Armour* by Mrs. Belloc Lowndes. New York: Longmans, Green, 1937. A facsimile of a typewritten letter on the front cover reads: A PETITION | Longmans, Green & Co. | New York, N.Y. | It is lamentable that "THE | CHINK IN THE ARMOUR"—that un- | canny masterpiece of dread and | suspense—should be so little | known in this country and vir- | tually unobtainable here. We beg | you to publish it so that we | may get it when we want it and | give it to our friends. | Ernest Hemingway | Alexander Woollcott | Edmund Pearson. Note: Hemingway writes of Gertrude Stein introducing him to Marie Belloc Lowndes' work in *A Moveable Feast*, p. 27. [Used by permission of David McKay Company, Inc.]

61   Advertisement. *Two Wars and More to Come* by Herbert L. Matthews. New York: Carrick & Evans, 1938. The publisher's advertisement in the *N.Y. Times Book Review* (Jan. 30, 1938), p. 28, quotes a cablegram from Hemingway, from Paris, praising this book. Note: Facsimiles of Hemingway's cablegram, stamped: DEL 1310 JAN 8 38, were also issued. They measure 9¼ x 8½.

62   Dust jacket. *Moon Over Miami* by Jack Kofoed. New York: Random House, 1955. A short blurb by Hemingway appears on the back cover.

63   Dust jacket. *The Restlessness of Shanti Andia and Other Writings* by Pio Baroja. Ann Arbor: Univ. of Michigan Press, 1959. A photograph of Hemingway and Pio Baroja appears on the back cover and a tribute to Baroja by Hemingway is quoted from *Time*, LXVIII (Oct. 29, 1956), 47.

269

164   Dust jacket. *Out of My League* by George Plimpton. New York: Harper, 1961. A blurb by Hemingway on the front cover reads: "Beautifully observed and incredibly conceived, this ac- | count of a self-imposed ordeal has the chilling quality of a | true nightmare. It is the dark side of the moon of Walter Mitty."—ERNEST HEMINGWAY. On the back cover: "After reading *Out of My League* it is very hard to wait for the true | story of George and Archie Moore." —Ernest Hemingway. [Used by permission of Harper & Row, Publishers.]

PART TWO
BIOGRAPHICAL
AND CRITICAL
MATERIAL ON
ERNEST HEMINGWAY

CHRONOLOGICAL LIST OF SOME
PRINCIPAL BOOKS ON HEMINGWAY

1931. *A Bibliography of the Works of Ernest Hemingway.*
Louis Henry Cohn. (B9).

1950. *Ernest Hemingway: The Man and His Work.* Edited by
John K. M. McCaffery. (G255).

1951. *A Hemingway Check List.* Lee Samuels. (B51).

1952. *Hemingway: The Writer as Artist.* Carlos Baker. (G26).

1952. *Ernest Hemingway.* Philip Young. (G460).

1952. *The Art of Ernest Hemingway.* John Atkins. (G22).

1954. *The Apprenticeship of Ernest Hemingway.*
Charles A. Fenton. (G143).

1959. *Hemingway par lui-même.* G.-A. Astre. (G21).

1960. *Hemingway: eine Bildbiographie.* Leo Lania. (G226).

1961. *Portrait of Hemingway.* Lillian Ross. (G342).

1961. *My Brother, Ernest Hemingway.*
Leicester Hemingway. (G188).

1961. *Hemingway and His Critics: An International Anthology.*
Edited by Carlos Baker. (G27).

1961. *Hemingway.* Edited by John Brown. (G67).

1962. *At the Hemingways.* Marcelline Hemingway Sanford. (G350).

1962. *Hemingway: A Collection of Critical Essays.* Edited by
Robert P. Weeks. (G439).

1962. *Ernest Hemingway: Critiques of Four Major Novels.*
Edited by Carlos Baker. (G28).

1963. *Ernest Hemingway in Übersetzungen.* Hans W. Bentz. (G41).

1963. *Ernest Hemingway.* Earl Rovit. (G345).

1965. *The Literary Reputation of Hemingway in Europe.*
Edited by Roger Asselineau. (G20).

1966. *Papa Hemingway: A Personal Memoir.*
A. E. Hotchner. (G198).

1966. *Hemingway in Michigan.* Constance Cappel Montgomery.
(B61).

SECTION G
BOOKS ON OR SIGNIFICANTLY MENTIONING HEMINGWAY

G1 Aamot, Per. *Streiftog: Essays*. Oslo: Dreyer, 1948. Pamphlet. pp. 67-85: "Ernest Hemingway."

2 Adams, J. Donald. *The Shape of Books to Come*. New York: Viking Press, 1944. pp. 103-113, 141, 181-182. [Published under the title *The Writer's Responsibility*. London: Secker & Warburg, 1946.] pp. 103-113: Ch. VI: "The Tough Guys." Mainly on Hemingway.

3 Adams, J. Donald. *Speaking of Books—and Life*. New York: Holt, Rinehart & Winston, 1965. pp. 8, 18, 21, 22, 23, 25, 37, 62, 64, 123, 174-176.
  pp. 174-176: "The Sun Also Sets," reprinted from the *N.Y. Times Book Review* (July 16, 1961).

4 Aldridge, John W. *After the Lost Generation: A Critical Study of the Writers of Two Wars*. New York: McGraw-Hill, 1951. pp. 11, 14, 23-43, 107-116. [Paperback edition: New York: Noonday Press, 1958.]
  pp. 23-43: Ch. III: "Hemingway: Nightmare and the Correlative of Loss." pp. 107-116: Ch. VII: "The Neo-Hemingways: and the Failure of Protest."

5 Aldridge, John W., ed. *Critiques and Essays on Modern Fiction: 1920-1951*. New York: Ronald Press, 1952. pp. 447-473, 588-591.
  pp. 447-473: "Ernest Hemingway" by Robert Penn Warren. See Warren's *Selected Essays* for reprint notes. pp. 588-591: A selected bibliography of critical studies of Hemingway's work, compiled by Robert W. Stallman.

6 Aldridge, John W. *In Search of Heresy: American Literature in an Age of Conformity*. New York: McGraw-Hill, 1956. pp. 149-165.
  Ch. VI: "Hemingway: the etiquette of the berserk," reprinted from *Mandrake*, II (Autumn–Winter 1954–1955).

7 Aldridge, John W. *Time to Murder and Create: The Contemporary Novel in Crisis*. New York: David McKay, 1966. pp. 153-155, 185-191.
  pp. 185-191: Ch. [XII]: "A Last Look at the Old Man," a review of the Scribner Library edition of *OMATS*.

8 Algren, Nelson. *Notes from A Sea Diary: Hemingway All the Way*. New York: Putnam, 1965. pp. 11, 15, 16, 18, 30-39, 87-95, 105, 167-171, 177, 207-210, 250-251.
  The novelist intersperses his defense of Hemingway against certain critics with an account of a trip to the Orient.

9 Allen, Walter. *The Modern Novel: In Britain and the United States*. New York: Dutton, 1964. pp. 92-98.

Discussion of Hemingway's work in the chapter "The Twenties: American."

10 Anderson, Carl L. *The Swedish Acceptance of American Literature.* Stockholm: Almqvist & Wiksell, 1957. pp. 82, 92, 98-99. Bibliographical footnotes.

pp. 98-99: Hemingway's influence on Swedish authors, especially short story writers.

11 Anderson, Margaret C. *My Thirty Years' War: An Autobiography.* New York: Covici, Friede, 1930. pp. 258-260. Photograph of Hemingway by Man Ray.

The founder of the *Little Review* reminisces on Hemingway in Paris, in the spring of 1923.

12 Anderson, Sherwood. *Memoirs.* New York: Harcourt, Brace, 1942. pp. 356, 473-476.

pp. 473-476: Under the heading "Of Faulkner and Hemingway," Anderson refers to the letter which Hemingway wrote him following the publication of *TOS*, and describes his final meeting with Hemingway.

13 Anderson, Sherwood. *Letters.* Selected and edited by Howard Mumford Jones in association with Walter B. Rideout. Boston: Little, Brown, 1953. pp. 82-83, 85, 136, 146, 173, 205, 295, 345, 392, 397.

p. 85: Letter to Gertrude Stein (1921), introducing the Hemingways. p. 146: Letter to Gertrude Stein (1925), regarding the blurb he wrote for the dust jacket of *IOT*.

14 Angoff, Allan, ed. *American Writing Today: Its Independence and Vigor.* New York: New York Univ. Press, 1957. pp. 61-63, 164, 165-166, 167, 168, 170, 184, 201, 205, 370-372.

pp. 370-372: Review of *FTA*, reprinted from the *Times Literary Supplement* (Nov. 28, 1929).

15 Ankenbrand, Frank, Jr. *By Their Works Shall Ye Know Them:* (*Ernest Hemingway, 18 -1961*). Torrance, Calif.: Hors Commerce Press, 1964. (No. 3.) Pamphlet. 16 pages. Drawing of Hemingway by Ben Tibbs.

Poems, titled after Hemingway's novels. Note: First limited edition of 400 copies.

16 Antheil, George. *Bad Boy of Music.* Garden City, N.Y.: Doubleday, Doran, 1945. pp. 146, 147, 148, 155. [London: Hurst & Blackett, 1947.]

p. 148: The composer recalls arranging for publication of Hemingway's work in *Der Querschnitt*, in 1925.

17 Arnavon, Cyrille. *Histoire Littéraire des États-Unis*. Paris: Librairie Hachette, 1953. pp. 326-328.
Discussion of Hemingway's work from the chapter "Témoins de la 'Génération Perdue.' "

18 Aronowitz, Alfred G. and Peter Hamill. *Ernest Hemingway*: *The Life and Death of a Man*. New York: Lancer, 1961. Original paperback. 222 pages. Cover drawing of Hemingway by Oscar Liebman.
Sections of this biography are reprinted from a series of eleven articles which appeared in the *N.Y. Post* (July 3-16, 1961).

19 Ashley, Schuyler. *Essay Reviews*. Kansas City: Lowell Press, 1929. pp. 67, 102.
p. 67: Review of *IOT*, reprinted from the *K.C. Star* (Dec. 12, 1925). p. 102: Review of *SAR*, reprinted from the *K.C. Star* (Dec. 4, 1926).

20 Asselineau, Roger, ed. *The Literary Reputation of Hemingway in Europe*. Paris: Minard, 1965. (Lettres Modernes. Situation, No.' 5.) 212 pages. Text in English. [New York: New York Univ. Press, 1965. Paperback.]
This collection of essays is from a symposium on the critical reception of Hemingway's work, held at the Villa Serbelloni in Bellagio, Italy, during September 1960. Two additional essays have been included: Stephen Jan Parker's essay on Hemingway's reception by Russian critics and Arturo Barea's essay on *FWBT*.
Contents: pp. 3-7: Introduction by Heinrich Straumann.
pp. 9-36: "Hemingway's English Reputation" by D.S.R. Welland. Notes on pp. 36-38.
pp. 39-65: "French Reactions to Hemingway's Work between the two World Wars" by Roger Asselineau. Notes on pp. 66-72.
pp. 73-91: "The Critical Reception of Hemingway's Work in Germany since 1920" by Helmut Papajewski. Notes on pp. 91-92.
pp. 93-123: "Hemingway in Italy" by Mario Praz. Notes on pp. 124-125.
pp. 127-148: "Hemingway in Norway" by Sigmund Skard. Notes on pp. 148-149.
pp. 151-170: "Hemingway in Sweden" by Lars Åhnebrink. Notes on pp. 171-174. Checklist of Swedish translations on p. 175.
pp. 177-193: "Hemingway's Revival in the Soviet Union: 1955-1962" by Stephen Jan Parker. Reprinted from *American Literature*, XXXV (Jan. 1964). Notes on pp. 193-195.
Appendix: pp. 197-210: "Not Spain but Hemingway" by Arturo Barea. First published in *Horizon*, III (May 1941).

21 Astre, G.-A. (Georges-Albert). *Hemingway par lui-même*. Paris: Éditions du Seuil, 1959. (Écrivains de Toujours series, No. 46.)

277

189 pages. Photographs. [(a) Translated into German, *Ernest Hemingway in Selbstzeugnissen und Bilddokumenten*. Hamburg: Rowohlt, 1961. 180 pages. (b) Revised edition, 1961, with a new three-page "Epitaphe."]

A study of Hemingway as seen through extracts of his writings. Bibliography on pp. 181-183, and "filmographie" on pp. 185-186.

22 Atkins, John. *The Art of Ernest Hemingway: His Work and Personality*. London: Peter Nevill, 1952. [viii] + 245 pages. Photographs. [(a) New York: Roy Publishers, 1953. (b) Revised edition: London: Spring Books, 1964. x + 258 pages. A preface by the author has been added on pp. vii-x.]

A study of the significant events in Hemingway's life and the manner in which his work reflects the man and his experience. Appendix A, on pp. 233-234, includes a partial checklist of Hemingway's work. Appendix B, on pp. 235-239, "Hemingway on the English." Appendix C, on pp. 240-245, "Old Soldier Goes Sour" by Bernard Raymund, expresses the belief that Hemingway actively disliked wars.

23 Baden, Hans Jürgen. *Literatur und Selbstmord: Cesare Pavese, Klaus Mann, Ernest Hemingway*. Stuttgart: Ernst Klett, 1965. pp. 147-213.

In four parts: "Die letzte Handlung," "Der Sieger geht leer aus," "Liebe," and "Tod."

24 Baiwir, Albert. *Le déclin de l'individualisme chez les romanciers américains contemporains*. Paris: E. Droz, 1943. pp. 291-312.

Ch. VII: "Ernest Hemingway."

25 Baiwir, Albert. *Abrégé de l'histoire du roman américain*. Brussels: Éditions Lumière, 1946. Pamphlet. Photograph. pp. 85-87.

Discussion on Hemingway's work from the chapter "Les principaux romanciers américains."

26 Baker, Carlos. *Hemingway: The Writer as Artist*. Princeton: Princeton Univ. Press, 1952. xx + 322 pages. [(a) Toronto: Saunders, 1952. (b) Translated into Italian by Guglielmo Ambrosoli, *Hemingway: scrittore e artista*. Parma: Ugo Guanda, 1954. (c) Translated into Arabic by Ihsan Abbas, reviser: Mohammed Najm, *Arnst Haminkhway*. Beirut, Lebanon: Dar Maktabat al-Hayat, 1959. (d) Translated into German by Helmut Hirsch. Hamburg: Rowohlt, 1967. (e) Second edition, enlarged, 1956. xx + 355 pages. Includes a new chapter on *OMATS*, pp. 289-310. (f) Third edition, enlarged, 1963. xx + 379 pages. Includes a new last chapter covering the last ten years of Hemingway's life and work, pp. 329-348.]

A study of Hemingway as artist, stylist, and craftsman, with an analysis and evaluation of his work from 1920 to 1952. Appended is a "Working Check-List of Hemingway's Prose, Poetry, and Journalism—with Notes," on pp. 299-310. Excerpts are reprinted in *Modern American Fiction*, ed. A. Walton Litz, New York, 1963, pp. 228-243; in *Concise American Composition and Rhetoric*, ed. Donald Davidson, New York, 1964, pp. 90-92; in *Weeks collection*, pp. 118-126; and in *Baker critiques*, pp. 11-17, 47-60, 108-130, 156-172.

27 Baker, Carlos, ed. *Hemingway and His Critics: An International Anthology*. New York: Hill & Wang, 1961. (American Century Series.) [xiv] + 298 pages. [(a) Paperback edition: same publisher, 1961. AC 36. (b) Toronto: Copp Clark, 1961.]

Contents: pp. 1-18: "Introduction: Citizen of the World" by Carlos Baker.

pp. 19-37: "An Interview with Ernest Hemingway" by George Plimpton. Reprinted from the *Paris Review*, v (Spring 1958).

pp. 38-54: "Ernest Hemingway" by André Maurois. First published in *Revue de Paris*, LXII (March 1955), translated from the French by Joseph M. Bernstein.

pp. 55-60: "Emergence of Ernest Hemingway" by Edmund Wilson, reprinted from *The Shores of Light*, New York, 1952, pp. 115-124.

pp. 61-70: "Hemingway and His Critics" by Lionel Trilling, reprinted from the *Partisan Review*, VI (Winter 1939).

pp. 71-79: "Hemingway's Short Stories" by H. E. Bates, reprinted from *The Modern Short Story*, London, 1941, pp. 167-178.

pp. 80-92: "The Death of Love in *The Sun Also Rises*" by Mark Spilka, reprinted from *Twelve Original Essays on Great American Novels*, ed. Charles Shapiro, Detroit, 1958, pp. 238-256.

pp. 93-115: "Observations on the Style of Ernest Hemingway" by Harry Levin. First published in *Kenyon Review*, XIII (Autumn 1951).

pp. 116-130: "Hemingway in Italy" by Mario Praz. First published in the *Partisan Review*, xv (Oct. 1948).

pp. 131-144: "The Hemingway of the Major Works" by Pier Francesco Paolini. First published in *Letterature Moderne*, VI (Nov.–Dec. 1956), translated from the Italian by Joseph M. Bernstein.

pp. 145-161: "Hemingway in Russia" by Deming Brown, reprinted from *American Quarterly*, v (Summer 1953).

pp. 162-179: "Alive in the Midst of Death: Ernest Hemingway" by Ivan Kashkeen. First published in *Soviet Literature*, No. 7 (July 1956).

pp. 180-191: "Ernest Hemingway: The Missing Third Dimension" by Michael F. Moloney, reprinted from *Fifty Years of the American Novel*, ed. Harold C. Gardner, New York, 1951, pp. 183-196.

pp. 192-201: "Hemingway Achieves the Fifth Dimension" by F. I. Carpenter, reprinted from *American Literature and the Dream*, New York, 1955, pp. 185-193.

pp. 202-212: "Not Spain but Hemingway" by Arturo Barea. First published in *Horizon*, III (May 1941), translated from the Spanish by Ilsa Barea.

pp. 213-226: "Hemingway's *Across the River and Into the Trees*" by Horst Oppel. First published in *Neueren Sprachen*, No. 11, [1952], translated from the German by Joseph M. Bernstein.

pp. 227-244: "How Do You Like It Now, Gentlemen?" by Joseph Warren Beach, reprinted from the *Sewanee Review*, LIX (Spring 1951).

pp. 245-258: "Hemingway: The Matador and the Crucified" by Melvin Backman, reprinted from *Modern Fiction Studies*, I (Aug. 1955).

pp. 259-268: "*The Old Man and the Sea*: Hemingway's Tragic Vision of Man" by Clinton S. Burhans, Jr., reprinted from *American Literature*, XXXI (Jan. 1960).

pp. 269-276: "The Marlin and the Shark: A Note on *The Old Man and the Sea*" by Keiichi Harada. First published in the *Journal of the College of Literature*, Aoyama Gakuin University, Tokyo, No. 4 (March 1960).

pp. 279-298: A Checklist of Hemingway Criticism.

28 Baker, Carlos, ed. *Ernest Hemingway: Critiques of Four Major Novels*. New York: Scribner's, 1962. (A Scribner Research Anthology.) Paperbound. 204 pages. For description of this book, see (B59).
Contents: p. 1: Introduction by the editor.

Part One: *The Sun Also Rises*
pp. 4-6: "*The Sun Also Rises*" by James T. Farrell, reprinted from *The League of Frightened Philistines*, New York, 1945, pp. 20-24.

pp. 7-10: "*The Sun Also Rises*: A Commentary" by Philip Young, reprinted from *Ernest Hemingway*, New York, 1952, pp. 54-60.

pp. 11-17: "Place, Fact, and Scene in *The Sun Also Rises*" by Carlos Baker, reprinted from *Hemingway: The Writer as Artist*, Princeton, 1956 edition, pp. 48-59.

pp. 18-25: "The Death of Love in *The Sun Also Rises*" by Mark Spilka, reprinted from *Twelve Original Essays on Great American Novels*, ed. Charles Shapiro, Detroit, 1958, pp. 238-256.

Part Two: *A Farewell to Arms*
pp. 28-36: "*A Farewell to Arms*" by Ray B. West, reprinted from *The Art of Modern Fiction*, New York, 1949, pp. 622-633.

pp. 37-40: "The Religion of Death in *A Farewell to Arms*" by

James F. Light, reprinted from *Modern Fiction Studies*, vii (Summer 1961).

pp. 41-46: "Hemingway's Other Style" by Charles R. Anderson, reprinted from *Modern Language Notes*, lxxvi (May 1961).

pp. 47-60: "The Mountain and the Plain" by Carlos Baker, reprinted from *Hemingway: The Writer as Artist*, Princeton, 1956 edition, pp. 94-116.

pp. 61-74: "Hemingway's Ambiguity: Symbolism and Irony" by E. M. Halliday, reprinted from *American Literature*, xxviii (March 1956).

p. 75: The Original Conclusion to *A Farewell to Arms*. See (B59).

Part Three: *For Whom the Bell Tolls*

pp. 78-81: "An American in Spain" by Lionel Trilling, reprinted from *The Partisan Reader*, ed. William Phillips and Philip Rahv, New York, 1946, pp. 639-644.

pp. 82-86: "Style in *For Whom the Bell Tolls*" by Joseph Warren Beach, reprinted from *American Fiction*, New York, 1941, pp. 111-119.

pp. 87-89: "The Background of a Style" by Mark Schorer, reprinted from the *Kenyon Review*, iii (Winter 1941).

pp. 90-94: Review of *FWBT* by Alvah C. Bessie, reprinted from *New Masses*, xxxvii (Nov. 5, 1940).

pp. 95-107: " 'Mechanized Doom': Ernest Hemingway and the American View of the Spanish Civil War" by Allen Guttmann. This is the revision of an article which first appeared in the *Massachusetts Review*, i (May 1960).

pp. 108-130: "The Spanish Tragedy" by Carlos Baker, reprinted from *Hemingway: The Writer as Artist*, Princeton, 1956 edition, pp. 223-263.

Part Four: *The Old Man and the Sea*

pp. 132-134: "With Grace Under Pressure" by Mark Schorer. Review of *OMATS*, reprinted from *New Republic*, cxxvii (Oct. 6, 1952).

pp. 135-143: "Hemingway: The Matador and the Crucified" by Melvin Backman. This is a corrected version of an article which first appeared in *Modern Fiction Studies*, i (Aug. 1955).

pp. 144-149: "*Confiteor Hominem*: Ernest Hemingway's Religion of Man" by Joseph Waldmeir, reprinted from the *Papers of the Michigan Academy of Science, Arts, and Letters*, xlii [1956].

pp. 150-155: "*The Old Man and the Sea*: Hemingway's Tragic Vision of Man" by Clinton S. Burhans, Jr., reprinted from *American Literature*, xxxi (Jan. 1960).

pp. 156-172: "Hemingway's Ancient Mariner" by Carlos Baker.

This is a revised version of Ch. xii of *Hemingway: The Writer as Artist*, Princeton, 1956 edition, pp. 289-320.

Part Five: Synoptic Essays
pp. 174-182: "Hemingway's Narrative Perspective" by E. M. Halliday, reprinted from the *Sewanee Review*, lx (Spring 1952).
pp. 183-192: "Ernest Hemingway: The Meaning of Style" by John Graham, reprinted from *Modern Fiction Studies*, vi (Winter 1960–1961).

29 Baker, Charles Henry, Jr. *The Gentleman's Companion*. New York: Derrydale Press, 1939. Vol. i: *Being an Exotic Cookery Book*, pp. xvii, 66, 168. Vol. ii: *Being an Exotic Drinking Book*. pp. xvi, 31-32, 34. [Reissued: New York: Crown, 1946.]
p. 66: "Smothered Conch, Ernest Hemingway, as Prepared by Carlos then Head Gaffer on Good Ship *Pilar*, while Sailfishing off Sombrero Light in the Gulf Stream; and which Fed Six." pp. 31-32: "Ernest Hemingway's *Reviver* on Mornings after Anything, Made of Hollands & other Things, which We Called 'Death in the Gulf Stream,' but Found Most Valuable." p. 34: "A Farewell to Hemingway, Being a Sort of *Kirsch* Collins We Invented on the Night We Saw Hemingway & Bullfighter Sidney Franklin off on the Plane for New York, & Loyalist Spain." Note: Issued in a numbered edition of 1250 copies; boxed.

30 Baker, Denys Val, ed. *Writers of Today*. Vol. ii. London: Sidgwick & Jackson, 1948. pp. 3-18.
"Ernest Hemingway" by Malcolm Cowley, reprinted from the Introduction to the Viking Portable *Hemingway*, pp. vii-xxiv.

31 Barea, Arturo. *The Forge*. London: Faber & Faber, 1941. [Translated by Ilsa Barea from the Spanish, *La forja de un rebelde*. Published under the title: *The Forging of a Rebel*. New York: Reynal & Hitchcock, 1946. pp. 643, 664, 685.]
Brief reminiscences of Hemingway, in Madrid, during the Spanish Civil War.

32 Barrett, C. Waller. *Italian Influence on American Literature*. New York: Grolier Club, 1962. An Address and a Catalogue of an Exhibition of Books, Manuscripts and Art showing this influence on American Literature and Art. Held at the Grolier Club, October 17 to December 10, 1961. pp. 28, 49, 90-91.
p. 49: List of Hemingway items in the exhibit. pp. 90-91: Facsimile of first page of *FTA* in *Scribner's Magazine*, lxxxv (May 1929), inscribed by Hemingway. Opposite is a photograph of Hemingway by Helen Breaker.

33 [Bartlett's]. *Familiar Quotations by John Bartlett: A Collection of Passages, Phrases and Proverbs Traced to Their Sources in Ancient and Modern Literature.* Boston: Little, Brown, 1955. [Thirteenth edition.] Centennial Edition. pp. 982-983.

Short quotations from *DIA, GHOA, FWBT, Men at War, Baker,* etc.

34 Bates, H. E. *The Modern Short Story: A Critical Survey.* London: Nelson, 1941. pp. 167-178.

This study was reprinted in *Baker anthology,* pp. 71-79, under the title "Hemingway's Short Stories."

35 Beach, Joseph Warren. *The Outlook for American Prose.* Chicago: Univ. of Chicago Press, 1926. pp. 11, 277-278.

pp. 277-278: Discussion of Hemingway's short chapters in *IOT*.

36 Beach, Joseph Warren. *The Twentieth Century Novel: Studies in Technique.* New York: Appleton-Century-Crofts, 1932. pp. 280, 396, 476-477, 532-537. [Translated into Italian by Aldo Camerino and Carlo Izzo. *Tecnica del romanzo novecentesco.* Milan: Bompiani, 1948.]

pp. 532-537: Discussion of Hemingway's work from the chapter "The Cult of the Simple."

37 Beach, Joseph Warren. *American Fiction: 1920-1940.* New York: Macmillan, 1941. pp. 9, 69-93, 97-119, 359. [(a) Translated into German, *Amerikanische Prosadichtung: 1920-1940.* Aschaffenburg: Pettloch, 1947. pp. 65-114. (b) Reissued: New York: Russell & Russell, 1960.]

pp. 69-93: Ch. IV: "Ernest Hemingway: Empirical Ethics." Discussion of the "ethical system" in *SAR, FTA,* and *FWBT.* pp. 97-119: Ch. V: "Ernest Hemingway: The Esthetics of Simplicity." Discussion of Hemingway's rejection of "proud words." Partly reprinted in *Baker critiques,* pp. 82-86.

38 Beach, Sylvia. *Shakespeare and Company.* New York: Harcourt, Brace, 1959. pp. 33, 40, 51, 77-83, 86, 88, 111, 112, 120, 121, 124, 127, 128, 132, 138, 182, 206, 211, 219-220. Photographs. [(a) London: Faber & Faber, 1960. (b) Translated into French by George Adam. Paris: Mercure de France, 1962. (c) Translated into Italian by Elena Spagnol Vaccari. Milan: Rizzoli, 1962. (d) Translated into German by Lilly v. Sauter. Munich: P. List Verlag, 1962.]

pp. 77-83: Ch. IX: "My Best Customer." The title refers to Hemingway's patronage of the author's bookshop in Paris, during the 1920s. pp. 219-220: Ch. XXIII: "Hemingway Liberates the Rue de l'Odéon." Describes Hemingway's arrival during the liberation of Paris, in August 1944.

39 [Beach, Sylvia.] *Les Années Vingt, Les Écrivains Américains à Paris et leurs amis: 1920–1930.* Paris: Centre Culturel Américain, 1959. pp. 9, 25, 43, 44, 47, 50, 65, 69, 70, 71, 74, 79, 80, 81, 83, 85, 91, 102-104, 131. Photographs.

Catalogue of the Exposition sponsored by the American Cultural Center of the United States Embassy, March 11 to April 25, 1959, in Paris. pp. 102-104: List of photographs, letters, inscribed books, and periodical pieces by Hemingway, which were included in the exhibit.

40 Beaver, Harold, ed. *American Critical Essays: Twentieth Century.* London: Oxford Univ. Press, 1959. pp. 286-313.

"Observations on the Style of Ernest Hemingway" by Harry Levin, reprinted from *Contexts of Criticism*, Cambridge, 1957, pp. 140-167.

41 Bentz, Hans W. *Ernest Hemingway in Übersetzungen.* Frankfurt a.M., Germany: Hans W. Bentz Verlag, 1963. (Weltliteratur in Übersetzungen, VIII. Amerikanische Autoren, Band I.) 34 pages. In German, French, and English.

Lists translations of Hemingway's work in forty-five languages; includes translator, publisher, year published, and price. Also indexed by publisher, translator, and language. Note: Numbered edition of 335 copies. Note: Item 367 A, "Animals of Farmer Johns," is not a translation of Hemingway's work.

42 Bessie, Alvah. *Men in Battle.* New York: Scribner's, 1939. pp. 135-137.

Relates his meeting with Hemingway and Herbert Matthews during the war in Spain, in April 1938.

43 Bessie, Alvah, ed. *The Heart of Spain: An Anthology of Fiction, Non-fiction and Poetry.* New York: Veterans of the Abraham Lincoln Brigade, 1951. p. vi.

Commentary in the Editor's Preface, regarding the reasons for the omission of work by Hemingway. [Cf. "The Abraham Lincoln Brigade Revisited" by Brock Brower in *Esquire*, LVII, March 1962.]

44 Bishop, Jim. *The Mark Hellinger Story: A Biography of Broadway and Hollywood.* New York: Appleton-Century-Crofts, 1952. pp. 312-318, 343, 347-352, 354. Photograph.

pp. 312-318: Regarding Hellinger's production of "The Killers" and Hemingway's favorable reaction to the film. pp. 347-352: Regarding Hellinger's trips to Havana and Sun Valley, Idaho, to confer with Hemingway concerning the film rights for his short stories.

45 Bishop, John Peale. *The Collected Essays of John Peale Bishop.*

Edited and with an Introduction by Edmund Wilson. New York: Scribner's, 1948. pp. 37-46, 66-77.

pp. 37-46: "Homage to Hemingway," reprinted from the *New Republic*, LXXXIX (Nov. 11, 1936). Reprinted in *After the Genteel Tradition*, ed. Malcolm Cowley, New York, 1937, pp. 186-201. pp. 66-77: "The Missing All," reprinted from the *Virginia Quarterly Review*, XIII (Winter 1937). Reprinted in *McCaffery*, pp. 292-307.

46 Blackmur, R. P. *Language as Gesture: Essays in Poetry*. New York: Harcourt, Brace, 1952. pp. 341-343.

Review of Allen Tate's book *Reactionary Essays on Poetry and Ideas*, New York, 1936, in which the sensibilities of Hemingway and Tate are compared.

47 Blankenship, Russell. *American Literature: As an Expression of the National Mind*. New York: Holt, Rinehart & Winston, 1949. Revised edition. pp. 731-742.

Discussion of Hemingway's work in the new chapter "The Present Confusion." Refers to "the authentic Hemingway down to 1937."

48 Blixen-Finecke, Bror von. *African Hunter*. New York: Knopf, 1938. Translated by F. H. Lyon from the Swedish, *Nyama*. pp. 226, 228-232.

The author, who was the husband of Izak Dinesen, relates the details of a day's deep-sea fishing with Hemingway, during a month spent as his guest at Bimini, in 1935.

49 Blöcker, Gunter. *Die neuen Wirklichkeiten: Linien und Profile der modernen Literatur*. Berlin: Argon, 1957. pp. 241-249 and *passim*.

pp. 241-249: "Ernest Hemingway."

50 Bode, Carl, ed. *The Great Experiment in American Literature: Six Lectures*. London: Heinemann, 1961. [New York: Praeger, 1961. pp. 135-151.]

"The Two Hemingways" by Arthur Mizener. One of a series of lectures organized by the Cultural Section of the American Embassy to Great Britain, in 1958.

51 Booth, Wayne C. *The Rhetoric of Fiction*. Chicago: Univ. of Chicago Press, 1961. pp. 151-152, 198, 299-300, 386.

pp. 151-152: "The Killers" is used as an example of the undramatized narrator. pp. 299-300: "A Clean, Well-Lighted Place" is used as an example of the reliable narrator in a "nihilistic" short story.

52 Bove, Charles F., with Dana Lee Thomas. *A Paris Surgeon's Story*. Boston: Little, Brown, 1956. pp. vii, 60.

Recollections of Hemingway in Paris, in the mid-1920s.

53 Bowers, Claude G. *My Mission to Spain: Watching the Rehearsal*

for World War II. New York: Simon & Schuster, 1954. pp. 336, 371-373, 422.

The U.S. Ambassador to Spain, during 1933 to 1939, relates his encounters with Hemingway in the shell-rocked Hotel Florida, in Madrid, and under fire during the battle for Teruel.

54 Braatøy, Trygve. *Kjaerlighet og åndslov: Essays.* Oslo: Fabritius & Sonners, 1934. pp. 132-147.
Psychoanalytical criticism of Hemingway's work.

55 Breit, Harvey. *The Writer Observed.* Cleveland: World, 1956. pp. 12, 19, 32-33, 82, 85, 148, 169, 216, 249, 263-265, 275-279. [Paperback edition: New York: Collier Books, 1961, No. AS-115.]
pp. 263-265: An interview with Hemingway on the occasion of the publication of *OMATS*, reprinted from the *N.Y. Times Book Review* (Sept. 7, 1952). pp. 275-279: Article on the occasion of the Nobel prize being awarded Hemingway, reprinted from the *N.Y. Times Book Review* (Nov. 7, 1954).

56 Briggs, Ellis O. *Shots Heard Round the World: An Ambassador's Hunting Adventures on Four Continents.* New York: Viking Press, 1957. pp. 55-73.
Ch. [IV]: "No Hasta El Postre: Meaning You Can't Throw Rolls until Dessert." Describes Hemingway's submarine hunting activities in the Caribbean, in 1943, and his forty-fourth birthday party at Finca Vigia.

57 Brinnin, John Malcolm. *The Third Rose: Gertrude Stein and Her World.* Boston: Atlantic–Little, Brown, 1959. pp. xv, 232, 233, 249-263, 264. Photograph of Hemingway by Man Ray.
pp. 249-263: An account of Gertrude Stein's meeting with Hemingway in Paris, in 1922; her influence on his early writings, and their references to each other in their later books.

58 Brodin, Pierre. *Les écrivains américains de l'entre-deux-guerres.* Paris: Horizons de France, 1946. pp. 127-147. [New York: Brentano's, 1946. Paperback.]
"Ernest Hemingway." Includes a brief chronology.

59 Brooks, Cleanth. *The Hidden God: Studies in Hemingway, Faulkner, Yeats, Eliot, and Warren.* New Haven: Yale Univ. Press, 1963. pp. 6-21, 46.
pp. 6-21: Ch. II: "Ernest Hemingway: Man on His Moral Uppers." A lecture given in 1955 at the Conference in Theology for College Faculty, at Trinity College, Hartford, Conn.

60 Brooks, Van Wyck. *The Confident Years: 1885-1915.* New York: Dutton, 1952. pp. 324, 325, 486, 561, 566, 570-576, 607, 608. [London: Dent, 1952.]

pp. 570-576: Discussion of Hemingway's work in the chapter "The Religion of Art."

61 Brooks, Van Wyck. *The Writer in America*. New York: Dutton, 1953. pp. 11, 69, 71, 92, 115, 161, 188.

62 Brown, Deming. *Soviet Attitudes toward American Writing*. Princeton: Princeton Univ. Press, 1962. pp. 53, 54, 88, 121, 171, 176, 177, 179, 194, 297-315, 323, 327. Bibliographical footnotes.

pp. 297-315: Ch. XII: "Ernest Hemingway." A slightly enlarged version of the essay "Hemingway in Russia," which appeared in *American Quarterly*, v (Summer 1953). Reprinted in *Baker anthology*, pp. 145-161. Includes translated excerpts from various reviews and critiques of Hemingway's work which have appeared in Russian periodicals.

63 Brown, Deming B. and Glenora Brown. *A Guide to Soviet Russian Translations of American Literature*. New York: King's Crown Press (Columbia Univ.), 1954. pp. 21, 24, 40, 42, 43, 92-95.

p. 21: Notes that stories and excerpts from Hemingway's novels "appeared at least 25 times in Soviet periodicals from 1934 to 1939." pp. 92-95: Checklist of Russian translations of Hemingway's work.

64 Brown, [Ernest] Francis, ed. *Highlights of Modern Literature*: *A Permanent Collection of Memorable Essays from The New York Times Book Review*. New York: New American Library, 1954. Paperback. pp. 10, 18-19, 59, 65-66, 74, 85, 87, 100, 106-109.

pp. 106-109: "Twenty-Eight Years of a Hemingway Classic" by Carlos Baker. Essay on *SAR*, reprinted from the *N.Y. Times Book Review* (April 29, 1951).

65 Brown, [Ernest] Francis, ed. *Opinions and Perspectives: From The New York Times Book Review*. Boston: Houghton Mifflin, 1964. pp. ix, 9, 15-16, 162-168, 207, 208, 209, 239, 282.

pp. 162-168: "Was 'Papa' Truly a Great Writer?" by Maxwell Geismar, reprinted from the *N.Y. Times Book Review* (July 1, 1962).

66 Brown, John [Lackey]. *Panorama de la Littérature contemporaine aux États-Unis*. Paris: Gallimard, [1954]. pp. 111-129. Photographs. "Ernest Hemingway." Discussion of his work. See also (E190).

67 Brown, John [Lackey], ed. *Hemingway*. Paris: Gallimard, 1961. (La Bibliothèque Idéale.) 304 pages. Photographs. Text in French.

Includes excerpts from biographical articles about Hemingway; a study of his work by the editor, on pp. 51-153; a checklist of his work translated into French; excerpts from the novels and short stories; short excerpts from critical studies; and a bibliography and filmography.

68 Brown, John [Lackey] and Livia Livi, eds. *Hemingway*. Milan: Feltrinelli, 1964. (La Biblioteca Ideale, No. 3.) 264 pages. Photographs. Text in Italian. Translated and revised from the French edition.

Includes excerpts from biographical articles; a study of Hemingway's work by John Brown, on pp. 41-130; excerpts from critical studies by Italian critics; résumés of the novels; a checklist of his work translated into Italian; and a checklist of critical studies.

69 Browne, Ray B. and Martin Light, eds. *Critical Approaches to American Literature*. Vol. II. New York: Crowell, 1965. pp. 275-291.

"The Hero and the Code" by Philip Young, reprinted from *Ernest Hemingway*, New York, 1952, pp. 28-50.

70 Bryher [Annie Winifred Ellerman]. *The Heart to Artemis: A Writer's Memoirs*. London: Collins, 1963. pp. 206, 216-217.

Reminiscences of Hemingway in Paris, in the early 1920s.

71 Buckley, Henry. *Life and Death of the Spanish Republic*. London: Hamish Hamilton, 1940. p. 289. Photograph opp. p. 392.

Reference to Hemingway during the Spanish Civil War.

72 Burgum, Edwin Berry. *The Novel and the World's Dilemma*. New York: Oxford Univ. Press, 1947. pp. 17, 171-172, 184-204, 244-246, 248, 284, 292, 304, 343. [Reissued: New York: Russell & Russell, 1963.]

pp. 171-172: Portrait of Hemingway by Gertrude Stein, reprinted from *Portraits and Prayers*, New York, 1934, p. 193. pp. 184-204: Ch. XI: "Ernest Hemingway and the Psychology of the Lost Generation," reprinted in *McCaffery*, pp. 308-328. pp. 244-246: Discussion on the influence of Hemingway on Richard Wright's work.

73 Burlingame, Roger. *Of Making Many Books: A Hundred Years of Reading, Writing and Publishing, 1846–1946*. New York: Scribner's, 1946. pp. 15, 16, 17, 47, 73-74, 87, 88, 123, 137, 138, 323, 324.

Published on the occasion of Charles Scribner's Sons centennial. Relates the circumstances which caused Hemingway to leave Boni & Liveright, in 1926, and become associated with Scribner's, who remained his publishers until his death.

74 Burnett, Whit. *The Literary Life and the Hell with It*. New York: Harper, 1939. pp. 173-178, 198-199, 206, 213.

pp. 173-178: An account of Hemingway's first public speech, before the American Writers' Congress, in New York, June 4, 1937. pp. 198-199: A letter from William Saroyan is quoted, in which he refers to "The Snows of Kilimanjaro" as "one of the few truly great stories of our time." Saroyan also refers to Hemingway's criticism of his writing, which appeared in *Esquire*, III (Jan. 1935).

75 Busch, Ernst, ed. *Canciones de las Brigadas Internacionales*. Barcelona, [1938]. Photograph of Hemingway on p. 55.

76 Caillois, Roger. *Les Littératures contemporaines à travers le monde*. Paris: Librairie Hachette, 1961. pp. 295-298. Photograph of Hemingway by Yousuf Karsh.
   "La libération du Ritz" by Michel Mohrt. Relates Hemingway's role in the liberation of Paris, in August 1944.

77 Callaghan, Morley. *That Summer in Paris: Memories of Tangled Friendships with Hemingway, Fitzgerald, and some others*. New York: Coward-McCann, 1963. 256 pages. Photograph. [Paperback edition: New York: Dell, 1964, Laurel Edition, 8664.]
   Recollections of Hemingway in Toronto, in 1923, and in Paris during the summer of 1929.

78 Canby, Henry Seidel, Amy Loveman, William Rose Benét, *et al.*, eds. *Designed for Reading: An Anthology Drawn from the Saturday Review of Literature—1924–1934*. New York: Macmillan, 1934. pp. 221-227.
   "Story of the Brave," review of *FTA* by Canby, reprinted from *SRL*, VI (Oct. 12, 1929).

79 Canby, Henry Seidel. *Seven Years' Harvest: Notes on Contemporary Literature*. New York: Farrar & Rinehart, 1936. pp. 5, 77, 123-125, 130-131, 150-154, 300.
   pp. 123-125, 130-131: Discussion of Hemingway's style from the chapter "Fiction Tells All," reprinted from *Harper's Magazine*, CLXXI (Aug. 1935). pp. 150-154: "Farewell to the Nineties," review of *WTN*, reprinted from *SRL*, X (Oct. 28, 1933).

80 Canby, Henry Seidel. *American Memoir*. Boston: Houghton Mifflin, 1947. pp. 332, 334, 339-344, 347, 410.
   pp. 339-344: Discussion of *SAR*.

81 Capa, Robert. *Slightly Out of Focus*. New York: Henry Holt, 1947. pp. 137-138, 166-171. Photographs.
   The photographer writes of Hemingway in London, in 1944, and with the 4th Infantry, 4th Division, in France, before and after the liberation of Paris.

82 Cargill, Oscar. *Intellectual America: Ideas on the March*. New York: Macmillan, 1941. pp. 351-370.
   On Hemingway's work, from the chapter "The Primitivists."

83 Carpenter, Frederic I. *American Literature and the Dream*. New York: Philosophical Library, 1955. pp. 185-193, 194.

pp. 185-193: Ch. xx: "Hemingway Achieves the Fifth Dimension," first published in *PMLA*, LXIX (Sept. 1954). Reprinted in *Baker anthology*, pp. 192-201.

84 Castellet, José María. *La evolución espiritual de Ernest Hemingway*. Madrid: Cuadernos Taurus, 1958. Pamphlet. 32 pages.

85 Cecchi, Emilio. *Scrittori inglesi e americani*. Vol. II. Milan: Mondadori, 1946. pp. 420-437. [Reissued: 1954. pp. 165-178.]
"Ernest Hemingway," reprinted from *Mercurio*, II (Oct. 1945).

86 Cestre, Charles. *La Littérature américaine*. Paris: Librairie Armand Colin, 1946. p. 172. [Third edition, 1957.]
A short critical appraisal of Hemingway's work.

87 Charters, James. *This Must Be the Place*: *Memoirs of Montparnasse*. London: Herbert Joseph, 1934. See (B15).

88 [Cliff's Notes]. *A Farewell to Arms*: *Notes*. Lincoln, Nebr.: Cliff's Notes, 1963. 62 pages. *The Sun Also Rises*: *Notes*. 1964. 58 pages. *For Whom the Bell Tolls*: *Notes*. 1965. 62 pages.

89 Cloete, Stuart. *The African Giant: the Story of a Journey*. Boston: Houghton Mifflin, 1955. pp. 327, 337, 358-359.
Recollections of Hemingway recuperating in Nairobi following the two African plane crashes, in 1954.

90 Cockburn, Claud. *A Discord of Trumpets*: *An Autobiography*. New York: Simon & Schuster, 1956. pp. 302-303. [Published under the title *In Time of Trouble*. London: Hart-Davis, 1956.]
The British journalist writes of Hemingway in Spain, during the Spanish Civil War.

91 Codman, Col. Charles R. *Drive*: *The General Patton Story*. Boston: Little, Brown, 1957. pp. 170, 255-256.
pp. 255-256: The author recalls a dinner conversation about *SAR*, with Hemingway, in Paris, in February 1945.

92 Cohn, Louis Henry. *A Bibliography of the Works of Ernest Hemingway*. New York: Random House, 1931. 116 pages.
For contents and description of this book, see (B9).

93 [Cohn, Louis Henry]. *First Editions of Modern Authors*: *With a Notable Hemingway Collection*. New York: House of Books, [1946]. Catalogue. pp. 29-40.
118 Hemingway items, including the manuscript of "The Snows of Kilimanjaro." See William White's article in *American Book Collector*, VII (Nov. 1956).

94 Coindreau, Maurice-Edgar. *Aperçus de littérature américaine*. Paris: Gallimard, 1946. pp. 26-27, 76-94, 142, 175.

pp. 76-94: On Hemingway, from the chapter "Romans al-
cooliques et exaltation de la brutalité," reprinted from *Cahiers du
Sud*, XIX (April 1932).

95 Connolly, Cyril. *Enemies of Promise*. London: Routledge, 1938.
[Boston: Little, Brown, 1939. pp. 9, 52, 75, 80-85, 89-90, 122, 163-
164.]
   pp. 80-85: Discussion of Hemingway's style and his use of the
colloquial language.

96 Connolly, Cyril. *Previous Convictions*. London: Hamish Hamilton,
1963. pp. 287, 288, 289, 290-298, 305, 306, 307. [New York: Harper
& Row, 1964.]
   pp. 290-292: "Ernest Hemingway: 1." Review of *ARIT*, reprinted
from the *Sunday Times*, London (Sept. 3, 1950). pp. 293-298:
"Ernest Hemingway: 2." Essay written on the occasion of Hemingway's death, reprinted from the *Sunday Times*, London (July 9,
1961).

97 Connolly, Cyril. *The Modern Movement: One Hundred Key Books
from England, France and America, 1880–1950*. London: Hamish
Hamilton, 1966. [New York: Atheneum, 1966. p. 153.]
   In Our Time is listed as number 49. The annotation under *The
Sun Also Rises*, which is number 50, refers to a "suppressed first
chapter" of the novel being recently published; the bibliographer
believes this reference to publication to be an error.

98 Connolly, Thomas E. *The Personal Library of James Joyce: A Descriptive Bibliography*. Buffalo: University Bookstore, 1957. p. 19.
   Regarding an inscribed copy of *FTA*, in which Hemingway had
filled in the publisher's dashes with the original obscenities.

99 Cooperman, Stanley. *Hemingway's Farewell to Arms: Review Notes
and Study Guide*. New York: Monarch Press, 1964. (No. 621.) 96
pages.
   Review notes on *FTA, SAR, FWBT,* and *OMATS*. Bibliographical suggestions on pp. 95-96.

00 Cossío, José María de. *Los Toros*. Vol. II: *Tratado, Técnico e His-
tórico*. Madrid: Espasa-Calpe, 1947. p. 633.
   "Ernest Hemingway." Brief biography, including appraisal of
DIA.

01 Cournos, John and Sybil Norton. *Famous Modern American Nov-
elists*. New York: Dodd, Mead, 1952. (The Famous Biographies for
Young People series.) pp. 129-135. Photograph.
   "Ernest Miller Hemingway: Fighting Author."

102 Cowles, Virginia. *Looking For Trouble.* New York: Harper, 1941. pp. 18, 30-31, 33-34, 38-39.
Recollections of Hemingway in Spain during the civil war.

103 Cowley, Malcolm. *Exile's Return: A Narrative of Ideas.* New York: W. W. Norton, 1934. [Revised edition: New York: Viking Press, 1951. New subtitle: *A Literary Odyssey of the 1920s.* pp. 3, 44-46, 105, 114, 120, 292, 299.]
pp. 44-46: Discussion of the war and *FTA.* p. 120: An account of the author's meeting with Hemingway, at Ezra Pound's apartment in Paris, during the summer of 1923.

104 Cowley, Malcolm, ed. *After the Genteel Tradition: American Writers Since 1910.* New York: W. W. Norton, 1937. pp. 186-201. [Reissued: Carbondale: Southern Illinois Univ. Press, 1964. (Crosscurrents Modern Critiques.) pp. 147-158.]
"Homage to Hemingway" by John Peale Bishop, reprinted from the *New Republic,* LXXXIX (Nov. 11, 1936).

105 Cowley, Malcolm. *The Literary Situation.* New York: Viking Press, 1954. pp. 34, 36, 113, 184-185, 189, 191.
p. 36: *iot* is quoted in an essay on war novels. pp. 184-185: Discussion of Hemingway's disciplined working habits.

106 Cranston, J. Herbert. *Ink On My Fingers.* Toronto: Ryerson Press, 1953. pp. 107-110.
Ch. XXVII: "His Hero Was a Matador." Reminiscences by the editor of the *Toronto Star Weekly* when Hemingway was on the staff, during 1920-1923.

107 Crosby, Caresse. *The Passionate Years.* New York: Dial Press, 1953. pp. 284-288. [London: Redman, 1955. pp. 170, 274, 293-300. Appendix, p. 354: Facsimile of a letter from Hemingway, written in 1929. See (F72).]
Reminiscences of Hemingway in San Sebastian, Spain, in July 1929, and in Paris, in the early thirties, when the author obtained permission to publish the Crosby Continental Editions of *TOS* and *IOT.*

108 Crosby, John. *With Love and Loathing.* New York: McGraw-Hill, 1963. pp. 11-15.
"Aranjuez, Spain." Relates an afternoon at the bullfights with Hemingway, to watch Antonio Ordoñez. Reprinted from two columns in the *N.Y. Herald Tribune* (June 8 and June 10, 1959).

109 cummings, e. e. *Poems, 1923–1954.* New York: Harcourt, Brace, 1954. p. 294.

Number "26," of "No Thanks," is a four-line poem about Hemingway.

10 Cunliffe, Marcus. *The Literature of the United States.* London: Penguin, 1954. Paperback. Bibliography. pp. 168, 270-275, 277, 279, 290, 355, 358, 359.

11 Daley, Robert. *The Swords of Spain.* New York: Dial Press, 1966. pp. 84-85, 89, 132-135. Photograph.

pp. 84-85: Regarding Hemingway's role in the feud between the bullfighters Antonio Ordoñez and Luis Miguel Dominguín.

12 Davidson, Donald. *The Spyglass: Views and Reviews, 1924–1930.* Selected and edited by John Tyree Fain. Nashville, Tenn.: Vanderbilt Univ. Press, 1963. pp. 75-79, 88-92.

pp. 75-79: "Tragedy of Limitation: Tarkington and Hemingway." Review of *MWW*, reprinted from the *Nashville Tennessean* (Jan. 28, 1928). pp. 88-92: "Perfect Behavior." Review of *FTA*, reprinted from the *Nashville Tennessean* (Nov. 3, 1929).

13 Davidson, Donald, ed. *Concise American Composition and Rhetoric.* New York: Scribner's, 1964. pp. 90-92.

"Landscape in Gorizia" by Carlos Baker. A critical appraisal of the opening chapter of *FTA*, reprinted from *Baker*, pp. 94-96.

14 DeFalco, Joseph. *The Hero in Hemingway's Short Stories.* Pittsburgh: Univ. of Pittsburgh Press, 1963. (Critical Essays in Modern Literature series.) 226 pages. Bibliographical references included in "Notes" on pp. 221-224.

A psychoanalytical study of Hemingway's short stories, which examines the relationship between structure and theme.

15 Denny, Margaret and William H. Gilman, eds. *The American Writer and the European Tradition.* Minneapolis: Univ. of Minnesota Press, 1950. pp. 111, 146-150, 153, 170, 173.

pp. 146-150: Discussion on the importance of ideas in Hemingway's and William Faulkner's work, from "Contemporary American Literature in Its Relation to Ideas" by Lionel Trilling. Reprinted from the *American Quarterly*, 1 (Fall 1949).

16 DeVoto, Bernard. *Forays and Rebuttals.* Boston: Little, Brown, 1936. pp. 340-344.

Review of *GHOA*, reprinted from *SRL*, XII (Oct. 26, 1935).

17 DeVoto, Bernard. *Minority Report.* Boston: Little, Brown, 1940. pp. 257-261.

An editorial, "Tiger, Tiger!" on *THAHN*, reprinted from *SRL*, XVI (Oct. 16, 1937).

118 DeVoto, Bernard. *The Literary Fallacy*. Boston: Little, Brown, 1944. pp. 104-108.
Discussion regarding Hemingway's work, from the chapter "Waste Land."

119 *Dictionnaire Biographique des Auteurs de tous les temps et de tous les pays*. Vol. I. Paris: Laffont-Bompiani, 1956. pp. 641-642. Photographs.
"Ernest Hemingway" by Salvatore Rosati.

120 *Dizionario Universale della Letteratura Contemporanea*. Vol. II. Milan: Mondadori, 1960. pp. 696-700. Photographs.
"Ernest Hemingway."

121 Dos Passos, John. *The Best Times: An Informal Memoir*. New York: New American Library, 1966. pp. 140-145, 153-159, 197-205, 210-220.
Reminiscences of Hemingway in Europe, in the 1920s, and in Key West, in the 1930s.

122 [Drew, Fraser B.] *Thirty-five Years of Ernest Hemingway: A Catalogue of the Hemingway Collection of Dr. Fraser B. Drew*. 8 mimeographed pages. Exhibited in the Edward H. Butler Library of the State University of New York College for Teachers at Buffalo, November 1-19, 1958.
Ninety-eight items, including inscribed first editions, periodicals containing first appearances, letters, photographs, and translations.

123 Dudley, Lavinia P. and John J. Smith, eds. *The Americana Annual: 1962*. New York: Americana, 1962. pp. 333-334. Photographs.
"Ernest Miller Hemingway" by Carlos Baker.

124 Durham, Philip and Tauno F. Mustanoja. *American Fiction in Finland: An Essay and Bibliography*. Helsinki: Société Néophilologique, 1960. pp. 17, 23, 24, 28-30, 51, 111, 147.

125 Dutourd, Jean. *La mort du chasseur, Hemingway*. Liége: Éditions Dynamo, 1961. (Babioles Cynégétiques, 34.) Pamphlet. 16 pages. Photograph of Hemingway by Yousuf Karsh.
pp. 7-8: "La mort du chasseur." pp. 9-10: "Les trois vieillards et la mer." Note: 56 copies printed.

126 Dutourd, Jean. *"Papa" Hemingway*. Liége: Éditions Dynamo, 1961. (Brimborious, 80.) Pamphlet. 24 pages. Frontispiece photograph of Hemingway and Dutourd. 51 copies printed.

127 Dyboski, Roman. *Wielcy pisarze amerykańscy*. Warsaw: Pax, [1958]. pp. 495-497, 616-618.
pp. 495-497: Discussion of Hemingway's work. pp. 616-618: "Ernest Hemingway" by Stanislaw Helsztynski.

128 Eastman, Max. *Art and the Life of Action: with other essays.* New York: Knopf, 1934. pp. 87-101.

Part II, Ch. I: "Bull in the Afternoon," reprinted from the *New Republic*, LXXV (June 7, 1933). This is the essay over which Hemingway and Eastman fought in Maxwell Perkins' office at Scribner's, August 11, 1937. Reprinted in *McCaffery*, pp. 66-75.

129 Eastman, Max. *Great Companions: Critical Memoirs of Some Famous Friends.* New York: Farrar, Straus & Cudahy, 1959. pp. 41-76. Photograph. [Paperback edition: *Einstein, Trotsky, Hemingway, Freud and Other Great Companions.* New York: Collier Books, 1962. No. AS-137X.]

Ch. III: "The Great and Small in Ernest Hemingway." Partially reprinted in the *Saturday Review*, XLII (April 4, 1959). Includes a letter from Hemingway, regarding the essay in the above entry. See (F87).

130 Edgar, Pelham. *The Art of the Novel: From 1700 to the Present Time.* New York: Macmillan, 1933. pp. 338-351.

Ch. XXVIII: "Four American Writers: Anderson, Hemingway, Dos Passos, Faulkner."

131 Ehrenburg, Ilya. *Memoirs: 1921–1941.* Cleveland: World, 1964. Translated from the Russian by Tatania Shebunina in collaboration with Yvonne Kapp. pp. 128, 302, 378, 379, 383-391, 404, 405, 418.

pp. 383-391: Regarding his meeting with Hemingway in Madrid, in March 1937, during the Spanish Civil War.

132 Eichholz, Armin. *In flagranti: Parodien.* Munich: Pohl, 1954. pp. 18-26: "Der alte Mann und das Motto."

133 Ellison, Ralph. *Shadow and Act.* New York: Random House, 1964. pp. 25, 34-41, 140-141, 144-145, 168.

pp. 140-141: Regarding Hemingway's influence on his work, reprinted from the *New Leader*, XLVII (Feb. 3, 1964).

134 Ellmann, Richard. *James Joyce.* New York: Oxford Univ. Press, 1959. pp. 521, 529, 543, 569, 598-599, 708.

p. 543: A letter from Hemingway to Sherwood Anderson about *Ulysses* is quoted. See (F44). p. 598: Letter protesting the pirating of *Ulysses*. See (C173). p. 708: An evaluation of Hemingway by Joyce.

35 Eppelsheimer, Hanns W. *Handbuch der Weltliteratur: von den anfängen bis zur gegenwart.* Frankfurt a.M., Germany: Klostermann, 1960. Bibliographical references. p. 673.

136 Escarpit, Robert. *Hemingway.* Paris: A.-G. Nizet, 1964. (La Renaissance du Livre.) 154 pages. In French.

137 Falk, Robert P., ed. *American Literature in Parody.* New York: Twayne, 1955. pp. 241-244. [Paperback edition: *The Antic Muse: American Writers in Parody.* New York: Grove Press, 1956.]
   "When the Gong Sounded" by Cornelia Otis Skinner. Reprinted from *Soap Behind the Ears,* New York, 1941, pp. 89-96.

138 Farrell, James T. *The League of Frightened Philistines: and other papers.* New York: Vanguard Press, 1945. pp. 20-24.
   "Ernest Hemingway's *The Sun Also Rises.*" First published in the *N.Y. Times Book Review* (Aug. 1, 1943). Reprinted in *McCaffery,* pp. 221-225; and in *Baker critiques,* pp. 4-6.

139 Farrington, Chisie. *Women Can Fish.* New York: Coward-McCann, 1951. pp. 8, 9, 24-25, 58. Photograph.
   References to Hemingway's fishing at Bimini, in the mid-1930s.

140 Farrington, S. Kip, Jr. *Fishing the Atlantic: Offshore and On.* New York: Coward-McCann, 1949. pp. 11, 223, 232, 259, 270.

141 Faulkner, William. *Essays, Speeches and Public Letters.* Edited by James B. Meriwether. New York: Random House, 1965. pp. 193, 210-211.
   p. 193: Review of *OMATS,* reprinted from *Shenandoah,* III (Autumn 1952). pp. 210-211: Letter regarding Evelyn Waugh's view of *ARIT,* reprinted from *Time,* LVI (Nov. 13, 1950).

142 Feidelson, Charles, Jr. and Paul Brodtkorb, Jr., eds. *Interpretations of American Literature.* New York: Oxford Univ. Press, 1959. pp. 297-331.
   pp. 297-319: "Hemingway's Ambiguity: Symbolism and Irony" by E. M. Halliday, reprinted from *American Literature,* XXVIII (March 1956). pp. 320-331: "No Beginning and No End: Hemingway and Death" by Frederick J. Hoffman, reprinted from *Essays in Criticism,* III (Jan. 1953).

143 Fenton, Charles A. *The Apprenticeship of Ernest Hemingway: The Early Years.* New York: Farrar, Straus & Young, 1954. [xii] + 302 pages. Bibliographical Notes on pp. 265-290. [Paperback editions: (a) New York: Viking Press, 1958. Compass Books, No. C 34. [xii] + 302 pages. (b) New York: New American Library, 1961. Mentor Book, No. MP 385. x + 240 pages. (c) Translated into Korean by Yun-Sup Shim. Seoul: Chang Mun Sa, 1958. 338 pages.]
   A detailed study of Hemingway during the years 1916-1924, covering his high school work, his cub-reporting on the *Kansas City Star,* his World War I experiences, his reporting for the *Toronto*

Star (both in Canada and Europe), and his abandonment of journalism for creative writing. Sections of this book first appeared, in somewhat different form, in *American Quarterly*, IV (Winter 1952); *New World Writing*, No. 2 (1952); and the *Atlantic*, CXCIII (March–May 1954).

144 Fiedler, Leslie, ed. *The Art of the Essay.* New York: Crowell, 1958. pp. 86-92, 612, 616-617.

pp. 86-92: Excerpt about Hemingway from *The Autobiography of Alice B. Toklas* by Gertrude Stein, New York, 1933, pp. 261-271.

145 Fiedler, Leslie A. *Love and Death in the American Novel.* New York: Criterion Books, 1960. pp. 304-309, 350-352.

pp. 304-309: Discussion of the Hemingway heroine. pp. 350-352: Discussion of death and murder in Hemingway's work. Reprinted in *Weeks collection,* pp. 86-92, under the title "Men Without Women."

146 Fiedler, Leslie. *Waiting for the End.* New York: Stein & Day, 1964. pp. 9-19, 20-21, 34, 63, 64, 98, 121-122.

pp. 9-19: Ch. 1: "The Death of the Old Men," about Hemingway and William Faulkner, "the two great presences who made possible both homage and blasphemy, both imitation and resistance." This chapter appeared in *Arts & Sciences*, LXIV (Winter 1963–1964).

147 Fitzgerald, F. Scott. *The Crack-Up.* Edited by Edmund Wilson. New York: Laughlin, 1945. (A New Directions Book.) pp. 25, 50, 79 (n. 3), 125, 176, 181, 189, 270, 272, 277, 284-285, 324-325.

Mainly references to Hemingway in Fitzgerald's Notebooks. pp. 284-285: Letter to Hemingway, regarding *FWBT*, written November 8, 1940.

148 Fitzgerald, F. Scott. *The Letters of F. Scott Fitzgerald.* Edited by Andrew Turnbull. New York: Scribner's, 1963. pp. 167, 179, 195-198, 200, 205-206, 208, 229, 233, 247, 267, 273, 275, 277, 295-313, 342, 345, 484. [(a) London: Bodley Head, 1964. (b) Paperback edition: New York: Delta Books, 1965.]

pp. 295-313: Part IV: "Letters to Ernest Hemingway." Eighteen letters, dated [Nov. 30, 1925]–Nov. 8, 1940.

149 Ford, Ford Madox. *It Was the Nightingale.* Philadelphia: Lippincott, 1933. pp. 9, 31, 289, 295-296, 323, 333-335, 337-338, 340. [London: Heinemann, 1934.]

pp. 333-335: Regarding Hemingway as "sub-editor" of the *Transatlantic Review*, in Paris, in 1924.

150 Forsythe, Robert [pseudonym of Kyle Crichton]. *Redder Than the Rose.* New York: Covici-Friede, 1935. pp. 44-48.

Ch. [XIII]: "In This Corner, Mr. Hemingway." A reply to Hemingway's article in *Esquire*, II (Dec. 1934), regarding Heywood Broun.

151 Frahne, Karl Heinrich. *Eine Einführung in die Literatur Nordamerika: Von Franklin bis Hemingway.* Hamburg: Toth, 1949. pp. 123, 125-126, 229-230.

pp. 229-230: "Ernest Hemingway." Biographical and critical commentary.

152 Franklin, Sidney. *Bullfighter From Brooklyn.* New York: Prentice-Hall, 1952. pp. 170-181, 205, 213-235. Photographs. [Translated into French by Françoise Vernan, *Ma Vie de Torero,* Paris: Corrêa, 1953. See note below.]

pp. 170-181: Relates his meeting with Hemingway in Madrid, in 1929, and the tour they took through Spain before he learned of Hemingway's identity. pp. 213-235: Relates his trip to Spain, in 1937, to help Hemingway cover the Spanish Civil War for the North American Newspaper Alliance. The book is a condensed version of the installments in *Town & Country,* CVI (Jan.–April 1952). Note: Hemingway's "Sidney Franklin as a Matador" is reprinted, on pp. 241-245, from *DIA.* It serves as an introduction to the French edition, on pp. [7]–11.

153 Friede, Donald. *The Mechanical Angel: His Adventures and Enterprises in the Glittering 1920's.* New York: Knopf, 1948. pp. 27-28, 237.

pp. 27-28: The author, who was with Boni & Liveright when they published *IOT,* handled the motion picture sale of *FWBT,* in 1940.

154 Frohock, Wilbur M. *The Novel of Violence in America: 1920–1950.* Dallas: Southern Methodist Univ. Press, 1950. pp. 167-199. Drawing of Hemingway. [Second edition, revised and enlarged, 1957.]

Ch. IX: "Ernest Hemingway: The River and the Hawk," reprinted from the *Southwest Review,* XXXII (Winter 1947) and (Spring 1947). Reprinted in *McCaffery,* pp. 262-291, under the title "Violence and Discipline."

155 Gardiner, Harold C., S.J., ed. *Fifty Years of the American Novel: A Christian Appraisal.* New York: Scribner's, 1951. pp. 183-196.

Ch. [XI]: "Ernest Hemingway: The Missing Third Dimension" by Michael F. Moloney, reprinted in *Baker anthology,* pp. 180-191.

156 Gardiner, Harold C., S.J. *In All Conscience: Reflections on Books and Culture.* Garden City, N.Y.: Hanover House, 1959. pp. 124-126.

pp. 124-125: "He-Man Whimpering," review of *ARIT,* reprinted from *America,* LXXXIII (Sept. 16, 1950). pp. 125-126: "Pathetic Fallacy," review of *OMATS*, reprinted from *America*, LXXXVII (Sept. 13, 1952).

57 Gates, Theodore J. and Austin Wright, eds. *College Prose*. Boston: D. C. Heath, 1942. pp. 416-423.

pp. 416-421: "Ernest Hemingway Crosses the Bridge" by Clifton Fadiman, a review of *FWBT*, reprinted from the *New Yorker*, XVI (Oct. 26, 1940). pp. 422-423: "A Review of *For Whom the Bell Tolls*" by J. N. Vaughan, reprinted from *Commonweal*, XXXIII (Dec. 13, 1940).

58 Geismar, Maxwell. *Writers in Crisis: The American Novel Between Two Wars*. Boston: Houghton Mifflin, 1942. pp. 39-85, 89-90, 100, 167.

pp. 39-85: Ch. II: "Ernest Hemingway: You Could Always Come Back." A condensation of this chapter first appeared in the *Virginia Quarterly Review*, XVII (Autumn 1941). Reprinted in *McCaffery*, pp. 143-189.

59 Geismar, Maxwell. *American Moderns: From Rebellion to Conformity*. New York: Hill & Wang, 1958. pp. 54-64.

pp. 54-58: "At the Crossroads," reprinted from the *N.Y. Times Book Review* (July 31, 1949), where it appeared under the title "Notes from a Critic on a Novelist's Work." pp. 59-61: "A Year Later," review of *ARIT*, reprinted from *SRL*, XXXIII (Sept. 9, 1950). pp. 61-64: "The Nobel Prize," an editorial, reprinted from *Saturday Review*, XXXVII (Nov. 13, 1954).

60 Gerstenberger, Donna and George Hendrick. *The American Novel, 1789-1959: A Checklist of Twentieth-Century Criticism*. Denver: Alan Swallow, 1961. pp. 119-127.

61 Gibbs, Wolcott. *Bed of Neuroses*. New York: Dodd, Mead, 1937. pp. 261-265.

"Death in the Rumble Seat" (With the Usual Apologies to Ernest Hemingway). This parody first appeared in the *New Yorker*, VIII (Oct. 8, 1932). Reprinted in *More in Sorrow*, New York, 1958, pp. 20-23; and in *Parodies*, ed. Dwight Macdonald, New York, 1960, pp. 248-250.

62 Gingrich, Arnold. *The Well-Tempered Angler*. New York: Knopf, 1965. pp. 20-27, 33, 307-308.

pp. 20-27: Ch. II: "Horsing Them in with Hemingway." These recollections of fishing out of Key West and Bimini with Hemingway, in the 1930s, first appeared in *Playboy*, XII (Sept. 1965).

163 Goldhurst, William. *F. Scott Fitzgerald and His Contemporaries.*
Cleveland: World, 1963. pp. 23-26, 31, 155-216, 219. Bibliography
on pp. 237-242.
A study of the part Edmund Wilson, H. L. Mencken, Ring Lardner, and Hemingway played in Scott Fitzgerald's life and career. pp.
155-216: Ch. v: "Ernest Hemingway." The author shows, by use
of comparative readings, the influence of Hemingway and Fitzgerald on each other's work.

164 González, Miguel. *Canto a Hemingway.* Havana, 1957. 12 pages.
Photograph of Hemingway on the cover.
Poem on pp. 7-12.

165 Gordon, Caroline. *How to Read a Novel.* New York: Viking Press,
1957. pp. 78-79, 99-102, 146-147.
"Today Is Friday" and *FTA* are used as examples of the "effaced
narrator."

166 Grant, Douglas. *Purpose and Place: Essays on American Writers.*
London: Macmillan, New York: St Martin's Press, 1965. pp. 169-
182.
pp. 169-174: "Ernest Hemingway [Part] I: The Bruiser and the
Poet," a review of *AMF*, reprinted from *TLS* (May 21, 1964). pp.
175-182: "Ernest Hemingway [Part] II: Men without Women."

167 Graves, Robert and Alan Hodge. *The Reader Over Your Shoulder:
A Handbook for Writers of English Prose.* New York: Macmillan,
1944. pp. 304-306.
Examination and comment on a brief passage from *FWBT*, and
an analysis of Hemingway's rendering of Spanish colloquialisms.

168 Gray, James. *On Second Thought.* Minneapolis: Univ. of Minne-
sota Press, 1946. pp. 59, 60, 74-81, 82. [Translated into German by
Paula Saatmann. *Halbgötter auf der literarischen Bühne.* Munich:
Kurt Desch, 1950. pp. 99-109.]
pp. 74-81: Discussion of Hemingway's work in Ch. [IV]: "Tenderly
Tolls the Bell for Three Soldiers" (F. Scott Fitzgerald, John Dos
Passos, and Ernest Hemingway). Reprinted in *McCaffery*, pp.
226-235.

169 Grenzmann, Wilhelm. *Weltdichtung der Gegenwart: Probleme und
Gestalten.* Bonn: Athenäum, 1955. pp. 403-425, 453, 460.
pp. 403-425: "Ernest Hemingway."

170 Grieg, Harald. *På fisketur med Hemingway.* Oslo, 1951. Pamphlet.
52 pages.
The director of Gyldendal's, Hemingway's Norwegian publishers,
relates a visit to Finca Vigia and a fishing trip with Hemingway.

G1 Grieg, Harald. *En forleggers erindringer.* Vol. I. Oslo: Gyldendal, 1958. pp. 272-282, 499, 798.

pp. 272-282: Regarding his visit to Finca Vigia.

G2 Grigson, Geoffrey, ed. *The Concise Encyclopedia of Modern World Literature.* New York: Hawthorn Books, 1963. pp. 32, 39, 46, 200, 205-206, 442, 497. Photograph of Hemingway on p. 176.

pp. 205-206: "Hemingway."

G3 Guérard, Albert J., Maclin B. Guérard, John Hawkes, and Claire Rosenfield. *The Personal Voice: A Contemporary Prose Reader.* Philadelphia: Lippincott, 1964. pp. 428, 431-455, 609-610.

pp. 431-444: "Observations on the Style of Ernest Hemingway" by Harry Levin, reprinted from *Contexts of Criticism,* Cambridge, 1957, pp. 140-167. pp. 444-455: "Nightmare and Ritual in Hemingway" by Malcolm Cowley, reprinted from the Introduction to the Viking Portable *Hemingway,* pp. vii-xxiv.

G4 [Guffey, Don Carlos]. *First Editions of English and American Authors: The Library of Dr. Don Carlos Guffey.* New York: Parke-Bernet Galleries, 1958. Auction catalogue. (Oct. 14, 1958.) Facsimiles of manuscript pages from *DIA* on the frontispiece and p. 27. Facsimile of inscription to Dr. Guffey on p. 31.

pp. 26-41: "An Important Collection of Ernest Hemingway Featuring the Major Portion of the MS of *Death in the Afternoon.*"

G5 Gurko, Leo. *The Angry Decade.* New York: Dodd, Mead, 1947. pp. 54-55, 163, 164, 187-190, 270.

pp. 187-190: About Hemingway in the 1930s, reprinted in *McCaffery,* on pp. 258-261, under the title "Hemingway in Spain."

G6 Gurko, Leo. *Heroes, Highbrows and the Popular Mind.* Indianapolis: Bobbs-Merrill, 1953. pp. 186-187, 270-272, 282.

pp. 186-187: Discussion on Hemingway's heroes. pp. 270-272: Discussion on the "disbelief in human improvability" in *FTA* and *THAHN.*

G7 Guyot, Charly. *Les Romanciers américains d'aujourd'hui.* Paris: Éditions Labergerie, 1948. pp. 13, 61-76, 120. Photograph.

pp. 61-76: Ch. [IV] on Hemingway.

G8 Gwynn, Frederick L. and Joseph L. Blotner, eds. *Faulkner in the University: Class Conferences at the University of Virginia, 1957–1958.* Charlottesville: Univ. of Virginia Press, 1959. pp. 15, 118, 143-144, 149, 161, 182-183, 206.

p. 149: Faulkner's assessment of Hemingway's writing, when queried by a student at the University of Virginia.

179 Haight, Anne Lyon. *Banned Books: Informal Notes on Some Books Banned for Various Reasons at Various Times and in Various Places*. New York: Bowker, 1935. pp. [vi], 72. [Second edition, revised and enlarged, 1955. pp. 102-103, 121.]

pp. 102-103: List of Hemingway's work banned in the United States and other countries. In regard to the banning of *THAHN* in Detroit, in 1938, it is noted that this was the only book suppressed in the United States during that year.

180 Hale, Nancy. *The Realities of Fiction: A Book about Writing*. Boston: Little, Brown, 1962. pp. 85-112, 129, 175-177.

pp. 85-112: "Hemingway and the Courage to Be," reprinted from the *Virginia Quarterly Review*, xxxviii (Autumn 1962).

181 Hanemann, H. W. *The Facts of Life: A Book of Brighter Biography Executed in the Manner of Some of Our Best-Known Writers* . . . New York: Farrar & Rinehart, 1930. pp. 131-159.

"A Farewell to Josephine's Arms—The Hemingway of All Flesh," reprinted in *Twentieth Century Parody*, ed. Burling Lowrey, New York, 1960, pp. 59-70.

182 Hartwick, Harry, *The Foreground of American Fiction*. New York: American Book, 1934. pp. 37, 151-159, 166.

pp. 151-159: Ch. [vii]: "Grace Under Pressure."

183 Hatcher, Harlan. *Creating the Modern American Novel*. New York: Farrar & Rinehart, 1935. pp. 228-233. [London: Williams & Norgate, 1936.]

Discussion of Hemingway's work from the chapter "The War Generation."

184 Heimburg, Carol. *Etched Portraits of Ernest Hemingway*. Northampton, Mass.: Apiary Press, 1961. 20 unnumbered pages. 7 etchings. Printed in a limited edition of 50 copies. Brief excerpt from "Banal Story" on p. [3].

185 Heiney, Donald. *Barron's Simplified Approach to Ernest Hemingway*. Woodbury, N.Y.: Barron's Educational Series, 1965. 120 pages.

186 Helfgen, Heinz. *Ich radle um die Welt*. Vol. ii. Gütersloh: Bertelsmann, 1954. pp. 297-306.

"Besuch bei Ernest Hemingway." Interview with Hemingway in Cuba.

187 Helmstadter, Frances. *Picture Book of American Authors*. New York: Sterling, 1962. (Visual History Series.) pp. 55-57. Juvenile. Photograph of Hemingway in Italy.

"Ernest Hemingway."

88 Hemingway, Leicester. *My Brother, Ernest Hemingway.* Cleveland: World, 1962. 283 pages. Photographs. [(a) Toronto: Nelson, Foster & Scott, 1962. (b) London: Weidenfeld & Nicolson, 1962. (c) Paperback edition: Fawcett World Library, 1963 (Crest Reprint, No. T-593.) 256 pages. Photographs. (d) Translated into French by Jean-Marc Pelorson. *Hemingway, Mon Frère.* Paris: Robert Laffont, 1962. 370 pages. (e) Translated into German. *Mein Bruder Ernest.* Hamburg: Rowohlt, 1962. 272 pages. (f) Translated into Danish by Torben W. Langer. *Min bror Ernest Hemingway.* Copenhagen: Hasselbalch, 1962. 320 pages. (g) Translated into Finnish by Jouko Linturi. *Veljeni Ernest Hemingway.* Helsinki: Tammi, 1962. 330 pages. (h) Translated into Norwegian by Per Wollebaek. *Min bror, Ernest Hemingway.* Oslo: Cappelen, 1962. 289 pages. (i) Translated into Swedish by Håkan Bergstedt. *Min bror, Ernest Hemingway.* Stockholm: Bonnier, 1962. 253 pages. (j) Translated into Spanish by Miguel Giménez Sales. *Mi hermano Ernest Hemingway.* Barcelona: Plaza y Janés, 1962. 368 pages. (k) Translated into Japanese. Tokyo: Chuon Koron Sha, 1963.] This biography first appeared in *Playboy*, VIII (Dec. 1961), IX (Jan., Feb., March 1962).

89 Herzberg, Max J., ed. *The Reader's Encyclopedia of American Literature.* New York: Crowell, 1962. pp. 450-456. Photograph.
"Ernest (Miller) Hemingway" by Philip Young.

90 Hicks, Granville. *The Great Tradition: An Interpretation of American Literature since the Civil War.* New York: Macmillan, 1933. pp. 273-277, 291.

91 Hoel, Sigurd. *50 gule.* Oslo: Gyldendal, 1939. pp. 20-36. Photograph.
Introductions reprinted from the Norwegian editions of *SAR*, *FTA*, and *THAHN*.

92 Hoel, Sigurd. *De siste 51 gule.* Oslo: Gyldendal, 1959. pp. 30-32.
Introduction reprinted from the Norwegian edition of *FWBT*.

93 Hoffman, Frederick J., Charles Allen, and Carolyn F. Ulrich, eds. *The Little Magazine: A History and a Bibliography.* Princeton: Princeton Univ. Press, 1946. pp. 12, 14, 262, 275, 279, 284, 311. Facsimile, opp. p. 28, of the first page of "A Divine Gesture," reproduced from the *Double Dealer*, III (May 1922).

94 Hoffman, Frederick J. *The Modern Novel in America: 1900–1950.* Chicago: Regnery, 1951. pp. 89-103. [(a) Reissued: 1956 (Gateway Edition). (b) Translated into Italian by Augusto Guidi. *Il romanzo in America: 1900–1950.* Rome: Storia e Letteratura, 1953. (c) Translated into Spanish by José María Castellet. *La novela moderna en Norteamerica.* Barcelona: Seix y Barral, 1955. (d) Translated into Arabic. Beirut, Lebanon, 1961.]

195 Hoffman, Frederick J. *The Twenties: American Writing in the Postwar Decade*. New York: Viking Press, 1955. pp. xi, 32, 52, 55, 56, 66-76, 80-85, 186-189, 193-196.

pp. 66-76: Part 4 of Ch. II: "The Unreasonable Wound." pp. 80-85: Part 6 of Ch. II: "The Text: Hemingway's *The Sun Also Rises.*"

196 Hohenberg, John. *Foreign Correspondence: The Great Reporters and Their Times*. New York: Columbia Univ. Press, 1964. pp. 283-284, 312-313, 362.

pp. 283-284: Regarding Hemingway's European dispatches for the *Toronto Star*. pp. 312-313: Regarding Hemingway's Spanish Civil War dispatches.

197 Holmes, John and Carroll S. Towle, eds. *A Complete College Reader*. Boston: Houghton Mifflin, 1950. pp. 244-247.

"*A Farewell to Arms*, A Review" by Henry Seidel Canby, reprinted from *SRL*, VI (Oct. 12, 1929).

198 Hotchner, A. E. *Papa Hemingway: A Personal Memoir*. New York: Random House, 1966. 304 pages. Photographs. [Translated into Italian by Ettore Caprioli. Milan: Bompiani, 1966. 340 pages.]

An account of the author's friendship with Hemingway from 1949 to 1961. Serialized in the *Saturday Evening Post*, CCXXXIX (March 12, 1966), 32-41, 45-48; (March 26, 1966), 36-44, 48, 52, 77-78, 83; (April 9, 1966), 34-47, 50. Note: Three lines from a Hemingway poem, titled "Across the Board," are quoted in the galleys, on p. 42, but did not appear in the book.

199 Houm, Philip. *Norsk Litteratur Historie*. Vol. VI: *Norges Litteratur fra 1914 til 1950-årene*. Oslo: Aschehoug, 1955. pp. 361-363, 440-441, 484.

Commentary on Hemingway's style and his influence on Norwegian writers.

200 Howe, Irving. *A World More Attractive: A View of Modern Literature and Politics*. New York: Horizon Press, 1963. pp. 59-76.

Ch. [III]: "The Quest for Moral Style." A study of Hemingway's writing and influence.

201 Huddleston, Sisley. *Paris Salons, Cafés, Studios: Being Social, Artistic and Literary Memories*. Philadelphia: Lippincott, 1928. pp. 121-123. [Published under the title *Bohemian Literary and Social Life in Paris*. London: Harrap, 1928.]

A critical estimate of Hemingway's short stories and *SAR*.

202 Huddleston, Sisley. *Back to Montparnasse: Glimpses of Broadway in Bohemia*. Philadelphia and London: Lippincott, 1931. pp. 106, 131, 132, 134, 180, 278.

p. 106: Regarding the little magazine *Exile.* Hemingway's "Neothomist Poem" is quoted. The title is incorrectly spelled "Nothoemist Poem," as it appeared in the magazine.

3 Hughes, Langston. *I Wonder as I Wander.* New York: Rinehart, 1956. pp. 333, 342, 362-365, 391, 393.

pp. 362-365: "A Hemingway Story." The poet relates the real-life episode of a shooting in the Aquarium Bar in Madrid, in 1937, on which Hemingway based his short story "The Butterfly and the Tank."

4 Hummel, Edwin. *The Calculus of Hemingway.* [n.p.], 1961. 29 pages. Drawing of Hemingway by the author on the front paper cover.

This study sets out to prove that the "true, lifelong influence" on Hemingway was *Essays on Authorship* by Frank Norris, "which he read when he was fourteen."

5 Huxley, Aldous. *Music at Night and Other Essays.* London: Chatto & Windus, 1931. [New York: Fountain Press, 1931. pp. 111-115.]

In the essay "Foreheads Villainous Low," Huxley discusses "the present trend of stupidity-snobbery" and cites as an example a phrase, "quite admirably expressive," from *FTA,* before Hemingway "passes on shamefacedly to speak once more of Lower Things." For Hemingway's comments on this essay, see *DIA,* p. 190.

6 Isabelle, Julanne. *Hemingway's Religious Experience.* New York: Vantage Press, 1964. 114 pages. Bibliographical Notes on pp. 99-106. A Selected Bibliography on pp. 107-114.

The author states in the Introduction that she has "probed into the soul of a man and found beauty and courage dedicated to God."

7 Ishi, Ichiro. [A Study of Hemingway.] Tokyo: Nanundo, 1955. 240 pages.

8 Johansen, Niels Kaas. *Ernest Hemingway.* Copenhagen: Haase, 1940. Pamphlet. 60 pages. Bibliography on p. 60. In Danish.

9 Jonsson, Thorsten. *Sex amerikaner: Hemingway, Faulkner, Steinbeck, Caldwell, Farrell, Saroyan.* Stockholm: Bonnier, 1942. pp. 7-37. Chapter on Hemingway, "Dödens närhet."

0 Karsh, Yousuf. *Portraits of Greatness.* London: Nelson, 1959. pp. 96-97. Photograph of Hemingway on p. 97.

p. 96: "Ernest Hemingway." An account of his visit to Finca Vigía, in 1957, to photograph Hemingway. Reprinted, with slight revisions, from the *Atlantic,* cc (Dec. 1957).

1 Kazin, Alfred. *On Native Grounds: An Interpretation of Modern American Prose Literature.* New York: Harcourt, Brace, 1942. pp.

215, 312-315, 327-341, 342-344, 450. [Paperback edition: Garden City, N.Y.: Doubleday, 1956. Anchor Books, A 69.]

pp. 327-341: A study of Hemingway's values and style, the influences upon his work, and his influence upon the work of younger writers. Reprinted in *McCaffery*, pp. 190-204, under the title "Hemingway: Synopsis of a Career."

212 Kelly, Frank K. *Reporters Around the World.* Boston: Little, Brown, 1957. Juvenile biography. pp. 155-166.
"Under Fire in Italy, Hemingway Finds He Is Mortal."

213 Kempton, Kenneth Payson. *The Short Story.* Cambridge: Harvard Univ. Press, 1948. pp. 20, 22, 39-41, 43, 44, 109-112, 126.
Explication of "The Killers."

214 Kiley, Jed. *Hemingway: An Old Friend Remembers.* New York: Hawthorn Books, 1965. 198 pages. Photographs. [Published in England under the title *Hemingway: A Title Fight in Ten Rounds.* London: Methuen, 1965.]
Memories of Hemingway in Paris, during the 1920s, and later in Bimini and Key West, Fla., which first appeared in eight installments in *Playboy*, see (H1000). Note: Kiley was one of the editors of *Boulevardier*, a magazine published in Paris, to which Hemingway contributed the article "The Real Spaniard." See (C183). The article was reprinted in the galleys of this book, on pp. 52-53, but was omitted from the final book.

215 Killinger, John. *Hemingway and the Dead Gods: A Study in Existentialism.* Lexington: Univ. of Kentucky Press, 1960. [x] + 114 pages. [Paperback edition: New York: Citadel Press, 1965. No. C-191. 128 pages.]
A study of the fictional world of Hemingway as it is related to the world view of existentialism.

216 Killinger, John. *The Failure of Theology in Modern Literature.* New York and Nashville: Abingdon Press, 1963. pp. 41-42, 53, 71-74, 111, 124-125, 132-135.

217 Knoll, Robert E. *Robert McAlmon: Expatriate Publisher and Writer.* Lincoln, 1957. (Univ. of Nebraska Studies, new series, No. 18.) Pamphlet. pp. 14, 33-34, 41, 78.
References to Hemingway in Paris, in the 1920s, in a study of the publisher of *TSTP*.

218 Kreymborg, Alfred. *The Little World: 1914 and After.* New York: Coward-McCann, 1932. p. 142.
A four-line verse "E. H.," in the series "Initials Abroad."

9 Kristensen, Sven Moeller. *Amerikansk litteratur: 1920–1940.* Copenhagen: Athenaeum, 1942. [Revised edition, 1948, covering 1920-1947. pp. 25, 43-55, 74, 142, 143, 220.]
pp. 43-55: "Ernest Hemingway."

0 Krzyżanowski, Jerzy R. *Ernest Hemingway.* Warsaw: Wiedza Powszechna, 1963. 176 pages. Photographs. Bibliography on pp. 163-166. Text in Polish.

1 [Kunitz, Stanley J.] "Dilly Tante," ed. *Living Authors: A Book of Biographies.* New York: Wilson, 1931. pp. 175-176. Photograph.
"Ernest Hemingway." A biographical sketch, which relates an incident in a Spanish bullring when a "disaster was averted" by Hemingway.

2 Kunitz, Stanley J. and Howard Haycraft, eds. *Twentieth Century Authors: A Biographical Dictionary of Modern Literature.* New York: Wilson, 1942. pp. 635-636. Photograph.

3 Kunitz, Stanley J. and Vineta Colby, eds. *Twentieth Century Authors.* New York: Wilson, 1955. First Supplement. pp. 433-434.

4 Land, Myrick. *The Fine Art of Literary Mayhem*: *A Lively Account of Famous Writers and Their Feuds.* New York: Holt, Rinehart & Winston, 1962. pp. 180-204.
Ch. x: "Mr. Hemingway Proves a Good Sport—but Only to Himself." Accounts of Hemingway's controversies with Sherwood Anderson, Gertrude Stein, Harold Loeb, Morley Callaghan, and Max Eastman.

5 Langford, Richard E. and William E. Taylor, eds. *The Twenties Poetry and Prose*: *20 Critical Essays.* Deland, Fla.: Everett Edwards Press, 1966. pp. 82-98.
pp. 82-86: "Ernest Hemingway and the Rhetoric of Escape" by Robert O. Stephens. pp. 87-91: "Implications of Form in *The Sun Also Rises*" by William L. Vance. pp. 92-94: "Hemingway as Moral Thinker: A Look at Two Novels" by Paul Ramsey. About *SAR* and *FWBT*. pp. 95-98: "Faulkner, Hemingway, and the 1920's" by William Van O'Connor.

6 Lania, Leo [pseudonym of Lazar Herrmann]. *Hemingway: eine Bildbiographie.* Munich: Kindler, 1960. (Kindlers Klassische Bildbiographien.) 142 pages. [(a) Translated into English by Joan Bradley. *Hemingway: a pictorial biography.* New York: Viking Press, 1961. (A Studio Book.) 142 pages. Chronology on pp. 129-131. (b) London: Thames & Hudson, 1961. (c) Translated into Spanish by Emilio Donato. *Hemingway: Biografía ilustrada.* Barcelona: Edi-

ciones Destino, 1963. 140 pages. (d) Translated into French by Claire Guinchat. Paris: Hachette, 1963. (Les Écrivains par l'image.) 140 pages.]

227 Larrabee, Eric, ed. *American Panorama: Essays by Fifteen American Critics on 350 Books Past and Present which Portray the U.S.A. in its Many Aspects.* New York: New York Univ. Press, 1957. pp. 53, 155.
p. 155: "The Short Stories of Ernest Hemingway" by "C. F." [Clifton Fadiman].

228 Lawrence, D. H. *Phoenix: The Posthumous Papers of D. H. Lawrence.* Edited by Edward D. McDonald. London: Heinemann, 1936. p. 365. [New York: Viking Press, 1936.]
Review of *In Our Time*, reprinted from the *Calendar of Modern Letters*, IV (April 1927). Reprinted in *The Portable D. H. Lawrence*, ed. Diana Trilling, New York: Viking Press, 1947, pp. 644-645; in *Selected Literary Criticism*, ed. Anthony Beal, London: Heinemann, 1955, pp. 427-428; in *Weeks collection*, pp. 93-94.

229 Leary, Lewis. *Articles on American Literature: 1900–1950.* Durham, N.C.: Duke Univ. Press, 1954. pp. 137-139. Bibliography.
Checklist of critical studies of Hemingway's work.

230 Leary, Lewis, ed. *The Teacher and American Literature: Papers Presented at the 1964 Convention of the National Council of Teachers of English.* Champaign, Ill.: National Council of Teachers of English, 1965. pp. 149-162.
pp. 149-156: "Recent Scholarship on Faulkner and Hemingway" by Richard P. Adams. pp. 157-162: "Faulkner and Hemingway: Implications for School Programs" by John N. Terrey.

231 Legman, Gershon. *Love and Death: A Study in Censorship.* New York: Breaking Point, 1949. pp. 86-90.
Discussion of Hemingway's heroes and heroines.

232 Lerner, Max. *Public Journal: Marginal Notes on Wartime America.* New York: Viking Press, 1945. pp. 44-46, 87-89.
pp. 44-46: "On Hemingway," reprinted from *PM* (Sept. 28, 1944). pp. 87-89: "No Man Is An Island," reprinted from *PM* (July 18, 1943).

233 Levin, Harry. *Contexts of Criticism.* Cambridge: Harvard Univ. Press, 1957. pp. 50, 140-167, 190-207, 231, 237, 239.
pp. 140-167: Ch. [x]: "Observations on the Style of Ernest Hemingway." This essay first appeared in *Kenyon Review*, XIII (Autumn 1951). Reprinted in *American Critical Essays*, ed. Harold Beaver, London, 1959, pp. 286-313; in *The Personal Voice*, Albert J. Gué-

rard *et al.*, Philadelphia, 1964, pp. 431-444; in *Baker anthology,* pp. 93-115; and in *Weeks collection*, in an abridged form, pp. 72-85. pp. 190-207: Ch. [xii]: "Symbolism and Fiction," reprinted from the book of the same title, Charlottesville: Univ. of Virginia Press, 1956.

34 Lewis, Robert W., Jr. *Hemingway on Love*. Austin and London: Univ. of Texas Press, 1965. 252 pages. Selected Reading List on pp. 229-235.
A study "to consider the subject of love as treated by Hemingway in major and representative works."

35 Lewis, Wyndham. *Men Without Art*. London: Cassell, 1934. pp. 17-40. [New York: Russell & Russell, 1964.]
"The Dumb Ox, A Study of Ernest Hemingway," reprinted from *Life & Letters*, x (April 1934).

36 Lewis, Wyndham. *Rude Assignment: A narrative of my career up-to-date*. London: Hutchinson, [1950]. pp. 18, 203-204, 205, 218.
pp. 203-204: An appraisal of Hemingway's work. Quotes a letter from Hemingway. See (F70).

37 Lewisohn, Ludwig. *The Story of American Literature*. New York: Harper, 1932. pp. 518-520.
Discussion of Hemingway's originality and style.

38 Linati, Carlo. *Scrittori anglo-americani d'oggi*. Milan: Corticelli, 1932. pp. 201-210. [Second edition, 1944. pp. 189-197.]
"Ernest Hemingway." A discussion of *IOT* and *FTA*.

39 *Litteraturhandboken: Tredje utökade och omarbetade upplagan.* Stockholm: Forum, 1959. pp. 208-209, 233-234. Photograph.
pp. 233-234: "Ernest Hemingway." Short biographical sketch and a checklist of Hemingway's work translated into Swedish.

40 Litz, A. Walton, ed. *Modern American Fiction: Essays in Criticism*. New York: Oxford Univ. Press, 1963. pp. 201-255.
pp. 201-214: "Hemingway: The Matador and the Crucified" by Melvin Backman, reprinted from *Modern Fiction Studies*, i (Aug. 1955). pp. 215-227: "Hemingway's Narrative Perspective" by E. M. Halliday, reprinted from *Sewanee Review*, lx (April–June 1952). pp. 228-243: "First Forty-five Stories" by Carlos Baker, reprinted from *Baker*, pp. 117-127. pp. 244-255: "Ernest Hemingway: The Failure of Sensibility" by R. B. West, Jr., reprinted from *Sewanee Review*, liii (Jan.–March 1945).

41 Llona, Victor, ed. *Les Romanciers américains*. Paris: Denoël et Steele, 1931. pp. 193-197.
"Ernest Hemingway" by André Maurois. See also (E25).

242 Loeb, Harold. *The Way It Was*. New York: Criterion, 1959. pp. 190, 193-194, 215-220, 228-231, 237-238, 281, 285-298, 300. Photographs.

p. 190: Relates his meeting with Hemingway in Paris, in 1923. pp. 285-298: Relates details of the trip to Pamplona by a group of American and English expatriates, in the summer of 1924, on which Hemingway based his fictional account in *SAR*. By the author's account, he is the original of Robert Cohn in *SAR*.

243 Loggins, Vernon. *I Hear America . . . Literature in the United States Since 1900*. New York: Crowell, 1937. pp. 12, 118, 134-138.

pp. 134-138: On Hemingway, from Ch. v: "Dominant Primordial: Frank Norris, Theodore Dreiser, Ernest Hemingway, and Thomas Wolfe."

244 Lombardo, Agostino. *Realismo e Simbolismo*. Rome: Edizioni di Storia e Letteratura, 1957. (Biblioteca di Studi Americani, No. 3.) pp. 12, 13, 14-17, 193.

pp. 14-17: The author quotes from *OMATS* as an example of Hemingway's evocative prose and from *FTA* as an example of his use of dialogue.

245 Lowrey, Burling, ed. *Twentieth Century Parody: American and British*. New York: Harcourt, Brace, 1960. pp. 59-70, 265-267.

pp. 59-70: "A Farewell to Josephine's Arms—The Hemingway of All Flesh" by H. W. Hanemann, reprinted from *The Facts of Life*, New York, 1930, pp. 131-159. pp. 265-267: "Thou Tellest Me, Comrade" by Gilbert Highet, reprinted from the *Nation*, CLII (March 1, 1941).

246 Lucas, John. *To Papa from Pamplona Plus*. Northfield, Minn.: College City Press, 1961. pp. [47]-[48].

The title poem is "To Papa from Pamplona."

247 Luccock, Halford E. *Contemporary American Literature and Religion*. Chicago: Willett-Clark, 1934. pp. 4, 148, 150-152, 159, 177, 179-180, 196.

The author deplores the lack of "meaningful significance" in Hemingway's work, especially in *SAR*.

248 Lüdeke, Henry. *Geschichte der amerikanischen Literatur*. Bern: A. Francke, 1952. pp. 497, 514-516.

249 Ludovici, Laurence J., ed. *Nobel Prize Winners*. London: Arco, 1957. pp. 85-100. [Westport, Conn.: Associated Booksellers, 1957.] "Ernest Hemingway" by M.J.C. Hodgart.

250 Ludwig, Richard M., ed. *Literary History of the United States: Bibliography Supplement*. New York: Macmillan, 1959. pp. 137-139.

Checklist of biographical and critical studies on Hemingway, from 1947 to 1957. See also (G387).

51 Lundkvist, Artur. *Atlantvind*. Stockholm: Bonnier, 1932. pp. 70-75. Evaluation of Hemingway's work.

52 Lundkvist, Artur. *Diktare och avslöjare i Amerikas moderna litteratur*. Stockholm: Kooperativa förbundents bokförlag, 1942. pp. 149-159.
Ch. xii: "Ernest Hemingway."

53 McAlmon, Robert. *Being Geniuses Together: An Autobiography*. London: Secker & Warburg, 1938. pp. 155-156, 159-162, 163, 191-192, 212-215, 230-231.
pp. 155-156: Hemingway's first publisher relates meeting him in Rapallo, Italy, early in 1923. pp. 159-162: "Let's Be Shadow-Boxers." Describes a trip with Hemingway to Madrid, in 1924, to see their first bullfight, followed by a tour of Spain, accompanied by William Bird. Reprinted in *McAlmon and the Lost Generation*, pp. 225-240.

54 McAlmon, Robert. *McAlmon and the Lost Generation: A Self-Portrait*. Edited by Robert E. Knoll. Lincoln: Univ. of Nebraska Press, 1962. pp. 192-193, 225-240, 353-354, 374. Photographs.

55 McCaffery, John K. M., ed. *Ernest Hemingway: The Man and His Work*, Cleveland and New York: World, 1950. 352 pages. [(a) Toronto: McClelland, 1950. (b) Paperback edition: New York: Avon Books, 1961. No. v 2041. 319 pages.]
Contents: pp. 9-15: Introduction by the editor.

[Part i] The Man
pp. 19-24: "A Note on Ernest Hemingway" by John Groth, reprinted from the Living Library edition of *MWW*, Cleveland, 1946, pp. 11-16.

pp. 25-33: "Hemingway in Paris" by Gertrude Stein, reprinted from *The Autobiography of Alice B. Toklas*, New York, 1933, pp. 261-271.

pp. 34-56: "A Portrait of Mister Papa" by Malcolm Cowley, reprinted from *Life*, xxv (Jan. 10, 1949). Slightly revised by the author.

[Part ii] His Work
pp. 59-65: "The Canon of Death" by Lincoln Kirstein, reprinted from *Hound & Horn*, vi (Jan.–March 1933).

pp. 66-75: "Bull in the Afternoon" by Max Eastman, reprinted from *Art and the Life of Action*, New York, 1934, pp. 87-101.

pp. 76-108: "Ernest Hemingway: A Tragedy of Craftsmanship" by J. [Ivan] Kashkeen, reprinted from *International Literature*, No. 5 (May 1935).

pp. 109-113: "Hemingway and the Critics" by Elliot Paul, reprinted from *SRL*, xvii (Nov. 6, 1937).

pp. 114-129: "Ernest Hemingway's Literary Situation" by Delmore Schwartz, reprinted from the *Southern Review*, iii (Spring 1938).

pp. 130-142: "Farewell the Separate Peace: The Rejections of Ernest Hemingway" by Edgar Johnson, reprinted from the *Sewanee Review*, xlviii (July–Sept. 1940).

pp. 143-189: "Ernest Hemingway: You Could Always Come Back" by Maxwell Geismar, reprinted from *Writers in Crisis*, Boston, 1942, pp. 39-85.

pp. 190-204: "Hemingway: Synopsis of a Career" by Alfred Kazin, reprinted, in slightly revised form, from *On Native Grounds*, New York, 1942, pp. 327-341.

pp. 205-220: "English and Spanish in *For Whom the Bell Tolls*" by Edward Fenimore, reprinted from the *ELH*, x (March 1943).

pp. 221-225: "*The Sun Also Rises*" by James T. Farrell, reprinted from *The League of Frightened Philistines*, New York, 1945, pp. 20-24.

pp. 226-235: "Tenderly Tolls the Bell" by James Gray, reprinted from *On Second Thought*, Minneapolis, 1946, pp. 74-81.

pp. 236-257: "Hemingway: Gauge of Morale" by Edmund Wilson, reprinted from *The Wound and the Bow*, New York: Oxford Univ. Press, 1947, pp. 214-242.

pp. 258-261: "Hemingway in Spain" by Leo Gurko, reprinted from *The Angry Decade*, New York, 1947, pp. 187-190.

pp. 262-291: "Violence and Discipline" by W. M. Frohock, reprinted from *The Novel of Violence in America*, Dallas, 1950, pp. 167-199.

pp. 292-307: "The Missing All" by John Peale Bishop, reprinted from *The Collected Essays of John Peale Bishop*, New York, 1948, pp. 66-77.

pp. 308-328: "Ernest Hemingway and the Psychology of the Lost Generation" by Edwin Berry Burgum, reprinted from *The Novel and the World's Dilemma*, New York, 1947, pp. 184-204.

pp. 329-339: "Hemingway and James" by George Hemphill, reprinted from the *Kenyon Review*, xi (Winter 1949).

pp. 340-351: "Hemingway's Women" by Theodore Bardacke. Not previously published.

256 McCole, C. John. *Lucifer at Large*. London & New York: Longmans, Green, 1937. pp. 153-172. Bibliographical references.

"Ernest Hemingway: Spokesman For His Generation." A study of Hemingway's originality and individuality of style, particularly in "Big Two-Hearted River" and *FTA*.

257 McCormick, John. *Catastrophe and Imagination*: *An Interpretation of the Recent English and American Novel*. London & New York: Longmans, Green, 1957. pp. 77, 95-96, 204, 207, 208-214, 219, 220-221, 242, 256.

pp. 95-96: Discussion of Henry James's influence on Hemingway's work. pp. 208-214: Discussion of Hemingway's war novels.

258 Macdonald, Dwight. *Parodies*: *From Chaucer to Beerbohm—and After*. New York: Random House, 1960. pp. 248-254. [Modern Library edition, 1965.]

pp. 248-250: "Death in the Rumble Seat" by Wolcott Gibbs, reprinted from *More in Sorrow*, New York, 1958, pp. 20-23. pp. 251-254: "Across the Street and Into the Grill" by E. B. White, reprinted from *The Second Tree from the Corner*, New York, 1954, pp. 140-143.

259 Macdonald, Dwight. *Against the American Grain: essays on the effects of mass culture*. New York: Random House, 1962. pp. 167-184.

pp. 167-179: "Ernest Hemingway," reprinted from *Encounter*, XVIII (Jan. 1962). pp. 179-184: Appendix: "Dissenting Opinion." A letter from George Plimpton in reply to Macdonald's essay.

260 Machlin, Milt. *The Private Hell of Hemingway*. New York: Paperback Library, 1962. 222 pages. Cover photograph of Hemingway by Yousuf Karsh.

The blurb on the cover states: "The brawling, boozing, battling years of America's greatest writer."

261 McKay, Claude. *A Long Way From Home*. New York: Furman, 1937. pp. 249-252. Autobiographical.

The poet discusses Hemingway's work and his impact on fellow writers in Paris, in 1924, following the publication of *in our time*.

262 MacLeish, Archibald. *Act Five and Other Poems*. New York: Random House, 1948. p. 53.

"Years of the Dog." Partially quoted in *Baker*, p. 19. Translated into French in *Hemingway*, ed. John Brown, Paris, 1961, pp. 14-16.

263 MacLeish, Archibald. *Songs for Eve*. Boston: Houghton Mifflin, 1954. p. 51.

"Poet" (for Ernest Hemingway).

264 [MacLeish, Archibald]. *The Dialogues of Archibald MacLeish and Mark Van Doren*. Edited by Warren V. Bush. New York: Dutton, 1964. pp. 85-87, 146.

MacLeish speaks of his friendship with Hemingway in Paris, in the 1920s, and of Hemingway's visit to his farm in Massachusetts, in 1930.

265 McNeir, Waldo F., ed. *Studies in Comparative Literature.* Baton Rouge: Louisiana State Univ. Press, 1962. pp. 260, 262-263, 268.

Discussion of Hemingway, from the chapter "American Literature in Postwar Germany: Impact or Alienation?" by Horst Oppel.

266 Magill, Frank N., ed. *Masterplots.* New York: Salem Press, 1949. [Reissued under the title *Masterpieces of World Literature*: *In Digest Form.* New York: Harper & Row, 1952.] First Series: pp. 269-271: *FTA*; pp. 282-284: *FWBT*; pp. 941-943: *SAR.* Second Series: pp. 764-766: *OMATS.*

267 Magill, Frank N., ed. *Cyclopedia of World Authors.* New York: Harper & Row, 1958. pp. 499-502. Bibliographical references.

268 Magill, Frank N., ed. *Cyclopedia of Literary Characters.* New York: Harper & Row, 1963. pp. 357-358: *FTA*; pp. 374-376: *FWBT*; p. 804: *OMATS*; pp. 1093-94: *SAR.*

269 Magny, Claude-Edmonde. *L'Âge du Roman américain.* Paris: Éditions du Seuil, 1948. pp. 159-178.

"Hemingway ou l'exaltation de l'instant."

270 Malcolmson, David. *Ten Heroes.* New York: Duell, Sloan & Pearce, 1941. pp. 23-24, 156-159.

pp. 156-159: On the death of Robert Jordan's father, in the chapter "The Escape from the Devouring Mother."

271 Mallett, Richard. *Literary Upshots or Split Reading.* London: Cape, 1951. pp. 44-47.

Parody. "Purple Bits of Hemingway: A sort of reminiscence of *Green Hills of Africa.*"

272 Martone, Maria and Edoardo Bizzarri. *Novellieri inglesi e americani.* Rome: DeCarlo, 1944. pp. 733-748.

273 Matthews, Herbert L. *Two Wars and More to Come.* New York: Carrick & Evans, 1938. pp. 282, 300, 309-311.

Personal narratives of the Spanish Civil War by the foreign correspondent for the *N.Y. Times.* See also (F161).

274 Matthews, Herbert L. *The Education of a Correspondent.* New York: Harcourt, Brace, 1946. pp. 7, 95-106, 122, 132-134, 138.

pp. 95-106: Describes the assault on Teruel, in December 1937, which the author and Hemingway covered together.

275 Maurois, André. *Portraits.* Ottawa: Bernard Grasset, 1955. (Le cercle du livre de France.) pp. 155-174. Text in French.

"Ernest Hemingway," reprinted from *Revue de Paris*, LXII (March 1955).

276 Meaker, M. J. [Marijane.] *Sudden Endings.* Garden City, N.Y.: Doubleday, 1964. pp. 1-25. Bibliography, p. 270.

Thirteen profiles of famous suicides. Ch. 1: "A Wow at the End." A study of Hemingway's work as relating to suicide.

277 Mehring, Walter. *The Lost Library: The Autobiography of a Culture.* Indianapolis: Bobbs-Merrill, 1951. Translated from the German by Richard and Clara Winston. pp. 190-191.

Describes the American cultural background from which Hemingway emerged to become "a lover of Latin culture."

278 Michaud, Régis. *Panorama de la littérature américaine contemporaine.* Paris: Simon Kra, 1926. pp. 244, 246, 255.

Brief critical commentary on Hemingway's work.

279 Miller, Lee G. *The Story of Ernie Pyle.* New York: Viking Press, 1950. pp. 342, 351, 355.

References to Hemingway when he and Pyle and other war correspondents lived in a press camp near Omaha Beach, in Normandy, in June 1944.

280 Millett, Fred B. [Introduction and Revision.] *Contemporary American Literature: Bibliographies and Study Outlines.* By John Matthews Manly and Edith Rickert. New York: Harcourt, Brace, [1929]. New and enlarged edition. pp. 40, 195-196.

Brief critical appraisal of Hemingway's work.

281 Millett, Fred B. *Contemporary American Authors.* New York: Harcourt, Brace, 1940. pp. 385-388.

282 Mizener, Arthur. *The Far Side of Paradise: A Biography of F. Scott Fitzgerald.* Boston: Houghton Mifflin, 1949. pp. 152, 180, 195-198, 212-213, 231, 238-240, 252, 270-271, 342 (n. 3), 346 (n. 3). [Second edition, revised, 1965.]

Letters from Hemingway to Fitzgerald are quoted. See (F60), (F63), (F65), (F89), (F91). p. 252: Regarding Fitzgerald's portrayal of Hemingway as the hero, Phillipe, in his novel about medieval life, "The Count of Darkness," published in four installments in *Redbook* magazine.

283 Mizener, Arthur. *The Sense of Life in the Modern Novel.* Boston: Houghton Mifflin, 1964. pp. 119, 131-133, 150, 180, 205-226.

pp. 205-226: Ch. x: "The American Hero as Leatherstocking: Nick Adams."

284 Mohrt, Michel. *Le nouveau Roman américain.* Paris: Gallimard, 1955. pp. 45-70.

Ch. [II]: "La vie heureuse et bien remplie d'Ernest Hemingway."

285 [Mondadori, Arnoldo]. *Il Cinquantennio Editoriale di Arnoldo Mondadori, 1907-1957.* Verona: Mondadori, 1957. pp. 47, 50, 53, 206, 207, 219, 228, 239. Photograph.

p. 206: Regarding the "Premio Hemingway" instituted by Hemingway's Italian publishers, Mondadori, in 1949. Letters from Hemingway to Arnoldo Mondadori are reprinted, in Italian, on pp. 219, 228, and 239. See (F108), (F112), (F128). Note: This book measures 13 5/8 x 9 3/4. An edition of 3500 copies was published in November 1957; boxed.

286 Montgomery, Constance Cappel. *Hemingway in Michigan.* New York: Fleet, 1966. 224 pages. Photographs.

Regarding the years 1900-1921, when the Hemingway family spent their summers in northern Michigan, and Hemingway's later use of this setting in his novels and short stories. For contents and description of this book, see (B61).

287 Mora, Constancia de la. *In Place of Splendor: The Autobiography of a Spanish Woman.* New York: Harcourt, Brace, 1939. pp. 290-291.
Recollections of Hemingway during the Spanish Civil War.

288 Moravia, Alberto. *L'Uomo Come Fine a Altri Saggi.* Milan: Bompiani, 1964. pp. 369-375. [Translated into English by Bernard Wall. *Man as an End: A Defense of Humanism.* New York: Farrar, Straus & Giroux, 1966. pp. 231-236.]
"Amici dei morte e nemici dei vivi," reprinted from *L'Espresso* (Aug. 20, 1961). An English translation appeared in *Status*, 1 (Nov. 1965), under the title "Nothing Amen."

289 Morris, Lloyd. *Postscript to Yesterday: America: The Last Fifty Years.* New York: Random House, 1947. pp. 154-157.
"Salvage." A discussion of Hemingway's views of American life as seen through his characters.

290 Morris, Wright. *The Territory Ahead.* New York: Harcourt, Brace, 1958. pp. 133-146.
"The Function of Style: Ernest Hemingway." This essay appeared in *New World Writing*, No. 13 (June 1958).

291 Moseley, Edwin M. *Pseudonyms of Christ in the Modern Novel: Motifs and Methods.* Pittsburgh: Univ. of Pittsburgh Press, 1962. pp. ix, 3-6, 16, 93-94, 107-113, 125, 205-213.
pp. 205-213: Ch. XIII: "Christ As The Old Champion: Hemingway's *The Old Man and the Sea*."

292 Mucharowski, Hans-Günter. *Die werke von Ernest Hemingway: Eine Bibliographie der deutschsprachigen Hemingway—Literatur*

und der Originalwerke, von 1923 bis 1954. Hamburg, 1955. 48 pages. Mimeographed.

293 Muller, Herbert J. *Modern Fiction: A Study of Values.* New York: Funk & Wagnalls, 1937. pp. 17, 29, 383-403. [Paperback edition: New York: McGraw-Hill, 1964.]

pp. 383-403: Ch. XXI: "Apostles of the Lost Generation: Huxley, Hemingway."

294 Myklebost, Tor. *Drommen om Amerika: Den amerikanske roman gjennom femti år.* Oslo: Gyldendal, 1953. pp. 92-99.

Ch. [XI]: "Ernest Hemingway: artisten."

295 Nathan, George Jean, Ernest Boyd, Theodore Dreiser, Sherwood Anderson, James Branch Cabell, and Eugene O'Neill, eds. *American Spectator Year Book.* New York: Stokes, 1934. pp. 231-235.

"Death at 5:45 P.M." by Thomas Beer. Review of *DIA*, reprinted from the *American Spectator*, 1 (Feb. 1933).

296 Nebot, Frank. *Hemingway.* Madrid: S.A.E. Gráficas Espejo, 1961. (Colección Hechos y Figuras.) 64 pages. In Spanish.

297 Norman, Charles. *Ezra Pound.* New York: Macmillan, 1960. pp. 16, 256, 257, 258-259, 269, 274, 275, 278, 288, 322, 453, 461.

p. 256: Hemingway's inscription regarding the publication of *iot* is reprinted from *The Library of Dr. Don Carlos Guffey*, New York, 1958, p. 32. p. 322: Reference to Hemingway's last visit with Pound, in Paris, in 1934.

298 North, Joseph. *No Men are Strangers.* New York: International Publishers, 1958. pp. 142-145, 146-147, 149.

pp. 142-145: Relates an argument on communism which he had with Hemingway in Madrid, on May Day of 1938. pp. 146-147: The author, who is a former editor of *New Masses*, quotes from the article Hemingway sent him for the special edition on the anniversary of the Popular Front victory of 1936. See (C313).

299 Nyren, Dorothy, ed. *A Library of Literary Criticism: Modern American Literature.* New York: Ungar, 1961. Second Edition with Index to Critics. pp. 226-231.

Sixteen short excerpts from critical studies of Hemingway are included in this survey of significant criticism of 170 American authors.

300 O'Brien, Edward J. *The Advance of the American Short Story.* New York: Dodd, Mead, 1931. Revised Edition. pp. 269-275.

Discussion of Hemingway's contribution to the American short story. Quotes a letter from Hemingway on what he tries to do in his writing. See (F45).

301 O'Connor, Frank. *The Lonely Voice: A Study of the Short Story.* Cleveland: World, 1963. pp. 23, 24, 25, 26, 156-169.

pp. 156-169: "A Clean Well-Lighted Place," an essay on Hemingway's short stories.

302 O'Connor, William Van, ed. *Forms of Modern Fiction.* Minneapolis: Univ. of Minnesota Press, 1948. pp. 7, 26-28, 86, 87-101, 152, 154. [Paperback edition: Bloomington: Indiana Univ. Press, 1948.]

pp. 87-101: "Ernest Hemingway: The Failure of Sensibility" by Ray B. West, Jr., reprinted from the *Sewanee Review,* LIII (Jan.–March 1945).

303 O'Connor, William Van. *The Grotesque: An American Genre and Other Essays.* Carbondale: Southern Illinois Univ. Press, 1962. (Crosscurrents Modern Critiques.) pp. 27-28, 36, 56, 115-117, 119-124.

pp. 119-124: Ch. XI: "Two Views of Kilimanjaro." A study examining "The Snows of Kilimanjaro" and Bayard Taylor's poem, "Kilimanjaro," written in the early 1850s. Reprinted from *History of Ideas Newsletter,* II (Oct. 1956).

304 O'Connor, William Van, ed. *Seven Modern American Novelists: An Introduction.* Minneapolis: Univ. of Minnesota Press, 1964. pp. 4, 5, 9, 153-188.

pp. 153-188: "Ernest Hemingway" by Philip Young. A revised version of Number I of the Pamphlets on American Writers series, Minneapolis, 1959.

305 O'Faolain, Sean. *The Vanishing Hero: Studies in Novelists of the Twenties.* London: Eyre & Spottiswoode, 1956. pp. 137-165. [Boston: Atlantic–Little, Brown, 1957, pp. 112-145.]

"Ernest Hemingway or Men Without Memories."

306 O'Hara, John. *Sweet and Sour: Comments on Books and People.* New York: Random House, 1954. pp. 39-44, 73.

pp. 39-44: Ch. VII on Hemingway.

307 Oldfield, Col. Barney. *Never a Shot in Anger.* New York: Duell, Sloan & Pearce, 1956. pp. 94, 108-109.

References to Hemingway in an account of the activities of war correspondents during World War II.

308 Orvis, Mary Burchard. *The Art of Writing Fiction.* New York: Prentice-Hall, 1948. pp. 26-27, 99-101, 108, 129-132, 167, 205-210, 211.

pp. 99-101, 129-132: Discussion of "Macomber." pp. 205-210: Regarding *FTA* and *FWBT.*

309 Otero, Lisandro. *Hemingway.* Havana: Editorial Nacional de

Cuba, 1963. (Cuadernos de la Casa de las Américas, No. 2.) Pamphlet. 44 pages.

310 Overton, Grant. *An Hour of the American Novel.* Philadelphia: Lippincott, 1929. pp. 142-143.
Brief critical commentary on Hemingway's work.

311 Pater, Alan F. and Milton Landau, eds. *What They Said In 1937: The Yearbook of Oral Opinion.* New York: Paebar, 1938. p. 89.
Quotes Hemingway on the probable duration of the Spanish Civil War, from an interview in the *N.Y. Times* (May 19, 1937).

312 Patmore, Derek. *Private History: An Autobiography.* London: Cape, 1960. pp. 28, 99-101, 181.
pp. 99-101: Relates a visit to the Hemingways, in the rue Notre Dame des Champs, with Ezra Pound, in 1925.

313 [Peirce, Waldo]. *Waldo Peirce.* New York: American Artists Group, 1945. (Monograph No. 5.) p. [43].
Portrait of Ernest Hemingway. Painted by Peirce for the cover of *Time,* xxx (Oct. 18, 1937).

314 [Pennsylvania, University of]. *Index to Articles on American Literature: 1951–1959.* Prepared in The Reference Department, University of Pennsylvania, University Library. Philadelphia, 1960. pp. 228-235.
Photocopies of cards listing critical studies and biographical articles on Hemingway.

315 Perkins, Maxwell E. *Editor to Author: The Letters of Maxwell E. Perkins.* Edited by John Hall Wheelock. New York: Scribner's, 1950. pp. 48, 58, 73, 77-80, 90-91, 94-98, 117-119, 152-157, 159, 164, 174-175, 193, 200-207, 209, 228, 233, 234-236, 251, 264, 266, 299. [Paperback edition: 1965. Scribner Library No. SL 107.]
Included are fifteen letters to Hemingway, written between 1932 and 1945.

316 Phillips, William and Philip Rahv, eds. *The Partisan Reader: Ten Years of Partisan Review, 1934–1944.* New York: Dial Press, 1946. pp. 639-644.
"An American in Spain" by Lionel Trilling. Review of *FWBT,* reprinted from *Partisan Review,* VIII (Jan.–Feb. 1941). Reprinted in *Baker critiques,* pp. 78-81.

317 Pivano, Fernanda. *La balena bianca e altri miti.* Milan: Mondadori, 1961. pp. 125-136.
"Il balletto della morte." Preface to *Morte nel pomeriggio (DIA)* reprinted.

318 Pivano, Fernanda. *America rossa e nera*. Florence: Vallecchi, 1964. pp. 78, 80, 81, 128, 132-150, 201, 224, 227, 234, 238.

pp. 132-150: "Ormai tutti sanno tutto: anche la storia del suo antifascismo." This essay on Hemingway was reprinted from *Aut Aut* (Sept. 1961).

319 [Plimpton, George]. *Writers at Work: The Paris Review Interviews*. Second Series. Introduced by Van Wyck Brooks. New York: Viking Press, 1963. pp. 215-239. Facsimile of manuscript page from "The Battler." [Paperback edition: Compass Book No. C-175.]

p. 215: Biographical note. pp. 217-239: "Ernest Hemingway" by George Plimpton. This interview was reprinted from the *Paris Review*, V (Spring 1958). Reprinted in *Baker anthology*, pp. 19-37.

320 Pongs, Hermann. *Im Umbruch der Zeit: das Romanschaffen der Gegenwart*. [Göttingen, Germany]: Göttinger, 1952. pp. 167-170. "Ernest Hemingways *Wem die Stunde schlägt*."

321 Portuondo, José Antonio. *El Heroismo Intelectual*. Mexico City: Tezontle, 1955. pp. 140-161. "Proceso Literario de Ernest Hemingway."

322 Pound, Ezra. *The Letters of Ezra Pound: 1907–1941*. Edited by D. D. Paige. New York: Harcourt, Brace, 1950. pp. 186, 199, 223, 283.

p. 283: Letter to Hemingway, in 1936, commending an article of his which appeared in *Esquire*.

323 Praz, Mario. *Cronache letterarie anglosassoni*. Vol. II: *Cronache inglesi e americane*. Rome: Edizioni di Storia e Letteratura, 1951. pp. 190-195, 202-231, 240, 274.

pp. 190-195: "Parodia di *Riso nero*," review of *TOS*. pp. 202-212: "Ernest Hemingway." Discussion of *IOT*, *WTN*, and *GHOA*. pp. 213-231: "Hemingway e alcuni scrittori italiani contemporanei," reprinted from *Partisan Review*, XV (Oct. 1948). Reprinted in *Baker anthology*, pp. 116-130.

324 Prescott, Orville. *In My Opinion: An Inquiry into the Contemporary Novel*. Indianapolis: Bobbs-Merrill, 1952. pp. 50, 65-71.

On Hemingway, from the chapter "Squandered Talents: Lewis, Steinbeck, Hemingway, O'Hara."

325 Prezzolini, Giuseppe. *America con gli stivali*. Florence: Vallecchi, 1954. pp. 606-620. Photograph.

"Hemingway e l'Italia," reprinted from *Tempo* (Oct. 18, 1952) and (Aug. 3, 1954).

326 Putnam, Samuel. *Paris Was Our Mistress: Memoirs of a Lost and*

Found Generation. New York: Viking Press, 1947. pp. 69-70, 110, 121, 127-134.

pp. 127-134: "Hard-Boiled Young Man Going Places (Ernest Hemingway)." Reminisces on his first meeting with Hemingway, in Chicago, in the early 1920s, and later meetings in Paris, in the mid-1920s.

27 Quinn, Arthur Hobson, ed. *The Literature of the American People: An Historical and Critical Survey.* New York: Appleton-Century-Crofts, 1951. pp. 882-884.

On Hemingway, from the chapter "The Twentieth Century" by George F. Whicher.

28 Rahv, Philip. *Image and Idea: Twenty Essays on Literary Themes.* New York: New Directions, 1957. pp. 11-12, 150, 188-195.

pp. 188-192: Review of *ARIT*, reprinted from *Commentary*, x (Oct. 1950). pp. 192-195: Review of *OMATS*, reprinted from *Commentary*, xiv (Oct. 1952). Under the heading "Hemingway in the 1950's." Both reviews are reprinted in *The Myth and the Powerhouse.* New York: Farrar, Straus & Giroux, 1964, pp. 193-201. Under the heading "Hemingway in the Early 1950's."

29 Rascoe, Burton. *A Bookman's Daybook.* New York: Liveright, 1929. pp. 253-254.

Entry for June 5 [1924]: "Ellis, Whitehead and Hemingway." Discusses *iot* and *TSTP* briefly. Quotes Ch. ix of *iot*. Reprinted from the *N.Y. Herald Tribune* (June 15, 1924).

30 Rascoe, Burton. *We Were Interrupted.* Garden City, N.Y.: Doubleday, 1947. pp. 184-186, 191.

In Part Two of his autobiography, Rascoe reminisces on his meeting with Hemingway in Paris, in 1924.

31 Ray, Man. *Self Portrait.* Boston: Atlantic–Little, Brown, 1963. pp. 156, 182, 184-185, 191.

pp. 184-185: The photographer relates the occasion in Paris, in the early 1920s, when a bathroom skylight fell on Hemingway, and he photographed him with a bandaged head and alpine hat.

32 Regler, Gustav. *The Owl of Minerva: Autobiography.* London: Hart-Davis, 1959. Translated from the German by Norman Denny. pp. 290-299. [New York: Farrar, Straus & Cudahy, 1960.]

Recollections of Hemingway during the Spanish Civil War.

33 Richards, Robert F., ed. *Concise Dictionary of American Literature.* New York: Philosophical Library, 1955. pp. 103-105. Photograph.

34 Rideout, Walter B. and James K. Robinson, eds. *A College Book*

of Modern Fiction. Evanston, Ill.: Row, Peterson, 1961. pp. 552-565.

"Hills Like White Elephants" and "Ten Indians" are used as examples in "What Makes a Short Story Short" by Norman Friedman. Reprinted from *Modern Fiction Studies,* IV (Summer 1958).

335 Rink, Paul. *Ernest Hemingway: Remaking Modern Fiction.* Chicago: Encyclopaedia Britannica Press, 1962. (Britannica Bookshelf: Great Lives for Young Americans.) Juvenile. 191 pages. Illustrated by Robert Boehmer.

336 Ritzen, Quentin. *Ernest Hemingway.* Paris: Éditions Universitaires, 1962. (Classiques du XXᵉ siècle, 46.) 120 pages.
A critical study.

337 Robinson, Donald. *The 100 Most Important People in the World Today.* Boston: Little, Brown, 1952. pp. 364-367. Pen portrait. [Paperback edition: New York: Pocket Books, 1953. pp. 372-376.]
"Ernest Hemingway." Biographical sketch.

338 Rosati, Salvatore. *Storia della Letteratura Americana.* Turin: Edizioni Radio Italiana, 1956. (Letteratura e civilta, No. 5.) pp. 8, 242, 247-249, 279-280.
pp. 247-249: Discussion of Hemingway's work, with a long excerpt from *OMATS.* pp. 279-280: Biographical note.

339 Rosenfeld, Isaac. *An Age of Enormity: Life and Writing in the Forties and Fifties.* Edited by Theodore Solotaroff. Cleveland: World, 1962. pp. 258-267.
"A Farewell to Hemingway," review of *ARIT,* reprinted from *Kenyon Review,* XIII (Winter 1951).

340 Rosenfeld, Paul. *By Way of Art: Criticisms of Music, Literature, Painting, Sculpture and the Dance.* New York: Coward-McCann, 1928. pp. 151-163.
"Hemingway's Perspective." Describes Hemingway as a "prose Goya" and compares the "violent world" which he created in *MWW* with the world of Goya's time.

341 Ross, Danforth. *The American Short Story.* Minneapolis: Univ. of Minnesota Press, 1961. (Pamphlets on American Writers, No. 14.) pp. 34-35, 36, 41.

342 Ross, Lillian. *Portrait of Hemingway.* New York: Simon & Schuster, 1961. 66 pages. Photograph of Hemingway by Paul Radkai. [Paperback editions: (a) Harmondsworth: Penguin Books, 1962. (b) New York: Avon Books, 1965. No. SS 3. 94 pages.]
Reprinted, with slight revisions, from the Profile in the *New*

Yorker, XXVI (May 13, 1950). A new preface by the author is on pp. 11-19. Reprinted in *Weeks collection*, pp. 17-39. See also next entry.

43 Ross, Lillian. *Reporting*. New York: Simon & Schuster, 1964. pp. 144, 148, 149, 150-151, 152, 155, 158, 160-161, 162, 182-183, 187-222.

pp. 144-183: Regarding Hemingway in the Profile of Sidney Franklin, reprinted from the *New Yorker*, xxv (March 12 and March 26, 1949). pp. 187-194: Preface, reprinted from *Portrait of Hemingway*, New York, 1961. pp. 194-222: Ch. VI: "Portrait of Hemingway." See above entry.

44 Rousseaux, André. *Littérature du vingtième Siècle*. Paris: Albin Michel, 1949. pp. 247-253.

"Le jeu avec la mort chez Hemingway."

45 Rovit, Earl. *Ernest Hemingway*. New York: Twayne, 1963. (Twayne's United States Authors, No. 41.) 192 pages. Notes and References on pp. 184-188. [Paperback edition: New Haven: College & Univ. Press, 1964.]

An analysis of Hemingway's achievements and his significance in literary history.

46 [Rowohlt, Ernst]. *Rowohlt's Rotblonder Roman: Eine story in gedichten, briefen fragmenten und dokumenten aus dem leben des autorenvaters zusammengestellt. Zu seinem 60. Geburtstag und herausgegeben von seinen freunden für Ernst Rowohlt*. [Hamburg, 1947.] p. 44.

Letter from Hemingway to Ernst Rowohlt, his German publisher, dated: December 18, 1946. See (F104).

47 St. John, Robert. *This Was My World*. Garden City, N.Y.: Doubleday, 1953. pp. 17, 21, 31, 49, 263.

Recollections of his boyhood in Oak Park, Ill., include incidents in which Hemingway took part.

48 Samuels, Lee. *A Hemingway Check List*. New York: Scribner's, 1951. 64 pages. For contents and description, see (B51).

49 Sanderson, Stewart, F. *Ernest Hemingway*. Edinburgh and London: Oliver & Boyd, 1961. (Writers and Critics series, No. 7.) 120 pages. [New York: Grove Press, 1961. Evergreen Pilot Books, No. EP-7.]

A critical study of Hemingway's work.

50 Sanford, Marcelline Hemingway. *At the Hemingways: A Family Portrait*. Boston: Atlantic–Little, Brown, 1962. xii + 244 pages. Photographs. [London: Putnam, 1963.]

Hemingway's older sister writes of their childhood in Oak Park, the summers spent in Northern Michigan, Ernest's return from World War I, and the family's reception to his writing. The dust

323

jacket is subtitled: *The Years of Innocence*. First appeared serialized in the *Atlantic*, CCVIII (Dec. 1961); CCIX (Jan. and Feb. 1962).

351 Saroyan, William. *The Daring Young Man on the Flying Trapeze and other stories*. New York: Random House, 1934. p. 34.
References to *GHOA*.

352 Sartre, Jean-Paul. *Literary and Philosophical Essays*. New York: Criterion Books, 1955. pp. 16, 20, 34, 35, 38. [Translated from the French by Annette Michelson. *Situations*. Vol. I. Paris: Gallimard, 1947-1949.]
pp. 34, 35, 38: Compares Albert Camus's style with Hemingway's.

353 Savage, Derek S. *The Withered Branch: Six Studies in the Modern Novel*. London: Eyre & Spottiswoode, 1950. pp. 23-43. [New York: Pellegrini & Cudahy, 1952.]
"Ernest Hemingway," reprinted from *Focus*, II (1946).

354 Scherman, David E. and Rosemarie Redlich. *Literary America: A Chronicle of American Writers with Photographs of the American Scene that Inspired Them*. New York: Dodd, Mead, 1952. pp. 152-154.
Scenes in Key West, Fla., and Horton Bay, Mich., which were the settings for *THAHN* and several of Hemingway's short stories.

355 Schevill, James. *Sherwood Anderson: His Life and Work*. Denver, Colo.: Univ. of Denver Press, 1951. pp. 153, 159, 207, 226-227, 238.
pp. 226-227: Regarding *TOS*, and Hemingway's subsequent letter to Anderson, from Madrid, in 1926.

356 Schlesinger, Arthur M., Jr. *A Thousand Days: John F. Kennedy in the White House*. Boston: Houghton Mifflin, 1965. pp. 105, 372.
p. 372: A message from Hemingway, from Rochester, Minn., regarding the 1961 inauguration, is quoted.

357 Schmidt, Adalbert. *Literaturgeschichte: Wege und Wandlungen moderner Dichtung*. Salzburg and Stuttgart: Bergland-Buch, 1957. pp. 215, 234, 392-393, 408, 465. Photograph of the Hemingways in Italy, opp. p. 384.
pp. 392-393: Discussion of Hemingway's work. p. 465: Checklist of Hemingway's work translated into German.

358 Schorer, Mark. *Sinclair Lewis: An American Life*. New York: McGraw-Hill, 1961. pp. 512, 546, 549, 550, 574, 616-617, 623, 633, 659, 671-672, 680, 780-781. Photograph.
pp. 616-617: Regarding Lewis's essay in the *Yale Literary Magazine*, CI (Feb. 1936), containing criticism of *GHOA* and a ten-line verse on Hemingway's use of four-letter words. pp. 671-672: Relates Lewis's first meeting with Hemingway, in Key West, in 1940,

and their trip to Cuba. pp. 780-781: About the Hemingways' meetings with Lewis in Venice, in March 1949, and the lampoon of Lewis in *ARIT*.

359 Schwartz, Harry and Paul Romaine. *Checklists of Twentieth Century Authors.* Milwaukee: Casanova Booksellers, 1931. First series. Catalogue. pp. 10-11.
   Brief checklist of Hemingway first editions to 1931.

360 Schyberg, Frederik. *Moderne amerikansk Litteratur: 1900–1930.* Copenhagen: Gyldendalske Boghandel, 1930. pp. 135-138.
   On Hemingway, from the chapter "Efterkrigstidens Digtning: 1920-1930."

361 Scott, Nathan A., Jr., ed. *Forms of Extremity in the Modern Novel.* Richmond, Va.: John Knox Press, 1965. pp. 35-54.
   "Hemingway and Our 'Essential Worldliness' " by John Killinger.

362 Sevareid, Eric. *This Is Eric Sevareid.* New York: McGraw-Hill, 1964. pp. 296-303.
   "Mano a Mano." Dateline: Málaga, Spain. Describes his meeting with the Hemingways in Málaga, and the rivalry between Antonio Ordoñez and Luis Miguel Dominguín. Reprinted from *Esquire*, LII (Nov. 1959).

363 Shapiro, Charles, ed. *Twelve Original Essays on Great American Novels.* Detroit: Wayne State Univ. Press, 1958. pp. 238-256.
   "The Death of Love in *The Sun Also Rises*" by Mark Spilka. Reprinted in *Baker anthology,* pp. 80-92; in *Weeks collection,* pp. 127-138; and in *Baker critiques,* pp. 18-25.

364 Sheean, Vincent. *Personal History.* New York: Doubleday, Doran, 1935. pp. 280-281.
   A chance meeting with Hemingway in Berlin, in 1927, sets the author to analyzing Hemingway's work.

365 Sheean, Vincent. *Not Peace But a Sword.* New York: Doubleday, Doran, 1939. pp. 73-80, 82, 235-240, 247-249, 328-338, 339.
   pp. 235-240: The author traveled with Hemingway and James Lardner from Paris to Barcelona, in March 1938. pp. 328-338: Relates how Hemingway averted a boat catastrophe, in November 1938, in Spain.

366 Shiga, Masaru. [A Study of Hemingway.] Tokyo: Eihosha, 1955. 200 pages.

367 Shipley, Joseph T., ed. *The Encyclopedia of Literature.* New York: Philosophical Library, 1946. pp. 990, 1104.
   "Ernest Hemingway" by "E.C.S." [Emerson C. Shuck].

368 Shklovski, Viktor. *Khudozhestvennaya proza: razmyshleniya i razbory*. Moscow, 1959. pp. 597-605.
"Kheminguei v yevo poiskakh ot yunosti do starosti."

369 Siciliano, Enzo, ed. *Antologia di Solaria*. Milan: Lerici, 1958. pp. 377-380.
Review of *FTA* by Umberto Morra, reprinted from *Solaria*, No. 2, [1930].

370 Sieburg, Friedrich. *Nur für Leser: Jahre und Bücher*. Stuttgart: Deutsche Verlags-Anstalt, 1955. pp. 71, 111, 193-196, 244, 328-333.
pp. 193-196: "Ein tod in Venedig," review of *ARIT*. pp. 328-333: "Mann ist mann," review of *OMATS*.

371 Silveira, Brenno. *Pequena História da Literatura Norte-Americana*. São Paulo: Livraria Martins Editora, 1943. (A Mancha do Espírito, No. XI.) pp. 215-219: "Ernest Hemingway."

372 Simon, Jean. *Le Roman américain au XXᵉ Siècle*. Paris: Boivin, 1950. pp. 108-118, 187, 195. Bibliographical checklists.
pp. 108-118: Untitled chapter on Hemingway.

373 Simpson, James Beasley. *Best Quotes of '54, '55, '56*. New York: Crowell, 1957. pp. 8, 9-10, 267-268.
Hemingway is quoted regarding the African airplane crashes, the Nobel prize, etc.

374 Singer, Kurt D. *Hemingway*: *Life and Death of a Giant*. Los Angeles: Holloway House, 1961. Illustrated by Ben Kudo. Paperback. 224 pages. [London: World Distributors, 1962. (Consul Books.)]

375 Singer, Kurt and Jane Sherrod. *Ernest Hemingway, Man of Courage: A Biographical Sketch of a Nobel Prize Winner in Literature*. Minneapolis: Denison, 1963. (Men of Achievement Series.) Cover photograph. Juvenile.

376 Skinner, Cornelia Otis. *Soap Behind the Ears*. New York: Dodd, Mead, 1941. pp. 89-96.
"When the Gong Sounded," reprinted in *American Literature in Parody*, ed. Robert P. Falk, New York, 1955, pp. 241-244.

377 Slochower, Harry. *No Voice Is Wholly Lost: Writers and Thinkers in War and Peace*. New York: Creative Age Press, 1945. pp. 36-40.
On Hemingway, from the chapter "Bourgeois Bohemia: Huxley and Hemingway."

378 Slocombe, George. *The Tumult and the Shouting*. London: Heinemann, 1936. [New York: Macmillan, 1936. pp. 168, 175.]
p. 168: Relates his meeting with Hemingway, in 1922, on the train en route to the Genoa Peace Conference, which both men

were covering for their newspapers. p. 175: Relates a visit made by Hemingway, Max Eastman, and himself to Max Beerbohm, in Rapallo, Italy.

79 Smith, Rex, ed. *Biography of the Bulls*. New York: Rinehart, 1957. pp. 369, 371.

"Papa Goes to the Fights" by Robert Ruark, reprinted from the *N.Y. World Telegram & The Sun* (Aug. 10, 1953). See also (E233).

80 Smith, Thelma M. and Ward L. Miner. *Transatlantic Migration: The Contemporary American Novel in France*. Durham, N.C.: Duke Univ. Press, 1955. pp. 99-121, 221-227.

pp. 99-121: Ch. VIII: "Ernest Hemingway." pp. 221-227: Checklist of translations, critical articles, and reviews of Hemingway's work appearing in French periodicals. French translation in *Revue des Lettres Modernes*, IV (1957).

81 Snell, George. *The Shapers of American Fiction: 1798–1947*. New York: Dutton, 1947. pp. 140, 302, 156-172.

pp. 156-172: "Ernest Hemingway and the 'Fifth Dimension.' "

82 Somma, Luigi. *Storia della letteratura americana*. Rome: Libraria Corso, 1946. pp. 205-208.

83 Sordo, Enrique. *Hemingway el Fabuloso*. Barcelona: Ediciones G. P., 1962. (Las Musas, No. 1.) Paperback. 80 pages. Drawings by Pradera. Cover portrait of Hemingway by Gracia.

84 Spender, Stephen. *The Destructive Element: A Study of Modern Writers and Beliefs*. London: Cape, 1935. pp. 42, 205-206. [Boston: Houghton Mifflin, 1936.]

85 Spender, Stephen. *World Within World*. New York: Harcourt, Brace, 1951. pp. 87, 208-210, 217. [London: Hamilton, 1951.]

pp. 208-210: Relates a conversation with Hemingway in Spain, in 1937, during which he "caught a glimpse of the esthetic Hemingway, whose presence I suspected."

86 Spiller, Robert E. *The Cycle of American Literature: An Essay in Historical Criticism*. New York: Macmillan, 1955. pp. 269-274.

Discussion on Hemingway's work from the chapter "Full Circle: O'Neill, Hemingway."

87 Spiller, Robert E., Willard Thorp, Thomas H. Johnson, and Henry Seidel Canby. *Literary History of the United States*. New York: Macmillan, 1960. pp. 1297, 1300-02, 1375, 1380, 1381, 1386, 1387, 1390, 1398. [Translated into German, *Literaturgeschichte der Vereinigten Staaten*. Mainz: Matthias-Grünewald, 1959.]

See also the *Bibliography Supplement* (G250).

388 Spiller, Robert E., ed. *A Time of Harvest: American Literature, 1910–1960*. New York: Hill & Wang, 1962. pp. 73-82.
"The 'Lost Generation' " by Arthur Mizener. General article.

389 Spiller, Robert E. *The Third Dimension: Studies in Literary History*. New York: Macmillan, 1965. pp. 153, 168-171, 185-186.
pp. 168-171: On Hemingway's work, from a paper read at the University of London, in 1958.

390 Springer, Anne M. *The American Novel in Germany*. Hamburg: Cram, de Gruyter, 1960. (Britannica et Americana, Band 7.) pp. 7, 80-84, 98, 112.
A study of the importance of eight American novelists (Jack London, Upton Sinclair, Sinclair Lewis, Theodore Dreiser, Ernest Hemingway, John Dos Passos, William Faulkner, and Thomas Wolfe) in Germany, during the period between the two World Wars.

391 Stallman, R. W. *The Houses That James Built and Other Literary Studies*. East Lansing: Michigan State Univ. Press, 1961. pp. vii, 173-199.
pp. 173-193: "*The Sun Also Rises*—But No Bells Ring." A study of the narrator's biased point-of-view and how *SAR* would read from Robert Cohn's point-of-view. First presented, in shortened form, as a lecture in Paris, in 1959. pp. 193-199: "A New Reading of 'The Snows of Kilimanjaro' " (1960).

392 Starrett, Vincent. *Best Loved Books of the Twentieth Century*. New York: Bantam Books, 1955. Original paperback edition. pp. 125-127.
Essay on *A Farewell to Arms*.

393 Stearns, Harold E. *The Street I Know*. New York: Furman, 1935. pp. 251, 256, 301, 396, 399.
Autobiographical. References to Hemingway in Paris, in the 1920s.

394 Steen, Jos van der. *Ernest Hemingway, de sten van het verloren Geslacht*. Antwerp: N.V. Standaard-Boekhandel, 1947. (Katholieke Vlaamse Hogeschooluitbreiding Verhandling, 395.) 46 pages. Bibliography on p. 46.

395 Steffens, Lincoln. *The Autobiography of Lincoln Steffens*. New York: Harcourt, Brace, 1931. pp. 834, 835, 836. Photograph of Hemingway by Helen Breaker, opp. p. 821.
Recollections of Hemingway in Paris, in the early 1920s.

396 Steffens, Lincoln. *The Letters of Lincoln Steffens: 1920–1936*. Vol. II. Edited by Ella Winter and Granville Hicks. New York: Harcourt, Brace, 1938. pp. 625, 799, 868.
p. 868: Letter to the Committee of Admissions of The Players

Club, in New York, in 1930, recommending Hemingway as a member.

•7 Stegner, Wallace, ed. *The American Novel: From James Fenimore Cooper to William Faulkner.* New York: Basic Books, 1965. pp. 192-205.

Ch. XVII: "Ernest Hemingway: *A Farewell to Arms*" by Carlos Baker. Note: The essays in this book were written for oral presentation over the Voice of America.

•8 Stein, Gertrude. *The Autobiography of Alice B. Toklas.* New York: Harcourt, Brace, 1933. pp. 261-271. [(a) New York: Literary Guild, 1933. (b) Translated into French. Paris: Gallimard, 1934. (c) Translated into Italian by Cesare Pavese. Turin: Einaudi, 1948.]

The section on Hemingway appeared in a slightly condensed form in the *Atlantic,* CLII (Aug. 1933). Reprinted in *Selected Writings of Gertrude Stein,* ed. Carl Van Vechten, New York: Random House, 1946, pp. 175-182; in *McCaffery,* pp. 25-33, under the title "Hemingway in Paris."

•9 Stein, Gertrude. *Portraits and Prayers.* New York: Random House, 1934. p. 193.

"He and They, Hemingway." Reprinted, with an interpretation, in *The Novel and the World's Dilemma* by E. B. Burgum, New York, 1947, pp. 171-172.

•0 Stein, Gertrude. *The Flowers of Friendship: Letters Written to Gertrude Stein.* Edited by Donald C. Gallup. New York: Knopf, 1953. pp. 158, 163-164, 166-167, 173, 174, 191, 360.

pp. 163-164, 166-167: Letters from Hemingway, written in Paris, in 1924. See (F49), (F51), (F52), (F54).

•1 Stovall, Floyd. *American Idealism.* Norman: Univ. of Oklahoma Press, 1943. pp. 149-152.

On Hemingway, from the chapter "Contemporary Fiction."

•2 Straumann, Heinrich. *American Literature in the Twentieth Century.* London: Hutchinson's University Library, 1951. pp. 79, 94, 95-104. [Revised edition, 1962.]

On Hemingway, from the chapter "The Fate of Man."

•3 Stresau, Hermann. *Ernest Hemingway.* Berlin: Colloquium, 1958. (Köpfe des XX Jahrhunderts, Band 6.) 94 pages.

•4 Suarez, Silvano. *El Esqueleto del Leopardo: Notas sobre la obra de Ernest Hemingway.* Havana: Neptuno, 1955. Pamphlet. 104 pages.

•5 Sutherland, William O. S., Jr., ed. *Six Contemporary Novels: Six Introductory Essays in Modern Fiction.* Austin: Dept. of English,

Univ. of Texas, 1962. Paperback. pp. 58-75. Drawing of Hemingway by Cyril Satorsky.

Ch. [IV]: "A New Dimension for a Hero: Santiago of *The Old Man and the Sea*" by William J. Handy.

406 [Swann Galleries, Inc.] *Hemingway in Depth: A Remarkably Complete Collection . . .* New York: Swann Galleries, Inc., October 6, 1966. Auction catalogue. (Sale No. 711. Lots No. 1-170.) pp. 1-17.
See "Record Prices for Hemingway," *Antiquarian Bookman,* XXXVIII (Oct. 24, 1966), 1603.

407 Takamura, Katsuji. [A Study of Hemingway.] Tokyo: Kenkyusha, 1955. 177 pages.

408 Taniguchi, Rikuo. [A Portrait of Hemingway.] Tokyo: Nanundo, 1956. 164 pages.

409 Taniguchi, Rikuo. [A Study of Hemingway.] Tokyo: Mikasa-shobo, 1956. 282 pages.

410 Tanner, Tony. *The Reign of Wonder: Naivety and Reality in American Literature.* Cambridge: Cambridge Univ. Press, 1965. pp. 228-257, 339.
pp. 228-257: Ch. XIII: "Ernest Hemingway's Unhurried Sensations."

411 Targ, William, ed. *Carrousel for Bibliophiles.* New York: Duschnes, 1947. pp. 31-35.
"Why Does Nobody Collect Me?" by Robert Benchley. Reprinted from the *Colophon,* Part 18 (Sept. 1934). Humorous references to Hemingway first editions.

412 Taylor, Walter F. *A History of American Letters.* New York: American Book, 1936. pp. 433, 440-441, 596-597.
pp. 596-597: Bibliography of critical studies of Hemingway's work compiled by Harry Hartwick.

413 Taylor, Walter Fuller. *The Story of American Letters.* Chicago: Regnery, 1956. pp. 397, 400-406.
On Hemingway, from Ch. II: "Pioneers of the Second Generation: F. Scott Fitzgerald (1896-1940) and Ernest Hemingway (1899-   )."

414 [Texas, University of]. *A Creative Century: Selections from the Twentieth Century Collections at the University of Texas.* Austin: University of Texas, 1964. Catalogue of an Exhibit held in November 1964 at the Academic Center and Undergraduate Library. pp. 29-30.
p. 29: A letter from Hemingway to "Dear Old Carper," [Howell

G. Jenkins], is briefly quoted. See (F62). p. 30: Facsimile of three Hemingway items, including the first page of the manuscript of *DIA*.

5 Thomas, Hugh. *The Spanish Civil War*. New York: Harper, 1961. pp. 176, 262n., 387-388, 392, 444n., 500.
    References to Hemingway during the war and brief excerpts from his dispatches.

6 Thorp, Willard. *American Writing in the Twentieth Century*. Cambridge: Harvard Univ. Press, 1960. pp. 129, 130, 133, 185-195, 298. [Translated into Spanish by C. Vázquez de Parga, *La literatura norteamericana en el Siglo XX*. Madrid: Editorial Tecnos, S.A., 1962.]
    pp. 185-195: Discussion on naturalism in Hemingway's work.

7 Thurston, Jarvis, O. B. Emerson, Carl Hartman, and Elizabeth V. Wright. *Short Fiction Criticism: A Checklist of Interpretation since 1925 of Stories and Novelettes (American, British, Continental) 1800–1958*. Denver: Alan Swallow, 1960. pp. 82-90.
    Checklist of explications of Hemingway's short stories.

8 Tinker, F. G., Jr. *Some Still Live*. New York: Funk & Wagnalls, 1938. pp. 110-111, 112, 197, 311.
    Autobiographical. Recollections of Hemingway in Spain, in 1937.

9 Trevisani, Giuseppe. *Ernest Hemingway*. Milan: Edizione Internazionale, 1966. (No. 7.) 78 pages. Photographs.
    Note: This study of Hemingway by one of his Italian translators is bound back to back with Roberto Fanesi's study of T. S. Eliot.

10 Turnbull, Andrew. *Scott Fitzgerald*. New York: Scribner's, 1962. pp. 152-153, 158-160, 163, 188-191, 228-229, 238, 244-246, 276-279, 310-312.
    pp. 152-153: Describes Fitzgerald's meeting with Hemingway in Paris, in the autumn of 1924. pp. 277-279: Reference to Hemingway's use of Fitzgerald's name in the first printing of "The Snows of Kilimanjaro." See (A16a). Excerpts regarding Hemingway were reprinted in *Esquire*, LVII (March 1962).

21 Untermeyer, Louis. *Makers of the Modern World: The Lives of Ninety-two Writers, Artists, Scientists, Statesmen, Inventors, Philosophers, Composers, and other Creators Who Formed the Pattern of Our Century*. New York: Simon & Schuster, 1955. pp. 717-725.
    "Ernest Hemingway."

22 Valverde, José María. *Historia de la literatura universal*. Vol. III. Barcelona: Noguer, 1959. pp. 545-547.

On Hemingway, from the chapter "Prosa de los 'años veinte': Dos Passos, Hemingway, etc."

423 Vanderschaeghe, Paul. *Ernest Hemingway*. Bruges: Desclée de Brouwer, 1958. (Ontmoetingen, No. 7.) 51 pages. Bibliography on pp. 47-49. Photograph of Hemingway on the cover.

424 Van Doren, Carl. *The American Novel: 1789–1939*. New York: Macmillan, 1940. Revised and enlarged edition. pp. 324, 340-343.

pp. 340-343: An evaluation of Hemingway's work from the chapter "New Realisms."

425 van Gelder, Robert. *Writers and Writing*. New York: Scribner's, 1946. pp. 95-98.

"Ernest Hemingway Talks of Work and War." An interview reprinted from the *N.Y. Times Book Review* (Aug. 11, 1940).

426 Varga, Margit. *Waldo Peirce*. New York: Hyperion Press, 1941. pp. 28, 37, 38, 70. Color reproduction of Peirce's portrait of Hemingway.

References to the artist's trip to Spain with Hemingway, in 1927, and his visits to Key West.

427 Vasudevan Nair, M. T. *Hemiṅgvē*. [n.p., n.d.] iv + 100 pages. Text in Malayalam. Biographical and critical study.

428 Vaucher-Zananiri, Nelly. *Voix d'Amérique: Études sur la littérature américaine d'aujourd'hui*. Cairo: Schindler, 1945. pp. 32-35.

"Ernest Hemingway: du journalisme à la littérature."

429 Vittorini, Elio. *Diario in pubblico*. Milan: Bompiani, 1957. pp. 146, 238-239, 266-267, 317-318.

pp. 238-239: Entry for November 1946: "Uno scrittore non può perdere tempo a correggere in se stesso i 'difetti' che sono della sua epoca. (Hemingway come Stendhal)." pp. 317-318: Entry for November 1950: "Hemingway e Tolstoi. (A proposito d'un libro che pur è il meno buono dell'americano)."

430 Wagenknecht, Edward C. *Cavalcade of the American Novel*. New York: Holt, 1952. pp. 368-381.

Ch. xx: "Ernest Hemingway: Legend and Reality."

431 Wagenknecht, Edward C. *A Preface to Literature*. New York: Holt, 1954. pp. 90, 138-139, 205, 341-344.

pp. 341-344: Review of *OMATS* by Carlos Baker, reprinted from the *Saturday Review*, xxxv (Sept. 6, 1952).

432 Walcutt, Charles Child. *American Literary Naturalism, A Divided Stream*. Minneapolis: Univ. of Minnesota Press, 1956. pp. 270-280.

Ch. xi: "Later Trends in Form: Steinbeck, Hemingway, Dos Passos."

33 [Walden Bookshop]. *Bibliographical Notes on Ernest Hemingway.* Chicago: Walden Bookshop, 1930. Leaflet. 4 pages.

Contains excerpts from a Hemingway letter in reply to questions concerning various editions of his work. See (F69). The leaflet is dated October 1930, but was actually issued in November 1930. [See *Cohn's Bibliography*, pp. 75-76.]

34 Walker, Warren S., compiler. *Twentieth-Century Short Story Explication: Interpretations, 1900–1960 Inclusive, of Short Fiction Since 1800.* Hamden, Conn.: Shoe String Press, 1961. pp. 146-160.

Checklist of explications of Hemingway's short stories.

35 Walter, Erich A., ed. *Essay Annual: 1941.* Chicago: Scott, Foresman, 1941. pp. 149-152.

Review of *FWBT* by Clifton Fadiman, reprinted from the *New Yorker*, XVI (Oct. 26, 1940).

36 Ward, A. C. *The Nineteen-twenties: Literature and Ideas in the post-War Decade.* London: Methuen, 1930. pp. 128-129, 146.

37 Ward, A. C. *American Literature: 1880-1930.* London: Methuen, 1932. [New York: Dial Press, 1932. pp. 151-153.]

38 Warren, Robert Penn. *Selected Essays.* New York: Random House, 1958. pp. 80-118.

"Ernest Hemingway." This essay originally appeared in the *Kenyon Review*, IX (Winter 1947). Reprinted in *Horizon*, XV (April 1947), 156-179. Swedish translation in *Bonniers Litterära Magasin*, XVI (Sept. 1947), 563-574. German translation in *Amerikanische Rundschau*, III (Dec. 1947), 89-104. It was reprinted, in slightly different form, as the Introduction to Scribner's Modern Standard Authors edition of *FTA*, 1949, pp. vii-xxxvii. Reprinted in *Literary Opinion in America*, ed. Morton Dauwen Zabel, New York, 1951 edition, pp. 444-463; in *Critiques and Essays on Modern Fiction*, ed. John W. Aldridge, New York, 1952, pp. 447-473. French translation in *Revue des Lettres Modernes*, IV (1957). Reprinted as the Introduction to *FTA* in *Three Novels*, pp. iii-xl.

39 Weeks, Robert P., ed. *Hemingway: A Collection of Critical Essays.* Englewood Cliffs, N.J.: Prentice-Hall, 1962. (Twentieth Century Views series.) 180 pages. [Paperback edition: 1962. Spectrum. No. S-TC-8.]

Contents: pp. 1-16: Introduction by the editor. Includes Hemingway's poem "Valentine," on p. 4, reprinted from the *Little Review*, XII (May 1929).

pp. 17-39: "How Do You Like It Now, Gentlemen?" by Lillian Ross. Profile, reprinted from the *New Yorker*, XXVI (May 13, 1950).

pp. 40-51: "Nightmare and Ritual in Hemingway" by Malcolm

Cowley, reprinted from the Introduction to the Viking Portable *Hemingway*, pp. vii-xxiv.

pp. 52-71: "Hemingway's Ambiguity: Symbolism and Irony" by E. M. Halliday, reprinted from *American Literature*, xxvIII (March 1956). Includes Hemingway's poem "Champs d'Honneur," on p. 64.

pp. 72-85: "Observations on the Style of Ernest Hemingway" by Harry Levin, reprinted, in an abridged form, from *Contexts of Criticism*, Cambridge, 1957, pp. 140-167.

pp. 86-92: "Men Without Women" by Leslie Fiedler, reprinted from *Love and Death in the American Novel*, New York, 1959, pp. 304-309; 350-352.

pp. 93-94: "*In Our Time*: A Review" by D. H. Lawrence, reprinted from *Phoenix*, New York, 1936, p. 365.

pp. 95-111: "Adventures of Nick Adams" by Philip Young, reprinted from *Ernest Hemingway*, New York, 1952. pp. 1-27.

pp. 112-113: "A Clean Well-Lighted Place" by Sean O'Faolain, reprinted from *Short Stories: A Study in Pleasure*, Boston, 1961, pp. 76-79.

pp. 114-117: "The Discovery of Evil: An Analysis of 'The Killers'" by Cleanth Brooks and Robert Penn Warren, reprinted from *Understanding Fiction*, New York, 1959, pp. 303-312.

pp. 118-126: "The Two African Stories" by Carlos Baker, reprinted from *Hemingway: The Writer as Artist*, Princeton, 1952, pp. 186-196.

pp. 127-138: "The Death of Love in *The Sun Also Rises*" by Mark Spilka, reprinted from *Twelve Original Essays on Great Novels*, ed. Charles Shapiro, Detroit, 1958, pp. 238-256.

pp. 139-151: "The Biological Trap," an essay on *FTA*, by Ray B. West, Jr., reprinted from *The Art of Modern Fiction*, New York, 1949, pp. 622-634.

pp. 152-160: "The Later Hemingway" by Nemi D'Agostino, reprinted from the *Sewanee Review*, LXVIII (Summer 1960).

pp. 161-168: "*Confiteor Hominem*: Ernest Hemingway's Religion of Man" by Joseph Waldmeir, reprinted from the *Papers of the Michigan Academy of Science, Arts, and Letters*, XLII [1956].

pp. 169-171: "The Art of Evasion" by Leon Edel, reprinted from *Folio*, xx (Spring 1955).

pp. 172-174: "Hemingway: A Defense" by Philip Young, reprinted from *Folio*, xx (Spring 1955).

pp. 175-176: Chronology of Important Dates.

pp. 179-180: Selected Bibliography.

440 West, Paul. *The Modern Novel*. London: Hutchinson, 1963, pp. 220-227 and *passim*.

441 West, Ray B., Jr. and Robert W. Stallman, eds. *The Art of Modern*

Fiction. New York: Rinehart, 1949. pp. 622-634.

"Analysis of *A Farewell to Arms*" by Ray B. West, Jr. Reprinted in *Weeks collection,* pp. 139-151; in *Baker critiques,* pp. 28-36. See also (E162).

442 West, Ray B., Jr. *The Short Story in America: 1900–1950.* Chicago: Regnery, 1952. pp. 23-24, 25-26, 45, 60, 61-63, 85-106.

pp. 85-106: Ch. IV: "Hemingway and Faulkner: Two Masters of the Modern Short Story."

443 Wheeler, John. *I've Got News for You.* New York: Dutton, 1961. pp. 183-187.

The author, an executive of the North American Newspaper Alliance news syndicate, comments briefly on Hemingway's NANA dispatches on the Spanish Civil War. A letter from Hemingway, regarding publication of "Fifty Grand," is quoted.

444 White, E. B. *The Second Tree from the Corner.* New York: Harper, 1954. pp. 140-143.

"Across the Street and Into the Grill." This parody originally appeared in the *New Yorker,* XXVI (Oct. 14, 1950). Reprinted in *Parodies,* ed. Dwight Macdonald, New York, 1960, pp. 251-254; in *An Anthology of American Humor,* ed. Brom Weber, New York, 1962, pp. 551-553.

445 White, William. *Ernest Hemingway (21 July 1899–2 July 1961): Guide to a Memorial Exhibition.* Detroit: University of Detroit Library, July 14–August 12, 1961. 8 pages. [Detroit: Wayne State University Library, September 18–October 28, 1961. Windsor, Ontario: Friends of the University Library, Assumption University of Windsor, November 5, 1961.]

A catalogue of an exhibition of manuscripts and presentation copies of books from the collection of Charles F. Feinberg, and of periodicals, translations, and ephemera from William White's collection.

446 Williams, Stanley T. *The Spanish Background of American Literature.* Vol. I. New Haven: Yale Univ. Press, 1955. pp. 237, 238, 239-241, 260.

447 Williams, William Carlos. *The Autobiography of William Carlos Williams.* New York: Random House, 1951. pp. 212, 218, 226, 227.

Recollections of Hemingway in Paris, in 1924.

448 Wilson, Colin. *The Outsider.* London: Gollancz, 1956. pp. 31-39, 46. [Boston: Houghton Mifflin, 1956.]

Discussion of the relevance of Hemingway's work to the problem of the "existentialist outsider."

449 Wilson, Edmund. *The Wound and the Bow: Seven Studies in Literature.* Boston: Houghton Mifflin, 1941. pp. 214-242. [(a) London: Secker & Warburg, 1942. (b) New York: Oxford Univ. Press, 1947. (c) Translated into Italian by Nemi D'Agostino. *La ferita e l'arco.* Milan: Garzanti, 1956.]

"Hemingway: Gauge of Morale." This essay originally appeared in the *Atlantic*, CLXIV (July 1939), under the title "Ernest Hemingway: Bourdon Gauge of Morale." Reprinted in *Readings from the Americas: An Introduction to Democratic Thought*, ed. Guy A. Cardwell, New York: Ronald Press, 1947, pp. 246-248; in *McCaffery*, pp. 236-257; in Wilson's *Eight Essays*, Garden City, N.Y.: Doubleday, 1954, pp. 92-114; in *Literature in America: An Anthology of Literary Criticism*, ed. Philip Rahv, New York: Meridian, 1957, pp. 373-390.

450 Wilson, Edmund. *Classics and Commercials: A Literary Chronicle of the Forties.* New York: Farrar, Straus, 1950. pp. 3-9.

Commentary on Archibald MacLeish's article in the *New Republic*, CII (June 10, 1940), in which MacLeish criticized the war novels of Hemingway and Dos Passos as lacking in terms of conviction and belief.

451 Wilson, Edmund. *The Shores of Light: A Literary Chronicle of the Twenties and Thirties.* New York: Farrar, Straus & Young, 1952. pp. 115-124, 339-344, 616-629.

pp. 115-124: "Emergence of Ernest Hemingway." This essay contains three letters from Hemingway to Wilson, written in 1923 and 1924. See (F47), (F48), (F55). It also contains Wilson's reviews of *TSTP* and *iot*, reprinted from the *Dial*, LXXVII (Oct. 1924). The essay is reprinted in *Baker anthology*, pp. 55-60. pp. 339-344: "The Sportsman's Tragedy," reprinted from the *New Republic*, LIII (Dec. 14, 1927). pp. 616-629: "Letter to the Russians About Hemingway." A prefatory note relates how the essay came to be written. The essay originally appeared in the *New Republic*, LXXXV (Dec. 11, 1935). A Russian translation appeared in *Internatsionalnaya Literatura*, No. 2 (Feb. 1936). The editorial which accompanied the translation is translated by Wilson and reprinted on pp. 625-629.

452 Wilson, Edmund. *The Bit Between My Teeth: A Literary Chronicle of 1950–65.* New York: Farrar, Straus & Giroux, 1965. pp. 515-525.

Review of Morley Callaghan's *That Summer in Paris*, reprinted from the *New Yorker*, XXXIX (Feb. 23, 1963).

453 Wiśniowski, Bronislaw. *William Faulkner, Ernest Hemingway, John Steinbeck.* Warsaw: Czytelnik, 1961. pp. 109-197. Bibliography on Hemingway, pp. 295-296.

54 Witham, W. Tasker. *Panorama of American Literature*. New York: Stephen Daye Press, 1947. pp. 327-333.

55 Woodress, James. *Dissertations in American Literature: 1891–1955. With Supplement: 1956–1961*. Durham, N.C.: Duke Univ. Press, 1962. pp. 23, 93.
Checklists of dissertations on Hemingway's work.

56 Woolf, Virginia. *Granite and Rainbow: Essays*. London: Hogarth, 1958. [New York: Harcourt, Brace, 1958. pp. 85-92.]
"An Essay in Criticism," review of *MWW*, reprinted from the *N.Y. Herald Tribune Books* (Oct. 9, 1927).

57 Wright, Austin McGiffert. *The American Short Story in the Twenties*. Chicago: Univ. of Chicago Press, 1961. pp. 254-256, 370-373, 383, 391-393, 400-402 and *passim*. Bibliographical references. [Toronto: Univ. of Toronto Press, 1961.]
Analysis and discussion of Hemingway's short stories. Appendix D, on pp. 391-393: "The Use of the First Person in 'Cross-Country Snow' and 'An Alpine Idyll.'" Appendix H, on pp. 400-401: "A Scene from 'The Doctor and the Doctor's Wife.'" Appendix I, on pp. 401-402: "The Chronology of 'In Another Country.'"

58 Wyrick, Green D. *The World of Ernest Hemingway: A Critical Study*. Emporia, Kansas: Graduate Division of the Kansas State Teachers College, 1953. (Emporia State Research Studies, II.) 32 pages. Bibliographical footnotes.

59 Yevtushenko, Yevgeny. *Yevtushenko: Selected Poems*. New York: Dutton, 1962. Translated from the Russian by Robin Milner-Gulland and Peter Levi, S.J. pp. 79-80, 91.
pp. 79-80: "Encounter." This poem, written in 1960, was originally titled "Vstrecha v Kopengagene." It appeared in *Iunost'*, No. 4 (April 1961). A translation of the poem by Stephen Jan Parker, titled "Meeting," appears in *The Literary Reputation of Hemingway in Europe*, ed. Roger Asselineau, Paris, 1965, p. 192. A translation of the poem by George Reavey, titled "A Meeting in Copenhagen" and dated April 1960, appears in *The Poetry of Yevgeny Yevtushenko, 1953 to 1965*, New York: October House, 1965, pp. 113, 115. This is a bilingual edition and the poem appears in Russian on pp. 112, 114. This translation appeared in *Playboy*, x (Jan. 1963).

60 Young, Philip. *Ernest Hemingway*. New York and Toronto: Rinehart, 1952. (Rinehart Critical Studies.) xii + 244 pages. Bibliographical notes on pp. 233-240. [(a) London: Bell, 1953. (Critical Handbook series.) 252 pages. (b) Paperback edition: New York: Rinehart, 1953. (c) Translated into German by Hans Dietrich

Berendt. Dusseldorf: Diederichs, 1954. 199 pages. (d) Revised edition. University Park and London: Pennsylvania State Univ. Press, 1966. *Ernest Hemingway: A Reconsideration.* [x] + 298 pages. Includes a new Foreword and an Afterword.]
A critical analysis of Hemingway's work. Excerpt from Ch. III, pp. 54-60, reprinted in *Baker critiques*, pp. 7-10. Ch. I is reprinted in *Weeks collection*, pp. 95-111. Ch. II is reprinted in *Critical Approaches to American Literature*, Vol. II, ed. Ray B. Browne and Martin Light, New York, 1965, pp. 275-291.

461 Young, Philip. *Ernest Hemingway.* Minneapolis: Univ. of Minnesota Press, 1959. (Pamphlets on American Writers, No. 1.) 44 pages. Bibliographical references on pp. 42-44. [(a) Translated into Korean by Lee Cheol-mo. Seoul: Yeo'weon'sa, 1959. 82 pages. (b) Translated into Spanish by Angela Figuera, in *Tres Escritores Norteamericanos*, Madrid: Editorial Gredos, 1961, pp. 7-49. (c) Translated into Hindi by Rakhalchandra Bhattacharya. Calcutta: Asia Publishing Co., 1961. 56 pages. (d) Translated into Arabic by Mahmoud As-Samra and Mohammed Najm. Beirut: Al-Maktaba Al-Ahlia, 1961. (e) Translated into Japanese, with notes by Ichiro Ishi. Tokyo: Kenkyusha, 1961. (f) Translated into Italian by Salvatore Bottino. Milan: Ugo Mursia Editore, 1962. (g) Translated into Portuguese by Alex Severino. São Paulo: Livraria Martins Editôra, 1963. (h) Second Korean translation by Seuk-Joo Kim. Seoul: Korean Society of English Language and Literature, 1963. 82 pages. Text in English and Korean, on opposite pages. (i) Second Japanese translation by Keiichi Harada. Tokyo: Hokuseido, 1965. (j) Revised edition, 1965.]
A critical and biographical introduction to Hemingway's work. Reprinted, in a revised version, in *Seven Modern American Novelists*, ed. William Van O'Connor, Minneapolis, 1964, pp. 153-188.

462 Zabel, Morton Dauwen, ed. *Literary Opinion in America.* New York: Harper, 1937. pp. 506-511. [(a) Translated into Italian, *Antologia della critica americana del novecento*. Rome: Edizioni di Storia e Letteratura, 1957. (b) Second edition, revised, 1951. pp. 444-463: "Hemingway" by Robert Penn Warren. See (G438). (c) Third edition, revised, 1962. Same pagination as second edition for Warren's essay.]
"Ernest Hemingway: A Farewell to Spain" by Malcolm Cowley. Review of *DIA*, reprinted from the *New Republic*, LXXIII (Nov. 30, 1932).

463 Zabel, Morton Dauwen. *Craft and Character in Modern Fiction: Texts, Method and Vocation.* New York: Viking Press, 1957. pp. 317-326.
"Hemingway: 1950 and 1952." pp. 317-321: Review of *ARIT*,

reprinted from the *Nation*, CLXXI (Sept. 9, 1950). pp. 321-326: Essay on *OMATS*, based on material from the *TLS* (Sept. 17, 1954).

4 Zabel, Morton Dauwen. *Historia de la Literatura Norteamericana: Desde los Orígenes hasta el Dia*. Buenos Aires: Losada, 1950. Translated into Spanish by Luis Echavarri. pp. 361-362, 550, 565-567. Photograph.

5 Zardoya, Concha and Carmen Iglesias. *Historia de la Literatura Norteamericana*. Barcelona: Editorial Labor, 1956. pp. 268-276.

6 Zink, Capt. D. D. *Ernest Hemingway*. [Denver]: U.S. Air Force Academy Library, 1959. (Special bibliography series, No. 8.) Pamphlet. 8 pages.

A selective checklist of critical studies of Hemingway's work.

SECTION H
NEWSPAPER AND
PERIODICAL MATERIAL
ON HEMINGWAY
(1918-1965)

All items on Hemingway appearing in the *N.Y. Times* have been included in this section because of that newspaper's availability in libraries. Whenever possible an article from a local newspaper where a newsworthy event occurred is included. However, the *K.C. Star* is given as the source of many news items datelined in other parts of the United States and abroad owing to the bibliographer's access to the files of that newspaper.

Among the main sources for items in this section were the *Readers' Guide to Periodical Literature, PMLA* (Publication of the Modern Language Association), the *Annual Bibliography of English Language and Literature, International Index to Periodicals, Book Review Digest,* and the *N.Y. Times Index.*

The foreign listings were greatly enlarged by items from the following: Deming Brown's bibliographical references to Russian articles in the *American Quarterly,* v (Summer 1953), and Stephen Jan Parker's bibliographical references to Russian articles in *American Literature,* xxxv (Jan. 1964). Thelma M. Smith and Ward L. Miner's checklist of French articles in *Transatlantic Migration* (Duke Univ. Press, 1955). Hans-Günter Mucharowski's bibliography of German articles in *Die Werke von Ernest Hemingway* (Hamburg, 1955). Cándido Pérez Gállego's checklist of Spanish articles in *Filología Moderna,* ii (Oct. 1961). And Anna Pandolfi's checklist of Italian articles in *Studi Americani,* viii (1962). All of these sources bear checking for other items of interest in their particular language.

H1 "Go Together from the *Star* to the Italian Front," *K.C. Star* (May 13, 1918), p. 4. Drawing of Hemingway.

Hemingway and Theodore Brumback, members of the editorial staff of the *K.C. Star,* sailed from an Atlantic port for Italy, to join a Red Cross ambulance unit.

2 "Wounded on Italy Front," *K.C. Star* (July 14, 1918), p. 5 A.

Reports that a telegram was received from the Red Cross stating that Hemingway had been wounded. Also quotes extracts from cards received from Hemingway, in Milan, in June.

3 "Valor Cross to Hemingway," *K.C. Times* (July 17, 1918), p. 8.

Italian Army Headquarters news release: Ernest Miller Hemingway recommended for the Italian Cross for Valor for bravery in action. Despite wounds received by the explosion of a trench mortar, he brought into a dressing station "several wounded Italian soldiers."

4 "Three are Wounded," *Oak Leaves* (July 20, 1918), p. 1. Photograph of Hemingway, from the high school yearbook.

Reports telegram received from Washington stating that Ernest had been wounded while doing rolling canteen work in Italy. Quotes a cable from Ernest and a letter, written June 9, in Milan. The article mentions that "Hemingway will be 19 tomorrow."

4₁ Photograph, "A. T. [Anson Tyler] Hemingway | In uniform of Civil War captain, whose grandson was wounded and cited for valor this week," *ibid.*, p. 2.

5 "Wins Italian Medal | Ernest Hemingway to Receive Valor Badge for Exploit at Piave River—Recovering in Milan," *Oak Leaves* (Aug. 10, 1918), p. 56.

Contains a letter to Dr. C. E. Hemingway from Theodore Brumback, telling of his visits with Ernest in the American Red Cross Hospital in Milan. Recounts the circumstances of Hemingway's being wounded. A postscript was added by Ernest. Reprinted in the *K.C. Star* (Aug. 11, 1918).

6 "With our Wounded | Hemingway Is Italian Hero. . . ," *Oak Leaves* (Sept. 7, 1918), p. 22.

Reports that Lieut. Hemingway "cabled his parents last week that the last operation had been performed on him, and the last bullet removed. . . . it is probable that it will be another month before he is able to use his legs again."

7 "Wounded 227 Times," *Oak Leaves* (Oct. 5, 1918), pp. 12-13. Photograph of Ernest in Milan hospital bed.

Contains a long letter from Ernest to his family, telling of his discharge from the hospital and of being sent to an Italian resort to recuperate. Reprinted in the *K.C. Star* (Oct. 29, 1918), p. 7. See (F43).

8 "Worst Shot-up Man in U.S. on Way Home," *Chicago American* (Jan. 21, 1919), p. 3.

A report on Hemingway's return from Italy.

9 "Has 227 Wounds, But Is Looking For Job | Kansas City Boy First to Return From Italian Front," *N.Y. Sun* (Jan. 22, 1919), p. 8.

Long interview in New York, following Hemingway's arrival on the steamship *Giuseppe Verdi*.

10 "Two Who Knew Combat | Ernest Hemingway Back Home From Italian Front. . . ," *Oak Leaves* (Jan. 25, 1919), p. 11.

11 Pettigrew, Stewar[t]. "Ernie Hemingway Speaks At the Big Meeting of Hanna Club, Tonight," *Trapeze*, VIII (Jan. 31, 1919), [1].

Hemingway to speak at high school social club.

12 Dean, Roselle. Interview, *Oak Parker* (Feb. 1, 1919).

Interview with Hemingway, in Oak Park, on his return from Italy.

13 "Southern Club Activities," *Oak Leaves* (Feb. 22, 1919), p. 2.

Lieut. Hemingway addressed the club members and showed souvenirs of the battlefields of Italy.

14 "Learn this for Assembly," *Trapeze*, VIII (March 14, 1919), [1].

Contains a seven-line song to be sung to Hemingway when he spoke at the high school assembly. It begins: "Hemingway, we hail you the victor, | Hemingway, ever winning the game. . . ."

15 Wells, Edwin. "Hemingway Speaks To High School" *Trapeze,* VIII (March 21, 1919), [1], [3]. Photograph of Hemingway, in uniform.

This account of Hemingway's talk before the Oak Park High School assembly is reprinted in *My Brother, Ernest Hemingway* by Leicester Hemingway, Cleveland, 1962, pp. 54-56.

16 "Ernest M. Hemingway Decorated by General Diaz," *Chicago Sunday Tribune* (Nov. 20, 1921), I, 2. Photograph.

Hemingway to be presented with Italy's Medal of Valor at a banquet in Chicago.

17 "Shop Talk: Something About Ernest M. Hemingway, Who Is Taking the Lid Off Europe," *Toronto Star Weekly* (April 14, 1923), p. 2.

Announcement concerning Hemingway's forthcoming European dispatches.

18 Stein, Gertrude. Poem, "Hemingway: A Portrait," *Ex Libris,* 1 (Dec. 1923), 192.

19 "K.J." Review of *TSTP, Transatlantic Review,* 1 (April 1924), 246.

"Mr. Hemingway's *Three Stories* shows a sensitive feeling for the emotional possibilities of a situation. His method is realistic, but unlike most of his school he has not killed his work on the shallow hardness of photography."

9₁ "M. R." [Marjorie Reid]. Review of *iot, ibid.,* pp. 247-248.

"[Hemingway] projects the moments when life is condensed and clean-cut and significant, presenting them in minute narratives that eliminate every useless word. Each tale is much longer than the measure of its lines. . . ."

20 Rascoe, Burton. A Bookman's Day Book column, *N.Y. Herald Tribune* (June 15, 1924), Book section, p. 20.

The entry for "June 5" mentions discussing Hemingway with Edmund Wilson. Also, *iot* is quoted. Reprinted in *A Bookman's Daybook,* New York, 1929, pp. 253-254.

21 "Bull Gores 2 Yanks Acting as Toreadores," *Chicago Daily Tribune* (July 29, 1924), p. 1. Dateline: Madrid, July 28.

Reports that MacDonald Ogden Stewart [*sic*] and Hemingway were gored in the bullring at Pamplona, Spain. Stewart had two ribs broken and Hemingway, who had rushed in to rescue his friend, was bruised. Appended to the article is a paragraph about Hemingway, titled "Hero of World War." Partly reprinted in *My Brother, Ernest Hemingway* by Leicester Hemingway, Cleveland, 1962, p. 90.

22 Photograph of Ernest and Hadley Hemingway, "Bull Gores Toronto Writer in Annual Pamplona Fiesta," *Toronto Daily Star* (July 30, 1924).

23 "Hooked by Spanish Bull | Oak Park Man and Group of Wits Horn Into Iberian Festival and Are Injured," *Oak Leaves* (Aug. 2, 1924), p. 34.

24 "Tackling a Spanish Bull is 'Just Like Rugby' | Hemingway Tells How He Surprised the Natives," *Toronto Star Weekly* (Sept. 13, 1924), Magazine section, p. 18. Photographs.

A letter from Hemingway to friends on the *Toronto Star Weekly*, regarding the bullfight fiesta at Pamplona, is paraphrased.

25 Wilson, Edmund. "Mr. Hemingway's Dry Points," review of *TSTP* and *iot*, *Dial*, LXXVII (Oct. 1924), 340-341.

"Mr. Hemingway's poems are not particularly important, but his prose is of the first distinction. He must be counted as the only American writer but one—Mr. Sherwood Anderson—who has felt the genius of Gertrude Stein's *Three Lives* and has been evidently influenced by it. . . . Not, however, that Mr. Hemingway is imitative. On the contrary, he is rather strikingly original, and in the dry compressed little vignettes of *in our time* has almost invented a form of his own."

26 Review of *TSTP*, *K.C. Star* (Dec. 20, 1924), p. 6.

"The stories, simple, direct, revealing, one of them set in the middle West, the other two in Europe, are the real stuff. . . . In them are vividness and the firm sure texture of reality."

27 Hickok, Guy. "Hemingway First Lives Wild Stories Then He Writes Them," *Brooklyn Daily Eagle* (May 17, 1925), p. 12. Photograph. Dateline: Paris.

Relates some of Hemingway's war experiences and incidents of the Hemingways honeymoon in Horton's Bay, Mich., in September 1921.

28 Brickell, Herschel. Review of *IOT*, *N.Y. Evening Post Literary Review* (Oct. 17, 1925), p. 3.

"Mr. Hemingway's book carries on its dust-covers the enthusiastic recommendation of nearly everybody. . . . Sherwood Anderson is there leading the chorus, and Mr. Hemingway's work is most like his. It is an attempt to get at minds and souls and what goes on within. . . . the best of the lot is a beautifully executed tale of the racetracks which Mr. Anderson himself could not have bettered."

29 Review of *IOT*, *N.Y. Times Book Review* (Oct. 18, 1925), p. 8.

"Hemingway has a lean, pleasing, tough resilience. His language is fibrous and athletic, colloquial and fresh, hard and clean; his very prose seems to have an organic being of its own. . . . Mr. Hemingway packs a whole character into a phrase, an entire situation into a sentence or two. He makes each word count three or four ways."

30 Rascoe, Burton. "Contemporary Reminiscences," *Arts & Decoration*, XXIV (Nov. 1925), 57. Photograph.
    General article.

31 Rosenfeld, Paul. Review of *IOT*, *New Republic*, XLV (Nov. 25, 1925), 22-23.

"Hemingway's short stories belong with cubist painting . . . bringing a feeling of positive forces through primitive modern idiom. . . . There is something of Sherwood Anderson, of his fine bare effects and values coined from simplest words, in Hemingway's clear medium. There is Gertrude Stein equally obvious. . . . Wanting some of the warmth of Anderson and some of the pathos of Gertrude Stein, Hemingway's style . . . shows the outline of a new, tough, severe and satisfying beauty."

32 Ashley, Schuyler. Review of *IOT*, *K.C. Star* (Dec. 12, 1925), p. 6.

"His phrases are brittle, with mordant edges, and he has the inestimable gift of concrete visualization. In lean, spare sentences he always makes you see the thing he writes about. . . . By this collection he has established himself as a colorful and competent performer; when he tackles a real subject he should bring all the stands up cheering." Reprinted in *Essay Reviews*, Kansas City, 1929, p. 67.

33 Walsh, Ernest. Poem, "Ernest Hemingway," *This Quarter*, 1 (Autumn–Winter 1925–1926), 67.

33₁ Photograph of Hemingway with his son, John, in Switzerland, *ibid.*, following p. 107.

33₂ "E. W." [Ernest Walsh]. Review of *IOT*, *ibid.*, pp. 319-321.

"The first impression one gets on reading a story by Hemingway is that this writer has been getting ready inside himself and outside himself for a long time before he began to write. . . . what sets him apart from most living writers, namely: His clarity of heart. . . .

Hemingway's vocabulary is mean and bare as a poor monastery and out of this he makes patterns of monastic austerity and richness. . . . It is the piling up of word for word in the right order to give a homely word more than its meaning, it is the use of 'speech' as distinguished from language that puts Hemingway among the first men writing today."

34 Review of *IOT*, *Time*, vii (Jan. 18, 1926), 38.
"[Hemingway] is that rare bird, an intelligent young man who is not introspective on paper. . . . Make no mistake, Ernest Hemingway is somebody; a new, honest, un-'literary' transcriber of life— a Writer."

35 Tate, Allen. Review of *IOT*, *Nation*, cxxii (Feb. 10, 1926), 160-162.
"Mr. Hemingway and Mr. Dos Passos . . . share . . . a seriousness, a care for good prose in itself."

36 Kronenberger, Louis. Review of *IOT*, *SRL*, ii (Feb. 13, 1926), 555.
"There are obvious traces of Sherwood Anderson and there are subtler traces of Gertrude Stein. His work is experimental and very modern. But much more significantly, it has sound merit of a personal, non-derivative nature; it shows no important affinity with any other writer, and it represents the achievement of unique personal experience. . . . his stories are experiments demanding further discipline and art."

37 Wolf, Robert. Review of *IOT*, *N.Y. Herald Tribune Books* (Feb. 14, 1926), p. 3.
"I know of no American writer with a more startling ear for colloquial conversation, or a more poetic sensitiveness to woods and hills. *In Our Time* has perhaps not enough energy to be a great book, but Ernest Hemingway has promise of genius."

38 Fitzgerald, F. Scott. "How to Waste Material: A Note on My Generation," *Bookman*, lxiii (May 1926), 262-265.
General article. In discussing *IOT*, Fitzgerald writes: ". . . many of us who have grown weary of admonitions to 'watch this man or that' have felt a sort of renewal of excitement at these stories wherein Ernest Hemingway turns a corner into the street."

39 Hansen, Harry. Review of *TOS*, *N.Y. World* (May 30, 1926), p. 4 M.
". . . when Hemingway published *In Our Time* it was Sherwood Anderson who turned handsprings and welcomed this newcomer to the ranks of America's great men. Anderson trumpeted loudly, and now Hemingway pays him back by making him the principal butt of his parody. . . . [He] has caught, I think, a glint of Anderson's professional naiveté. Beyond that, however, parody is a gift of

the gods. Few are blessed with it. It missed Hemingway. He is better as a writer of short stories."

40 Boyd, Ernest. Review of *TOS, Independent*, CXVI (June 12, 1926),
694.

"[Mr. Hemingway's] most recent book is an elaborate and ex-
ceedingly witty parody of the Chicago school of literature in general, and of Sherwood Anderson in particular. It is the kind of
parody, however, which is real criticism, and I can think of no subject more urgently in need of criticism. . . . With good humor, but
unerringly, he has put his finger upon all the shoddy and thread-
bare patches in the material so endlessly and complacently woven
by Mr. Anderson's divagating fancy. . . . Mr. Hemingway is a genuine humorist, and a critic so shrewd that I almost hope he may
cure the disease he so well diagnoses."

41 Review of *TOS, N.Y. Times Book Review* (June 13, 1926), p. 8.

"The delightful entertainment of *The Torrents of Spring*, if not
precisely what might have been expected of the author of *In Our
Time*, is full-blooded comedy, with a sting of satire at the expense
of certain literary affectations. . . . In the last analysis, the book sets
out to amuse. This it does."

42 Review of *TOS, Time*, VII (June 28, 1926), 31.

"Mr. Hemingway has sat down and written a not altogether re-
spectful parody of Mr. Anderson's vein."

43 Latimer, Margery. Review of *TOS, N.Y. Herald Tribune Books*
(July 18, 1926), p. 16.

"*The Torrents of Spring* gives just the right degree of self-consciousness and humor to the reader of Anderson and in its superficial way seems to mark the passing of the naive realists. . . . Perhaps Mr. Hemingway's name, which one hears everywhere now, is
more familiar than his prose, which is narrow, robust and excellent
in its limited area. . . . But his robust rites in honor of Mr. Anderson are, in places, as tedious as that writer himself."

44 Tate, Allen. Review of *TOS, Nation*, CXXIII (July 28, 1926), 89-90.

". . . these characters and places focus the best genial satire of the
'spirituality' of roughnecks, the most deftly tempered ribaldry, and
the most economically realized humor of disproportion that this
reviewer has read in American prose."

45 Brief review of *TOS, New Yorker*, II (July 31, 1926), 50.

"*The Torrents of Spring* is a burlesque, almost wholly of Sherwood Anderson. It doesn't work too hard at being funny—a great
merit."

46 Review of *TOS*, *SRL*, III (July 31, 1926), 12.

"In his book of short stories *In Our Time*, he presented some fiction of more than average merit, though the influence of Sherwood Anderson was discernible. *The Torrents of Spring*, inasmuch as it burlesques the Andersonian manner, may be taken as a sign that Hemingway is freeing himself of an influence of which he is obviously conscious. . . . the complimentary character of parody must also be considered. . . . Anderson's status among modern writers being assured, the younger writer's half-hour of humor can hardly be said to work to his injury."

47 Morris, Lawrence S. Review of *TOS*, *New Republic*, XLVIII (Sept. 15, 1926), 101.

"[Hemingway] has written a parody of *Dark Laughter*, with sideswipes at Gertrude Stein, which is also a parody of himself. Psychologically, it is clearly a declaration of independence. . . . That he had to do it so vigorously is the finest tribute Sherwood Anderson has received yet. That he chose to do it wittily is our good luck."

48 O'Brien, Edward J. Review of *IOT*, *Now & Then*, No. 21 (Autumn 1926), pp. 30-32.

"You may regard [Hemingway] as brutal. If you do, I shall disagree with you. His outward brutality is designed to conceal the reactions of a very sensitive mind. It is obvious that he has been influenced by Sherwood Anderson, and that he in turn has influenced Anderson. I regard him as the more significant writer of the two because he has succeeded in freeing himself completely from the sentimentality of American life and also from the fear of sentimentality."

49 Aiken, Conrad. Review of *SAR*, *N.Y. Herald Tribune Books* (Oct. 31, 1926), p. 4. Drawing.

"The dialogue is brilliant. If there is better dialogue being written today I do not know where to find it. It is alive with the rhythms and idioms, the pauses and suspensions and innuendoes and shorthands, of living speech. It is in the dialogue, almost entirely, that Mr. Hemingway tells his story and makes the people live and act."

50 Review of *SAR*, *N.Y. Times Book Review* (Oct. 31, 1926), p. 7.

"No amount of analysis can convey the quality of *The Sun Also Rises*. It is a truly gripping story, told in a lean, hard athletic narrative prose that puts more literary English to shame. . . . It is magnificent writing, filled with that organic action which gives a compelling picture of character. This novel is unquestionably one of the events of an unusually rich year in literature."

51 Review of *SAR*, *Time*, VIII (Nov. 1, 1926), 48.

"A lot of people expected a big novel from burly young Author Hemingway. His short work [*IOT*] bit deeply into life. He said things naturally, calmly, tersely, accurately. . . . Now his first novel is published and while his writing has acquired only a few affectations, his interests appear to have grown soggy with much sitting around sloppy café tables in . . . Paris. He has chosen to immortalize the semi-humorous love tragedy of an insatiable young English War widow and an unmanned U.S. soldier. . . . The ironic witticisms are amusing, for a few chapters. There is considerable emotion, consciously restrained, quite subtle. . . . But the reader is very much inclined to echo a remark that is one of Jake's favorites, and, presumably, Author Hemingway's too, 'Oh, what the hell!' "

52 Review of *IOT*, *TLS* (Nov. 4, 1926), p. 766.

"Mr. Ernest Hemingway, a young American writer living in Paris, is definitely of the 'moderns.' It is not merely a deliberate taste for writing ungrammatically now and again which points the way to Mr. Hemingway's literary camp; it is rather his unconcern for the conventional features of good writing. The short stories in the volume entitled *In Our Time* . . . achieve their effect by novel and rather puzzling means. . . . Only one story in the book—'Indian Camp,' the first—has anything like a straightforward appeal, and even here the actual method is as elusive as in the rest of the tales."

53 Rascoe, Burton. Review of *SAR*, *N.Y. Sun* (Nov. 6, 1926), p. 10. Drawing.

"Every sentence that [Hemingway] writes is fresh and alive. There is no one writing whose prose has more of the force and vibrancy of good, direct, natural, colloquial speech. . . . It seems to me that Hemingway is highly successful in presenting the effect that a sensual love for the same woman might have on the temperaments of three men who are utterly different in disposition and training. . . . Some Americans familiar around the Dôme and Rotondo in Paris appear in the novel in the thinnest of disguises, and remarkably true to character."

54 Gould, Gerald. Review of *IOT*, *Observer* (Nov. 7, 1926), p. 8.

"[Hemingway] is a new writer, with a vision and a technique of his own. He has a touch of genius: for the technique follows the vision. But the very first story in his collection raises the question of how cruel art can allow itself to be. . . . But in some of his later stories [cites 'The Battler'] he calls up the reserves of human love."

55 Gorman, Herbert S. Review of *SAR*, *N.Y. World* (Nov. 14, 1926), p. 10 M.

"Here, at last, is a writer who can assume (or, at least, appear to assume) an entirely impartial attitude toward his characters, drawing them with a surprising clarity through which no shadow of the author falls. . . . The sentences are cold and direct. They are always statements. The characters themselves are evolved from their conversations mainly, and it is a tribute to the uncanny skill of Hemingway to note that these people live with an almost painful reality."

56 Boyd, Ernest. Review of *SAR, Independent*, cxvii (Nov. 20, 1926), 594.
"The technique of this book is fascinating. When one is not swept along by astonishing dialogue, subtle, obvious, profound, and commonplace,—but always alive,—one is listening to careful enumeration of little facts whose cumulative effect is to give them the importance of remarkable incidents."

57 Review of *SAR, Chicago Daily Tribune* (Nov. 27, 1926), p. 13.
"*The Sun Also Rises* is the kind of book that makes this reviewer at least almost plain angry, not for the obvious reason that it is about utterly degraded people, but for the reason that it shows an immense skill, a very honest and unimpassioned conviction about how writing should be done, a remarkably restrained style, and is done in an amusing and clever modern technique, a sketching in with conversation and few modelings of description and none of rumination. . . . Ernest Hemingway can be a distinguished writer if he wishes to be. He is, even in this book, but it is a distinction hidden under a bushel of sensationalism and triviality."

58 Ashley, Schuyler. Review of *SAR, K.C. Star* (Dec. 4, 1926), p. 8.
"Mr. Hemingway . . . writes with a swinging, effortless precision that puts him in the very first flight of American stylists. . . . it is a mannerism of Hemingway's to recount exactly his characters' physical evolutions, through doors, up and down stairs, in and out of bed, as though establishing alibis. . . . He savors the taste and feel and smell of living with a sort of hard-boiled gusto."

59 Chase, Cleveland B. Review of *SAR, SRL*, iii (Dec. 11, 1926), 420-421.
"Written in terse, precise and aggressively fresh prose, and containing some of the finest dialogue yet written in this country, the story achieves a vividness and a sustained tension that makes it unquestionably one of the events of a year rich in interesting books. . . . There is a truly Shakespearian absoluteness about his writing. . . . It is an interesting fact that neither in his short stories nor in this novel does Hemingway make use of a single simile. To him

things are not 'like' other things. He does not write about them until he has been able to grasp their essential qualities."

60 Tate, Allen. Review of *SAR*, *Nation*, CXXIII (Dec. 15, 1926), 642, 644.

"Mr. Hemingway has produced a successful novel, but not without returning some violence upon the integrity achieved in his first book [*IOT*]. . . . he is not hard-boiled enough, in the artistic sense. . . . Hemingway doesn't fill out his characters and let them stand by themselves; he isolates one or two chief traits which reduce them to caricature. His perception of the physical object is direct and accurate; his vision of character, singularly oblique."

61 Morris, Lawrence S. Review of *SAR*, *New Republic*, XLVIII (Dec. 22, 1926), 142-143.

"Ernest Hemingway's short stories in the volume, *In Our Time*, were the most stirring pages of imaginative prose by an American which appeared last year. . . . Now comes his first novel, *The Sun Also Rises*, and it is clear that the shorter tales were merely a preparation. . . . He has shown that he can not only state a theme, but develop it. . . . He loves all the hard, stinging experiences of the senses, he loves skill, he can laugh. He knows the intonations and obliquenesses of human speech. No other American writing today can match his dialogue for its apparent naturalness, its intimacy and its concealed power of revealing emotion."

62 Brief review of *SAR*, *Dial*, LXXXII (Jan. 1927), 73.

"His characters are as shallow as the saucers in which they stack their daily emotions, and instead of interpreting his material—or even challenging—he has been content merely to make a carbon copy of a not particularly significant surface of life in Paris."

63 Kronenberger, Louis. Review of *The Best Short Stories of 1926*, edited by Edward J. O'Brien, *N.Y. Herald Tribune Books* (Jan. 16, 1927), p. 4.

Appraises "The Undefeated."

64 "Four More Americans Get Divorces in Paris," *N.Y. Times* (March 11, 1927), p. 2.

Hadley Richardson Hemingway received a divorce, in Paris, on the grounds of desertion. She and Hemingway were married in Horton's Bay, Mich., on September 3, 1921, and had one son, John.

65 Barton, Bruce. Review of *SAR*, *Atlantic*, CXXXIX (April 1927), 12, 14.

"A writer named Hemingway has arisen, who writes as if he had never read anybody's writing, as if he had fashioned the art of writing himself. . . . It is true that his book deals with people who have no morals. They drink too much. . . . They have no religion, and no ideals in the accepted sense of the word. But they have courage and friendship, and mental honestness. And they are *alive*. Amazingly real and alive."

66 Portrait, *Bookman*, LXV (April 1927), 235.

A woodcut of Hemingway from a portrait by Henry Strater.

67 Lawrence, D. H. Review of *IOT*, *Calendar of Modern Letters*, IV (April 1927), 72-73.

"*In Our Time* calls itself a book of stories, but it isn't that. It is a series of successive sketches from a man's life, and makes a fragmentary novel. . . . It is a short book: and it does not pretend to be about one man. But it is. It is as much as we need know of the man's life. The sketches are short, sharp, vivid, and most of them excellent." Reprinted in *Phoenix*, London, 1936, p. 365; *Selected Literary Criticism*, London, 1955, pp. 427-428; and in *Weeks collection*, pp. 93-94.

68 Ford, Ford Madox. "Some American Expatriates," *Vanity Fair*, XXVIII (April 1, 1927), 64, 98. Photograph on p. 65.

General article. Discusses *SAR*.

69 Ferguson, Charles W. "Five Rising Stars in American Fiction," *Bookman*, LXV (May 1927), 251-257.

Commentary on Eleanor Carroll Chilton, John Gunther, Hemingway, Leonard Nason, and Elizabeth Madox Roberts.

70 Eisenberg, Emanuel. Parody, "The Importance of Being Ernest: Irresponsibly inscribed after a perusal of *The Sun Also Rises*," *N.Y. World* (May 9, 1927), p. 13.

71 Walpole, Hugh. "Contemporary American Letters," *Nation & Athenaeum*, XLI (June 4, 1927), 302-303.

General article. Refers to Hemingway as "the most interesting figure in American letters in the last ten years."

72 Review of *Fiesta*, *Observer* (June 12, 1927), p. 8.

"Mr. Hemingway began brilliantly, with a set of short stories called *In Our Time*. But *Fiesta* gives us neither people nor atmosphere; the maudlin, staccato conversations—evidently meant to be realistic in their brokenness and boringness—convey no impression of reality; and the characters, both men and women, in Paris and in Spain, are so consistently soaking themselves with alcohol as to lose all human interest. . . . O that wearisome, drenching deluge of drink! . . . Why does Mr. Hemingway, who *can* draw flesh-and-blood, waste his time on these bibulous shadows?"

73 Review of *Fiesta*, *TLS* (June 30, 1927), 454.

"Now comes a novel, *Fiesta* . . . more obviously an experiment in story-making [than *IOT*], and in which he abandons his vivid impressionism for something much less interesting. There are moments of sudden illumination in the story, and throughout it displays a determined reticence; but it is frankly tedious after one has read the first hundred pages and ceased to hope for anything different. . . . The Spanish scenes give us something of the quality of Mr. Hemingway's earlier book, but they hardly qualify the general impression of an unsuccessful experiment."

74 Muir, Edwin. Review of *Fiesta, Nation & Athenaeum*, XLI (July 2, 1927), 450, 452.
 "Mr. Hemingway is a writer of quite unusual talent. . . . His dialogue is by turns extraordinarily natural and brilliant, and impossibly melodramatic; when he has to describe anything he has a sureness and economy which recall Maupassant; he neither turns away from unpleasant details, nor does he stress them. . . . The original merits of the book are striking; its faults, equally apparent . . . is a lack of artistic significance. We see the lives of a group of people laid bare, and we feel that it does not matter to us. . . . But he is still a young writer; his gifts are original; and this first novel raises hopes of remarkable achievement."

75 Littell, Robert. "Notes on Ernest Hemingway," *New Republic*, LI (Aug. 10, 1927), 303-306.
 Biographical and critical essay. For Ezra Pound's reply, regarding *TOS*, see *NR*, LIII (Oct. 5, 1927), 177a.

76 Rascoe, Burton. Review of *MWW*, *Bookman*, LXVI (Sept. 1927), 90.
 "['Fifty Grand'] is a brutally ironic story, as real as life. . . . The book also includes 'The Killers,' the most talked-of story of the year. The other stories in the collection are of varying worth, but all of them are written in Hemingway's admirably clean and incisive style."

77 Drawing of Hemingway and announcement of publication of *MWW*, *N.Y. Times Book Review* (Sept. 25, 1927), p. 7.

78 Woolf, Virginia. "An Essay in Criticism," review of *MWW*, *N.Y. Herald Tribune Books* (Oct. 9, 1927), pp. 1, 8.
 "*Men Without Women* consists of short stories in the French rather than in the Russian manner. . . . There is never a thread left hanging: indeed so contracted are they, that when the last sentence of the last page flares up, as it so often does, we see by its light the whole circumference and significance of the story revealed. . . . Mr. Hemingway, then, is courageous; he is candid; he is highly skilled; he plants words precisely where he wishes; he has moments of bare and nervous beauty; he is modern in manner but not in vision;

355

he is self-consciously virile; his talent has contracted rather than expanded; compared with his novel his stories are a little dry and sterile." Reprinted in *Granite and Rainbow*, New York, 1958, pp. 85-92.

79 Hutchison, Percy. Review of *MWW, N.Y. Times Book Review* (Oct. 16, 1927), pp. 9, 27.
"Hemingway's is the art of the reporter carried to the highest degree. . . . His facts may be from experience, and they may be compounded solely of imagination; but he so presents them that they stand out with all the clearness and sharpness (and also the coldness) of pinnacles of ice in clear, frosty air. To sum up in a figure, Hemingway's is a stark naked style."

80 Review of *MWW, Time*, x (Oct. 24, 1927), 38. Photograph.
"*The Sun Also Rises*, published last winter, made critics realize that at least one of the Americans who live in Paris can do something more important than sit about in restaurants. Its little hard sentences were like round stones polished by rain and wind, not a Mason's grading. The book had the sharp determined rhythm of a person walking upstairs; there was no literary gesticulation, no wasted energy, no flourishing. The stories in *Men Without Women* have the same qualities. . . . Totally objective, they are as clear and crisp and perfectly shaped as icicles, as sharp as splinters of glass."

81 Review of *MWW, New Yorker*, iii (Oct. 29, 1927), 92-94.
". . . a truly magnificent work. . . . I do not know where a greater collection of stories can be found. . . . Hemingway has an unerring sense of selection. . . . His is, as any reader knows, a dangerous influence. The simple thing he does looks so easy to do. But look at the boys who try to do it."

82 Photograph of Hemingway in Paris, *Town & Country*, LXXXII (Nov. 1, 1927), 68.

83 Krutch, Joseph Wood. Review of *MWW, Nation*, cxxv (Nov. 16, 1927), 548.
"These stories are painfully good . . . no one can deny their brilliance."

84 Dodd, Lee Wilson. Review of *MWW, SRL*, iv (Nov. 19, 1927), 322-323.
"To the present critic, who is amazed by and genuinely admires the lean virtuosity of Mr. Hemingway, the second most astonishing thing about him is the narrowness of his selective range. . . . I can easily conceive of a great writer choosing to write the short and simple annals of the hard-boiled; what I can not conceive is his doing so virtually without reference to other possible aspects of hu-

man existence." Hemingway's poem "Valentine," which appeared in the *Little Review*, XII (May 1929), is a reply to this review.

85 Connolly, Cyril. Review of *MWW*, *New Statesman*, XXX (Nov. 26, 1927), 208.

"*Men Without Women* is a collection of grim little stories told in admirable colloquial dialogue with no point, no moral and no ornamentation."

86 Wilson, Edmund. "The Sportsman's Tragedy," *New Republic*, LIII (Dec. 14, 1927), 102-103.

Wilson discusses the short stories in *MWW* and advances the opinion that Hemingway's world is not quite so rudimentary as certain reviewers represent it. "Mr. Hemingway's feelings about this world, his criticism of what goes on in it, are, for all his misleadingly simple and matter-of-fact style, rather subtle and complicated. . . . His point of view, his state of mind, is a curious one, and one typical, I think, of 'our time'; he seems so broken in to the human agonies, and, though even against his will, so impassively, so hopelessly, resigned to them, that the only protest of which he is capable is, as it were, the grin and the curse of the sportsman who loses the game." Reprinted in *The Shores of Light*, New York, 1952, pp. 339-344.

87 Curtis, William. Review of *MWW*, *Town & Country*, LXXXII (Dec. 15, 1927), 59.

"It is probably the best volume of short stories published since the days of the younger Kipling. . . . Each sentence says something, crisply, sharply, incisively. Says something and then moves on. . . . Any future anthology of the American short story which does not include 'The Killers' will not be complete."

88 Smyth, Joseph Hilton. "He Drank With Them, Played With Them, Wrote A Book About Them | Ernest Hemingway of Boston [*sic*] Put His Playfellows of Montparnasse Into His Stories," *Boston Globe* (Dec. 18, 1927), Feature section, p. 3. Photograph.

89 Caricature by Saravi, *Bookman*, LXVI (Jan. 1928), opp. p. 560.

90 Riddell, John [Corey Ford]. "A Parody Interview with Mr. Hemingway," *Vanity Fair*, XXIX (Jan. 1928), 78. Caricature of Hemingway by Ralph Barton.

91 "Roark Bradford Wins O. Henry Story Prize | First Award Goes for 'Child of God'—Hemingway and Bromfield Honored," *N.Y. Times* (Jan. 20, 1928), p. 12.

Hemingway was awarded second prize of O. Henry Memorial Award for "The Killers."

92 "Oak Park Writer Wins Prize for Second Best Magazine Story of Year in 'The Killers,' " *Oak Leaves* (Feb. 4, 1928), p. 8.

Reports that Hemingway, "one of the most noted young writers of fiction in the country today . . . was honored by the [O. Henry] memorial prize commission with the $250 cash prize for the second best magazine story of 1927."

93 Matthews, T. S. Parody, "Flatteries: Pretty Grand: By a sincere flatterer of Ernest Hemingway," *New Republic*, LIII (Feb. 8, 1928), 323-324.

94 Faÿ, Bernard. Review of *MWW* [Scribner's edition], *Revue Européenne*, No. 3 (March 1928), pp. 322-323.

95 Hickok, Guy. "Paris Won't Let Hemingway Live a Private Life," *Brooklyn Daily Eagle* (March 4, 1928), p. 2 F. Dateline: Paris.

96 Rothman, N. L. Review of *MWW*, *Dial*, LXXXIV (April 1, 1928), 336-338.

". . . there is no hope and no suspense in any of Hemingway's work." [The reviewer cites the tragedies of Shakespeare as a precedent for such a lack.] "I find this in Hemingway, singing out under the constant beat of conversation and reiteration. . . some modern version of 'to be or not to be.' . . . I venture to say that he could write a great tragedy. He remains, I think, our outstanding realist."

97 Mencken, H. L. Review of *MWW*, *American Mercury*, XIV (May 1928), 127.

"Mr. Hemingway and Mr. [Thornton] Wilder have made huge successes of late, and received a great deal of uncritical homage. I believe that both are too sagacious to let it fool them. It is technical virtuosity that has won them attention; it is hard and fundamental thinking that must get them on, if they are to make good their high promise."

98 Barrett, Richmond. "Babes in the Bois," *Harper's Magazine*, CLVI (May 1928), 724-736.

General article. *SAR* is used as a starting point to write of American expatriates in Paris.

99 Photograph of Hemingway by Helen Breaker, *N.Y. Times Book Review* (June 10, 1928), p. 4.

100 Orvitt, Lenore. "Ernest Hemingway, One of Ours," *Oak Parker* (June 29, 1928), p. 32.

"Whatever his intrinsic worth, it must be admitted that Hemingway is the village genius. There is no other Oak Park writer who has made so definite and overwhelming a contribution to literature."

Cowley, Malcolm. "The Hemingway Legend," *Brentano's Book Chat* (Sept.–Oct. 1928), pp. 25-29. Sketch of Hemingway by Waldo Peirce.

This article is subtitled "the first real pen-picture of Ernest Hemingway that has ever appeared in print."

Photograph of Hemingway in Florida, *transition*, No. 14 (Fall 1928), opp. p. 96.

Lania, Leo. "Mr. Hemingway vagabondiert in Europa," *Tagebuch*, ix (Dec. 1928), 2178-80.

"Dr. Hemingway, Writer's Father, Ends Own Life," *Chicago Tribune* (Dec. 7, 1928), p. 4. Photograph of Dr. Hemingway on p. 46.

Obituary of Hemingway's father. Dr. Clarence Edmunds Hemingway, 57, shot and killed himself at his home, 600 North Kenilworth Avenue, Oak Park, Ill.

Llona, Victor. Review of *Cinquante mille dollars* (short stories), *Nouvelle Revue Française*, xxxii (Jan. 1, 1929), 123-124.

Caricature of Hemingway by Eva Herrmann, *Bookman*, lxviii (Feb. 1929), 683.

McIntyre, O. O. "Drop in Again, Ernest!" *K.C. Times* (March 9, 1929), p. 28. Dateline: New York.

"New York had a visiting novelist this winter who made no effort to be a bright boy at the tea table. . . ." Comments mainly on Hemingway's disregard for the "financial rewards of his trade."

Photograph of Hemingway by Helen Breaker, *Scribner's Magazine*, lxxxv (May 1929), 492. See (C188).

Photograph of Hemingway in Florida, *Scribner's Magazine*, lxxxv (June 1929), 41.

Praz, Mario. "Un giovane narratore americano," *Stampa* (June 14, 1929), p. 3.

This article is quoted extensively in Praz's "Hemingway in Italy," *Partisan Review*, xv (Oct. 1948).

"Boston Police Bar Scribner's Magazine | Superintendent Acts on Objections to Ernest Hemingway's Serial, 'Farewell to Arms,'" *N.Y. Times* (June 21, 1929), p. 2.

Reports that "some persons deemed part of the instalment salacious." Statement from Scribner's quoted.

"Boston Bans Scribner's for July," *N.Y. Times* (June 29, 1929), p. 8.

A second issue of *Scribner's Magazine* was banned from Boston news stands because of the serial *A Farewell to Arms*.

113 Wister, Owen. Letter to the editor, *Scribner's Magazine*, LXXXVI (July 1929), 27.
Letter praising *FTA*.

114 Burke, Kenneth. "A Decade of American Fiction," *Bookman*, LXIX (Aug. 1929), 561-567.
General article. Commentary on Hemingway on pp. 562-563.

115 Capers, Julian, Jr. Letter to the editor, *Scribner's Magazine*, LXXXVI (Sept. 1929), 52-53.
Regarding Hemingway's work on the *K.C. Star* and with the Red Cross ambulance unit in Italy.

116 Butcher, Fanny. Review of *FTA*, *Chicago Daily Tribune* (Sept. 28, 1929), p. 11.
"Technically and stylistically the most interesting novel of the year is a judgment which any keenly critical reader would pass on *A Farewell to Arms*. Anyone who thus has watched American writing cannot but find in it a blossoming of a most unusual genius of our day. . . . It is brutal, it is terrific, it is awesome, it is coarse, it is vulgar, it is beautiful, it is all sorts of contradictory things."

117 Hazlitt, Henry. Review of *FTA*, *N.Y. Sun* (Sept. 28, 1929), p. 38.
Drawing of Hemingway.
"Many things in the novel are magnificently done. The account of the retreat, which never goes beyond Henry's personal experiences, is unforgettable. . . . The scenes are vividly realized, and the passage of time is conveyed with uncanny skill. . . . In depth, in range, in drama, *A Farewell to Arms* is the finest thing Hemingway has yet done. The dialogue is what we have come to expect. It is brilliantly authentic; one listens to it rather than reads it. There is no more convincing dialogue being written anywhere. . . . With so much that is admirable it may seem ungrateful to speak of Hemingway's limitations, or of the limitations of his style and method. . . . It is not merely his dialogue that is simple and bare, but his writing in between. . . . In *A Farewell to Arms* he has often carried this simplicity to a point where it becomes palpably artificial, with the result that the prose falls off from the level achieved in *The Sun Also Rises*. . . . even Hemingway's dialogue, brilliant as it is, has important limitations. It is not sharply enough individualized."

118 Hutchison, Percy. Review of *FTA*, *N.Y. Times Book Review* (Sept. 29, 1929), p. 5.
"It is not impossible that Ernest Hemingway has developed his style to the extreme to which he carries it because in it he finds a sort of protective covering for a nature more sensitive than he would have one know. . . . a moving and beautiful book."

19 Photograph of Hemingway at Gstaad, Switzerland, in 1927, *Scribner's Magazine*, LXXXVI (Oct. 1929), 372.

20 Maurois, André. Review of *FTA, This Quarter*, II (Oct.–Dec. 1929), 212.

21 Cowley, Malcolm. Review of *FTA, N.Y. Herald Tribune Books* (Oct. 6, 1929), pp. 1, 16.

"One cannot help thinking that *A Farewell to Arms* is a symbolic title; that it is Hemingway's farewell to a period, an attitude, and perhaps to a method also. . . . As the process of demobilization draws slowly to its end the simple standards of wartime are being forgotten. Pity, love, adventurousness, anger, the emotions on which his earlier books were based, almost to the entire exclusion of idea, are less violently stimulated in a world at peace. The emotions as a whole are more colored by thought. . . . They seem to demand expression in a subtler and richer prose. The present novel shows a change in this direction, and perhaps the change may extend still further. . . . Perhaps even Hemingway may decide in the end that being deliberately un-sophisticated is not the height of sophistication."

22 Matthews, T. S. Review of *FTA, New Republic*, LX (Oct. 9, 1929), 208-210.

"The writings of Ernest Hemingway have very quickly put him in a prominent place among American writers, and his numerous admirers have looked forward with impatience and great expectations to his second novel. They should not be disappointed: *A Farewell to Arms* is worthy of their hopes and of its author's promise. The book is cast in the form which Hemingway has apparently delimited for himself in the novel—a diary form. It is written in the first person . . . in that tone which suggests a roughly educated but sensitive poet who is prouder of his muscles than of his vocabulary, which we are now accustomed to associate with Hemingway's name."

23 "A.W.S." Review of *FTA, New Yorker*, V (Oct. 12, 1929), 120.

"If you do not think there is any poetry left in the modern idiom, I suggest that you read some of the dialogue in the final tragic episode of *A Farewell to Arms*. Its eloquent simplicity makes all other dialogue sound smirking and stilted."

24 Canby, Henry Seidel. "Story of the Brave," review of *FTA, SRL*, VI (Oct. 12, 1929), 231-232. Drawing of Hemingway by Waldo Peirce.

"You cannot take too seriously a novel of such vivid reality as *Farewell to Arms*, nor an observer and auditor of such uncanny powers. . . . Hemingway works almost entirely through a simple record of incident and dialogue which he stretches to include meditation in the rhythm of thought. It is a fine art. . . . [He] is after voice rhythms and voice contrasts. It is the way these people talk not what they say that lifts the scene into reality. . . . Let his imitators beware lest they copy him, twisting syntax, not as he does to fit necessity, but out of bravado and freakishness." Reprinted in *Designed for Reading*, New York, 1934, pp. 221-227; *A Quarto of Modern Literature*, ed. Leonard Brown and Porter G. Perrin, New York, 1940 edition, pp. 425-427; *A Complete College Reader*, ed. John Holmes and Carroll S. Towle, Boston, 1950, pp. 244-247.

125 Review of *FTA*, *Time*, XIV (Oct. 14, 1929), 80.

"In its sustained, inexorable movement, its throbbing preoccupation with flesh and blood and nerves rather than the fanciful fabrics of intellect, it fulfills the prophecies that his most excited admirers have made about Ernest Hemingway."

126 Fadiman, Clifton P. Review of *FTA*, *Nation*, CXXIX (Oct. 30, 1929), 497-498.

"*A Farewell to Arms* revolves about two strong, simple feelings: love for a beautiful and noble woman, affection for one's comrades. . . . It is certainly Hemingway's best book to date. There seems no reason why it should not secure the Pulitzer Prize for, despite the Italian setting, it is as American as Times Square. It is a real occasion for patriotic rejoicing."

127 Rascoe, Burton. Review of *FTA*, *Arts & Decoration*, XXXII (Nov. 1929), 124. Photograph of Hemingway by Helen Breaker.

". . . a distinguished work of fiction by a writer who is to be counted among the best we have. . . . When the story first began to appear serially in a magazine it was accorded the distinction of being banned in Boston. It has other merits beside this, however. The story of the Italian retreat is superbly done."

128 Ross, Mary. Brief review of *FTA*, *Atlantic*, CXLIV (Nov. 1929), 20.

"[*A Farewell to Arms*] has the strange power of his earlier books in suggesting overtones through laconic dialogue; and beyond this technical mastery a wider and deeper reach of emotion than Hemingway has dared before."

129 Herrick, Robert. "What is dirt?" *Bookman*, LXX (Nov. 1929), 258-262.

For replies to this highly critical article, see [Henry Seidel Canby's] Chronicle and Comment column in the *Bookman*, LXX (Feb. 1930), 641-647; M. K. Hare's "Is It Dirt or Is It Art?" in Scribner's advertisement in the *Bookman*, LXXI (March 1930) xiv-xv; and the foreword, "In Spite of Robert Herrick," in *Cohn's Bibliography,* p. 9.

130 DeVoto, Bernard. Review of *FTA, Bookwise,* I (Nov. 1929), 5-9.

"The new book has what its predecessor [*SAR*] lacked, passion. It has, too, a kind of sublimity. The clipped sentences, the almost completely maintained objective of style, are here employed on material of greater importance and to a finer end. . . . In *A Farewell to Arms* Mr. Hemingway for the first time justifies his despair and gives it the dignity of a tragic emotion."

131 Curtis, William. Review of *FTA, Town & Country,* LXXXIV (Nov. 1, 1929), 86. Photograph of Hemingway by Helen Breaker.

"I perhaps, as much as any other man, have done my frothing at the mouth about Mr. Hemingway. I still think his short story, 'The Killers' is one of the most perfect pieces of work in the language. . . . *A Farewell to Arms* is one of those things you simply have to read, because everybody else will be reading it. But, as you read, remember that even Mr. Hemingway is not yet God." The last reference is in regard to his not being infallible.

132 Bennett, Arnold. Review of *FTA, Evening Standard,* London (Nov. 14, 1929).

"The book is hard, almost metallic, glittering, blinding by the reflections of its bright surface, utterly free of any sentimentality. But imbued through and through with genuine sentiment. A strange and original book. Whatever it may not do to you, it will convince you of its honesty and veracity. You will never be able to say as you read: 'This isn't true. This is exaggerated. This is forced.' The book is a superb performance."

133 Review of *FTA, Times,* London (Nov. 15, 1929), p. 20.

"Mr. Ernest Hemingway has found in the War a finer scope for his very powerful talent than he has ever found before. *A Farewell to Arms,* even in these days of many War novels, stands out as something entirely original with the grim dryness of its humour, the sensual realism of its episodes, and the unrelieved pessimism of its view of life. . . . Rinaldi, a surgeon, whose portrait, drawn entirely in dialogue, is the most brilliant achievement in a brilliant book."

34 Todd, B. E. Review of *FTA, Spectator* (Nov. 16, 1929), p. 727.

"There is no glamour here, and few thrills: even the physical horrors described are not quite so ghastly as those in many war books. It is an epic of weariness. . . . There may be cruder war books, but there are none gloomier than this very great one, which deserves a shelf of its own on that space on the wall, so that it can be used as an antidote to the sickly poison of glory and glamour."

135 Gould, Gerald. Review of *FTA*, *Observer* (Nov. 17, 1929), p. 8.

"*A Farewell to Arms* is not a war-novel . . . it is a novel of adventure and passion which happens to touch a corner of the war. The hero, it is true, is wounded . . . and the stark description of the desperate senselessness of pain is the best, the most awful, the most memorable, thing in the book. . . . The hero is a typical Hemingway creation: gallant, cruel, selfish, sensual, direct . . . the sort of man who would have found this sort of adventure and suffering somewhere in the world, waiting for him round some corner, war or no war. . . . I have read few books more terrible; but the beauty survives."

136 Carroll, Raymond G. "Hemingway Gives Up Old Life With Literary Success," *N.Y. Evening Post* (Nov. 18, 1929), p. 6. Dateline: Paris.

Mentions that Pauline and Ernest and their son, Patrick, lived in a six-room apartment on the top floor of a house in the Rue Ferou. Includes a short parody to prove that "the Hemingway who sat nightly in the Latin Quarter cafés is no more."

137 "I.M.P." [Isabel M. Paterson]. Turns With a Bookworm column, *N.Y. Herald Tribune Books* (Nov. 24, 1929), p. 27.

Quotes Caroline Bancroft in the *Denver Post*, regarding a boxing match between Hemingway and Morley Callaghan in Paris. See Callaghan's reply in the *NYHTB* (Dec. 8, 1929), p. 29. This letter to Isabel Paterson, denying that he ever knocked out Hemingway, is reprinted in *That Summer in Paris*, New York, 1963, p. 242.

138 Review of *FTA*, *TLS* (Nov. 28, 1929), p. 998.

". . . a novel of great power. Though it adds one to the now many novels of war, it is unlike any other. . . . The actual scenes of war are biting and brilliant. . . . the end is unbelievably painful, for no horror of that tragic maternity is left to the imagination. And with that death and Henry walking back to the hotel in the rain this gripping story ends abruptly, leaving all its pain raw. Mr. Hemingway's pessimism is his own affair: we can only recognize that it animates an extremely talented and original artist." Reprinted in *TLS* (Sept. 17, 1954), p. lxxxvii; and in *American Writing Today*, Allen Angoff, ed., New York, 1957, pp. 370-372.

139 "E. S." Review of *FTA*, *New Statesman*, xxxiv (Nov. 30, 1929), 267.

"His tale is not about racial characteristics or their manifestation in war, but about human individuals, Henry and Catherine, and their associates, and it is a convincing and a moving tale. Mr. Hemingway does not indulge in even as much explanation of motive as might be justified by the method of first-person narration. He presents the fact and the reader believes him. . . . To make one phrase of it, Mr. Hemingway communicates his experience whole and un-impaired."

40 Parker, Dorothy. Profile, "The Artist's Reward," *New Yorker*, v (Nov. 30, 1929), 28-31. Drawing of Hemingway.

Relates the occasion when Hemingway defined courage as "grace under pressure." The title is taken from a letter Hemingway wrote to F. Scott Fitzgerald.

41 Dos Passos, John. Review of *FTA*, *New Masses*, v (Dec. 1, 1929), 16.

"The book is a firstrate piece of craftsmanship by a man who knows his job. It gives you the sort of pleasure line by line that you get from handling a piece of wellfinished carpenter's work. . . . The stuff will match up as narrative prose with anything that's been written since there was any English language."

42 Redman, Ben Ray. "Spokesman For a Generation," *Spur*, XLIV (Dec. 1, 1929), 77, 186. Photograph.

Writes of Hemingway in Pamplona, during the week of the San Fermin fiesta. Also discusses *SAR* and *FTA*.

43 Hartley, L. P. Review of *FTA*, *Saturday Review*, London, CXLVIII (Dec. 7, 1929), 684, 686.

"Mr. Hemingway is a novelist of the expatriated. . . . There is the Continental scene as envisaged by a thirsty Anglo-Saxon: cafés, vermouths, drinks—unlimited drinks. There is the same dialogue between the lovers. . . . *A Farewell to Arms* contains most of the ingredients of its predecessor [*SAR*], but it has others as well, and it is a much better book. The Italian officers, with whom the hero was on intimate terms (Mr. Hemingway has a gift for portraying friendship as well as love), are excellently drawn and the war passages are vivid and exciting."

44 Review of *FTA*, *Illustrated London News* (Dec. 21, 1929), p. 1092.

"His genius declares itself in the perfection of detail, on the one hand, and in a profound discernment on the other. Dualism runs through the narrative, and it runs deep. It lies at the very foundations of the brilliant construction."

45 Walpole, Hugh. "The Best Books of 1929," *Saturday Review*, London, CXLVIII (Dec. 21, 1929), 747-748.

". . . the finest novel of the year for myself is Ernest Hemingway's *A Farewell to Arms*, a most moving and beautiful story."

46 Hope, Edward. The Lantern column, *N.Y. Herald Tribune* (Dec. 23, 1929), p. 14.

An appraisal of *FTA* is included in this year-end summation of the books published in 1929.

147 Priestley, J. B. Review of *FTA*, *Now & Then*, No. 34 (Winter 1929), pp. 11-12.

"Mr. Hemingway is really very American; though he may write about boulevards and bullfights, he could not possibly be mistaken for an English writer. He has a curious manner and idiom which are based on characteristic American speech. He tells his tales in a succession of short, direct sentences, piling up the facts, and avoiding all obvious 'literary' airs and graces. You feel as if he were riddling his subjects with a machine-gun. But through the medium of this bluff, masculine, 'hard-boiled', apparently insensitive style, he contrives to give you a very vivid and sometimes poignant picture of the life he knows. He has done this superbly in *A Farewell to Arms*." Reprinted from the *Book Society's Review* (Nov. 1929).

148 Mencken, H. L. Review of *FTA*, *American Mercury*, XIX (Jan. 1930), 127.

"Mr. Hemingway's dialogue, as always, is fresh and vivid. Otherwise his tricks begin to wear thin."

149 Galantière, Lewis. Review of *FTA*, *Hound & Horn*, III (Jan.-March 1930), 259-262.

"Our knowledge of [Catherine and Frederic] is limited to their sensations. . . . of their personality, their common humanity, we know nothing. . . . The war story . . . is much more successful. . . . As for the writing, it seems to me the best Hemingway has done. The book is welded together with great care and scrupulous attention to detail. There are surprises in the novel, but only because we do not read attentively enough: the tone of each situation is sounded in advance; the colour of each character is indicated somewhere before he moves completely into view."

150 Orton, Vrest. "Some Notes Bibliographical and Otherwise on the Books of Ernest Hemingway," *Publishers' Weekly*, CXVII (Feb. 15, 1930), 884-886.

151 Hicks, Granville. "The World of Hemingway," *New Freeman*, I (March 22, 1930), 40-42.

This study traces the "spiritual history" of the Hemingway hero from Nick Adams to Jake Barnes to Frederic Henry.

152 "Visit by Ernest Hemingway," *K.C. Star* (July 6, 1930), p. 3.

Interview with Hemingway, in Kansas City, Mo., where he was visiting his cousin, Mrs. W. Malcolm Lowry, en route to Wyoming to continue work on *DIA*.

153 Joachim, Hans A. "Romans aus Amerika," *Neue Rundschau*, XLI (Sept. 1930), 396-409.

General article. Hemingway's work is discussed on pp. 405-407.

54 Hammond, Percy. Review of the play, *FTA, N.Y. Herald Tribune* (Sept. 23, 1930), p. 14.

". . . the play, though of course inferior to the book, is a reasonably life-like imitation. This was scarcely to be expected since Mr. Hemingway's ironic chronicle of romance and the War seemed hostile to the Theater, so real are its people, speech, and incidents. . . . Mr. [Laurence] Stallings . . . manages to salvage much of the story's quality."

55 Atkinson, J. Brooks. Review of the play, *FTA, N.Y. Times* (Sept. 23, 1930), p. 30.

"In his adaptation of *A Farewell to Arms* . . . Laurence Stallings has done as well by the novel as any one could, yet what he has done is not very much. Hemingway's novel of wartime is a virtuoso achievement—fierce, swift, brilliant. Story and style are fused. In the play Mr. Stallings has been reasonably faithful to the story. . . . What is memorable in the novel becomes vivid and touching here. Nevertheless, the play is not the novel; and as a play it is diffuse and disconnected. . . . The second act lives by virtue of Mr. Stallings' brisk adaptation. He maunders in the first act and seems rather bewildered in the last, but in the second act his touch is sure. . . . As a play, *A Farewell to Arms* lacks structure and lacks unity of mood."

56 Polgar, Alfred. Review of *In einem andern Land (FTA)*, *Tagebuch*, XI (Oct. 1930), 1646-47.

57 Young, Stark. Review of the play, *FTA, New Republic*, LXIV (Oct. 8, 1930), 208-209.

". . . the surface of Mr. Hemingway's style is always realistic, even though his work may be always at bottom poetic and distilled. On the stage a large portion of this effect is impossible. . . . In the hospital scene of the second act Mr. [Laurence] Stallings achieved some brilliant play writing, every bit as good as the novel, and to my mind much better, as well as being much more difficult to contrive in theater terms than it was in fiction. . . . On the whole I found the play, despite the drag of much of the last act, interesting all through."

58 Fergusson, Francis. Review of the play, *FTA, Bookman*, LXXII (Nov. 1930), 296.

"The love-story is made the center of interest in the stage version. Thanks to Mr. [Rouben] Mamoulian's direction and the acting of Elissa Landi and Glenn Anders, something authentic is established. . . . it is when one comes to look for the Hemingway sensibility, which gives the novel its importance, that one is most disappointed. Mr. Stallings has tried to save it by keeping the dialogue intact; but the Hemingway laconic remarks lose their flavor when they are not imbedded in the Hemingway prose."

159 "Hemingway Hurt," *N.Y. Times* (Nov. 3, 1930), p. 29.
Hemingway suffered a fractured right arm in an automobile accident near Billings, Mont. He was accompanied by John Dos Passos, who escaped injury.

160 Redman, Ben Ray. Review of *IOT* (Scribner's edition), *N.Y. Herald Tribune Books* (Nov. 16, 1930), p. 22.

161 Review of *IOT* (Scribner's edition), *SRL*, VII (Jan. 24, 1931), 548.

162 Schneider, Isidor. "The Fetish of Simplicity," *Nation*, CXXXII (Feb. 18, 1931), 184-186.
General article. The writer comments that "It is the writers of the Hemingway school . . . who have been chiefly responsible for the present over-accent on simplicity. . . . the Hemingway picture of a hard and disillusioned generation is a flattery. . . .'" See Josephine Herbst's "Counterblast," in the *Nation,* CXXXII (March 11, 1931), 275-276.

163 Mann, Klaus. "Ernest Hemingway," *Neue Schweizer Rundschau,* XXIV (April 1, 1931), 272-277.

164 Fallada, Hans. "Ernest Hemingway oder Woram liegt es?" *Literatur,* XXXIII (Sept. 1931), 672-674. Photograph.

165 "Hemingway's 8-Year-Old Boy Stirs Spain as *Toreador,*" *N.Y. Herald Tribune* [European Edition] (Sept. 17, 1931), p. 2.
Interview with Hemingway in Paris. He tells about his son, John, learning the art of bullfighting from Sidney Franklin, the American bullfighter.

166 Dewing, Arthur. "The Mistake About Hemingway," *North American Review*, CCXXXII (Oct. 1931), 364-371.
The writer notes that Hemingway has been accused of "lacking joy and vigor. Were such an estimate correct, Hemingway could never have produced the work he has. . . . Not many contemporary writers are as vitally alive."

167 Item, *Publishers' Weekly*, CXX (Oct. 3, 1931), 1580.
Brief mention of the Hemingways' arrival in New York, aboard the liner *Ile de France*, on September 29.

168 "Brick Salesman? Bootlegger? No Sir! Hemingway's Just Expectant Daddy!" *N.Y. Herald Tribune* [European Edition] (Oct. 14, 1931), p. 2.

Interview with Hemingway in New York. The Hemingways were en route to Kansas City, Mo., for the birth of their second child.

69 "The Ghost of a Writer," *K.C. Star* (Oct. 21, 1931), p. 17.
Interview with Hemingway in Kansas City. He tells of an impersonator who has been passing himself off as Hemingway in Europe and America.

70 Rascoe, Burton. A Bookman's Daybook column, "Random Thoughts About F. Scott Fitzgerald, Hemingway and Others," *N.Y. Sun* (Nov. 2, 1931), p. 37.

71 Item, *Time*, XVIII (Nov. 30, 1931), 46.
Brief item noting the birth of a second son, Gregory Hancock, to Ernest and Pauline Hemingway, in Kansas City, Missouri.

72 Seligo, Irene. "Mr. Hemingway und der Tod," *Frankfurter Zeitung* [1932], pp. 969-970.

73 Pieritz, Hilde. "Ernest Hemingway und sein Werk," *Hefte für Büchereiwesen*, XVI, [1932], 313-316.

74 Mackall, Leonard L. Notes for Bibliophiles column, *N.Y. Herald Tribune Books* (Jan. 31, 1932), p. 19.
Review of Louis Henry Cohn's *Bibliography of the Works of Ernest Hemingway*.

75 Review of *TOS* (Crosby Continental Edition), *Town & Country*, LXXXVII (Feb. 15, 1932), 21. Photograph of Hemingway at Dry Tortugas.

76 Johnson, Merle. "American First Editions: Ernest Hemingway," *Publishers' Weekly*, CXXI (Feb. 20, 1932), 870.
Brief checklist.

77 Coindreau, Maurice-Edgar. "L'Amérique et le roman alcoolique," *Cahiers du Sud*, XIX (April 1932), 166-172.
A denunciation of Hemingway's work by the French translator of *FTA* and *SAR*. Reprinted in *Aperçus de littérature américaine*, Paris, 1946, pp. 76-94.

78 Pound, Ezra. Letter, "Pound to Rascoe," *N.Y. Sun* (June 11, 1932), p. 36.
Regarding Hemingway's work. Also includes a reply by Burton Rascoe, "Rascoe's Riposte," regarding his early championing of Hemingway.

79 Leighton, Lawrence. "An Autopsy and a Prescription," *Hound & Horn*, V (July-Sept. 1932), 520-539.

For reply, see Hemingway's letter in the *Hound & Horn*, VI (Oct.–Dec. 1932).

180 Franzen, Erich. Review of *In unserer Zeit (IOT)*, *Vossische Zeitung* (Aug. 7, 1932).

181 "G. S." [Georg Svensson]. "Hemingways mästerverk pa svenska," *Bonniers Litterära Magasin*, 1 (Sept. 1932), 73-74. Photograph.
This review of *Farväl till vapnen (FTA)* is one of the earliest Swedish efforts to define Hemingway's style.

182 Kracauer, Siegfried. Review of *In unserer Zeit (IOT)*, *Frankfurter Zeitung* (Sept. 4, 1932).

183 Stallings, Laurence. Review of *DIA*, *N.Y. Sun* (Sept. 23, 1932), p. 34. Photograph.
"Ernest Hemingway's new book is a basic treatise on the art of the bullfighter, but it is also a superbly colored and capricious essay on human pride. It has grand flashes of ribaldry and wit, with brutal humors and frank compassions, and is shot through with a ruthless profundity. . . . [*Death in the Afternoon*] is concerned with the Pagan virtues rather than the Christian moralities. It has been long since such a note has been heard in an essay on life and death."

184 Redman, Ben Ray. Review of *DIA*, *SRL*, IX (Sept. 24, 1932), 121. Photograph.
"Hemingway has done his best to write a book that will prove at least intelligible to the reader who has not seen a bullfight. . . . He has written of the art in all its aspects, from every point of view; historical, critical, emotional and esthetic. . . . couched in a prose that must be called perfect because it states with absolute precision what it is meant to state, explains what it is meant to explain beyond possibility of misunderstanding, and communicates to the reader the emotion with which it is so heavily charged. . . . no reader can put down [*DIA*] ignorant of the fact that bullfighting is a tragic art."

185 Brickell, Herschel. Review of *DIA*, *N.Y. Herald Tribune Books* (Sept. 25, 1932), pp. 3, 12.
"If *Death in the Afternoon* were no more than a book on bullfighting it would be excellent reading, full of the vigor and forthrightness of the author's personality, his humor, his strong opinions —and language—and his great skill in conveying his undiluted emotions to his readers. . . . it is a book teeming with life, vigorous, powerful, moving and consistently entertaining. In short it is the essence of Hemingway."

86 Duffus, R. L. Review of *DIA*, *N.Y. Times Book Review* (Sept. 25, 1932), pp. 5, 17.

"The book is not only a careful, even a meticulous explanation of the way bull-fighting is done, but is also a picturing of the spirit in which it is done and seen. . . . the famous Hemingway style is neither so clear nor so forceful in most passages of *Death in the Afternoon* as it is in his novels and short stories."

87 Review of *DIA*, *Time*, xx (Sept. 26, 1932), 47. Portrait of Hemingway by Luis Quintanilla.

"*Death in the Afternoon* is all about bullfighting: a complete, compendious, appreciative guide."

88 "S. C." [Seward Collins]. Review of *DIA*, *Bookman*, LXXV (Oct. 1932), 622-624.

"Hemingway has gone past the spectator's viewpoint and made his way to the viewpoint of the torero himself—a feat which surely cannot be achieved by a non-Spaniard more than once in a generation, and which has never before been coupled, in English at least, with such skill in writing."

8₁ Photograph of Hemingway and caricature by Luis Quintanilla, *ibid.*, p. 567.

89 Lovett, Robert Morss. "Ernest Hemingway," *English Journal*, xxi (Oct. 1932), 609-617.

90 Fallada, Hans. "Gespräch zwischen Ihr und Ihm über Ernest Hemingway: *In unserer Zeit*," *Literatur*, xxxv (Oct. 1932), 21-24.

91 Coates, Robert M. Review of *DIA*, *New Yorker*, viii (Oct. 1, 1932), 61-63.

"The book is an exhaustive treatise on bullfighting in all its aspects. . . . Hemingway creates in your image a mythical Old Lady, who . . . acts as his interlocutor while he expresses some pretty bitter opinions on readers, writers, and things in general. There are passages in which his bitterness descends to petulance (as in his gibes at William Faulkner, who has done him no harm save to come under his influence, T. S. Eliot, Aldous Huxley, Jean Cocteau, and others, living and dead), there are also passages of bright, appealing honesty. . . ." See Hemingway's letter to Coates in the *New Yorker*, viii (Nov. 5, 1932).

92 Gibbs, Wolcott. Parody, "Death in the Rumble Seat," *New Yorker*, viii (Oct. 8, 1932), 15.

Subtitled: "With the usual apologies to Ernest Hemingway, who must be pretty sick of this sort of thing." Reprinted in *Bed of Neuroses*, New York, 1937, pp. 261-265.

193 Patterson, Curtis. Review of *DIA, Town & Country*, LXXXVII (Oct. 15, 1932), 50. Portrait of Hemingway by Luis Quintanilla.

"It is a tri-partite work: bull-fighting in Spain, plus semi-autobiographical details of the author, plus smut. . . . [Hemingway] has abandoned the short, loose sentence for an overlong, highly involved, extremely intricate periodic sentence that is supremely unsuccessful."

194 Coindreau, Maurice-Edgar. Review of *DIA, Nouvelle Revue Française*, XXXIX (Nov. 1, 1932), 778-781.

195 Hicks, Granville. Review of *DIA, Nation*, CXXXV (Nov. 9, 1932), 461.

". . . more people will read the book because they are interested in Hemingway than will read it because they are interested in bull-fighting. . . . Fortunately the author, fully aware of the interest in his personality, has made a vigorous effort to put as much of himself as possible into this book. . . . We have, then, a series of observations on life and letters that provide glimpses of the mind of Ernest Hemingway; and there are, of course, other less premeditated revelations."

196 Cowley, Malcolm. "A Farewell to Spain," review of *DIA, New Republic*, LXXIII (Nov. 30, 1932), 76-77.

"Just why did Ernest Hemingway write a book on bull-fighting? It is, make no mistake, a good book on bull-fighting, full of technical writing as accurate as anything printed in Spanish newspapers like *El Sol* or *A.B.C.* and general information presented more vividly and completely than ever before in Spanish or English. . . . Being a good artist, he does a good job, never faking, skimping or pretending. He often talks about himself, but meanwhile keeps his eye on the thing outside, the object to be portrayed. . . . His book about bull-fighting thus becomes . . . a book about artistic appreciation and literary criticism, and the art of living, of drinking, of dying, of loving the Spanish land. . . . In a sense, every book he has written has been an elegy. . . . Will he ever give us, I wonder, his farewell to farewells?" Reprinted in *Literary Opinion in America*, ed. Morton Dauwen Zabel, New York, 1937 edition, pp. 506-511.

197 Mencken, H. L. Review of *DIA, American Mercury*, XXVII (Dec. 1932), 506-507.

"In [*Death in the Afternoon*], which is not fiction but fact, his characteristic merits and defects are clearly revealed. It is, on the one hand, an extraordinarily fine piece of expository writing, but on the other hand it often descends to a gross and irritating cheapness. . . . The narrative is full of the vividness of something really seen, felt, experienced. It is done simply, in English that is often bald and graceless, but it is done nevertheless with great skill. Take out the interludes behind the barn . . . and it would be a really first-rate book."

98 Photograph of Hemingway by Helen Breaker, *Bookman*, LXXV (Dec. 1932), 783.

99 "Refuses to See Film of His Novel," *N.Y. Times* (Dec. 6, 1932), p. 27.
Hemingway refuses to see the movie, *FTA*, which was being rushed to Piggott, Arkansas, where he was visiting, for a "world premiere."

00 Review of *DIA*, *TLS* (Dec. 8, 1932), p. 936.
"Praise can scarcely be too high for Mr. Hemingway's exposition of the technique of the *corrida* or his description of the slow un-rolling of the three-act tragedy that is the bullfight. His prose style is irritating, his supercharged 'he-manishness' is brutal and infuriat-ing, but his description of the various *suertes* is extremely felicitous. . . . In fine, it is an irritatingly written book . . . but a valuable one."

01 Review of *DIA*, *Times*, London (Dec. 16, 1932), p. 8.
"Mr. Hemingway is an expert on the art of the bull-fight, an en-thusiast who knows what he is talking about. His book describes with great felicity—of course, his personal predilections are open to personal criticisms—the various *suertes* which go to make up the *corrida*. He shows forth the ritual, the pageantry, the beauty, the commercialism, and the brutality of the *Fiesta Nacional*. . . . If one wishes to understand the technique of the bull-fight . . . this is the man and the book. . . ."

02 Hall, Mordaunt. "A Hemingway Novel in Film Form," *N.Y. Times* (Dec. 18, 1932), X, p. 7.
"Although Frank Borzage's pictorial version of Ernest Heming-way's trenchant novel *A Farewell to Arms* does not reflect the real and gripping quality of the author's work, it should be stated that it is an earnest and occasionally affecting film. . . . Helen Hayes is restrained and lovely as Catherine Barkley, the English nurse, Gary Cooper is sympathetic as Lieutenant Frederic Henry, and Adolphe Menjou is excellent as Captain Rinaldi. Although the film does not capture the spirit of the book, many a tear will be shed over the tragic romance. . . ."

03 Photograph of Hemingway "in Montana this autumn," *N.Y. Times Book Review* (Dec. 25, 1932), p. 4.

04 Fadiman, Clifton. "Ernest Hemingway: An American Byron," *Na-tion*, CXXXVI (Jan. 18, 1933), 63-64.
Translated into German in *Querschnitt*, XIII (April 1933), 235-

373

240. A condensed version appears in *Reading I've Liked*, New York, 1941, pp. 426-430.

205 Kirstein, Lincoln. "The Canon of Death," *Hound & Horn*, VI (Jan.–March 1933), 336-341. Reprinted in *McCaffery*, pp. 59-65.

206 Beer, Thomas. "Death at 5:45 P.M.," review of *DIA*, *American Spectator*, I (Feb. 1933), 1, 4. Reprinted in *The American Spectator Yearbook*, New York, 1934, pp. 231-235.

207 Ford, Terence. Parody, "Men Without Sales: The Trailers of Mr. Hemingway," *Bookman*, LXXVI (Feb. 1933), 140.

208 Quennell, Peter. Review of *TOS*, *New Statesman & Nation*, V (Feb. 18, 1933), 196.
"*The Torrents of Spring* . . . caricatures Anderson's naive romanticism and his various irritating, yet occasionally persuasive, verbal tricks. It reproduces his habit of repetition. . . . besides being a satire on Sherwood Anderson, good-humoured if mercilessly acute, it is also a satire on Anderson's method as Hemingway himself has seen fit to adapt it. . . . [Hemingway] is perhaps the finest story-teller now writing in English. . . . Mr. [David] Garnett adds a sympathetic foreword. He points out, as I have indicated above, that Hemingway's laughter is double-edged."

209 Review of *TOS*, *TLS* (March 30, 1933), p. 222.
"This is the first English publication of *The Torrents of Spring*. . . . It is a parody of those notions summed up in Mr. Sherwood Anderson's *Dark Laughter*. . . . the reader who is unfamiliar with Mr. Anderson's work should need no more information than Mr. [David] Garnett supplies [in the preface] to appreciate this amusing mime. . . . much of *The Torrents of Spring* may be enjoyed as a parody of badness common to a good deal of contemporary fiction: rambling introspection, repetition as padding, shallow lyricism. . . . Efficient and valuable as a corrective, *The Torrents of Spring* is nicely calculated to provoke laughter, be it dark or light; as a story it has its own lively merits and is not a page too long."

210 Dietrich, Max. "Ernest Hemingway," *Hochland*, XXX (April 1933), 89-91. In German.

211 "T.S.E." [T. S. Eliot]. "A Commentary," *Criterion*, XII (April 1933), 468-473.
General article, by the editor. Commentary on Hemingway on p. 471.

212 Eastman, Max. "Bull in the Afternoon," *New Republic*, LXXV (June 7, 1933), 94-97.

This is the essay which provoked the encounter between Hemingway and Eastman, in Maxwell Perkins' office, on August 11, 1937. See Eastman's letter, "Red Blood and Hemingway," in the *NR*, LXXV (June 28, 1933), 184. The essay was reprinted in *Art and the Life of Action*, New York, 1934, pp. 87-101; in *McCaffery*, pp. 66-75.

13 "Prowess in Action," *Time*, XXII (July 24, 1933), 24. Photograph.

Hemingway boats 468-pound black marlin, the biggest marlin ever caught off the Cuban coast with rod and line.

14 Stein, Gertrude. "Ernest Hemingway and the Post-War Decade," *Atlantic*, CLII (Aug. 1933), 197-208.

A slightly revised version of this article appeared in *The Autobiography of Alice B. Toklas*, New York, 1933, pp. 261-271.

15 Soupault, Philippe. Review of *Cinquante mille dollars* (short stories), *L'adieu aux armes* (*FTA*), and *Le Soleil se lève aussi* (*SAR*), *Europe*, XXXIII (Sept. 1933), 140-141.

16 Hart, Henry. "I Come Not to Bury Hemingway," *Contempo*, III (Oct. 25, 1933), 1, 2.

Discusses the "inevitable human necessity to smash the idol that has been worshipped."

17 Fadiman, Clifton. "A Letter to Mr. Hemingway," review of *WTN*, *New Yorker*, IX (Oct. 28, 1933), 74-75.

". . . these short stories [are] as honest and as uncompromising as anything you've done. But that's not enough. Somehow, they are unsatisfactory. They contain strong echoes of earlier work. . . . I can't feel that your stories about sport and sudden death lead to anything large or profound. As literary material, you have developed these things to the saturation point. Why not go on with something else?"

18 Canby, Henry Seidel. "Farewell to the Nineties," review of *WTN*, *SRL*, X (Oct. 28, 1933), 217.

"His staccato style has had the compliment of much imitation. . . . Hemingway, like Ring Lardner, like O. Henry, like Kipling, has created his world and his technique of making it articulate. . . . And what does one find in a collection of short stories such as this new volume? On the plus side, an extraordinary power of observation, worthy of comparison with Kipling's, an observation that knows no inhibitions, but is as limited as was that earlier master's who could do the sensational, but not nuances and subtleties of a matured culture. . . . But the two belong to the same wave of historical culture. Kipling began what Hemingway, perhaps, is ending. The path seems to lead into a swamp." Reprinted in *Seven Years' Harvest*, New York, 1936, pp. 150-154.

219 Gregory, Horace. Review of *WTN, N.Y. Herald Tribune Books* (Oct. 29, 1933), p. 5.

"In this book of fourteen very short narratives, the young man has grown considerably older, has lost something of his boyish, two-fisted, middle-western manner, is revealed for a half hour as the sensitive, disciplined, entirely civilized person that he is today."

220 Svensson, Georg. "Prisromanerna," *Bonniers Litterära Magasin*, II (Nov. 1933), 8-14.

General article. Discusses Hemingway's influence on the work of Walter Ljungquist, on pp. 10-11.

221 Erskine, John. Review of *WTN, Brooklyn Daily Eagle* (Nov. 5, 1933), Sunday Review, p. 17. Portrait of Hemingway by Henry Strater.

"I find so many brilliant things about [*Winner Take Nothing*], in spite of the fact that it is one of the most disagreeable books I have ever read. . . . The book is a collection of stories about derelicts, and waifs, and ne'er-do-wells, every one of whom is a failure, and few, if any, have a single redeeming trait. . . . If [Hemingway] would take a long breath, and laugh a little at us all, himself included, then I would ask nothing better than to see him paint life as it is. No one is better equipped than he for telling the whole truth."

222 Kronenberger, Louis. Review of *WTN, N.Y. Times Book Review* (Nov. 5, 1933), p. 6.

"Without Hemingway there could hardly have been, for example, a gangster literature as we know it, or so much melodrama disguised as realism or sentimentality disguised as bravado. . . . He has superb drive but no gusto, fine perceptions but little sense of identification. One feels that he learns about people by listening to them, not by talking to them. In the end he probably learns more that way, but he remains in some subtle sense a stranger among his characters."

223 Review of *WTN, Time*, XXII (Nov. 6, 1933), 59-60.

"Nobody now could mistake a Hemingway story for anything else. . . . His subjects, as carefully chosen as his style, are almost always illustrations of the same theme: the sportsman caught in an unsportingly tight place and, with various versions of the Hemingway stiff upper lip, taking it like a sportsman."

224 Troy, William. Review of *WTN, Nation*, CXXXVII (Nov. 15, 1933), 570.

"Unless Mr. Hemingway realizes within the next few years that fiction based on action as catharsis is becoming less and less potent as an opium, he will not be able to hold the championship much longer."

225 Matthews, T. S. Review of *WTN, New Republic*, LXXVII (Nov. 15, 1933), 24.

"Sensitive adolescents whose feelings have been hurt take refuge and revenge in ruthless imaginary adventures, often fatal to themselves but always obscurely heroic. The winner may take nothing (in fact, he may glory in it), but he is still the winner. Hemingway has put that adolescent into American literature. This may sound like an attack on Hemingway, and it is. I think he is one of the few exciting writers we have and that consequently we ought to see, if we can, what all the excitement is about. And I think that what it is about is adolescence."

226 "Hemingway Plans to Hunt Big Game in Tanganyika," *N.Y. Herald Tribune* [European Edition] (Nov. 17, 1933), p. 3.

Interview with Hemingway in Paris. Mentions that the Hemingways reached Santander, Spain, from Havana, in mid-August and had been in Paris nearly a month.

227 Rebora, Piero. Review of *TOS* (Cape edition), *Leonardo*, No. 12 (Dec. 1933), pp. 538-539. In Italian.

228 Photograph of Ernest, Pauline, and John Hemingway "leaving Paris bound for Africa," *N.Y. Herald Tribune* (Dec. 10, 1933), VI, 8.

The caption is erroneous in part, as his son, John, did not accompany them on the trip.

229 Jameson, Storm. "The Craft of the Novelist," *English Review*, LVIII (Jan. 1934), 28-43.

General article. Discusses Hemingway's "simplicity," on pp. 37-39, and compares his work with that of D. H. Lawrence, on pp. 41-42.

230 Rascoe, Burton. Review of *WTN, Esquire*, I (Jan. 1934), 86.

". . . at his best, [Hemingway] records life with an expert reportorial cleverness. I wish the war and life had not done so many things to him that he should find it necessary to put his virility so much on parade, because he is a genius."

231 Kashkeen, Ivan. "Dve novelly Khemingueya," *Internatsionalnaya Literatura*, No. 1 (Jan. 1934), pp. 92-93.

232 Review of *WTN, TLS* (Feb. 8, 1934), p. 90.

"The somewhat pessimistic title of Mr. Ernest Hemingway's new collection of stories . . . is appropriate enough: a melancholy note predominates in these tales. The protagonist of the first, 'After the Storm,' literally takes nothing, and that is the burden of the story he tells. . . . A similar effect is more starkly contrived in 'God Rest You, Merry Gentlemen,' a really terrible story in which two doctors describe a case of self-mutilation to a friend. . . . 'Wine of Wyoming' is among the pleasanter stories. In this study of a charming elderly couple we can enjoy Mr. Hemingway's talent for communicating simple pleasures—the pleasures of vague and genial talk, of courtesy and hospitality. . . . There is perhaps nothing in this collection so good as the best in *Men Without Women* and *In Our Time*. . . . But on the whole Mr. Hemingway's singular merits as a story-teller are well sustained."

233 Review of *WTN, Times,* London (Feb. 9, 1934), p. 9.
"Mr. Hemingway's is a somewhat gloomy book. The ironic bitterness of 'A Natural History of the Dead' . . . is reflected to some extent in most of the other stories. . . . A subtler melancholy of spirit is evoked in 'A Clean, Well-Lighted Place' and 'The Gambler, the Nun, and the Radio.' The mood is happier in 'Wine of Wyoming.' Madame Fontan is a delightful character, and her wild mingling of two languages gives us some gay and extraordinary dialogue. Mr. Hemingway's use of dialogue is peculiarly his own. . . . there are few unsuccessful stories. The brutal frankness of some of them will not be to every reader's taste; but the whole will maintain Mr. Hemingway's high reputation."

234 Garnett, David. Review of *WTN, New Statesman & Nation,* VII (Feb. 10, 1934), 192.
This review consists mainly of an explanation of Hemingway's literary manner. "*Winner Take Nothing* is certainly a disappointing collection but we have to be grateful for what our favourite artists give us. . . . Hemingway seems to me to be like a Dutch painter: a master of still life who is at his best in pictures of game and birds, and in describing the things that he has actually seen with his own eyes. His weakness is in dramatic effects. . . . But every one of these stories has something beautiful in it for which one must be grateful."

235 Plomer, William. Review of *WTN, Now & Then,* No. 47 (Spring 1934), pp. 22-23. Photograph of Hemingway on p. 17.
"Mr. Hemingway writes as an artist, in many ways representative of his race and time. . . . His writings belong, quite as much as the writings of, say, D. H. Lawrence, to the literature of protest and escape. . . . To me he is the most interesting contemporary American short-story writer. Vivid, adroit, and an expert in brevity. . . ."

236 Lundkvist, Artur. Review of *WTN* (Cape edition), *Bonniers Litterära Magasin,* III (April 1934), 43-46.

237 Lewis, Wyndham. "The Dumb Ox: A Study of Ernest Hemingway," *Life & Letters,* X (April 1934), 33-45.

Reprinted in *American Review,* III (June 1934), 289-312; and in *Men Without Art,* London, 1934, pp. 17-40.

238 "Hemingway Here, Avid for Lion Hunt," *N.Y. Times* (April 4, 1934), p. 18.

Interview with Hemingway in New York, upon his arrival on the French liner *Paris,* after a three-month safari in Kenya Colony, East Africa.

239 "Stalking Lions Was Exciting to Hemingway," *N.Y. Herald Tribune* (April 4, 1934), p. 4. Photograph.

". . . enthusiastic over the three months he had passed in East Africa stalking big game with rifle and camera. . . . Mr. Hemingway was in such high spirits that he granted an interview, something unusual for him."

240 Praz, Mario. "Hemingway o dell'economia narrativa," *Stampa* (April 6, 1934), p. 3.

241 Photograph of the Hemingways with Baron G. Hoyningen-Huené, *Town & Country,* LXXXIX (June 15, 1934), 43.

242 Photograph of the Hemingways, on board the liner *Paris,* by Hoyningen-Huené, *Vanity Fair,* XLII (July 1934), 25.

Brief item concerning the Hemingways frequent travels.

243 Bütow, Hans. "Ernest Hemingway, ein Schriftsteller aus U.S.A.," *Frankfurter Zeitung* (July 5, 1934), pp. 335-336.

244 Riccio, Attilio. "Ritratti americani (Ernest Hemingway)," *Occidente,* VIII (July–Sept. 1934), 111-117.

245 Conrad, Lawrence H. "Ernest Hemingway," *Landmark,* XVI (Aug. 1934), 397-400.

An analysis of Hemingway's values.

246 Benchley, Robert. "Why Does Nobody Collect Me?" *Colophon,* Part 18 (Sept. 1934), four-page article, pages unnumbered.

Humorous account of Hemingway's inscribing the first editions of his work in Benchley's collection. Reprinted in *Carrousel for Bibliophiles,* ed. William Targ, New York, 1947, pp. 31-35.

247 Kashkeen, Ivan. "Smert' posle poludnya," *Literaturny Kritik,* No. 9 (Sept. 1934), pp. 121-148.

379

248 Rosene, M. R. "The Five Best American Books Published since 1900," *Writer*, XLVI (Oct. 1934), 370-371.

Selects *MWW*; refers to "The Undefeated" as "the best American short story since [Stephen] Crane's 'Open Boat.'" Works by T. S. Eliot, Sherwood Anderson, Theodore Dreiser, and H. L. Mencken were also selected.

249 Hofmann, W.J.V. Contemporary Portraits, III: "Ernest Hemingway," *Literary America*, II (Feb. 1935), 111-113. Caricature of Hemingway by Herbert Fouts, on p. 110.

250 Kashkeen, J. [Ivan]. "Ernest Hemingway: A Tragedy of Craftsmanship," *International Literature*, No. 5 (May 1935), pp. 72-90.

Reprinted in *McCaffery*, pp. 76-108.

251 Nemerovskaya, Olga. "Sud'ba amerikanskoi novelly," *Literaturnaya Ucheba*, No. 5 (May 1935), pp. 99-104.

252 Abramov, Al. "Molodost veka," *Internatsionalnaya Literatura*, No. 6 (June 1935), p. 141.

253 Samuelson, Arnold. "Beating Sharks to a Marlin," *Outdoor Life*, LXXV (June 1935), 30-31, 54. Photographs.

An account of several fishing trips with Hemingway, in marlin waters off Cuba.

254 Cohn, Louis Henry. "A Note on Ernest Hemingway," *Colophon*, I, new series (Summer 1935), 119-122.

The compiler of *A Bibliography of the Works of Ernest Hemingway* points out a number of errors and differences in a dummy copy of *DIA* that had been made to look like an advance issue and sold to a collector as such.

255 Preston, John Hyde. "A Conversation," *Atlantic*, CLVI (Aug. 1935), 187-194.

An interview with Gertrude Stein, on May 3, 1935, during which she gave her views on Hemingway.

256 Canby, Henry Seidel. "Fiction Tells All," *Harper's Magazine*, CLXXI (Aug. 1935), 308-315.

General article. Discusses Hemingway's style. Reprinted in *Seven Years' Harvest*, New York, 1936, pp. 118-132.

257 "Catastrophe...," *Time*, XXVI (Sept. 23, 1935), 17.

Quotes from Hemingway's article in *New Masses*, XVI (Sept. 17, 1935), concerning the hurricane which struck the Florida Keys, destroying the C.C.C. work-camp and killing 458 veterans.

258 "New American and Atlantic Record," *Outdoor Life*, LXXVI (Oct. 1935), 87.

Brief item, "Mako, 786 pounds, [caught] by Ernest Hemingway, at Bimini, aboard his own boat the *Pilar* in June. This mako is only 12 pounds less than the New Zealand world's record."

259 Adams, J. Donald. Review of Morley Callaghan's novel, *They Shall Inherit the Earth, N.Y. Times Book Review* (Oct. 16, 1935), p. 6.

Comments on Hemingway's "unfortunate" influence on Callaghan's work.

260 Chamberlain, John. Review of *GHOA, N.Y. Times* (Oct. 25, 1935), p. 19.

"Mr. Hemingway's *Green Hills of Africa* is pretty evenly divided between big game lore and salon controversy. . . . There are some memorable passages. . . . For example, the one in which Hemingway draws the analogy between the Gulf Stream and the stream of human history. Or the passages about Tolstoy and the Russian countryside. Or the section on skies of Spain, Italy and Northern Michigan. . . . For all his talk about seeing things 'truly,' [Hemingway] is not really interested in the underlying aspects, the fundamental meaning of the human comedy—or tragedy. His book is all attitude—all Byronic posturing."

261 Review of *GHOA, Newsweek,* VI (Oct. 26, 1935), 39-40.

"His enormous technical skill at writing lifts *Green Hills of Africa* far above the usual ruck of big game hunting records. Few books have ever brought African scenery so vividly to life."

262 DeVoto, Bernard. Review of *GHOA, SRL,* XII (Oct. 26, 1935), 5. Cover photograph of Hemingway.

"*Green Hills of Africa* cannot compete with his works of the imagination. . . . The prize sentence in the book runs forty-six lines. . . . The five word sentences of *The Sun Also Rises* were better. . . . A pretty small book for a big man to write." Reprinted in *Forays and Rebuttals*, Boston, 1936, pp. 340-344.

263 Van Doren, Carl. Review of *GHOA, N.Y. Herald Tribune Books* (Oct. 27, 1935), p. 3.

"*Green Hills* makes it plain once more that Mr. Hemingway is not tough and strong, as in the legend about him. . . . he is what is better for him to be, a very sensitive man, subtle and articulate beneath his swaggering surfaces. . . . When he reflects or argues, he is often as boyish as Byron, and he is often tiresome when he goes in for talking and writing tough. He is mature only as an artist, expounding his own art and exhibiting it in prose that sings like poetry without ever ceasing to be prose, easy, intricate, magical."

264 Poore, C. G. Review of *GHOA, N.Y. Times Book Review* (Oct. 27, 1935), pp. 3, 27.

". . . it is the best-written story of big-game hunting anywhere I have read. And more than that. It's a book about people in unacknowledged conflict and about the pleasures of travel and the pleasures of drinking and war and peace and writing."

265 Weeks, Edward. Review of *GHOA, Atlantic,* CLVI (Nov. 1935), 30.
". . . it holds, more than any of his other works, the philosophy of the writer. . . . dialogue which is at once so natural and so unexpected that it swiftly reveals the people speaking. . . . passages of 'landscape painting' in which Hemingway, intent on the perfection of his style, fuses together the sensual and the intellectual. . . . a self-portrait which is masterful."

266 Fadiman, Clifton. Review of *GHOA, New Yorker,* XI (Nov. 2, 1935), 96, 98.
"Not all of this one . . . is about Mr. Hemingway's happy days among antelopes, rhinoceroses, and reedbuck. There are a few amusing conversations, very truculent, in which Mr. Hemingway carries on his feud with the reviewers and insists on his right—I have never heard anyone deny it—to lead his own life in his own way. There's some talk, very well done, too, about war and revolution. . . ."

267 Review of *GHOA, Time,* XXVI (Nov. 4, 1935), 81. Photograph of Ernest and Pauline Hemingway.
"The author writes candidly and with delicacy of his love for his wife, of a minor family squabble, of his affection for the guide, pictures himself as a forthright man with a weakness for bragging, easily irritated and easily calmed. . . . a successful experiment. With its swift narrative and its human conflicts, it is as carefully organized as a good novel."

268 Photograph of Hemingway with Charles Scribner, Maxwell Perkins, and S. S. Van Dine, *SRL,* XIII (Nov. 16, 1935), 10.

269 Hicks, Granville. Review of *GHOA, New Masses,* XVII (Nov. 19, 1935), 23.
"Hunting is probably exciting to do; it is not exciting to read about. . . . The ten interesting pages in the book are all given over to discussions of the nature of literature and the function of the author. It is a subject on which Mr. Hemingway feels deeply, and when he feels deeply he writes well. Would Hemingway write better books if he wrote on different themes? . . . a great theme is important: it calls out so much more of what is in an author. I should like to have Hemingway write a novel about a strike, to use an obvious example, not because a strike is the only thing worth writing about, but because it would do something to Hemingway. If he

would just let himself look squarely at the contemporary American scene, he would be bound to grow."

270 Matthews, T. S. Review of *GHOA, New Republic,* LXXXV (Nov. 27, 1935), 79-80.

"It used to be pretty exciting, sitting down to read a new book by Hemingway, but now it's damn near alarming. . . . the things he says in [*GHOA*] would have gone just as well (better) in a letter to some pal. He thinks he can write a piece about anything and get away with it. He probably can, too. But it isn't the hot stuff he says he knows it is."

271 Harris, Paul. "Please, Mr. Ernest Hemingway!: A Letter," *American Criterion,* I (Dec. 1935), 13-16.
Regarding Hemingway's *Esquire* articles.

272 Wilson, Edmund. "Letter to the Russians About Hemingway," *New Republic,* LXXXV (Dec. 11, 1935), 135-136.
A Russian translation of this article appeared in *Internatsionalnaya Literatura,* No. 2 (Feb. 1936), pp. 151-154. The English version was reprinted in *The Shores of Light,* New York, 1952, pp. 616-629.

273 Silman, T. "Ernest Kheminguei," *Literaturny Sovremennik,* No. 3 (1936), pp. 181-182.

274 Lewis, Sinclair. "Rambling Thoughts on Literature as a Business," *Yale Literary Magazine,* CI (Feb. 1936), 43-47. Centennial Number.
General article. Contains some incidental criticism of *GHOA* and "Lines to a College Professor," a ten-line verse on Hemingway's use of four-letter words, on pp. 46-47. The verse is reprinted in *Sinclair Lewis: An American Life* by Mark Schorer, New York, 1961, p. 617.

275 Fleming, Peter. Review of *GHOA, Now & Then,* No. 53 (Spring 1936), pp. 18-19. Photograph of Hemingway on p. 35.
"Buffalo, rhino, kudu, sable—their pursuit and slaughter Mr. Hemingway ennobles with a kind of savage poetry. Neither hunters nor hunted are romanticized: rather the reverse. The result is several passages of swift, brutal, but above all honest and exciting, narrative."

276 Review of *GHOA, Times,* London (April 3, 1936), p. 10.
"When he tells of the search for game, of the long walks out from camp and long walks back in the evening, we share with him and his party, all of whom we come to know so well during their trip, much of the pleasure of being in such country. . . . It is this fundamental enjoyment which he brings out so well and which makes the

book good reading. . . . Through the thread of the story the author has woven his theory of living a full life and enjoying it."

277 Garnett, David. Review of *GHOA*, *New Statesman & Nation*, XI (April 4, 1936), 529.

"It is not that the subject isn't big enough. . . . It is the author's horizon which is limited here. . . . Perhaps it is partly my own fault that I was disappointed, since I was hoping for a book on Big Game that would have the solidity and specialist accuracy of Hemingway's monograph on bull-fighting, *Death in the Afternoon*."

278 Review of *GHOA*, *TLS* (April 4, 1936), p. 291.

"*Green Hills of Africa* is a promising title, to begin with, for it evokes at once a typical aspect of the country, and one that may be surprising; for in the untravelled imagination Africa is apt to be all yellow ochre. The book has definite design: it is arranged in four sections . . . each written in a rather different mood and tempo. . . . Certainly the book is the expression of a deep enjoyment and appreciation of being alive in Africa."

279 Cook, C. N. "The Silver Parade," *Field & Stream*, XLI (June 1936), 42, 70-71.

The writer tells of tuna fishing off Cuba with Hemingway, who uses "his pet elephant gun" to kill two tiger sharks but in the end other sharks get the big tuna.

280 McIntyre, O. O. "New Eyes on Key West," *K.C. Times* (June 2, 1936), p. 18.

Description of Hemingway's home in Key West, his working habits, and the fishing trips he arranges for his guests.

281 Salpeter, Harry. "Rabelais in a Smock," *Esquire*, VI (July 1936), 101, 118, 121-123.

Article on Waldo Peirce; with some observations on the artist by Hemingway.

282 Dinamov, Serge. "Roman Khemingueya o voine," *Internatsional-naya Literatura*, No. 7 (July 1936), pp. 165-170.

283 Praz, Mario. Review of *GHOA* (Cape edition), *Stampa* (July 31, 1936), p. 3.

284 Item, *Time*, XXVIII (Aug. 17, 1936), 36.

Brief item about Hemingway in Fort Worth, Texas, motoring to the Pacific Coast to fish.

285 La Cour, Paul. Review of *WTN* (Cape edition), *Tilskueren* (Sept. 1936), pp. 172-185.

86 Wimberly, Lowry Charles. "Hemingway and Horatio Alger, Jr.," *Prairie Schooner*, x (Fall 1936), 208-211.
Compares passages from "The Killers" with *Jed, the Poor House Boy*, for traces of Alger's influence on Hemingway's style.

87 Lundkvist, Artur. Review of *GHOA* (Cape edition), *Bonniers Litterära Magasin*, v (Oct. 1936), 622-623.

88 Lewis, Sinclair. Short parody of *GHOA*, "Literary Felonies: Obtaining Game under False Pretensions," *SRL*, xiv (Oct. 3, 1936), 3.

89 Sylvester, Harry. "Ernest Hemingway—A Note," *Commonweal*, xxv (Oct. 30, 1936), 10-12.
Regarding Hemingway's war experiences, his conversion to Catholicism, and the writer's estimate of Hemingway as a boxer.

90 Bishop, John Peale. "Homage to Hemingway," *New Republic*, LXXXIX (Nov. 11, 1936), 39-42.
The writer recalls meeting Hemingway in the summer of 1922, in Paris, when Ezra Pound took him to Hemingway's room in the rue Cardinal Lemoine. Reprinted in *After the Genteel Tradition*, ed. Malcolm Cowley, New York, 1937, pp. 186-201; in *The Collected Essays of John Peale Bishop*, New York, 1948, pp. 37-46; and in the *New Republic*, CXXXI (Nov. 22, 1954), 109-111.

91 Brumback, Theodore. "With Hemingway Before *A Farewell to Arms*," *K.C. Star* (Dec. 6, 1936), pp. 1 C–2 C. Photographs.
The writer recalls his friendship with Hemingway when both were reporters on the *K.C. Star*. During World War I, they sailed together to France to join Red Cross ambulance units. Brumback, who served in the French ambulance corps, tells of visiting Hemingway in the Milan hospital after he was wounded.

92 Bishop, John Peale. "The Missing All," *Virginia Quarterly Review*, XIII (Winter 1937), 106-121. Reprinted in *The Collected Essays of John Peale Bishop*, New York, 1948, pp. 66-77; in *McCaffery*, pp. 292-307.

93 "Writer to Aid Loyalists," *N.Y. Times* (Jan. 12, 1937), p. 4.
Hemingway was named chairman of the ambulance committee for the Medical Bureau of American Friends of Spanish Democracy.

94 Editorial, "Reviving the practice of salutes to the living," *Esquire*, VII (Feb. 1937), 5, 28.
A tribute to Hemingway.

95 "Hemingway Off to Spain," *N.Y. Times* (Feb. 28, 1937), p. 30.
Hemingway, who sailed Feb. 27, 1937, on his way to Spain to report the civil war for the North American Newspaper Alliance

(NANA), was accompanied by the American bullfighter, Sidney Franklin.

296 Chambers, Canby. "America's Southern-most City," *Travel* (March 1937), pp. 32-35.
In this article about Key West, Fla., the writer recalls fishing the Gulf Stream with Hemingway.

297 Photograph of Hemingway and Sidney Franklin departing for Spain, *Newsweek*, IX (March 6, 1937), 38.

298 Photograph of Hemingway with André Malraux and Robert Haas, in New York, *SRL*, XVI (March 6, 1937), 12.

299 [Wright, Donald M.] "A Mid-Western Ad Man Remembers," *Advertising & Selling*, XXVIII (March 25, 1937), 54. Photograph.
Recalls when Hemingway was assistant editor of the *Co-operative Commonwealth*, in Chicago, in 1920.

300 Delpech, Jeanine. "Ernest Hemingway, romancier de la vie dangereuse," *Nouvelles Littéraires*, No. 755 (April 3, 1937), p. 9. Photograph.

301 "Spain Chewed Up," *Time*, XXIX (April 5, 1937), 21-22, 24. Drawing of Hemingway by Luis Quintanilla.
Quotes from Hemingway's NANA dispatch on the Brihuega battlefield.

302 Reid, John T. "Spain As Seen By Some Contemporary American Writers," *Hispania*, XX (May 1937), 139-150.
General article.

303 Ford, Corey. Parody, ". . . And So They Lived Happily Ever After. Part IV: In the manner of *Death in the Afternoon, Death Without Women, Death in Esquire.* Mr. Ernest Hemingway," *Scribner's Magazine*, CI (May 1937), 31.

304 Smith, Francis. "Hemingway Curses, Kisses, Reads At Sylvia Beach Literary Session," *N.Y. Herald Tribune* [European Edition] (May 14, 1937), p. 5. Dateline: Paris.
Hemingway read ["Fathers and Sons"] at a gathering in Sylvia Beach's bookshop in Paris, on May 12, 1937. See facsimile inscription in *WTN* in the *Princeton Alumni Weekly*, LXV (Feb. 16, 1965), 13.

305 "Hemingway Sees Defeat of Franco," *N.Y. Times* (May 19, 1937), p. 10.
Interview with Hemingway in New York, on his return from Spain.

306 Photograph, "Ernest Hemingway Returns from Spain," *Life,* II (May 31, 1937), 76.

307 Editorial, "A Farewell to the Lead-off Man," *Esquire,* VII (June 1937), 5.
Regarding Hemingway's work in the early issues of *Esquire.* Partially reprinted in *The Esquire Treasury,* New York, 1953, pp. 86-87.

308 Miller-Budnitskaya, R. "Ernest Kheminguei," *Internatsionalnaya Literatura,* No. 6 (June 1937), p. 219.

309 "Creator's Congress," *Time,* XXIX (June 21, 1937), 79-80. Photograph.
Report on the Second Writers' Congress, held in New York, on June 4, 1937. Reports Hemingway's nervousness prior to his first big public speech. "But as he began to describe what he had seen reporting the Spanish war, he warmed up eloquently." For Walter Duranty's letter regarding the mixup between his and Hemingway's photographs, see *Time,* XXX (July 12, 1937), 8.

310 "The President to View New Film at White House Tonight," *Washington Evening Star* (July 8, 1937), p. 3 B.
Hemingway and Joris Ivens were guests of the President and Mrs. Roosevelt at dinner at the White House. Afterward the film *The Spanish Earth* was shown.

311 "President Sees War Film | Hemingway Picture of the Spanish Revolt Shown at White House," *N.Y. Times* (July 9, 1937), p. 19.

312 "Hemingway Here by Plane," *K.C. Star* (July 11, 1937), p. 3 A.
Interview with Hemingway aboard a sleeper plane, in Kansas City, Mo., en route to Los Angeles.

313 "Hemingway Links Fate of Democracy with Spain," *Los Angeles Times* (July 12, 1937), p. 1. Photograph.
Interview with Hemingway in Los Angeles. The film *The Spanish Earth* was to be shown for the benefit of the Spanish ambulance corps.

314 Interview, *San Francisco Chronicle* (July 15, 1937), p. 13. Photograph.
Interview with Hemingway, on his first visit to San Francisco.

315 McManus, John T. "Down to Earth in Spain," *N.Y. Times* (July 25, 1937), X, 4.
Interview with Joris Ivens regarding the filming of *The Spanish Earth,* and the benefit showings in Los Angeles.

316 Mingulina, A. "Ernest Kheminguei," *Kniga i Proletarskaya Revolutsiya,* No. 8 (Aug. 1937), pp. 122-125.

317 "Hemingway Slaps Eastman in Face | Clash in Publisher's Office Has to Do With 'Bull' and 'Death' Both 'in Afternóon,'" *N.Y. Times* (Aug. 14, 1937), p. 15.

Hemingway discusses his fight with Max Eastman in Maxwell Perkins' office at Scribner's, on August 11, 1937, over Eastman's essay "Bull in the Afternoon" from *Art and the Life of Action* (New York, 1934). This account is reprinted in Eastman's *Great Companions*, New York, 1959, pp. 65-67.

318 "Hemingway Off to Spain," *N.Y. Times* (Aug. 15, 1937), p. 31.

Hemingway sailed on August 14, on the French liner *Champlain*.

319 "Eastman Claims Title," *N.Y. Times* (Aug. 16, 1937), p. 21.

Max Eastman gives his version of his encounter with Hemingway.

320 Editorial, "Literary Slug Fests," *N.Y. Times* (Aug. 17, 1937), p. 18.

Regarding the Hemingway-Eastman encounter.

321 Item, *Newsweek*, x (Aug. 21, 1937), 4. Photograph.

Item about the Hemingway-Eastman encounter.

322 "J.T.M." [John T. McManus]. Review of the film, *The Spanish Earth*, *N.Y. Times* (Aug. 21, 1937), p. 7.

"By comparison with the picture's commentary, written and presented by Ernest Hemingway, the camera would seem to be mightier than the pen. Hemingway's narrative is, of course, superb. It is terse, powerful, and at times informative; but it is vengeful, bitter and unreasoning. In its contemplative way, the film argues its point much more effectively. Its technique is that of the film document, but Hemingway's narrative makes it a definitely propagandist effort." Hemingway's narrative is quoted extensively.

323 McManus, John T. Review of the film, *The Spanish Earth*, *N.Y. Times* (Aug. 22, 1937), x, 3.

"As it stands it is a great propaganda picture. . . . The bellicose Ernest Hemingway saw to that. His sardonic, vengeful narration, reducing the issues to one-syllable dimensions, converts Mr. [Joris] Ivens's mass of collected cinema fact into a direct, concise and not easily refuted argument."

324 Review of the film, *The Spanish Earth*, *Time*, xxx (Aug. 23, 1937), 48-49.

"It would have been surprising if *The Spanish Earth* had not turned out as well as it did. . . . Besides Author Hemingway, who wrote and recites the infrequent but unforgettably eloquent narrative lines, there were five other unusually meritorious contributors."

324₁ Item, *ibid.*, p. 66.

Item regarding the Hemingway-Eastman encounter. For John

O'Hara's letter, regarding a reference to Hemingway's scars, see *Time*, xxx (Sept. 6, 1937), 8.

25 Root, E. Merrill. "Aesthetic Puritans," *Christian Century*, LIV (Aug. 25, 1937), 1043-45.
General article.

26 "MacLeish on Spain," *Cinema Arts*, I (Sept. 1937), 59, 104.
Interview with Archibald MacLeish, regarding the film, *The Spanish Earth.*

27 Ferguson, Otis. Review of the film, *The Spanish Earth, New Republic*, XCII (Sept. 1, 1937), 103.
"Much of the carrying power in understatement should be credited to Ernest Hemingway's commentary. His voice doesn't come over too well . . . but with his knowledge and quiet statement of the odds against survival, that feeling for the people of Spain which comes from his heart, the combination of experience and intuition directing your attention quietly to the mortal truth you might well have missed in the frame, there could hardly be a better choice. . . . And though it is not a great film, it has been made so that somehow the power of meaning of its subject matter is there to feed the imagination of those who have any."

28 Review of *THAHN, Times*, London (Oct. 8, 1937), p. 20.
". . . this is hardly the book for an introduction to Mr. Hemingway's writing, which spends itself here in an attempt to justify a plain and unscrupulous rascal. His adventures, however, are wonderful . . . the action has an excitement that the novel as a whole lacks. . . . and there are several descriptive passages that seem to have no purpose but to affront the squeamish."

29 Review of *THAHN, TLS* (Oct. 9, 1937), p. 733.
"Within the narrow limits which Mr. Hemingway's scale of values imposes on his material, this is an absorbing and moving story. . . . Mr. Hemingway's gift for dialogue, for effective understatement, and for communicating such emotions as the tough allow themselves, has never been more conspicuous."

30 Connolly, Cyril. Review of *THAHN, New Statesman & Nation*, XIV (Oct. 16, 1937), 606.
"*To Have and Have Not*, while a much better book than *Green Hills of Africa*, and very exciting and readable, represents no sort of advance on his other short stories. . . . In this book Hemingway is the victim of his style. He does not parody himself, but he is unable to tackle anything that does not fit into it."

31 Fadiman, Clifton. Review of *THAHN, New Yorker*, XIII (Oct. 16, 1937), 100-101.

389

"... there are a few episodes that may rank with the billiard scene and the closing pages of *A Farewell to Arms*. One is the conversation in bed between Harry Morgan and his wife, a conversation as beautiful as it is unashamed. Just three pages; unforgettable; poetry, with 'cojones.' ... I think the best stuff in it should have been planed and chiselled into short stories and let go at that."

332 Stevens, George. Review of *THAHN, SRL,* xvi (Oct. 16, 1937), 6-7.

"It is the talk as much as the action that carries you along, if not breathless, certainly well stimulated. ... The idea of the book seems to be that you either live dangerously or you walk around dead. This idea doesn't have to be phony ... and it isn't phony in Hemingway; but it is less than profound and short of impressive."

332₁ [DeVoto, Bernard.] Editorial, "Tiger, Tiger!" *ibid.,* p. 8.

Regarding the lack of consciousness in Hemingway's characters, including those in *THAHN*. Reprinted in *Minority Report*, Boston, 1940, pp. 257-261.

333 Kazin, Alfred. Review of *THAHN, N.Y. Herald Tribune Books,* (Oct. 17, 1937), p. 3. Photograph of Hemingway, in Spain, by Joris Ivens.

"... troubled, sketchy, feverishly brilliant and flat by turns, and only a little heartening. ... [*To Have and Have Not*] happens to be the first full-length book Hemingway has ever written about his own country and his own people. ... it is Key West, apparently, that remains America in cross-section to him: the noisy, shabby, deeply moving rancor and tumult of all those human wrecks, the fishermen and the Cuban revolutionaries; the veterans and the alcoholics, the gilt-edged snobs and the hungry natives ... this is a Hemingway who can get angry and snarl with his heart open. ... where before there was one style for one chill elegy on the war and wasted youth, here there are many new twists and turns; even an unusual clumsiness, for this is a Hemingway who is rather less sure of himself than usual, but a good deal more intense."

334 Adams, J. Donald. Review of *THAHN, N.Y. Times Book Review* (Oct. 17, 1937), p. 2.

"In spite of its frequent strength as narrative writing, *To Have and Have Not* is a novel distinctly inferior to *A Farewell to Arms.* ... Mr. Hemingway's record as a creative writer would be stronger if it had never been published."

335 Lewis, Sinclair. Review of *THAHN, Newsweek,* x (Oct. 18, 1937), 34.

"... in this alleged novel, which is not a novel at all but a group of thinly connected tales ... [Hemingway] demonstrates that all excellently educated men and women are boresome and cowardly degenerates, while un-lettered men engaged in rum running and the importation of Chinese coolies are wise and good and attractive. . . . this thin screaming, this little book of not more than 75,000 words, is Mr. Hemingway's first novel in eight years—the first since the rich and exhilarating *A Farewell to Arms*."

336 Cover story and review of *THAHN*, *Time*, xxx (Oct. 18, 1937), 79-85. Cover painting of Hemingway by Waldo Peirce. Photographs.

"The story is a sort of saga, disconnected and episodic, of one Harry Morgan . . . whose life has been spent in the single-minded effort to keep himself and his family at least on the upper fringes of the 'have-nots.' . . . most readers will agree that Author Hemingway can rest well content with the knowledge that in Harry Morgan, hard, ruthless, implacable in his lonely struggle, he has created by far his most thoroughly consistent, deeply understandable character."

337 Cowley, Malcolm. "Hemingway: Work in Progress," review of *THAHN*, *New Republic*, xcii (Oct. 20, 1937), 305-306.

"His new novel I found easy to read, impossible to lay down before it was finished, and very hard to review. It contains some of the best writing he has ever done . . . as a whole it lacks unity and sureness of effect."

338 Kronenberger, Louis. Review of *THAHN*, *Nation*, cxlv (Oct. 23, 1937), 439-440.

". . . despite a living hero and a handful of superb scenes, it is a book with neither poise nor integration, and with shocking lapses from professional skill. It splits up in the middle, not simply as a narrative, but also as a conception for a narrative: Hemingway, having told the story of a man, suddenly reinterprets it, and finds it necessary to contrast his hero with other men. . . . Structurally all this is awkward and incompetent."

339 Muir, Edwin. Review of *THAHN*, *Listener*, xviii (Oct. 27, 1937), 925.

"The main contrast in *To Have and Have Not* is between Harry Morgan, a fisherman of Key West in Florida, and a crowd of rootless intellectuals who sprawl about the place. . . . Several of the violent scenes are described with Mr. Hemingway's usual brilliant economy. The account of Harry's return in his boat from Cuba with a broken arm is an especially fine piece of imagination. The dialogue occasionally produces an effect of caricature, but it is very good, nevertheless. The account of Harry's death is disfigured by a first-class piece of hard-boiled sentimentality, supplied by the widow. The contrast between the haves and the have nots is unconvincing. But the story of Harry himself is extraordinary simply as a story."

340 Weeks, Edward. Review of *THAHN*, *Atlantic*, CLX (Nov. 1937), front section.

"Three elements are conspicuously present in *To Have and Have Not*. First, action, swift-moving and wholly absorbing while it is on. . . . characterization, whether by word of mouth . . . or by short flashes of introspection in the idiom of the thinker. And social satire. . . . This is not always a pretty world, and in mirroring its brutality Hemingway is only doing with his prose what Hogarth did with his brush."

341 "Autores contemporaneos: Ernest Hemingway," *Hoy*, VI (Nov. 4, 1937), 70-74.

342 Paul, Elliot. "Hemingway and the Critics," *SRL*, XVII (Nov. 6, 1937), 3-4. Photograph of Hemingway in Madrid.

A defense of Hemingway against the critics' reception to *THAHN*. Reprinted in *McCaffery*, pp. 109-113. For Herschel Brickell's reply, see *SRL*, XVII (Nov. 20, 1937), 9.

343 "Hemingway Writes Play in Shell-Rocked Madrid," *N.Y. Times* (Nov. 15, 1937), p. 2. Dateline: Madrid, Nov. 14.

"Hemingway's first play, *The Fifth Column*, was finished here today. It was all written here in the Florida, the famous hotel which has been so severely punished by Rebel shells."

344 Editorial, "Hot Observation Spot," *N.Y. Times* (Nov. 16, 1937), p. 22.

Regarding Hemingway's play, *The Fifth Column*, written in Madrid.

345 Item, *Fortune*, XVI (Dec. 1937), 224. Photograph.

Brief item about the critics' reception to *THAHN*.

346 "E. B." [Earle Birney]. Parody review of *THAHN*, "The Importance of Being Ernest Hemingway," *Canadian Forum*, XVII (Dec. 1937), 322-323.

347 Calverton, V. F. "Ernest Hemingway: *Primevalite*," *Modern Monthly*, X (Dec. 1937), 6-7.

348 Rahv, Philip. Review of *THAHN*, *Partisan Review*, IV (Dec. 1937), 62-64.

"*To Have and Have Not* is among the least successful of Hemingway's works, although in some of the scenes, as in the description of the veterans running amuck, the writing is superb."

49 Photograph of Hemingway in the reserve trenches in Madrid, on December 14, 1937, "Former Reporters for *The Star* Cover the War in Spain," *K.C. Star* (Dec. 31, 1937), p. 4.

50 Pritchett, V. S. Review of *THAHN*, *Now & Then*, No. 58 (Winter 1937), pp. 29-30.

"[Hemingway] has too great a dose of American herd instinct in him to care for prolonged thought about anything. Thought leads to radicalism and he is American enough to pretend to himself that he doesn't like that because radicals are not generally noted for being tough. . . . So Harry Morgan is created, a huge ugly perfect animal, trying to make money out of his boat down at Key West."

51 Druzin, V. "V poiskakh nastoyashchevo cheloveka," review of *THAHN*, *Rezets*, No. 18, [1938], p. 22.

52 Baker, Howard. "The Contemporary Short Story," *Southern Review*, III (Winter 1938), 576-596.

General article. Discusses "The Snows of Kilimanjaro," on pp. 585-589.

53 Cohn, Capt. Louis Henry. "Collecting Hemingway," *Avocations*, I (Jan. 1938), 346-355. Photographs.

The compiler of *A Bibliography of the Works of Ernest Hemingway* comments on rare items and first editions of Hemingway's books.

54 Mirrielees, Edith. "Those College Writing Courses," *SRL*, XVII (Jan. 15, 1938), 3-4, 16.

General article. Discusses the four major influences: O. Henry, Joseph Conrad, Katherine Mansfield, and Hemingway. "So far, no writer later than Hemingway has established an influence even to be compared with him. . . ."

55 "Hemingway Back From Spain," *N.Y. Times* (Jan. 28, 1938), p. 19. Interview with Hemingway in Miami.

56 Coindreau, Maurice-Edgar. Review of *THAHN*, *Nouvelle Revue Française*, XXVI (March 1938), 501-504.

57 "Hemingway Wins Bout | Enters Key West Ring as the Referee, Winds Up as Fighter," *N.Y. Times* (March 14, 1938), p. 17. Dateline: Key West, Fla.

58 "Hemingway Off to Spain," *N.Y. Times* (March 19, 1938), p. 3.

"The author tried to sail secretly and had his name kept from the list of passengers. He boarded the ship hatless and with no overcoat."

359 Schwartz, Delmore. "Ernest Hemingway's Literary Situation," *Southern Review*, III (Spring 1938), 769-782. Reprinted in *McCaffery*, pp. 114-129.

360 "Ot redaktsii," review of *THAHN*, *Internatsionalnaya Literatura*, No. 4 (April 1938), p. 23.

361 Solow, Herbert. "Substitution at Left Tackle: Hemingway for Dos Passos," *Partisan Review*, IV (April 1938), 62-64.

362 "Three-Way *Ken*," *Business Week*, No. 448 (April 2, 1938), p. 37. Photograph.
Regarding Hemingway's role as "editor" on *Ken* magazine.

363 "Air Raid Siren Halts Showing of War Film," *N.Y. Times* (April 25, 1938), p. 6. Dateline: Barcelona.
A showing of the film, *The Spanish Earth*, attended by Hemingway, was interrupted by an air raid for forty minutes. Hemingway was "applauded for five minutes when somebody pointed him out."

364 Item, *Time*, XXXI (May 2, 1938), 24.
Item about production plans for Hemingway's play, *The Fifth Column*.

365 "Adjournment in Book Trial," *Detroit News* (May 14, 1938), p. 2.
Alvin C. Hamer, Detroit book dealer, sought to have the prosecutor's office and the Police Department enjoined from interfering with the sale of *To Have and Have Not*.

366 "Hamer Fights Hemingway Ban," *Publishers' Weekly*, CXXXIII (May 14, 1938), 1935.
Regarding Alvin C. Hamer's efforts to obtain an injunction which would end the banning of *THAHN* in Detroit.

367 "Hemingway Returns Tired of War in Spain," *N.Y. Times* (May 31, 1938), p. 12.
Interview with Hemingway in New York.

368 Nemerovskaya, Olga. "V poiskakh geroizma," *Znamya*, No. 6 (June 1938), pp. 275-287.

369 "Prosecutor Wins Hemingway Battle," *Detroit News* (June 19, 1938), p. 8.
The judge refused to issue a temporary injunction restraining the Prosecutor and Police from interfering with the sale of *THAHN* in Detroit.

370 Item, *Publishers' Weekly*, CXXXIII (June 25, 1938), 2434.
Item about the judge's ruling on *THAHN* in Detroit.

394

71 Brooks, Van Wyck, Archibald MacLeish, and Thornton Wilder. Letter to the editor, *Nation*, CXLVII (July 23, 1938), 96.
Regarding the banning of *THAHN* in Detroit.

72 Marsh, W. Ward. "One Moment, Please!" *Cleveland Plain Dealer* (July 24, 1938), p. 9 B.
Article about Clevelander Jasper Wood's publication of *The Spanish Earth* and Hemingway's objections to the book. Reprinted in pamphlet form by the J. B. Savage Co., Cleveland, 1938.

73 "Ernest Hemingway Sails for Europe," *N.Y. Times* (Sept. 1, 1938), p. 5.
Hemingway planned to visit Paris and spend some time in Spain.

74 Delpech, Jeanine. "Un musicien, un comédien, un écrivain et un peintre nous parlent des livres de Hemingway et de Peyré sur la *fiesta brava*," *Nouvelles Littéraires* (Sept. 3, 1938), p. 8.
SAR and *DIA* and Joseph Peyré's *Sang et Lumière* and *De Cape et d'Epée* are discussed by Louis Buydts, Marcelle Auclair, Alerme, and Roger Wild.

75 Davis, Elmer. Review of *First 49*, *SRL*, XVIII (Oct. 15, 1938), p. 6.
"Hemingway had [*The Fifth Column*] published because he thought it might read well, and he is right. . . . these people are all alive. . . . these people (except Dorothy) are all doing something; whether you agree with what they are doing a hundred per cent . . . or no per cent, they are worth reading about. There is not much to say about [the stories] except that nobody else now living could show forty-nine stories that good."

76 Kazin, Alfred. Review of *First 49*, *N.Y. Herald Tribune Books* (Oct. 16, 1938), p. 5.
"*The Fifth Column* is hardly a great play; it is an interesting Hemingway period piece—I almost said Hemingway short story, so nimbly do his stage people talk the clipped Hemingway speech—for it tells us more about him than it does about Spain. . . . What it comes to is that this play—witty, noisy, full of crackle and home-driven insight—fails to master, because Hemingway has not yet mastered, that contemporary drama of which the Spanish war is but the most violent episode."

77 Review of *First 49*, *Time*, XXXII (Oct. 17, 1938), 75.
"Best of the new tales, 'The Short Happy Life of Francis Macomber,' sums up Hemingway's fundamental credo as well as anything he has written. In comparison with such brief and finished works which combine psychological subtlety with adventure, *The Fifth Column* seems ragged and confused."

378 Fadiman, Clifton. Review of *First 49, New Yorker*, XIV (Oct. 22, 1938), 94-95.

"I don't see how you can go through this book without being convinced that Hemingway is the best short-story writer now using English."

379 Jack, Peter Monro. Review of *First 49, N.Y. Times Book Review* (Oct. 23, 1938), p. 4.

"From 1921 to 1938 it has been the same short story, love and pity and pride and loneliness concealed in a brief reportage of the cruel facts. . . . Professional from the first, their functioning is letter-perfect. But where it was only the surgery that seemed to interest him, there is now, I think, a growing tendency to realize the importance of the patient. . . . [*The Fifth Column*] reads well, it reads like a collection of his stories. There are some fine scenes and at least two characters whose dialect and manners will be amusing on the stage, and of course the dialogue does exactly what it has to do; but it begins and ends casually, neither with a bang nor a whimper, and though this casual but perfect understatement is Hemingway's gift to story-writing, it is doubtful if this is to be his gift to the stage."

380 Platonov, A. "Navstrechu lyudyam," review of *THAHN, Literaturny Kritik*, No. 11 (Nov. 1938), p. 171.

381 Cowley, Malcolm. "Hemingway in Madrid," review of *First 49, New Republic*, XCVI (Nov. 2, 1938), 367-368.

"Hemingway's violence seemed excessive during the relatively quiet decade that followed the War. But now, after the fighting in Spain and China and the great surrender at Munich, it seems a simple and accurate description of the world in which we live."

382 Burgum, Edwin Berry. Review of *First 49, New Masses*, XXIX (Nov. 22, 1938), 21-24.

". . . the play makes good reading. . . . If *The Fifth Column* were only another story of violence and intrigue in time of war, it would be of little moment. But its sensational events are the mechanism through which a typical Hemingway character gets a grip on himself. . . . this collection of his short stories is the record of the road that Hemingway has traveled through the confusions of modern life to a clearer insight into the relation between democracy and art."

383 "Hemingway Back, Sees Food Key to Spanish War," *N.Y. Herald Tribune* (Nov. 25, 1938), p. 3.

Interview with Hemingway in New York, on his arrival aboard the *Normandie*.

384 Wilson, Edmund. "Hemingway and the Wars," review of *First 49* and "The Spanish War" dispatches, *Nation*, CXLVII (Dec. 10, 1938), 628, 630.

"[*The Fifth Column*] opens very amusingly and rather dramatically, and it is good reading for the way the characters talk. But one can't see that it does very much either for Hemingway or for the revolution. . . . The book contains four new short stories which are among the best that Hemingway has written. 'The Short Happy Life of Francis Macomber' seems to me to be one of his masterpieces. . . . this omnibus volume . . . represents one of the most considerable achievements of the American writing of our time." The reviewer also discusses the Spanish War dispatches, published in *Fact* [London] No. 16 (July 1938).

385 Trilling, Lionel. "Hemingway and His Critics," review of *First 49*, *Partisan Review*, VI (Winter 1939), 52-60.

"Between *The Fifth Column*, the play which makes the occasion for this large volume, and *The First Forty-Nine Stories*, which makes its bulk and its virtue, there is a difference of essence. For the play is the work of Hemingway the 'man' and the stories are by Hemingway the 'artist.' . . . Hemingway the 'artist' is conscious, Hemingway the 'man' is self-conscious; the 'artist' has a kind of innocence, the 'man' a kind of naivety. . . . In *To Have and Have Not* and now in *The Fifth Column* the 'first person' dominates and is the source of the failure of both works." The reviewer discusses at length the important part that "critical tradition" has played in Hemingway's career. Reprinted in *Baker anthology*, pp. 61-70.

386 Kashkeen, Ivan. "Ernest Kheminguei," *Internatsionalnaya Literatura*, No. 7-8, [1939], pp. 319-333.

386₁ Fedin, Konstantin. "O knigakh Khemingueya," *ibid.*, p. 217.

387 Bleiman, M. "Poeziya borby i gumanizma," review of *TFC*, *Iskusstvo i zhizn*, No. 5, [1939], pp. 15-17.

388 Pesis, B. "Pyataya kolonna," review of *TFC*, *Literaturnoye Obozreniye*, No. 11, [1939], pp. 33-36.

389 Frid, Ya. "Rasskazy Khemingueya," *Literaturnoye Obozreniye*, No. 18, [1939], pp. 48-53.

390 Berestov, O. "Vecher E. Khemingueya," *Rezets*, No. 7, [1939], pp. 23-24.

391 Grinberg, I. "Geroi beryotsya za oruzhiye," *Rezets*, No. 9-10, [1939], 28-30.

392 Abramov, Al. "Novoye v amerikanskoi dramaturgii," review of *TFC*, *Teatr*, No. 2-3, [1939], pp. 39-50.

393 "Hemingway by K. O. in Big Night Club Card," *N.Y. Sunday Mirror* (Jan. 15, 1939), p. 3. Photo. Dateline: New York.

Accosted by a belligerent lawyer in the Stork Club, Hemingway knocked him out.

394 Adams, J. Donald. "Ernest Hemingway," *English Journal*, XXVIII (Feb. 1939), 87-94.

395 Kashkeen, Ivan. "Slovo o neizvestnom kritike," *Literaturnaya Gazeta* (Feb. 26, 1939).

396 Lundkvist, Artur. Review of *First 49* (Scribner's edition), *Bonniers Litterära Magasin*, VIII (March 1939), 198-204. Portrait of Hemingway by Waldo Peirce.

397 Monchak, Stephen J. Interview with Herbert L. Matthews, *Editor & Publisher*, LXXII (March 4, 1939), 7.

Matthews, *N.Y. Times* correspondent, relates how war writers in Spain were saved from a possible boat crash by Hemingway.

398 Svensson, Georg. "Hemingways tredje roman," review of *Att ha och inte ha [THAHN]*, *Bonniers Litterära Magasin*, VIII (June–Aug. 1939), 481-483.

399 Review of *First 49*, *TLS* (June 17, 1939), p. 359.

"To read it straight through—which is not the way to read it, but a reviewer has no time for sipping—very forcibly reveals Mr. Hemingway's faults and virtues. . . . Mr. Hemingway is a great technician. He has made the 'dumb ox' speak, but, as Mr. Wyndham Lewis has pointed out, what the dumb ox says is so peculiarly uninteresting; and all that goring does get monotonous. So much blood is tedious. But what technique! The interest never flags in watching that exquisitely subtle exposure of brutally unsubtle specimens. . . . But when . . . Mr. Hemingway absents himself from brutality awhile, he can perform prodigies. He can fascinate us by pure evocation, by the tensity of a situation as in that brilliant story 'Hills Like White Elephants,' or by mere actuality. For twenty-three pages in 'Big Two-Hearted River' he can tell us how he pitches camp and goes fishing and catches two trout—that is all—and hold us absolutely." [For review of *TFC*, see *TLS* (July 1, 1939).]

400 Wilson, Edmund. "Ernest Hemingway: Bourdon Gauge of Morale," *Atlantic*, CLXIV (July 1939), 36-46.

For reprints of this essay, see *The Wound and the Bow* (G449).

401 Kashkeen, Ivan. "Pereklichka cherez okean," *Krasnaya nov'*, No. 7 (July 1939), pp. 196-201.

₂ Review of *First 49*, *TLS* (July 1, 1939), p. 385.

"The scene of the play which opens the volume holds possibilities of peculiar drama. Besieged Madrid is a theatre of war in which the action is not restricted to soldiers. . . . In spite of the title, 'the fifth column' has essentially a secondary part. . . . The subsidiary events are exciting and carefully arranged to bring out the characters of one or two persons." [For review of the short stories, see *TLS* (June 17, 1939).]

₃ Maloney, Russell. "A Footnote to a Footnote," *New Yorker*, xv (July 15, 1939), 26.

Regarding Hemingway's footnote on humanism in "A Natural History of the Dead" in the *First 49*, p. 543.

₄ Calverton, V. F. "Steinbeck, Hemingway and Faulkner," *Modern Quarterly*, xi (Fall 1939), 36-44.

₅ Item, *Time*, xxxiv (Oct. 2, 1939), 54.

Brief item mentioning that Hemingway was "at his ranch in Montana, working on a new book."

₆ Mellers, W. H. Review of *First 49*, *Scrutiny*, viii (Dec. 1939), 335-344.

This long review of the short stories concludes: "It is Mr. Hemingway's achievement that, in a fashion rather different from his intention, he really has presented us with the picture of a kind of death, and that he has done so without 'blur.' The death which is the Hemingway mentality is closer to us to-day than it has ever been, and it is stated in his art with the greatest possible neatness and condensation. We can take it or leave it; but we run the risk of being blurred ourselves if we try to be grateful to him and sad about him at one and the same time."

₇ Editorial, *N.Y. Times* (Dec. 7, 1939), p. 26.

Hemingway to be co-chairman of the American Committee for Protection of Foreign Born conference.

₈ "Hemingway Has His Way," *K.C. Star* (Dec. 22, 1939), p. 18.

"*The Fifth Column* at last has found a producer [Theater Guild] who will stage the play as the author [then at his home in Key West, Fla.] wants it staged."

₉ Tucker, George. Man About Manhattan column, *K.C. Times* (Jan. 18, 1940), p. 18.

Regarding the play, *The Fifth Column*, making the rounds of the New York theatrical producers.

₁₀ Allen, Hugh. "The Dark Night of Ernest Hemingway," *Catholic World*, cl (Feb. 1940), 522-529.

411 Watts, Richard, Jr. Review of the play, *The Fifth Column, N.Y. Herald Tribune* (March 7, 1940), p. 16.

". . . after a long and troubled sojourn in Philadelphia, Boston and Baltimore, [*The Fifth Column*] reaches town in an adaptation by Benjamin Glazer as a Theater Guild production, and it can be said that the result is surprisingly impressive. Something of Hemingway has gone out of it and something of Hollywood has gone in. . . . Unquestionably *The Fifth Column* is at its best in its earlier sections, although it pulls itself together in time for a proper ending. . . . It is truly a happy ending in that it saves the play."

412 Brown, John Mason. Review of the play, *The Fifth Column, N.Y. Post* (March 7, 1940), p. 10.

". . . the sorry truth is that, though the script is excellently acted in most cases and holds the attention fairly well, its virtues are mainly deceptive because of the lack of distinction and genuine relevance in its writing."

413 Atkinson, Brooks. Review of the play, *The Fifth Column, N.Y. Times* (March 7, 1940), p. 18.

"During the last few years Ernest Hemingway's *The Fifth Column* has passed through so many hands that most of us have despaired of it. Obviously, we despaired too early. . . . Most of it rings true with the kind of metallic echo Mr. Hemingway can strike off a contemporary subject, and it is notably well acted by an excellent company. . . . Although *The Fifth Column* is an uneven play that never recovers in the second act the grim candor of the beginning, it manages to make a statement that is always impressive and sometimes poignant or shattering."

414 Krutch, Joseph Wood. Review of the play, *The Fifth Column, Nation,* CL (March 16, 1940), 371-372.

"If a consensus of reviewers' opinions is sufficient evidence, it is a fine play and ought to be a great success. In my judgment, however, it is not quite the first nor very likely to become quite the second. Mr. Hemingway's report on the war in Spain begins well. In fact, the first of the two acts is, in its entirety, tense and absorbing. But the expectations created by the first act are never fulfilled . . . and what has begun as a complex picture of life in a war-torn city ends stagily as the love story of a hard-boiled hero whose grandiose gestures may be authentic but are too familiar. . . ."

415 Gibbs, Wolcott. "Saint Dorothy," review of the play, *The Fifth Column, New Yorker,* XVI (March 16, 1940), 44.

"That was Dorothy, beautiful and expensive, a little bit out of Anita Loos, a little bit out of *Vogue* and *Harper's Bazaar*—Mr. Hemingway's half-contemptuous, half-rueful symbol of what has to be given up by men who have dedicated the rest of their lives to an idea. . . . there is certainly not much left of the original Dorothy in the play at the Alvin. . . . I think *The Fifth Column* is astonishingly good."

416 Nathan, George Jean. Review of the play, *The Fifth Column, Newsweek*, xv (March 18, 1940), 52.

"When the voice of Hemingway is allowed its solo say, the play now and again has an honest ring."

417 Review of the play, *The Fifth Column, Time*, xxxv (March 18, 1940), 65-67.

"The acting version is far more dramatic—the first half, indeed, is often extremely exciting theatre. But the new version is also much more romantic, and bulging with high ethical conflicts. . . . Despite its bold beginning, the love affair is flimsy, vaporous, unreal, nearly sinks the play. Only eloquent rhetoric holds the second half of *The Fifth Column* together. And nothing could be less characteristic of Hemingway than eloquent rhetoric."

418 Vernon, Grenville. Review of the play, *The Fifth Column, Commonweal*, xxxi (March 22, 1940), 475-476.

"There is . . . a love story concerning the newspaper man and an American girl, but it is a very weak and trite story indeed and proves that Mr. Hemingway has not yet learned how to write love scenes. . . . Though in some scenes Hemingway shows that he can write dramatic dialogue, the success of the play, if success occurs, will be due to the admirable cast furnished by the Theatre Guild."

419 Review of the play, *The Fifth Column, Life*, viii (March 25, 1940), 100-101. Photographs.

420 Young, Stark. Review of the play, *The Fifth Column, New Republic*, cii (March 25, 1940), 408.

"As compared with the published text, Mr. [Benjamin] Glazer has rewritten the play with more space given to the love story, and has added rape. These love scenes often lack the character and excitement and so on of Mr. Hemingway's style; but the point of view, or attitude toward love between men and women, the approach to the subject, seem to me quite in accord with that found in the novels."

421 Gilder, Rosamond. Review of the play, *The Fifth Column, Theatre Arts*, xxiv (May 1940), 310-314.

"It is far from being a perfect play, but it is a good play, if a good play is one that rivets the attention of the listener, enlists his sympathy and draws him into participation in the spiritual combat which takes place on the stage. The nature of that combat is clearly defined in Ernest Hemingway's text and further clarified—if somewhat sentimentalized—in Mr. [Benjamin] Glazer's adaptation. . . . Much of the effectiveness of the play lies in the forthright, pungent impact of Hemingway's dialogue. . . . Structurally Mr. Glazer's play is far more theatre-worthy than Mr. Hemingway's original version."

422 MacLeish, Archibald. "Post-war Writers and Pre-war Readers," *New Republic*, cii (June 10, 1940), 789.

This speech was delivered before the American Association for Adult Education, in New York. MacLeish blamed the war books of Hemingway, John Dos Passos and other writers for leaving the "conclusion that not only the war and the war issues but *all* issues, all moral issues, were false—were fraudulent—were intended to deceive." See Hemingway's letter to *Life*, viii (June 24, 1940).

423 Baker, Carlos. "The Hard Trade of Mr. Hemingway," *Delphian Quarterly*, xxiii (July 1940), 12-17.

424 Johnson, Edgar. "Farewell the Separate Peace," *Sewanee Review*, xlviii (July–Sept. 1940), 289-300. Reprinted in *McCaffery*, pp. 130-142.

425 van Gelder, Robert. "Ernest Hemingway Talks of Work and War," *N.Y. Times Book Review* (Aug. 11, 1940), p. 2. Photograph.

Interview with Hemingway during his visit to New York, in July, when he was copyreading the final draft of *FWBT*. Reprinted in *Writers and Writing*, New York, 1946, pp. 95-98.

426 Canby, Henry Seidel. Review of *FWBT*, *Book-of-the-Month Club News* (Oct. 1940), pp. 2-3.

For Whom the Bell Tolls was the November selection of the Book-of-the-Month Club. "This is Hemingway's best book since *Farewell to Arms*. . . . As in *Farewell to Arms*, a love story enters, quite accidentally, and becomes a vital part of the narrative. . . . [Hemingway has written] one of the most touching and perfect love stories in modern literature—a love story with a tragic ending which lifts rather than depresses the imagination." Note: This review was reprinted in a four-page leaflet, which was sent to subscribers.

426₁ Perkins, Max. "Ernest Hemingway," *ibid.*, p. 4. Photograph.

A biographical sketch of Hemingway by his editor at Charles Scribner's Sons. Reprinted in *Current History & Forum*, lii (Nov. 7, 1940), 27-28; and in *Book-of-the-Month Club News* (May 1964).

427 Seaver, Edwin. Review of *FWBT*, *Direction*, iii (Oct. 1940), 18-19.

"Hemingway has written truly of real events; he was in Spain and he knew that country and the defenders of the Republic, knew them as a poet knows them, which is what counts. . . . [Hemingway] owes much to the war in Spain; it enormously deepened his experience, widened his horizons. It saved him from 'death in the afternoon.' Now he has repaid some of that debt and we are all the richer for it."

28 Parker, Dorothy. Review of *FWBT*, *PM* (Oct. 20, 1940), p. 42.

"This is a book about love and courage and innocence and strength and decency and glory. It is about stubbornness and stupidity and selfishness and treachery and death. It is a book about all those things that go on in the world night and day and always; those things that are only heightened and deepened by war. It is written with justice that is blood brother to brutality. It is written with a wisdom that washes the mind and cools it. It is written with an understanding that rips the heart with compassion for those who live. . . . It is a great thing to see a fine writer grow finer before your eyes."

29 Chamberlain, John. Review of *FWBT*, *N.Y. Herald Tribune Books* (Oct. 20, 1940), pp. 1, 2. Photograph.

"The new 'return to arms' is a story that has something for everybody. On one level it is a thriller which yields nothing to Malraux's *Man's Fate*—or, for that matter, to Nick Carter. . . . It moves along from high spot to high spot with tumultuous abandon, the style purged of all the early Hemingway preoccupation with finicky Steinesque internal rhyme schemes. . . . On another level *For Whom the Bell Tolls* is a political novel . . . and on still another level the novel is a paean to the landscape and spirit of Spain, a country which Hemingway knows far more intimately than he does his own."

30 Adams, J. Donald. Review of *FWBT*, *N.Y. Times Book Review* (Oct. 20, 1940), p. 1.

"This is the best book Ernest Hemingway has written, the fullest, the deepest, the truest. It will, I think, be one of the major novels in American literature. . . . It is a fine title, and an apt one, for this is a book filled with the imminence of death, and the manner of man's meeting it. . . . Hemingway has struck universal chords, and he has struck them vibrantly. . . . *For Whom the Bell Tolls* is the book of a man who knows what life is about, and who can convey his knowledge."

31 Review of *FWBT*, *Newsweek*, XVI (Oct. 21, 1940), 50.

"For more than 400 pages, in which he builds up a terrific suspense, Hemingway develops his characters, dissecting the anatomies of their fear and bravery, breaking down their emotions like some spiritual chemist. By the time the little band is ready for the final action at the bridge, the reader is so completely one with them that reading the few intense pages describing the end is almost a physical experience. And that is great writing."

432 Thompson, Ralph. Review of *FWBT*, *N.Y. Times* (Oct. 21, 1940), p. 15.

". . . a tremendous piece of work. . . . As a story, it is superb, packed with the matter of picaresque romance: blood, lust, adventure, vulgarity, comedy, tragedy. . . . The dialogue, handled as though in translation from the Spanish is incomparable."

433 Review of *FWBT*, *Time*, xxxvi (Oct. 21, 1940), 94-95. Photograph of Hemingway by Robert Capa.

"*For Whom the Bell Tolls* is 1) a great Hemingway love story; 2) a tense story of adventure in war; 3) a grave and sombre tragedy of Spanish peasants fighting for their lives. But above all it is about death. . . . The bell in this book tolls for all mankind."

434 "Novel Brings $110,000," *N.Y. Times* (Oct. 25, 1940), p. 25.

FWBT purchased by Paramount, for reputedly the highest price ever paid for a novel for film use.

435 Marshall, Margaret. Review of *FWBT*, *Nation*, CLI (Oct. 26, 1940), 395-396.

"It is a long book; it has obviously been written with care and love; it is in a straight line from *A Farewell to Arms* and superior to it; and happily it not only removes the bad taste left in the mouth by *The Fifth Column* but sets a new standard for Hemingway in characterization, dialogue, suspense, and compassion for the human being faced with death—and with the necessity for imposing death on other human beings."

436 Fadiman, Clifton. "Ernest Hemingway Crosses the Bridge," review of *FWBT*, *New Yorker*, xvi (Oct. 26, 1940), 82-85.

"I do not much care whether or not this is a 'great' book. I feel that it is what Hemingway wanted it to be: a true book. It is written with only one prejudice—a prejudice in favor of the common human being. But that is a prejudice not easy to arrive at and which only major writers can movingly express." Reprinted in *Essay Annual*, ed. Erich A. Walter, Chicago, 1941, pp. 149-152; *College Prose*, ed. Theodore J. Gates and Austin Wright, Boston, 1942, pp. 416-421; in *Reading I've Liked*, New York, 1941, pp. 430-434.

437 Jones, Howard Mumford. Review of *FWBT*, *SRL*, xxiii (Oct. 26, 1940), 5, 19. Cover photograph of Hemingway.

"It is . . . the finest and richest novel which Mr. Hemingway has written. . . . Manner has been replaced by style, and the mere author has died out in the artist. . . . Hemingway has done for the

Spanish Civil War the sort of thing that Tolstoy did for the Napoleonic campaign in *War and Peace*. At the end of *For Whom the Bell Tolls*, the reader has not lived in Spain, he has lived Spain."

38 Wilson, Edmund. Review of *FWBT*, *New Republic*, CIII (Oct. 28, 1940), 591-592.

"Hemingway the artist is with us again; and it is like having an old friend back. This book is also a new departure. It is Hemingway's first attempt to compose a full-length novel, with real characters and a built-up story. . . . There is in *For Whom the Bell Tolls* an imagination for social and political phenomena such as he has hardly given evidence of before. . . . The author has begun to externalize the elements of a complex personality in human figures that have a more complete existence than those of his previous stories."

39 Sherwood, Robert E. Review of *FWBT*, *Atlantic*, CLXVI (Nov. 1940), front section.

"Ernest Hemingway is an artist, and his new novel . . . is a rare and beautiful piece of work. It contains all the strength and brutality, the 'blood and guts' of all the previous Hemingway books. . . . he has achieved the true union of passion and reason, and that is why it is so pre-eminently a work of art."

40 "Hemingway Novel a Smash," *Publishers' Weekly*, CXXXVIII (Nov. 2, 1940), 1751.

Item about sales of *FWBT*.

40₁ "Selling the Hemingway Novel to the Movies," *ibid.*, p. 1752.

Item about *FWBT* being purchased by Paramount.

41 Benét, Stephen Vincent and Rosemary Benét. "Ernest Hemingway: Byron of Our Day," *N.Y. Herald Tribune Books* (Nov. 3, 1940), p. 7. Photograph.

42 Bessie, Alvah. Review of *FWBT*, *New Masses*, XXXVII (Nov. 5, 1940), 25-29.

"[*For Whom the Bell Tolls*] is his finest achievement only in the sense that he has now perfected his extraordinary technical facility and touched some moments of action with a fictional suspense that is literally unbearable. But depth of understanding there is none, breadth of conception is heart-breakingly lacking; there is no searching, no probing, no grappling with the truths of human life that is more than superficial." Reprinted in *Baker critiques*, pp. 90-94.

43 "Ernest Hemingway is Divorced," *N.Y. Times* (Nov. 5, 1940), p. 13.

Hemingway was divorced in Miami by his second wife, the former Pauline Pfeiffer, on grounds of desertion.

444 "Hemingway Weds Magazine Writer," *N.Y. Times* (Nov. 22, 1940), p. 25. Dateline: Cheyenne, Wyoming.

Hemingway and Martha Gellhorn were married on November 21 by the Justice of the Peace in Cheyenne.

445 "Hemingways on Way Here," *N.Y. Times* (Nov. 23, 1940), p. 15.

The Hemingways were motoring to New York, on a cross-country wedding trip.

446 [Fisher, Paul W.] "Back to His First Field," *K.C. Times* (Nov. 26, 1940), p. 1. Photograph.

Interview with Hemingway in Kansas City, Missouri. Hemingway reminisced about his days as a reporter on the *K.C. Star* and about World War I. Also present was his friend Luis Quintanilla, artist-in-residence at the University of Kansas City.

447 Rascoe, Burton. Review of *FWBT, American Mercury,* LI (Dec. 1940), 493-498.

". . . Hemingway's most recent melodrama, quite entertaining, yet surprisingly dull in spots, somewhat absurdly pretentious."

448 Chamberlain, John. Review of *FWBT, Harper's Magazine,* CLXXXII (Dec. 1940), front section.

"*The Sun Also Rises* and *A Farewell to Arms* were brilliant evocations of a post-war mood; *For Whom the Bell Tolls* is an equally brilliant evocation of the crusading mood of 1940."

449 Vandercook, Dorothy I. Letter, "For Whom the School Bell Tolled," *Chicago Daily Tribune* (Dec. 3, 1940), p. 14.

Recalls the days when Hemingway was a classmate at the Oliver Wendell Holmes grade school in Oak Park, Ill.

450 Vaughan, J. N. Review of *FWBT, Commonweal,* XXXIII (Dec. 13, 1940), 210.

"As a conservative estimate, one million dollars will be spent by American readers for this book. They will get for their money 34 pages of permanent value. These 34 pages tell of a massacre happening in a little Spanish town in the early days of the Civil War. . . . Personal participation in massacre in order to know it 'from the inside' is no longer indispensable. You can get it from pages 96 to 130 of *For Whom the Bell Tolls.* . . . Of the main story little need be said. It is infinitely inferior to Hemingway's prior work." Reprinted in *College Prose,* ed. Theodore J. Gates and Austin Wright, Boston, 1942, pp. 422-423.

451 Schorer, Mark. "The Background of a Style," review of *FWBT, Kenyon Review,* III (Winter 1941), 101-105.

"In *For Whom the Bell Tolls* we may witness a new style, less brilliant but more flexible, as it integrates itself. . . . If the early books pled for sporting conduct on violent occasions, this book pleads the moral necessity of political violence. A different thing; indeed, a different writer. . . . Because it is another story, this story could not have been told in the older style, and, so, in the future, the flexibility of this new style, with its broader subject matter, gives us a bigger writer." Reprinted in *Baker critiques*, pp. 87-89.

452 Littell, Robert. Review of *FWBT*, *Yale Review*, xxx (Winter 1941), vi, viii.

"It is Mr. Hemingway's best novel, and one of the best novels about that carrion angel, man, which any American has written. . . . [*For Whom the Bell Tolls*] is a succession of crises so sharply, deeply described that they are often a test of the reader's own physical courage. . . . I don't know anyone who so well as Mr. Hemingway forces one to share the intimate, personal, dry-in-the-mouth, pit-of-the-stomach feelings of a character in a very tight corner."

453 Macdonald, Dwight. "Reading from Left to Right," *Partisan Review*, viii (Jan.–Feb. 1941), 24-28.

A footnote explains that: "Elsewhere in this issue, Lionel Trilling reviews *For Whom the Bell Tolls* at length. Here I am concerned primarily with its political rather than its literary significance—as I shall try to show, its shortcomings in both respects are organically connected."

454 Trilling, Lionel. "An American in Spain," review of *FWBT*, *ibid.*, pp. 63-67.

"To anyone at all interested in its author's career—and who is not?—*For Whom the Bell Tolls* will first give a literary emotion. For here, we feel at once, is a restored Hemingway writing to the top of his bent. . . . no one else can make so memorable the events of physical experience, how things look and move and are related to each other. From the beginning of the novel to the end, one has the happy sense of the author's unremitting and successful poetic effort. So great is this effort, indeed, that one is inclined to feel that it is at times even too great. . . . Yet the virtuosity and the lapses of taste are but excesses of an effort which is, on the whole, remarkably successful." Reprinted in *The Partisan Reader*, ed. William Phillips and Philip Rahv, New York, 1946, pp. 639-644; in *Baker critiques*, pp. 78-81. German translation in *Monat*, 1 (Feb. 1949), 90-93.

455 Isherwood, Christopher. "Hemingway, Death, and the Devil," *Decision*, 1 (Jan. 1941), 58-60.

456 "The Hemingways in Sun Valley: The Novelist Takes a Wife," *Life*, x (Jan. 6, 1941), 49-51. Photographs of Martha Gellhorn and Hemingway by Robert Capa.

456₁ *"Life* Documents His New Novel [*FWBT*] with War Shots," *ibid.,* pp. 52-57.

457 Cowley, Malcolm. Review of *FWBT, New Republic,* CIV (Jan. 20, 1941), 89-90.

"In addition to being a fine novel, *For Whom the Bell Tolls* is also an interesting and very complicated and moral document. . . . [Hemingway] is trying here not only to write his best novel, but also to state and justify an attitude toward the Spanish revolution, and toward the whole set of beliefs that dominated the 1930's, besides implying an attitude toward what has happened since his story ended. It is an ambitious undertaking, but then Hemingway has written a very long book, and everything is there if you look for it."

458 Ingersoll, Ralph. "Hemingway Is on the Way to Far East for *PM* | Accompanied by Wife, He Returns to the Wars As Our Correspondent," *PM* (Jan. 31, 1941), p. 12. Photograph.

Hemingway was to report on the war in China for *PM,* a New York daily newspaper. His wife, Martha Gellhorn, was a correspondent for *Collier's.*

459 Delaplane, Stanton. "For the Hemingways, There'll Be no Farewell to Arms," *San Francisco Chronicle* (Jan. 31, 1941), p. 13. Photograph.

Interview with Hemingway in San Francisco. The Hemingways "sail today on the *Matsonia* for Hawaii. From there they will clipper to Hong Kong."

460 Lundkvist, Artur. Review of *FWBT* (Scribner's edition), *Bonniers Litterära Magasin,* x (Feb. 1941), 127-129.

461 Photograph of the Hemingways, "Hawaiian Welcome, on Way to Far East," *PM* (Feb. 11, 1941), p. 6.

462 "Ernest Hemingway Meets Ingrid Bergman," *Life,* x (Feb. 24, 1941), 48, 51. Photographs.

Hemingway and Miss Bergman, who was his choice to portray Maria in the movie version of *FWBT,* met in San Francisco, prior to the Hemingways leaving for China.

463 Guterman, Norbert. Review of *FWBT* (Scribner's edition), *Bonniers Litterära Magasin,* x (March 1941), 215-217.

464 Daiches, David. "Ernest Hemingway," *English Journal,* xxx (March 1941), 175-186.

This study of Hemingway's work was reprinted in *College English,* II (May 1941), 725-736.

465 Photograph of the Hemingways, en route to the Far East, *Town & Country,* xcvi (March 1941), 101.

466 Highet, Gilbert. Parody, "Thou Tellest Me, Comrade," *Nation*, CLII (March 1, 1941), 242.

Objects to Hemingway's use of Spanish colloquialisms in *FWBT*. Reprinted in *20th Century Parody*, ed. Burling Lowry, New York, 1960, pp. 265-267.

467 Greene, Graham. Review of *FWBT*, *Spectator*, CLXVI (March 7, 1941), 258.

"[Hemingway] has brought out of the Spanish war a subtlety and sympathy which were not there before and an expression which no longer fights shy of anything that literature can lend him. . . . Nobody need be afraid that this will be propaganda first and literature only second. It stands with [André] Malraux's magnificent novel of the Republican air force as a record more truthful than history, because it deals with the emotions of men, with the ugliness of their idealism, and the cynicism and jealousy that are mixed up in the best causes. . . ."

468 Review of *FWBT*, *TLS* (March 8, 1941), p. 113.

"[The demolition of the bridge] is an episode full of drama that rings very true. Yet the story, for all its passion, is less successful than Mr. Hemingway might have made it. . . . the style is something of a problem. . . . The habitual use of the second person singular is by itself a bit of a strain, but in conjunction with English, not to speak of American, colloquialisms it is a little absurd. . . . Then there is the unwearied suggestion of oath-besprinkled Spanish speech in the remorseless use of words like 'unprintable,' 'unnameable,' 'obscenity,' and the like. . . . Nevertheless, despite these irritants, Mr. Hemingway holds the reader. The excitement gathers pace, and through it all Jordan's personal drama, the drama of a civilized soul on the losing side in war with only courage to sustain his hope of victory, has pathos and poignancy."

469 Flower, Desmond. Review of *FWBT*, *Observer* (March 9, 1941), p. 4.

"*For Whom the Bell Tolls* is, I think, a greater sustained effort, a more mature, more tightly constructed work [than *FTA*]. It never drops below its own extraordinarily high level; it is moving, breathlessly exciting, and the perfect simplicity and exactitude of Mr. Hemingway's style is once more astonishing. It seems impossible that this book should not be one of the greatest novels which our troubled age will produce."

470 Pritchett, V. S. Review of *FWBT*, *New Statesman & Nation*, XXI (March 15, 1941), 275-276.

"The great quality, as we should expect, is in the talk. We know by now Hemingway's power with the words and accent of dialogue;

but here, in his astonishingly real Spanish conversation, he has surpassed anything I have ever seen. . . . The political portraits are short but they are packed with life, sceptical observation and shrewdness."

471 Photograph of the Hemingways in Honolulu, "Literary Honeymoon," *N.Y. Times* (March 16, 1941), IX, 3.

472 Squire, Sir John. Review of *FWBT*, *Illustrated London News* (March 29, 1941), p. 420. Photographs of Hemingway in Spain, by Robert Capa.
"The 'stuff' is here, as usual with Mr. Hemingway. But, as usual, one has the feeling that he is holding himself in. A naturally sensitive man, he compels himself to describe the worst horrors as though he were telling the time of a train's departure. . . . Even when he is feeling most lyrical about love and natural beauty he holds himself in check, and grunts out short sentences instead of singing. . . . Think what Conrad would have made of this theme!"

473 Cecchi, Emilio. "Pane al pane e vino al vino," *Corriere della Sera* (March 30, 1941), p. 3.
General article. Discusses Hemingway's use of dialogue.

474 Spender, Stephen. "Books and the War. Part IV: The Short Story To-day," *Penguin New Writing*, No. 5 (April 1941), pp. 131-142.
General article. Discusses "Under the Ridge."

475 "Hemingway Novel Wins Critics' Vote," *N.Y. Times* (April 26, 1941), p. 13.
FWBT headed a *SRL* survey, by a panel of thirty-nine literary critics, of possible Pulitzer prize winners.

476 "The Nation's Book Reviewers Nominate Their Pulitzer Prize Favorites," *SRL*, XXIV (April 26, 1941), 7.
FWBT was first choice by a large majority; however, Hemingway did not receive the Pulitzer prize for 1940.

477 Barea, Arturo. "Not Spain but Hemingway," review of *FWBT*, *Horizon*, III (May 1941), 350-361.
". . . as a novel about Spaniards and their war, it is unreal and, in the last analysis, deeply untruthful . . . Ernest Hemingway does know 'his Spain.' But it is precisely his intimate knowledge of this narrow section of Spain which has blinded him to a wider and deeper understanding . . . Hemingway has understood the emotions which our 'people as a whole' felt in the bull ring, but not those which it felt in the collective action of war and revolution. . . . The erroneous use of blasphemy and obscene language reveals very neatly how Hemingway has failed to grasp certain subtleties of

Spanish language and psychology." Reprinted in *Baker anthology*, pp. 202-212; in *The Literary Reputation of Hemingway in Europe*, ed. Roger Asselineau, Paris, 1965, pp. 197-210.

78 Photograph of the Hemingways in Chungking, having tea with representatives of Chinese cultural societies, *China Weekly Review*, xcvi (May 10, 1941), 314.

79 "Hemingway, Here for a Visit, Says He'd Think He Was Slipping If He Had Won Pulitzer Prize," *St. Louis Star & Times* (May 23, 1941), p. 3.

Interview with Hemingway in St. Louis, where he was visiting his mother-in-law, Mrs. George Gellhorn, en route to New York.

80 Mellers, W. H. Review of *FWBT*, *Scrutiny*, x (June 1941), 93-99.

"The Spanish war [has] enabled him to elaborate his stock counters and typical situations with a detailed precision and authenticity which came from first-hand experience—to turn reporting, as he has so often done, into a small kind of art. . . . I think Mr. Hemingway should restrict himself to short stories where the accuracy of his reporter's eye and his limitation of emotional range help rather than hinder him. . . . Actually this book itself contains a number of excellent shorts—for instance some of the political portraits and, finest of all, the terrifying objective account of the massacre of Sordo and his band."

81 "Ernest Hemingway Interviewed by Ralph Ingersoll," *PM* (June 9, 1941), pp. 6-10. Photographs and facsimile of a page of the interview edited by Hemingway, with his penciled revisions.

This interview, in New York, preceded the publication of Hemingway's seven Far East dispatches in *PM*. A map, on p. 7, shows the Hemingways' route and indicates their various modes of transportation.

82 "Eire Bans Hemingway Book," *N.Y. Times* (June 12, 1941), p. 3.

FWBT banned by the censors from circulation in Ireland.

83 Gellhorn, Martha. "These, Our Mountains," *Collier's*, cvii (June 28, 1941), 16-17, 38-44. Photographs by Hemingway.

Of the six Far East articles which Martha Gellhorn wrote for *Collier's*, only this one refers directly to Hemingway. Here, she relates their trip to the Canton fighting front, by way of plane, truck, motorboat, and horseback.

84 Baker, Charles, H., Jr. "Tropical Coolers for Torrid Days," *Town & Country*, xcvi (July 1941), 39, 68. Photograph.

The writer tells of fishing with Hemingway off American Shoals Light and gives a recipe for a drink which Hemingway concocted and named 'Death in the Gulf Stream.'

485 Forster, E. M. Brief review of *FWBT, Listener*, xxvi (July 10, 1941), 63.

"It is full of courage and brutality and foul language. It is also full of tenderness and decent values, and the idea running through it is that, though there must be war in which we must all take part, there will have to be some sort of penance after the war if the human race is to get straight again."

486 Photograph of the Hemingways with Mme. Chiang Kai-shek, in Chungking, *Collier's*, cviii (Aug. 30, 1941), 16.

487 Ferguson, Otis. Parody, "Double-Talk Tales: For Whom is That Bell For?" *SRL*, xxiv (Sept. 27, 1941), 10.

488 Geismar, Maxwell. "No Man Alone Now," *Virginia Quarterly Review*, xvii (Autumn 1941), 517-534.

An enlarged version of this essay appeared in *Writers in Crisis*, Boston, 1942. Reprinted in *McCaffery*, pp. 143-189.

489 Sickels, Eleanor M. "Farewell to Cynicism," *College English*, iii (Oct. 1941), 31-38.

Discusses the "new spirit of affirmation" in *FWBT*.

490 "Hunting at Sun Valley," *Life*, xi (Nov. 24, 1941), 116-119. Photographs.

About the Hemingways, Hemingway's three sons, and the Gary Coopers at Sun Valley, Idaho.

491 "Hemingway Gets Medal for Book," *N.Y. Times* (Nov. 27, 1941), p. 21.

FWBT wins Limited Editions Club Award. Charles Scribner accepted the gold medal—awarded to the book (published in the three previous years) most likely to become a classic—for Hemingway, who was vacationing at Sun Valley, Idaho. In his address at the presentation luncheon, Sinclair Lewis ranked Hemingway with the half dozen leaders of writing at the time: Theodore Dreiser, Willa Cather, Somerset Maugham, H. G. Wells, and Jules Romaine.

492 Lindberger, Örjan. "Svenska romaner och noveller 1941," *Ord och Bild*, li (1942), 418-431.

Discusses Hemingway's influence on Swedish authors, on pp. 423-424.

493 Brooks, Cleanth and Robert Penn Warren. "The Killers," *American Prefaces*, vii (Spring 1942), 195-209.

Reprinted, with revisions, in *Understanding Fiction*, New York, 1943, pp. 316-324.

494 Frankenburg, Lloyd. "Themes and Characters in Hemingway's Latest Period," *Southern Review*, VII (Spring 1942), 776-788.
Essay on *TFC* and *FWBT*.

495 Item, *Newsweek*, XIX (May 11, 1942), 12.
Brief item mentioning that Hemingway was in Mexico.

496 "Out of Oak Park by Madrid," *Monthly Letter of the Limited Editions Club*, No. 149 (Sept. 1942), 4 pages.
Regarding the selection of *FWBT* for the Limited Editions Club's Gold Medal, and publication of their illustrated edition of the book. See (A18c).

497 Item, *Time*, XL (Sept. 28, 1942), 41.
Brief item noting that Hemingway had informed a reporter, at Finca Vigia, that he was going to get into the war.

498 McHugh, Vincent. Review of *Men at War*, *New Yorker*, XVIII (Oct. 24, 1942), 80-81.
"The editor [Hemingway] contributes a twenty-page introduction, in which, as usual, he says some profound things and some that are extraordinary."

499 Millis, Walter. Review of *Men at War*, *N.Y. Herald Tribune Books* (Oct. 25, 1942), p. 3.
"This remarkable anthology presents in one volume the red face of war as it has been recorded upon the imaginations of men. . . . I confess that I liked Hemingway's introduction the least of any article in the book. . . . It seemed to me . . . angry, chaotic, rambling and pointless. . . . Through his shrewd and sound remarks on war literature and war writers, he scatters at random his resentments against the whole business of war and his convictions as to the necessity of fighting this one."

500 Lundkvist, Artur. "Hemingways noveller," review of *Snön på Kilimandjaro och andra noveller*, *Bonniers Litterära Magasin*, XI (Nov. 1942), 733-734.

501 Gorman, Herbert. Review of *Men at War*, *N.Y. Times Book Review* (Nov. 8, 1942), pp. 1, 37.
"It is a thundering panorama that Mr. Ernest Hemingway unrolls before us in *Men at War*. . . . There is hardly an aspect of man's bravery, tenacity and endurance under fire and the threat of immediate and violent death that is not pictured here either in fictional form or in memoirs or in straight history. . . . To cap it all Mr. Hemingway has written a twenty-one-page introduction that is interesting but badly put together and discursive."

502 Brief review of *Men at War, Newsweek,* xx (Nov. 16, 1942), 92.
"Subtitled 'The Best War Stories of All Time,' and who is to question Hemingway, who himself owes his literary life to war. An excellent collection. . . ."

503 Jones, Howard Mumford. Review of *Men at War, SRL,* xxv (Dec. 12, 1942), 11.
". . . what we have is a collection of pieces to satisfy Mr. Hemingway's curious obsession with death. . . . I think Mr. Hemingway is too important an artist to permit himself to 'author' (the book deserves the word) so shapeless a collection."

504 Baker, Carlos. Review of *Men at War, Sewanee Review,* LI (Jan.–March 1943), 160-163.
". . . this anthology of men at war is evidently a compromise between what Mr. Hemingway wanted to include, and what the times made it expedient to exclude; between what Mr. Hemingway thought was sentimental trash, and what his publishers . . . were set on putting in. . . . insofar as it falls short of his hopes, it corroborates his standards—those (I mean) that underlie the best of his own writing. The latest restatement of these standards is what renders valuable Hemingway's introduction to the anthology."

505 Fenimore, Edward. "English and Spanish in *For Whom the Bell Tolls,*" *ELH,* x (March 1943), 73-86. Reprinted in *McCaffery,* pp. 205-220.

506 Item, *N.Y. Times* (March 10, 1943), p. 4.
The Spanish Ambassador to the U.S. protests the filming of *FWBT* as propaganda against the Franco regime.

507 Kirkwood, M. M. "Value in the Novel Today," *University of Toronto Quarterly,* xii (April 1943), 282-296.
General article. Discusses *FWBT* on pp. 290-296.

508 Lerner, Max. "It Tolls for Thee," review of the film, *FWBT, PM* (July 18, 1943), p. 2.
"Hemingway's novel is far greater as a book than the movie is as a movie." Reprinted in *Public Journal,* New York, 1945, pp. 87-89.

509 Adams, J. Donald. Speaking of Books column, *N.Y. Times Book Review* (Aug. 1, 1943), p. 2.
Discusses *FWBT.*

510 Farrell, James T. "Ernest Hemingway, Apostle of a 'Lost Generation,'" *ibid.,* pp. 6, 14. Photograph.
A revaluation of *SAR.* For reprints of this critique, see *The League of Frightened Philistines* (G138).

511 Adams, J. Donald. Speaking of Books column, *N.Y. Times Book Review* (Oct. 24, 1943), p. 2.
Draws a comparison between Hemingway's novels.

512 Cowley, Malcolm. "The Generation That Wasn't Lost," *College English*, v (Feb. 1944), 233-239.
General article.

513 Wilson, Earl. "This Is Ernest Hemingway—In Beard and Bare Feet," *N.Y. Post* (May 2, 1944), p. 17.
Tells of Hemingway boxing at George Brown's gym, in New York, before going to England as a war correspondent for *Collier's*.

514 "Hemingway Is Injured," *N.Y. Times* (May 26, 1944), p. 6. Dateline: London.
Hemingway suffered head injuries when the automobile in which he was riding struck a water tank. He was reported as progressing well after a minor operation.

515 "Hemingway Leaves Hospital," *N.Y. Times* (May 30, 1944), p. 5. Dateline: London.
Regarding Hemingway's release from the hospital following an automobile accident in the blackout.

516 Photograph of Hemingway in a London hospital, by Robert Capa, *Life*, xvi (June 26, 1944), p. 37.
"Five days after his accident . . . Hemingway was out of his hospital bed and, over the protests of his doctors, in an attack transport headed for the invasion beachhead."

517 Shoop, Duke. "Dine on Chili and Wine," *K.C. Times* (July 31, 1944), pp. 1, 2. Dateline: With the American Troops in Normandy.
Relates how Hemingway "led the capture of a fancy German motorcycle, a Nazi staff officer's sedan and a Nazi officer's cache of vintage wine."

518 "Hemingway 'Captures' Six," *N.Y. Times* (Aug. 4, 1944), p. 3. Dateline: United States First Army Headquarters.
Hemingway was credited with sharing in the capture of six German Panzer soldiers, in a small French village in the battle area.

519 "*SRL* Poll on Novels and Novelists," *SRL*, xxvii (Aug. 5, 1944), 61. Twentieth Anniversary Issue.
Hemingway received twice as many votes for the leading American novelist as Ellen Glasgow, the runner-up. However, Sinclair Lewis's *Arrowsmith* was chosen as the outstanding novel. *FTA* was a close second and *FWBT* was fifth choice. A short biographical and critical note on Hemingway is included.

520 Gorrell, Henry T. "A Close Hemingway Call," *K.C. Star* (Aug. 6, 1944), p. 6. Dateline: With U.S. Infantry in the Vicinity of St. Pois [France].

Reports that when Hemingway, Robert Capa, the photographer, and three others approached the town of St. Pois, an antitank shell exploded in the road three yards from Hemingway, who was blown into a ditch.

521 Cowley, Malcolm. "Hemingway at Midnight," *New Republic*, cxi (Aug. 14, 1944), 190-195.

This essay was incorporated into the introduction to the Viking Portable *Hemingway*. French translation appeared in *Revue Internationale* (June–July 1946), 549-554; German translation in *Umschau*, ii (1947), 542-550.

522 Cowley, Malcolm. "Notes for a Hemingway Omnibus: The Pattern of His Work and Its Relation to His Life," *SRL*, xxvii (Sept. 23, 1944), 7-8, 23-25.

This article is drawn from the introduction to the Viking Portable *Hemingway*.

523 Lerner, Max. "On Hemingway," review of the Viking Portable *Hemingway*, *PM* (Sept. 28, 1944), p. 2.

Reprinted in *Public Journal*, New York, 1945, pp. 44-46.

524 Norton, Dan S. "Eclectic Hemingway," review of the Viking Portable *Hemingway*, *N.Y. Times Book Review* (Oct. 8, 1944), p. 3. Photograph.

525 Hicks, Granville. "Twenty Years of Hemingway," review of the Viking Portable *Hemingway*, *New Republic*, cxi (Oct. 23, 1944), 524, 526.

526 "Hemingway's Son Captured," *K.C. Times* (Nov. 15, 1944), p. 1.

Lieut. John H. Hemingway, 20 years old, was captured by the Germans on the Seventh Army front, October 28th.

527 "Hemingway Still at Front," *N.Y. Times* (Nov. 25, 1944), p. 7.

Supreme Headquarters report to quiet rumors circulating in London that Hemingway had been taken prisoner.

528 Cowley, Malcolm. "Hemingway and the Hero," *New Republic*, cxi (Dec. 4, 1944), 754-758.

529 West, Ray B., Jr. "Ernest Hemingway: Death in the Evening," *Antioch Review*, iv (Winter 1944–1945), 569-580.

530 Lundkvist, Artur. "Novellens förnyelse," *Stockholms-Tidningen* (Jan. 14, 1945), p. 6.

A brief survey of modern Swedish short story writing and its debt to Hemingway and William Saroyan.

531 West, Ray B., Jr. "Ernest Hemingway: The Failure of Sensibility," *Sewanee Review*, LIII (Jan.–March 1945), 120-135.

This essay on *FWBT* was reprinted in *Forms of Modern Fiction*, ed. W. V. O'Connor, Minneapolis, 1948, pp. 87-101; and in *Modern American Fiction*, ed. A. Walton Litz, New York, 1963, pp. 244-255.

532 Tavernier, René. "Ernest Hemingway ou la jeunesse du monde," *Confluences*, II (March 1945), 143-172.

533 People Who Read and Write column, "War and Mr. Hemingway," *N.Y. Times Book Review* (April 8, 1945), p. 23.

A war correspondent relates an incident in France and describes Hemingway as "about as battle wise as a man can be."

534 "Hemingway's Son is Liberated," *N.Y. Times* (May 2, 1945), p. 4.

Lieut. Jack Hemingway was liberated from a German prison camp. He was captured at St. Die, in France, on October 28, 1944.

535 Schneider, Marcel. "Ernest Hemingway," *Espace* (June 1945), pp. 98-105.

536 "Herido el gran novelista americano Hemingway en un accidente ayer," *Diario de la Marina* (June 21, 1945), p. 2.

537 "Hemingway Injured in Havana," *N.Y. Times* (June 21, 1945), p. 17.

Hemingway was slightly injured when the automobile in which he was riding overturned on the outskirts of Havana.

538 Cowley, Malcolm. "The Middle American Style: Davy Crockett to Ernest Hemingway," *N.Y. Times Book Review* (July 15, 1945), pp. 3, 14. Photograph.

"Hemingway read [*Three Lives*], and in Paris after the war he adopted Miss Stein as his teacher and critic. He also felt an early, fervent and brief admiration for Sherwood Anderson. His style was not acquired from either of them—from the first it was largely his own invention—but Miss Stein in particular encouraged him to write a strictly Midwestern prose. . . . Most writers of standard English prose keep looking for synonyms, in order not to repeat the same words over and over. This Midwestern style, on the other hand, is based on a pattern of repetitions."

539 "Hemingways to Get Divorce," *N.Y. Times* (July 27, 1945), p. 17.

Martha Gellhorn announced that she and Hemingway would seek a divorce in the fall of 1945.

540 Magny, Claude-Edmonde. Review of *Pour qui sonne la glas* (*FWBT*), *Gavroche* (Aug. 16, 1945), p. 4.

541 Cecchi, Emilio. "Ernest Hemingway," *Mercurio*, II (Oct. 1945), 111-123.
Reprinted in *Scrittori inglesi e americani*, Vol. II, Milan, 1954, pp. 165-178.

542 "Hemingway fait un roman chaque fois qu'il risque sa vie," *Samedi-Soir* (Oct. 6, 1945), p. 3.

543 Cranston, Herbert. "Hemingway's Early Days," [Midland, Ontario] *Free Press Herald* (Oct. 17, 1945), p. 2.
Reminiscences by the editor of the *Toronto Star Weekly*, when Hemingway was on the staff in the early 1920s.

544 Las Vergnas, Raymond. "Deux romanciers de la liberté," *Nouvelles Littéraires* (Oct. 18, 1945), p. 1.
Discussion and comparison of *FWBT* and André Malraux's *L'Espoir*.

545 "Hemingway Wins Divorce," *N.Y. Times* (Dec. 22, 1945), p. 17. Dateline: Havana.
Hemingway granted divorce from Martha Gellhorn on grounds of abandonment.

546 Savage, D. S. "The Realist Novel in the Thirties: Ernest Hemingway," *Focus*, II (1946), 7-27.
Reprinted in *The Withered Branch*, London, 1950, pp. 23-43.

547 Guilleminault. "Un 'Don Quichotte' américain," review of *Pour qui sonne la glas* (*FWBT*), *Bataille* (Jan. 3, 1946), p. 5.

548 Svensson, Georg. "Den siste Hemingway?" *Bonniers Litterära Magasin*, XV (Feb. 1946), 101-102.

549 Anglès, Auguste. "Hemingway ou l'américain tel qu'on le parle," *Temps Présent* (Feb. 1, 1946), p. 5.

550 "Ernest Hemingway Marries Miss Mary Welsh of Chicago," *Havana Post* (March 15, 1946), p. 3.
Hemingway was married in a civil ceremony, in Havana, to Mary Welsh of Chicago, Ill., and Bemidji, Minn.

551 "Ernest Hemingway Weds Writer in Cuba," *N.Y. Times* (March 15, 1946), p. 12. Dateline: Havana, March 14.
Hemingway was married to Mary Welsh, a correspondent in the London bureau of *Time* during World War II.

552 Sigaux, Gilbert. "Ernest Hemingway," *Gazette des Lettres* (March 16, 1946), p. 7.

53 Lévy, Yves. Review of *Pour qui sonne le glas* (*FWBT*) and *En avoir ou pas* (*THAHN*), *Paru*, No. 17 (April 1946), pp. 41-46.

54 De Caro, Lucio. "Hemingway o la disperazione," *Società Nuova,* ii (April 1946), 31-35.

55 Bizzari, Edoardo. "Croce con prefazione di Hemingway," *Fiera Letteraria,* ii (May 2, 1946), 4.
   Regarding Hemingway's preface to *Treasury of the Free World.* See (B44).

56 Rousseaux, André. "Les nouveaux romans d'Hemingway," *Littéraire* (May 4, 1946), p. 2.
   Discusses *FWBT* and *THAHN*.

57 "l. m." "Ernest Hemingway," *Emporium*, civ (July 1946) , 29-31. Photograph. In Italian.

58 Sartre, Jean-Paul. "American Novelists in French Eyes," *Atlantic*, clxxviii (Aug. 1946), 114-118.
   General article. "The greatest literary development in France between 1929 and 1939 was the discovery of Faulkner, Dos Passos, Hemingway, Caldwell, Steinbeck. The choice of these authors, many people have told me, was due to Professor Maurice Coindreau of Princeton, who sent us their works in translation with excellent prefaces. . . ."

59 "Hemingway's Wife in Hospital," *N.Y. Times* (Aug. 21, 1946), p. 29. Dateline: Casper, Wyoming.
   Mary Hemingway was hospitalized on their trip from Cuba to Ketchum, Idaho.

60 McNulty, John. Review of the film, *The Killers, New Yorker*, xxii (Sept. 7, 1946), 49-50.
   "The movie starts with a terrifying quietness and maintains throughout the intensity that distinguished Hemingway's story."

61 Cowley, Malcolm. "U.S. Books Abroad," *Life*, xxi (Sept. 16, 1946), 6.
   General article. "Of all American authors, Ernest Hemingway is the most widely admired and imitated for his technique."

62 Lévy, Yves. Review of *Dix indiens* (short stories), *Paru,* No. 24 (Nov. 1946), pp. 51-53.

63 Las Vergnas, Raymond. "Romanciers américains contemporains," *Cahiers des Langues Modernes* (Dec. 1946), pp. 165-181.
   General article.

64 Item, *Time*, xlviii (Dec. 16, 1946), 45.
   Item about Hemingway shooting ducks on Gardiner's Island, following his arrival in New York from Idaho.

565 Linscott, Roger Bourne. On the Books column, *N.Y. Herald Tribune Book Review* (Dec. 29, 1946), p. 13.
Interview with Hemingway, in New York, prior to his return to Cuba for Christmas.

566 Warren, Robert Penn. "Hemingway," *Kenyon Review*, IX (Winter 1947), 1-28.
For reprints of this essay, see *Selected Essays* (G438).

567 Frohock, W. M. "Ernest Hemingway: Violence and Discipline," *Southwest Review*, XXXII (Winter 1947), 89-97, Part I; (Spring 1947), 184-193, Part II. Reprinted in *McCaffery*, pp. 262-291.

568 Desternes, Jean. "Que pensez-vous de la littérature américaine?" *Combat* (Jan. 4, 1947), p. 2; (Jan. 5–6, 1947), p. 2; (Jan. 17, 1947), p. 2; (Jan. 26–27, 1947), p. 2; (Feb. 2–3, 1947), p. 2.
Replies by Louis-René des Forêts, Georges Charensol, Albert Camus, François Mauriac, and Emile Henriot, respectively. Hemingway's work is discussed in each article in the series.

569 "Indestructible," Talk of the Town column, *New Yorker*, XXII (Jan. 4, 1947), 20.
Interview with Hemingway in New York.

570 Chadourne, Marc. "Rencontre avec Hemingway," *Carrefour* (Jan. 30, 1947), pp. 1, 2.

571 Butcher, Fanny. The Literary Spotlight column, *Chicago Sunday Tribune* (March 30, 1947), Magazine of Books, p. 10. Dateline: Havana.
Regarding a visit with the Hemingways at Finca Vigia.

571₁ "Thalia." "Saints Days in Cuba Are Days of Gaiety and Entertainment," *ibid.*, VII, 1.
Includes a description of Finca Vigia.

572 Astre, Georges-Albert. "Sur le roman américain," *Critique*, II (April 1947), 302-315.
General article.

573 Wallace, Henry. "Bronze Star Awarded to Ernest Hemingway," *Havana Post* (June 14, 1947), p. 1. Photograph.
Hemingway received the United States War Department's Bronze Star Medal for meritorious service during the war, at a ceremony held at the United States Embassy in Havana.

574 "Hemingway Receives U.S. Award," *N.Y. Times* (June 14, 1947), p. 16. Dateline: Havana.
See above entry.

575 Peyre, Henri. "American Literature Through French Eyes," *Virginia Quarterly Review*, XXIII (Summer 1947), 421-438.
General article. "The great names of American fiction are thus in French eyes Hemingway, Steinbeck, Dos Passos, and Faulkner."

576 de Fels, Marthe. "A la recherche d'Hemingway," *Bataille* (July 16, 1947), p. 6.
Interview with Hemingway in Havana.

577 Las Vergnas, Raymond. "Ernest Hemingway," *Nouvelles Littéraires* (Sept. 4, 1947), pp. 1, 2.

578 Anderssen, Odd-Stein. "Ernest Hemingway," *Vinduet*, I (Nov. 1947), 253-267. In Swedish.

579 Item, *Newsweek*, XXX (Nov. 24, 1947), 16.
Item about Hemingway in Sun Valley, Idaho, working on his new book.

580 Savelli, Giovanni. "Hemingway e il Novecento-americano," *Humanitas*, II (Dec. 1947), 1230-1233.

581 McMahon, T. "Hemingway: Philosophy of Action," *Yale Literary Magazine*, CXV (Dec. 1947), 16-20.

582 Daniel, Robert A. "Hemingway and His Heroes," *Queen's Quarterly*, LIV (Winter 1947–1948), 471-485.

583 Photograph of Hemingway in Cuba, *Holiday*, III (Jan. 1948), 52.

584 Wilson, Earl. It Happened Last Night column, *N.Y. Post* (Feb. 26, 1948), p. 30. Dateline: Havana.
Relates details of a visit with the Hemingways at Finca Vigia.

585 Schorer, Mark. "Technique as Discovery," *Hudson Review*, I (Spring 1948), 67-87.
General article. Hemingway's work is discussed on pp. 84-86.

586 Photograph of the Hemingways at Sun Valley, Idaho, *Town & Country*, CII (April 1948), 90.

587 Lavergne, Edouard. "Der Dichter Ernest Hemingway," *Neue Zeitung* (April 13, 1948).

588 Ekelöf, Gunnar. "Tjugu år efteråt," review of *Och solen har sin gång* (*SAR*), *Bonniers Litterära Magasin*, XVII (July–Aug. 1948), 449.

589 Savage, D. S. "Ernest Hemingway," *Hudson Review*, I (Autumn 1948), 380-401.

590 Young, Philip. "Hemingway's *A Farewell to Arms*," *Explicator*, VII (Oct. 1948), Item 7.

591 Praz, Mario. "Hemingway in Italy," *Partisan Review*, xv (Oct. 1948), 1086-1100. Reprinted in *Cronache letterie anglossasoni*, Rome, 1951, pp. 202-212; in *Baker anthology*, pp. 116-130.

592 Photograph of the Hemingways vacationing in Italy, *Time*, lii (Oct. 25, 1948), 40.

593 "Hemingway cherche les glas perdus," *Bataille* (Oct. 27, 1948), p. 5. Interview with Hemingway in Paris.

594 Photograph of the Hemingways in Venice, *N.Y. Times Magazine* (Nov. 14, 1948), p. 9.

595 Hemphill, George. "Hemingway and James," *Kenyon Review*, xi (Winter 1949), 50-60.
This essay on Hemingway and Henry James was reprinted in *McCaffery*, pp. 329-339.

596 Cowley, Malcolm. "A Portrait of Mister Papa," *Life*, xxv (Jan. 10, 1949), 86-101. Photographs. Reprinted in *McCaffery*, pp. 34-56. A German translation appeared in *Monat*, vii (Dec. 1954), 204-210.

597 Halliday, E. M. "Hemingway's *In Our Time*," *Explicator*, vii (March 1949), Item 35.

598 Ross, Lillian. Profile, "El Único Matador," *New Yorker*, xxv (March 12, 1949), 34-45, Part i; (March 26, 1949), 32-56, Part iii.
Hemingway was one of the people interviewed for this Profile of Sidney Franklin, the American bullfighter. Reprinted in *Reporting*, New York, 1964, pp. 143-186.

599 Photographic essay, "Giant of the Storytellers," *Coronet*, xxv (April 1949), 16-17.

600 Walcutt, Charles C. "Hemingway's 'The Snows of Kilimanjaro,' " *Explicator*, vii (April 1949), Item 43.

601 "Ernest Hemingway in Hospital," *St. Louis Post-Dispatch* (April 1, 1949), p. 2 A. Dateline: Venice.
Hemingway entered Padua Hospital for treatment of a slight facial infection.

602 Gordon, Caroline. "Notes on Hemingway and Kafka," *Sewanee Review*, lvii (April–June 1949), 215-226.

603 "Ernest Hemingway in Cristobal," *N.Y. Times* (May 23, 1949), p. 9. Dateline: Canal Zone.
Hemingway arrived from Italy, en route to Cuba.

604 Silvi, Valeria. Review of *I quarantanove racconti* (*First 49*), *Ponte*, v (June 1949), 776-778.

05 Forestier, Marie. "Un grand romantique: Ernest Hemingway," *Revue Nouvelle* (June 15, 1949), pp. 570-579.

06 Photograph of the Hemingways in Venice, "For Whom the Gondolier Poles," *N.Y. Times Book Review* (June 19, 1949), p. 6.

07 Geismar, Maxwell. "The Position of Ernest Hemingway. Part II: Notes from a Critic on a Novelist's Work," *N.Y. Times Book Review* (July 31, 1949), p. 1. Photograph.

For Part I: "Notes from a Novelist on His System of Work" by Hemingway, see (C352). Part II was reprinted in *American Moderns*, New York, 1958, pp. 54-58. A German translation appeared in *Amerikanische Rundschau*, v (Oct.–Nov. 1949), 118-121.

08 Hackett, Francis. "Hemingway: *A Farewell to Arms*," SRL, XXXII (Aug. 6, 1949), 32-33.

A reappraisal.

8₁ Photographs of writers of the twenties, including Hemingway, *ibid.*, pp. 108-109.

8₂ Photograph of Hemingway with fellow war correspondents, during World War II, *ibid.*, p. 120.

09 Wallenstein, Marcel. "When Ernest Hemingway Led Troops to Free France," *K.C. Star* (Sept. 4, 1949), p. 1 C. Photographs.

An account of Hemingway's actions from August 14 to August 25, 1944, the day that Paris was liberated, and of subsequent efforts by the U.S. Army to have him court-martialed for taking an active part in the hostilities at Rambouillet.

10 Morris, Lloyd. "Heritage of a Generation of Novelists: Anderson and Dreiser, Hemingway, Faulkner, Farrell and Steinbeck," *N.Y. Herald Tribune Book Review* (Sept. 25, 1949), p. 12. Twenty-Fifth Anniversary Issue.

10₁ Kazin, Alfred. Brief appraisal, *ibid.*, p. 25.

Gives his reasons for choosing *FTA* as one of the three most memorable books of the previous twenty-five years.

11 Trilling, Lionel. "Contemporary American Literature and Its Relation to Ideas," *American Quarterly*, 1 (Fall 1949), 195-208.

General article. Reprinted in *The American Writer and the European Tradition*, ed. Margaret Denny and William H. Gilman, Minneapolis, 1950, pp. 146-150.

12 Tedlock, E. W., Jr. "Hemingway's 'The Snows of Kilimanjaro,' " *Explicator*, VIII (Oct. 1949), Item 7.

13 "Hemingway Novel Slated for March," *N.Y. Times* (Oct. 13, 1949), p. 25.

Announcement by Scribner's of forthcoming publication of *Across the River and Into the Trees.* Hemingway's publishers disclosed that during the previous winter, in Italy, a fragment of shotgun wadding had lodged in his eye, causing blood poisoning, and the doctors had despaired of his recovery.

614 Lyons, Leonard. The Lyons Den column, *N.Y. Post* (Nov. 18, 1949), p. 38.

Regarding the Hemingways visit to New York.

615 Trilling, Diana. Review of Elio Vittorini's *In Sicily, N.Y. Times Book Review* (Nov. 27, 1949), pp. 1, 37.

Appraises Hemingway's introduction as "endlessly suggestive, and vulgar. . . . He makes it an occasion for an attack upon criticism."

616 Mostly About People column, *N.Y. Herald Tribune* [European Edition] (Dec. 26, 1949), p. 4.

Hemingway finished his new novel, *ARIT*, in the Paris Ritz, then left for Venice.

617 Halliday, Ernest Milton. "Narrative Technique in the Novels of Ernest Hemingway," *Microfilm Abstracts*, x, ii (1950), 110-111.

Abstract from doctoral dissertation, University of Michigan, 1950.

618 Gallup, Donald C. "The Making of *The Making of Americans*," *New Colophon*, III (1950), 54-74. Facsimile of Hemingway letter, on p. 65.

Quotes correspondence between Gertrude Stein and Hemingway, in the early 1920s, regarding publication of her book in the *Transatlantic Review.* See (F49), (F50), (F51), (F53), (F54).

619 Wallenstein, Marcel. "A Tip From Gertrude Stein Started Hemingway to Top," *K.C. Times* (Jan. 5, 1950), p. 13. Dateline: Paris.

About Hemingway finishing *ARIT* in Paris, and about his years there in the 1920s, when Gertrude Stein advised him to give up newspaper work if he wished to become a writer.

620 Photograph, "Roaring Charm," *Flair*, 1 (Feb. 1950), 110-111.

621 Engstrom, Alfred G. "Dante, Flaubert, and 'The Snows of Kilimanjaro,'" *Modern Language Notes*, LXV (March 1950), 203-205.

"The Holy Hill for Dante is that of Righteousness. For Flaubert, it is Art in its perfection. But for Hemingway, in 'The Snows of Kilimanjaro,' it is Death."

622 "The Hemingways in Cuba," *Harper's Bazaar*, LXXXIV (March 1, 1950), 172-173. Photographs by Paul Radkai.

23 Lyons, Leonard. The Lyons Den column, *N.Y. Post* (March 30, 1950), p. 30.

Quotes a letter from Hemingway regarding his five "home towns": Paris, Venice, Ketchum, Key West, and Havana. Partially reprinted in *Time*, LV (April 10, 1950), 36.

24 "Shapers of the Modern Novel: A Catalog of an Exhibition," *Princeton University Library Chronicle*, XII (Spring 1950), 134-141.

Fifteen Hemingway items are listed on pp. 136-137.

25 Hansen, Harry. "Hemingway Back, Carrying His Hush-Hush Manuscript," *Chicago Sunday Tribune* (April 9, 1950), IV, 10. Dateline: New York.

Hemingway arrived in New York, on March 27, to confer with Wallace Meyer, his editor at Scribner's, regarding changes in *ARIT* for book publication.

26 "Title Defender," *Newsweek*, XXXV (April 10, 1950), 46. Photograph.

Item about Hemingway defending his title as "the World's Worst Dressed Man," at the Stork Club.

27 Ross, Lillian. Profile, "How Do You Like It Now, Gentlemen?" *New Yorker*, XXVI (May 13, 1950), 36-62. Drawing of Hemingway by Reginald Marsh.

The title is taken from an oft-repeated phrase of Hemingway's. Reprinted, with some revisions, in *Portrait of Hemingway*, New York, 1961; in *Weeks collection*, pp. 17-39; in *Reporting*, New York, 1964, pp. 194-222. Translated into Italian by Alfredo Todisco, "L'atleta Hemingway," *Mondo*, II (Dec. 2, 1950), 11-12.

28 Sigaux, Gilbert. "Le Monde Hemingway," *Gazette des Lettres* (May 27, 1950), p. 7.

29 Photograph of Hemingway at Finca Vigia, "El Hombre," *N.Y. Times Book Review* (June 11, 1950), p. 4.

30 Brereton, Geoffrey. Review of *DIA* (new Cape edition), *New Statesman & Nation*, XXXIX (June 24, 1950), 716-717.

31 Williams, Tennessee. "A Writer's Quest For a Parnassus," *N.Y. Times Magazine* (Aug. 13, 1950), pp. 16, 35. Caricature.

General article. Includes a long paragraph on Hemingway, Venice, and *ARIT*.

32 Rovere, Richard H. Review of *ARIT*, *Harper's Magazine*, CCI (Sept. 1950), 104-106.

"Ernest Hemingway's *Across the River and Into the Trees* is a disappointing novel. Though it has moments of strength and beauty, it also has moments of tawdriness. . . . It is an incredibly talky book. It is almost garrulous, a strange thing for a Hemingway novel to be. The reason, I think, is that Hemingway is here using dialogue not as a tool of narrative but simply as a means for the author to unburden himself of opinions."

633 Connolly, Cyril. Review of *ARIT, Sunday Times*, London (Sept. 3, 1950), p. 3.
"It is not uncommon for a famous writer to produce one thoroughly bad book. . . . Alas and in fact, *Across the River and Into the Trees* can be summed up in one word, lamentable. . . . The novel fails because it is constructed from a false sense of values. . . . If Mr. Hemingway is to turn the corner he will have to cease to be a repressed intellectual, as ashamed of the mind as he is outspoken about the body; he will have to study chess instead of baseball. . . ."
Reprinted in *Previous Convictions*, London, 1963, pp. 290-292.

634 Gannett, Lewis. Review of *ARIT, N.Y. Herald Tribune* (Sept. 7, 1950), p. 23.
"There are wonderful flashes of the old Hemingway in the book —the tacit understanding between the colonel and his American driver, for instance. . . . There is the old Hemingway passion for good shooting, and there is the dream-girl who is a dream of all fair women and never more than a dream, like almost all the Hemingway women. . . . Some of the book is Hemingway at his worst, and the whole does not add up to Hemingway at his best."

635 Poore, Charles. Review of *ARIT, N.Y. Times* (Sept. 7, 1950), p. 29.
"After a decade of reading road-company-Hemingways, it is a great pleasure to be reading Hemingway himself again. . . . The swarming Hemingwayfarers have never matched his gift for stinging comedy, his cadences and his profoundly tragic sense of life. . . . Here, then, is Hemingway's new novel, a little less than perfect, but proof positive that he is still the old master."

636 Jackson, Joseph Henry. Review of *ARIT, San Francisco Chronicle* (Sept. 7, 1950), p. 18.
"There is no question about the Hemingway touch. . . . That is here, though too often it resembles a parody of Hemingway at his best. . . . along with many others who have lived and read through the decades in which Mr. Hemingway has been a unique literary influence, I shall wait for the longer, more important novel on which he is reported to have been engaged for some time. It should provide the clue to whether the old Hemingway is still—as the Colonel might put it—'operating.' "

637 Strong, L.A.G. Review of *ARIT, Spectator*, CLXXXV (Sept. 8, 1950), 279.

"Mr. Hemingway has not won his reputation for nothing, and his great gifts survive. The descriptive writing is assured, the dialogue, as always, excellent. . . . the colonel is immature . . . still in the secret-society, schoolboy stage of development, and his reaction to the threat of death is to drink himself more swiftly towards it. This is a perfectly understandable reaction, but it does not qualify him as a tragic figure."

38 Zabel, Morton Dauwen. Review of *ARIT*, *Nation*, CLXXI (Sept. 9, 1950), 230.

". . . an occasion for little but exasperated depression. But we are promised another novel soon. We must wait for it. And see." Reprinted in *Craft and Character in Modern Fiction*, New York, 1957, pp. 317-321.

39 Kazin, Alfred. Review of *ARIT*, *New Yorker*, XXVI (Sept. 9. 1950), 101-103.

"The book was obviously written under great tension . . . and can only distress anyone who admires Hemingway. . . . It is wonderful to know . . . that this book is not his last word."

40 Geismar, Maxwell. Review of *ARIT*, *SRL*, XXXIII (Sept. 9, 1950), 18, 19. Photograph by Paul Radkai.

"It is not only Hemingway's worst novel; it is a synthesis of everything that is bad in his previous work and it throws a doubtful light on the future. It is so dreadful, in fact, that it begins to have its own morbid fascination and is almost impossible, as they say, to put down." Reprinted in *American Moderns*, New York, 1958, pp. 59-61.

41 Meyer, Ben F. "Hemingway Novel of Venice Completed at Home in Cuba," *K.C. Star* (Sept. 10, 1950), p. 1 C. Dateline: San Francisco de Paula, Cuba.

Interview with Hemingway at Finca Vigia.

42 Cowley, Malcolm. Review of *ARIT*, *N.Y. Herald Tribune Book Review* (Sept. 10, 1950), pp. 1, 16.

"It is beautifully finished as a piece of writing; in that sense it is what we expect of Hemingway; but it is still below the level of his earlier novels, which we studied so eagerly and from which we learned so much. . . . For all its skill and honesty, *Across the River and Into the Trees* is a tired book compared with those others. To see what the new Hemingway can do we still have to wait for his big novel."

43 O'Hara, John. Review of *ARIT*, *N.Y. Times Book Review* (Sept. 10, 1950), pp. 1, 30-31. Photographs.

"The most important author living today, the outstanding author since the death of Shakespeare, has brought out a new novel. The title of the novel is *Across the River and Into the Trees*. The author, of course, is Ernest Hemingway, the most important, the outstanding author out of the millions of writers who have lived since 1616. . . . The novel was written as a serial for *Cosmopolitan*, whose demands and restrictions are, I should say, almost precisely those of the movies. Now that the novel is available between boards, a great many touches that most likely were in Hemingway's working manuscript have been restored. They don't add much, they don't take much away. At the same time they do make a difference: they make the bound volume authentically Hemingway, and not Hemingway plus (or maybe minus is the word) the *Cosmopolitan* editors. . . . To use his own favorite metaphor, he may not be able to go the full distance, but he can still hurt you. Always dangerous. Always in there with that right cocked. Real class." For replies to this review, see *N.Y.T.B.R.* (Oct. 1, 1950), p. 37.

644 "Profile: Ernest Hemingway," *Observer* (Sept. 10, 1950), p. 2.

645 Paul, Elliot. Review of *ARIT, Providence Sunday Journal* (Sept. 10, 1950), VI, 8.
". . . this magnificent story . . . the decades of experience Hemingway has gathered goes into his best telling of the familiar, touching, sad story. . . . Hemingway will, no doubt, get the usual disrespectful reception from the boys of English 'A' who have spent their years in New York offices and hate those who have seen or felt other things. Thanks to Ernest and nuts to his disparagers."

646 "The New Hemingway," article and review of *ARIT, Newsweek*, XXXVI (Sept. 11, 1950), 90-95. Photographs.
"There are few characters. It is a novel of atmosphere, blues and grays, shaded lights, quiet talk, a sense of ease and friendliness, suddenly captured and suddenly lost, against the magical loveliness of the ancient city. . . . The lyricism of Hemingway's early books . . . is almost entirely lacking in the colonel's story. It would be too poignant if they were there. . . . Thus at 52, with thirteen books behind him, Hemingway has mastered a new subject and a new style."

647 Review of *ARIT, Time*, LVI (Sept. 11, 1950), 110, 113.
"However thin his story, he keeps it in motion and even invests it with a sense of potential explosion, though the explosion never comes off. The famed Hemingway style, once a poetic blend of tension and despair, is hardly more than a parody of itself."

648 Gardiner, Harold C., S.J. Review of *ARIT, America*, LXXXIII (Sept. 16, 1950), 628, 630.
"The 'great bronze god' of American fiction for so many years

has definitely lost his sheen in this utterly trivial book. . . . Hemingway, to be sure, still has some of the old touches for which he was laudable. There is the sense of human fellowship, especially that of men under stress and agony. There is the bitter realization of the futility of war. . . . But all these traits are here subordinated to an un-manly atmosphere of griping and whining. The colonel is a beaten man from the start of the book, and he knows it—and so does the reader." Reprinted in *In All Conscience*, New York, 1959, pp. 124-125.

9 Butcher, Fanny. Review of *ARIT*, *Chicago Sunday Tribune* (Sept. 17, 1950), Magazine of Books, pp. 3, 14. Photograph.
  "The end of [*ARIT*] dominates and motivates the whole novel. The reader senses it almost from the first. . . . Ernest Hemingway has that old black magic with words which few writers have ever had, a magic which his imitators have dreamed of but which is truly his alone. . . . *Across the River and Into the Trees* will hold countless readers in a kind of literary vise by the sheer power of his technique."

91 "British Call Hemingway Book 'Evil, Adolescent,' " *ibid.*, p. 14.
  Regarding the British critics' reception to *ARIT*.

50 Breit, Harvey. "Talk With Mr. Hemingway," *N.Y. Times Book Review* (Sept. 17, 1950), p. 14.
  "Extracts from a series of exchanges" between Hemingway and Breit.

51 Simon, Kate. Review of *ARIT*, *New Republic*, CXXIII (Sept. 18, 1950), 20-21.
  "It is a slight, sad book, quieter and more muted than his others. . . . The artful, rhythmic sentences with their compelling stresses, the words that bear many echoes and undertones, the phrases that quiver with emotion, blur the border between prose and poetry. . . . Here and there the high art lapses and one finds the usual Hemingway flaws . . . the useless obscenities and the spots of repetition which serve no artistic purpose . . . and always irritating is the firm rejection of cerebration so characteristic of Hemingway people. . . . although the canvas is now smaller and painted in grayed tones, there is no less art. The mixture is, on a minor scale, as before and still magical; the Hemingway spell still holds."

52 Item, *Commonweal*, LII (Sept. 22, 1950), 572-573.
  Item about the critics' reception to *ARIT*.

53 Hutchens, John K. "Nobody on the Fence," *N.Y. Herald Tribune Book Review* (Sept. 24, 1950), p. 3.
  Item about the critics' reception to *ARIT*.

654 Adams, J. Donald. Speaking of Books column, *N.Y. Times Book Review* (Sept. 24, 1950), p. 2.
Regarding the critics' reception to *ARIT*.

655 Poore, Charles. Review of John K. M. McCaffery's *Ernest Hemingway: The Man and His Work, N.Y. Times* (Sept. 30, 1950), p. 15.

656 Waugh, Evelyn. Review of *ARIT, Tablet,* cxcvi (Sept. 30, 1950), 290, 292.
"Mr. Ernest Hemingway's long-expected novel has been out for some weeks, and has already been conspicuously reviewed by all the leading critics. It is now impossible to approach it without some prejudice either against the book itself or against its critics, for their disapproval has been unanimous. . . . What, in fact, [Hemingway] has done is to write a story entirely characteristic of himself, not his best book, perhaps his worst, but still something very much better than most of the work to which the same critics give their tepid applause. . . . The book is largely a monologue. The veteran ruminates bitterly over old battles. He exults in his young mistress. And all is written in that pungent vernacular which Mr. Hemingway should have patented." A German translation appeared in *Universitas,* vi (March 1951), 291-293.

657 Weeks, Edward. Review of *ARIT, Atlantic,* clxxxvi (Oct. 1950), 80, 81.
"The hero of Ernest Hemingway's new novel, *Across the River and Into the Trees,* is a truculent American Colonel who in December, 1946, goes to Venice on a short leave to see his nineteen-year-old mistress and to shoot ducks on the icy marshes. He enjoys both pleasures to the full: he keeps going on drugs with the realization that he has had three heart attacks and that the next excess may kill him. It is a mordant story. . . . Not unnaturally the dialogue is peppered with the Colonel's Army talk, coarse, unbridled, offensive to some in its repetition. . . . What's best in this story is its love: its heartfelt love of the Infantry, its bantering, affectionate love of Venice and the Venetians, its gusty love of sea food and wine, and its love of gondolas with Renata in the lee."

658 Rahv, Philip. Review of *ARIT, Commentary,* x (Oct. 1950), 400-402.
"The first thing to be said about this novel is that it is so egregiously bad as to render all comment on it positively embarrassing to anyone who esteems Hemingway as one of the more considerable prose-artists of our time and as the author of some of the finest short stories in the language. . . . This novel reads like a parody by the author of his own manner—a parody so biting that it virtually destroys the mixed social and literary legend of Hemingway that

has now endured for nearly three decades. . . . The stated themes of love and death are unrealized . . . the story turns on no significant principle of honor or valor or compassion such as invested some of Hemingway's earlier narratives with value and meaning." Reprinted in *Image and Idea,* New York, 1957, pp. 188-192; in *The Myth and the Powerhouse,* New York, 1964, pp. 193-198.

59 Driscoll, Joseph. "Hemingway Takes Shine Off High Brass," *St. Louis Post-Dispatch* (Oct. 1, 1950), p. 2 G.

This article, subtitled: Author Ranks Ten Best Generals in New Book, largely quotes from *ARIT.*

60 "M. B." Review of *ARIT, Saturday Night,* LXV (Oct. 3, 1950), 24.

"Plot, here, is virtually non-existent. . . . What can be seen is Hemingway's unique power of presenting a picture of universal sadness without a coincidental feeling of futility. The Colonel becomes alive through the very pattern and process of his thinking. . . . Here is the sure touch of the literary artist."

61 Review of *ARIT, TLS* (Oct. 6, 1950), p. 628.

"It is almost as if Mr. Hemingway were writing his swan-song. . . . But it is only 'as if,' for all passion is not spent, however it may seem. Rather, for the first time passion is under control. At last Mr. Hemingway knows his own strength, and at last he has learned that there is no need to waste it by using it all at once. *Across the River and Into the Trees* is the first of his novels of which that could be said; but there is no reason why it should be the last."

62 White, E. B. Parody, "Across the Street and Into the Grill," *New Yorker,* XXVI (Oct. 14, 1950), 28.

For reprints, see *The Second Tree from the Corner* (G444).

63 Rugoff, Milton. "Much Smoke, Some Sparks," review of *McCaffery, N.Y. Herald Tribune Book Review* (Oct. 15, 1950), p. 12.

64 Hicks, Granville. "The Critics Have Never Been Easy on Hemingway," review of *McCaffery, N.Y. Times Book Review* (Oct. 15, 1950), pp. 5, 32.

65 Montale, Eugenio. "Un americano a Venezia," review of *ARIT* (Cape edition), *Corriere della Sera* (Oct. 26, 1950), p. 3.

66 Redman, Ben Ray. "The Champ and the Referees," *SRL,* XXXIII (Oct. 28, 1950), 15-16, 38. Photograph.

Assesses the diverse reception accorded *ARIT* by the reviewers.

66₁ Smith, Harrison. "A Titan To Task," review of *McCaffery, ibid.,* pp. 17, 39.

666₂ "N. C." [Norman Cousins]. Editorial, "Hemingway and Steinbeck," *ibid.*, pp. 26-27.

Compares *ARIT* with John Steinbeck's *Burning Bright*. States that Steinbeck "reveals moral values where Hemingway reveals monomaniac meanderings."

667 Item, *Time*, LIV (Oct. 30, 1950), 44.

Quotes from Evelyn Waugh's criticism of Hemingway's critics in the *Tablet*, CXCVI (Sept. 30, 1950). For William Faulkner's letter supporting Waugh, see *Time*, LVI (Nov. 13, 1950), 6. The letter is reprinted in *Essays, Speeches & Public Letters*, New York, 1965, pp. 210-211.

668 Angoff, Charles. Review of *ARIT*, *American Mercury*, LXXI (Nov. 1950), 619-625.

"[Hemingway] has reached the dead end of his brand of realism. . . . It seems incredible that the school he founded will be able to outlive the disgrace of *Across the River*."

669 Einsiedel, Wolfgang von. "Ein Komet verblasst," review of *ARIT, Merkur,* IV (Nov. 1950), 1220-25.

670 Young, Philip. Review of *ARIT, Tomorrow,* x (Nov. 1950), 55-56.

"The situation in the novel . . . is perilous. But that fact does not fully explain why, using the methods and materials which have been in other Hemingway novels so satisfying, this is a pretty bad book. The failure is the sum of many errors—the outrageous and irrelevant attacks on recognizable living writers for instance; and the wholly embarrassing conversations with Renata's portrait, and —nearly as discomforting—with Renata herself."

671 Waugh, Evelyn. "The Case of Mr. Hemingway," *Commonweal*, LIII (Nov. 3, 1950), 97-98.

Concerning the critics' reception to *ARIT*, Waugh writes: "They have been smug, condescending, derisive . . . all are agreed that there is a great failure to celebrate. . . . Why do they all hate him so? I believe the truth is that they have detected in him something they find quite unforgivable—Decent Feeling. Behind all the bluster and cursing and fisticuffs he has an elementary sense of chivalry —respect for women, pity for the weak, love of honor—which keeps breaking in. There is a form of high supercilious caddishness which is all the rage nowadays in literary circles. That is what the critics seek in vain in this book, and that is why their complaints are so loud and confident."

672 Clark, Gregory. "Hemingway Slept Here," *Montreal Standard* (Nov. 4, 1950), pp. 13-14.

Reminiscences by the Feature Editor of the *Toronto Star Weekly* when Hemingway was on the staff, during the early 1920s.

73 Reed, Henry. Review of *ARIT, Listener*, XLIV (Nov. 9, 1950), 515.

The reviewer compares *ARIT* with Alberto Moravia's *Disobedience*. "The styles of these two writers indicate clearly enough the difference between them as artists: there is an honestly earned richness and certainty in Moravia; in Hemingway there is only an affected roughness which suggests a quick-return evasion of all difficult problems. . . . Mr. Hemingway gives us a duck-shoot on the wintry lagoon of Venice because he seems to know what that is like, and such knowledge is not to be lightly ignored or wasted. . . . He gives us the old man's war reminiscences and his animadversions on contemporary generalship because if such things are not used now, they will soon be useless. It is curious how false and hollow all these things come to be when they are forced into relationship with each other."

74 Moravia, Alberto. "Lettere Americane: Il colonello Hemingway," review of *ARIT, Mondo*, II (Nov. 11, 1950), 9.

Elio Vittorini's reply in *Mondo*, II (Nov. 25, 1950), 8, is followed by a note by Moravia.

75 Cecchi, Emilio. "Meno ponci, Signor Hemingway," review of *ARIT, Europeo* (Nov. 12, 1950), p. 11.

76 Photograph of Hemingway in Cuba, *Vogue*, CXVI (Nov. 15, 1950), 105.

77 Editorial, "and New Champion," *Collier's*, CXXVI (Nov. 18, 1950), 86. Caricature of Hemingway.

78 Warshow, Robert. Review of *ARIT, Partisan Review*, XVII (Nov.–Dec. 1950), 876-884.

"The book is a compendium of Hemingway's habitual themes, opinions, and prejudices—death, war, hunting, love, good food, good wine, the true comradeship of 'combat men,' the true *noblesse* of waiters and boatmen, the vileness of intellectuals, journalists, and members of the middle class—all so vulgarized that one wonders how the writer himself can possibly be taken in. . . . The prose is that of Hemingway's most misguided imitators. . . . This is the saddest story Hemingway has written."

79 Boal, Sam. "I Tell You True," *Park East*, X (Dec. 1950), 18-19, 46-47, Part I; XI (Jan. 1951), 36, 48-49, Part II.

The title of this biographical portrait is taken from an oft-repeated phrase of Hemingway's.

680 Mazars, Pierre. "Les généraux et leurs romanciers," *Table Ronde* (Dec. 1950), pp. 145-148.
General article. Discusses the work of Hemingway, Norman Mailer, and Robert Frost.

681 Frye, Northrop. Review of *ARIT*, *Hudson Review*, III (Winter 1951), 611-612.
"The theme of *Across the River and Into the Trees* is death in Venice, with Colonel Cantwell . . . as a military counterpart to [Thomas] Mann's beat-up old novelist. The colonel is a lonely man. Around him is an impersonal hatred directed, like a salute, at his uniform; behind him is the wreck of a marriage and of the career of a good professional soldier; in front of him is his next and last heart attack. . . . It is a great theme, and in the hands of someone competent to deal with it—say Ernest Hemingway—it might have been a long short story of overwhelming power. . . . In the opening scene and in the curt description of the colonel's death, there is something of the old Hemingway grip. In between, however, the story lies around in bits and pieces, with no serious effort to articulate it."

682 Rosenfeld, Isaac. "A Farewell to Hemingway," review of *ARIT*, *Kenyon Review*, XIII (Winter 1951), 147-155.
The reviewer is critical of the "false attitude toward life" which he believes Hemingway expresses in his work. "For once the hero, a man of the same cut and cloth as all the rest, is identified for what he is. . . . He is a man on his own, lonely, grown old, demoted from the rank of General to nobody . . . prattling of war, of the good life and the true love with an unfeeling, monotonous, heartsick narcissism . . . having learned nothing from life, nothing beyond the one thing he knows now—that he is about to die. . . . This is the most touching thing that Hemingway has done. For all the trash and foolishness of this book, perhaps even because of it, because he let himself be lulled and dulled by the fable of himself, he gave away some of his usual caution and let a little grief, more than ordinarily and not all of it stuck in the throat, come through his careful style." Reprinted in *An Age of Enormity*, Cleveland, 1962, pp. 258-267.

683 Papajewski, Helmut. "Die Frage nach der Sinnhaftigkeit bei Hemingway," *Anglia*, LXX, ii (1951), 186-209.
Essay on the question of meaningfulness in Hemingway's work.

684 Politizer, Heinz. "Der neue Hemingway," review of *ARIT*, *Neue Rundschau*, LXII, [1951], 136-139.

685 West, Ray B., Jr. "Three Methods of Modern Fiction: Ernest Hemingway, Eudora Welty, Thomas Mann," *College English*, XII (Jan. 1951), 193-203.

Explication of "The Short Happy Life of Francis Macomber," on pp. 194-196. Reprinted in *Introduction to Literature*, ed. Louis G. Locke *et al.*, New York, 1952, Second edition, pp. 479-481.

86 Hemingway, Mary. "Life with Papa: A Portrait of Ernest Hemingway," *Flair*, ii (Jan. 1951), 29, 116-117. Photograph.

An account of life at Finca Vigia.

87 Antonini, Giacomo. "Hemingway dopo Shakespeare," *Fiera Letteraria* (Jan. 14, 1951), p. 2. Photograph.

The title of this article about Hemingway, Venice, and *ARIT*, is taken from John O'Hara's review in the *N.Y. Times Book Review* (Sept. 10, 1950).

88 Morrow, Elise. "The Hemingway View of His Critics," *St. Louis Post-Dispatch* (Jan. 15, 1951), p. 1 C.

Quotes a letter from Hemingway regarding the critics' reception to *ARIT*. See (F114).

89 Vallette, Jacques. "Le dernier roman de Hemingway," review of *ARIT* (Cape edition), *Mercure de France*, No. 1050 (Feb. 1, 1951), pp. 333-335.

90 Janzon, Åke. "Älskad i Venedig," review of *Över floden in bland träden* (*ARIT*), *BLM*, xx (March 1951), 229-231.

91 Carroll, Jock. "I Never Knocked Out Hemingway," *Montreal Standard* (March 31, 1951), pp. 9, 25.

Interview with Morley Callaghan.

92 White, Leigh. The Cities of America series, "Havana," *Saturday Evening Post*, ccliii (March 31, 1951), 24. Photograph of Hemingway heading the *Pilar* out of Havana harbor.

93 Wylder, Deb. Review of *ARIT*, *Western Review*, xv (Spring 1951), 237-240.

". . . the dialogue of *Across the River and Into the Trees* sounds like an imitation of Hemingway's worst imitators. The dialogue, moreover, is often used as a device to allow the unbelievable Colonel Cantwell to make Hemingway-inspired remarks about war and literature. . . . The result is a failure, for the imposition of such authoritative (and Hemingway *is* authority in this novel) material disrupts the novel form."

94 de Montalet, R.-H. "Le dernier Roman d'Hemingway et la critique Anglo-Saxonne," review of *ARIT*, *Critique*, vii (April 15, 1951), 301-307.

95 Baker, Carlos. "Twenty-five Years of a Hemingway Classic," *N.Y. Times Book Review* (April 29, 1951), pp. 5, 31.

This reappraisal of *SAR* was reprinted in *Highlights of Modern Literature*, ed. Francis Brown, New York, 1954, pp. 106-109.

696 Beach, Joseph Warren. "How Do You Like It Now, Gentlemen?" *Sewanee Review*, LIX (April-June 1951), 311-328.
   Essay on *ARIT*. Reprinted in *Baker anthology*, pp. 227-244.

697 Whit, Joseph. "Hemingway's 'The End of Something,' " *Explicator*, IX (June 1951), Item 58.

698 "Mrs. Hemingway | Funeral To Be Held Tomorrow," *Chicago Tribune* (June 29, 1951), p. 16.
   Obituary of Hemingway's mother. Mrs. Grace Hall Hemingway, 79, of River Forest, Ill., died on June 27, in Memphis, Tenn., while visiting her daughter.

699 Baker, Carlos. "The Mountain and the Plain," *Virginia Quarterly Review*, XXVII (Summer 1951), 410-418.
   This essay became part of Chapter V of *Hemingway: The Writer as Artist*, Princeton, 1952.

700 Poore, Charles. Brief review of Lee Samuels' *A Hemingway Check List*, *N.Y. Times* (July 27, 1951), p. 17.

701 Soria, Regina. "The American Writer and the European Tradition: *Ernest Hemingway, the Man and His Work*," review of *McCaffery*, *Letteratura Moderna*, II (July–Sept. 1951), 377-385.

702 Gullón, Ricardo. "La irrupción de la novela norteamericana," *Insula*, No. 69 (Sept. 15, 1951), pp. 1, 6, 7.

703 Levin, Harry. "Observations on the Style of Ernest Hemingway," *Kenyon Review*, XIII (Autumn 1951), 581-609.
   For reprints of this essay, see *Contexts of Criticism* (G233).

704 D'Argo, Silvio. "Hemingway," *Paragone*, No. 22 (Oct. 1951), p. 77. In Italian.

705 Adams, J. Donald. Speaking of Books column, *N.Y. Times Book Review* (Oct. 25, 1951), p. 2.
   Discussion of *ARIT*.

706 Orrok, Douglas Hall. "Hemingway, Hugo, and Revelation," *Modern Language Notes*, LXVI (Nov. 1951), 441-445.

707 Šimić, S. "Preporni Hemingway," *Republika*, VII (Dec. 1951), 919-925.

708 Duesberg, Jacques. "Grandeur et décadence d'Ernest Hemingway," *Synthèses*, VI (Dec. 1951), 90-91.

709 Hoel, Sigurd. "Hemingway," *Vinduet*, v (Dec. 1951), 761-767. Photograph. In Swedish.

710 "Cuban Court Clears Hemingway," *N.Y. Times* (Dec. 11, 1951), p. 20.
Hemingway had been charged with possession of a twenty-two-caliber rifle without a license.

711 Neumann, John. "Ich packe dieses Herz bei den Hornern," *Literatur*, I, [1952], 1.
Interview with Hemingway.

712 Oppel, Horst. "Hemingway's *Across the River and Into the Trees*," *Neueren Sprachen*, I, new series [1952], 473-486. In German. Reprinted in *Baker anthology*, pp. 213-226.

713 Fenton, Charles A. "Hemingway's Kansas City Apprenticeship," *New World Writing*, No. 2 (1952), pp. 316-326.
This article became part of Chapter II of *The Apprenticeship of Ernest Hemingway*, New York, 1954.

714 Lyons, Leonard. The Lyons Den column, "Lunch at Papa Hemingway's," *N.Y. Post* (Jan. 7, 1952), p. 22. Dateline: Havana.
Regarding a visit to Finca Vigia.

715 Cranston, Herbert. "When Hemingway Earned Half a Cent a Word on the *Toronto Star*," *N.Y. Herald Tribune Book Review*, (Jan. 13, 1952), p. 6.
Reminiscences by the editor of the *Toronto Star Weekly* when Hemingway was on the staff, during the early 1920s.

716 Franklin, Sidney. "Bullfighter from Brooklyn," *Town & Country*, CVI (Feb. 1952), 112-115, 126-134, Part II; (April 1952), 74-77, 130-134, Part IV. Photographs.
In Part II, Franklin relates his meeting with Hemingway in Madrid, in 1929, and their tour of the bullfights. He describes the impact that Anna Pavlova made on Hemingway when she danced for them in Sevilla. Part IV describes Franklin's trip, in 1937, to cover the Spanish Civil War with Hemingway. This article appeared, with some revisions, in *Bullfighter from Brooklyn*, New York, 1952.

717 Parker, Alice. "Hemingway's 'The End of Something,'" *Explicator*, X (March 1952), Item 36.

718 Gurko, Leo. "The Achievement of Ernest Hemingway," *College English*, XIII (April 1952), 368-375. Reprinted in the *English Journal*, XLI (June 1952), 291-298.

719 Young, Philip. "Hemingway's *In Our Time*," *Explicator*, X (April 1952), Item 43.

720 Halliday, E. M. "Hemingway's Narrative Perspective," *Sewanee Review*, LX (April–June 1952), 202-218. Reprinted in *Baker critiques*, pp. 174-182; in *Modern American Fiction*, ed. A. Walton Litz, New York, 1963, pp. 215-227.

721 Ynduráin, Francisco. "La novela norteamericana en los últimos veinte años," *Arbor*, No. 77 (May 1952), pp. 67-68.
General article.

722 Hutchens, John K. On the Books column, " 'Luck' and Mr. Hemingway," *N.Y. Herald Tribune Book Review* (June 22, 1952), p. 2.
Item about Hemingway's forthcoming novel, *OMATS*. Briefly quotes a letter from Hemingway. See (F123).

723 Baker, Carlos. "Hemingway's Wastelanders," *Virginia Quarterly Review*, XXVIII (Summer 1952), 373-392.
This essay became part of Ch. IV of *Hemingway: The Writer as Artist*, Princeton, 1952.

724 Canby, Henry Seidel. "A Report on *The Old Man and the Sea*," *Book-of-the-Month Club News* (Aug. 1952), pp. 2-3.
OMATS was chosen as part of a dual selection for September, 1952, by the Book-of-the-Month Club. Canby describes the book as: "An unforgettable picture of man against the sea and man against fate." Note: This review was reprinted in a four-page leaflet, which was sent to subscribers.

724₁ Rodman, Selden. "Ernest Hemingway," *ibid.*, pp. 6-7.
Recalls a visit with Hemingway in Cuba.

725 Hobson, Laura Z. Trade Winds column, "Momentary Scoop," *Saturday Review*, XXXV (Aug. 23, 1952), 4.
Item regarding the circumstances which led to the publication of *OMATS* in *Life* magazine.

726 Advertisement, *Life*, XXXIII (Aug. 25, 1952), 124.
Regarding the forthcoming publication of *OMATS* in *Life*. Quotes a letter from Hemingway. See (F124). Also quoted in *Time*, LX (Sept. 1, 1952), 48.

727 Prescott, Orville. Review of *OMATS*, *N.Y. Times* (Aug. 28, 1952), p. 21.
"Within the sharp restrictions imposed by the very nature of his story Mr. Hemingway has written with sure skill. Here is the master technician once more at the top of his form, doing superbly what he can do better than anyone else."

727₁ Advertisement, *ibid.*, p. 14.
Full page ad announcing the publication of *OMATS* in *Life*,

XXXIII (Sept. 1, 1952), with comments on the story by W. Somerset Maugham, Eric Sevareid, *et al.*

728 Cannon, Jimmy. Jimmy Cannon Says column, *N.Y. Post* (Aug. 29, 1952), p. 54.

"Hemingway is a sports writer who uses the medium of the short story and the novel. . . . The athlete who is true to the standards of his sport has always been admired by Hemingway. In [*The Old Man and the Sea*] the old man, who dreams of lions, worships Joe DiMaggio. . . . We, who write of sports, should be grateful that the greatest writer honors us with his interest in our beat."

729 Sann, Paul. Parody review of *OMATS*, *N.Y. Post* (Aug. 31, 1952), p. 12 M.

730 Weeks, Edward. Review of *OMATS*, *Atlantic*, CXC (Sept. 1952), 72.

"In *The Old Man and the Sea*, Ernest Hemingway has returned to the stripped, lean, objective narrative so characteristic of him at his best. . . . a story which is beautiful in its description, and of clean thrusting power in its pursuit." Reprinted in *Adventures in American Literature*, ed. John Gehlmann and Mary Rives Bowman, New York, 1958, pp. 208-209.

731 Editorial, "A Great American Storyteller," *Life*, XXXIII (Sept. 1, 1952), 20. Cover photograph by Alfred Eisenstaedt.

OMATS appeared in full in this issue. For letter from William Saroyan, see *Life*, XXXIII (Sept. 22, 1952), 12; letter from A. N. Brabrook, a schoolmate of Hemingway's, *ibid.*, p. 14.

732 Breit, Harvey. Review of *OMATS*, *Nation*, CLXXV (Sept. 6, 1952), 194.

"It is Hemingway's great art that he teaches whatever it is he is concerned with, whether it be shooting game, fighting bulls, planning a military campaign, or plotting a prize fight. It has little to do with pedantry; it has everything to do with reality and concreteness. And more: in all his best work, and it is true of the new novel, these special areas, these particular professions and occupations, are transposed inexorably into universal meanings. In *The Old Man* the mystique of fishing, with its limited triumphs and tragedies, is transposed into a universal condition of life, with its success and shame, its morality and pride and potential loss of pride."

733 Gill, Brendan. Review of *OMATS*, *New Yorker*, XXVIII (Sept. 6, 1952), 115.

"*The Old Man and the Sea* . . . shows a great writer in a mood of unprecedented tenderness. The story he tells is short and simple— so simple that we run the risk of seeing it as a parable, and thus diminishing and vulgarizing it. The wise reader, leaving parables to the professors, will take the story on its own spare terms; its dimensions and meanings will prove as big and as many as he can make them."

734 Baker, Carlos. "The Marvel Who Must Die," review of *OMATS, Saturday Review*, xxxv (Sept. 6, 1952), 10-11. Cover drawing of Hemingway by Norkin.

"What Santiago has at the close of his story is what all the heroes of Hemingway have had—the proud, quiet knowledge of having fought the fight, of having lasted it out, of having done a great thing to the bitter end of human strength. . . . Hemingway has enhanced the native power of his tragic parable by engaging, though unobtrusively, the further power of Christian symbolism. . . . *The Old Man and the Sea* is a great short novel, told with consummate artistry and destined to become a classic in its kind." Reprinted in *A Preface to Literature*, ed. Edward C. Wagenknecht, New York, 1954, pp. 341-344.

735 Butcher, Fanny. Review of *OMATS, Chicago Sunday Tribune* (Sept. 7, 1952), Magazine of Books, p. 1.

"Ernest Hemingway, whose pen seemed less mighty than the sword in his last book *Across the River and Into the Trees*, has touched again the eternal source of his incomparable descriptive writing nature."

736 Cowley, Malcolm. Review of *OMATS, N.Y. Herald Tribune Book Review* (Sept. 7, 1952), pp. 1, 17. Photo by Lee Samuels.

"Hemingway has a peculiar manner of typing: in his manuscripts each word is separated from the following by three or four spaces. That may be the result of a defective space bar on his typewriter, but I like to believe that it has something to do with his feeling that each word has a special value and should stand out separately and clearly on the page. That is what the words seem to do in *The Old Man and the Sea*. The writing has the quality of being familiar and yet perpetually new that is the essence of classical prose."

737 Davis, Robert Gorham. Review of *OMATS, N.Y. Times Book Review* (Sept. 7, 1952), pp. 1, 20.

"It is a tale superbly told and in the telling Ernest Hemingway uses all the craft his hard, disciplined trying over so many years has given him. . . . [His] heroes have nearly always been defeated, or have died, and have lost what they loved. . . . The important thing was the code fought by, and keeping the right feeling toward what was fought for, and when something had been won, not to let the sharks have it. . . . In *The Old Man and the Sea*, it is all quite different. The old man has learned humility. . . . Hemingway has, like the young man in 'Big Two-Hearted River,' got back to something good and true in himself, that has always been there. And with it are new indications of humility and maturity and a deeper sense of being at home in life which promise well for the novel in the making."

37₁ Breit, Harvey. "Talk with Ernest Hemingway," *ibid.*, p. 20.

"A set of answers to a set of questions that [Hemingway] himself devised." Reprinted in *The Writer Observed*, Cleveland, 1956, pp. 263-265.

738 Muir, Edwin. Review of *OMATS, Observer* (Sept. 7, 1952), p. 7.

". . . *The Old Man and the Sea*, told with a simplicity which shows that Mr. Hemingway has forgotten that he is a tough writer. . . . Mr. Hemingway is essentially an imaginative writer, and his imagination has never displayed itself more powerfully than in this simple and tragic story."

739 Jackson, Joseph Henry. Review of *OMATS, San Francisco Chronicle* (Sept. 7, 1952), pp. 20, 22. Drawing of Hemingway by Bert Buel.

"In the sense of the plain story, this is a fishing yarn, a sharply and cleanly told tale of conflict between a fisherman and a great fish. . . . What Hemingway is talking about, however, is what has always been in one way or another his theme when he is at his best. He is talking about courage, but he is also saying something else. . . . As he has always said, it is the striving that is important . . . putting up the fight, and going on with the fight with all a man has, and Hemingway means 'all.' . . . Here, because he knows so well the background against which he stages his miracle-play of Man against Fate, he evokes both struggle and sea with a skill that very few—oh, well, what few, then? no one else writing today— could touch."

740 Connolly, Cyril. Review of *OMATS, Sunday Times*, London (Sept. 7, 1952), p. 5.

"What is remarkable about Hemingway is that, while many can write beautiful description, he can also depict action beautifully; a long physical struggle is described with the dynamic right words even as the changing qualities of the static sea are portrayed in their true colours, and the soul of the old man—humble, fearless, aromatic—is described perfectly too. . . . I believe this is the best story Hemingway has ever written. Get it at once, read it, wait a few days, read it again, and you will find (except for an occasional loose 'now' or 'until') that no page of this beautiful master-work could have been done better or differently."

441

741 Review of *OMATS, Newsweek*, XL (Sept. 8, 1952), 102-103.

"He handles with casual sympathy the central character of an old Cuban fisherman who hooks an 18-foot, 1,500-pound blue marlin . . . the false note appearing only when he tries to deepen the emotion from sympathy to tragic intensity."

742 Review of *OMATS, Time*, LX (Sept. 8, 1952), 114.

"As a story, it is clean and straight. Those who admire craftsmanship will be right in calling it a masterpiece. . . . But *The Old Man* is only better Hemingway, not fundamentally different. It is a poem of action, praising a brave man, a magnificent fish and the sea, with perhaps a new underlying reverence for the Creator of such wonders."

743 Hormel, Olive Deane. Review of *OMATS, Christian Science Monitor* (Sept. 11, 1952), p. 11.

". . . will these millions [of *Life* readers] see this as defeat or triumph? In a work of art of the dimensions the critics now acclaim there could be no possible uncertainty upon so all-important a point. But even the critics disagree. . . . I believe that Hemingway meant this as a triumph for the old man, and that it marks a definite advance in his philosophy. His god, however, is still only 'the principle of good sportsmanship,' as Mr. Edmund Wilson once said—and his man just 'a guy that can take it.' "

744 Gary, Romain. "Le retour du champion," review of *OMATS Nouvelles Littéraires*, XXXI (Sept. 11, 1952), 1. Reprinted in *NL* (July 6, 1961), p. 7.

745 Review of *OMATS, TLS* (Sept. 12, 1952), p. 593.

"Mr. Hemingway has always sailed near the wind of the style he mocked in *The Torrents of Spring*. The present 'conte' does not always escape the precious in its sometimes ponderous simplicity and tendency to imply an inner meaning."

746 Gardiner, Harold C., S.J. Review of *OMATS, America*, LXXXVII (Sept. 13, 1952), 569.

". . . Hemingway has here woven one of his better stories. *The Old Man and the Sea* is very simple, as most of his master stories are. . . . There is . . . not a wasted word in the lean, tense, utterly functional narrative. There is the atmosphere of struggle even in the rhythm of his sentences. There is the extraordinary feel for the cleanness of the sea winds, the mysterious life under the waves, the lone majesty of the sunset. And there is, above all, the feeling of kinship between the two elemental creatures—fisherman and fish —each noble in his own way. The trouble is . . . that the respective nobility tends to get blurred, and Hemingway is the one who does the blurring. . . . Long ago, Ruskin used the term 'pathetic fallacy' to describe the 'undue attribution of personality to impersonal objects.' It is this quality in this story, and indeed in most of Hemingway's work, that militates against true greatness." Reprinted in *In All Conscience*, New York, 1959, pp. 125-126.

747   Brief review of *OMATS*, *Times*, London (Sept. 13, 1952), p. 8.
"Mr. Hemingway has written a tale of endeavor and endurance in a style of biblical simplicity and purity. . . . It is written with great care, and Mr. Hemingway conveys not only the strangeness which the old fisherman sensed in his ordeal but the excitement and importance of his struggle. He has often tackled and sometimes achieved more, but rarely has he written less pretentiously or more pleasantly, or within the limits of a small compass shown greater mastery."

748   Item, "about 'the old man' and his book," *Publishers' Weekly*, CLXII (Sept. 13, 1952), 1011.

749   Breen, Melwyn. Review of *OMATS*, *Saturday Night*, LXVII (Sept. 13, 1952), 26.
"There is nothing in the new book that was not there before. There is the same pre-occupation with suffering, violence and death. . . . The story is simple. . . . In action and narrative it is superb, always controlled by Hemingway's certain authority over the subject matter. In style it is Hemingway at his most stripped, exercising the peculiar discipline he inherited with a difference from Flaubert."

750   Calder-Marshall, Arthur. Review of *OMATS*, *Listener*, XLVIII (Sept. 18, 1952), 477.
"Mr. Hemingway is once again 'the champ.' Apart from the opening pages, which are too solemnly simple, as if the author had to induce the mood for his story by incantation, *The Old Man and the Sea* is not only the finest long short story which Mr. Hemingway has ever written, but one of the finest written by anyone anywhere. . . . He has thrown away the story-teller's favourite weapon, suspense, so confident is he of his other powers. We know from the very beginning what is going to happen. . . . What holds us is the perfection of composition and execution. . . . Mr. Hemingway intends and achieves the perfection of a lyric poem."

751   Krim, Seymour. Review of *OMATS*, *Commonweal*, LVI (Sept. 19, 1952), 584-586.
"This intense and brilliant artist—and we must never forget that he is above all an artist, and quite as intense, though less demonstrative, than Faulkner—has only a smallish range in which he

can do his best work, and it is the familiarity of the range which makes his new book . . . slightly 'old hat.' This is not to say that the book isn't moving, or written and felt with that romantic dignity which has become Hemingway's seal. . . . He may write several more good or even fine books of a kind, but it is very doubtful if they will extend our sensibilities and refresh our vision of life as the earlier works did; and the chances are that they will merely repeat or embellish the best of his earlier work, as does *The Old Man and the Sea.*"

752 Adams, J. Donald. Speaking of Books column, *N.Y. Times Book Review* (Sept. 21, 1952), p. 2.

Discussion of *OMATS*. Reprinted in *Rendezvous: A Prose Reader*, ed. John J. McShea and Joseph W. Ratigan, New York, 1960, pp. 216-218.

753 "Condecora el Instituto Cubano del Turismo hoy al escritor Hemingway," *Diario de la Marina* (Sept. 23, 1952), p. 3.

754 "Hemingway Gets Medal," *N.Y. Times* (Sept. 24, 1952), p. 7. Dateline: Havana.

Hemingway received the Medal of Honor from the Cuban Tourist Institute for *OMATS*. Speaking in Spanish, he accepted the medal "in the name of all commercial fishermen of the north coast of Cuba."

755 Photograph of Hemingway receiving the Cuban Tourist Institute medal, *Diario de la Marina* (Sept. 25, 1952), Rotogravure, p. 1.

756 Review excerpts, *Now & Then*, No. 87 (Autumn 1952), pp. 10-11.

Excerpts from reviews of *OMATS*, which appeared in English periodicals.

757 Faulkner, William. Review of *OMATS*, *Shenandoah*, III (Autumn 1952), 55.

"His best. Time may show it to be the best single piece of any of us, I mean his and my contemporaries. This time, he discovered God, a creator. . . . It's all right. Praise God that whatever made and loves and pities Hemingway and me kept him from touching it any further." Reprinted in *Essays, Speeches & Public Letters*, New York, 1965, p. 193.

758 Pickrel, Paul. Review of *OMATS*, *Yale Review*, XLII (Autumn 1952), viii.

"This is the Hemingway who can sweep the slime of words off things and give us—separate, erect, bright in their fresh-created newness—the objects of the physical world and the feelings of men. . . . *The Old Man and the Sea* offers in a high degree the kind of pleasure proper to fiction: an image of life, intense and passionate, its meaning self-contained yet universal."

59 Rahv, Philip. Review of *OMATS*, *Commentary*, XIV (Oct. 1952), 390-391.

". . . if one is to judge by what some of the reviewers have been saying and by the talk among literary people, the meaning of *The Old Man and the Sea* is to be sought in its profound symbolism. It may be that the symbolism is really there, though I for one have been unable to locate it. . . . Hemingway's big marlin is no Moby Dick, and his fisherman is not Captain Ahab nor was meant to be. It is enough praise to say that their existence is real, and that their encounter is described in a language, at once relaxed and disciplined, which is a source of pleasure." Reprinted in *Image and Idea*, New York, 1957, pp. 192-195; in *The Myth and the Powerhouse*, New York, 1964, pp. 198-201.

60 Parsons, Louella O. "Hemingway's Magic Touch," *Cosmopolitan*, CXXXIII (Oct. 1952), 15-16. Photograph.

Regarding the movie version of "The Snows of Kilimanjaro."

61 Sampson, Edward C. "Hemingway's 'The Killers,' " *Explicator*, XI (Oct. 1952), Item 2.

62 Highet, Gilbert. Review of *OMATS*, *Harper's Magazine*, CCV (Oct. 1952), 102, 104.

"*The Old Man and the Sea* is a good story. It is about courage. It tells of a fisherman who fights old age and the loss of his strength, poverty and the loss of his luck, loneliness and the gigantic sea in which he hunts. . . . This always was a good story. It was good when Mr. Hemingway first told it, in an essay called 'On the Blue Water,' on page 184 of *Esquire* for April 1936."

63 Neumann, John. "Kompromisz ist reine Illusion: Gespräch mit Ernest Hemingway auf seiner Ranch in Cuba," *Kultur*, 1 (Oct. 1, 1952), 1.

64 Schorer, Mark. "With Grace Under Pressure," review of *OMATS*, *New Republic*, CXXVII (Oct. 6, 1952), 19-20.

". . . for those who, like this reviewer, believe that Hemingway's art, when it is art, is absolutely incomparable, and that he is unquestionably the greatest craftsman in the American novel in this century . . . this appears to be not only a moral fable, but a parable, and all the controlled passion in the story, all the taut excitement in the prose come, I believe, from the parable. It is an old man catching a fish, yes; but it is also a great artist in the act of mastering his subject, and, more than that, of actually writing about that struggle." Reprinted in *Baker critiques*, pp. 132-134.

445

765 "Hemingway, l'Européen," *Réforme* (Oct. 11, 1952), p. 7.

766 Hicks, Granville. "Hemingway's 'Happy Conspiracy with Permanence,'" review of Carlos Baker's *Hemingway: The Writer as Artist, N.Y. Times Book Review* (Oct. 12, 1952), p. 4. Photographs of the original dust jackets of *SAR, FTA, ARIT,* and *OMATS.*

767 Mayberry, George. "Truth and Poetry," review of *Baker, New Republic,* CXXVII (Oct. 13, 1952), 21-22.

768 Dutourd, Jean. Review of *OMATS, Arts* (Oct. 17, 1952), p. 5.

769 Mizener, Arthur. "Prodigy Into Peer," review of *Baker, Saturday Review,* XXXV (Oct. 18, 1952), 25.

770 Prezzolini, Giuseppe. Review of *Il vecchio e il mare (OMATS), Tempo* (Oct. 18, 1952), p. 3.
   Reprinted in *America con gli stivali,* Florence, 1954.

771 Quinn, Patrick F. "Measure of Hemingway," review of *Baker, Commonweal,* LVI (Oct. 24, 1952), 73-75.

772 Calvo, Lino Novás. "A Cuban Looks at Hemingway," review of *OMATS, Américas,* IV (Nov. 1952), 37-38.
   "The author has lived among us for some time. . . . From that living a novel has emerged that is Cuban to the small extent that a few names and allusions locate it here, but that is of all lands and all times in the universal quality that Hemingway always gives his work. . . . In Hemingway, man's supreme quality is his moral courage. This leitmotiv appears in all his works and is strikingly present in this latest one. . . . *The Old Man and the Sea* possesses some of the best qualities of Hemingway's best work (of the African stories, for example), and it proves that the author is still full of creative vigor."

773 Hughes, Riley. Review of *OMATS, Catholic World,* CLXXVI (Nov. 1952), 151.
   "This brief novel is Hemingway at his best; theme, tone, and action come together in a wholeness of dignity and power."

774 Ynduráin, Francisco. "La literatura norteamericana," *Insula,* VII (Nov. 15, 1952), 3.
   General article.

774₁ Gullón, Ricardo. "Las novelas de Hemingway," *ibid.,* p. 5.

775 Rugoff, Milton. "A Major Work of Literary Evaluation," review of *Baker, N.Y. Herald Tribune Book Review* (Nov. 23, 1952), p. 8.

776 Schwartz, Delmore. Review of *OMATS, Partisan Review,* XIX (Nov.–Dec. 1952), 702-703.

"The experience of literature is always comparative, and we have only to remember a story like 'The Undefeated,' which has almost the same theme as *The Old Man and the Sea*, or the account of the Caporetto retreat in *A Farewell to Arms*, to see exactly how the new book falls short. Whenever . . . the narrative is concerned wholly with fishing, there is a pure vividness of presentation. But when the old man's emotions are explicitly dealt with, there is a margin of self-consciousness and a mannerism of assertion which is perhaps inevitable whenever a great writer cannot get free of his knowledge that he is a great writer."

776₁ Advertisement, *ibid.*, p. 732.
Brief appraisal by Bernard Berenson of *OMATS*, in Scribner's advertisement.

777 Portuondo, José Antonio. "The Old Man and Society," *Américas*, IV (Dec. 1952), 6-8, 42-44. Photographs.
Assesses Hemingway's contribution to literature.

778 Repo, Ville. "Hemingwayn kalajuttu," review of *OMATS*, *Parnasso*, II (Dec. 1952), 375-377.

779 Mohrt, Michel. "Hemingway, les héros et les dieux," *Table Ronde*, No. 606 (Dec. 1952), pp. 122-128.

780 Cary, Joyce. "I Wish I Had Written That," *N.Y. Times Book Review* (Dec. 7, 1952), p. 4.
In this article by various authors, Joyce Cary writes on *OMATS*.

781 Tinkle, Lon. "Year of the Long Autumn: A Reviewer Wanders Through 1952," *Saturday Review*, XXXV (Dec. 27, 1952), 7-9.
General article. ". . . the suggestion of the wisdom of Jesus's humility and courage was present in *The Old Man and the Sea* and it remained for Carlos Baker in the *Saturday Review* [XXXV, Sept. 6, 1952] (in what was probably the best book review of the year) to state most clearly the symbols of Hemingway's present brooding over Christian thought."

782 Fenton, Charles A. "No Money for the Kingbird: Hemingway's Prizefight Stories," *American Quarterly*, IV (Winter 1952), 339-350. Reprinted, in a different form, in *The Apprenticeship of Ernest Hemingway*, New York, 1954.

783 White, William. "Father and Son: Comments on Hemingway's Psychology," *Dalhousie Review*, XXXI (Winter 1952), 276-284.

784 Dupee, F. W. Review of *OMATS*, *Kenyon Review*, XV (Winter 1953), 150-155.

"Hemingway's next to last book, *Across the River and Through the Trees* [*sic*], may some day be admired more liberally than it seems to have been on its first appearance. That novel was at least a powerful expression of Hemingway's legend. His new novel, *The Old Man and the Sea*, has nothing to do with the legend, except as it registers a determination to shake the legend off. In this story the author is revealed rather than exposed. He is shown in what are no doubt his original capacities: as an exacting artist, a visionary of nature and human nature, a man committed to self-reliance *jusqu'au feu* and beyond."

785 Barnes, Lois L. "The Helpless Hero of Ernest Hemingway," *Science & Society*, XVII (Winter 1953), 1-25.

A German translation of this essay appeared in *Heute und Morgen*, No. 9, [1953], pp. 671-679.

786 Frohock, W. M. "Mr. Hemingway's Truly Tragic Bones," review of *OMATS*, *Southwest Review*, XXXVIII (Winter 1953), 74-77.

787 McCormick, John. "Hemingway and History," *Western Review*, XVII (Winter 1953), 87-98.

788 Strauss, Stuart H. "Hemingway and Tomorrow," *Kansas Magazine* (1953), pp. 31-32.

789 Forssell, Lars. "Den heroiska stilen: Ñagra anteckningar till Hemingway," *BLM*, XXII (Jan. 1953), 43-47.

790 Hoffman, Frederick J. "No Beginning and No End: Hemingway and Death," *Essays in Criticism*, III (Jan. 1953), 73-84. Reprinted in *Interpretations of American Literature,* ed. Charles Feidelson, Jr. and Paul Brodtkorb, Jr., New York, 1959, pp. 320-331.

791 Vallette, Jacques. "Dernier État de Hemingway," review of *OMATS* (Cape edition), *Mercure de France*, No. 1073 (Jan. 1, 1953), pp. 151-156.

792 Camilucci, Marcello. Review of *Il vecchio e il mare (OMATS)*, *Osservatore Romano* (Jan. 23, 1953), p. 3.

Includes summation of Hemingway's work.

793 Erval, François. "Transformations de Hemingway," *Temps Modernes*, VIII (Jan.–Feb. 1953), 1248-53.

794 Freehof, Solomon B. Review of *OMATS*, *Carnegie Magazine*, XXVII (Feb. 1953), 44-48.

"It is beautifully written with a sort of unintended tenderness. It has the same clear vivid style, one that you could paint in a modern painting, the same struggle which from the beginning you know is going to be hopeless. . . . The style is still strong, the noun and verbs create a dynamic prose which is unequalled. There is a sense of energy and power in all that he writes—but the meanings, alas the meanings! What is he trying to say in all these powerfully written novels? His novels have more power than depth, more action than thought. There is no introspection, there is only outer action."

795 Cournot, Michel. Review of *Le vieil homme et la mer* (*OMATS*), *Nouvelle Revue Française*, I (Feb. 1953), 351-353.

796 Sigaux, Gilbert. "Avec Hemingway," *Preuves*, III (Feb. 1953), 95-99. Photograph.

797 Hemingway, Mary. The Man I Married series, "Ernest Hemingway," *Today's Woman* (Feb. 1953), pp. 30-31, 46-48. Photographs.

798 Raimondi, Giuseppe. "Il vecchio Hemingway," *Mondo*, V (Feb. 7, 1953), 7. Discussion of *OMATS*.

799 Connolly, Cyril. "Earnest Work," review of John Atkins' *The Art of Ernest Hemingway* and *Baker, Sunday Times*, London (Feb. 8, 1953), p. 5.

800 "Concerning Mr. Hemingway," review of John Atkins' *The Art of Ernest Hemingway* and *Baker, TLS* (Feb. 20, 1953), p. 122.

801 Beaver, Joseph. " 'Technique' in Hemingway," *College English*, XIV (March 1953), 325-328.

802 Bataille, Georges. "Hemingway à la lumière de Hegel," review of *Le vieil homme et la mer* (*OMATS*) and *Baker, Critique*, IX (March 1953), 195-201.

803 Spector, Robert D. "Hemingway's *The Old Man and the Sea*," *Explicator*, XI (March 1953), Item 38.

804 Ekström, Kjell. "Ernest Hemingway," *Samtid och Framtid*, X (March 1953), 153-158.

805 Duesberg, Jacques. "Une Victoire par k.o. technique: *The Old Man and the Sea*," *Synthèses*, VII (March 1953), 219-222.

806 Item, *Time*, LXI (March 2, 1953), 33.
Quotes a letter from Hemingway to Louisville, Kentucky, high school students, regarding *OMATS*.

807 Duggan, Francis X. "The Obsession of Violence," review of Philip Young's *Ernest Hemingway, Commonweal*, LVII (March 13, 1953), 583-584.

808 Montejo, Alberto Delgado. Review of *El viejo y el mar* (*OMATS*), *Bohemia*, XLV (March 15, 1953), 58, 111-112. Cover drawing and photograph.

449

This issue also contains the Spanish translation of *OMATS*. See (C376).

809 Aberg, Gilbert. "White Hope—Somewhat Sunburned: The Maturity of Hemingway," *Chicago Review*, VII (Spring 1953), 18-24.

810 Lewis, R.W.B. Review of *OMATS*, *Hudson Review*, VI (Spring 1953), 146-148.

"Hemingway's brief parable of the old fisherman, the giant marlin and the sharks has an authentic beauty, but I doubt if the book can bear the amount of critical weight already piled upon it. . . . The work is not, somehow, altogether and finally *serio* (the Italian word distinguishes, better than its English translation, between the good quality and its corruptions into the stuffy and pretentious); and our assent has to be partially withheld. Yet it has its rare and gentle humanities."

811 Black, Frederick. Parody review of *OMATS*, "The Cuban Fish Problem," *New Mexico Quarterly*, XXIII (Spring 1953), 106-108.

812 Dupee, F. W. Review of *OMATS*, *Perspectives U.S.A.*, No. 3 (Spring 1953), pp. 127-130.

"One of his best stories, *The Old Man and the Sea,* is also a first-rate example of that literature of the big hunt to which so many American writers have contributed, affirming through this image the frontier virtues and the natural basis of our life. . . . the old fisherman's portrait . . . emerges from the swiftly presented minutiae of his conduct in the process of the action. The portrait brings to a high pitch of consciousness that humane naturalism which Hemingway professes, in common with Faulkner and other American writers of their generation." A German translation appeared in *Perspektiven*, No. 3 (May 1953), pp. 130-134.

813 Aldridge, John W. Review of *OMATS*, *Virginia Quarterly Review*, XXIX (Spring 1953), 311-320.

"I confess that I am unable to share in the prevailing wild enthusiasm for . . . *The Old Man and the Sea.* It is of course a remarkable advance over his last novel; and it has a purity of line and a benignity, a downright saintliness, of tone which would seem to indicate not merely that he has sloughed off his former emotional pettiness but that he has expanded and deepened his spiritual perspective in a way that must strike us as extraordinary . . . [it] seems to me a work of distinctly minor Hemingway fiction."

814 West, Ray B. "The Sham Battle over Ernest Hemingway," reviews of *OMATS*, *Baker*, and Philip Young's *Ernest Hemingway*, *Western Review*, XVII (Spring 1953), 234-240.

315 Daniel, Robert. Review of *Baker, Yale Review*, XLII (Spring 1953), 443-445.

316 Strage, Mark. "Ernest Hemingway: Wars, Women, Wine, Words," *Pageant*, VIII (April 1953), 18-29. Photographs.

317 Whitfield, E. "Hemingway: The Man," *Why*, I (April 1953), 10-19. A psychoanalytical study.

318 Colten, L. "Hemingway's *The Old Man and the Sea*," *Explicator*, XI (May 1953), Item 38.

319 Bellow, Saul. "Hemingway and the Image of Man," review of Philip Young's *Ernest Hemingway*, *Partisan Review*, XX (May–June 1953), 338-342.

320 Halliday, E. M. "Hemingway's Hero," *University of Chicago Magazine*, XLV (May 1953), 10-14.

321 "Hemingway Awarded Pulitzer Prize," *N.Y. Times* (May 5, 1953), pp. 1, 24. Photograph of Hemingway by Lee Samuels.
Hemingway was awarded his first Pulitzer prize, for *OMATS*.

322 Editorial, "A Souvenir from a Pulitzer Prize Novelist," *Life*, XXXIV (May 11, 1953), 25.
Quotes a letter from Hemingway, regarding *OMATS*. See (F124).

323 Daiber, H. "Der alte Mann und Kapitän Ahab," *Deutsche Rundschau*, LXXIX (June 1953), 618-620.

324 Photograph of Hemingway, Spencer Tracy, and an old Cuban fisherman, Anselmo [Hernandez], by Leland Hayward, "Three Men and *The Old Man and the Sea*," *Vogue*, CXXI (June 1953), 106-107.

325 Redman, Ben Ray. "Gallantry in the Face of Death," *Saturday Review*, XXXVI (June 6, 1953), 18.
New Scribner's editions of *SAR*, *FTA*, *THAHN*, and *GHOA* reviewed.

326 "Hemingway Going to Africa," *K.C. Star* (June 16, 1953), p. 5. Dateline: Key West, Florida.
Announced that he and his wife were going on an African safari.

327 Lyons, Leonard. The Lyons Den column, "A Day in Town with Hemingway," *N.Y. Post* (June 26, 1953), p. 26. Dateline: New York.

328 Brown, Deming. "Hemingway in Russia," *American Quarterly*, V (Summer 1953), 143-156.
A slightly enlarged version of this article, on the Russian translations of Hemingway's work, appears in *Soviet Attitudes toward American Writing*, Princeton, 1962, pp. 297-315. Reprinted in *Baker anthology*, pp. 145-161.

451

829 McClennen, Joshua. "Ernest Hemingway and His Audience," *Michigan Alumnus Quarterly Review*, LIX (Summer 1953), 335-340.

830 Baker, Carlos. "When the Warriors Sleep," *Saturday Review*, XXXVI (July 4, 1953), 13.
A re-review of *SAR*.

831 Item, "Across the Ocean and into the Ritz," *Time*, LXII (July 13, 1953), 46. Photograph.
Brief item about Hemingway in Paris.

832 Valverde, José María. Review of *El viejo y el mar (OMATS)*, *Indice de Artes y Letras*, Nos. 65-66 (July 30, 1953), pp. 3-4.

833 Blanchet, André. Review of *Le vieil homme et la mer (OMATS)*, *Études*, CCLXXVIII (July–Aug. 1953), 102-104.

834 Dworkin, Martin S. "A Dead Leopard and an Empty Grail: Three Ernest Hemingways," review of the film, *The Snows of Kilimanjaro*, *Humanist*, XIII (July–Aug. 1953), 164-165.

835 Buchwald, Art. "For Whom the Bloody Marys Toll," *N.Y. Herald Tribune* [European Edition] (Aug. 5, 1953), p. 6. Dateline: Paris.
Interview with Hemingway, who had just returned to Paris from Spain and was about to depart for Africa.

836 Ruark, Robert C. "Papa in Spain," *N.Y. World-Telegram & Sun* (Aug. 10, 1953), p. 13. Dateline: Pamplona, Spain. Reprinted in *Biography of the Bulls*, ed. Rex Smith, New York, 1957, pp. 369, 371.

837 "Il 'Premio Bancarella' assegnato a Ernest Hemingway," *Corriere della Sera* [Pomeriggio edition] (Aug. 17–18, 1953), p. 6. Dateline: Pontremoli, Italy.
Hemingway was awarded the 1953 Bancarella Award for *OMATS*.

838 Sordo, Enrique. "El retorno de Hemingway," *Cuadernos Hispanoamericanos*, No. 45 (Sept. 1953), pp. 358-361.

839 Hyman, Stanley Edgar. "A Hemingway Sampler," review of *The Hemingway Reader*, *N.Y. Times Book Review* (Sept. 13, 1953), p. 28.

840 Antonini, Giacomo. "Hemingway, uno dei maestri della letteratura americana," *Fiera Letteraria*, VIII (Sept. 27, 1953), 1-2.

841 Whicher, George F. Review of *The Hemingway Reader*, *N.Y. Herald Tribune Book Review* (Sept. 27, 1953), p. 21.

842 "Churchill May Get Prize," *N.Y. Times* (Oct. 9, 1953), p. 9.

Winston Churchill and Hemingway were reported as the strongest candidates for the Nobel prize for literature in 1953. Note: The award went to Sir Winston.

43 Stobie, Margaret. "Ernest Hemingway, Craftsman," *Canadian Forum*, XXXIII (Nov. 1953), 179, 181-182.

44 Vandercook, Dorothy Powell. "Pictures with a Past," *Saturday Evening Post*, CCXXVI (Nov. 21, 1953), 17. Photograph of Ernest at fourteen, dressed in a Japanese kimono for his role in a Sunday-school play.

45 Hotchner, A. E. "Hemingway Ballet: Venice to Broadway," *N.Y. Herald Tribune* (Dec. 27, 1953), IV, 3.
An account of the four years of preparation for the adaptation of "The Capital of the World" into a ballet.

46 Terry, Walter. Review of the ballet, "The Capital of the World," *N.Y. Herald Tribune* (Dec. 28, 1953), p. 14.
Presented by the Ballet Theatre, at the Metropolitan Opera House, on Dec. 27, 1953. Score by George Antheil; choreography by Eugene Loring. The work was commissioned by the Ford Foundation's Television Workshop and first presented on Omnibus, on December 6, 1953.

47 Clavería, A. "Arte y artesanía en Hemingway," *Correo Literario*, No. 89, [1954], pp. 1, 14.

48 "Ernest Agent," *Newsweek*, XLIII (Jan. 4, 1954), 35.
Spruille Braden, former Assistant Secretary of State, disclosed that Hemingway's wartime duty in the Caribbean was part of a counterespionage organization set up to help American agents combat saboteurs who were sinking Allied ships.

49 "Hunt Hemingway in Jungle," *Chicago Daily Tribune* (Jan. 25, 1954), pp. 1, 2. Dateline: Kampala, Uganda, Jan. 24.
A chartered plane carrying Hemingway and his wife crashed near Murchison Falls, in the upper Nile country of East Africa, on January 23.

49₁ "Born in Oak Park," *ibid.*, p. 2.

50 "Lo scrittore Hemingway con la moglie precipita con un aereo nell' Uganda," *Corriere della Sera* (Jan. 25, 1954), p. 1. Dateline: Nairobi, Jan. 25.

50₁ "e. m." [Eugenio Montale]. "L'uomo e le opere," *ibid.*, p. 1.

51 "Seek Hemingway," *K.C. Times* (Jan. 25, 1954), p. 1.
A bulletin, on p. 1, announced that following a plane crash, on

January 23, the Hemingways had been picked up by a tourist launch which took them to Butiaba, where they boarded another plane. They escaped from the second plane, which crashed and burned on take-off.

851₁ "Reporter Here Before Writing Novels," *ibid.*, p. 18. Photographs.

852 Wilson, Earl. "Fans Hail Hemingway As Invulnerable 'Papa,' " *N.Y. Post* (Jan. 25, 1954), p. 3.

852₁ Wilson, Earl. It Happened Last Night column, *ibid.*, p. 10.
Reminisces on visits with the Hemingways, in Cuba, during the past fifteen years.

852₂ Lyons, Leonard. "Papa," *ibid.*, p. 20.
Reminiscences of his friendship with Hemingway.

853 "Hemingway and Wife Are Reported Safe After Two Plane Crashes in East Africa | Rescue Craft Cracks Up After First Flight Falls in Jungle Near Nile," *N.Y. Times* (Jan. 25, 1954), pp. 1, 13. Dateline: Kampala, Uganda, Jan. 25.

854 "Hemingway Out of the Jungle: Arm Hurt, He Says Luck Holds," *N.Y. Times* (Jan. 26, 1954), pp. 1, 25. Dateline: Entebbe, Uganda.

855 Photograph of Hemingway, in Entebbe, Uganda, *N.Y. Times* (Jan. 27, 1954), p. 14.

856 Photograph, "Rescued After Having Survived Two Aeroplane Crashes in Uganda," *Illustrated London News* (Jan. 30, 1954), p. 163.

857 Laird, Landon. About Town column, *K.C. Times* (Jan. 30, 1954), p. 5.
Herbert R. Schindler recalls Hemingway's bravery in the no-man's-land of the Huertgen Forest, during World War II.

858 Carstensen, Broder. "Evelyn Waugh und Ernest Hemingway," *Archiv für das Studium der Neueren Sprachen*, CXC (Feb. 1954), 193-203.

858₁ Happel, Nikolaus. "Äusserungen Hemingways zur Darstellung der Wirklichkeit und Wahrheit," *ibid.*, pp. 204-213.

859 "Only His Heroes Die," *Newsweek*, XLIII (Feb. 1, 1954), 19. Photograph.
Item about the African plane crashes.

860 Item, *Time*, LXIII (Feb. 1, 1954), 31. Photographs.
Item about the African plane crashes.

61 "Hemingway Ends Stay in Bed," *N.Y. Times* (Feb. 2, 1954), p. 16. Dateline: Nairobi, Kenya.

Hemingway ended a three-day stay in bed after suffering "minor injuries" in the two airplane crashes.

62 Talk of the Town column, "Dead or Alive," *New Yorker*, xxix (Feb. 6, 1954), 21.

A report on the New York newspapers' obituary notices on Hemingway, when he was believed to have perished in the plane crash in East Africa, on January 23, 1954.

63 "'Papa' Pops Up Again," *Life*, xxxvi (Feb. 8, 1954), 41. Photographs.

Regarding the two African plane crashes.

64 Fenton, Charles A. "Ernest Hemingway: The Young Years," *Atlantic*, xcxiii (March 1954), 25-34, Part i; (April 1954), 49-57, Part ii; (May 1954), 39-44, Part iii: "The Paris Years." Cover drawing of Hemingway by Russell Carpenter. Reprinted in *The Apprenticeship of Ernest Hemingway*, New York, 1954.

65 Antonini, Giacomo. "Retrospettiva di Hemingway: *Addiò alle armi* venticinque anni dopo," *Fiera Letteraria*, ix (March 21, 1954), 1, 2. Photograph.

66 "Hemingways in Venice," *St. Louis Post-Dispatch* (March 23, 1954), p. 7 A.

Brief item regarding the Hemingways arrival in Venice, from Africa.

67 "A Medal for Hemingway," *N.Y. Times* (March 24, 1954), p. 55.

Hemingway was chosen to receive the Award of Merit medal and $1000, from the American Academy of Arts and Letters.

68 Montale, Eugenio. "Abbruciacchiato e felice Hemingway è tornato a Venezia," *Corriere della Sera* (March 26, 1954), p. 3. Dateline: Venice.

69 Pivano, Fernanda. "Ritratto di Hemingway," *Smeraldo*, viii (March 30, 1954), 22-26.

70 "Gave Up On Hemingway," *K.C. Times* (May 15, 1954), p. 7. Dateline: Madrid.

Report on the extent of the injuries which Hemingway received in the African plane crashes.

71 Garnett, E. B. "A New Book Tells of Work on the *Star* That Helped Hemingway to Fame," review of Charles A. Fenton's *The Apprenticeship of Ernest Hemingway*, *K.C. Star* (May 16, 1954), p. 4 D.

872 "Hemingway: Making of a Master," review of Charles A. Fenton's *The Apprenticeship of Ernest Hemingway, Newsweek*, XLIII (May 17, 1954), 104, 106. Photograph.

873 Item, *Time*, LXIII (May 24, 1954), 43.
Brief item about Hemingway in Madrid.

874 Baker, Carlos. "The Palmy Days of Papa," review of John Atkins' *The Art of Ernest Hemingway* and Charles A. Fenton's *The Apprenticeship of Ernest Hemingway, Saturday Review*, XXXVII (May 29, 1954), 14-15.

875 Photograph of the Hemingways at a bullfight in Madrid, *N.Y. Times Magazine* (June 6, 1954), p. 4.

876 "Hemingway Sails for Cuba," *N.Y. Times* (June 7, 1954), p. 17. Dateline: Genoa, Italy, June 6.
Brief report that Hemingway "sailed today aboard the *Francesco Morosini*, bound for Havana."

877 Item, *Time*, LXIII (June 21, 1954), 45. Photograph.
Brief item about Hemingway in Genoa, Italy.

878 Fussell, Edwin. "Hemingway and Mark Twain," *Accent*, XIV (Summer 1954), 199-206.

879 Aldridge, John W. "Before the Sun Began to Rise," review of Charles A. Fenton's *The Apprenticeship of Ernest Hemingway, N.Y. Times Book Review* (July 11, 1954), p. 4.

880 "Cuba Honors Hemingway," *N.Y. Times* (July 22, 1954), p. 3. Dateline: Havana, July 21.
The highest award that Cuba gives to a foreigner, the Order of Carlos Manuel de Céspedes, was awarded Hemingway, on his fifty-fifth birthday.

881 "Ernest Hemingway's School Days," *Chicago*, I (Aug. 1954), 57-60. Photographs.
Includes the Class Prophecy which Hemingway wrote for the high school Yearbook, *Senior Tabula* (June 1917).

882 Item, *Time*, LXIV (Aug. 2, 1954), 31. Photograph.
Item about Hemingway receiving the Cuban Order of Carlos Manuel de Céspedes.

883 Prezzolini, Giuseppe. "Hemingway e l'Italia," *Tempo* (Aug. 3, 1954), p. 3. Reprinted in *America con gli stivali*, Florence, 1954.

884 Hotchner, A. E. "All-Star Bullfight," *This Week* (Aug. 8, 1954), pp. 10-11. Dateline: Madrid. Photographs.

An account of the Hemingways and Ava Gardner watching bull-fighter Luis Miguel Dominguín at a practice session.

85 Carpenter, Frederic I. "Hemingway Achieves the Fifth Dimension," *PMLA*, LXIX (Sept. 1954), 711-718. Reprinted in *American Literature and the Dream*, New York, 1955, pp. 185-193; and in *Baker anthology*, pp. 192-201. A French translation appeared in *Revue des Lettres Modernes*, IV (1957), 599-613.

86 Photograph of Hemingway with his houseguest Luis Miguel Dominguín, *Time*, LXIV (Sept. 20, 1954), 46.

87 Dupee, F. W. Item, *Perspectives U.S.A.*, No. 9 (Autumn 1954), pp. 154-155.
   Regarding Hemingway's award from the National Institute of Arts and Letters.

88 Aldridge, John W. "Hemingway: The Etiquette of the Berserk," *Mandrake*, II (Autumn–Winter 1954–1955), 331-341. Reprinted in *In Search of Heresy*, New York, 1956, pp. 149-165.

89 Bache, William. "Hemingway's 'The Battler,'" *Explicator*, XIII (Oct. 1954), Item 4.

90 Photographic essay, "Sportsman: Ernest Hemingway," *Sports Illustrated*, I (Oct. 4, 1954), 9-10.
   See Winston McCrea's letter, regarding Hemingway's trips to Sun Valley, Idaho, in *Sports Illustrated*, I (Nov. 1, 1954), 79.

91 Selander, Sten. Review of *Afrikas gröna berg* (GHOA), *Svenska Dagbladet* (Oct. 4, 1954), p. 4.

92 Lagercrantz, Olof. Review of *Afrikas gröna berg* (GHOA), *Dagens Nyheter* (Oct. 24, 1954), p. 4.

93 "Hemingway Is the Winner of Nobel Literature Prize," *N.Y. Times* (Oct. 29, 1954), p. 1. Photograph.
   Hemingway received the news, at Finca Vigia, that he had been awarded the Nobel prize for literature for 1954. The gold medal and $35,000 to be presented in Stockholm, on December 10.

93₁ Matthews, Herbert L. "Winner Rules Out Trip to Stockholm," *ibid.*, p. 10. Dateline: Havana.
   Interview with Hemingway, who related the extent of his injuries from the two African plane crashes, and his plans "to stay in Cuba and keep on working through the winter."

93₂ Poore, Charles. "Hemingway's Quality Built on a Stern Apprenticeship," *ibid.*, p. 10.

93₃ "Career Marked by Wars," biographical sketch, *ibid.*, p. 10.

894 "Nobel priset i litteratur till Ernest Hemingway," *Dagens Nyheter* (Oct. 29, 1954), p. 1. Photographs.

894₁ Ahman, Sven. "Roman med Afrikamotic snart klar i Kubahem-met," *ibid.*, pp. 1, 6. Dateline: Havana.

894₂ Lagercrantz, Olof. "Hemingway, soldaten som aldrig kom hem," *ibid.*, p. 4.

894₃ "Mårten Edlund: 'Inte hårdkokt,' " *ibid.*, p. 6.
Regarding Hemingway's Swedish translator.

895 "Ernest Hemingway nobelpristagare," *Svenska Dagbladet* (Oct. 29, 1954), p. 3.

895₁ Persson, Per. "Skador hindrar Hemingway Att komma till Stockholm," *ibid.*, pp. 3, 15. Dateline: San Francisco de Paulo, Kuba.

895₂ Selander, Sten. "Ernest Hemingway," *ibid.*, p. 17.

896 "Giv at Stal en penning aven!" *BLM*, XXIII (Nov. 1954), 683-685. Photograph.
Regarding Hemingway's receiving the Nobel prize.

897 Gérard, Albert. "Ernest Hemingway, prix Nobel 1954," *Revue Générale Belge* (Nov. 1954), pp. 11-20.

898 "Schriftsteller: Hemingway," review of Philip Young's *Ernest Hemingway* (German translation), *Spiegel*, XLV (Nov. 3, 1954), 36-38. Photograph.

899 Maurice, François. "Hemingway Prix Nobel: propose l'exemple d'un cow-boy d'épopée," *Arts*, No. 488 (Nov. 3-9, 1954), pp. 1, 6.

900 Las Vergnas, Raymond. "Un Classique américain: Hemingway," *Nouvelles Littéraires*, No. 1418 (Nov. 4, 1954), p. 1.

901 Castellet, José María. "Hemingway, Premio Nobel 1954," *Revista*, No. 134 (Nov. 4-10, 1954), p. 1.

902 Fouchet, Max-Pol. "Hemingway: Un catcheur avec des myosotis dans le ventre," *Figaro Littéraire*, IX (Nov. 6, 1954), 1, 5. Photographs.

902₁ Guth, Paul. "En pêchant l'espadon en compagnie d'Hemingway," *ibid.*, p. 5.

903 Photograph of Hemingway receiving the news of the Nobel prize, at Finca Vigia, *Illustrated London News* (Nov. 6, 1954), p. 807.

904 Gonzalez, Lisandro Otero. "Ernest Hemingway: Riesgo y Ventura de Un Gran Escritor," *Bohemia*, XLVI (Nov. 7, 1954), 56-58, 81-83. Photographs.

5 Breit, Harvey. "The Sun Also Rises in Stockholm," *N.Y. Times Book Review* (Nov. 7, 1954), p. 1. Photograph.

Telephoned interview with Hemingway, on October 28, regarding the Nobel prize. Reprinted in *The Writer Observed*, Cleveland, 1956, pp. 275-279. A Swedish translation appeared in *Aikamme*, No. 4 (April 1955), pp. 8, 10.

6 "The Old Man Lands the Biggest Fish," *Life*, xxxvii (Nov. 8, 1954), 25-29. Photographs.

Regarding Hemingway's Nobel prize.

7 "Nobel's Hemingway: The Rock," *Newsweek*, xliv (Nov. 8, 1954), 88-89. Photograph.

8 "Heroes: Life with Papa," *Time*, lxiv (Nov. 8, 1954), 27. Photograph.

Regarding Hemingway's Nobel prize.

9 "B.A.Y." Poem, "The Old Man and the Prize" (For Ernest Hemingway), *Punch*, ccxxvii (Nov. 10, 1954), 593. Caricature of Hemingway by Ronald Searle.

10 Cooke, Alistair. "Hemingway: Master of the Mid-West Vernacular," *Guardian*, Manchester (Nov. 11, 1954), p. 7.

11 Calvino, Italo. "Hemingway e noi," *Contemporaneo* (Nov. 13, 1954), p. 3.

12 Geismar, Maxwell. Editorial, "Hemingway and the Nobel Prize," *Saturday Review*, xxxvii (Nov. 13, 1954), 24, 34.

Reprinted in *American Moderns*, New York, 1958, pp. 61-64. See letter from Emmett B. McGeever in *SR*, xxxvii (Dec. 25, 1954), 21.

13 Castillo-Puche, José Luis. "Hemingway, quinto Nobel yanquí," *Ateneo*, No. 70 (Nov. 15, 1954), pp. 20-22.

14 "Hemingway, premio Nobel," *Insula*, No. 107 (Nov. 15, 1954), p. 1.

15 Schorer, Mark. "Mr. Hemingway and His Critics," review of Charles A. Fenton's *The Apprenticeship of Ernest Hemingway* and John Atkins' *The Art of Ernest Hemingway*, *New Republic*, cxxxi (Nov. 15, 1954), 18-20.

16 Brion, Marcel. "Ernest Hemingway Prix Nobel," *Revue des Deux Mondes* (Nov. 15, 1954), pp. 309-317.

17 "Homage to the Old Man," *Reporter*, xi (Nov. 18, 1954), 6-7.

Regarding Hemingway's Nobel prize.

918 Sullivan, Ed. "Papa Was Overdue: New Yorkers Glad Famed Nobel Prize went to Hemingway," *St. Louis Globe-Democrat* (Nov. 28, 1954), p. 1 F.

919 Rosati, Salvatore. "Lettere Americane: Hemingway premio Nobel," *Mondo* (Nov. 30, 1954), p. 8.

920 von Rosen, Björn. "Hemingway och de gröna bergen," review of *Afrikas gröna berg (GHOA), BLM*, XXIII (Dec. 1954), 800-804.

921 Krishnan, T. V. Kunhi. "Ernest Hemingway: His Life and Works," *Indian Review*, LV (Dec. 1954), 543-545.

922 Ynduráin, Francisco. "Hemingway, espectador de la muerte," *Nuestro Tiempo*, No. 6 (Dec. 1954), pp. 10-20.

923 Lévy, Yves. "Hemingway, chevalier du Graal," *Preuves*, IV (Dec. 1954), 60-63.

924 Las Vergnas, Raymond. "Hemingway, prix Nobel," *Revue Hommes et Mondes*, IX (Dec. 1954), 143-145.

925 Soby, James Thrall. "Hemingway and Painting," *Saturday Review*, XXXVII (Dec. 4, 1954), 60-61.

926 "[19]54 Nobel Prizes Awarded by King | Hemingway, Unable to Attend in Stockholm, Asserts That Writing Is a Lonely Life," *N.Y. Times* (Dec. 11, 1954), p. 5.
   Quotes from Hemingway's Nobel prize acceptance speech, which was read by the American Ambassador to Sweden, John Moors Cabot.

927 "Hemingways budskap: En god författare ställes varje dag inför evigheten," *Svenska Dagbladet* (Dec. 11, 1954), pp. 3, 8.
   Includes Hemingway's Nobel prize acceptance speech, translated into Swedish.

928 Cover story, "An American Storyteller," *Time*, LXIV (Dec. 13, 1954), 70-77. Cover drawing of Hemingway by Artzybasheff. Photographs.
   For the background of this article, see Robert Manning's "Hemingway in Cuba," in the *Atlantic*, CCXVI (Aug. 1965). See also letters from Philip Young in *Time*, LXV (Jan. 3, 1955), 2; and from George Sumner Albee in *Time*, LXV (Jan. 10, 1955), 2, 4.

929 Fenton, Charles A. "Hemingway's Apprenticeship," *Saturday Night*, LXX (Dec. 18, 1954), 17-19; (Dec. 25, 1954), 14-18; (Jan. 1, 1955), 11-12; (Jan. 8, 1955), 14-18; (Jan. 15, 1955), 16-18. Photographs.
   Serialized in five parts from *The Apprenticeship of Ernest Hemingway*, New York, 1954.

930 Harling, Robert. "A Journey to Hemingway," *Sunday Times,* London (Dec. 19, 1954), p. 10. Photograph of Hemingway by Leonard McCombs.

Interview with Hemingway at Finca Vigia.

931 Gould, Jack. Radio in Review column, "NBC Salutes Hemingway As Man Who 'Lived it Up to Write it Down,'" *N.Y. Times* (Dec. 22, 1954), p. 34.

Review of the hour-long documentary "Meet Ernest Hemingway," presented by the National Broadcasting Company, on December 19, 1954. Participants included Lester Pearson, narrator, Charles A. Fenton, James T. Farrell, John Mason Brown, Max Eastman, Leonard Lyons, and Malcolm Cowley. Marlon Brando read excerpts from *OMATS.* A tape was played of Hemingway reading his Nobel prize acceptance speech.

932 MacLeish, Archibald. "Presentation to Ernest Hemingway of the Award of Merit Medal for the Novel," *American Academy of Arts and Letters and the National Institute of Arts and Letters Proceedings,* New York, Second Series, No. 5 (1955), pp. 28-29.

933 [Lorenzo, Emilio]. "Hemingway, Premio Nobel de Literatura," *Arbor* (Jan. 1955), pp. 102-106.

934 Richter, W. "Hemingway und die Helden," *Deutsche Rundschau,* LXXXI (Jan. 1955), 54-56.

935 Phillips, William L. "Sherwood Anderson's Two Prize Pupils," *University of Chicago Magazine,* XLVII (Jan. 1955), 9-12. Photograph.

Regarding Anderson's influence on Hemingway and Faulkner.

936 Aranda, Joaquín. "La novela de Ernest Hemingway," *Revista de Estudios Americanos,* Nos. 40-41 (Jan.–Feb. 1955), pp. 63-72.

937 Antonini, Giacomo. "Hemingway grande e meno grande," *Fiera Letteraria,* x (Jan. 16, 1955), 1, 2. Photograph.

938 Breit, Harvey. "A Walk With Faulkner," *N.Y. Times Book Review* (Jan. 30, 1955), pp. 4, 12.

Regarding William Faulkner's listing Hemingway last, when asked to rate the five best contemporary writers.

939 Guérard, Albert. "Ernest Hemingway," *Revue des Langues Vivantes,* XXI (Feb. 1955), 35-50.

940 Pizzetti, Ippolito. "Un addio a Hemingway," *Società,* XI (Feb. 1955), 23-45.

941 Dietrich, Marlene. "The Most Fascinating Man I Know," *This Week* (Feb. 13, 1955), pp. 8-9. Photograph.

Relates her meeting with Hemingway on a transatlantic crossing on the *Ile de France*, in 1934, and their subsequent friendship.

942 Troilo, Nicola. "Ernest Hemingway premio Nobel," *Nuova Antologia*, xc (March 1955), 423-428.

943 Photographic essay, "The Old Man by the Sea," *Pageant*, x (March 1955), 114-119. Photographs by Hans Malmberg.

944 Maurois, André. "Ernest Hemingway," *Revue de Paris*, LXII (March 1955), 3-16.
   Reprinted in *Portraits*, Ottawa, 1955, pp. 155-174. An English translation appeared in *Baker anthology*, pp. 38-54.

945 Karst, Roman. "*Casus* Hemingway," *Twórczość*, xi (March 1955), 98-105.

946 Holthusen, Hans Egon. "Hemingways Darstellungskunst, "*Universitas*, x (March 1955), 257-260.

947 Frauenfelden, William. "Ernest Hemingway, l'uomo e il suo eroe," *Umana* (March–April 1955), pp. 28-32.

948 Edel, Leon and Philip Young. "Hemingway and the Nobel Prize," *Folio*, xx (Spring 1955), 18-22.
   A debate: "The Art of Evasion" by Edel, pp. 18-19; and "A Defense" by Young, pp. 20-22. Reprinted in *Weeks collection*: Edel, pp. 169-171; Young, pp. 172-174.

949 Happel, Nikolaus. "Chapter V aus Hemingways Kurzgeschichtenband *In Our Time*," *Archiv für das Studium der Neueren Sprachen*, CXCI (April 1955), 324-325.

950 Photograph of Hemingway with U.S. airmen, at Finca Vigía, *Look*, XIX (April 19, 1955), 106-107.

951 Pérez Navarro, Francisco. "*El viejo y el mar* y la crítica inglesa," *Cuadernos Hispanoamericanos*, No. 65 (May 1955), pp. 251-252.

952 Waggoner, Hyatt H. "Ernest Hemingway," *Christian Scholar*, XXXVIII (June 1955), 114-120.

953 Moylan, Thomas J. "Violence in Hemingway," *Catholic World*, CLXXXI (July 1955), 287-293. Photograph.

954 Gaston-Cherau, Françoise. "Ernest Hemingway et le 'catholicisme sceptique,'" *Esprit*, XXIII (July 1955), 1130-43.

955 Pritchett, V. S. "Ernest Hemingway," *New Statesman & Nation*, L (July 30, 1955), 137-138.
   Regarding the Penguin editions of *FTA*, *MWW*, *FWBT*, and

THAHN. For reply by H. Quiller, see *NS&N*, L (Aug. 6, 1955), 163.

56 Backman, Melvin. "Hemingway: The Matador and the Crucified," *Modern Fiction Studies*, I (Aug. 1955), 2-11. Hemingway Number edited by William Bache. Reprinted in *Baker anthology*, pp. 245-258; in *Baker critiques*, pp. 135-143; in *Modern American Fiction*, ed. A. Walton Litz, New York, 1963, pp. 201-214. A French translation appeared in *Revue des Lettres Modernes*, IV (1957), 521-543.

56₁ Holman, C. Hugh. "Hemingway and Emerson: Notes on the Continuity of an Aesthetic Tradition," *ibid.*, pp. 12-16.

56₂ Wyrick, Green D. "Hemingway and Bergson: The *Élan Vital*," *ibid.*, pp. 17-19.

56₃ Burnam, Tom. "Primitivism and Masculinity in the Work of Ernest Hemingway," *ibid.*, pp. 20-24.

56₄ Russell, H. K. "The Catharsis in *A Farewell to Arms*," *ibid.*, pp. 25-30.
A French translation appeared in *Revue des Lettres Modernes*, IV (1957), 563-576.

56₅ Oldsey, Bernard S. "Hemingway's Old Men," *ibid.*, pp. 31-35.

56₆ Beebe, Maurice. "Criticism of Ernest Hemingway: A Selected Checklist With an Index to Studies of Separate Works," *ibid.*, pp. 36-45.

57 Gorokhov, Viktor. "Kheminguei i ego novaia kniga," review of *OMATS* (Cape edition), *Novoe Vremia*, No. 37 (Sept. 8, 1955), pp. 27-28.

58 Allen, Charles A. "Ernest Hemingway's Clean, Well-Lighted Heroes," *Pacific Spectator*, IX (Autumn 1955), 383-389.

59 Schwartz, Delmore. "The Fiction of Ernest Hemingway," *Perspectives U.S.A.*, No. 13 (Autumn 1955), pp. 70-88.

60 Lindner, Sven. "Hårdkokthetens grammatik," review of *Noveller* (short stories), *BLM*, XXIV (Oct. 1955), 643-644.

61 Gurko, Leo. "The Heroic Impulse in *The Old Man and the Sea*," *English Journal*, XLIV (Oct. 1955), 377-382.
Reprinted in *College English*, XVII (Oct. 1955), 11-15. A French translation appeared in *Revue des Lettres Modernes*, IV (1957), 614-625.

62 Flanagan, John T. "Hemingway's Debt to Sherwood Anderson," *Journal of English and Germanic Philology*, LIV (Oct. 1955), 507-520.

963 "Hemingway y Adolfo Luque, condecorados la Medalla de oro de San Cristobal," *Diario de la Marina* (Oct. 27, 1955), p. 14 A.

964 Lvov, Sergei. "Mesto cheloveka v zhizni," review of *OMATS* (Cape edition), *Literaturnaya Gazeta* (Oct. 27, 1955), p. 2.

965 "Cuba Decorates Hemingway," *N.Y. Times* (Oct. 28, 1955), p. 15. Dateline: Havana.
   Hemingway received the Order of San Cristobal in recognition of his interest in Cuba.

966 Colvert, James B. "Ernest Hemingway's Morality in Action," *American Literature*, XXVII (Nov. 1955), 372-385.
   A French translation appeared in *Revue des Lettres Modernes*, IV (1957), 544-562.

967 Beck, Warren. "The Shorter Happy Life of Mrs. Macomber," *Modern Fiction Studies*, I (Nov. 1955), 28-37.
   A French translation appeared in *Revue des Lettres Modernes*, IV (1957), 577-598.

968 Wilson, Earl. "Hemingway . . . About to Bank Another Book," *N.Y. Post* (Nov. 9, 1955), p. 17. Dateline: Havana.
   Regarding a visit to the Hemingways.

969 Spivey, Ted R. "Hemingway's Pursuit of Happiness on the Open Road," *Emory University Quarterly*, XI (Dec. 1955), 240-252.

970 Clark, John Abbott. "A Footnote to a Footnote to a Footnote," *National Review*, I (Dec. 28, 1955), 19-21.
   Regarding Russell Maloney's article in the *New Yorker*, XV (July 15, 1939), concerning Hemingway's footnote on humanists in "A Natural History of the Dead," in the *First 49*, p. 543.

971 Bache, William B. "Craftsmanship in 'A Clean, Well-Lighted Place,'" *Personalist*, XXXVII (Winter 1956), 60-64.

972 Björneboe, Jens. "Hemingway og Dyrene," *Danske Magasin*, IV, No. 4-5, [1956], 225-235.

973 Happel, Nikolaus. "Stilbetrachtung an *The Old Man and the Sea*," *Neueren Sprachen*, V (1956), 71-78.

974 Waldmeir, Joseph. "*Confiteor Hominem*: Ernest Hemingway's Religion of Man," *Papers of the Michigan Academy of Science, Arts, and Letters*, XLII (1956 Meeting), 349-356.
   Reprinted in *Weeks collection*, pp. 161-168; and in *Baker critiques*, pp. 144-149.

975 D'Agostino, Nemi. "Ernest Hemingway," *Belfagor*, XI (Jan. 1956), 54-73. In Italian.

An English translation, titled "The Later Hemingway," appeared in *Sewanee Review*, LXVIII (Summer 1960), 482-493. Reprinted in *Weeks collection*, pp. 152-160.

176 Agrikolyanski, V., A. Krasnovski, and D. Rachkov. "Pis'mo studentov Ernestu Khemingueya," *Inostrannaya Literatura*, No. 1 (Jan. 1956), p. 233.

An open letter to Hemingway about *OMATS*, from three Moscow University students. For translated excerpt, see *Soviet Attitudes toward American Writing*, Deming Brown, Princeton, 1962, p. 311.

177 Dorgelès, Roland. "Ce rude Hemingway," *Figaro Littéraire*, No. 509 (Jan. 21, 1956), p. 7. Photograph.

178 Blumenberg, Hans. "Die Peripatie des Mannes: Über das Werk Ernest Hemingways," *Hochland*, XLVIII (Feb. 1956), 220-233.

179 Ishi, Ichiro. "Understanding Ernest Hemingway," *Hototogisu*, V (Feb. 1956), 11-12.

180 [Hemingway, Mary, John O'Hara, Malcolm Cowley, John Groth, *et al.*] "Who the Hell is Hemingway?" *True*, XXXVI (Feb. 1956), 14-19, 25-31, 68. Cover drawing and photographs.

A symposium comprised of reprinted excerpts.

181 Wilson, Earl. "Hemingway In Bed 40 Days But Whips Hepatitis Virus," *N.Y. Post* (Feb. 6, 1956), p. 15. Dateline: Havana.

182 Parks, Edd Winfield. "Hemingway and Faulkner: The Pattern of Their Thought," *Dagens Nyheder* (Feb. 12, 1956), pp. 4-5. In Danish.

An English translation appeared in *South Atlantic Bulletin*, XXII (March 1957), 1-2.

183 Sordo, Enrique. Review of *Adiós a las armas* (*FTA*), *Revista*, No. 202 (Feb. 23-29, 1956), p. 14.

184 Halliday, E. M. "Hemingway's Ambiguity: Symbolism and Irony," *American Literature*, XXVIII (March 1956), 1-22.

Reprinted in *Interpretations of American Literature*, ed. Charles Feidelson, Jr. and Paul Brodtkorb, Jr., New York, 1959, pp. 297-319; in *Weeks collection*, pp. 52-71; in *Baker critiques*, pp. 61-74. A French translation appeared in *Revue des Lettres Modernes*, IV (1957), 626-658.

185 Photograph of Hemingway and Gary Cooper, in Havana, *Newsweek*, XLVII (March 12, 1956), 62.

186 Kashkeen, Ivan. "Perechityvaya Khemingueya," *Inostrannaya Literatura*, No. 4 (April 1956), pp. 194-206.

987 Bernheim, Kurt. *McCall's* Visits series, "Ernest Hemingway," *McCall's* (May 1956), pp. 6, 8, 10. Photographs.
Interview with Hemingway at Finca Vigia.

988 Drobyshevski, Vladislav. "Nepobedimy," review of *Starik i more* (*OMATS*), *Zvezda*, No. 5 (May 1956), pp. 166-170.
For Sergei Lvov's reply, see *Zvezda*, No. 8 (Aug. 1956), pp. 188-189.

989 "Hemingway's Big Catch," *St. Louis Post-Dispatch* (May 4, 1956), p. 6 A. Dateline: Cabo Blanco, Peru.
After a forty-five-minute fight, Hemingway landed a 750-pound black marlin as cameramen recorded the catch for the film version of *OMATS*.

990 "Search: the truly big one," *Newsweek*, XLVII (May 7, 1956), 53. Photograph.
Item about Hemingway fishing off the coast of Peru, at Talara, during filming of *OMATS*.

991 Sosin, Milt. "Novelist Hemingway Puts Books in 'Bank,'" *Miami Daily News* (May 22, 1956), p. 2. Photograph on p. 1.
Interview with Hemingway in Miami, on his arrival by plane from Peru.

992 "Papa and Old Man Ramirez," *Time*, LXVII (June 18, 1956), 47. Photograph.
Regarding the news stories in the Havana *Excelsior* claiming that Miguel Ramirez, an old Cuban fisherman, was the old man in *OMATS*; a fact which he later denied.

993 Holman, C. Hugh. "Hemingway and *Vanity Fair*, *Carolina Quarterly*, VIII (Summer 1956), 31-37.

994 "Americans in Paris: Catalogue of an Exhibition," Princeton University Library, May 4–June 30, 1956, *Princeton University Library Chronicle*, XVII (Summer 1956).
Hemingway items are listed on pp. 247, 248, 256. Quotes a letter from Hemingway to F. Scott Fitzgerald, on p. 248. See (F66).

995 Kashkeen, Ivan. "Alive in the Midst of Death," *Soviet Literature*, No. 7 (July 1956), pp. 160-172.
Reprinted in *Baker anthology*, pp. 162-179.

996 Bienkowski, Zbigniew. "Opowiadania Hemingwaya," *Twórczość*, No. 8 (Aug. 1956), pp. 153-157.
An essay on Hemingway's short stories.

997 "Gift to a Shrine," *Newsweek*, XLVIII (Aug. 27, 1956), 58. Photograph.

Item about Hemingway donating his Nobel prize gold medal to the Shrine of Our Lady of Charity of Cobre, the patron saint of Cuba.

98 Lyons, Leonard. The Lyons Den column, "Papa's Back in Town," *N.Y. Post* (Aug. 28, 1956), p. 24. Dateline: New York.

Relates a conversation with the Hemingways, at Toots Shor's restaurant.

99 Campoamor, Fernando G. "Homenaje Cubano a Hemingway," *Boletín Comisión Nacional Cubano de la UNESCO*, v (Sept. 1956), 11-13.

00 Kiley, Jed. "Hemingway: a title bout in ten rounds," *Playboy*, III (Sept. 1956), 19, 28, 34-38; (Oct. 1956), 55-56; (Nov. 1956), 67, 70, 84-86; (Dec. 1956), 61-62, 75; IV (March 1957), 51-52, 60, 66; (April 1957), 63, 66; (Aug. 1957), 45-46, 50, 52, 60, 66-67; (Sept. 1957), 65-66.

Published in book form as *Hemingway: An Old Friend Remembers*, New York, 1965. See also Playbill in the September 1956 issue, pp. 2, 4; and Arthur Moss's letter in the March 1957 issue, p. 5, regarding Hemingway's contribution to *Boulevardier*.

01 D'Incecco, Nick and Joe P. Faulkner. "Hemingways Sail, End 'Incognito' Stay Here," *N.Y. Journal-American* (Sept. 2, 1956), p. 3. Dateline: New York.

Regarding the Hemingways' two-week stay in New York, prior to sailing on the *Ile de France* to Le Havre.

02 "Hemingway in France," *K.C. Star* (Sept. 8, 1956), p. 9. Dateline: Le Havre.

Brief item regarding the Hemingways arrival in France, and their plans to travel to the Riviera and Italy.

03 "Hemingway in Spain," *St. Louis Post-Dispatch* (Sept. 22, 1956), p. 2 A. Dateline: Logrono, Spain.

Brief item that the Hemingways had arrived to see the bullfights of the Logrono Fair.

04 Goodheart, Eugene. "The Legacy of Ernest Hemingway," *Prairie Schooner*, XXX (Fall 1956), 212-218.

05 Hertzel, Leo J. "Hemingway and the Problem of Belief," *Catholic World*, CLXXXIV (Oct. 1956), 29-33.

06 O'Connor, William Van. "Two Views of Kilimanjaro," *History of Ideas News Letter*, II (Oct. 1956), 76-80. Reprinted in *The Grotesque*, Carbondale, Ill., 962, pp. 119-124.

07 Photograph, "Fifteen Americans who made Literary History," *N.Y. Times Book Review* (Oct. 7, 1956), p. 8.

1008 Strandberg, Olle. "Livets säkra faktum är döden: porträtt ar Ernest Hemingway," *Vi*, No. 43 (Oct. 26, 1956), pp. 15-17. Cover photograph of Hemingway by Rune Hassner. Photographs. Interview with Hemingway at Finca Vigia.

1009 Item, "Campaigning," *Newsweek*, XLVIII (Oct. 29, 1956), 57. Quotes a letter from Hemingway to students of the University of Glasgow, who had nominated him for the honorary job of university Lord Rector.

1010 Item, *Time*, LXVIII (Oct. 29, 1956), 47. Photograph. Regarding Hemingway's visit to Pio Baroja, in Madrid.

1011 White, William. "On Collecting Hemingway," *American Book Collector*, VII (Nov. 1956), 21-23. Discusses various items of interest in his Hemingway collection. See Fraser Drew's letter in *ABC*, VII (Dec. 1956), 2; and Adrian Goldstone's letter in *ABC*, VII (Feb. 1957), 20.

1012 Paolini, Pier Francesco. "Lo Hemingway dei grandi racconti," *Letteratura Moderne*, VI (Nov.–Dec. 1956), 742-750. An English translation, titled "The Hemingway of the Major Works," appeared in *Baker anthology*, pp. 131-144.

1013 Wandruszka, Mario. "Strukturen moderner Prosa," *Deutschunterricht*, IX (1957), 89-104. Essay on *OMATS*.

1014 Beebe, Maurice, ed. Preface, "Configuration Critique d'Ernest Hemingway," *Revue des Lettres Modernes*, IV, xxxi-xxxiv (1957), 469-472. Hemingway Number.

1014₁ Warren, Robert Penn. "Introduction a *L'adieu aux armes*," *ibid.*, pp. 473-520. Translated from the introduction to *FTA*. See (A81).

1014₂ Backman, Melvin. "Le Matador et le crucifié," *ibid.*, pp. 521-543. Translated from *Modern Fiction Studies*, I (Aug. 1955).

1014₃ Colvert, James B. "La morale dans l'action," *ibid.*, pp. 544-562. Translated from *American Literature*, XXVII (Nov. 1955).

1014₄ Russell, H. K. "Étude de la catharsis dans *L'adieu aux armes*," *ibid.*, pp. 563-576. Translated from *Modern Fiction Studies*, I (Aug. 1955).

1014₅ Beck, Warren. "Une interprétation de L'heure triomphale de Francis Macomber,'" *ibid.*, pp. 577-598. Translated from *Modern Fiction Studies*, I (Nov. 1955).

146 Carpenter, Frederic I. "Hemingway et la cinquième dimension," *ibid.*, pp. 599-613.
Translated from *PMLA*, LXIX (Sept. 1954).

147 Gurko, Leo. "L'élan héroïque dans *Le vieil homme et la mer*," *ibid.*, pp. 614-625.
Translated from the *English Journal*, XLIV (Oct. 1955).

148 Halliday, E. M. "Symbolisme et ironie chez Hemingway," *ibid.*, pp. 626-658.
Translated from *American Literature*, XXVIII (March 1956).

149 Beebe, Maurice. "Critique d'Ernest Hemingway," *ibid.*, pp. 659-679.
A checklist of English and American articles on Hemingway.

1410 Smith, Thelma M. and Ward L. Miner. "La Critique de Hemingway en France," *ibid.*, pp. 681-700.
Translated from *Transatlantic Migration: The Contemporary American Novel in France,* Durham, N.C., 1955, pp. 99-121.

1411 Esquisse Bibliographique (d'articles et de comptes rendus), *ibid.*, pp. 702-705.

015 Duffy, Charles. "Ernest Hemingway," *Sprache und Literatur Englands und Amerikas*, II (1957), 151-164.

016 Bache, William B. "*Nostromo* and 'The Snows of Kilimanjaro,' " *Modern Language Notes*, LXXII (Jan. 1957), 32-34.

017 Lyons, Leonard. "Last Day in Europe," *N.Y. Post* (Jan. 21, 1957), p. 26. Dateline: Paris. Photograph, on p. 2, of Hemingway and Lyons in Paris Lido nightclub.
Relates a day spent in Paris with Hemingway.

018 Photograph of Hemingway, in formal attire, dancing with Ingrid Bergman, in Paris, "Hemingway danse avec son Heroïne," *Paris Match*, No. 407 (Jan. 26, 1957), p. 39.

019 "Hemingway In After Europe Trip," *N.Y. Herald Tribune* (Jan. 31, 1957), II, 1. Photograph.
Interview in New York, en route to Cuba.

020 Seyppel, Joachim H. "Two Variations on a Theme: Dying in Venice," *Literature & Psychology*, VII (Feb. 1957), 8-12.
Essay on *ARIT* and Thomas Mann's *Death in Venice*.

021 Guérard, Albert. "Hemingway's Lehrjahre," *Revue des Langues Vivantes*, XXIII (Feb. 1957), 89-91.

022 Scott, Arthur L. "In Defense of Robert Cohn," *College English*, XVIII (March 1957), 309-314.

469

Describes Robert Cohn, in *SAR*, as "the most fashionable whipping boy of modern American literature."

1022₁ Hart, Robert C. "Hemingway on Writing," *ibid.*, pp. 314-320.

1022₂ Wagner, Vern. Round Table, "A Note for Ernest Hemingway," *ibid.*, p. 327.
Appeals to Hemingway to write about America.

1023 Photograph of Hemingway with Spencer Tracy, during the filming of *OMATS, Newsweek*, XLIX (March 18, 1957), 117.

1024 Shockley, Martin S. "Hemingway's Moment of Truth," *Colorado Quarterly*, V (Spring 1957), 380-388.

1025 Roberts, MacLean. "An Afternoon with Papa Hemingway," *Bachelor*, II (May 1957), 38-41, 72. Photographs.
Regarding a visit to Finca Vigia.

1026 Bovie, Verne H. "The Evolution of a Myth: A Study of the Major Symbols in the Works of Ernest Hemingway," *Dissertation Abstracts*, XVII (May 1957), 1080.
Abstract of doctoral dissertation, University of Pennsylvania, 1957.

1027 Weeks, Robert P. "Hemingway's 'The Killers,'" *Explicator*, XV (May 1957), Item 53.

1028 Wilson, Earl. "A Visit With 'Papa,'" *N.Y. Post* (May 26, 1957), p. M-3. Dateline: Havana.

1029 "Hollywood Goes Hemingway," *N.Y. Times Magazine* (May 26, 1957), pp. 66-67.
Regarding the filming of Hemingway's novels.

1030 Zumalde, Ignacio. "La novela de guerra," *Nuestro Tiempo*, No. 36 (June 1957), pp. 749-753.
Discussion of *FTA*.

1031 Kashkeen, Ivan. "Kheminguei na puti k masterstvu," *Voprosi Literaturi*, No. 6 (June 1957), pp. 184-204.
Essay on "Hemingway on the path to mastery."

1032 Castellet, José María. "El diálogo en los relatos de Ernest Hemingway," *Revista*, No. 271 (June 22–28, 1957), p. 15.

1033 Thody, Philip. "A Note on Camus and the American Novel," *Comparative Literature*, IX (Summer 1957), 243-249.
General article. Discusses Hemingway's influence on Albert Camus's work.

034 Weeks, Robert P. "Hemingway and the Spectatorial Attitude," *Western Humanities Review*, XI (Summer 1957), 277-281.

035 Wyka, Jan. Review of *Komu biji dzwon (FWBT)*, *Twórczość*, XIII (July 1957), 144-147.

036 Shearer, Lloyd. "Hollywood Goes Hemingway," *Parade* (July 28, 1957), pp. 6, 7, 9. Cover photograph of Hemingway by Yousuf Karsh.

Regarding the filming of *SAR*, *FTA*, and *OMATS*, and the seven previously filmed Hemingway stories.

037 Rolo, Charles J. "Venetian Hotel," *Atlantic*, CC (Aug. 1957), 94-96.

Regarding the Gritti, in Venice, and its part in *ARIT*.

038 James, T. F. "Hemingway at Work," *Cosmopolitan*, CXLIII (Aug. 1957), 52-55. Photographs.

039 Fenton, Charles A. "The Writers Who Came Out of the War," *Saturday Review*, XL (Aug. 3, 1957), 5-7, 24.

General article. Regarding World War I.

040 "Hemingway Dog Slain; Cuba Patrol Denies Act," *N.Y. Times* (Aug. 22, 1957), p. 8. Dateline: Havana.

Hemingway's dog, Machakosa, was found dead following a night visit to Finca Vigia by a patrol of soldiers.

041 "Hemingway's Lost Souls," review of the film, *SAR*, *Life*, XLIII (Sept. 16, 1957), 61-66.

Excerpts from the novel are used as captions under scenes from the film.

042 Friedrich, Otto. "Ernest Hemingway: Joy Through Strength," *American Scholar*, XXVI (Autumn 1957), 470, 518-530.

For Sheldon Grebstein's reply, see *American Scholar*, XXVII (Spring 1958), 229-231.

043 Fagan, Edward R. "Teaching Enigmas of *The Old Man and the Sea*," *English Record*, VIII (Autumn 1957), 13-20.

044 Item, *Time*, LXX (Oct. 7, 1957), 44.

Brief item about the Hemingways in New York.

045 Meyer, Charles R. Boatman of the Month series, "Hemingway and the *Pilar*," *Popular Boating*, II (Nov. 1957), 27-31, 81, 83. Cover drawing of Hemingway by Robert T. McCall. Photographs.

046 Riccio, Attilio. "Una storia difficile," *Mondo*, IX (Nov. 12, 1957), 14.

Regarding the movie version of *SAR*.

1047 Karsh, Yousuf. "The Camera's Eye: Ernest Hemingway," *Atlantic*, cc (Dec. 1957), 102-103. Photograph of Hemingway by Karsh.

Regarding Karsh's photographic session with Hemingway, at Finca Vigia. Reprinted in *Portraits of Greatness*, London, 1959, p. 96.

1048 Rondi, Gian Luigi. "Hemingway e il cinema," *Mondo Occidentale*, IV (Dec. 1957), 50-61.

1049 Happel, Nikolaus. "Ein Beitrag zur 'discipline' in Hemingways Stil," *Neueren Sprachen*, VI (Dec. 1957), 583-587.

1050 Weeks, Robert P. "Hemingway and the Uses of Isolation," *University of Kansas City Review*, XXIV (Dec. 1957), 119-125.

Discusses Hemingway's pronouncement on the writer's need to stand alone, and his "vision of man isolated," as delineated in his fictive world.

1051 Lyons, Leonard. The Lyons Den column, *N.Y. Post* (Dec. 12, 1957), p. M-8. Dateline: Havana.

Relates details of a visit with the Hemingways in Cuba. Mentions that Hemingway was working on a series of portrait sketches of his early years in Paris.

1052 "It's Hemingway's Year," *Newsweek*, L (Dec. 16, 1957), 116-119. Photograph.

Regarding the filming of *SAR*, *FTA*, and *OMATS*.

1053 Kreymborg, Alfred. "Exit Vachel Lindsay—Enter Ernest Hemingway," *Literary Review*, I (Winter 1957–1958), 208-219.

Reminiscences of Hemingway in the 1920s.

1054 Bartlett, Phyllis. "Other Countries, Other Wenches," *Modern Fiction Studies*, III (Winter 1957–1958), 345-349.

1055 Dawson, William Forrest. "Ernest Hemingway: Petoskey Interview," *Michigan Alumnus Quarterly Review*, LXIV (Winter 1958), 114-123.

Regarding Hemingway's early summers spent in northern Michigan. Reprinted, under the title "Hemingway at Walloon Lake," in *Best Articles & Stories*, II (Oct. 1958), 46-51.

1056 Stephens, Robert O. "Hemingway's *Across the River and Into the Trees*: A Reprise," *University of Texas Studies in English*, XXXVII (1958), 92-101.

1057 Dunlop, Blanche. "Hemingway's Hectic Stint with the *Star*," *Canadian Journalist & Press Photographer*, II (Jan. 1958), 8-11.

Regarding Hemingway's work on the *Toronto Star*, in the early 1920s.

58 Kemp, Tom. "The Fishing Times of a Great Author," *Fisherman*, IX (Jan. 1958), 34-35, 78-81. Cover photograph of Hemingway.

81 Dos Passos, John, Waldo Peirce, and Taylor Williams. "Hemingway in the Eyes of Some Friends," *ibid.*, pp. 37, 83-86.

82 Photographs, "Hemingway in Pictures," *ibid.*, pp. 38-41.

59 Caricature by Al Hirschfeld, "Harry's Bar in Venice," *Holiday*, XXIII (Jan. 1958), 48-49.

60 Corin, Fernand. "Steinbeck and Hemingway: A Study in Literary Economy," *Revue des Langues Vivantes*, XXIV (Jan.–Feb. 1958), 60-75, Part I; (March–April 1958), 153-163, Part II.

61 Lange, Per-Adolf. "Hemingways poesi," *BLM*, XXVII (Feb. 1958), 133-138.

62 Young, Leo Vernon. "Values of the Young Characters in the Fiction of Dos Passos, Hemingway, and Steinbeck," *Dissertation Abstracts*, XVIII (Feb. 1958), 518-519.
   Abstract from doctoral dissertation, Stanford University, 1957.

63 Plimpton, George. "Hemingway—Dix Conseils aux Jeunes Écrivains," *Arts*, No. 662 (March 19–25, 1958), pp. 1, 2, Part I; No. 663 (March 26–April 1, 1958), pp. 1, 3, Part II; No. 664 (April 2–8, 1958), p. 3, Part III. Photographs.
   For Jean Hougron's reply, see *Arts*, No. 664 (April 2–8, 1958), pp. 1, 5.

64 Sapin, Louis. "Un colosse qui triomphe des éléments et des hommes," *Arts*, No. 662 (March 19–25, 1958), p. 4.

65 Sapin, Louis. "Les deux sources vives de son oeuvre: l'amour et la mort," *Arts*, No. 663 (March 26–April 1, 1958), p. 3.

66 Plimpton, George. "The Art of Fiction, XXI: Ernest Hemingway," *Paris Review*, V (Spring 1958), 60-89. Drawing of Hemingway by Bee W. Dabney. Facsimile of manuscript page from "The Battler."
   Plimpton notes, on pp. 64-65, that "many of the replies in this interview [Hemingway] preferred to work out on his reading-board." Reprinted in *Horizon*, I (Jan. 1959), 82-85, 132-135; in *Baker anthology*, pp. 19-37; and in *Writers at Work: The Paris Review Interviews*, New York, 1963, pp. 215-239. A German translation appeared in *Merkur*, XIII (1959), 526-544. A Russian translation appeared in *Inostrannaya Literatura*, No. 1 (Jan. 1962), pp. 212-218. Note: The 42-page manuscript of the original questions and Hemingway's holograph answers is among the holdings of the Rare Book Division of the New York Public Library.

473

1067 Avril, François. "Depuis 20 ans, Hemingway est resté fidèle à ses idées," *Arts*, No. 665 (April 9–15, 1958), p. 10.

1068 "Hemingway . . . Writes in an Icy Mood," *Newsweek*, LI (April 21, 1958), 122-123. Photograph.
Regarding the interview in the *Paris Review*, V (Spring 1958).

1069 Moore, Harry T. "An Earnest Hemingwaiad," *Encounter*, X (June 1958), 15-18.
A verse account of Hemingway's career.

1070 Morris, Wright. "The Ability to Function: A Reappraisal of Fitzgerald and Hemingway," *New World Writing*, No. 13 (June 1958), pp. 34-51.
"Hemingway: The Function of Style," pp. 43-51, was reprinted in *The Territory Ahead*, New York, 1958, pp. 133-146.

1071 Atkins, John. "Hemingway and the American Novel," *Wisdom*, III, No. 26 (June 1958), 5-9. Front and back cover photographs of Hemingway by Yousuf Karsh. Reprinted, in a different form, from *The Art of Ernest Hemingway*, London, 1952.

1071₁ "Hemingway and the Motion Picture," *ibid.*, pp. 10-13.

1071₂ "Hemingway and the Great Outdoors," *ibid.*, pp. 14-15.

1071₃ "Hemingway: *The Old Man and the Sea.*," *ibid.*, pp. 16-17.
Regarding the filming of the movie.

1072 Cimatti, Pietro. "L'altro Hemingway," *Fiera Letteraria*, XIII (June 8, 1958), 6.

1073 Friedman, Norman. "What Makes a Short Story Short?" *Modern Fiction Studies*, IV (Summer 1958), 103-117.
General article. On pp. 107-108, "Hills Like White Elephants" and "Ten Indians" are used as examples. Reprinted in *A College Book of Modern Fiction*, ed. Walter B. Rideout and James K. Robinson, Evanston, Ill., 1961, pp. 552-565.

1074 "Recall Casualty Report on Ernest Hemingway," *K.C. Star* (July 14, 1958), p. 5. Drawing of Hemingway, at eighteen.
Article about Hemingway being wounded during World War I, in Italy.

1075 Robinson, Layhmond. "Hemingway Brings Suit to Stop Reprint of Spanish War Stories," *N.Y. Times* (Aug. 6, 1958), p. 1.
Hemingway's lawyer brought suit, in the New York Supreme Court, to block *Esquire* from reprinting three of his Spanish Civil War stories in an anthology.

076 Robinson, Layhmond. "Hemingway Says He Will Drop Suit | Asserts that Political Fear Did Not Spur Attempt to Bar Reprints of Stories," *N.Y. Times* (Aug. 7, 1958), p. 27.

Note: Only one story, "The Butterfly and the Tank," was included in the anthology, see (B58).

077 "Same Old Papa," *Newsweek*, LII (Aug. 18, 1958), 27-28.

Regarding the suit against *Esquire*.

078 "Hemingway Stories Outagin', Inagin' *Esquire* Tome," *Publishers' Weekly*, CLXXIV (Aug. 18, 1958), 28-29.

079 Beatty, Jerome, Jr. "Hemingway vs *Esquire*," *Saturday Review*, XLI (Aug. 23, 1958), 9, 11, 36.

080 Machlin, Milt. "Hemingway Talking," *Argosy* (Sept. 1958), pp. 34-37, 84-86. Photographs.

Interview with Hemingway at Finca Vigia.

081 "The Old Man and His Big Catch," pictorial review of the film, *OMATS*, *Look*, XXII (Sept. 2, 1958), 66-67.

082 Friedman, Norman. "Criticism and the Novel: Hardy, Hemingway, Crane, Woolf, Conrad," *Antioch Review*, XVIII (Fall 1958), 343-370.

Discusses Hemingway's work on pp. 352-356.

083 Lange, Per-Adolf. "Tjugofem år efteråt," review of *Döden på eftermiddagen (DIA)*, *BLM*, XXVII (Oct. 1958), 682-684.

084 Drummond, Ann. "The Hemingway Code as Seen in the Early Short Stories," *Discourse*, I (Oct. 1958), 248-252.

085 Knight, Arthur. "The Old Man on the Screen," review of the film, *OMATS*, *Saturday Review*, XLI (Oct. 4, 1958), 26.

086 Raines, Halsey. "Movie Log of a Famed Fish Story," *N.Y. Times* (Oct. 5, 1958), II, 7.

An account of the filming of *OMATS*.

087 "Hemingway's Old Man and His Movie Epic," *Life*, XLV (Oct. 6, 1958), 124-129.

Pictorial essay on the film, *OMATS*. ". . . the first successful effort to get Hemingway's flavor on film . . . retains all of the beauty of Hemingway's noted prose style."

088 Beckley, Paul V. " 'Old Man and Sea' Is a Movie Poem," review of the film, *OMATS*, *N.Y. Herald Tribune* (Oct. 12, 1958), IV, 1, 4.

089 Crowther, Bosley. "One-Man Show," review of the film, *OMATS*, *N.Y. Times* (Oct. 12, 1958), II, 1.

475

1090 "Trouble, Then Triumph," review of the film, *OMATS*, *Newsweek*, LII (Oct. 13, 1958), 118-119.
"Summing up: Magnificent."

1091 "Hemingway Manuscript Sold," *N.Y. Times* (Oct. 15, 1958), p. 36.
Regarding the Parke-Bernet Galleries auction of the library of Dr. Don Carlos Guffey, at which a holograph manuscript of *DIA* was purchased by House of Books, Ltd., for $13,000. For catalogue of the sale, see (G174).

1092 Item, *Time*, LXXII (Oct. 27, 1958), 40.
Regarding the auction of the library of Dr. Don Carlos Guffey.

1092₁ "Two with Tracy," review of the film, *OMATS, ibid.*, p. 42.

1093 Evans, Oliver. "The Protagonist of Hemingway's 'The Killers,'" *Modern Language Notes*, LXXIII (Dec. 1958), 589-591.

1094 "Offer by Hemingway," *N.Y.Times* (Dec. 3, 1958), p. 34.
Brief item regarding Hemingway's offer of $1000 for the "best novel" by a Polish author.

1095 Hicks, Granville. "The Shape of a Career," *Saturday Review*, XLI (Dec. 13, 1958), 16, 38.

1096 Todd, Harold W., Jr. "Natural Elements in Hemingway's Novels," *Wingover*, I (Autumn–Winter 1958–1959), 25-27.

1096₁ Wood, Dean C. "The Significance of Bulls and Bullfighters in *The Sun Also Rises*," *ibid.*, pp. 28-30.

1097 Richardson, H. Edward. "The 'Hemingwaves' in Faulkner's *Wild Palms*," *Modern Fiction Studies*, IV (Winter 1958–1959), 357-360.
Discusses William Faulkner's coinage of the word "hemingwaves" and parallels in the work of Hemingway and Faulkner.

1098 Baker, Sheridan. "Hemingway's 'Two-Hearted River,'" *Michigan Alumnus Quarterly Review*, LXV (Winter 1959), 142-149.

1099 Hagopian, John V. "Style and Meaning in Hemingway and Faulkner," *Jahrbuch für Amerikastudien*, IV (1959), 170-179.

1099₁ Carstensen, Broder. "Das Zeitmoment und einige charakteristische Motive in Ernest Hemingways Kurzgeschichte 'The Killers,'" *ibid.*, pp. 180-190.

1100 Wiśniowski, Bronislaw. "Ernest Hemingway," *Przegląd Humanistyczny*, III, No. 1 (1959), pp. 91-123, Part I; No. 2 (1959), pp. 77-106, Part II. In Polish.

1101 Adams, Richard P. "Sunrise out of the Waste Land," *Tulane Studies in English*, IX (1959), 119-131.

102 Fleming, Eugene D. "People Who Avoided the Ruts of Life, *Cosmopolitan*, CXLVI (Jan. 1959), 31. Photograph.
Short biographical sketch of Hemingway's life.

103 Soler, María de los Angeles. "Hemingway y la victoria de la juventud," *Cuadernos Hispanoamericanos*, XXXVII (Jan. 1959), 49-58.

104 "Trials in Cuba Are Defended by Hemingway," *K.C. Star* (Jan. 23, 1959), pp. 1, 2.
In a telephoned interview from Ketchum, Idaho, with the Associated Press, Hemingway gave his views on the trials of Batista supporters in Cuba.

105 Kroeger, F. P. "The Dialogue in 'A Clean, Well-Lighted Place,' " *College English*, XX (Feb. 1959), 240-241.
For reply by Otto Reinert, see *CE*, XX (May 1959), 417-418.

105₁ Colburn, William E. "Confusion in 'A Clean, Well-Lighted Place,' " *ibid.*, pp. 241-242.
For reply by Otto Reinert, see *CE*, XX (May 1959), 417-418.

106 Bury, John P. "Hemingway in Spain," *Contemporary Review*, CXCV (Feb. 1959), 103-105.

107 Levy, Alfred J. "Hemingway's *The Sun Also Rises*," *Explicator*, XVII (Feb. 1959), Item 37.

108 Photograph of Hemingway with Gary Cooper, in Sun Valley, "Playful Papa's Pitch," *Life*, XLVI (Feb. 16, 1959), 28.

109 Knox, Sanka. "Painting Proves Hard to Borrow | Museum Has a Hectic Time Getting Hemingway Loan Out of Cuba in Revolt," *N.Y. Times* (Feb. 24, 1959), p. 26.
Regarding Joan Miró's painting, The Farm, which Hemingway loaned to the Museum of Modern Art, in New York.

110 Facsimiles, *American Book Collector*, IX (March 1959), 4.
Facsimiles of the first page of the corrected typescript of *DIA* and the cover of *TSTP*, which were in the auction of the library of Dr. Don Carlos Guffey. See (G174).

111 Shanley, John P. "Hard Work as 'The Bell' Tolls," *N.Y. Times* (March 8, 1959), II, 11.
Regarding the Columbia Broadcasting System's television presentation of *FWBT*.

112 Flanner, Janet. "Americans in Paris," *N.Y. Times Book Review* (March 8, 1959), p. 44. Photograph.
Regarding the exposition sponsored by the cultural section of the American Embassy in Paris. For catalogue of the exposition, see (G39).

1113 Drawing of Hemingway by Ben Shahn, *N.Y. Times* (March 12, 1959), p. 60.
Advertisement for Playhouse 90's television presentation of *FWBT*.

1114 Item, *Newsweek*, LIII (March 30, 1959), 57.
Brief item about Hemingway in Las Vegas.

1115 Cohen, Joseph. "Wouk's *Morningstar* and Hemingway's *Sun*," *South Atlantic Quarterly*, LVIII (Spring 1959), 213-224.
Comparison of Herman Wouk's *Marjorie Morningstar* and *SAR*.

1116 Kinnamon, Keneth. "Hemingway, The *Corrida*, and Spain," *Texas Studies in Literature and Language*, I (Spring 1959), 44-61.

1117 Lillich, Richard B. "Hemingway on the Screen," *Films in Review*, X (April 1959), 208-218.

1118 Eastman, Max. "The Great and Small in Ernest Hemingway," *Saturday Review*, XLII (April 4, 1959), 13-15, 50-51. Photograph and cover portrait of Hemingway by Yousuf Karsh. Reprinted from *Great Companions*, New York, 1959, pp. 41-76.

1118₁ Shayon, Robert Lewis. "It Tolls for TV," *ibid.*, p. 31.
Regarding Playhouse 90's television adaptation of *FWBT*.

1119 "Hemingway Off to Europe," *N.Y. Herald Tribune* (April 26, 1959), p. 5. Photograph.
Quotes Hemingway's words of praise for Cuban Premier Fidel Castro. The Hemingways sailed on the liner *Constitution* for a vacation in Spain.

1120 Lyons, Leonard. "Papa Comes to Town," *N.Y. Post* (April 26, 1959), II, 7. Dateline: New York.

1121 Photograph of Hemingway with Alec Guinness and Noel Coward in Sloppy Joe's bar, in Havana, *Time*, LXXIII (April 27, 1959), 28.

1122 Photograph of Hemingway at the ringside, in Madrid, *N.Y. Times* (May 21, 1959), p. 5.

1123 "Rostros Famosos en Las Ventas," *Ruedo*, XVI (May 21, 1959), 13-14. Photograph.
Interview with Hemingway, in Las Ventas, Spain.

1124 Photograph of Antonio Ordoñez dedicating a bull to Hemingway, during a bullfight in Madrid, *Stampa* (May 22, 1959), p. 7.

1125 Babcock, Frederic. Among the Authors column, *Chicago Tribune* (May 24, 1959), Magazine of Books, p. 8.

Hemingway's poem, "The Worker," is reprinted from *Tabula,* XXIII (March 1917).

126 Paddleford, Clementine. "Cooking à la Hemingway," *This Week* (May 24, 1959), pp. 30-33. Photographs.
Regarding a visit with the Hemingways, at their home in Ketchum, Idaho.

127 "A la cathédrale de Madrid, Hemingway, écrivain barbu, a retrouvé sa passion," *Paris Match,* No. 529 (May 30, 1959), p. 87. Photographs.

128 Nakaza, Gensuke. "Hemingway and the Sea," *Bulletin of the Arts and Sciences Division,* IV (June 1959), 1-28.

129 Olay, Lionel. "Ernest Hemingway's Last Revolution," *Pageant,* XIV (June 1959), 86-90.

130 Photograph of Hemingway at a bullfight, in Madrid, *Newsweek,* LIII (June 8, 1959), 53.

131 Crosby, John. "The Son Rises," *N.Y. Herald Tribune* (June 8, 1959), II, 1. Dateline: Aranjuez, Spain.
Regarding Hemingway and his favorite bullfighter, Antonio Ordoñez, the son of Nino de la Palma, whom Hemingway portrayed as Pedro Romero in *SAR.* Reprinted in *With Love and Loathing,* New York, 1963, pp. 11-13.

132 Crosby, John. "Afternoon With the Bulls," *N.Y. Herald Tribune* (June 10, 1959), II, 1. Dateline: Aranjuez, Spain. Reprinted in *With Love and Loathing,* New York, 1963, pp. 13-15.

133 Ray, David. "A Talk on the Wild Side," *Reporter,* XX (June 11, 1959), 31-33.
Interview with Nelson Algren, during which he comments on a visit with Hemingway in Cuba.

134 Item, *Ruedo,* XVI (June 25, 1959), 12-13. Photograph.
Regarding Hemingway at the bullfights of the *feria* of Algeciras.

135 Holmes, John Clellon. "Existentialism and the Novel: Notes and Questions," *Chicago Review,* XIII (Summer 1959), 144-151.
General article.

136 Moses, W. R. "Water, Water, Everywhere: *Old Man* and *A Farewell to.Arms,*" *Modern Fiction Studies,* V (Summer 1959), 172-174.

137 Labor, Earle. "Crane and Hemingway: Anatomy of Trauma," *Renascence,* XI (Summer 1959), 189-196.
A study of the differences between *The Red Badge of Courage* and *FTA.*

1138 Freedman, Richard. "Hemingway's Spanish Civil War Dispatches," *Texas Studies in Literature and Language*, I (Summer 1959), 171-180.

1139 Zielinski, Bronislaw. "Hemingway: A Polish Writer," *Poland* [American edition], No. 7 (July 1959), p. 30. Photograph.

1140 Zavaleta, Carlos E. "La novela de Hemingway," *Estudios Americanos*, XVI (July–Aug. 1959), 47-52.

1141 Photograph of Hemingway in Zaragoza, Spain, *Ruedo*, XVI (July 3, 1959), 3.

1141₁ Photograph of Hemingway at the *feria* in Burgos, Spain, *ibid.*, p. 18.

1142 Daley, Robert. "Dominguín: Torero with Ego," *N.Y. Times* (July 19, 1959), V, 12. Photograph. Dateline: Pamplona, Spain.
Regarding the feud between Luis Miguel Dominguín and Antonio Ordóñez, and Hemingway's admiration for Ordóñez.

1143 Blashill, John. "Report from Valencia: Ordóñez vs. Dominguín," *Sports Illustrated*, XI (Aug. 17, 1959), 42-43.
Regarding the *mano a mano* in Valencia, on July 30, 1959, in which Luis Miguel Dominguín was gored.

1143₁ Hemingway, Mary. "Holiday for a Wounded Torero," *ibid.*, pp. 44-51. Photographs.
An account of the convalescence of Antonio Ordóñez, who was gored in the bullring in Aranjuez, on May 30, 1959. Quotes Hemingway's explanation of the goring. See also (C404).

1144 "N.C." [Norman Cousins]. Editorial, "For Whom the Bells Ring," *Saturday Review*, XLII (Aug. 22, 1959), 18.
Regarding Hemingway's popularity in the Soviet Union.

1145 Garlington, Jack. "The Intelligence Quotient of Lady Brett Ashley," *San Francisco Review*, I (Sept. 1959), 23-28.

1146 "Winner's Flawless Form and 'Papa's' High Praise," *Life*, XLVII (Sept. 7, 1959), 28-29. Photograph.
Regarding Hemingway and the bullfighter, Antonio Ordóñez.

1147 "Hemingway Prefers Bulls to Soviet Trip," *N.Y. Times* (Sept. 10, 1959), p. 5. Dateline: Murcia, Spain.
The Soviet newspaper *Literaturnaya Gazeta* invited Hemingway to visit the Soviet Union with President Eisenhower, but he preferred to remain in Spain to watch the bullfights.

1148 Photograph of Hemingway at a bullfight, in Madrid, "Famous Fan," *N.Y. Times Magazine* (Sept. 13, 1959), p. 54.

1149 Photograph, "Public School Products," *Time*, LXXIV (Sept. 14, 1959), 71.

Hemingway is included in a group of successful men who attended public high schools.

1150 "Hemingway Asks Thief to Return His Wallet," *St. Louis Post-Dispatch* (Sept. 16, 1959), p. 22 A. Dateline: Madrid.

Hemingway appealed to the thief who stole his wallet, while he was signing autographs at a bullfight festival at Murcia, in southern Spain, to return it. See next entry.

1151 "Thief Heeds Hemingway," *N.Y. Times* (Sept. 23, 1959), p. 15. Dateline: Madrid.

Thief complies with Hemingway's plea to return his wallet, which was stolen at a festival in Murcia, Spain.

1152 Jones, John A. "Hemingway: The Critics and the Public Legend," *Western Humanities Review*, XIII (Autumn 1959), 387-400.

1153 Runnquist, Ake. "Stackars Robert Cohn," review of Harold Loeb's *The Way It Was*, BLM, XXVIII (Oct. 1959), 643-645.

1154 Morris, William E. "Hemingway's 'The Killers,'" *Explicator*, XVIII (Oct. 1959), Item 1.

1155 Haas, Rudolf. "Zum Todesmotiv im Werk Hemingways," *Neueren Sprachen*, VIII (Oct. 1959), 455-465.

1156 Nozaki, Takashi. "An Embodiment of Sensibility—The Works of Ernest Hemingway," *Studies in English Literature*, XXXVI (Oct. 1959), 93-108. In English and Japanese.

1157 Photograph of Hemingway in Nîmes, France, *Ruedo*, XVI (Oct. 1, 1959), 19.

1158 Nichols, Lewis. In and Out of Books column, "Appendix," *N.Y. Times Book Review* (Oct. 4, 1959), p. 8.

Brief item about Hemingway working on an appendix to *DIA*. Briefly quotes a letter from Hemingway to his publishers.

1159 "Moscow Marks Hemingway's 6oth," *N.Y. World Telegram & Sun* (Oct. 10, 1959), p. 3.

Moscow Museum of Literature was filled to capacity for a lecture on Hemingway by Ivan Kashkeen.

1160 Adams, Val. " 'The Killers' to Have Double Exposure," *N.Y. Times* (Oct. 18, 1959), II, 19.

A re-run of the 1946 film version of "The Killers" and the Buick Playhouse television adaptation were both scheduled for November 19, 1959.

1161 Hotchner, A. E. "Hemingway Talks to American Youth," *This Week* (Oct. 18, 1959), pp. 10-11, 24-26. Cover photograph of Hemingway by Ken Heyman. Photographs by John Bryson.

Report on Hemingway's meeting with high school students in Hailey, Idaho. Mainly in the form of questions and answers.

1162 Barucca, Primo. "Il messaggio di Ernest Hemingway," *Ausonia,* XIV (Nov.–Dec. 1959), 46-51.

1163 Sevareid, Eric. "*Mano a Mano*: Dominguín vs Ordoñez," *Esquire,* LII (Nov. 1959), 40-44. Reprinted in *This Is Eric Sevareid,* New York, 1964, pp. 296-303.

1164 "Hemingway Here," *N.Y. Herald Tribune* (Nov. 3, 1959), p. 3. Photograph of Hemingway by Morris Warman.

Regarding Hemingway's arrival from Europe, aboard the *Liberté.*

1165 Huguenin, Jean-René. "Une journée avec Hemingway," *Arts* (Nov. 4–10, 1959), p. 4. Photograph.

1166 "Hemingway Back in Cuba," *N.Y. Times* (Nov. 6, 1959), p. 9.

Regarding Hemingway's return to Cuba after a year's absence.

1167 Photograph of Hemingway, by Yousuf Karsh, *Life,* XLVII (Nov. 30, 1959), 13.

1168 Moynihan, William T. "The Martyrdom of Robert Jordan," *College English,* XXI (Dec. 1959), 127-132.

1169 Bluefarb, Sam. "The Sea—Mirror and Maker of Character in Fiction and Drama," *English Journal,* XLVIII (Dec. 1959), 501-510.

General article. Includes discussion of Santiago in *OMATS.*

1170 McCullers, Carson. "The Flowering Dream: Notes on Writing," *Esquire,* LII (Dec. 1959), 162-164.

General article. Discusses Hemingway's style.

1171 Rao, K. S. Narayana. "Women, Violence and Darkness in the World of Hemingway's Short Stories," *Literary Criterion,* IV (Winter 1960), 32-38.

1172 Galinsky, Hans. "Beharrende Strukturzüge in Wandel eines Jahrhunderts amerikanischer Kurzgeschichte (dargelegt an Poe und Hemingway)," *Stil und Formprobleme,* V (1960), 442-447.

1173 Burhans, Clinton S., Jr. "*The Old Man and the Sea*: Hemingway's Tragic Vision of Man," *American Literature,* XXXI (Jan. 1960), 446-455.

Translated into Italian, "La concezione tragica di Ernest Hemingway," in *Mondo Occidentale*, VII (Nov. 1960), 39-50. Reprinted in *Baker anthology*, pp. 259-268; in *Baker critiques*, pp. 150-155.

174 Belyaev, V. "Novye izdaniya amerikanskikh knig," *Inostrannaya Literatura*, No. 1 (Jan. 1960), p. 248.

175 Castillo-Puche, José Luis. "El verdadero Hemingway y su mito," *Estafeta Literaria*, No. 184 (Jan. 1, 1960), pp. 16-19.

176 "Getting a Head of 'Papa,'" *This Week* (Jan. 24, 1960), p. 16. Photograph.
Regarding the bust of Hemingway by sculptor Robert Berks.

177 Tynan, Kenneth. "A Visit to Havana," *Holiday*, XXVII (Feb. 1960), 50-58.
Includes an account of a visit with the Hemingways at Finca Vigia, and a visit to Havana, where Tynan introduced Hemingway to Tennessee Williams.

178 Mazzaro, Jerome L. "George Peele and *A Farewell to Arms*: A Thematic Tie?" *Modern Language Notes*, LXXV (Feb. 1960), 118-119.
Discusses several parallels between Hemingway's novel and Peele's poem of the same title.

179 Photograph, "Hemingway Host to Mikoyan in Cuba," *St. Louis Post-Dispatch* (Feb. 9, 1960), p. 2.
Soviet Deputy Premier Anastas Mikoyan visited Finca Vigia and presented Hemingway with a set of his works in Russian translation.

180 "Tass Reports Hemingway Pact," *N.Y. Times* (Feb. 21, 1960), p. 11.
Report that the authorized serialization of *FWBT* is to appear in the Leningrad literary journal, *Neva*.

181 Stephens, Robert O. "Hemingway's Riddle of Kilimanjaro: Idea and Image," *American Literature*, XXXII (March 1960), 84-87.

182 Arnold, Aerol. "Hemingway's 'The Doctor and the Doctor's Wife,'" *Explicator*, XVIII (March 1960), Item 36.

183 Harada, Keiichi. "The Marlin and the Shark: A Note on *The Old Man and the Sea*," *Journal of the College of Literature*, No. 4 (March 1960), pp. 49-54. Reprinted in *Baker anthology*, pp. 269-276.

184 Kashkeen, Ivan. "O samom glavnom," *Oktiabr'*, No. 3 (March 1960), pp. 215-223.

1185 Hulin, J.–P. "Le nombre trois: superstition du procédé tragique dans *L'adieu aux armes*," *Langues Modernes*, LIV (March–April 1960), 103-108.

1186 Alsop, Joseph. "A Cuban Visit With Hemingway," *N.Y. Herald Tribune* (March 9, 1960), p. 18. Dateline: Havana.
Regarding a visit to Finca Vigia and an afternoon spent at a cock fight with Hemingway.

1187 Soucie, Gary. "Reflections on Hemingway," *Carolina Quarterly*, XI (Spring 1960), 57-63.

1188 Herbst, Josephine. "The Starched Blue Sky of Spain," *Noble Savage*, No. 1 (Spring 1960), pp. 76-117.
Reminiscences of Hemingway during the Spanish Civil War.

1189 Lehan, Richard. "Camus and Hemingway," *Wisconsin Studies in Contemporary Literature*, I (Spring–Summer 1960), 37-48.
A French translation appeared in *Revue des Lettres Modernes*, VIII (Autumn 1961), 55-71.

1190 Borovik, Genrikh. "U Ernesta Khemingueya," *Ogoniok*, No. 14 (April 1960), pp. 26-29. Photographs.
Interview with Hemingway at Finca Vigia.

1191 Harrison, James M. "Hemingway's *In Our Time*," *Explicator*, XVIII (May 1960), Item 51.

1192 Hashiguchi, Yasuo. "*A Farewell to Arms*," *Kyusha American Literature*, No. 3 (May 1960), pp. 1-8.

1193 Guttmann, Allen. "Mechanized Doom: Ernest Hemingway and the Spanish Civil War," *Massachusetts Review*, I (May 1960), 541-561.
Reprinted in *Baker critiques*, pp. 95-107.

1194 Photograph, "Lucky Novice, Famous Pro," *Life*, XLVIII (May 30, 1960), 35.
Fidel Castro placed first in the annual Hemingway fishing tournament in Havana.

1195 Sanders, David. "Ernest Hemingway's Spanish Civil War Experiences," *American Quarterly*, XII (Summer 1960), 133-143.

1196 Seidensticker, Edward. "Redskins in Japan," *Kenyon Review*, XXII (Summer 1960), 374-391.
General article. Discusses the reception of American writing in Japan and comments on Hemingway's popularity.

1197 Lair, Robert L. "Hemingway and Cézanne: An Indebtedness," *Modern Fiction Studies*, VI (Summer 1960), 165-168.

98 Bartres, J. Raymundo. "De Poe a Hemingway pasando por Baroja," *Torre*, VIII (July–Sept. 1960), 165-171.

99 Barker, Garry. "Glum Hemingway Stays Mum on Cuban Troubles in Interview," *Detroit News* (July 20, 1960), p. 12-A. Dateline: Havana.

00 Jackson, C. D. "Publishers' Preview," *Life*, XLIX (Aug. 29, 1960), 69. Facsimile of a tally sheet of words written by Hemingway "last March, in Spain."
Regarding the forthcoming serialization of "The Dangerous Summer," in *Life*. See (C407).

01 Nishiyama, Tamotsu. "Hemingway's Post-War Generation Reconsidered," *North Dakota Quarterly*, XXVIII (Autumn 1960), 129-133.

02 Tate, Allen. "Random Thoughts on the Twenties," *Minnesota Review*, I (Fall 1960), 46-56.
General article.

03 Owen, Charles A., Jr. "Time and the Contagion of Flight in 'The Killers,'" *Forum*, III (Fall–Winter 1960), 45-46.

04 Gullón, Ricardo. "The Old Man and the Business," *Insula*, No. 168 (Nov. 1960), p. 7. In Spanish.

05 Merlin, Olivier. "Dominguín à Hemingway: je suis le meilleur," *Paris Match*, No. 604 (Nov. 5, 1960), pp. 22-30. Photographs.

06 MacShane, Frank. "*The Transatlantic Review*," *London Magazine*, VII (Dec. 1960), 49-59.
General article. Comments on Hemingway's twofold role on the short-lived little magazine, which was published in Paris, from January 1924 to January 1925.

07 Stein, William Bysshe. "Ritual in Hemingway's 'Big Two-Hearted River,'" *Texas Studies in Literature and Language*, I (Winter 1960), 555-561.

08 Graham, John. "Ernest Hemingway: The Meaning of Style," *Modern Fiction Studies*, VI (Winter 1960–1961), 298-313. Reprinted in *Baker critiques*, pp. 183-192.

09 Bache, William B. "*The Red Badge of Courage* and 'The Short Happy Life of Francis Macomber,'" *Western Humanities Review*, XV (Winter 1961), 83-84.

10 Miglior, Giorgio. "L'idillio in Hemingway," *Studi Americani*, VII (1961), 195-214.

11 Gerstenberger, Donna. "*The Waste Land* in *A Farewell to Arms*," *Modern Language Notes*, LXXVI (Jan. 1961), 24-25.

1212 "Hemingway in Hospital," *N.Y. Times* (Jan. 11, 1961), p. 14. Dateline: Rochester, Minn.

Report that Hemingway had been hospitalized at St. Mary's Hospital, under the care of physicians from Mayo Clinic, since November 30, 1960. The nature of his illness was not revealed.

1213 "Hemingway Has Hypertension," *N.Y. Times* (Jan. 12, 1961), p. 12. Dateline: Rochester, Minn.

Report that Hemingway was under treatment for high blood pressure.

1214 Item, *Time*, LXXVII (Jan. 20, 1961), 37. Photograph.

Regarding Hemingway's six weeks' stay at the Mayo Clinic, under the name of "George Saviers."

1215 Barolini, Antonio. "Hemingway sentì che la mano tremava," *Epoca*, XLII (Jan. 22, 1961), 30-31.

1216 "Hemingway in Sun Valley," *N.Y. Times* (Jan. 24, 1961), p. 10. Dateline: Sun Valley, Idaho.

Hemingway returned to Sun Valley, after a 53-day stay at Mayo Clinic.

1217 Hutchens, John K. Review of *Hemingway and His Critics* edited by Carlos Baker, *N.Y. Herald Tribune* (March 31, 1961), p. 19.

1218 Marcus, Mordecai. "*A Farewell to Arms*: Novel into Film," *Journal of the Central Mississippi Valley American Studies Association*, II (Spring 1961), 69-71.

1219 Aldridge, John W. "Hemingway and Europe," *Shenandoah*, XII (Spring 1961), 11-24.

1220 Stein, William Bysshe. "Hemingway's 'The Short Happy Life of Francis Macomber,' " *Explicator*, XIX (April 1961), Item 47.

1221 Yevtushenko, Yevgeny. Poem, "Vstrecha," *Iunost'*, No. 4 (April 1961), p. 7.

For translations of this poem, see (G459).

1222 "Hemingway Back in Hospital," *N.Y. Times* (April 27, 1961), p. 3. Dateline: Rochester, Minn.

Hemingway returned to St. Mary's Hospital, on April 25, for further treatment for hypertension.

1223 Gabriel, Joseph F. "The Logic of Confusion in Hemingway's 'A Clean, Well-Lighted Place,' " *College English*, XXII (May 1961), 539-546.

24 Anderson, Charles R. "Hemingway's Other Style," *Modern Language Notes*, LXXVI (May 1961), 434-442. Reprinted in *Baker critiques*, pp. 41-46.

25 Davis, Robert Gorham. "Speaking of 'Papa,'" review of *Hemingway and His Critics*, ed. Carlos Baker, *N.Y. Times Book Review* (May 14, 1961), p. 4.

26 "A Hemingway Gain," *K.C. Star* (May 31, 1961), p. 2. Dateline: Rochester, Minn.
   Mayo Clinic reported an improvement in Hemingway's condition.

27 Parsons, Thornton H. "Hemingway's Tyrannous Plot," *University of Kansas City Review*, XXVII (June 1961), 261-266.

27₁ Montgomery, Marion. "The Leopard and the Hyena: Symbol and Meaning in 'The Snows of Kilimanjaro,'" *ibid.*, pp. 277-282.

228 "Hemingway Leaves Hospital," *N.Y. Times* (June 28, 1961), p. 7. Dateline: Rochester, Minn.
   Hemingway returned to his home in Ketchum, Idaho.

229 Light, James F. "The Religion of Death in *A Farewell to Arms*," *Modern Fiction Studies*, VII (Summer 1961), 169-173. Reprinted in *Baker critiques*, pp. 37-40.

230 Stein, William Bysshe. "Love and Lust in Hemingway's Short Stories," *Texas Studies in Literature and Language*, III (Summer 1961), 234-242.

231 Taylor, J. Golden. "Hemingway on the Flesh and the Spirit," *Western Humanities Review*, XV (Summer 1961), 273-275.

232 "Own Gun Kills Hemingway | Author Slain in Home; Accident, Says Wife | Idaho Officials Weigh Inquest Into Death," *Chicago Daily Tribune* (July 3, 1961), pp. 1, 2. Dateline: Ketchum, Idaho, July 2.

32₁ Butcher, Fanny. "Hemingway's Maxim: Live Life to Hilt," *ibid.*, pp. 1, 2.
   Reminiscences of Hemingway, since the 1920s.

32₂ "Genius Hinted by Hemingway As School Boy | Oak Park Classmate Recalls Author," *ibid.*, p. 2.
   Reminiscences of Hemingway by a classmate, Earle Pashley.

32₃ "Great Citizen, Kennedy Says of Hemingway," *ibid.*, p. 2. Dateline: Hyannis Port, Mass.
   President John F. Kennedy's tribute to Hemingway.

1233 Nordell, Rod. "The Two Hemingways," *Christian Science Monitor* (July 3, 1961), p. 4.

Compares Hemingway, the public personality, and Hemingway, the writer.

1234 McManis, John. "State Gave Inspiration to Author | Early Hemingway Works Reflect Days in Michigan," *Detroit News* (July 3, 1961), pp. 1, 2.

1235 "Hemingway Dead | Accident while cleaning gun," *Guardian*, Manchester (July 3, 1961), p. 1.

1235₁ "The Hero in Modern Literature | Ernest Hemingway's art and life," *ibid.*, p. 18.

1236 "Hemingway Killed By Shot: 'Accident,'" *N.Y. Herald Tribune* (July 3, 1961), pp. 1, 10.

1236₁ "Life of Hemingway: Works Controversial," *ibid.*, p. 10.

1236₂ Editorial, "Hemingway and His World," *ibid.*, p. 12.

1237 "The Bell Tolls for Ernest Hemingway," *N.Y. Post* (July 3, 1961), p. 3.

1237₁ "The President's Eulogy," *ibid.*, p. 3.

1237₂ Lyons, Leonard. The Lyons Den column, "I Remember Papa," *ibid.*, pp. 3, 17.

1237₃ Wilson, Earl. It Happened Last Night column, "Hemingway: The Gentle Genius," *ibid.*, p. 8.

1237₄ Lerner, Max. "Papa," *ibid.*, p. 19.

1238 "Hemingway Dead of Shotgun Wound; Wife Says He Was Cleaning Weapon," *N.Y. Times* (July 3, 1961), pp. 1, 6. Dateline: Ketchum, Idaho, July 2.

1238₁ "[19]54 Nobel Award Honored Career," *ibid.*, p. 6.

For Lillian Ross's letter, regarding references to her Profile of Hemingway in the *New Yorker*, xxvi (May 13, 1950), see the *N.Y. Times* (July 5, 1961), p. 32.

1238₂ "Mourned by Kennedy," *ibid.*, p. 6.

1238₃ Poore, Charles. "Books: Hemingway," *ibid.*, p. 6.

1238₄ "Authors and Critics Appraise Works," *ibid.*, p. 6.

Estimates of Hemingway's work given to the *N.Y. Times* by Archibald MacLeish, Lionel Trilling, Alfred Kazin, James Thurber, John Dos Passos, Van Wyck Brooks, Lillian Hellman, Oliver La-

Farge, Tennessee Williams, J. B. Priestley, Cyril Connolly, Carl Sandburg, V. S. Pritchett, C. P. Snow, Harvey Breit, William Faulkner, John O'Hara, and Robert Frost.

1238₅ "Letter to Youth Offered Advice," *ibid.*, p. 6. [City Edition].
Quotes a letter from Hemingway to Jack Hirschman, from Cuba, [Jan. 9] 1953. See (F131).

1238₆ Editorial, "A Giant Passes," *ibid.*, p. 14.

1239 "Tragica morte di Hemingway," *Osservatore Romano* (July 3–4, 1961), p. 3.

1240 "Mr. Hemingway Dies in Gun Accident," *Times*, London (July 3, 1961), p. 12.

1240₁ Leading article, "Ernest Hemingway," *ibid.*, p. 13.

1240₂ "Mr. Ernest Hemingway An Outstanding Creative Writer," *ibid.*, p. 16.

1241 Photographs, "Recuerdos Graficos de Hemingway en España," *ABC* (July 4, 1961), Rotogravure section.

1241₁ Massip, José María. "A Hemingway Tendremos que recordarlo conmovidos por lo que amo a España y a los Españoles," *ibid.*, p. 39.

1241₂ "Datos biográficos," *ibid.*, pp. 40-41.

1241₃ "Todo el bronco sabor de la existencia," *ibid.*, p. 41.

1241₄ Caranillas, Julián Cortes. "Italia Asocia a Hemingway con España," *ibid.*, p. 42. Dateline: Rome.

1241₅ Ruano, César Gonzalez. "La Importancia de Llamarse Ernesto," *ibid.*, pp. 42-43.

1242 "Nessuno forse potra far luce sulla drammatica morte di Hemingway," *Corriere della Sera* (July 4, 1961), p. 3.

1242₁ Montale, Eugenio. "Schietta umanità," *ibid.*, p. 3.

1243 Dutourd, Jean. "La mort du chasseur," *Figaro* (July 4, 1961), p. 1.

1243₁ "Hemingway s'est tué en nettoyant un fusil," *ibid.*, p. 2.

1243₂ "Le President Kennedy: 'Hemingway a apporté le gloire aux États-Unis,' " *ibid.*, p. 2.

1243₃ "Du réportage vécu," *ibid.*, p. 2. (Chronology.)

1243₄ Brief estimates of Hemingway's work from François Mauriac, Gerard Bauer, William Faulkner, Eyvind Johnson, and Alberto Mondadori, *ibid.*, **p. 2.**

1244 Aranda, Joaquín. "Hemingway en Zaragoza," *Heraldo de Aragón* (July 4, 1961), p. 7.

1244₁ Liria, Luis Horno. "Hemingway," *ibid.*, p. 7. In Spanish.

1245 Editorial, "Bolshoi pisatel," *Izvestia* (July 4, 1961), p. 4.
An English translation, titled "A Tribute to Hemingway," appeared in *Soviet Review*, II (Sept. 1961), 72.

1246 "Ernest Hemingway est mort," *Monde* (July 4, 1961), p. 1.

1246₁ Escarpit, Robert. "Un lyrique de l'action," *ibid.*, pp. 1, 7.

1246₂ "J.G.D." "La passion des toros," *ibid.*, p. 7.

1247 Crosby, John. "This Is the Word for Him," *N.Y. Herald Tribune* (July 4, 1961), pp. 1, 10.
Recalls his first meeting with Hemingway, in Venice. The word that the title refers to is "true . . . one of his words."

1247₁ "Wave of Tribute Follows News of Hemingway's Death," *ibid.*, p. 10.
Regarding tributes in newspapers and on radio broadcasts throughout the world.

1248 "France Shocked Over Hemingway," *N.Y. Times* (July 4, 1961), p. 9.

1248₁ "Praised by Vatican Paper," "[Manchester] *Guardian* Cites Influence," "Mourned in Madrid," "Tributes from Lisbon," "Work Lauded in Norway," "Stockholm is Stunned," "Top Influence in Poland," " 'One of Us' to Cubans," and "Brazilian Hails Greatness," *ibid.*, p. 9.

1248₂ "Hemingway Inquest Is Ruled Out After Authorities Talk to Family," *ibid.*, p. 9. Dateline: Ketchum, Idaho, July 3.

1248₃ "Ordoñez Kills Two Bulls in Honor of Hemingway," *ibid.*, p. 9.

1249 Leonov, Leonid. "Pisatel s mirovym golosom," *Pravda* (July 4, 1961), p. 4.

1250 "Non era tempo di caccia nell' Idaho quando Hemingway volle pulire il fucile," *Corriere della Sera* (July 5, 1961), p. 7. Dateline: Ketchum, Idaho.

1251 Alsop, Joseph. "Hemingway," *N.Y. Herald Tribune* (July 5, 1961), p. 18.
Reminiscences of a visit to Finca Vigia, in 1960. Reprinted in the *Guardian*, Manchester (July 10, 1961), p. 18.

1252 Wilson, Earl. It Happened Last Night column, " 'Papa' Couldn't Spell," *N.Y. Post* (July 5, 1961), p. 14.
Quotes excerpts from letters from Hemingway. See (F125).

253 "Services Slated for Hemingway," *N.Y. Times* (July 5, 1961), p. 68. Dateline: Ketchum, Idaho.

A private graveside service in the Ketchum Cemetery planned, pending arrival of Hemingway's son, Patrick, from Africa.

254 Neville, Edgar. "Adiós a Hemingway," *ABC* (July 6, 1961), p. 48.

255 Aranda, Joaquín. "El otro Hemingway," *Heraldo de Aragón* (July 6, 1961), p. 9.

256 "Hemingway Rites Scheduled Today," *N.Y. Times* (July 6, 1961), p. 27. Dateline: Ketchum, Idaho.

257 Ruark, Robert C. "Papa's Death Reaches Africa," *N.Y. World-Telegram & Sun* (July 6, 1961), p. 21. Dateline: Nairobi, Kenya.

57₁ Starnes, Richard. "The Old Man and the Gun," *ibid.*, p. 21.

258 Diolé, Philippe. "Le Vieil Homme et la Mort," *Nouvelles Litté-raires*, No. 1766 (July 6, 1961), p. 7. General heading: "Hommage à Hemingway."

58₁ Brown, John. "Le style d'une époque," *ibid.*, p. 7. Reprinted in *Ernest Hemingway*, Paris, 1961.

58₂ Gary, Romain. "Le retour du champion," review of *OMATS*, *ibid.*, p. 7. Reprinted from *NL* (Sept. 11, 1952).

58₃ "Dates d'une vie," *ibid.*, p. 7.

58₄ Delpech, Jeanine. "Notre ami," *ibid.*, p. 7.

259 Editorial, "Ernest Hemingway," *Oak Leaves* (July 6, 1961), p. 3.

59₁ "Writer Ernest Hemingway Is Dead at 62," *ibid.*, pp. 5, 12.
Note: Hemingway would have been sixty-two on July 21, 1961.

260 "La salma di Hemingway riposa in un piccolo cimitero di campagna," *Corriere della Sera* (July 7, 1961), p. 9. Dateline: Ketchum, Idaho.

261 Miller, Karl. "Hemingway," *New Statesman*, LXII (July 7, 1961), 23.

262 "Service is Held for Hemingway," *N.Y. Times* (July 7, 1961), p. 13. Dateline: Ketchum, Idaho, July 6.

The graveside service was conducted by the Rev. Robert J. Waldmann, pastor of the Roman Catholic church in Ketchum.

263 Sordo, Enrique. "Hemingway: riesgo, amor y muerte," *Revista Gran Via*, No. 482 (July 7, 1961), p. 10.

1264 Leading article, "Tones of Voice," *TLS* (July 7, 1961), p. 417.
Discusses Arthur Mizener's lecture on Hemingway in *The Great Experiment in American Literature*, ed. Carl Bode, London, 1961.

1265 Beach, Sylvia. "Mon meilleur client," *Figaro Littéraire*, No. 794 (July 8, 1961), p. 4.

1265₁ Châtelain, Nicolas. "Comment l'Amérique a réagi devant sa mort," *ibid.*, p. 4.

1265₂ Mohrt, Michel. "L'homme des bois," *ibid.*, p. 5.

1265₃ Lauwick, Hervé. "A la corrida!" *ibid.*, p. 5.

1265₄ "Hemingway vous a-t-il marqué?" *ibid.*, p. 5.
Replies by André Bay, Jean-Louis Curtis, Roger Grenier, Jean Bloch-Michel, Jacques Brenner, Guy Le Clec'h, Georges Conchon, Gisèle Prassinos, Alain Robbe-Grillet, and Robert Sabatier.

1266 "Una notizia che ha sconvolto il mondo: Hemingway e morto," *Fiera Letteraria*, xvi (July 9, 1961), 1.

1267 Cowley, Malcolm. "One Man's Hemingway," *N.Y. Herald Tribune Book Review* (July 9, 1961), pp. 3, 15.

1268 "Widow Describes Hemingway Manuscripts," *N.Y. Times* (July 9, 1961), p. 45. Dateline: Ketchum, Idaho.
Interview with Mary Hemingway, regarding Hemingway's unpublished work and his death.

1269 Wain, John. "Ernest Hemingway: Aim and Achievement: Heroes with Wounds," *Observer* (July 9, 1961), Weekend Review, p. 21.

1270 Connolly, Cyril. "Death of a Titan: Hemingway's Moments of Truth," *Sunday Times*, London (July 9, 1961), Magazine Section, p. 27. Reprinted in *Previous Convictions*, London, 1963, pp. 293-298.

1271 "The Bell Tolls," *Newsweek*, LVIII (July 10, 1961), 32. Photographs.

1272 Obituary Notes, *Publishers' Weekly*, CLXXX (July 10, 1961), 48-49.

1273 "Schriftsteller: Hemingway, Wem die Stunde schlägt," *Spiegel*, xv (July 12, 1961), 45-52. Cover photograph of Hemingway.
A survey of Hemingway's life and work, including his significance in Germany.

1274 Editorial, "Our Warmest Memories of Hemingway," *Life*, LI (July 14, 1961), p. 2. Cover photograph of Hemingway.
A Spanish translation appeared in *Life, en Español*, XVIII (Aug. 7, 1961), 2.

74₁ Photographic essay, "Hemingway: Driving Force of a Great Artist," *ibid.*, pp. 59-69.

74₂ MacLeish, Archibald. "His Mirror Was Danger," *ibid.*, pp. 71-72.
A Spanish translation appeared in *Life, en Español*, xviii (Aug. 7, 1961), 23-24.

275 Holman, Adrian. Letter, "Hemingway, the man," *New Statesman*, lxii (July 14, 1961), 51.
The former British Ambassador to Cuba recalls an incident that shows it was "quite untrue that [Hemingway] bore any ill feeling toward our country."

276 "The Hero of the Code," *Time*, lxxviii (July 14, 1961), 87-90. Photographs.

76₁ Auer, Bernhard M. A Letter from the Publisher column, *ibid.*, p. 10.
Includes excerpts from reviews of Hemingway's books in *Time*.

277 Garcia, Padre Félix. "País para vivir," *ABC* (July 15, 1961), p. 1.

278 "Notes and Comment," *New Yorker*, xxxvii (July 15, 1961), p. 17.

279 Feo, José Rodríquez. "Ernest Hemingway: Una nota discrepante," *Bohemia*, liii (July 16, 1961), 36-37, 83.

280 Lazzero, Ricciotti. "L'ultima domenica mattina," *Epoca*, xliv (July 16, 1961), 40-42. Cover photograph of Hemingway. Photographs on pp. 44-57.

281 Adams, J. Donald. Speaking of Books column, *N.Y. Times Book Review* (July 16, 1961), p. 2.
Regarding correspondence with Hemingway. Reprinted in *Speaking of Books—and Life*, New York, 1965, pp. 174-176.

282 Crawford, Kenneth. "Good Man in a Fight," *Newsweek*, lviii (July 17, 1961), 32.

283 Cantwell, Robert. "The River That Will Flow Forever," *Sports Illustrated*, xv (July 17, 1961), 52-59. Drawing of Hemingway by John Groth.
An account of a trip to the country around the Two Hearted River, in northern Michigan, to record the changes since Hemingway wrote "Big Two-Hearted River."

284 Bianchini, Angela. "La Guerra di Hemingway," *Mondo*, xiii (July 18, 1961), 9.

285 "The Bell Tolls for Hemingway," *Christian Century*, lxxviii (July 19, 1961), 869.

286 "Farewell," *Reporter*, xxv (July 20, 1961), 10.

1287 Brady, Charles A. "Portrait of Hemingway," *America*, cv (July 22, 1961), 546-548.

1288 "Zum Tode Hemingways: Ihm schlug die Stunde," *Bunte Illustrierte* (July 22, 1961), pp. 12-15. Photographs.

1289 "A Farewell to Hemingway," *Editor & Publisher*, xciv (July 22, 1961), 43.

1290 Edlund, Mårten. "Ernest Hemingway," *Vi*, No. 29-30 (July 22–29, 1961), p. 12. In Swedish.

1291 Napolitano, Giangaspare, Walter Chiari, Randolfo Pacciardi, and Giuseppe Trevisani. "Quattro istantanee—ricordo della vita di Ernest Hemingway," *Epoca*, xliv (July 23, 1961), 7.

1292 Lyons, Leonard. The Lyons Den column, *N.Y. Post* (July 23, 1961), p. M-7.
Reminiscences of Hemingway.

1293 Howe, Irving. "Hemingway: The Conquest of Panic," *New Republic*, cxlv (July 24, 1961), 19-20.
For Lillian Ross's reply, regarding references to her Profile of Hemingway in the *New Yorker*, xxvi (May 13, 1950), see *NR*, cxlv (Aug. 7, 1961), 30-31.

1294 "The Death of Hemingway," *Commonweal*, lxxiv (July 28, 1961), 413.

1295 Lyons, Leonard. Trade Winds column, *Saturday Review*, xliv (July 29, 1961), 6, 8. Special issue: Hemingway: A World View.
Recalls his friendship with Hemingway.

1295₁ Photograph of Hemingway, by Yousuf Karsh, *ibid.*, p. 10.

1295₂ Baker, Carlos. "Hemingway," *ibid.*, pp. 11-13.
An appraisal of Hemingway's work.

1295₃ Editor's Note, *ibid.*, p. 12.
Regarding the special Hemingway issue. Hemingway's birth date is given as July 21, 1898. See Keith Hanson's reply in *SR*, xliv (Sept. 2, 1961), 23, which quotes a one-line letter from Hemingway giving the correct date as July 21, 1899. See (F148).

1295₄ Photographs, "A Man, A Writer, A Legend," *ibid.*, pp. 14-17.

1295₅ "The World Weighs a Writer's Influence," *ibid.*, pp. 18-22.
Brief estimates by Salvador de Madariaga of Spain, Frank Moraes in India, Carlo Levi of Italy, Ilya Ehrenburg of USSR, Alan Pryce-Jones of England, and Edward Seidensticker in Japan.

95₆ Betsky, Seymour, "A Last Visit," *ibid.*, p. 22.
Report of a visit to Hemingway, in Ketchum, Idaho, in November 1960, with Leslie Fiedler.

95₇ Stein, Gertrude. Excerpt from *The Autobiography of Alice B. Toklas, ibid.*, pp. 23-24.

95₈ Loeb, Harold. "The Young Writer in Paris and Pamplona," *ibid.*, pp. 25-26.

95₉ "Milestones on a Literary Journey," *ibid.*, pp. 27-29, 35-36.
Excerpts from reviews of Hemingway's books.

95₁₀ Hicks, Granville. Editorial, "A Feeling About Life," *ibid.*, pp. 30, 38.

95₁₁ Ciardi, John. Manner of Speaking column, "The Language of an Age," *ibid.*, p. 32.
Discusses Hemingway's style and dialogue.

95₁₂ Knight, Arthur. "Hemingway Into Film," *ibid.*, pp. 33-34.

296 "Mrs. Hemingway is Cautious on Publication of Manuscripts," *N.Y. Times* (July 29, 1961), p. 21.
Interview with Mary Hemingway, in Cuba, where she was examining and sorting Hemingway's papers. See Glenway Wescott's letter in the *N.Y. Times* (Aug. 9, 1961), p. 32, urging that all unpublished material be preserved for future biographers and students.

297 Cela, Camilo José. "En la muerte violente de un amigo," *Papeles de Son Armadans,* No. 64 (July 1961), p. 1.

297₁ Pacheco, Manuel. "Poema para la muerte de Ernest Hemingway," *ibid.*, p. 1.

298 Brown, John. "Hemingway e la sua opera," *Ponte,* XVII (July 1961), 1047-60.

299 "E. F." "Necrologi per Hemingway," *Tempo Presente,* VI (July 1961), 535-536.

300 Grebstein, Sheldon. "Sex, Hemingway, and the Critics," *Humanist,* XXI (July–Aug. 1961), 212-218.

301 Smith, Norman. "Ernest Hemingway," *Nostro Tempo,* X (July–Aug. 1961), 1-2. In Italian.

302 Vientós Gastón, Nilita. "Ernest Hemingway, 1899-1961," *Asomante,* XVII (July–Sept. 1961), 37-39. In Spanish.

303 Vázquez Amaral, José. "Hemingway: Bridge Between Two Worlds," *Américas,* XIII (Aug. 1961), 2-5. Photographs.

1304 Jens, Walter. "Marginalien: Zum Tode Ernest Hemingways," *Merkur*, xv (Aug. 1961), 797-800.

1305 Eisner, Alexei. "On byl s nami v Ispanii," *Novyi Mir*, No. 8 (Aug. 1961), pp. 169-172.

1306 Camerino, Aldo. "Morte di Hemingway," *Osservatore*, vii (Aug. 1961), 63-66.

1306₁ Excerpts from the foreign press on Hemingway's death, *ibid.*, pp. 67-70. In Italian.

1307 Misrahi, Victor. "Hemingway au delà de sa légende," *Revue Générale Belge* (Aug. 1961), pp. 11-20.

1308 Bigongiari, Piero. Poem, "In morte di Ernest Hemingway," *Tempo Presente*, vi (Aug. 1961), 571-572.

1309 Franconeri, Francesco. "Hemingway, uomo e scrittore," *Vita e Pensiero*, xliv (Aug. 1961), 549-555.

1310 Schmied, Wieland. "Der Tod war sein Thema: Ernest Hemingway, Mann ohne Dämmerung," *Wort in der Zeit*, vii (Aug. 1961), 2-5.

1311 "Ernest Hemingway," *Writer's Digest*, xlii (Aug. 1961), 10, 80. Cover photograph of Hemingway.

1312 Lavergne, Édouard. "Hemingway ou la passion de la vie," *Revue des Deux Mondes*, cxxx (Aug. 1, 1961), 467.

1313 Ruark, Robert. "Ernest Was Very Simple," *N.Y. World Telegram* (Aug. 4, 1961), pp. 15, 17. Dateline: Baragoi, Kenya.

1314 Hyman, Stanley Edgar. Writers and Writing column, "The Best of Hemingway," *New Leader*, xliv (Aug. 14–21, 1961), 22-24.

1315 Moravia, Alberto. "Amici dei morte e nemici dei vivi," *Espresso* (Aug. 20, 1961), p. 8.

1316 "Last Words Hemingway Wrote," *Life*, li (Aug. 25, 1961), 7.
Includes a facsimile of a two-page letter from Hemingway to Fritz Saviers, a nine-year-old friend in Ketchum, Idaho. See (F147).

1317 Maiorana, Ronald. "Hemingway Wrote His Will in Legal Style," *N.Y. Times* (Aug. 25, 1961), p. 27. Facsimile.
Regarding Hemingway's "Last Will and Testament," dated September 1955 and signed Ernest Miller Hemingway.

1318 "Hemingway Manuscripts Are Shipped Here," *N.Y. Times* (Aug. 31, 1961), p. 29. Dateline: Tampa, Florida.
Reports that Mary Hemingway "gave Cuban home to the people of Cuba."

19 Pivano, Fernanda. "Ritratto di Hemingway," *Aut Aut* (Sept. 1961), pp. 397-413. Reprinted in *America rossa e nera*, Florence, 1964, pp. 132-150.

20 "In Memoriam: Av allt att doma. . . ," *BLM*, xxx (Sept. 1961), 500-501.

21 Lauras, Antoine. "Ernest Hemingway est mort," *Études*, cccx (Sept. 1961), 278-281.

22 Arnavon, Cyrille. "Mort d'Ernest Hemingway," *Europe*, ccclxxxix (Sept. 1961), 103-105.

23 Waterman, Arthur E. "Hemingway's 'The Short Happy Life of Francis Macomber,' " *Explicator*, xx (Sept. 1961), Item 2.

24 Greacen, Robert. "Homage to Hemingway," *Humanist*, London, lxxvi (Sept. 1961), 266-267.

25 "Public Meeting to Mourn Death of Ernest Hemingway," *Indian P.E.N.*, xxvii (Sept. 1961), 287-288.

26 Marra López, José R. "Hemingway: la última singladura," *Insula*, xvi (Sept. 1961), 13, 16.

26₁ Fuente, Pablo de la. "Recuerdo de Hemingway," *ibid.*, p. 13.

27 "Hemingway Postscript: Newsman Provides *Quill* With Story-Telling Photo," *Quill*, xlix (Sept. 1961), 15. Photograph by Carl E. Hayden.
   Photograph shows Hemingway holding the 12-gauge double-barrel shotgun that killed him. Both bolts had been pulled, revealing his care with guns.

28 Macdonald, Dwight. "Profilo di Hemingway," *Tempo Presente*, vi (Sept.–Oct. 1961), 712-718. Translated by Stefano Montenegro.
   This "parody biography" appeared in English in *Encounter*, xviii (Jan. 1962), 115-118, 120-121. Reprinted in *Against the American Grain*, New York, 1962, pp. 167-179. For Harvey Breit's reply, see *Encounter*, xviii (April 1962), 93.

29 Morris, Wright. "One Law for the Lion," *Partisan Review*, xxviii (Sept.–Nov. 1961), 541-551.

30 Crumpet, Peter. "Death One Afternoon: In Dominguín's Dressing Room," *National Review*, xi (Sept. 9, 1961), 169-170.
   Regarding the goring of Luis Miguel Dominguín, in August 1959, which Hemingway described in "The Dangerous Summer."

31 Hemingway, Mary. "Hemingway," *Look*, xxv (Sept. 12, 1961), 19-23. Photographs by Earl Theisen.

Regarding the 1953-1954 safari in East Africa and fishing from the *Pilar* in the Gulf Stream.

1332 Merton, Thomas. Poem, "An Elegy for Ernest Hemingway," *Commonweal*, LXXIV (Sept. 22, 1961), 513.

1333 Howe, Irving. "In Search of a Moral Style," *New Republic*, CXLV (Sept. 25, 1961), 21-23, 26-27.

1334 Farrell, James T. "Ernest Hemingway: The End of Something," *Thought*, XIII (Sept. 30, 1961), 13-15.
Reprinted in *Nugget*, VI (Dec. 1961), 44-45, 63-65.

1335 Strater, Henry. "Hemingway," *Art in America*, XLIX, No. 4 (1961), 84-85. Photographs, in color, of Strater's paintings of Hemingway.
Recalls his friendship with Hemingway, in Paris, and relates the three occasions on which he painted him: in 1922-1923, at Rapallo, Italy, and in 1930, at Key West, Florida.

1336 Castro, José Rodriquez. "Evocação de Hemingway," *Cadernos Brasileiros*, III, No. 3 (1961), 58-62.

1337 Kelly, John C. "Ernest Hemingway (1899–1961): Formulating the Data of Experience," *Studies: An Irish Quarterly Review*, L (Autumn 1961), 312-326.

1338 Toynbee, Philip. Review of *Hemingway and His Critics* edited by Carlos Baker, *Encounter*, XVII (Oct. 1961), 86-88.
Includes the reviewer's appraisal of Hemingway's work.

1339 Gingrich, Arnold. "Ernest Hemingway: A Coda from the Maestro," *Esquire*, LVI (Oct. 1961), 8.

1340 Glasser, William. "Hemingway's *A Farewell to Arms*," *Explicator*, XX (Oct. 1961), Item 18.

1341 Ruark, Bob. "Papa Had No Use for Sham," *Field & Stream*, LXVI (Oct. 1961), 8, 109-111.

1342 Pérez Gállego, Cándido. "Aportacion española al estudio de Hemingway: Notas para una bibliografia," *Filología Moderna*, II (Oct. 1961), 57-71.
A checklist of books and periodical articles on Hemingway, in Spanish, with commentary.

1343 Franzen, Erich. "Hemingways vierte und fünfte Dimension des Schreibens," *Merkur*, XV (Oct. 1961), 989-992.

1344 George, Manfred. "Ernest Hemingways Nachlass," *Universitas*, XVI (Oct. 1961), 1129-31.

45 Shanley, John P. "The Essence of Ernest Hemingway," *N.Y. Times* (Oct. 2, 1961), p. 63.

Regarding the television account of Hemingway's life, presented on the DuPont Show of the Week, on October 1, 1961; produced and directed by Julian Claman; narrated by Chet Huntley.

46 Callaghan, Morley. "Hemingway: A Man Trapped in His Own Legend," *Toronto Star Weekly* (Oct. 7, 1961), Magazine Section, pp. 2, 4-5. Photograph.

47 MacLeish, Archibald. Poem, "The Gunshot," *Atlantic*, ccviii (Nov. 1961), 46.

Reprinted in *Newsweek*, lviii (Nov. 6, 1961), 58, with the notation that the poem begins with a "poignant fragment of Mary Hemingway's statement to newsmen after her husband's death."

48 Schroeter, James. "Hemingway's *The Sun Also Rises*," *Explicator*, xx (Nov. 1961), Item 28.

49 Spinucci, Pietro. "Ernest Hemingway: Lo stile e la vita," *Humanitas*, xvi (Nov. 1961), 937-944.

50 Keeler, Clinton. "*A Farewell to Arms*: Hemingway and Peele," *Modern Language Notes*, lxxvi (Nov. 1961), 622-625.

Regarding Hemingway's novel and George Peele's poem of the same title.

51 Castillo-Puche, José Luis. " 'De profundis' a Hemingway," *Estafeta Literaria*, No. 228 (Nov. 1, 1961), pp. 16-17.

52 "Hemingway's Biographer," *N.Y. Times* (Nov. 4, 1961), p. 17.

Announcement by Scribner's that Professor Carlos Baker, of Princeton University, will write the authorized biography of Hemingway.

53 Algren, Nelson. "Hemingway: The Dye That Did Not Run," *Nation*, cxciii (Nov. 18, 1961), 387-390.

54 "Nick Adams Grows Up," *Newsweek*, lviii (Nov. 20, 1961), 106-107.

Regarding the negotiations for purchasing ten Hemingway short stories for the film, *Adventures of a Young Man*.

55 Sanford, Marcelline Hemingway. "At the Hemingways," *Atlantic*, ccviii (Dec. 1961), 31-39, Part i: "Walloon Lake"; ccix (Jan. 1962), 32-37. Part ii: "My Doctor Father"; (Feb. 1962), 60-66, Part iii: "Ernest Returns From War."

Reminiscences by Hemingway's older sister of the early years in Oak Park, Ill., and the summers spent in northern Michigan. Published in *At the Hemingways*, Boston, 1962.

499

1356 Stephens, Robert O. "Hemingway's Don Quixote in Pamplona," *College English*, XXIII (Dec. 1961), 216-218.
Regarding the Don Quixote code as applied to Jake Barnes in *SAR*.

1357 Hemingway, Leicester. "My Brother, Ernest Hemingway," *Playboy*, VIII (Dec. 1961), 48-78; IX (Jan. 1962), 36-48, 136-145; (Feb. 1962), 26-42; (March 1962), 32-42, 106-108. Photographs.
Published in *My Brother, Ernest Hemingway*, Cleveland, 1962.

1358 Evans, Oliver. " 'The Snows of Kilimanjaro': A Revaluation," *PMLA*, LXXVI (Dec. 1961), 601-607.

1359 Photograph of Hemingway in 1957, by Yousuf Karsh, *Réalités*, No. 133 (Dec. 1961), pp. 74-75.

1360 Palmer, Aileen. "Lament for the Death of a Bullfighter," *Overland*, No. 21 (Winter 1961), p. 32.
Regarding the renewed interest in Hemingway's work, in Australia.

1361 Stephens, Robert O. "Hemingway's Old Man and the Iceberg," *Modern Fiction Studies*, VII (Winter 1961–1962), 295-304.

1362 Holman, C. Hugh. "Ernest Hemingway: A Tribute," *Books Abroad*, XXXVI (Winter 1962), 5-8.

1363 Montgomery, Marion. "Hemingway's 'The Gambler, the Nun, and the Radio': A Reading and a Problem," *Forum*, III (Winter 1962), 36-40.

1364 McAleer, John J. "*A Farewell to Arms*: Frederic Henry's Rejected Passion," *Renascence*, Milwaukee, XIV (Winter 1962), 72-79, 89.
Discusses Hemingway's use of "Christ symbolism" in *FTA*.

1365 Clendenning, John. "Hemingway's Gods, Dead and Alive," *Texas Studies in Literature and Language*, III (Winter 1962), 489-502.

1366 Rodrigues, Eusebio L. " 'Hills Like White Elephants': An Analysis," *Literary Criterion*, V (1962), 105-109.

1367 Baužytė, G. "Ankstyvųjų Hemingvejaus romanų herojus," *Literatūra*, III (1962), 137-147.

1368 Photograph of Hemingway by John Bryson, *Photography Year Book* (1962), p. 172.

1369 Pandolfi, Anna. "La fortuna di Ernest Hemingway in Italia (1929–1961)," *Studi Americani*, VIII (1962), 151-199.
Bibliography of Italian translations and critical studies on pp. 159-199.

370 Lania, Leo. Essay on the occasion of the death of Hemingway, *Ukraine & the World* (1962), pp. 64-65. In Ukrainian. Reprinted from *Schönste* (Aug. 1961).

370₁ Korotytch, Vitaly. Poem in memory of Hemingway, "The Rock in the Moor," *ibid.*, pp. 65-66. In Ukrainian.

371 Traberg, Ebbe. Review of *Doden kommer om eftermiddagen (DIA)*, *Vindrösen*, IX (1962), 264-266.

372 Helman, Albert. "Dood in de voormiddag," *Gids*, CXXV (Jan. 1962), 14-22.

373 Longyear, Christopher Rudston. "Linguistically Determined Categories of Meanings: A Comparative Analysis of Meaning in 'The Snows of Kilimanjaro' in English and German," *Dissertation Abstracts*, XXII (Jan. 1962), 2391-92.
　　Abstract from doctoral dissertation, University of Michigan, 1961.

374 Krause, Sydney J. "Hemingway's 'My Old Man,'" *Explicator*, XX (Jan. 1962), Item 39.

375 Killinger, John. "When Papa Was Still in the Ring," review of Lillian Ross's *Portrait of Hemingway*, *Saturday Review*, XLV (Jan. 13, 1962), 59-60. Photograph.

376 Quarantotti Gambini, P. A. "Sinclair Lewis contro Hemingway," *Corriere della Sera* (Jan. 16, 1962), p. 3.
　　Reminiscence of the two authors in Venice, in 1949.

377 Ginna, Robert Emmett. "Life in the Afternoon," *Esquire*, LVII (Feb. 1962), 104-106, 136. Photograph of Hemingway by Ken Heyman.
　　Relates a visit with Hemingway in Cuba, in 1958.

378 Tanselle, G. Thomas. "Hemingway's 'Indian Camp,'" *Explicator*, XX (Feb. 1962), Item 53.

379 Turnbull, Andrew. "Scott Fitzgerald and Ernest Hemingway," *Esquire*, LVII (March 1962), 110-113, 115-124.
　　Excerpts from *Scott Fitzgerald*, New York, 1962.

379₁ Brower, Brock. "The Abraham Lincoln Brigade Revisited," *ibid.*, pp. 64-68, 127-130.
　　For commentary regarding the change of opinion about Hemingway's portrayal of André Marty in *FWBT*, see p. 129.

380 Drew, Fraser B. "Pupil, Teacher and Hemingway," *New York State Education* (March 1962), pp. 16-17, 37. Photographs.
　　Regarding his correspondence with Hemingway and his visit to Finca Vigía, in 1955.

1381 Evans, Oliver. "The Arrow Wounds of Count Mippipopolous," *PMLA*, LXXVII (March 1962), 175.

1382 Lederer, W. J. "What I Learned from Hemingway," *Reader's Digest*, LXXX (March 1962), 207-208.

While stationed on a U.S. Navy river gunboat at Chungking, China, in 1941, the author traded Hemingway "six bottles of whiskey" for "six lessons on how to become a writer."

1383 Ritzen, Quentin. "Hemingway à Paris," *Revue de Paris*, LXIX (March 1962), 100-113.

1384 Baker, Carlos. "Personal History: Before the Bell Tolled," review of Leicester Hemingway's *My Brother, Ernest Hemingway, Saturday Review*, XLV (March 3, 1962), 86. Photograph of Hemingway taken in 1918.

1385 Hindus, Milton. "The 'Papa' They Knew," review of Leicester Hemingway's *My Brother, Ernest Hemingway*, and Lillian Ross's *Portrait of Hemingway, N.Y. Times Book Review* (March 4, 1962), pp. 14, 16. Photographs.

1386 Talese, Gay. "Manuscripts Hemingway Left May Yield Four More Novels," *N.Y. Times* (March 9, 1962), p. 31.

Interview with Mary Hemingway, in New York.

1387 Review of Leicester Hemingway's *My Brother, Ernest Hemingway, Time*, LXXIX (March 16, 1962), 86. Photographs.

1388 Eastman, Max. "Thoughts about Ernest Hemingway," *Saturday Review*, XLV (March 24, 1962), 6, 8, 54.

Reminiscences of Hemingway as a "kid reporter" in Genoa, in 1922, and of the encounter in Maxwell Perkins' office, in 1937.

1389 Lyons, Leonard. "Hemingway si confessa," *Epoca*, XLVI (March 25, 1962), 78-83. Photographs.

1390 White, William. "Some Thoughts on the Hemingway Racket," *New Republic*, CXLVI (March 26, 1962), 24-25.

Comments on the publication of *The Secret Agent's Badge of Courage*. See (F153). A German translation, under the title "Clausewitz," appeared in *Welt* (April 3, 1962), p. 7.

1391 Marshall, S.L.A. "How Papa Liberated Paris," *American Heritage*, XIII (April 1962), 5-7, 92-101. Photographs.

The author was the U.S. Army's chief historian in the European theatre at the time of the events, in August 1944, which he relates here.

1392 "49 Nobel Prize Winners Honored at White House," *N.Y. Times* (April 30, 1962), pp. 1, 19.

Fredric March read a chapter from an unpublished work of Hemingway's, which was made available by Mary Hemingway, a guest at the dinner given by President and Mrs. John F. Kennedy. Mrs. Hemingway's introduction to the chapter from Hemingway's novel about the sea is quoted.

393 Spender, Stephen. "The Importance of Being Ernest," review of Leicester Hemingway's *My Brother, Ernest Hemingway, Sunday Times*, London (May 20, 1962), Magazine Section, p. 31.

394 Tanner, Tony. "Old Man and the River," review of Leicester Hemingway's *My Brother, Ernest Hemingway, Spectator*, CCVIII (May 25, 1962), 685-686.

395 Peterson, Richard Kenyon. "Hemingway: Direct and Oblique," *Dissertation Abstracts*, XXII (June 1962), 4353-54.

Abstract from a doctoral dissertation, University of Washington, 1961.

396 Newman, Paul B. "Hemingway's Grail Quest," *University of Kansas City Review*, XXVIII (June 1962), 295-303.

Critique on *SAR*.

397 Wyndham, Francis. "Stein," review of Leicester Hemingway's *My Brother, Ernest Hemingway, New Statesman*, LXIII (June 29, 1962), 947.

398 Kennedy, John F. "The President's Tribute," *Mark Twain Journal*, XI (Summer 1962), 1. Hemingway Memorial Number. Edited by Cyril Clemens. 20 pages. Facsimile of a letter from Hemingway, in 1930, on the cover. See (F74).

98₁ Hemingway, Mary. "My Husband's Black Dog," *ibid.*, p. 1.

98₂ Baker, Carlos. "Two Rivers: Mark Twain and Hemingway," *ibid.*, p. 2.

98₃ Dieckmann, Edward A., Jr. "The Hemingway Hypnosis," *ibid.*, pp. 3-4, 16.

98₄ Brocki, Sister Mary Damascene, C.S.S.F. "Faulkner and Hemingway: Values in a Modern World," *ibid.*, pp. 5-9, 15.

98₅ Hollowell, Grace. Poem, "Dearest Our Sons Ernest Hemingway and Boris Pasternak," *ibid.*, p. 10.

98₆ Maurois, André. "A Tribute from France," *ibid.*, p. 10.

98₇ White, William. "Hemingway-iana: Annotated," *ibid.*, pp. 11-13.

98₈ Swinnerton, Frank. "A Marvelous Thing for the Novel," *ibid.*, p. 13.

1398₉ Thomas, Lowell. "Larger Than Life," *ibid.*, p. 15.

1398₁₀ Chubb, Thomas Caldecot. "A Glimpse of Hemingway," *ibid.*, p. 15.
Brief reminiscence of Hemingway in France, in 1927.

1398₁₁ Derleth, August. "A Superb Short Story Writer," *ibid.*, p. 16.

1398₁₂ "Upton Sinclair, Homer Croy and Robert Graves Dissent," *ibid.*,
p. 17.

1398₁₃ Steen, Marguerite. "Interpreter of the Spanish Mystique," *ibid.*,
p. 17.

1398₁₄ Bottome, Phyllis. "Chronicler of the Modern-Minded," *ibid.*, p. 17.

1398₁₅ Bell, Neil. "Of The Company," *ibid.*, p. 18.

1398₁₆ Drew, Fraser. "Hemingway's Generosity and Humility," *ibid.*, p. 19.

1398₁₇ Hughes, Langston. "A Reader's Writer," *ibid.*, p. 19.

1399 Fiedler, Leslie. "An Almost Imaginary Interview: Hemingway in
Ketchum," *Partisan Review*, xxix (Summer 1962), 395-405.
Relates a visit with Hemingway in November 1960, in Idaho. For
Seymour Betsky's account of this visit, see (H1295₆). For reply by
Douglas Taylor, see *PR*, xxix (Fall 1962), 631-633.

1400 Barnes, Robert J. "Two Modes of Fiction: Hemingway and
Greene," *Renascence*, Milwaukee, xiv (Summer 1962), 193-198.
Draws a comparison between the styles of Hemingway and Gra-
ham Greene.

1401 Kruse, Horst. "Hinrich Kruses *Weg und Umweg* und die Tradition
der Short Story Ernest Hemingways," *Germanisch-romanische
Monatsschrift*, xii, new series (July 1962), 286-301.

1402 Ogawa, Jiro. "On *The Old Man and the Sea*," *Hiroshima Studies
in English Language and Literature*, viii (July 1962), 115-126.

1403 Randall, David A. "Dukedom Large Enough. Part ii: Hemingway,
Churchill and the Printed Word," *Papers of the Bibliographical
Society of America*, lvi (July-Sept. 1962), 346-353.
Regarding the "advance copies" of *ARIT*, see (A23a); and the
anti-Semitic deletions from the Bantam edition of *SAR*, see (A6g).

1404 Geismar, Maxwell. "Was 'Papa' a Truly Great Writer?" *N.Y. Times
Book Review* (July 1, 1962), pp. 1, 16. Photograph of Hemingway
by John Bryson.
An appraisal of the literary stature of Hemingway on the first an-
niversary of his death. Reprinted in *Opinions and Perspectives*, ed.
Francis Brown, Boston, 1964, pp. 162-168.

405 Ritzen, Quentin. "Il y a un an Un Coup de Feu . . . La Mort d'Hemingway," *Nouvelles Littéraires* (July 5, 1962), p. 3. Photograph.

406 Cubillas, Vicente. "Que 'Mató' a 'Papá' Hemingway?" *Bohemia*, LIV (July 6, 1962), 32-35, 85. Photographs.
Written on the first anniversary of Hemingway's death.

407 Ehrenburg, Ilya. "In Spagna con Hemingway," *Rinascita* (July 7, 1962), p. 32. Photographs.

408 Prudkov, O. "K tem, kto boretsia," *Literaturnaya Gazeta* (July 10, 1962).
Review of the play, *The Fifth Column*, which was presented by the Sovremennik Theatre company in Moscow on July 9, 1962.

409 Rodnon, Stewart. "Sports, Sporting Codes, and Sportsmanship in the Work of Ring Lardner, James T. Farrell, Ernest Hemingway, and William Faulkner," *Dissertation Abstracts*, XXIII (Aug. 1962), 634-635.
Abstract from a doctoral dissertation, New York University, 1961.

410 Crowther, Bosley. "Farewell to Ernest," review of the film, *Hemingway's Adventures of a Young Man*, N.Y. *Times* (Aug. 5, 1962), II, 1.
For Marcelline Hemingway Sanford's letter, approving this review, see the *N.Y. Times* (Aug. 12, 1962) II, 7.

411 Lombardo, Agostino. "Ricordo di Hemingway: L'innocenza, la paura e la morte," *Mondo*, XIV (Aug. 14, 1962), 10-11. Photographs.

412 Hicks, Granville. "The Number One Son," review of Marcelline Hemingway Sanford's *At the Hemingways*, *Saturday Review*, XLV (Aug. 18, 1962), 17.

413 Coleman, John. "Rape of Hemingway," review of the film, *Hemingway's Adventures of a Young Man*, *New Statesman*, LXIV (Aug. 31, 1962), 265-266.

414 Bergman, Petter. "Petoskey, Michigan," *BLM*, XXXI (Sept. 1962), 580-581.
Review of the Swedish translation of *TOS*, *Vårflod*.

415 Baker, Carlos. "When Ernie Was Just an Eldest Brother," review of Marcelline Hemingway Sanford's *At the Hemingways*, N.Y. *Times Book Review*, (Sept. 2, 1962), pp. 5, 18. Photographs.

416 Krzyżanowski, Jerzy R. "*For Whom the Bell Tolls*: The Origin of General Golz," *Polish Review*, VII (Autumn 1962), 69-74.

417 Floor, Richard. "Fate and Life: Determinism in Ernest Hemingway," *Renascence*, Milwaukee, XV (Fall 1962) 23-27.
An essay on "The Dangerous Summer."

1418 Hale, Nancy. "Hemingway and the Courage to Be," *Virginia Quarterly Review*, XXXVIII (Autumn 1962), 620-639. Reprinted in *The Realities of Fiction*, Boston, 1962, pp. 85-112.

1419 Stone, Edward. "Hemingway's Waiters Yet Once More," *American Speech*, XXXVII (Oct. 1962), 239-240.
    Regarding the linguistic reproduction in "A Clean, Well-Lighted Place."

1420 Cotter, Janet M. "*The Old Man and the Sea*: An 'Open' Literary Experience," *English Journal*, LI (Oct. 1962), 459-463.
    Discussion on teaching *OMATS* to high school students.

1421 Ehrenburg, Ilya. "Hemingway," *Soviet Review*, III (Oct. 1962), 22-26.
    Excerpt translated from *People, Years, Life: Memoirs of Ilya Ehrenburg*, Moscow, 1960. Relates his meeting with Hemingway in Madrid, in 1937, and quotes their conversation on writing.

1422 Foy, James L. Poem, "Cante hondo | For Ernest Hemingway | Requiescat in Pace," *Commonweal*, LXXVII (Oct. 5, 1962), 47.

1423 Nugent, John. "Vita col padre," *Europeo*, XVIII (Oct. 21, 1962), 82-87. Photographs.
    Interview with Patrick Hemingway.

1424 Yokelson, Joseph Bernard. "Symbolism in the Fiction of Ernest Hemingway," *Dissertation Abstracts*, XXIII (Nov. 1962), 1714.
    Abstract from a doctoral dissertation, Brown University, 1960.

1425 Marcus, Fred H. "*A Farewell to Arms*: The Impact of Irony and the Irrational," *English Journal*, LI (Nov. 1962), 527-535.

1426 Ostroff, Anthony. Short story, "The Hemingway Influence," *Harper's Magazine*, CCXXV (Nov. 1962), 92-96.

1427 Kashkeen, Ivan. "Letters of Ernest Hemingway to Soviet Writers," *Soviet Literature*, No. 11 (Nov. 1962), pp. 158-167.
    Two letters to Kashkeen, written in 1935 and 1939, and a letter to Konstantin Simonov, written in 1946, are quoted. See (F90), (F95), (F102).

1428 "Hemingway View of U. S. Explained | Biographer Says Author Was a 'Vicarious' Patriot," *N.Y. Times* (Nov. 11, 1962), p. 63.
    Carlos Baker comments on the collection of Hemingway-Lanham letters, which was given to the Princeton University Library by General Charles T. Lanham.

1429 Baker, Carlos. "Hemingway Among the Princetonians," *Princeton Alumni Weekly*, LXIII (Nov. 16, 1962), 6-9, 15.
    Transcript of a talk given at Princeton University, in June 1962.

429₁ "New Hemingway Letters," *ibid.*, p. 11. Photograph.

Regarding the 150 Hemingway-Lanham letters, written between 1945 and 1961, which General Charles T. Lanham presented to the Princeton University Library.

430 Weeks, Robert P. "Fakery in *The Old Man and the Sea*," *College English*, XXIV (Dec. 1962), 188-192.

430₁ O'Connor, William Van. "Faulkner's One-Sided 'Dialogue' with Hemingway," *ibid.*, pp. 208, 213-215.

430₂ Hagopian, John V. "Symmetry in 'Cat in the Rain,'" *ibid.*, pp. 220-222.

1431 Taylor, Zack. "The Special Outdoor World of Ernest Hemingway," *Sports Afield*, CXLVIII (Dec. 1962), 52-55, 105-108. Photographs.

1432 "Hemingway Items to Texas [University]," *N.Y. Times* (Dec. 4, 1962), p. 47.

Regarding the $50,000 collection of Hemingway books and articles given to the University of Texas by Lee Samuels.

1433 Rubin, Louis D., Jr. "*In Memoriam*: Ernest Hemingway," *Virginia Librarian*, VIII (Winter 1962), 43-45.

1434 Lid, Richard W. "Hemingway and the Need for Speech," *Modern Fiction Studies*, VIII (Winter 1962–1963), 401-407.

A study of "the barrier of articulation" in "Old Man at the Bridge" and "Hills Like White Elephants."

434₁ Weeks, Robert P. "The Power of the Tacit in Crane and Hemingway," *ibid.*, pp. 415-418.

Compares Stephen Crane's *The Red Badge of Courage* and *FWBT*.

1435 Yunck, John A. "The Natural History of a Dead Quarrel: Hemingway and the Humanists," *South Atlantic Quarterly*, LXII (Winter 1963), 29-42.

1436 Bhai, Indira. "Hemingway's Hero," *English Miscellany*, St. Stephen's College, Delhi, No. 2 [1963], pp. 57-62.

1437 Heissenbüttel, Helmut. "Versuch über den Ruhm Hemingways," *Deutsche Rundschau*, LXXXIX (Jan. 1963), 50-56.

1438 Yevtushenko, Yevgeny. Poem, "Meeting with Hemingway," *Playboy*, X (Jan. 1963), 123.

Translated from the Russian by George Reavey. For book publication and other translations, see (G459).

1439 Guidi, Augusto. "Ernest Hemingway, un classico della narrativa moderna," *Dialoghi*, XI (Jan.–April 1963), 29-35.

1440 Paulding, Gouverneur. "Long Count," review of Morley Callaghan's *That Summer in Paris, Reporter*, XXVIII (Jan. 17, 1963), 52, 54.

1441 Fischer, William J. "Hemingway poszukiwacz rzetelnych wartości moralnych," *Ameryka*, No. 49 [Feb. 1963], pp. 2-5. Cover photograph of Hemingway and other photographs.
Regarding Hemingway's "search for an honest morality."

1441₁ "Hemingway w ocenie innych pisarzy," *ibid.*, p. 5.
Short appraisals of Hemingway's work by various authors. See also (C416).

1442 Belfrage, Sally. "Haunted House of Ernest Hemingway," *Esquire*, LIX (Feb. 1963), 66-67. Photographs and a facsimile of penciled record of Hemingway's weight.
Relates a visit to Finca Vigia, which the Cuban government inaugurated as a museum in 1962.

1443 Markel, Helen. "A Look Back, A Look Ahead," *Good Housekeeping*, CLVI (Feb. 1963), 32-34, 36-37. Photographs.
Interview with Mary Hemingway.

1444 Katsurada, Shigetoshi. "An Explication of Hemingway's Literary Situation," *Kobe Gaidai Ronso*, XIII (Feb. 1963), 23-40. In Japanese.

1445 Dodd, Martha. "Hemingway in Cuba: A Home Away From Home," *Mainstream*, XVI (Feb. 1963), 25-30.

1446 White, William. Review of *The Wild Years, Quill*, LI (Feb. 1963), 27, 36.

1447 Zaphiro, Denis and Worth Bingham. "Hemingway's Last Safari," *Rogue*, VIII (Feb. 1963), 18-20, 87-88. Photographs.

1448 Van Dusen, William. "Hemingway's Longest Day," *True*, XLIV (Feb. 1963), 54-55, 62.
An account of Hemingway's participation in the invasion of Normandy, in June 1944.

1449 Butcher, Fanny. "At Mary Hemingway's, Mementos of a Great Writer," *Chicago Sunday Tribune* (Feb. 3, 1963), Magazine of Books, p. 6.

1450 "Mrs. Grace Hemingway Reveals . . . My Son, Ernest Hemingway," *National Insider* (Feb. 3, 1963), pp. 10-11. Photographs.
This article, under the by-line of Hemingway's mother, includes a description of the airplane crashes in Africa, in 1954, despite the fact that Mrs. Grace Hemingway died in 1951.

451 Farrell, James T. "A Preface to Ernest," *Chicago Daily News* (Feb. 9, 1963), p. 10.

452 Wilson, Edmund. Review of Morley Callaghan's *That Summer in Paris, New Yorker*, XXXIX (Feb. 23, 1963), 139-142, 145-148.
Reprinted in *The Bit Between My Teeth*, New York, 1964, pp. 515-525. For Mary Hemingway's reply, see the *New Yorker*, XXXIX (March 16, 1963), 160, 162-163.

453 Himuro, Misako. "*The Old Man and the Sea*," *English Literature*, No. 23 (March 1963), pp. 14-27. In Japanese.
A study of the "symbolic structure" of *OMATS*.

454 Takigawa, Motoo. "Hemingway and His View on Religion," *Journal of the Society of English and American Literature*, VII (March 1963), 57-67.

455 "Importance of Beating Ernest," review of Morley Callaghan's *That Summer in Paris, Time*, LXXXI (March 15, 1963), 106.

456 Reid, Stephen A. "The Oedipal Pattern in Hemingway's 'The Capital of the World,'" *Literature & Psychology*, XIII (Spring 1963), 37-43.

457 Oldsey, Bern. "The Snows of Ernest Hemingway," *Wisconsin Studies in Contemporary Literature*, IV (Spring–Summer 1963), 172-198.
A study of imagery in Hemingway's work.

458 Hemingway, Mary. "A Sentimental Safari," *Life*, LIV (April 19, 1963), 88-92, 95-96, 99. Photographs.
On a return visit to Africa, Mary Hemingway recalls their safari during the winter of 1953-1954.

458₁ Hunt, George P. Editor's Note: "How We Got to Know the Hemingways," *ibid.*, p. 3.

459 Malaquais, Jean. "Hemingway, ou le champion et la mort," *Preuves*, No. 147 (May 1963), pp. 32-41.

460 Thomas, Amory A. "Portrait pour un Lion," *Ruban Rouge*, No. 17 (June 1963), pp. 14-21. Photographs.

461 Hofling, Charles K. "Hemingway's *The Old Man and the Sea* and The Male Reader," *American Imago*, XX (Summer 1963), 161-173.
A psychoanalytical study.

462 Page, Alex. "Pakistan's Hemingway," *Antioch Review*, XXIII (Summer 1963), 203-211.
Regarding the response in Pakistan to Hemingway's work.

1463 Gray, James. "Hemingway in Piggott," *Approach*, No. 48 (Summer 1963), pp. 30-32.

Regarding Hemingway's visits to Piggott, Arkansas, where he worked on *FTA* and went duck hunting.

1464 Dillingham, William B. "Hemingway and Death," *Emory University Quarterly*, XIX (Summer 1963), 95-101.

1465 Gelfant, Blanche. "Language as a Moral Code in *A Farewell to Arms*," *Modern Fiction Studies*, IX (Summer 1963), 173-176.

1466 Mailer, Norman. "Punching Papa," review of Morley Callaghan's *That Summer in Paris*, *N.Y. Review of Books*, I [Aug. 1963], 13.

1467 La Forest, Sister Mary Austina. "La vogue de Hemingway en France," *Revue de l'Université Laval*, XVIII (Sept. 1963), 40-61. Bibliographical footnotes.

1468 Walters, Raymond, Jr. In and Out of Books column, "Mr. Way's Way," *N.Y. Times Book Review* (Sept. 8, 1963), p. 8.

Quotes Victor Franco, French journalist, regarding a recent visit to Cuba. For Mary Hemingway's reply, see the *N.Y.T.B.R.* (Oct. 20, 1963), p. 26.

1469 Christensen, Francis. "A Lesson from Hemingway," *College English*, XXV (Oct. 1963), 12-18.

Analysis of the sentence structure of "The Undefeated."

1470 Moore, Geoffrey. "*The Sun Also Rises*: Notes Toward an Extreme Fiction," *Review of English Literature*, IV (Oct. 1963), 31-46.

1471 Jacque, Valentina. "Soviet Scholars on Modern American Literature and Scholarship," *Soviet Literature*, No. 10 (Oct. 1963), pp. 161-166.

Review of *Modern American Literature* [Moscow, 1963], which contains the lecture "The Tragedy of Hemingway" by M. O. Mendelson.

1472 Holder, Alan. "The Other Hemingway," *Twentieth Century Fiction*, IX (Oct. 1963), 153-157.

A study of the women characters in Hemingway's work.

1473 Bryan, James E. "Hemingway as Vivisector," *University Review*, XXX (Oct. 1963), 3-12.

1474 Meriwether, James B. "The Text of Ernest Hemingway," *Papers of the Bibliographical Society of America*, LVII (Oct.–Dec. 1963), 403-421.

Regarding the need for a full-scale bibliographical and textual study of Hemingway's work.

1475 Mearns, David C. and John McDonough. "Acquisitions," *Library of Congress Information Bulletin,* XXII (Oct. 7, 1963), 533-534.

Regarding the fifteen-page manuscript that Hemingway wrote in connection with the showing of the film *The Spanish Earth,* in 1937, which was presented to the Library of Congress by Mrs. Fredric March.

1476 White, William. "The Hemingway Industry," *American Book Collector,* XIV (Nov. 1963), 8-10.

Regarding books about Hemingway published in the two years following his death.

1477 Sykes, Robert Howard. "Ernest Hemingway's Style: A Descriptive Analysis," *Dissertation Abstracts,* XXIV (Nov. 1963), 2043.

Abstract from a doctoral dissertation, University of Pittsburgh, 1962.

1478 Blum, Ralph. "A Play in Three Acts," *New Yorker,* XXXIX (Nov. 2, 1963), 55-88; (Nov. 9, 1963), 59-92; (Nov. 16, 1963), 59-112.

An account of the rehearsals and the opening night performance of *The Fifth Column,* which was translated into Russian by Evgenia Davidovna Kalashnikova and presented by the Sovremennik Theatre company in Moscow.

1479 Wilson, James Robert. "Responses of College Freshmen to Three Novels," *Dissertation Abstracts,* XXIV (Dec. 1963), 2465-66.

Abstract from a doctoral dissertation, University of California (Berkeley), 1963. The three novels are: *The Catcher in the Rye* by J. D. Salinger, *The Grapes of Wrath* by John Steinbeck, and *A Farewell to Arms.*

1480 Wells, Arvin R. "Ritual of Transfiguration: *The Old Man and the Sea,*" *University Review,* XXX (Dec. 1963), 95-101.

1481 Gilroy, Harry. "Hemingway Left Variety of Works," *N.Y. Times* (Dec. 10, 1963), p. 50.

Regarding Scribner's press conference for Mary Hemingway to discuss *A Moveable Feast,* Hemingway's first posthumously published work. Mrs. Hemingway reported that a novel, a travel book, some short stories (including one Nick Adams story), and "about half a pound of poems" were among her husband's unpublished papers.

1482 "Posthumous Hemingway," *Publishers' Weekly,* CLXXXIV (Dec. 16, 1963), 10.

Regarding Scribner's press conference to announce the publication of *AMF.*

1483 Kazin, Alfred. "Young Man, Old Man," *Reporter*, XXIX (Dec. 19, 1963), 33-36.

[Part] 1. "Hemingway: No Further Down the Stream." [Part] 2. "Faulkner: Back Into the Havoc."

1484 Baker, Carlos. "Letters from Hemingway," *Princeton University Library Chronicle*, XXIV (Winter 1963), 101-107.

Regarding Princeton University's collection of Hemingway letters and their biographical significance.

1485 Fiedler, Leslie A. "The Death of the Old Men," *Arts & Sciences*, LXIV (Winter 1963–1964), 1-5.

Ch. I, on Hemingway and Faulkner, reprinted from *Waiting for the End*, New York, 1964, pp. 9-19.

1486 Lauter, Paul. "Plato's Stepchildren, Gatsby and Cohn," *Modern Fiction Studies*, IX (Winter 1963–1964), 338-346.

Regarding the main character in F. Scott Fitzgerald's *The Great Gatsby* and Robert Cohn in *SAR*.

1487 Hemingway, Leicester. "Ernest Hemingway's Boyhood Reading," *Mark Twain Journal*, XII (Winter 1964), 4-5.

1488 Cooperman, Stanley. "Death and *Cojones*: Hemingway's *A Farewell to Arms*," *South Atlantic Quarterly*, LXIII (Winter 1964), 85-92.

1489 Hagopian, John V. "Tidying Up Hemingway's 'Clean, Well-Lighted Place,' " *Studies in Short Fiction*, I (Winter 1964), 140-146.

1490 Tatandziewicz-Glebko, Ewa. "Hemingway Translations in Poland," *Babel: International Journal of Translations*, X, ii (1964), 85-87.

Regarding Hemingway's Polish translators.

1491 Moss, Sidney P. "Character, Vision, and Theme in *The Sun Also Rises*," *Iowa English Yearbook*, No. 9 (1964), pp. 64-67.

1492 Gorlier, Claudio. "Ernest Hemingway," *Terzo Programma*, No. 3 (1964), pp. 93-151.

A study in six parts: 1. I vecchi e i giovani. 2. Il paragone Europa. 3. Dimensioni dell'eroe. 4. La morte e il tempo. 5. Un nuovo linguaggio. 6. L'età del compromesso.

1493 Parker, Stephen Jan. "Hemingway's Revival in the Soviet Union: 1955-1962," *American Literature*, XXXV (Jan. 1964), 485-501.

Reprinted in *The Literary Reputation of Hemingway in Europe*, Roger Asselineau, ed., Paris, 1965, pp. 177-195.

1494 Pérez Gállego, Cándido. "Los dos finales de *A Farewell to Arms*," *Filología Moderna*, IV (Jan. 1964), 152-153.

Regarding the original conclusion to *FTA*, which appears in *Baker critiques*, p. 75.

495 Hemingway, Mary. "To Africa with Love," *Harper's Bazaar,* XCVII (Jan. 1964), 110, 164.
Regarding the Hemingways' safari in 1953-54.

496 Bisol, Gaetano. "Ernest Hemingway: portavoce di una 'generazione perduta,' " *Letture,* XIX (Jan. 1964), 3-22.

497 El'jaševič, Ark. "Čeloveka nel'zja pobedit," *Voprosi Literaturi,* VIII (Jan. 1964), 107-127.

497₁ Kashkeen, Ivan. "Soderžanie—forma—soderžanie," *ibid.,* pp. 128-149.
Translated into English in *Soviet Literature,* No. 6 (June 1964), pp. 172-180, under the title "What Is Hemingway's Style."

498 Howell, John Michael. "The Waste Land Tradition in the American Novel," *Dissertation Abstracts,* XXIV (Feb. 1964), 3337.
Abstract from a doctoral dissertation, Tulane University, 1963. Discusses *SAR.*

499 Cunningham, Donald H. "Hemingway's 'The Snows of Kilimanjaro,' " *Explicator,* XXII (Feb. 1964), Item 41.

500 Houck, Marjorie C. "Hemingway House Becomes a Museum," *N.Y. Times* (Feb. 2, 1964), X, 3.
The present owners, Mr. and Mrs. Jack Daniel, have turned the house in Key West, Florida, where Hemingway lived during the 1930s, into a museum.

501 Tomasson, Robert. "Twain and Hemingway: Accounting of Two Estates," *N.Y. Times* (Feb. 22, 1964), pp. 1, 18.
Regarding Hemingway's royalties, stock holdings, and manuscripts.

502 White, William. "Violence, Blood, Death in the Writings of Ernest Hemingway," *T.A.L.S.,* No. 1 (March 1964), pp. 22-30.

503 "Kennedy Library Given Papers of Hemingway," *N.Y. Times* (March 31, 1964), p. 32.
Regarding Mary Hemingway's plans to give Hemingway's manuscripts, letters, notes, and memorabilia to the John F. Kennedy Library.

504 Simpson, Herbert. "The Problem of Structure in *A Farewell to Arms,*" *Forum,* IV (Spring 1964), 20-24.

505 Westbrook, Max. "Necessary Performance: The Hemingway Collection at Texas," *Library Chronicle of the University of Texas,* VII (Spring 1964), 26-31. Facsimile of manuscript page from *DIA.*
Regarding the 354 items in the Hemingway collection at the Uni-

versity of Texas; including the many books which Hemingway inscribed to Lee Samuels.

1506 White, William. "Ernest Hemingway and Nathanael West: How Well-Known Is Your Collector's 'Item'?" *American Book Collector*, XIV (May 1964), 29, 32.

1507 Fadiman, Clifton. Report on *AMF, Book-of-the-Month Club News* (May 1964), pp. 1-2, 4-5. Cover photograph by Yousuf Karsh.

"In these simple, flowing pages, written without much thought for the famous Hemingway 'effects,' is an invaluable portrait of the artist as a young man during that most interesting of all periods— the period when mere living and mere loving and mere writing were enough, and the contagion of the world's slow stain lay, though not far distant, still in the future." *A Moveable Feast* was the Book-of-the-Month Club selection for June 1964.

1507₁ Perkins, Max. "Ernest Hemingway," *ibid.*, pp. 6, 16.

A biographical sketch reprinted from the *Book-of-the-Month Club News* (Oct. 1940).

1508 Geismar, Maxwell. Review of *AMF, Cosmopolitan*, CLVI (May 1964), 8-9.

"It is always interesting to read a good writer on his own life and times. . . . it is Hemingway's great moments of fiction that we are still hungry for, as well as a new light on himself and his period. . . . the real tone of this book: under the nostalgic glow . . . is in actuality sharp, satiric, wholly self-centered and without compassion. It is really without understanding. . . ."

1509 Tynan, Kenneth. "Papa and the Playwright," *Playboy*, XI (May 1964), 97, 138-141.

The critic describes the meeting between Hemingway and Tennessee Williams in Havana, in 1959.

1510 Havighurst, Walter. Review of *AMF, Chicago Tribune Books Today* (May 3, 1964), p. 1.

"An American chapter in Paris. More than any other expatriate account, Hemingway's is American. Here he is writing his Michigan stories, recalling his American boyhood, and shaping an American language for it. . . . All of Hemingway's books are about himself. This one especially, and its last six pages most of all. . . . Those last pages, the only ones told in the third person, end this bittersweet book on a note of endless regret."

1510₁ Butcher, Fanny. "For Mary Hemingway, Steps in Ernest's Path," *ibid.*, p. 6.

Regarding Hemingway's unpublished manuscripts and the editing of *AMF*.

511 Plimpton, George. Review of *AMF*, *N.Y. Herald Tribune Book Week* (May 3, 1964), pp. 1, 12-13. Drawing.

"The Paris sketches are absolutely controlled, far enough removed in time so that the scenes and characters are observed in tranquility, and yet with astonishing immediacy—his remarkable gift—so that many of the sketches have the hard brilliance of his best fiction. Indeed, in a short prefatory note Hemingway says the book may be regarded as fiction—by which he means not that the incidents described are imaginary, but that the techniques utilized are those of the fiction writer."

512 Pryce-Jones, Alan. Review of *AMF*, *N.Y. Herald Tribune* (May 5, 1964), p. 23.

"In this absorbing book of Paris recollections there is a certain element of the *inaccrochable*, along with much that is bright-colored and occasionally touching. It covers 'the early days when we were very poor and very happy,' legendary days which have already been copiously recorded by everyone, it sometimes seemed, who ever bought a drink in the Select or Lipp's. But Hemingway's is the book we have been waiting for. . . . All the time he writes a bony, unwasteful prose which is a joy to read. . . . He is at his best in evocation of being young and in love, writing of wife, child and cat as though from a great distance, yet with a tenderness far more convincing than the nervous masculinity with which he faced the outer world. In the last chapter especially, where the scene shifts to the Austrian Alps, there is real poignancy in the contrast between desired tranquillity and the intrusive restlessness which finally wrecked the marriage."

513 Poore, Charles. Review of *AMF*, *N.Y. Times* (May 5, 1964), p. 41.

"Here is Hemingway at his best. No one has ever written about Paris in the nineteen-twenties as well as Hemingway. Thousands, of course, have given their own bright versions of that unaccountably perpetual springtime, but too many lost parts of their own identities in taking on some of Hemingway's. . . . the light these pages throw on what has been written by and around and about Hemingway is extraordinarily various. . . . once again, it is a greater pleasure, for the reader at large, to read Hemingway than to cope with the folklorists of his mythology."

514 Review of *AMF*, *Time*, LXXXIII (May 8, 1964), 98, 100. Photographs.

"Unlike the glum testaments and boring memorabilia most men bequeath to the world, Ernest Hemingway left behind an invitation to laugh with him amid the scenes of his youth, where he was happier than he would ever be again. . . . The gay and artless sketches (with a lifetime of craft behind each deceptively negligent line) have a heartbreaking quality when the reader recalls that these glittering trivia were cut and polished by a man soon to take his own life."

15¹5 Kauffmann, Stanley. Review of *AMF, New Republic*, CL (May 9, 1964), 17-18, 20-21, 23-24.

"This book, highly affecting and biographically invaluable, is an anomalous performance in literature. An author, who slipped in critical esteem during the second half of his writing life, reminds us after his death of his earlier claims to greatness. There are 20 sections, most of them self-contained but each one a glimpse that adds to a prospect. . . . these sketches give us, for the first time, an intimate view of him as he evolved his art, of his first marriage, of others around him. He provides (deliberately posthumously, one can assume) insight and information that, for all the publicity and public *persona*, he never afforded during his life." For Thomas Sturak's reply, see *NR*, CL (June 6, 1964), 29.

15¹6 Hicks, Granville. Review of *AMF, Saturday Review*, XLVII (May 9, 1964), 29-30.

"[*A Moveable Feast*] comes out of his last literary phase, and since it concerns his first literary phase, 1921-1926, during which he wrote *The Sun Also Rises* and some of his best short stories, the early Hemingway and the late are instructively juxtaposed. The comparison is not in favor of the later Hemingway. . . . [Quotes the opening paragraph.] This is Hemingway, all right, omission of commas and all; but it is Hemingway imitating himself, whereas there was once an inimitable Hemingway. . . . He remained a craftsman to the end, and there is some first-class Hemingway in the book, but there is little of the evocative power one finds in *The Sun Also Rises*."

15¹6₁ Danby-Smith, Valerie. "Reminiscence of Hemingway," *ibid.*, pp. 30-31, 57. Photograph.

Hemingway's secretary recalls his visit to Paris, in 1959, to recheck the places and scenes described in *AMF*.

15¹7 Galantière, Lewis. Review of *AMF, N.Y. Times Book Review* (May 10, 1964), pp. 1, 26. Photograph.

"*A Moveable Feast* is composed of 20 sketches, rewritten from Hemingway's notebooks of the years 1921-1926. Though the volume has the air of a random compilation, it is in fact a calculated production, and this for two reasons: first, because embedded in its pages are messages to the few readers who will know for whom they are meant; and, secondly, because as an artist Hemingway never allowed himself to appear in undress. . . . Written with that controlled lyricism of which he was master, these pages are marvelously evocative."

71 Hemingway, Mary. "The Making of the Book: A Chronicle and a Memoir," *ibid.*, pp. 26-27. Photograph.

Regarding the "conception and construction" of *AMF* and the degree of editing that was necessary.

18 Hyman, Stanley Edgar. Review of *AMF, New Leader*, XLVII (May 11, 1964), 8-9.

"It is Hemingway's most insignificant book, worse than *Green Hills of Africa*. . . . Some of the prose exaggerates Hemingway's mannerisms until it reads like self-parody. . . .'"

19 Review of *AMF, Newsweek*, LXIII (May 11, 1964), 102. Photograph.

". . . the glimpses we get of Gertrude Stein's personal life and artistic decline are harrowing; there is the expected affectionate portrait of Ezra Pound; the admiration for the brilliant James Joyce; a funny, malicious vignette of Ford Madox Ford; the tender, sad, exasperated memory of Scott Fitzgerald and the murderous judgment of Zelda as castrator, unmanning Fitzgerald, undoing him as a writer. . . . What is startling is not the judgments themselves, but rather the vividness of [Hemingway's] feelings, their intensity and immediacy. There lies the key to the book, and its abiding interest. . . . We are made to sense—despite the recurrent sentimentality, the passages of leaden dialogue, the unwitting self-parody—his feelings of utter fullness, of the good years, when he came into possession of all his powers as a man and writer."

20 "Fitzgerald le magnifique," *Figaro Littéraire* (May 14-20, 1964), p. 8.

Letters to Hemingway and Maxwell Perkins, translated into French, from *The Letters of F. Scott Fitzgerald*, ed. Andrew Turnbull, New York, 1963.

21 [Grant, Douglas]. Review of *AMF, TLS* (May 21, 1964), pp. 425-426.

". . . how far [Hemingway's] attempt to recall his own experience of Paris rises to fiction can be seen in one of the chapters, called 'A False Spring,' which, whatever its relation to fact, is a short story. . . . The chapter is among the best stories Hemingway had written for many years. . . . Hemingway's description of his years in Paris explains the dualism evident in his prose; viewed from one angle he is the tough young man . . . and from another the poet . . . 'I remember . . . I remember,' he exclaims in the tones of Mark Twain, and to remember with him is a pleasure in itself and a reminder of the flourishing time of his genius." Reprinted in *Purpose and Place*, London, 1965, pp. 169-174. For correspondence regarding this review, see W. J. Weatherby in *TLS* (May 28, 1964), p. 455; reply by Robert Wright in *TLS* (June 4, 1964), p. 483; reply by Weatherby in *TLS* (June 11, 1964), p. 511; reply by Wright in *TLS* (June 25, 1964), p. 556; reply to both writers by Frank W. Masterson in *TLS* (July 16, 1964), p. 631; and reply to Masterson by Norman Silverstein in *TLS* (Aug. 20, 1964), p. 754.

1522 Ellmann, Richard. Review of *AMF, New Statesman*, LXVII (May 22, 1964), 809-810.

"The book is made up of a series of short stories or near-stories, the form in which Hemingway always did his best. While autobiographical, they offer no direct self-portraiture, but look at the old comrades generally with a beady eye."

1523 Callaghan, Morley. Review of *AMF, Spectator*, CCXII (May 22, 1964), 696.

"[Hemingway] manages to give the impression that two star-crossed lovers, himself and Hadley, the *Farewell to Arms* theme again, had their happiness destroyed by the great enemy—people. . . . Some of the people to be looked down on are done in the book as set pieces, and not at all in the flow of memories. This faulty structure is the great weakness of the book. And what frightening sketches of people who at one time knew and liked him! . . . The touch he uses in these portraits is controlled, expert, humourous and apparently exact. . . . But underneath the surface humour—it's really a gallow's humour—there is a long-nourished savagery, or downright venom, and in his portraits there is the quick leap for the jugular vein."

1524 Toynbee, Philip. Review of *AMF, Observer* (May 24, 1964), p. 23.

"Reading these delicate, pared and yearning pages older readers will find themselves stirred again by the liberating joy they felt when they first read the early stories. . . . The marvel here is that before he died, stimulated, perhaps, by remembering his best days, Hemingway shed 40 years of 'Papa,' of building his legend and posturing inside it, of worse and worse writing accompanied by sweatier and sweatier sweat shirts—he got rid of all this and wrote again something of the arduous purity of his youth."

1525 Fiedler, Leslie A. "A Different View of the Hemingway Legend," *Chicago Tribune Books Today* (May 24, 1964), p. 3.

An excerpt condensed from *Waiting for the End*, New York, 1964.

1526 Kazin, Alfred. "Hemingway as His Own Fable," *Atlantic*, CCXIII (June 1964), 54-57. Photograph.

Reprinted in *Cornhill*, CLXXIV (Summer 1964), 139-147.

527 Lewis, Robert William, Jr. "Eros and Agape: Ernest Heming-way's Love Ethic," *Dissertation Abstracts*, XXIV (June 1964), 5411.

Abstract from a doctoral dissertation, University of Illinois, 1963. This dissertation was published, in a revised form, as *Hemingway on Love*, Austin, 1965.

528 DeMott, Benjamin. Review of *AMF*, *Harper's Magazine*, CCXXVIII (June 1964), 114, 116, 118.

"The book's period is 1921 to 1926, and, for reasons that are convincing even when abstractly stated, its quality is that of an idyl."

529 Thomas, Amory A. "La littérature américaine," *Ruban Rouge*, No. 21 (June 1964), pp. 67-73.

General article.

530 Hutton, Virgil. "The Short Happy Life of Macomber," *University Review*, XXX (June 1964), 253-263.

530₁ Adler, Jack. "Theme and Character in Hemingway: *For Whom the Bell Tolls*," *ibid.*, pp. 293-299.

531 Algren, Nelson. Review of *AMF*, *Nation*, CXCVIII (June 1, 1964), 560-561.

"The present reminiscence is pleasant, humorous—and evasive. . . . The light he throws here is upon others. It is the harsh light of exposure: he reserves a soft, blurring glow for himself."

532 Hart, Jeffrey. "Hemingway's Code," *National Review*, XVI (June 2, 1964), 450-452.

533 Paulding, Gouverneur. Review of *AMF*, *Reporter*, XXX (June 4, 1964), 40-43.

"These memories of Hemingway's young writing years in the Paris of the 1920's show a wonderful craftsman at his best; they are also cruel, devious, and at the end overwhelmingly sad."

534 Brien, Alan. "Afterthought," *Spectator*, CCXII (June 5, 1964), 774.

Recalls the difficulties he encountered trying to interview Hemingway, in 1956, on board the *Liberté*.

535 Kermode, Frank. Review of *AMF*, *N.Y. Review of Books*, II (June 11, 1964), 4-6. Caricatures by David Levine on pp. 1, 5.

"Much of what he says of Paris is generally familiar from other books. But no other book is of this authority and distinction, and no other so strongly conveys (largely by omission, of course) the sense of time regained. . . . There is malice here, recollected in tranquillity; as in the pages on Stein, and those on members of what she called the lost generation. . . . It is an ingenious and deliberate way of revisiting the sources of a great writer's strength; and it displays that strength as very little else of his had done in thirty years."

1536 Eder, Richard. "Hemingway's Memory Kept Alive in Cuba," *N.Y. Times* (June 11, 1964), p. 3. Photographs.
Regarding Finca Vigia and its caretaker, René Villareal.

1537 Dos Passos, John. "Old Hem Was a Sport," *Sports Illustrated*, xx (June 29, 1964), 58-60, 62, 65-67.
Recollections of fishing with Hemingway in Key West and Bimini, in the early 1930s.

1537₁ James, Sidney L. Letter from the Publisher, *ibid.*, p. 4. Photograph.
Regarding the friendship of Hemingway and John Dos Passos.

1538 Webster, Harvey Curtis. "Ernest Hemingway: The Pursuit of Death," *Texas Quarterly*, vii (Summer 1964), 149-159. Facsimile of manuscript page from *DIA*.

1539 Tanner, Tony. Review of *AMF* and Andrew Turnbull's *The Letters of F. Scott Fitzgerald, Encounter*, xxiii (July 1964), 71-75.
"[*A Moveable Feast*] is of course an exercise in nostalgia, but it is a controlled exercise: a few well-placed shadows prevent the vivid recollections from spilling over into deliquescent idealisation. . . . Even the humour in the book (and parts are very funny) is rather cutting—a weapon rather than a joy. Hemingway certainly reveals himself more nakedly than he can have intended."

1540 Bisol, Gaetano. Review of *Festa mobile* (*AMF*), *Letture*, xix (July 1964), 511-512.

1541 Meyer, Chuck. "Hemingway (the boatman)," *Motor Boating*, cxiv (July 1964), 21-23, 103, 105. Photographs.

1542 Atkinson, Brooks. Critic at Large column, *N.Y. Times* (July 7, 1964), p. 32.
Criticizes Hemingway for his "cruel and humiliating" recollections of Gertrude Stein and Scott Fitzgerald in *AMF*. Reprinted in *Brief Chronicles*, New York: Coward-McCann, 1966, pp. 176-178.

1543 Guenther, John. Letter to the editor, *TLS* (July 9, 1964), p. 613.
Regarding Jed Kiley's memoirs in *Playboy*, iii (Sept. 1956). See also the publishers' introduction to Kiley's *Hemingway: An Old Friend Remembers*, New York, 1965, p. 10. For Archibald MacLeish's reply, see *TLS* (Sept. 3, 1964), p. 803; for reply by Guenther, see *TLS* (Oct. 15, 1964), p. 939.

1544 Baker, Carlos. "A Search for the Man As He Really Was," *N.Y. Times Book Review* (July 26, 1964), pp. 4-5, 14. Photographs.
Regarding problems of Hemingway biography.

545 Porter, Katherine Anne. "Paris: A Little Incident in the Rue de l'Odéon," *Ladies' Home Journal*, LXXXI (Aug. 1964), 54-55.

Recalls meeting Hemingway at Sylvia Beach's book shop, "maybe in 1934."

546 Maclaren-Ross, J. Review of *AMF, London Magazine*, IV (Aug. 1964), 88-95.

"The real interest in the book lies . . . in his portraits of the famous contemporaries with whom he came in contact, and the self-revelation contained in the personal reactions which he now claims they aroused in him. . . ."

547 Winfrey, Lee. "An Empty Home—But Hemingway's Still There," *Chicago Daily News* (Aug. 24, 1964), p. 43.

Relates how René Villareal, the caretaker of Finca Vigía, keeps the house just as it was when Hemingway left it, on July 24, 1960.

548 Halverson, John. "Christian Resonance in *The Old Man and the Sea*," *English Language Notes*, II (Sept. 1964), 50-54.

549 White, William. "Novelist as Reporter: Ernest Hemingway," *Orient/West*, IX (Sept.–Oct. 1964), 77-92.

550 Broussard, Louis. "Hemingway as a Literary Critic," *Arizona Quarterly*, XX (Autumn 1964), 197-204.

551 Young, Philip. "Our Hemingway Man," *Kenyon Review*, XXVI (Autumn 1964), 676-707.

Part I: "The End of Compendium Reviewing." Brief reviews of books about Hemingway published since 1960. Part II: "Touching Down and Out: *A Moveable Feast*." Review of *AMF*. "Some of the dialogue with Hadley is unreal and a little embarrassing; sometimes the borders of sentimentality are skirted if not transgressed. But for the most part the prose glitters, warms, and delights. Hemingway is not remembering but re-experiencing; not describing, making. In several cases the results are comparable to his fiction."

551₁ Lattimore, Richmond. Poem, "Old Hemingway," *ibid.*, p. 674.

552 Gleaves, Edwin Sheffield, Jr. "The Spanish Influence on Ernest Hemingway's Concepts of Death, *Nada*, and Immortality," *Dissertation Abstracts*, XXV (Oct. 1964), 2511-12.

Abstract from a doctoral dissertation, Emory University, 1964.

553 Miller, Patrick. "Hemingway's 'A Way You'll Never Be,'" *Explicator*, XXIII (Oct. 1964), Item 18.

554 Callejas, Bernardo. "La Casa de Hemingway," *Pueblo y Cultura*, No. 28 (Oct. 1964).

1555 Wellershoff, Dieter. "Hemingway und seine Dichtung," *Universitas,* XIX (Oct. 1964), 1057-64.

1556 North, Joseph. "Hemingway: The Man and the Writer," *American Dialog,* I (Oct.–Nov. 1964), 7.

1556₁ Wolff, Milton. "We Met in Spain," *ibid.,* pp. 8-9.

The author, who was commander of the Abraham Lincoln Battalion, recalls his meetings with Hemingway during the Spanish Civil War. He also gives the background of the seven letters from Hemingway which are printed on pp. 11-13. See (C424₁).

1556₂ Kashkeen, Ivan. "Another View," *ibid.,* p. 14.

An excerpt from the book on Hemingway which Kashkeen was working on before his death, in 1963. For a longer excerpt, see (H1497₁).

1557 Meriwether, James B. "The Dashes in Hemingway's *A Farewell to Arms,*" *Papers of the Bibliographical Society of America,* LVIII (Oct.–Dec. 1964), 449-457.

In 1931, Hemingway filled in the publisher's deletions in fifteen places in the text of *FTA,* for Maurice-Edgar Coindreau's translation into French. Also, the deletions in the serialization in *Scribner's Magazine* are compared with those in the book publication, and the American and English editions are compared.

1558 Knieger, Bernard. "The Concept of Maturity in Hemingway's Short Stories," *CLA Journal,* VIII (Dec. 1964), 149-156.

1559 Stafford, Edward. "An Afternoon with Hemingway," *Writer's Digest,* XLIV (Dec. 1964), 18-22. Cover photograph of Hemingway.

Relates a visit to Finca Vigia and his discussion with Hemingway on writing.

1560 Amory, Cleveland. "A Moveable Interview," *N.Y. Times Book Review* (Dec. 6, 1964), p. 8.

A "posthumous interview," with Hemingway's answers taken from *AMF.*

1561 Cowley, Malcolm. "The 1930's Were An Age of Faith," *N.Y. Times Book Review* (Dec. 13, 1964), pp. 4-5, 14-17.

General Article.

1562 Hertzel, Leo J. "The Look of Religion: Hemingway and Catholicism," *Renascence,* XVII (Winter 1964), 77-81.

1563 Motola, Gabriel. "Hemingway's Code: Literature and Life," *Modern Fiction Studies,* X (Winter 1964–1965), 319-329.

564 Portz, John. "Allusion and Structure in Hemingway's 'A Natural History of the Dead,'" *Tennessee Studies in Literature*, x (1965), 27-41.

565 Fuchs, Daniel. "Ernest Hemingway: Literary Critic," *American Literature*, xxxvi (Jan. 1965), 431-451.

566 Nelson, Howard. "Hemingway Without Tears," *Fact*, New York, ii (Jan.–Feb. 1965), 44-47. Caricature of Hemingway.
Relates a visit to Finca Vigia, in 1949.

567 Bradbury, Ray. Short story, "The Kilimanjaro Machine," *Life*, lviii (Jan. 22, 1965), 68-79.
"A fantasy and a tribute" to Hemingway. See also George P. Hunt's Editors' Note, "The Man Who Drives the Kilimanjaro Machine," on p. 3.

568 Rice, Howard C., Jr. "The Papers of Sylvia Beach," *Princeton Alumni Weekly*, lxv (Feb. 16, 1965), 12-14, 17-18. Facsimile of inscription by Hemingway in *WTN*, dated Paris, August 25, 1944.

569 Bourjaily, Vance. "The Big Comeback," *N.Y. Times Book Review* (Feb. 28, 1965), pp. 1, 49. Photograph.
Review of *OMATS*, on the publication of the Scribner Library paperback edition.

570 Hovey, Richard B. *"The Torrents of Spring*: Prefigurations in the Early Hemingway," *College English*, xxvi (March 1965), 460-464.

571 deVries, Theun. "La Maison de Hemingway," *Nouvelle Critique*, No. 164 (March 1965), pp. 70-79.

572 Nolan, William F. "Last Days of the Lion," *Carte Blanche* (Spring 1965), pp. 24-29. Photographs.

573 Hovey, Richard B. "Hemingway's 'Now I Lay Me': A Psychological Interpretation," *Literature & Psychology*, xv (Spring 1965), 70-78.

574 Wegelin, Christof. "Hemingway and the Decline of International Fiction," *Sewanee Review*, lxxiii (Spring 1965), 285-298.

574₁ Lytle, Andrew. *"A Moveable Feast*: The Going To and Fro," *ibid.*, pp. 339-343.

575 Bernard, Kenneth. "Hemingway's 'Indian Camp,'" *Studies in Short Fiction*, ii (Spring 1965), 291.
For Philip Young's reply, see *SSF*, iii (Fall 1965), ii-iii.

576 Ueno, Naozo. "An Oriental View of *The Old Man and the Sea*," *East-West Review*, ii (Spring-Summer 1965), 67-76.

1577 White, William. "Paperback Hemingway," *American Book Collector*, xv (April 1965), 6.
Regarding the paperback editions of work by and about Hemingway.

1578 White, William. "Hemingway in Korea," *Papers of the Bibliographical Society of America*, LIX (April–June 1965), 190-192.
Regarding Korean translations of Hemingway's work.

1579 "Hemingway Shrine to Be Bigger," *N.Y. Times* (April 22, 1965), p. 29.
Regarding the Cuban Government's plans to build an annex to Finca Vigia to create additional exhibition space for the Hemingway Museum.

1580 Montale, Eugenio. "Hemingway di là dal fiume," *Corriere della Sera* (May 16, 1965), p. 11.
Regarding the Italian translations of *AMF* and *ARIT*.

1581 Pivano, Fernanda. "Incontri con Hemingway: Il romanzo di Venezia," *Mondo* (May 18, 1965), pp. 9-10. Photograph.
The author, one of Hemingway's Italian translators, recalls a visit with the Hemingways in Cortina d'Ampezzo.

1582 Baker, Carlos. "A Myth in the Making," review of Jed Kiley's *Hemingway: An Old Friend Remembers*, *N.Y. Times Book Review* (May 23, 1965), pp. 42-43.

1583 Merle, Robert. "Hemingway à Cuba," *Lettres françaises* (June 3-9, 1965), pp. 1, 6. Photograph.

1584 Drinnon, Richard. "In the American Heartland: Hemingway and Death," *Psychoanalytic Review*, LII (Summer 1965), 5-31.

1585 Sister Richard Mary, O.P. "Addition to the Hemingway Bibliography," *Papers of the Bibliographical Society of America*, LIX (July–Sept. 1965), 327.
Regarding Hemingway's letter on mutilated fish in *Outdoor Life*, LXXVII (June 1936).

1586 Renaud, Tristan. "Hemingway: Mourir à Venise," review of the French translation of *ARIT*, *Lettres françaises* (July 1–7, 1965), p. 3.

1587 Hofmann, Paul. "Speaking of Books: Hemingway's Finca," *N.Y. Times Book Review* (July 11, 1965), pp. 2, 22. Photographs. Facsimile of eight lines of an unpublished story, on Hemingway's clipboard.
Regarding the Hemingway Museum, as Finca Vigia was officially renamed, and its director, Fernando G. Campoamor.

588 Hemingway, Mary. "To Parajiso with Papa and 'Pilar,'" *Sports Illustrated*, XXIII (July 12, 1965), 62-70.

Recollections of fishing near a small island in the Caribbean. See also Sidney L. James's Letter from the Publisher, on p. 4.

589 Shepard, Richard F. "Hemingway Tapes Cut Into a Record," *N.Y. Times* (July 13, 1965), p. 31.

Regarding "Ernest Hemingway Reading" (Caedmon, TC 1185).

590 "Hemingway Speaking," *N.Y. Times* (July 18, 1965), IV, 2.

Regarding "Ernest Hemingway Reading" (Caedmon, TC 1185).

591 Biagini, Adriana Ivancich. "La Renata di Hemingway sono io," *Epoca*, LX (July 25, 1965), 68-73, 75.

Regarding her meeting with Hemingway in 1949, her visit to Finca Vigia in 1950, and her portrayal as Renata in *ARIT*. Four letters from Hemingway are briefly quoted. See (F117), (F122), (F127), (F136). See also "Hemingway's Heroine" in *Parade* (Oct. 10, 1965), p. 12, regarding this article.

592 Gilroy, Harry. "Mrs. Hemingway Releases Poems," *N.Y. Times* (July 27, 1965), p. 30.

Regarding publication of Hemingway's "Two Love Poems" in the *Atlantic*, CCXVI (Aug. 1965).

593 "Papa's Poems," *Time*, LXXXVI (July 30, 1965), 33.

Regarding Hemingway's poems in the *Atlantic*, CCXVI (Aug. 1965).

594 Hemingway, Mary. [Note], *Atlantic*, CCXVI (Aug. 1965), 96.

Regarding the circumstances in which Hemingway's "Two Love Poems," which appear in this issue, were written.

594₁ Manning, Robert. "Hemingway in Cuba," *ibid.*, pp. 101-108.

Relates details of his visit to Finca Vigia to interview Hemingway for the cover story in *Time*, LXIV (Dec. 13, 1954).

595 Krauss, William A. "Footnote from Hemingway's Paris, 1964," *Harper's Magazine*, CCXXXI (Aug. 1965), 91-95.

Regarding a pilgrimage to the places in Paris that Hemingway knew in the 1920s.

596 Clements, Robert J. "The European Literary Scene," review of Roger Asselineau's *The Literary Reputation of Hemingway in Europe*, *Saturday Review*, XLVIII (Aug. 7, 1965), 21-22.

597 Karlen, Arno. Review of Nelson Algren's *Notes from a Sea Diary*, *N.Y. Times Book Review* (Aug. 22, 1965), pp. 4-5.

1598 Poore, Charles. "Nelson Algren's Seaborne Defense of Hemingway," review of Algren's *Notes from a Sea Diary, N.Y. Times* (Aug. 24, 1965), p. 29.

1599 Callaghan, Morley. "Legends of the Old Man," review of Nelson Algren's *Notes from a Sea Diary* and Jed Kiley's *Hemingway: An Old Friend Remembers, Saturday Review,* XLVIII (Aug. 28, 1965), 43.

1600 Gingrich, Arnold. "Horsing Them in with Hemingway," *Playboy,* XII (Sept. 1965), 123, 256-258.
    Recollections of fishing with Hemingway in Key West and Bimini in the mid-1930s. Reprinted in *The Well-Tempered Angler,* New York, 1965, pp. 20-27.

1601 "Last Will and Testament," *Charles Hamilton Autographs, Inc.,* No. 9 (Sept. 30, 1965), p. 21.
    Descriptive entry regarding an early Hemingway will, which is dated: Chicago, December 3, 1921. Facsimile of signature reproduced.

1602 Canaday, Nicholas, Jr. "Is There Any Light in Hemingway's 'The Light of the World'?" *Studies in Short Fiction,* III (Fall 1965), 75-76.

1603 San Juan, Epifanio, Jr. "Integrity of Composition in the Poems of Ernest Hemingway," *University Review,* XXXII (Autumn 1965), 51-58.

1604 Kerr, Johnny F. "Hemingway's Use of Physical Setting and Stage Props in His Novels: A Study in Craftsmanship," *Dissertation Abstracts,* XXVI (Oct. 1965), 2217.
    Abstract from a doctoral dissertation, University of Texas, 1965.

1605 "Cubans Resume Their Exodus By Boat Across Florida Strait | Fisherman Among Arrivals at Key West Says He Is Model for 'Old Man and the Sea,' " *N.Y. Times* (Oct. 22, 1965), p. 20.
    Anselmo Hernandez, a ninety-two-year-old Cuban fisherman, claimed that he had been the inspiration for *The Old Man and the Sea.* Mary Hemingway stated that the novel was not about any one person.

1606 Vanderbilt, Kermit. "The Last Words of E. H.," *Nation,* CCI (Oct. 25, 1965), 284-285.
    Review of "Ernest Hemingway Reading" (Caedmon, TC 1185). Note: The cover title for this article is: "Hemingway's Last Laugh."

1607 Davies, Phillips G. and Rosemary R. Davies. "Hemingway's 'Fifty Grand' and the Jack Britton-Mickey Walker Prize Fight," *American Literature,* XXXVII (Nov. 1965), 251-258.

08 Moravia, Alberto. "Nothing Amen," *Status*, I (Nov. 1965), 28-29, 89. Reprinted from *Man as an End*, New York, 1966, pp. 231-236.

09 Sahl, Hans. "Hemingways Spätwerk," *Universitas*, xx (Nov. 1965), 1151-54.

10 Cooperman, Stanley. "Hemingway and Old Age: Santiago as Priest of Time," *College English*, xxvii (Dec. 1965), 215-220.

11 Morris, William E. "Hemingway's 'The Short Happy Life of Francis Macomber,' " *Explicator*, xxiv (Dec. 1965), Item 31.

12 Rouch, John S. "Jake Barnes as Narrator," *Modern Fiction Studies*, xi (Winter 1965–1966), 361-370.

12₁ Moore, L. Hugh, Jr. "Mrs. Hirsch and Mrs. Bell in Hemingway's 'The Killers,' " *ibid.*, pp. 427-428.

PART THREE

APPENDIX

LIST OF NEWSPAPERS AND PERIODICALS
CITED IN SECTIONS C AND H

APPENDIX

NOTE: An asterisk has been used to indicate newspapers.

ABC, Madrid
Accent, Urbana, Ill.
Advertising & Selling,
    New York
Aikamme, Helsinki
**Alcázar*, Madrid
America, New York
American Book Collector,
    Chicago
American Criterion, New York
American Dialog, New York
American Heritage,
    Marion, Ohio
American Imago, New York
American Literature,
    Durham, N.C.
American Mercury, New York
American Prefaces,
    Iowa City, Iowa
American Quarterly,
    Philadelphia
American Review, New York
American Scholar,
    Washington, D.C.
American Spectator, New York
American Speech, New York
Américas, Washington, D.C.
Amerikanische Rundschau,
    New York
Ameryka, Washington, D.C.
Among Friends, New York
Anglia, Bonn, Germany
Antioch Review,
    Yellow Springs, Ohio
Antiquarian Bookman,
    Newark, N.J.
Approach, Rosemont, Pa.
Arbalète, Lyon, France
Arbor, Madrid

*Archiv für das Studium der
    Neueren Sprachen*,
    Braunschweig, Germany
Argosy, New York
Arizona Quarterly,
    Tucson, Ariz.
Art in America, New York
**Arts*, Paris
Arts & Decoration, New York
Arts & Sciences, New York
Asomante, San Juan,
    Puerto Rico
Ateneo, Madrid
Atlantic, Boston
Aufbau, Zurich
Ausonia, Siena, Italy
Aut Aut, Milan
AVB: All världens Berättare,
    Stockholm
Avocations, New York

*Babel: International Journal
    of Translations*, Paris
Bachelor, New York
**Bataille*, Paris
Belfagor, Florence, Italy
Best Articles & Stories,
    Spencer, Ind.
Bifur, Paris
Blanco y Negro, Madrid
BLM, Stockholm (see
    Bonniers Litterära Magasin)
Bohemia, Havana
*Boletín Comisión Nacional
    Cubano de la UNESCO*,
    Paris
Bonniers Litterära Magasin,
    Stockholm (changed to
    BLM in January 1951)

Book Find News, New York
Bookman, New York
Book-of-the-Month Club News, New York
Books Abroad, Norman, Okla.
Books & Bookmen, London
Book Society's Review, London
Bookwise, Cambridge, Mass.
*Boston Globe, Boston
Boulevardier, Paris
Brentano's Book Chat, New York
*Brooklyn Daily Eagle, Brooklyn, N.Y.
Bulletin of the Arts & Sciences Division, Kyoto, Japan (University of Ryukus)
Bunte Illustrierte, Offenburg, Germany
Business Week, New York

Cadernos Brasileiros, Rio de Janeiro
Cahiers d'Art, Paris
Cahiers des Langues Modernes, Paris
Cahiers du Sud, Marseille
Calendar of Modern Letters, London
Canadian Forum, Toronto
Canadian Journalist & Press Photographer, Montreal
Carnegie Magazine, Pittsburgh
Carolina Quarterly, Chapel Hill, N.C.
*Carrefour, Paris
Carte Blanche, Chicago
Casa Belga (catalogue), Havana
Catholic World, New York
Charles Hamilton Autographs, Inc. (catalogue), New York
Chicago, Chicago
*Chicago American, Chicago

*Chicago Daily News, Chicago
Chicago Review, Chicago
*Chicago Tribune, Chicago (also *Chicago Tribune Books Today*)
China Weekly Review, Shanghai
Choix, London
Christian Century, Chicago
Christian Scholar, New York
*Christian Science Monitor, Boston
*Ciao, Vicenza, Italy
Cinema Arts, Jersey City, N.J.
CLA Journal, Baltimore, Md. (College Language Association)
*Cleveland Plain Dealer, Cleveland, Ohio
College English, Champaign, Ill.
Collier's, New York
Colophon, New York (also *New Colophon*)
Colorado Quarterly, Boulder, Colo.
*Combat, Paris
Commentary, New York
Commonweal, New York
Comparative Literature, Eugene, Ore.
Confluences, Lyon, France
Contact, New York
Contempo, Chapel Hill, N.C.
Contemporaneo, Rome (supplement of *Rinascita*)
Contempory Review, London
Co-operative Commonwealth, Chicago
Cornhill, London
Coronet, Chicago
Correo Literario, Madrid
*Corriere della Sera, Milan (also Pomeriggio edition)
Cosmopolitan, New York

Criterion, London
Critique, Paris
Cuadernos Hispano-
    americanos, Madrid
Current History & Forum,
    New York

*Dagens Nyheder, Copenhagen
*Dagens Nyheter, Stockholm
*Daily Express, London
Danske Magasin, Copenhagen
Dalhousie Review,
    Halifax, Nova Scotia
Decision, New York
Delphian Quarterly, Chicago
*Denver Post, Denver, Colo.
*Detroit News, Detroit, Mich.
Deutsche Rundschau, Berlin
Deutschunterricht,
    Stuttgart, Germany
Dial, New York
Dialoghi, Rome
*Diario de la Marina, Havana
Digest, New York
Direction, Darien, Conn.
Discourse, Moorhead, Minn.
Dissertation Abstracts,
    Ann Arbor, Mich.
Double Dealer,
    New Orleans, La.

East-West Review,
    Kyoto, Japan
Ecclesia, Madrid
Editor & Publisher, New York
ELH: Journal of English
    Literary History,
    Baltimore, Md.
Elle, Paris
Emory University Quarterly,
    Atlanta, Ga.
Emporium, Bergamo, Italy
Encounter, Indianapolis, Ind.
    (as noted)
Encounter, London

English "A" Analyst,
    Evanston, Ill.
English Journal, Chicago
English Language Notes,
    Boulder, Colo.
English Literature, Tokyo
English Miscellany,
    Delhi, India
English Record,
    Hamilton, N.Y.
English Review, London
Epoca, Milan
Espace, Paris
España Semanal,
    Tangier, Morocco
*Espresso, Rome
Esprit, Paris
Esquire, New York
Essays in Criticism,
    Oxford, England
Estafeta Literaria, Madrid
Estudios Americanos,
    Seville, Spain
Études, Paris
Europäische Revue, Leipzig
Europe, Paris
Europeo, Milan
*Evening Standard, London
Exile, Paris and Rapallo, Italy
Ex Libris, Paris
Explicator, Columbia, S.C.

Fact, London (as noted)
Fact, New York
Field & Stream, New York
*Fiera Letteraria, Rome
*Figaro, Paris
Figaro Littéraire, Paris
Films in Review, New York
Filología Moderna, Madrid
Fisherman, Oxford, Ohio
Flair, New York
Focus, London
Folio, Bloomington, Ind.
Folket i Bild, Stockholm

Fortune, Chicago
Forum, Houston, Tex.
*Frankfurter Zeitung,
   Frankfurt a.M., Germany
*Free Press Herald,
   Midland, Ontario
Free World,
   United Nations, N.Y.

Gavroche, Paris
Gazette des Lettres, Paris
Germanisch-romanische
   Monatsschrift, Heidelberg,
   Germany
Gids, Amsterdam
Golden Book Magazine,
   New York
Good Housekeeping,
   New York
*Guardian,
   Manchester, England

Harper's Bazaar, New York
Harper's Magazine, New York
*Havana Post, Havana
Hefte für Büchereiwesen,
   Leipzig
*Heraldo de Aragón,
   Zaragoza, Spain
Heute und Morgen,
   Düsseldorf, Germany
Hiroshima Studies in English
   Language and Literature,
   Hiroshima
Hispania, Stanford, Calif.
History of Ideas News Letter,
   New York
Hochland, Munich
Holiday, Philadelphia
Horizon, London
Hototogisu, Tokyo
Hound & Horn, New York
Hoy, Santiago, Chile
Hudson Review, New York

Humanist, London (as noted)
Humanist,
   Yellow Springs, Ohio
Humanitas, Brescia, Italy

Illustrated London News,
   London
Independent, Boston
Indian P.E.N., Bombay
Indian Review, Madras, India
Indice, Madrid
Indice de Artes y Letras,
   Madrid
Inostrannaya Literatura,
   Moscow
Insula, Madrid
International Literature,
   Moscow
Internatsionalnaya Literatura,
   Moscow
   (also English edition above)
Iowa English Yearbook,
   Iowa City, Iowa
Iskusstvo i zhizn, Moscow
Iunost', Moscow
*Izvestia, Moscow

Jahrbuch für Amerikastudien,
   Heidelberg, Germany
Journal of the Central
   Mississippi Valley American
   Studies, Parkville, Mo.
Journal of the College of
   Literature, Tokyo (Aoyama
   Gakuin University)
Journal of English &
   Germanic Philology,
   Urbana, Ill.
Journal of the Society of
   English & American
   Literature, Hyogo, Japan
Journalism Quarterly,
   Minneapolis, Minn.

K.C. Star, Kansas City, Mo.
K.C. Times, Kansas City, Mo.
(morning edition of the
K.C. Star)
Kansas Magazine, Manhattan,
Kans.
Ken, New York
Kenyon Review,
Gambier, Ohio
*Kniga i Proletarskaya
Revolutsiya*, Moscow
Kobe Gaidai Ronso,
Kobe, Japan
Krasnaya Nov', Moscow
Kultur, Munich
Kyusha American Literature,
Fukuoka, Japan

Ladies' Home Journal,
Philadelphia
Landmark, London
Langues Modernes, Paris
Leonardo, Florence, Italy
Letteratura Moderna, Milan
Lettres françaises, Paris
Letture, Milan
*Library Chronicle of the
University of Texas*,
Austin, Tex.
*Library of Congress
Information Bulletin*,
Washington, D.C.
Library Journal, New York
Life, New York
(also *Life* en Español)
Life & Letters, London
Listener, London
Literary America, New York
Literary Criterion,
Mysore, India
Literary Review,
Teaneck, N.J.
Literatur, Stuttgart and Berlin
Literatūra, Vilna, Lithuania

Literature & Psychology,
New York
Literaturnaya Gazeta, Moscow
Literaturnaya Ucheba,
Moscow
Literaturnoye Obozreniye,
Moscow
Literaturny Kritik, Moscow
Literaturny Sovremennik,
Moscow
Littéraire, Paris
Little Review, Chicago
London Magazine, London
Look, Des Moines, Iowa
Los Angeles Times,
Los Angeles, Calif.
Lovat Dickson's Magazine,
London

Mainstream, New York
Mandrake, London
Marginales, Brussels
Mark Twain Journal,
Kirkwood, Mo.
Massachusetts Review,
Amherst, Mass.
McCall's, Dayton, Ohio
Mercure de France, Paris
Mercurio, Rome
Merkur, Stuttgart, Germany
Miami Daily News,
Miami, Fla.
*Michigan Alumnus Quarterly
Review*, Ann Arbor, Mich.
Microfilm Abstracts,
Ann Arbor, Mich.
Minnesota Review,
Minneapolis, Minn.
Modern Fiction Studies,
Lafayette, Ind.
Modern Language Notes,
Baltimore, Md.
Modern Monthly, New York
Modern Quarterly, New York

Mois, Paris
Monat, Berlin
*Monde, Paris
*Mondo, Rome
Mondo Occidentale, Rome
*Monthly Letter of the
    Limited Editions Club*,
    New York
**Montreal Standard*, Montreal
*Montreal Star, Montreal
Moskva, Moscow
Motor Boating, New York

Nation, New York
National Geographic,
    Washington, D.C.
*National Insider, Chicago
National Police Gazette,
    New York
National Review, New York
**Nation & Athenaeum*, London
Navire d'Argent, Paris
Neue Deutsche Literatur,
    Berlin
Neueren Sprachen,
    Frankfurt a.M., Germany
Neue Rundschau,
    Frankfurt a.M., Germany
Neue Schweizer Rundschau,
    Zurich
Neue Zeitung, [Berlin?]
New Colophon, New York
    (also *Colophon*)
New Freeman, New York
New Leader, New York
New Masses, New York
New Mexico Quarterly,
    Albuquerque, N.M.
New Republic, New York
New Statesman & Nation,
    London (changed from
    New Statesman in February
    1931 and back to it in
    June 1957)
Newsweek, New York

New World Writing,
    New York
**N.Y. Daily Mirror*, New York
    (also *N.Y. Sunday Mirror*)
**N.Y. Daily News*, New York
New Yorker, New York
**N.Y. Evening Post*, New York
    (also *N.Y. Evening Post
    Literary Review*)
**N.Y. Herald Tribune*,
    New York (European
    edition, Paris) (also *N.Y.
    Herald Tribune Books,
    Book Review*, and
    Book Week)
**N.Y. Journal-American*,
    New York
**N.Y. Post*, New York
N.Y. Review of Books,
    New York
N.Y. State Education,
    Albany, N.Y.
**N.Y. Sun*, New York
**N.Y. Times*, New York (also
    N.Y. Times Book Review
    and *N.Y. Times Magazine*)
**N.Y. World*, New York
**N.Y. World-Telegram & Sun*,
    New York
Noble Savage, New York
North American Review,
    New York
North Dakota Quarterly,
    Grand Forks, N.D.
Nostro Tempo, Naples
Nouvelle Critique, Paris
Nouvelle Revue Française,
    Paris
**Nouvelles Littéraires*, Paris
Novoe Vremia, Moscow
Novyi Mir, Moscow
Now & Then, London
*Nowiny Literackiei
    Wydawnicze*, Warsaw
Nuestro Tiempo, Madrid

Nugget, New York
Nuova Antologia, Rome

*Oak Leaves, Oak Park, Ill.
*Oak Parker, Oak Park, Ill.
*Observer, London
Occidente, Rome
Ogoniok, Moscow
Oktiabr', Moscow
Omnibus, Berlin
Ord och Bild, Stockholm
Orient/West, Tokyo
Osservatore, Milan
*Osservatore Romano,
   Vatican City
Outdoor Life, Boulder, Colo.
Overland,
   Melbourne, Australia

Pacific Spectator,
   Palo Alto, Calif.
Pageant, New York
Papeles de Son Armadans,
   Palma de Mallorca, Spain
*Papers of the Bibliographical
   Society of America,*
   New York
*Papers of the Michigan
   Academy of Science, Arts,
   and Letters,*
   Ann Arbor, Mich.
*Parade, New York
   (a nationally distributed
   supplement in Sunday
   newspapers)
Paragone, Florence, Italy
Paris Match, Paris
*Paris-Matin, Paris
*Paris-Presse-l'Intransigeant,
   Paris
Paris Review, Paris and
   New York
Park East, New York
Parnasso, Helsinki
Partisan Review, New York

Paru, Monaco
Penguin New Writing,
   Harmondsworth, Middlesex,
   England
Personalist, Los Angeles, Calif.
Perspectives U.S.A., New York
   (also German edition,
   Perspektiven)
Photography Annual,
   New York
Photography Year Book,
   London
Playboy, Chicago
*PM, New York
PMLA, New York
   (Publication of the Modern
   Language Association)
Poetry: A Magazine of Verse,
   Chicago
Poland, Warsaw
   (American edition)
Polish Review, New York
Ponte, Florence, Italy
Popular Boating, New York
Prairie Schooner,
   Lincoln, Nebr.
*Pravda, Moscow
Preuves, Paris
Princeton Alumni Weekly,
   Princeton, N.J.
*Princeton University Library
   Chronicle,* Princeton, N.J.
*Providence Sunday Journal,
   Providence, R.I.
Przegląd Humanistyczny,
   Warsaw
Psychoanalytic Review,
   New York
Publishers' Weekly, New York
Pueblo y Cultura, Havana
Punch, London

Queen's Quarterly,
   Kingston, Ontario
Querschnitt, Berlin

537

APPENDIX

Quill, Chicago

Reader's Digest,
Pleasantville, N.Y.
Réalités, Paris
*Réforme, Paris
Renascence, Milwaukee, Wis.
(as noted)
Renascence, St. Mary-of-the-
Woods, Ind.
Reporter, New York
Republika,
Zagreb, Yugoslavia
Review of English Literature,
Leeds, Yorkshire, England
Revista, Barcelona
*Revista de Estudios
Americanos*, Seville, Spain
Revista Gran Vía, Madrid
Revue des Deux Mondes, Paris
Revue Européenne, Paris
Revue Générale Belge,
Brussels
Revue Hommes et Mondes,
Paris
Revue Internationale, Paris
Revue des Langues Vivantes,
Brussels
Revue des Lettres Modernes,
Paris
Revue Nouvelle, Brussels
Revue de Paris, Paris
Revue de l'Université Laval,
Quebec
Rezets, Moscow
Rinascita, Rome
Rogue, Chicago
Rotarian, Evanston, Ill.
Ruban Rouge, Paris
Ruedo, Madrid

*St. Louis Globe-Democrat,
St. Louis, Mo.
*St. Louis Post-Dispatch,
St. Louis, Mo.

*St. Louis Star & Times,
St. Louis, Mo.
*Samedi-Soir, Paris
Samtid och Framtid,
Stockholm
*San Francisco Chronicle,
San Francisco, Calif.
San Francisco Review,
San Francisco, Calif.
Saturday Evening Post,
Philadelphia
Saturday Night, Toronto
Saturday Review, London
(as noted)
Saturday Review, New York
(see *SRL*)
Schönste, Munich
Science & Society, New York
Scribner's Magazine, New York
Scrutiny, Cambridge, England
Senior Tabula, Oak Park, Ill.
(also *Tabula*)
Sewanee Review,
Sewanee, Tenn.
Shenandoah, Lexington, Va.
Smeraldo, Milan
Società, Rome
Società Nuova, Rome
South Atlantic Bulletin,
Chapel Hill, N.C.
South Atlantic Quarterly,
Durham, N.C.
Southern Review,
Baton Rouge, La.
Southwest Review,
Dallas, Tex.
Soviet Literature, Moscow
Soviet Review, Lancaster, Pa.
Spectator, London
Spiegel, Hamburg, Germany
Sports Afield, New York
Sports Illustrated, New York
*Sprache und Literatur
Englands und Amerikas*,
Tübingen, Germany

Spur, New York

SRL: Saturday Review of
Literature, New York
(changed to Saturday Review
in 1952)

*Stampa, Turin, Italy

Status, New York

Stil und Formprobleme,
[Heidelberg, Germany?]

*Stockholms-Tidningen,
Stockholm

Studi Americani, Rome

Studies: An Irish Quarterly
Review, Dublin

Studies in English Literature,
Tokyo

Studies in Short Fiction,
Newberry, S.C.

*Sunday Times, London

*Svenska Dagbladet, Stockholm

Synthèses, Brussels

Table Ronde, Paris

*Tablet, London

Tabula, Oak Park, Ill.
(also Senior Tabula)

Tagebuch, Berlin

T.A.L.S., Tokyo (Tokyo
American Literature Society)

*TDS: Toronto Daily Star,
Toronto (also Toronto Star
Weekly)

Teatr, Moscow

*Tempo, Milan

Tempo Presente, Rome

Temps Modernes, Paris

*Temps Présent, Paris

Tennessee Studies in
Literature, Knoxville, Tenn.

Terzo Programma, Rome

Texas Quarterly, Austin, Texas

Texas Studies in Literature &
Language, Austin, Tex.

Theatre Arts, New York

This Quarter, Paris and Milan

*This Week, New York
(a nationally distributed
supplement in Sunday newspapers)

Thought, Delhi, India

Tilskueren, Copenhagen

Time, New York

*Times, London (also TLS:
Times Literary Supplement)

*TLS, London
(see above entry)

Today's Woman, New York

Tomorrow, New York

Toros, Madrid

Torre, San Juan, Puerto Rico

Town & Country, New York

Transatlantic Review, Paris

transition, Paris

*Trapeze, Oak Park, Ill.

Travel, New York

True, New York

*TSW: Toronto Star Weekly,
Toronto (also Toronto Daily
Star)

Tulane Studies in English,
New Orleans, La.

Twentieth Century Fiction,
Denver, Colo.

Twórczość, Warsaw

Ukraine & The World, [Kiev?]

Umana, Trieste

Umschau, Mainz, Germany

Universitas,
Stuttgart, Germany

University of Chicago
Magazine, Chicago

University of Kansas City
Review, Kansas City, Mo.
(changed to University Review in 1963)

University Review,
Kansas City, Mo.
(see above entry)

University of Texas Studies in English, Austin, Tex.
University of Toronto Quarterly, Toronto

*Vanguardia Española, Barcelona
Vanity Fair, New York
Verve, Paris
Vi, Stockholm
Vindrôsen, Copenhagen
Vinduet, Oslo
Virginia Librarian, Norfolk, Va.
Virginia Quarterly Review, Charlottesville, Va.
Vita e Pensiero, Milan
Vogue, New York
Voprosi Literaturi, Moscow
*Vossische Zeitung, Berlin

*Washington Evening Star, Washington, D.C.
*Washington Post, Washington, D.C.
*Welt, Hamburg, Germany
Weltbühne, Berlin

Western Humanities Review, Salt Lake City, Utah
Western Review, Iowa City, Iowa
Why, (place of publication not known)
Wilson Library Bulletin, New York
Wingover (place of publication not known)
Wisconsin Studies in Contemporary Literature, Madison, Wis.
Wisdom, Beverly Hills, Calif.
Wort in der Zeit, Graz, Austria
Writer, Boston
Writer's Digest, Cincinnati, Ohio

Yale Literary Magazine, New Haven, Conn.
Yale Review, New Haven, Conn.

Znamya, Moscow
Zvezda, Leningrad

INDEX

INDEX

INDEX

INDEX

INDEX

INDEX

INDEX

Mirrielees, Edith, E17, H354
Misrahi, Victor, H1307
Mitchell, Edwin Valentine, E125
Mizener, Arthur, E313, F60, 63, 65, 89, 91, 107, G50, 282, 283, 388, H769, 1264
Mohrt, Michel, G76, 284, H779, 1265_2
Moloney, Michael F., G27, 155
Monchak, Stephen J., H397
Mondadori, Alberto, $H1243_4$
Mondadori, Arnoldo, F108, 112, 128, G285
Monicelli, Giorgio, D162, 172
Monnier, Adrienne, C169
Monroe, Harriet, F14a
Montale, Eugenio, H665, 850_1, 868, 1242_1, 1580
Montalet, R.-H. de, H694
Monteiro, Aldolfo Casais, D271
Montejo, Alberto Delgado, H808
Montgomery, Constance Cappel, B61, F43, G286
Montgomery, Marion, $H1227_1$, 1363
Moore, Archie, F164
Moore, Geoffrey, H1470
Moore, Harry T., H1069
Moore, John Rees, E302
Moore, L. Hugh, Jr., $H1612_1$
Moore, Marianne, B55
Moore, Nicholas, E144
Moorhead, Ethel, C165, F12a, 57, 59, 61, 64
Moqaddam, Rezā, D247
Mora, Constancia de la, G287
Moraes, Frank, $H1295_5$
Moravia, Alberto, G288, H673, 674, 1315, 1608
Morris, Alton C., E179, 341
Morris, John N., E311
Morris, Lawrence S., H47, 61
Morris, Lloyd, G289, H610
Morris, Richard B., B46, E161
Morris, William E., H1154, 1611
Morris, Wright, G290, H1070, 1329
Morrison, Theodore, B35, E72
Morrow, Elise, F114, H688
Moseley, Edwin M., G291
Moses, W. R., H1136
Moss, Arthur, H183, H1000
Moss, Sidney P., H1491
"Mother of a Queen, The," A12a, 16a
Motola, Gabriel, H1563
Mott, Frank Luther, E148
Motta, Virgínia, D278
Moveable Feast, A, A31a, 31b, 46a, 46b, C420-423, D45, 54, 68, 85, 112, 175, 214, 244, 263, 282, 342, 382; critical comment on, $H1571_1$, 1580; reviews of, G166, H1507, 1508, 1510-1519,

1521-1523, 1528, 1531, 1533, 1535, 1539, 1540, 1546, 1551; allusions to, F160, H1481, 1482, 1510_1, 1516_1, 1517_1, 1542, 1560
Mowrer, Edgar Ansel, B31
Moylan, Thomas J., H953
Moynihan, William T., E295, H1168
"Mr. and Mrs. Elliot," A3a, 16a, 20a, 32a, B53, C159, 210, 399, E127, 181, 216, 305
Mucharowski, Hans-Günter, G292
Muir, Edwin, H74, 339, 738
Mukherji, Dipali, D150
Muller, Herbert J., G293
Mumford, Lewis, B5, E6
Murtezai, Masar, D2
Mussey, Barrows, B38
Mussolini, Benito, C93, 122, 240
Muṣṭafā, Nūr-il-Dīn, D7
Mustanoja, Tauno F., G124
"My Old Man," A1a, 3a, 16a, 20a, 28a, B1, C194, 225, D40, E1, 9, 24, 26, 70, 73, 95, 117, 118, 157, 174, 183, 202, 229, 316, 327, 344; critical comment on, H1374
Myklebost, Tor, G294

Najm, Mohammed, G26c, 461d
Nakata, Kôji, D194-196, 200
Nakaza, Gensuke, H1128
Naly, Robert, D81, 82
Napolitano, Giangaspare, H1291
Nash, Ogden, B30
Nasif, Majdī al-Din, D6
Nason, Leonard, H69
Nathan, George Jean, G295, H416
"Natural History of the Dead, A," A12a, 16a, E158; manuscript, F6c; critical comment on, H1564; allusions to, H233, 403, 970
Neagoe, Peter, E29
Nebot, Frank, G296
Neely, A14a
Neider, Charles, E168, 193, 218
Nejgebauer, Aleksandar, D360
Nelson, Howard, H1566
Nelson, Roy C., B19, $C239_1$
Nemerovskaya, Olga, H251, 368
Németh, Andor, D130
Neumann, John, H711, 763
Neville, Edgar, H1254
Nevins, Allan, E86
Newell, David M., B18
Newman, Paul B., H1396
Nichols, Lewis, F140, H1158
"Night Before Battle," C311
Nikolajević, Kaliopa, D368
Nishimura, Kôji, D183
Nishiyama, Tamotsu, H1201

INDEX

INDEX

INDEX

INDEX

INDEX

1969

2nd Prtg

50⁰⁰